The Cinema of Attractions Reloaded

The Cinema of Attractions Reloaded

Edited by Wanda Strauven

AMSTERDAM UNIVERSITY PRESS

Cover illustration: Carrie-Anne Moss in *The Matrix* (1999). Directors: Andy and Carry Wachowski. © Photos 12

Cover design: Kok Korpershoek, Amsterdam
Lay-out: JAPES, Amsterdam
Production: Textcase, Hilversum, the Netherlands

ISBN-13   978 90 5356 944 3 (paperback)
ISBN-10   90 5356 944 8 (paperback)

ISBN-13   978 90 5356 945 0 (hardcover)
ISBN-10   90 5356 945 6 (hardcover)

NUR 674

Contents

ORDERING INFORMATION

Orders from the U.S.A. and Canada:

The University of Chicago Press
Order Department
11030 South Langley Avenue
Chicago, Illinois 60628
U.S.A.
Telephone: 1-800-621-2736 (U.S.A. only); (773) 568-1550
Facsimile: 1-800-621-8476 (U.S.A. only); (773) 660-2235
Pubnet @ 202-5280
WWW: http://www.press.uchicago.edu

Orders from the United Kingdom and Europe:

The University of Chicago Press
c/o John Wiley & Sons Ltd.
Distribution Centre
1 Oldlands Way
Bognor Regis, West Sussex PO22 9SA
UNITED KINGDOM
Telephone: (0) 1243 779777
Facsimile: (0) 1243 820250
Internet: cs-books@wiley.co.uk
WWW:
http://www.wiley.com/WorldWide/Europe.html

Orders from Japan:

Booksellers' orders should be placed with our agent:
United Publishers' Services, Ltd.
Kenkyu-sha Building
9, Kanda Surugadai 2-chome
Chiyoda-ku, Tokyo
JAPAN
Telephone: (03) 3291-4541
Facsimile: (03) 3293-3484
Libraries and individuals should place their orders with local booksellers.

Orders from Australia, New Zealand, South Pacific, Africa, the Middle East, China (P.R.C.), Southeast Asia, India, Mexico, Central and South America:

The University of Chicago Press
International Sales Manager
1427 E. 60th Street
Chicago, Illinois 60637
U.S.A.
Telephone: (773) 702-7740
Facsimile: (773) 702-9756
Internet: dblobaum@press.uchicago.edu

Orders from Korea, Hong Kong, and Taiwan, R.O.C.:

The American University Press Group
3-21-18-206 Higashi Shinagawa
Shinagawa-ku, Tokyo, 140
JAPAN
Telephone: (03) 3450-2857
Facsimile: (03) 3472-9706
Internet: andishig@po.iijnet.or.jp

THE UNIVERSITY OF CHICAGO PRESS

REVIEW COPY

The Cinema of Attractions Reloaded

Edited by Wanda Strauven

Published by Amsterdam University Press
Distributed by the University of Chicago Press

Domestic Publication Date: 15 March 2007

464 p.	•	Cloth	•	$75.00	ISBN 90-5356-945-6
		Paper	•	$47.50	ISBN 90-5356-944-8

For more information, please contact Kristi McGuire by phone at (773) 702-2548, by fax at (773) 702-9756, or by e-mail at kam@press.uchicago.edu

Please send two copies of your published review to:

Publicity Director, THE UNIVERSITY OF CHICAGO PRESS
1427 E. 60th Street, Chicago, Illinois 60637, U.S.A.   Telephone 773-702-7740

Dossier

Acknowledgments

First of all, I wish to thank Tom Gunning and André Gaudreault for their enthusiastic response to this commemorative book project, for their confidence and their inspiration, and for their willingness to participate. My gratitude also goes to Thomas Elsaesser with whom I had the opportunity to regularly brainstorm on film historiographical issues over the last four years at the University of Amsterdam and who promptly accepted to add this anthology to his series of "Film Culture in Transition." Furthermore, I am grateful to all the contributors, whose positive reactions and often intense e-mail discussions kept me persevering in this long venture. One of the real challenges of this project was to bring together scholars from both sides of the Atlantic and to bridge the gap between the Anglo-Saxon and Francophone worlds. A special thanks goes to all the translators and in particular to Joyce Goggin who was kindly enough to help me with the English translation of Gaudreault and Gunning's joint paper "Le cinéma des premiers temps: un défi à l'histoire du cinéma?" ("Early Cinema as a Challenge to Film History"). I also express my sincere thanks to Viva Paci for her assistance with the compilation of the general bibliography and to Jaap Kooijman for his valuable feedback. The Fédération Internationale des Archives du Film (FIAF) gently authorized the reprint of Donald Crafton's paper "Pie and Chase," which was originally presented at the 1985 FIAF Slapstick Symposium in New York City. For the other reprints in the dossier of this volume, I thank the authors for granting their permission. The publication of this book would not have been possible without the financial support of the University of Amsterdam, in particular the Department of Media Studies and the Amsterdam School for Cultural Analysis (ASCA), as well as the Groupe de recherche sur l'avènement et la formation des institutions cinématographique et scénique (GRAFICS) at Université de Montréal. And, last but not least, I thank Donato Montanari for his day to day support and for introducing me to the secrets of Newton's law of attraction.

Wanda Strauven
Amsterdam, August 2006

Introduction to an Attractive Concept

Wanda Strauven

DIE GROSSE ATTRAKTION (Max Reichmann, 1931), NIE YUAN (Keqing Chen & Kuang-chi Tu, 1952), NOVYY ATTRAKTSION (Boris Dolin, 1957), L'ATTRAZIONE (Mario Gariazzo, 1987), FATAL ATTRACTION (Adrian Lyne, 1987), ATRAÇÃO SATÂNICA (Fauzi Mansur, 1990), ATTRAZIONE PERICOLOSA (Bruno Mattei, 1993), FAMILY ATTRACTION (Brian Hecker, 1998), THE LAST BIG ATTRACTION (Hopwood DePree, 1999), THE RULES OF ATTRACTION (Roger Avary, 2002), ANIMAL ATTRACTION (Keith Hooker, 2004), FUTILE ATTRACTION (Mark Prebble, 2004), LAWS OF ATTRACTION (Peter Howitt, 2004). This is just a selection of movie titles that over the last seventy-five years have ensured the film spectator diegetic attractions; from shorts to feature length films; from comedy to romance, from drama and thriller to low-budget horror; from the USA to the USSR, from Hong Kong to Brazil. None of these films – not even the most popular one, FATAL ATTRACTION – is discussed in the present anthology. What is studied, however, is the attractiveness of the notion "attraction," its use and usefulness, within the field of cinema studies and beyond. This anthology specifically reflects on the term as employed in the phrase "cinema of attractions," coined in the mid-1980s by Tom Gunning and André Gaudreault in relation to early cinema and proven to be adequate, or at least "attractive," for the definition of contemporary special effect cinema as well. THE MATRIX (Andy and Larry Wachowski, 1999), for instance, can be conceived of as a reloaded form of cinema of attractions in that it is "dedicated to presenting discontinuous visual attractions, moments of spectacle rather than narrative."[1] Now, twenty years after the "birth" of the "cinema of attractions" (and, as I will discuss below, ten years after the "rebirth" of the "cinématographie-attraction"), it is the perfect time to look back upon the debate and question the relevance of the concept for the future.

A Complex Chronology

Twenty years ago, in 1986, two essays which were fundamental in the formation and launching of the concept of "cinema of attractions" were published. Firstly, the by now classic essay of Tom Gunning, "The Cinema of Attraction: Early Film, Its Spectator and the Avant-Garde," appeared in the discontinued film quarterly *Wide Angle*, illustrated with some stills from THE GAY SHOE

CLERK (1903) on its title page (Fig. 1). And, secondly, the joint paper by André Gaudreault and the same Tom Gunning, "Le cinéma des premiers temps: un défi à l'histoire du cinéma?," was printed in the Tokyo journal *Gendai Shiso. Revue de la pensée d'aujourd'hui* in Japanese translation "Eigashi No Hohoron" (Fig. 2).

The Cinema of Attraction:
Early Film, Its Spectator
and the Avant-Garde

The Gay Shoe Clerk *(1903)*

By Tom Gunning

Writing in 1922, flushed with the excitement of seeing Abel Gance's *La Roue*, Fernand Léger tried to define something of the radical possibilities of the cinema. The potential of the new art did not lay in "imitating the movements of nature" or in "the mistaken path" of its resemblance to theater. Its unique power was a "matter of *making images seen*."[1] It is precisely this harnessing of visibility,

Fig. 1. *Wide Angle* 8.3-4 (Fall 1986): "The Cinema of Attraction: Early Film, Its Spectator and the Avant-Garde"

Fig. 2. *Gendai Shiso* 14.12 (Nov. 1986): "Eigashi No Hohoron"

Whereas the first has been reprinted several times and translated into at least six different languages (Swedish, Danish, German, Finnish, Japanese, Hungarian, but, interestingly enough, not French), the latter appeared only once more after its Japanese première, in 1989, in its original French version.[2] One year later, Gunning revised his essay for its (first) reprint in what is now also a classic anthology edited by Thomas Elsaesser, *Early Cinema: Space Frame Narrative,*[3] adding one extra paragraph and changing the singular "attraction" of the title into plural. It is this 1990 reprint that Gunning considers the final (and correct) version. Thus, the French publication of "Un défi à l'histoire du cinéma" follows "The Cinema of Attraction," but precedes "The Cinema of Attractions."

The spoken version of the joint paper "Un défi à l'histoire du cinéma" also preceded "The Cinema of Attraction." It was delivered by Gaudreault in August 1985 at the Cerisy Conference "Nouvelles approches de l'histoire du cinéma" in Normandy, France. Gunning, from his side, gave his paper shortly after, in the fall, at the Ohio University Film and Video Conference. The chronology is getting really imbricate if we consider that both papers cited Donald Crafton's use of the term "attraction" in a paper he delivered in May 1985 at the FIAF Conference on Slapstick, which was held at the Museum of Modern Art in New York.[4] Since the Slapstick Symposium only published its proceedings two years later, Crafton is translated in Japanese *ante litteram* (Fig. 3).[5]

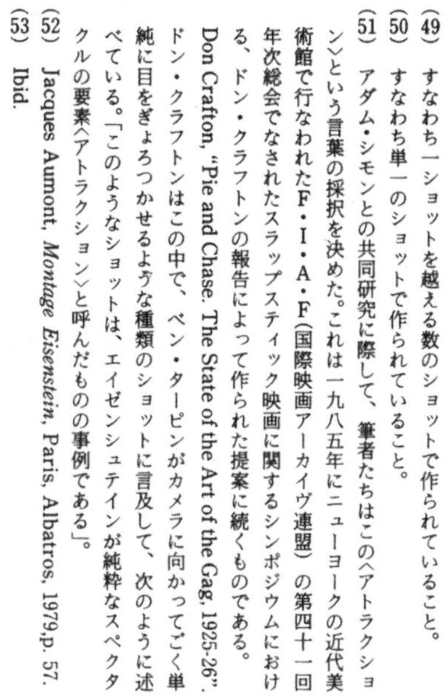

（49）すなわち一ショットを越える数のショットで作られていること。

（50）すなわち単一のショットで作られていること。

（51）アダム・シモンとの共同研究に際して、筆者たちはこのヘアトラクションという言葉の採択を決めた。これは一九八五年にニューヨークの近代美術館で行なわれたF・I・A・F〔国際映画アーカイヴ連盟〕の第四十一回年次総会でなされたスラップスティック映画に関するシンポジウムにおける、ドン・クラフトンの報告によって作られた提案に続くものである。Don Crafton, "Pie and Chase. The State of the Art of the Gag, 1925-26". ドン・クラフトンはこの中で、ベン・ターピンがカメラに向かってごく単純に目をぎょろつかせるような種類のショットに言及して、次のように述べている。「このようなショットは、エイゼンシュテインが純粋なスペクタクルの要素〈アトラクション〉と呼んだものの事例である」。

（52）Jacques Aumont, *Montage Eisenstein*, Paris, Albatros, 1979. p. 57.

（53）Ibid.

Fig. 3. "Eigashi No Hohoron," note 51

In the written version of his 1985 paper, Crafton himself incorporated, quite anachronistically, not only a response to some of the criticism[6] Gunning made during the conference in New York, but also a paragraph long quotation from his essay "The Cinema of Attraction," which had meanwhile been published in *Wide Angle*. Next to Crafton's paper as direct source of inspiration, I should also name Adam Simon, who is mentioned in both the Cerisy paper and Gunning's essay. On the role that Simon played in the theory formation I refer to Gunning's personal account of the facts in his opening essay of the present anthology.

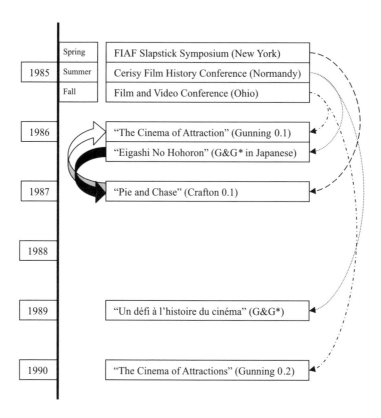

Fig. 4. Chronological Chart
(*G&G stands for Gaudreault & Gunning)

To complete my chronological chart (Fig. 4), I should specify that Gunning's "The Cinema of Attraction(s)" (in both its original and final version) refers to his collaboration with Gaudreault and their paper given at Cerisy. The Cerisy publication, on the contrary, does not take into account the *Wide Angle* article, which had not come out at the time of writing. "Un défi à l'histoire du cinéma" actually does not propose or include the phrase "cinema of attractions"! In this paper Gaudreault and Gunning suggest a distinction between two successive "modes of film practice": on the one hand, the "system of monstrative attractions" which covers *grosso modo* the period 1895-1908; and, on the other, the "system of narrative integration" which defines the period 1909-1914.[7] The term "monstrative" builds upon the concept of "monstration" that Gaudreault had introduced around 1984 in the field of early cinema.[8] Monstration (showing) is to narration (telling) what presentation is to representation or, in Gunning's terms, "exhibitionism" to voyeurism. It is all about the cinema's ability to *show* something, to *"make images seen,"*[9] to directly address the spectator. For the concept of the attraction, Gaudreault and Gunning rely upon Jacques Aumont's *Montage Eisenstein*, and more specifically upon his first definition of the Eisensteinian attraction, that is, as performance (which should, however, be considered in close relation to the second and the third definition of the attraction, that is, as association of ideas and as agitation of the spectator).[10] Although the reference to Aumont is missing in "The Cinema of Attraction(s)," Gunning does not overlook the fundamental question of the impact on the spectator. This question is actually central to his theorization of the "cinema of attractions," for which he cites not only Eisenstein's "Montage of Attractions" (1923), but also Marinetti's manifesto of "The Variety Theater" (1913).

These are some of the points of convergence and divergence between "The Cinema of Attraction(s)" and "Un défi à l'histoire du cinéma." There is much more to be said about the differences in approach, context and background, but what they have in common is that they are the product of a series of discussions between Gunning and Gaudreault; and that they were both published, in one form or another, in 1986. The present volume brings them together for the first time, with the first English translation of "Un défi à l'histoire du cinéma," making an actual comparison possible.

Yet this comparison should be contextualized: "The Cinema of Attraction(s)" and "Un défi à l'histoire du cinéma" are not only the outcome of a series of discussions between the two authors; they are also typical expressions of the post-Brighton movement. Both Gunning and Gaudreault relate in their respective contribution in this volume the importance of the legendary 34th FIAF Conference held in Brighton, England, in 1978. More particularly, they both stress the importance of the screening of all the surviving and in FIAF archives preserved films that were made between 1900 and 1906. It was this extensive and systematic viewing process that radically changed (Old) Film History.

Too young to participate in (or even know about) the Brighton Project, I had the opportunity to attend a less extensive, but equally systematic screening much later, in the summer of 1996, at the second Cerisy Conference on Georges Méliès.[11] There we watched in chronological order the integral oeuvre of Méliès, the by then 170 discovered films, which represent a third of his entire production. For my PhD dissertation on Futurism, this experience meant a point of no return. Thanks to its daily screenings and its inaugural live performance, this conference made me realize that in order to understand Marinetti's writings of the 1910s I had not only to look forward to the experimental cinema of the 1920s and 1960s (following for instance Dominique Noguez's path "From Futurism to

Underground"[12]), but also and especially backward to early cinema and its vaudeville origins. This does not mean that I had so far totally ignored early cinema,[13] but I had underestimated (and under-explored) the different meanings of its specific "language," on the one hand, and its exhibition practices, on the other, for Futurism in general and for Marinetti in particular.

At the same conference, in 1996, André Gaudreault gave a paper that questioned the teleological implications of certain historiographical notions, such as the French "cinéma des premiers temps," insisting instead on the importance of using terms that reflect historical realities. At the end of his paper he cautiously proposed for the first time G.-Michel Coissac's term "cinématographie-attraction," which he had found in Jean Giraud's *Lexique français du cinéma des origines à 1930*.[14] A linguist by training, this quest for "terminological correctness" certainly attracted me and offered me a concrete tool by which to rethink (Futurist) history.

However, eventually, it was Gunning's essay "The Cinema of Attraction(s)" that helped me in reinforcing my Futurist thesis, not least because of his explicit reference to Marinetti and his incitement, in the opening paragraph, to re-explore early cinema's inspiration for the historical avant-garde. One could say I took his words quite literally. The notion of attraction that refers both "backwards to a popular tradition and forwards to an avant-garde subversion,"[15] as Gunning explains in his follow up article "An Aesthetic of Astonishment," became the guiding principle for my research on Marinetti and his relation to cinema.[16]

Attraction vs. Attractions, Attraction vs. Monstration

As Gaudreault himself explains, the term "cinématographie-attraction," as borrowed from Coissac, has a couple of advantages with respect to Gunning's concept: first, it captures the phenomenon of "attraction" under the denomination of "cinematography" (instead of "cinema") and, second, it testifies to the fact that the phenomenon of "cinematography" was indeed received as such, that is, as attraction, at the time described by Coissac (which, however, corresponds more or less to the end of the cinema of attractions and the beginning of institutionalized cinema).[17] What is remarkable about Coissac's expression is the use of attraction in its singular form. This might be peculiar to the French language, if one considers more recent expressions such as Livio Belloï's "image-attraction"[18] or the common "cinéma-attraction." But does "cinéma-attraction" in French have the same meaning as "cinéma des attractions"? And, further, is the "image-attraction" just one of the attractions of a particular film or is it rather an image of attraction, that is, an image with the quality of attracting the gaze, a "dialectical image," as Belloï defines it, which exists only because we look at it?[19]

My next question would be: is there any fundamental difference between Gunning's "cinema of *attraction*" (as used in the *Wide Angle* version of 1986) and "cinema of *attractions*" (as in the revised version of 1990)? Is the first not inviting us more directly to consider the cinema itself, that is "the Cinématographe, the Biograph or the Vitascope,"[20] as an attraction, whereas the latter rather suggests (or focuses on) the cinema as a series of attractions, as a succession of astonishing numbers, be it the individual "animated views" or the magical tricks within one and the same view (or the special effects within one and the same feature length film)? This distinction, if it exists, could then be compared with the differentiation between the system of monstration and the system of monstrative attractions, which find their respective "opponent" in the system of narration and the system of narrative integration?

Attraction and monstration, albeit both equally "opposed" to narration, cannot simply be considered as synonyms. Whereas the concept of monstration implies a (narratological) instance that shows something, the notion of attraction emphasizes the magnetism of the spectacle shown. In the mode of attraction the spectator is *attracted* toward the filmic (or the apparatical); this direction is somehow reversed in the case of monstration, where the filmic (or the apparatical) is *monstrated* to the spectator. Attraction involves, more manifestly than monstration, the spectator; it is a force put upon the latter.

Laws of Attraction

The first definition of attraction given in the *Oxford English Dictionary* is "the action of drawing or sucking in." Etymologically the English term was adopted in the 16th century from the French *attraction*, which derived from the Latin *attractio*, meaning "'contraction,' and, grammatically, 'attraction' (from *trahere*, to pull)."[21] Conversely, the attraction in terms of spectacle or any other form of entertainment drawing crowds was adopted into French from English in the early 19th century. See also the *OED* quoting "Littré [who], in his Supplement, says that this 'English sense' of attraction began to be borrowed in French about the era of the Great Exhibitions, and had then, in 1869, become quite current."

In order to give a comprehensive definition of the term, at least three different levels of meaning should be distinguished: the grammatical, the spectacular and the physical. The grammatical significance of attraction is probably the less known one. It concerns, however, its original Latin use referring to the modification of one form under the influence of another form which stands in syntactical relation to the first. In French, there is for instance the attraction of genders, which is illustrated in *Le Petit Robert* with the following example: "un espèce d'idiot" (the article "une," that the feminine noun "espèce" requires, is transformed into "un" under the influence of the masculine noun "idiot"). In English a similar phenomenon can be found in the use of the expression "kind of," when (incorrectly) preceded by *these, those,* and the like, and followed by a plural verb and pronoun under the influence of the plural noun it defines. See the example given by the *OED*: "these kind of men have their use." As far as I know, this specific meaning of attraction has not been applied, at least not explicitly and intentionally, to (early) cinema; one could think of valid analyses that examine whether or not a non-fiction film was received as fictional under the influence of the fiction films that preceded or followed it; that is, whether or not the genre of a film was transformed by its particular (grammatical) position in the program.[22]

The second sense of attraction, on the other hand, is the most common one in our field: it concerns the attraction value of different forms of entertainment. Very generally, attraction stands for "center of interest," for that which attracts people (e.g. tourist attraction); more specifically, it can refer to a spectacle, a (variety, circus, cinema, etc.) show, or – in Eisenstein's theory – to one of the "peak moments"[23] of a (variety, circus, cinema, etc.) show. This second significance of attraction corresponds to its so-called "English sense," defined by the *OED* as follows: "A thing or feature which draws people by appealing to their desires, tastes, etc.; *esp.* any interesting or amusing exhibition which 'draws' crowds." The "English sense" is the most banal meaning of the cinema of attractions (in both its original and reloaded form), but the definition of Gunning's phrase, like Eisenstein's montage of attractions, implicates a direct, somewhat aggressive, address of the spectator; it goes beyond (or even against) a simple process of appealing to the taste of the public. According to Eisenstein, an attraction was supposed to produce "emotional shocks."[24] For this aggressive dimension of the spectacle, the Soviet director relies upon the tradition of the French Grand Guignol Theater that was notorious for its horror and special effects: e.g. "an eye is gouged out, an arm or leg amputated before the very eyes of the audience."[25] It is remarkable that this bodily violence characterizes early cinema as well. Numerous car accidents and cutting up of the body were exhibited to the early film spectator. These were attractions that attempted to shock, that is, to *épater les bourgeois* rather than appeal to their taste.

The spectacular dimension of attraction grounds itself on the literal and physical sense of the term, namely "the force that draws or sucks in." One of the most elementary substances that in this sense can be drawn in is air; hence, the obsolete meaning of attraction as "drawing in of the breath, inspiration, inhalation," to which Vivian Sobchack's contribution in this volume draws our attention, more particularly in relation to the (modern) "aesthetic of astonishment." More common, of course, is the force that draws together two distinct bodies, which leads us not only to the "fatal attraction" between human beings, but also and especially to Newton's law of attraction (Fig. 5). The *OED* speaks of the *"attraction* of *gravity,"* which is defined as "that which exists between all bodies, and acts at all distances, with a force proportional to their masses, and inversely proportional to the square of their distance apart." No further reference is made to Newton in the present anthology, although his law of attraction could prove to be stimulating and fruitful to map out the possible effects on the spectator according to his/her distance to the screen, to his/her own body mass and to the size of the image.

$$F_A \cong \frac{M_1 \times M_2}{r^2}$$

Fig. 5. Newton's law of attraction

And, what is more, this third physical (or scientific) meaning of attraction could help us to better understand Eisenstein's Constructivist film theory. In his "Montage of Attractions" (1923) the Soviet director talks about the attraction as "a molecular (i.e. compound) unity of the *efficiency* of the theater and of *theater in general.*"[26] In other words, should we not examine the laws of "molecular attraction" rather than the attractions of Coney Island? Because of his contacts with the Factory of the Eccentric Actor (FEKS), Eisenstein certainly was attracted to the fairground. But, in the end, he was less concerned with roller coasters than with a scientific approach to art. It should not be forgotten that Eisenstein was an engineer by training. And as an engineer he learned that "any approach becomes scientific when the domain of research acquires its own unit of measurement."[27] In his *Memoirs*, Eisenstein gives us insight into his theory formation:

Let us thus go in search for a unit that will measure the influence of art.

Science has its "ions," its "electrons," its "neutrons."

Art will have – its "attractions"!

From the production processes, a technical term has become part of everyday language, designating assemblages in terms of machines, water canalizations, machine tools, the beautiful word "montage," that designates – an assemblage.

Even if the word is not yet in vogue, it has potentially everything to work well.

Well, let us go!

And may *the combination of the units of influence in a whole* receive the double designation, half-production, half-music hall […]

This is how the term "montage of attractions" was born.[28]

Intriguingly enough, Eisenstein also makes the following confession: "If I had known more about Pavlov at that time, I would have called the theory of montage of attractions a 'theory of artistic stimulants.'"[29] On the one hand, the notion of "artistic stimulant" reveals once more Eisenstein's preoccupation with the spectator and the (Pavlovian) impact upon him or her. On the other, it also points to Eisenstein's conception of montage as a general, i.e. non-medium specific, artistic principle; to his ambition to conceive *art in general* as science.

Even if the concept of "cinema of attractions," when it was introduced in 1986, conflated types of cinema that had until then been considered as entirely divergent (fiction vs. non-fiction, narrative vs. non-narrative), Gunning certainly did not aim at a theory for *cinema in general*. The concept was conceived, first and foremost, as historical "mode of film practice" that would "cover the entire first period of film history until 1908" (according to the Cerisy paper) or at least be "dominant"[30] in films made "before 1906 (or so)" (according to Gunning's founding article). It is precisely this rather large demarcation in time, more or less an entire decade, that has been "severely" criticized by Charles Musser. In the early 1990s Musser pleaded for a more detailed periodization of early cinema, in which the novelty period (i.e. the period of cinema of attractions) is delimited to the very first theatrical season, "from late 1895 to early 1897," and the "rise of story film" (i.e. the system of narrative integration) is dated much earlier, around 1903-04.[31] Furthermore, Musser questions the nonnarrative dimension of the cinema of attractions, by closely examining the sequencing of early film programs and pointing out, as he does in his contribution to the present volume, the logical structures of these programs and the complex intertextuality at play.

Despite the fact that the cinema of attractions was clearly thought of as a time specific category of film practice (and more specifically of spectatorship), its real attraction consists of its applicability to other periods of film history, to other similar practices beyond early cinema (and even beyond cinema). Gunning himself is responsible for such a universalization of the concept by stating in his seminal essay: "In fact the cinema of attractions does not disappear with the dominance of narrative, but rather goes underground, both into certain avantgarde practices and as a component of narrative films, more evident in some genres (e.g. the musical) than in others."[32] Or again: "Clearly in some sense recent spectacle cinema has reaffirmed its roots in stimulus and carnival rides, in what might be called the Spielberg-Lucas-Coppola cinema of effects."[33]

One of the challenges of the present anthology is to interrogate this all-purpose applicability of the term. Why did the cinema of attractions become such a successful formula, such a buzzword? Is it because it can be considered as designating a specific period as well as a transhistorical style, a historical film practice as well as a universal film practice that appears, disappears and re-appears like a cyclical phenomenon? Is it because it filled certain gaps at the right time, offering for instance an alternative solution to talk about immersivity, interactivity, self-reflexivity?

The Anthology

To commemorate the twentieth anniversary of the "cinema of attractions," this anthology looks into its past and its future. Not only the past and the future of the concept itself are the object of analysis (from its conception in the early 1980s to its future validity in the field of film studies and beyond), but also the past and the future of the attraction as phenomenon are under discussion. Both pre-cinematic cultural series (from baroque painting to optical toys) and post-cinematic media (such as digital cinema, VR and computer games) are addressed from the viewpoint of attraction(s). This anthology, thus, is not or not merely about early cinema.

The book is structured in five parts, each of which comprises four essays and reflects upon one specific component of the title of Gunning's inspirational essay: "The Cinema of Attractions: Early Film, Its Spectator and the Avant-Garde." It opens with four contributions dealing with the theory formation of "The Cinema of Attractions" (Part 1), the first word being given to Tom Gunning, who traces the prehistory and "birth" of the concept from his own standpoint and memory. This personal chronicle is followed by the scientific dissection of "The Cinema of Attractions," operated by Warren Buckland on the basis of Rudolf Botha's study into the "conduct of inquiry" with the intention of investigating the empirical adequacy of Gunning's concept. Frank Kessler argues that the concept of the cinema of attractions should be seen as a mode of address rather than as a mode of representation and proposes therefore a reinterpretation of Jean-Louis Baudry's *dispositif* in terms of historical pragmatics. The concept of spectacle, from both historical and ideological viewpoints, is the central issue of Scott Bukatman's contribution that explores the affinities between Gunning's essay and the equally influential manifesto by Laura Mulvey, "Visual Pleasure and Narrative Cinema."

Part 2 is dedicated to attraction theories and terminologies from the perspective of "Early Film." It brings together four essays that are centered on historical and/or historiographical research. Whereas André Gaudreault disapproves of the terms "primitive cinema" and "early cinema" because of their teleological implications and puts forward a newly coined expression "Kine-Attractography" (modeled on Coissac's "cinématographie-attraction"), my own contribution pleads for a positively connoted use of "primitive cinema," inspired by

Marinetti, and for the introduction of the Futurist concept of "marvelous" in the field of early film studies. Viva Paci focuses on the first film theories of the 1910s and 20s (ranging from the French school of *photogénie* to Luigi Pirandello, Walter Benjamin and Dziga Vertov), demonstrating how during the period of narrative integration the fascination for the cinema of attractions, that is, for the cinema as "vision machine," persists. The *photogénie* school returns in Laurent Guido's contribution that addresses the attraction of the dancing body in early film culture, from the chronophotographic inscriptions by Georges Demenÿ to the general *Girl-Kultur*, from the important influence of Loïe Fuller to the emergence of a new montage principle.

In Part 3 the concept of attraction is questioned in relation to "Its Spectator." According to Charles Musser the early film spectator's reaction to cinema was not only visceral, but also and especially cerebral in so far as s/he was expected to make comparisons between living pictures and moving pictures, to discern among films of the same or similar view, in brief, to participate in a complex play of intertextuality. Germain Lacasse, on the other hand, stresses the role of the lecturer in this reading process; the lecturer is not only the mediator between the attraction and the spectator, but also the proof that the spectator had to be prepared in his/her consumption of the attractions. In the so-called transitional era of the 1910s, the role of the lecturer becomes obsolete because of the gradual narrativization of cinema. Yet this leaves the spectator somehow confused or conflicted, as Charlie Keil argues, between the remnants of the attraction system and the beginning of a new reading process, between the "spectatorial stance conditioned by modernity" and the disciplining of narrational logic. Discipline is the central topic of the contribution by Thomas Elsaesser, who exploits the genre of the (early and contemporary) rube film as case study to discuss the relation between auditorium space and screen space and to propose a redefinition of diegesis which could possibly bridge the opposition between the cinema of attractions and the cinema of narrative integration – that is, the diegesis as "the temporal, spatial and linguistic sited- and situated-ness of the cinematic event and its experience by a body and subject."

The relation between the cinema of attractions and "The Avant-Garde" is explored in the next two parts of the volume. Part 4 analyzes various attraction practices through history, which can be considered as pioneering, subversive or "traditionally" avant-garde. The contribution by Nicolas Dulac and André Gaudreault demonstrates how attraction was already the primary structuring principle of 19th-century optical toys, such as the phenakisticope and the zoetrope; because of their circularity, repetition, and brevity, these devices established the form of attraction as an endless loop. The figure of the loop recurs in Christa Blümlinger's analysis of recent avant-garde films centered on the attraction of the railway and the phantom ride, e.g. THE GEORGETOWN LOOP (Ken Jacobs,

1996), THE DEATH TRAIN (Bill Morrison, 1993), LUMIÈRE'S TRAIN (Al Razutis, 1979), L'ARRIVÉE (Peter Tscherkassky, 1998). These experimental films can be seen as reflections on the "spectacularity" of early cinema attractions which they incorporate and submit to endless repetition. In the subsequent essay, Malte Hagener looks at the programming practice of the avant-garde film clubs in the 1920s and 30s (such as the Dutch Filmliga, the German Volksfilmverband, the London Film Society and the Parisian Vieux Colombier) to point out their attractionist clash of styles and genres, which consisted, for instance, in mixing "absolute" cinema with Chaplin shorts, commercial art cinema with avant-garde "classics" or educational films. Pierre-Emmanuel Jaques closes this first section on the avant-garde with an original reading of the attraction numbers of the classical musical of the 1930s, indicating how these numbers are often based on a complex, associative play of (sexual) intertext and, thus, closer to Eisenstein's "intellectual cinema" than to Gunning's cinema of attractions.

Part 5 deals with "The Avant-Garde" in the digital realm. Precursors of first person and over-the-shoulder perspectives in today's 3D computer games can be found, according to Alison McMahan, in early cinema and more particularly in the genre of the "homunculus film," where a triangular relationship is created between the subject photographed, the photographer character and the camera (or spectator), transgressing therefore the classical exhibitionist set-up of the cinema of attractions. SPIDER-MAN 1 (2002) and SPIDER-MAN 2 (2004), on the other hand, seem to fulfill the perfect return to the cinema of attractions, as suggested by Dick Tomasovic, precisely because of their exhibitionism. This is a cinema of showing rather than telling, where the spectators are assailed by stunning views and rewarded with purely visual pleasure thanks to the virtuoso "spider-cam," yet at the same time find themselves caught in a complex cobweb of commodification. The last two contributions take the bullet time effect as starting-point to discuss the relation between mobility and immobility. Eivind Røssaak leads us from THE MATRIX (1999) back to Eadweard Muybridge via Francis Bacon's *Figure in Movement* (and the Deleuzian notion of "Figure") and back to Tintoretto via Eisenstein and his reading of Gotthold Ephraim Lessing's *Laocoön*. The tension between movement and immobility is of all ages, but thanks to cinema it is now turned into an attraction. Vivian Sobchack, lastly, undertakes a Heideggerian analysis of the attraction of slow motion in contemporary martial arts films, using as case study Zhang Yimou's HERO (2002). Dealing with the kinetic identification that contemporary spectators have to the digitized figuration of physical action on the micro-perceptual level, she gives full attention to the ritualized and meditative sword combat and the extreme slow motion of falling raindrops.

The anthology concludes with a dossier of four reprints: Donald Crafton's "Pie and Chase" (as published in the proceedings of the 1985 Slapstick Symposium), André Gaudreault and Tom Gunning's "Le cinéma des premiers temps: un défi à l'histoire du cinéma?" (appearing here in its first English translation: "Early Cinema as a Challenge to Film History"), Tom Gunning's "The Cinema of Attraction[s]: Early Film, Its Spectator and the Avant-Garde" (confronting the *Wide Angle* version with its 1990 version) and Charles Musser's polemical "Rethinking Early Cinema: Cinema of Attractions and Narrativity" (as published in 1994 in *The Yale Journal of Criticism*).[34]

All the texts in this anthology can be read as individual, autonomous "attractions," but the reader will discern many cross-references. Some are explicit, because openly acknowledged, as for instance Gunning's reply to Musser, my own follow up of Gaudreault's discourse or Lacasse's criticism of Dulac and Gaudreault's exclusion of the magic lantern tradition in their analysis of the optical toys. Others are to be read between the lines and between the various parts of the volume: from Kessler's reinterpretation of the *dispositif* to Elsaesser's redefinition of the diegesis, from Guido's analysis of dancing bodies in slow motion to Sobchack's sensitive "cutting to the quick."

The most cited "attractions" are, in chronological order, THE BIG SWALLOW (James Williamson, 1901), THE GREAT TRAIN ROBBERY (Edwin Porter, 1903), THE GAY SHOE CLERK (Edwin Porter, 1903), LA ROUE (Abel Gance, 1922), BALLET MÉCANIQUE (Fernand Léger, 1924) and THE MATRIX trilogy (Andy and Larry Wachowski, 1999-2003). This short list could be seen as the start of the canonization of the "cinema of attractions" or, more symptomatically, as an indication that this specific mode of film practice "returns" not only in the avant-garde cinema of the 1920s but also in New New Hollywood at the turn of the millennium. One of the obvious yet contestable (and contested) outcomes of this anthology is indeed the verification that some early attraction techniques re-emerge, in one form or another, in later periods of film history. The emblematic shot from THE GREAT TRAIN ROBBERY can be coupled with both its misogynic re-use in the classical Hollywood style (as "destroyed" by Mulvey and re-read by Bukatman) and its exploitation as logo according to Hollywood's laws of attraction (as demonstrated by Tomasovic's reading of SPIDER-MAN). The motif of the early rube films with their image touching characters such as Uncle Josh is recurring over the course of the 20th century up to Tom Cruise's character in MINORITY REPORT (as discussed by Elsaesser). And, last but not least, the technique of the bullet time which is based on an 1880s experiment by Muybridge is reloaded repeatedly, not only in THE MATRIX trilogy but also in HERO.

Does this mean that the cinema of attractions is the true nature of cinema and that we have to consider classical cinema as a detour or "intermezzo"? Gunning's concept certainly permits to connect early cinema with avant-garde cinema, on the one hand, and pre-classical (or pre-narrative) cinema with post-classical (or post-narrative) cinema, on the other, but the reasons behind the "return" of the attraction mode differ from epoch to epoch. Whereas for the avant-garde cinema (be it the historical avant-garde of the 1920s or later practices of the 1960s till 1990s) the link with early cinema is mainly to be understood in terms of aggression on the spectator, the digital "cinema of attractions" of the late 1990s shares with early cinema the fact that it cannot be isolated from the complex media network in which it is imbedded. Today, like hundred years ago, film should not be considered within the sole cultural series of film, but within a complex constellation of various and mutually interpenetrating cultural series. These surroundings, however, have drastically changed over the course of the years. While comparing Wachowski's bullet-arresting-Neo with Porter's bullet-firing-outlaw-leader, one should thus not forget to ask oneself in which constellation of old and new cultural series (from advertisement and fashion to DVDs, computer games and cyberspace) the early cinema figuration of frontality is re-used, re-mastered, re-loaded.

Notes

1. According to the definition of "cinema of attractions" given by Tom Gunning in the *Encyclopedia of Early Cinema*, ed. Richard Abel (London/New York: Routledge, 2005) 124.
2. André Gaudreault and Tom Gunning, "Le cinéma des premiers temps: un défi à l'histoire du cinéma?," *Histoire du cinéma. Nouvelles approches*, ed. Jacques Aumont, André Gaudreault and Michel Marie (Paris: Sorbonne, 1989) 49-63. In 1989, Gunning published his second essay on the term, namely "An Aesthetic of Astonishment: Early Film and the (In)Credulous Spectator," *Art and Text* 34 (Spring 1989): 31-45; rpt. in *Film Theory and Criticism*, ed. Leo Braudy and Marshall Cohen (Oxford: Oxford UP, 1999) 818-32.
3. Tom Gunning, "The Cinema of Attractions: Early Film, Its Spectator and the Avant-Garde," *Early Cinema: Space Frame Narrative*, ed. Thomas Elsaesser (London: British Film Institute, 1990) 56-62. Reprinted in the dossier of this volume.
4. This 1985 Slapstick Symposium, organized by Eileen Bowser, was commemorated last spring by my compatriot Tom Paulus who organized a second Slapstick Symposium at the Cinemathèque Royale de Belgique, with the participation of Bowser and Gunning, among others.
5. Donald Crafton, "Pie and Chase: Gag, Spectacle and Narrative in Slapstick Comedy," *The Slapstick Symposium*, ed. Eileen Bowser (Bruxelles: FIAF, 1988) 49-59. Reprinted in the dossier of this volume.
6. The reprint of Crafton's paper in *Classical Hollywood Comedy*, ed. Kristine Brunovska Karnick and Henry Jenkins (New York: Routledge, 1995) is followed by a postscript by Tom Gunning.

7.   This pair somehow replaces Noël Burch's distinction between the "primitive mode of representation" (PMR) and the "institutional mode of representation" (IMR). See Noël Burch, "Porter, or Ambivalence," *Screen* 19.4 (Winter 1978-79): 91-105; and "Un mode de représentation primitif?," *Iris* 2.1 (1984): 113-23. Burch, however, is not cited in the Cerisy article.

8.   André Gaudreault, "Film, récit, narration; le cinéma des frères Lumière," *Iris* 2.1 (1984): 61-70. English trans. "Film, Narrative, Narration: The Cinema of the Lumière Brothers," *Early Cinema: Space Frame Narrative* 68-75.

9.   Fernand Léger quoted in Gunning, "The Cinema of Attractions" 56.

10. Jacques Aumont, "Attraction/Stimulus/Influence," *Montage Eisenstein*, trans. Lee Mildreth, Constance Penley and Andrew Ross (1979; London/Bloomington: British Film Institute/Indiana UP, 1987) 41-51.

11. The conference was entitled "Georges Méliès et le deuxième siècle du cinéma" and organized by Jacques Malthête and Michel Marie. See also the proceedings *Georges Méliès, l'illusionniste fin de siècle?* (Paris: Sorbonne Nouvelle, 1997).

12. See Dominique Noguez, "Du futurisme à l'"underground,'" *Cinéma: Théorie, Lectures*, ed. Dominique Noguez (Paris: Klincksieck, 1978) 285-93; rpt. in *Eloge du cinéma experimentale* (Paris: Expérimental, 1999) 27-35.

13. In my conference paper, I discussed the phenomenon of the Fregoligraph and identified some points of contact between Méliès and Fregoli. See Wanda Strauven, "L'art de Georges Méliès et le futurisme italien," *Georges Méliès, l'illusionniste fin de siècle?* 331-55.

14. André Gaudreault, "Les *vues cinématographiques* selon Georges Méliès, ou: comment Mitry et Sadoul avaient peut-être raison d'avoir tort (même si c'est surtout Deslandes qu'il faut lire et relire)," *Georges Méliès, l'illusionniste fin de siècle?* 111-31.

15. Gunning, "An Aesthetic of Astonishment" 825.

16. See Wanda Strauven, *Marinetti e il cinema: tra attrazione e sperimentazione* (Udine: Campanotto, 2006). This book is a revised version of my PhD dissertation which I defended in January 2001 at the University of Antwerp, Belgium.

17. Coissac describes the Parisian boulevards as "center of the *cinématographie-attraction*" in the chapter dedicated to "Les salles de cinéma," which concerns the opening of fixed movie theaters in the period 1907-08. G.-Michel Coissac, *Histoire du cinématographe. De ses origines à nos jours* (Paris: Cinéopse/Gauthier-Villars, 1925) 359.

18. Livio Belloï, *Le regard retourné. Aspects du cinéma des premiers temps* (Québec/Paris: Nota Bene/Méridiens Klincksieck, 2001).

19. Belloï 388-89.

20. Gunning, "The Cinema of Attractions" 58.

21. Albert Dauzat, Jean Dubois and Henri Mitterand, *Nouveau dictionnaire étymologique et historique* (Paris: Larousse, 1989) 55. My translation.

22. A step in this direction is undertaken, for instance, by Yuri Tsivian in "Some Historical Footnotes to the Kuleshov Experiment," *Early Cinema: Space Frame Narrative* 247-55. See also my contribution in the present anthology.

23. Aumont 42.

24. S.M. Eisenstein, "Montage of Attractions [1923]," *The Film Sense*, trans. and ed. Jay Leyda (1947; San Diego/New York: Harcourt Brace, 1975) 231.

25. Eisenstein, "Montage of Attractions" 231.

26. Eisenstein, "Montage of Attractions" 231.

27. S.M. Eisenstein, "Comment je suis devenu réalisateur," *Mémoires*, trans. Jacques Aumont, Michèle Bokanowski and Claude Ibrahimoff (Paris: Julliard, 1989) 177. My translation from French.

28. Eisenstein, "Comment je suis devenu réalisateur" 177.

29. Eisenstein, "Comment je suis devenu réalisateur" 177.

30. "Dominant" should be understood in the Russian Formalist sense of the term. See Tom Gunning's opening essay in this volume.

31. See Charles Musser, "Rethinking Early Cinema: Cinema of Attractions and Narrativity," *Yale Journal of Criticism* 7.1 (1994): 203-32. Reprinted in the dossier of this volume.

32. Gunning, "The Cinema of Attractions" 57.

33. Gunning, "The Cinema of Attractions" 61.

34. Along with some typos, I "corrected" note 6 in Crafton, note 4 in Gunning, and note 1 in Musser. This last change was made on the demand of the author.

Theory Formation

["The Cinema of Attractions"]

Attractions: How They Came into the World

Tom Gunning

Someone once said (it might even have been me) that historians begin by studying history and end by becoming part of it. Bearing in mind that oblivion remains the ultimate fate of most writing (and even publishing), and hopefully
avoiding a hubristic perspective, I would like to embed my concept of the cinema of attractions, or at least the writing of the essays that launched it, in a
historical context, largely based on personal memory. That, rather than a de-
fense or further explanation of the term, forms the modest ambition of this essay, which will hopefully provide an additional context to the critical evalua-
tions (positive, negative or both) of the term's use and usefulness that appear in
this anthology. I thank Wanda Strauven for giving me this opportunity.

This is how I remember it. André Gaudreault visited me in the spring of 1985
(or maybe the winter of 1984) in Cambridge, Massachusetts (where I was teaching for the year in the Carpenter Center for Visual and Environment Studies at
Harvard University) to discuss our ongoing projects on early cinema, which
had grown out of our participation in the FIAF Brighton Project on Early Fiction
Film in 1978. These projects included a filmography and a discussion of the
lecture we were supposed to give together at the colloquium on Film History at
Cerisy, in Normandy, France, that summer. André lamented – as far as I recall
(but he may remember this differently) – that the phrase that sounds quite natural in English, "early cinema" (which, I believe, Charles Musser had introduced in his writings on Porter and Edison), did not translate especially well in
French. The equivalent expression "le cinéma des premiers temps" sounded
awkward to the ears of several French scholars. Gaudreault wished we could
find something that worked in both languages.

During that year at Harvard I had been teaching courses on Film Noir, Japanese Cinema and Melodrama and, as fortune had it, had been assigned an extraordinary Teaching Assistant, recently graduated from the Carpenter Center,
Adam Simon. Simon later left cinema studies for a career in filmmaking, directing the low budget dinosaur thriller CARNOSAUR (1993) and documentaries on
Samuel Fuller (THE TYPEWRITER, THE RIFLE & THE MOVIE CAMERA, 1996) and on
the American horror film of the 1960s and 1970s (THE AMERICAN NIGHTMARE,
2000), as well as pursuing detours into occult studies. Simon proved an inspiring
interlocutor, and together we had discussed the different ways genres like melo-

drama and the horror film addressed the cinematic spectator, and related this to my work on early cinema coming out of the Brighton Project. Simon and I had been developing a term I used in teaching, "the cinema of attractions," based on the work of Sergei Eisenstein. We suggested it as a term to Gaudreault, who thought about its French translation, went back and re-read Eisenstein, and Jacques Aumont's insightful treatment of the "attraction" in his book *Montage Eisenstein*, and decided it worked well; indeed, it fitted in very strongly with ideas Gaudreault himself was evolving about narrative and what he called monstration. He incorporated the term into our Cerisy lecture, "Le cinéma des premiers temps: un défi à l'histoire du cinéma?"[1] (which appears in this volume in English translation for the first time, and which is mainly the product of Gaudreault's pen, albeit incorporating passages I wrote, as well as our common ideas).

This return to Eisenstein held great significance for me. I felt at that time (and still do) a need to rediscover the Utopian promise the cinema offered, as it had been described by theorists and filmmakers in the 1920s (the Soviets, as well as the French "Impressionists" and, a bit later, into the 1930s, Benjamin and Kracauer). In contrast to the ideological critique of the cinematic apparatus that had dominated Film Theory post-1968, these earlier avant-garde thinkers and practitioners saw revolutionary possibilities (both political and aesthetic) in the novel ways cinema took hold of its spectator. In that era, the inheritance of 1970s High Theory still confined ideas about spectatorship to uncovering ideological complicity in the narrative construction of popular films, while describing cinema spectatorship technically as a process of unconscious enthrallment, drawing on inherently reactionary and regressive psychological states. Although aspects of this critique were (and remain) valuable, I felt it also led to a lack of curiosity about the range of film practices throughout film history (in popular as well as avant-garde work) and the sorts of spectatorial activities they cued. This monolithic description encouraged film students to hold a complacent sense of their own superiority in relation to the bulk of film practices. The work of Sergei Eisenstein, both as theorist and as filmmaker, presented an alternative: an excitement about the (then) new possibilities of cinema deriving from the Utopian confluence of modernist practice and political revolution that Russian Constructivism had allowed, combined with a concerted critique, both ideological and formal, of dominant practices. The 1970s had also witnessed a rediscovery of Soviet modernism, and I was fortunate to have taken courses with Annette Michelson at NYU that revealed the possibilities contained in this legacy. The concept of the attraction captured the potential energy of cinema's address to the spectator.

Our discussions with Gaudreault at Harvard and, over the next months, the passing back and forth and revising of drafts of our lecture, led to the formulation of early cinema as a "system of monstrative attractions" given in the Cerisy lecture (which Gaudreault had to deliver without me, partly because I was finally finishing my dissertation on D.W. Griffith at Biograph). However, I prepared my own statement of the concept for the Film and Video Conference at Ohio University in the fall of 1985. With some revision this paper was published in the journal *Wide Angle* and in its final form in the anthology *Early Cinema: Space Frame Narrative* edited by Thomas Elsaesser.[2] It is this slightly longer version that constitutes the final version of my essay. In the next few years I developed the concept in several other essays, primary among them: "An Aesthetic of Astonishment: Early Film and the (In)Credulous Spectator," *Art and Text* (Fall 1989); "'Now You See it, Now You Don't': The Temporality of the Cinema of Attractions," *Velvet Light Trap* 32 (Fall 1993); and "The Whole Town's Gawking: Early Cinema and the Visual Experience of Modernity," *Yale Journal of Criticism* 7.2 (Fall 1994).

Returning to the genealogy of the term, other progenitors than Gaudreault, Simon and I must be mentioned. Donald Crafton's powerful essay on slapstick comedy, "Pie and Chase" which he delivered in the spring of 1985 at the FIAF Slapstick Symposium, which I attended, also drew on Eisenstein's concept. Crafton described gags in slapstick comedy as "attractions" which often intrude on narrative development, and, as Crafton emphasized in his article, do not necessarily strive to become integrated into narrative structures. Although in the published version of his essay, Crafton refers to my "Cinema of Attractions" essay, his original presentation predated my publication and, in fact, discussions with Crafton influenced my own evolution of the term.[3] Therefore Crafton's simultaneous use of the term attraction played a very conscious role in my thinking. In contrast, it was only some years after having published my original article that I recalled Ben Brewster had also used the term in his important essay "A Scene at the Movies" published in *Screen* in 1982. At one point, discussing the role of the early close-up point of view structure in GRANDMA'S READING GLASS (1900), Brewster described it as the "pleasure point of the film, its attraction."[4] This observation very much paralleled – and indeed anticipated – my point that close-ups in early films, such as the shot of the lady's ankle in THE GAY SHOE CLERK (1903), operated not only as narrative punctuation (and therefore an anticipation of classical construction), but, equally importantly, provided a dose of visual pleasure in the act of display that visual enlargement facilitated and underscored.[5] I must add, contra Warren Buckland's reference to Musser in his essay in this anthology, that I still maintain this should be evident for any one who actually watches the film. On re-reading Brewster's article some years after I wrote mine, I realized I had not consciously remembered his use of this term. However, when I apologized to him for not acknowledging his use of "attraction" before mine, he paused and recalled that the term had not really been his first choice for the passage, but an amendment suggested by an editor.

A historiographic essay on the cinema of attractions (from, of course, an individual perspective) must include cultural geography. In the late 1970s a number of influences converged to produce the re-evaluation of early cinema and New York City, at least initially, formed the epicenter. The Museum of Modern Art with its outstanding archive of early films (especially American films by Edison and Biograph) provided material that opened up possibilities of rediscovery and re-evaluation, possibilities galvanized by the creative curatorship of the extraordinary Eileen Bowser. Along with David Francis of the National Film and Television Archive of the British Film Institute, Bowser had conceived of the FIAF Brighton Project and held extensive screening at MoMA in New York City to prepare for the event in 1978. Attended by, among others, Charles Musser, André Gaudreault, Russell Merritt, Jay Leyda, John Gartenberg and Paul Spehr (who brought the treasures of the Library of Congress' Paper Film Collection, perhaps the largest proportion of films), not only looked at the films, but also argued and exchanged ideas for a week. In the Seventies New York City had also produced an extraordinary school of avant-garde filmmakers, especially the unofficially named "Chambers Street Group" of Ernie Gehr, Hollis Frampton, and Ken Jacobs. Each of these filmmakers not only looked carefully at films from the period of early cinema, but incorporated them into their own works, often mining the Library of Congress' Paper Film Collection, as in Jacobs's TOM, TOM, THE PIPER'S SON (1969) and Frampton's PUBLIC DOMAIN (1972). Speaking personally, the influence of the fresh perspective on early cinema opened up by these filmmakers played a key role in not only refocusing my attention on this period, but re-contextualizing the films, liberating them from the teleological approach that classed them as "primitive" attempts at later forms. Finally, during this period Jay Leyda taught seminars in film history at New York University, including his seminars on Griffith's Biograph films, inspiring a number of young film scholars to rethink early American cinema.

It would be extremely ungenerous and unhistorical not to immediately acknowledge the influence of Noël Burch on my own approach to early cinema, an intellectual and critical influence of the highest order. Burch in his peripatetic career in the 1970s and 80s, moved between London, Paris, and New York City (as well as Columbus Ohio!), and taught at New York University where his lectures on early cinema had a strong influence on my work. I was already immersed in this period from my dissertation research and work with Leyda, but Burch's sense of the alterity of these early films penetrated deeply into my viewing of them. Burch then participated in the Brighton screenings and conference, bringing his work on Edwin Porter to its published form.[6] While deeply influenced by his lectures and writings, I think Burch would be the first to find differences in our approaches. While frequently emphasizing the difference between early film and later practices, Burch actually saw these films as fundamentally expressing the Urform of classical spectatorship, exposing some of the contradictions or impulses that became less evident later on, but participating in the same meta-psychology. Thus Burch's film CORRECTION, PLEASE OR HOW WE GOT INTO PICTURES (1979) used early films to indicate the roots of the processes of a fundamentally ideological construction of spectatorship. I do not think I would claim Burch's position to be in error, but I chose rather to stress the ways in which early cinema represented a much more polymorphous stage in which the potential for a variety of developments lay.

My essay written for the Brighton Project, "The Non-Continuous Style of Early Film," tried to express the radical alterity the fictional films made between 1900 and 1906 displayed from the development of Hollywood cinema's narrative form, and even from the one reel films that Griffith had produced for the Biograph Company starting in 1908, which formed the core of my doctoral research.[7] Although I still believe that my Brighton essay describes that alterity accurately, I felt dissatisfied with using a negative characterization ("non-continuous") for an important aspect of film development (very much like the equally unsatisfactory, but frequently used, terms "pre-classical" or "non-classical"). I felt I had to penetrate more deeply into what these early films were doing, analyzing them as intentional objects. The emphasis that 1970s theory had placed on spectatorship aided me enormously here, especially the feminist work of Laura Mulvey and others that opened up issues of spectatorship in terms of gender. My own attraction to Mulvey's classic essay "Visual Pleasure and Narrative Cinema"[8] lay less in its use of a Lacanian meta-psychology than in its more revolutionary (for me) thesis that spectatorship may not be determined by the nature of the cinematic apparatus (as Baudry claimed), but also shaped by its relation to filmic modes, such as spectacle and narrative. In short, Mulvey showed that spectatorship itself included possibilities of difference. If a gendered spectator had to be considered, then isn't a historical spectator also in need of discussion? Early films of the sort that had attracted my attention at Brighton, with their lack of integration of images into a continual narrative structure, addressed their spectators differently than films that created a strong sense of diegesis. Such early films managed rhetoric of display for the viewer rather than fashioning a process of narration and absorption.

Opposition or contrast between narrative and spectacle frequently re-appeared, of course, in discussions of film form throughout the 1970s and early 80s. Whereas Mulvey's essay presents its most famous and sophisticated version, the 1982 article on this opposition by Lea Jacobs and the late Richard DeCordova provides one of the most thorough treatments of this issue.[9] However, the most important predecessors in the use of the term "attraction," as Gaudreault points out in his essay in this volume, came from the showmen and filmmakers of the early era. I knew, of course, that Eisenstein had taken the term from the fairground and circus, and from the realm of popular entertainments, generally. I only gradually realized how widespread its use had been, usually referring to something close to my definition – the ability of a novel display to attract gawkers and spectators. Not the least of the virtues I feel the concept and term "attraction" carries is that it names (even if, as a theoretical and analytical term, it does not simply duplicate) a concept that would not be foreign to the practitioners of the era. I do not mean to claim this as a requirement for analytical concepts, which would limit our methods unduly. But I think it enhances the historical valiancy of the term.

Should the term "cinema of attractions" replace the term "early cinema," whose awkward French translation somewhat cued the first discussions that Gaudreault and I had? To my mind, it should not, although hopefully it does shape how we think about cinema's first decade. "Early Cinema" best describes a period basically encompassing the first decade of cinema, although arguably it could be extended (as in the time expanse of Domitor, the organization dedicated to the study of "Early Cinema") until World War I and the rise of the classical paradigm. This period by no means forms a monolithic era, and Musser's argument for the first years of cinema (perhaps as short a time as the period before 1900) as a unique "novelty period" makes a lot of sense. Enormous transformations in cinema occur during the years between the novelty period and the establishment of the classical paradigm in the late 1910s. Rather than naming a specific period as "the cinema of attractions," I use the term to refer to an approach to spectatorship that I felt *dominated* early cinema from the novelty period until the dominance of longer narrative films, around 1906-07. I will not rehearse my arguments for the dates here, but I do want to emphasize my use of the term "dominant" taken from the Russian Formalists.[10] The "dominant," far from indicating an exclusion of other aspects, describes a dynamic interplay between factors. The drive towards display, rather than creation of a fictional world; a tendency towards punctual temporality, rather than extended development; a lack of interest in character "psychology" or the development of motivation; and a direct, often marked, address to the spectator at the expense of the creation of a diegetic coherence, are attributes that define attractions, along with its power of "attraction," its ability to be attention-grabbing (usually by being exotic, unusual, unexpected, novel). In contrast to what I feel are hasty readings of my essay, I never claimed that attractions were the only aspect of early cinema, although I claim they do dominate the period, first numerically (the large number of films of vaudeville acts – including dances, acrobatic feats, and song numbers; trick films; tourist views; urban scenes; records of processions, and other public events). Secondly, attractions tend to dominate even those films which also involve narrative, detouring their energies from storytelling to display, either by including outright attractions (the outlaw Barnes firing his six shooter at the camera in THE GREAT TRAIN ROBBERY [1903]) in a "non-continual" fashion that interrupts narrative coherence, or, as in Méliès's more extended story films, structuring the action around a succession of attractions, with, as Méliès himself described it, the story serving basically as a pretext to move us through a scenography of spectacle and display.

Thus, rather than seeing attractions as simply a form of counter-narrative, I have proposed them as a different configuration of spectatorial involvement, an address that can, in fact, interact in complex and varied ways with other forms of involvement. I would therefore not deny Charles Musser's contention that narrative appears very early in film history.[11] I would agree that some impulse toward storytelling exists from the beginning of cinema, but I feel it does not dominate most films, rarely serving as the primary form in integrating their images until later (whether around 1903 as Musser would claim or 1906 as I see it). However, the role of gags or visual pranks in early cinema, which one could claim provides the first film narratives (such as Lumière's L'ARROSEUR ARROSÉ [1895]), does complicate things. With their self-contained, sudden, laughter-inducing incidents of surprise and disaster, gags exemplify attractions for Crafton (and it would seem this would very much correspond to Eisenstein's clown-inspired scenography of the montage of attractions). I tend to agree, but would also grant that the gag's temporal structure of anticipation and eventual payoff, also resembles a mini-narrative. Although it sounds perhaps too much like a mechanical compromise, I tend to class gags as a midpoint, even a relay, between attractions and narrative. The gag seems to me to pose a more important aspect of the narrative form of early cinema than Musser's claims about the presentation of early film with exhibitor supplied supplements.[12] In fact Musser's important work on exhibition strategies contributed greatly to my sense of a cinema of attractions. The role of the lecturer, outside the film, situated between the screen and the audience, explicating and mediating their relation, typifies the different sort of spectatorial involvement practiced in early cinema compared to the self-contained forms of later narrative films. Further, the commentary provided by early film lecturers, although often difficult to reconstruct, does not seem in all (or even most) cases to supply a story for the viewer to follow. Existing accounts of film lecturers indicate that frequently they served as monstrators as much as narrators, directing spectators' attention to points of interest, or as in Albert E. Smith's lecture for the film THE BLACK DIAMOND EXPRESS (1896), cueing and preparing the audience response to a powerful attraction.[13] Clearly many of Musser's points about the impulse to narrative in early film must be granted, but this does not necessarily eliminate the role of attractions. The close-up of the ankle in THE GAY SHOE CLERK certainly plays the narrative role of focusing attention on a motivating detail. But it also serves the role of reveling in the voyeuristic pleasure (of the audience as well as the shoe salesman) in visual display. Whether audiences were mainly amazed by the sets, costumes and camera tricks of LE VOYAGE DANS LA LUNE (1902), or primarily drawn into its narrative of exploration and discovery, can never be absolutely adjudicated. Both undoubtedly played a role and it is the relation between the two aspects that makes up the complex and multi-faceted process of early film spectatorship.

I proposed the cinema of attractions as a tool for critical analysis of early films and as a means of describing the differences between various periods of film history. Its value lies ultimately in how it opens up films and generates discussion, in a historically specific and analytically detailed manner, of the nature of film spectatorship. Disagreements undoubtedly will continue about how to resolve these discussions, but I think the concept of attractions continues to serve us well in keeping these discussions going.

Notes

1. André Gaudreault and Tom Gunning, "Le cinéma des premiers temps: un défi à l'histoire du cinéma?," *Histoire du cinéma. Nouvelles approches*, ed. Jacques Aumont, André Gaudreault and Michel Marie (Paris: Sorbonne, 1989) 49-63.

2. Tom Gunning, "The Cinema of Attractions: Early Film, Its Spectator and the Avant-Garde," *Early Cinema: Space Frame Narrative*, ed. Thomas Elsaesser (London: British Film Institute, 1990) 56-62.

3. Donald Crafton, "Pie and Chase: Gag, Spectacle and Narrative in Slapstick Comedy," *The Slapstick Symposium*, ed. Eileen Bowser (Bruxelles: FIAF, 1988) 49-59; reprinted in the dossier of this volume. Crafton's article and my own response were also published in the AFI anthology *Classical Hollywood Comedy*, ed. Kristine Brunovska Karnick and Henry Jenkins (New York: Routledge, 1995) 106-122.

4. Ben Brewster, "A Scene at the 'Movies,'" *Screen* 23.2 (July-August 1982): 7. Also in *Early Cinema: Space Frame Narrative* 320.

5. As Wanda Strauven has pointed out to me, this is especially true since the shot is not the POV of the male character in the film, but the POV of the spectator outside the film. Ben Brewster makes a similar point in his essay "A Scene at the 'Movies'" (320), contrasting the shot with the point of view shot in AS SEEN THROUGH THE TELESCOPE.

6. Noël Burch, "Porter or Ambivalence," *Screen* 19.4 (Winter 1978-79): 91-105.

7. Tom Gunning, "The Non-Continuous Style of Early Film (1900-1906)," *Cinema 1900-1906: An Analytical Study*, ed. Roger Holman (Bruxelles: FIAF, 1982) 219-30.

8. Laura Mulvey, "Visual Pleasure and Narrative Cinema," *Screen* 16.3 (1975): 6-18.

9. Lea Jacobs and Richard DeCordova, "Spectacle and Narrative Theory," *Quarterly Review of Film and Video* 7.4 (1982): 293-307.

10. See the discussion of the dominant in Roman Jakobson, "The Dominant," *Readings in Russian Poetics: Formalist and Structuralist Views*, ed. Ladislav Matejka and Krystyna Pomorska (Cambridge: MIT P, 1971). Different Formalists had slightly different

definitions of the dominant. The term is also used by Bordwell and Thompson during their "neo-Formalist" period, but Bordwell at least has indicated his current dissatisfaction with the concept.

11. Charles Musser, "Rethinking Early Cinema: Cinema of Attractions and Narrativity," *Yale Journal of Criticism* 7.2 (Fall 1994): 203-32. Reprinted in the dossier of this volume.

12. Musser 214-15.

13. Albert Smith, *Two Reels and a Crank* (Garden City: Doubleday, 1952) 39. On the role of the lecturer, as mediator of the attraction, see also the contribution by Germain Lacasse in this volume.

A Rational Reconstruction of "The Cinema of Attractions"

Warren Buckland

> One thing that one can do with a theory when it confronts empirical or
> conceptual difficulties is to engage in a process of constantly recasting it in a
> wide variety of reformulations. By rearranging the theory's structural parts
> in numerous ways, and constantly reorganizing the theory in terms of a
> variety of possible alternative fundamental principles, one can hope to gain
> new insight into the internal structure of a theory.[1]

In this chapter I aim to rationally reconstruct (in the sense defined by Sklar
above) the conceptual structure of, and assumptions underlying, Tom Gunning's essay "The Cinema of Attractions." I use Rudolf Botha's philosophical
study into the conduct of inquiry to analyze the way Gunning formulates conceptual and empirical problems and how he deproblematizes them.[2] In terms of
my reconstruction strategies, I shall rearrange the parts of Gunning's essay according to the four central activities Botha identifies in the formulation of theoretical problems: (1) Analyzing the problematic state of affairs; (2) Describing
the problematic state of affairs; (3) Constructing problems; and (4) Evaluating
problems with regard to well-formedness and significance. Although a contribution to film history, Gunning's essay is amenable to this type of analysis because it is theoretically-informed, and clearly constitutes problem-driven research that attempts to understand and explain – rather than simply describe –
a temporal sequence of historical events pertaining to early cinema.

Before introducing these four activities and systematically recasting Gunning's essay in terms of them, I shall briefly review a number of essays Gunning
wrote prior to "The Cinema of Attractions."

From Non-Continuity to Attractions

After watching over 500 fiction films from the 1900-1906 period at the Brighton
Symposium in 1978, Gunning initially systematized his experiences under the
cinematic concept of "non-continuity."[3] A non-continuous cinema "maintains

the separateness of its component parts, instead of absorbing them into an illusion of a continuous narrative flow."[4] Each shot is a complete unit in itself, and no attempt is made to integrate it into other shots to create a synthetic unity from the individual shots. Gunning lists seven characteristics of the non-continuity style (some of which reappear in his definition of the attraction),[5] and relates it to the popular arts of the time (comic strips, magic lanterns, and vaudeville). The term "non-continuity" is a forerunner to "attraction," and Gunning abandoned the first in favor of the second because "non-continuity" is a negative characterization of early cinema (it presupposes narrative coherence to be the prescriptive norm from which early cinema deviates), whereas "attraction" is a positive designation of early cinema's qualities (it is judged in its own terms as a distinct aesthetic system).[6] In 1978 we therefore witness Gunning formulating the concept of "attraction" under a different name, and comparing it to the popular arts. He makes no attempt at this stage to link early cinema to the avant-garde.

In 1984 Gunning expanded his study of non-continuity by identifying it as a "genre" of early cinema and by sketching out three other "genres": single shot films (which are complete in themselves); cinema of continuity (in which fragmented shots are linked together by a continuity of action from shot to shot); and cinema of discontinuity (exemplified by the use of parallel editing, which specifies the spatial and temporal relations between shots).[7] Gunning presents these genres as a straightforward historical progression, from single shots to non-continuity, continuity and finally discontinuity. His systematization of his own data therefore remains basic. However, I think his precise delineation of the four genres can be symbolized in a more rigorous fashion – in terms of A.J. Greimas's semiotic square.[8] The four corners – and the three relations established between them (opposite, contrary and imply) – represent the necessary logical possibilities and intelligibility of phenomena:

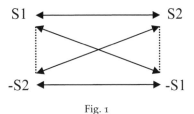

Fig. 1

The semiotic square consists of "a correlation between two pairs of opposed terms."[9] S1 and S2 are the first two opposed terms, while -S2 and -S1 are the second two opposed terms. When linked together, the two oppositions form additional relations – of implication and contradiction. S1 becomes the unmarked positive of the four terms. As well as being the opposite of S2, it is the contrary of -S1, while -S2 is implied by S1. Each term can be described in the same way – according to the term it opposes, contradicts, and implies.

Gunning's four genres fit into this model because all three relations rigorously hold up between them:

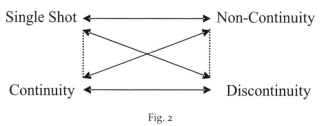

Fig. 2

The single shot is the unmarked positive term because it is the most basic unit (as it preserves spatial-temporal unity). The single shot therefore implies the concept of continuity, which can be slotted into the -S2 position. The single shot is the opposite of non-continuity (which therefore occupies the S2 position), because non-continuity creates a noticeable disruption in spatial-temporal unity. The single shot is the contrary of discontinuity, which also disrupts spatial-temporal unity by cutting between two spaces (as in parallel editing). But rather than creating a noticeable disruption, discontinuity can be used to create suspense. Similarly, we can start with any other term in the square and define its three relations. For example, discontinuity is the opposite of continuity; it is the contrary of the single shot; and it implies non-continuity, and so on.

At the very beginning and ending of his 1984 essay, Gunning mentions that his research into early cinema links up to his interest in avant-garde filmmaking. But he does not explore this link in this essay. Instead, he refers the reader to his earlier paper written in 1979: "An Unseen Energy Swallows Space."[10]

In this 1979 essay Gunning cautiously explores historical and conceptual links between early cinema and the avant-garde. He begins by noting that the impetus for the comparison comes from the American avant-garde filmmakers themselves, some of whom (Ken Jacobs, Ernie Gehr, Hollis Frampton) directly use early cinema techniques in their films. He also adds a personal note by saying that it is by watching avant-garde films that he came to appreciate early cinema as a distinct aesthetic practice. He then presents, via three case studies, reasons for accepting the links between early cinema and the avant-garde. His reasons are as follows: both create a contradictory space via multiple superimpositions (Méliès on the one hand, Deren and Brakhage on the other); both involve an acknowledgment of the spectator via the view of the camera; and both are known to explore space via the panoramic shot.

Gunning begins to generalize by referring to the way both types of cinema construct space and address the spectator in a manner different to classical filmmaking. He initially introduced the concept of attraction into this discussion in collaboration with André Gaudreault, in their joint 1985 conference paper "Le cinéma des premiers temps: un défi à l'histoire du cinéma?"[11] Developing the concept of attraction from Eisenstein, the authors distinguish "the system of monstrative attractions" (1895-1908) from "the system of narrative integration" (1909-1914). Gunning subsequently refined both concepts in his famous paper "The Cinema of Attraction" published in 1986.

The Cinema of Attractions

1. *Analyzing the problematic state of affairs.* Under this first heading we need to understand the problematic state of affairs Gunning addresses in "The Cinema of Attractions."[12] We shall investigate: What is problematic; isolate each component of the problematic state of affairs; determine how they are interrelated; and identify background assumptions.

From all the multitude of problematic aspects pertaining to early cinema, Gunning extracts one in order to simplify and delimit his research. In addressing this primary problematic state of affairs, he inevitably feels the need to address secondary ones. He formulates his primary problematic at the end of his essay's opening paragraph:

> Its [early cinema's] inspiration for the avant-garde of the early decades of this [the twentieth] century needs to be re-explored. (1986: 64/1990: 56) [problematic 1]

He uses the concept of the attraction to re-explore the relation between early cinema and the avant-garde. As we shall see, the concept of attraction has conceptual, psychological and explanatory import. In regard to explanation, Gunning attempts to demonstrate the generalizable nature of the concept of attraction: that is, it does not only apply to a few scattered examples, but is a general characteristic of early cinema and the avant-garde. It therefore has predictive capacity and can be tested and justified.[13] One of the key issues in evaluating the well-formedness and significance of the concept of attraction is whether Gunning has over-extended its range of applicability.

A secondary problematic state of affairs Gunning addresses involves periodization. He notices

> the strangely heterogeneous relation that film before 1906 (or so) bears to films that follow. (64/56) [problematic 2]

He thereby identifies 1906 as a crucial date in film's historical development. By calling this relation "strangely heterogeneous," he clearly identifies it as a problematic that needs to be addressed and solved.

This heterogeneity also exposes another (secondary) problematic that he addresses:

> The history of early cinema, like the history of cinema generally, has been written and theorized under the hegemony of narrative films. (64/56) [problematic 3]

The problematic Gunning addresses here is therefore the *hegemony* of film history, which relates all films positively or negatively to the monolith of narrative, as opposed to the *heterogeneity* of the actual relation between the films.

Now that we have identified what is problematic for Gunning and isolated each one (problematic 1, 2, and 3), we can begin to see how they are interrelated. Gunning uses the primary problematic (the link between early cinema and the avant-garde) to address and solve problematics 2 and 3 (periodization and heterogeneity/hegemony). The as-yet unstated concept of the attraction is the gel that binds together and solves these problematics.

Gunning isolates and lists the primary components of problematic 1 in the essay's sub-title: "Early Film, Its Spectator, and the Avant-Garde." These terms, simply organized as a list,[14] are brought together under the umbrella of the essay's title: "The Cinema of Attraction(s)." He does not discuss his four primary components – early film, its spectator, the avant-garde, and attractions – all at once. Instead, he begins with early cinema, before offering his initial definition of the cinema of attractions – a cinema of display, or exhibitionism, which naturally leads to a characterization of the spectator address implied by exhibitionism (an acknowledged spectator, in opposition to the unseen voyeur), before returning to the term "attractions" and fleshing out its definition: the term derives from Eisenstein (and his avant-garde theater and film practices), who in turn borrows it from the circus and the fairground – especially the fairground attraction and its sensual and psychological impact. Gunning ends by mentioning the cinema of "narrative integration," which does not simply replace the cinema of attractions, but absorbs it, as can be seen in some mainstream genres such as musicals, as well as contemporary blockbusters.[15] Rather than set up a relation of opposition between early and narrative cinema, Gunning establishes a relation of inclusion (before 1906 early cinema existed by itself; thereafter it becomes a subset of narrative cinema).

Determining how the primary components simply listed in the sub-title are conceptually and historically related is one of the principal aims of the essay – especially the relation between early cinema and its "inspiration" for avant-garde film movements (French Impressionism, Surrealism, German Expressionist, Soviet montage school, the American avant-garde). Gunning's use of the verb "inspire" is relevant here for understanding this interrelation: it literally means to breathe air into something. More generally, it means a procedure of internalizing (air) to give something life, or to animate it. By using "inspire" to relate early cinema to the avant-garde, Gunning is implying that the avant-garde internalized early cinema, which in turn animated the avant-garde.

This latter assumption can be located in Gunning's opening lines, where he quotes Fernand Léger praising the *montage court* in the first three sections of Abel Gance's LA ROUE (1922), a renowned avant-garde film from the French Impressionist movement. Gunning begins from Léger's background assumptions concerning the uniqueness of cinema in general, based on his reaction to an individual film. Léger's praise is governed by the specificity thesis, in which he locates film's specificity in its unique ability to harness the act of pure vision, of "making images seen."[16]

Noël Carroll identifies the specificity thesis as a prescriptive rather than de-scriptive theory with two components: "One component is the idea that there is something that each medium does best. The other is that each of the arts should do what differentiates it from the other arts."[17] Theorists and critics who uphold the specificity thesis therefore encourage filmmakers to identify and then ex-ploit film's essential defining qualities. The specificity thesis, therefore, is not only prescriptive, but also essentialist. Léger praises LA ROUE because it exploits what he considers to be the specific qualities of film.

Aware of the pitfalls of the specificity thesis, Gunning chooses his words care-fully to align himself with Léger. Gunning writes: "I want to *use* it [the specifi-city thesis]" (64/56; emphasis added). He therefore suggests he will employ the specificity thesis merely in an instrumentalist fashion; he will observe its habi-tual way of thinking without fully committing himself to it as a means to ex-plore his problematic states of affairs. Gunning therefore "uses" the specificity thesis (at a distance) when he writes immediately before formulating proble-matic number 1: "It is precisely this harnessing of visibility, this act of showing and exhibition which I feel cinema before 1906 displays most intensely" (63-4/56). Cinema's specificity, according to Gunning, lies in its "act of showing and exhibition," and early cinema and the avant-garde exploit this specificity.

Gunning's use of the word "inspire" also identifies two of his background assumptions: that early cinema did not simply die out after 1906, but became integrated into both narrative film and the avant-garde, and breathed life into them. This in turn leads to another background assumption: that cinema was borne out of a modernist aesthetic and mode of experience (an assumption he downplays in correspondence with David Bordwell, as we shall see below).

In summary, although Gunning delimits his argument to cinema before 1906, he implies that showing and exhibition are film's specific qualities, and that early cinema is special because it exploits this specific quality of film in an unadulterated form. Film after 1906 becomes enslaved to narrative, although it occasionally acknowledges its specificity in musicals, prolonged action sequences, or other moments of spectacle.

2. *Describing the problematic state of affairs*. This stage involves the accurate recording and formal description of each element of the problematic state of affairs. Under this second section heading we shall discuss how Gunning's essay records and formally describes the problematic state of affairs identified in the previous section. Describing involves collecting data, systematizing it, and symbolizing the results.

Collecting data. Gunning collects a total of 9 primary film examples (all are analyzed only briefly): La Roue (Gance, 1922), Le Voyage dans la lune (Méliès, 1902), The Bride Retires (France, 1902), The Gay Shoe Clerk (Porter, 1903), Photographing a Female Crook (Biograph, 1904), Hooligan in Jail (Biograph, 1903), Personal (Biograph, 1904), How a French Nobleman Got a Wife Through the New York Herald Personal Columns (Edison, 1904), and Ben Hur (1924). He also mentions the names of other filmmakers: Lumière, G.A. Smith, Griffith, Eisenstein, Keaton, and Jack Smith, plus a few films in passing (without discussing them): Le Déjeuner de bébé, The Black Diamond Express, and Un Chien andalou.

Systematizing data. One of the key innovative (and contentious) aspects of Gunning's essay is the way he uses classification to organize his data. His conceptual distinction between attraction/narrative enables him to rewrite the history of early cinema, by positing a break in its periodization (occurring around 1906), rather than its continuous linear teleological development towards narrative. This break defines early (pre-1906) cinema positively, by identifying it as a distinct unified practice with its own rules and conventions, rather than (as in the standard – continuous and linear – film history) negatively, as merely an imperfect narrative cinema.

Yet, while standard film history is predominately written under the aegis of narrative, it does, of course, posit a heterogeneous, discontinuous history – usually summed up as the opposition Lumière vs. Méliès (in which Lumière films are defined negatively, as non-narrative, rather than positively). What Gunning actually does is not replace a hegemonic film history with a heterogeneous one; instead, he replaces one heterogeneous history (albeit defined as narrative/non-narrative) with another more authentic heterogeneous history, in which the heterogeneity is located elsewhere. His heterogeneous history radically posits a homogeneous relation between Lumière and Méliès while locating heterogeneity between the cinema of attractions (before 1906) and cinema of narrative integration (after 1906). He unites Lumière and Méliès under the banner of the attraction:

Whatever differences one might find between Lumière and Méliès, they should not represent the opposition between narrative and non-narrative filmmaking, at least as it is understood today. Rather, one can unite them in a conception that sees cinema less as a way of telling stories than a way of presenting a series of views to an audience. (64/57)

Both Lumière and Méliès addressed spectators in the same way by presenting them with attractions. Gunning revises standard film history (which frames Méliès as a proto-narrative filmmaker), by arguing that, for Méliès, narrative is only a pretext for stringing together a series of attractions: "the trick film [...] is itself a series of displays, of magical attractions, rather than a primitive sketch of narrative continuity" (65/57-8).[18] Gunning even quotes Méliès making a statement to this effect (64/57).

Symbolizing the results. It is rare for humanities scholars to formally symbolize their results. Film historians occasionally use a timeline to symbolize film history and its various stages. Gunning simply makes his new film history timeline implicit in his statements that systematize his data.

3. *Constructing problems.* The researcher uses concepts to deproblematize the problematic state of affairs. Constructing problems involves: phenomenological concepts (factual data about problematic states of affairs); filmic concepts (background assumptions concerning the nature of individual films); cinematic concepts (background assumptions concerning the general nature of film); and metatheoretical concepts (reflections on the aims and nature of theoretical inquiry). It is in constructing problems that the concept of the attraction comes into play. The "attraction" is primarily a cinematic concept, concerning the general nature of film. Gunning's focus therefore falls on the cinematic, although he also uses phenomenological and metatheoretical concepts. Because he is not analyzing individual films per se, the filmic plays a negligible role in the essay.

Phenomenological concepts. Gunning challenges the intuitions of standard film historians and those who accept their histories as empirically sound. He reinterprets the same data used by traditional film historians and puts them under a different classification.

Cinematic concepts. We have already seen that Gunning inherits Léger's background assumptions concerning the nature of film in general (based on Léger's reaction to an individual film, Gance's LA ROUE): Léger locates film's specificity in its "act of showing and exhibition." Following Léger, Gunning implies that showing and exhibition are film's specific qualities, and that early cinema exploits this specific quality of film. Gunning labels this quality an "attraction," a cinematic concept that aims to deproblematize the primary problematic he addresses in his essay – early cinema's inspiration for the avant-garde – for the concept of attraction names the common feature they share.

But the concept of the attraction is not sufficient in itself to link early cinema to the avant-garde. To make the link viable, Gunning introduces a concept familiar to the modern or "contemporary film theory" of the 1970s: the abstract concept of the subject (or spectator) position. The contemporary film theorists defined the classical narrative film as a realist discourse that attempts to construct an illusory, coherent subject position – a voyeuristic position where meaning is realized. They then defined avant-garde and modernist film as a discourse that deconstructs meaning, narrative, and the illusory, coherent subject position through reflexive practices that foreground film's materiality.

It is the spectator's role in the equation that really holds the key to the relation between early cinema and the avant-garde. More specifically, Gunning introduces the concept of the deconstructed "spectator position" to link early cinema and the avant-garde. In the cinema of attractions, the spectator is not positioned as a voyeur absorbed into and spying on a self-enclosed narrative world; instead, it is exhibitionist, knowingly/reflexively addressing the spectator and providing him or her with a series of views.

Gunning then acknowledges the origin of the term, in Eisenstein's theatrical and filmic work, which fleshes out the desired impact of attractions on the audience:

> In his search for the "unit of impression" of theatrical art, the foundation of an analysis which would undermine realistic representational theater, Eisenstein hit upon the term "attraction." An attraction aggressively subjected the spectator to "sensual or psychological impact" [Eisenstein]. According to Eisenstein, theater should consist of a montage of such attractions, creating a relation to the spectator entirely different from the absorption in "illusory imitativeness" [Eisenstein]. (66/59)

Eisenstein is precise about the spectator effect an attraction should create: an attraction employs shock as an aesthetic and political strategy, an assault on the senses that also changes the audience's political consciousness. In fact, his theory is premised on the attraction's impact: adhering to a basic tenet of Constructivist art,[19] he argues that one cannot separate out attraction and its impact on the spectator. This in turn became the principle behind his montage theory, in which the juxtaposition of two attractions creates a third meaning, which is not contained in the attractions themselves but is actively constructed by the spectator (who is nonetheless strongly guided by the film).

The origin of the term "attraction" does not end with Eisenstein. Gunning reminds us that Eisenstein in turn borrows it from the circus – from fairground attraction, the mass form of entertainment that delivers a sensual and psychological impact (66/59). And it is, finally, in this impact created by a mass art form that Gunning presents arguments that address his main problematic – the relation between early cinema (the cinema of attractions) and the avant-garde. If early cinema can be defined as a cinema of attractions, then it is precisely this "exhibitionist confrontation rather than diegetic absorption" offered by both early cinema and the avant-garde that links the two together: "I believe that it was precisely the exhibitionist quality of turn of the century popular art that made it attractive to the avant-garde" (66/59). An attraction is non-illusionistic, non-deceptive, and non-voyeuristic.[20] Instead, it declares its intentions; it is exhibitionistic and aims to astonish rather than deceive.

Less dramatically, the concept of attraction also aims to solve Gunning's second and third problematics, of periodization and hegemony, because it is the demise of the attraction and the rise of narrative that creates "the strangely heterogeneous relation that film before 1906 (or so) bears to films that follow" (64/56).

In the same way, the concept of the attraction aims to unite Lumière and Méliès (and, more generally, the oppositions between formalism/realism, and documentary/fiction), thereby overturning their opposition as posited in standard histories and theories of film.

We have already seen that, for Gunning, early cinema did not simply die out after 1906, but became integrated into both narrative film and the avant-garde, and breathed life into them. This is one of his general background assumptions concerning the nature of film.

Metatheoretical concepts. Gunning makes four metatheoretical statements (reflections on the aims and nature of theoretical inquiry): 1) The history of cinema has been written under the hegemony of narrative (64/56); 2) By studying early cinema in the context of the archive and academy, we risk missing its vital relation to vaudeville, its original context of reception (66/59-60); 3) In positing a periodization that includes the cinema of attractions and cinema of narrative integration, Gunning points out that "it would be too easy to see this as a Cain and Abel story, with narrative strangling the nascent possibilities of a young iconoclastic form of entertainment" (68/60); 4) In a similar vein, he urges the reader not to conceive the cinema of attractions as a truly oppositional (avant-garde) program. "This view," he writes, "is too sentimental and too a-historical." (70/61)

The first two statements point to the problems of assuming that cinema was borne into a narrative tradition, and that studying the films in isolation from their original context of reception downplays their function as an attraction. (Charles Musser criticizes Gunning for not taking this far enough – he accuses him of only developing a textual analysis of the films shown in vaudeville, which downplays the lecturer's role of narrativizing the images on screen.[21]) The third statement avoids the simple logical inversion of the relation between attraction and narrative; instead Gunning implies the relation between them is more complex than a binary logic of opposition allows. The fourth statement similarly downplays the temptation to politicize early cinema as a negative, critical practice.

4. *Evaluating problems with regard to well-formedness and significance.* Finally, under this heading we shall investigate: the well-formedness of problems (whether they are solvable, based on correct assumptions, or clearly formulated); and the significance of problems (which expand our existing knowledge of film).

I pointed out above that one of the key issues in evaluating the concept of attraction is whether Gunning over-extends its applicability. All research that goes beyond mere description of data necessarily makes generalizations and relies on implicit assumptions, but such generalizations and assumptions need to be critically evaluated.

Problematic 1. Has Gunning clearly formulated and successfully solved his first problematic (re-exploring the relation between early cinema and the avant-garde by means of the concept of attraction)? And is it based on correct assumptions? Can early cinema (Lumière and Méliès), the avant-gardes (French Impressionism, German Expressionism, Soviet montage, Surrealism, the American avant-garde), as well as vaudeville, circuses and fairgrounds, and contemporary Hollywood blockbusters, really be discussed under the same concept? Is the concept of attraction not being stretched too far? This problematic raises two issues: (1) The uneasy relation between pre-classical and post-classical narrative cinema; (2) The thorny cultural generalization that early cinema and the avant-garde "expressed" the visual experience of modernity.

I shall address (1) below. In relation to (2), I shall defer to David Bordwell's commentary on several of Gunning's essays. Bordwell first summarizes how Gunning presents a cultural explanation of the cinema of attractions, and then expresses his concerns:

> Tom Gunning suggests that many tactics of the "cinema of attractions" reflect culturally determined modes of experience at the turn of the century. He adduces examples of an "aesthetics of astonishment" – locomotives hurtling to the viewer, early audiences' wonder at magical transformations, the charm of the very illusion of motion. The attraction, Gunning claims, at once epitomizes the fragmentation of modern experience and responds to alienation under capitalism. It reflects the atomized environment of urban experience and the new culture of consumption; like an advertisement, the movie's isolated gag or trick tries to grab attention.[22]

The more exactly Gunning ties modernity to this phase of stylistic history, however, the more problematic the case seems to become.[23]

Bordwell then criticizes Gunning's claims that not all early films express modernity, for the concept of attraction loses its explanatory power and becomes merely contingent. Bordwell's critique implies that Gunning artificially inflated the importance of attractions in early cinema as a way to justify his primary research problematic – his investigation of the influence of early cinema on the avant-garde. Other theoretically-informed film historians then presented counter-evidence (especially Charles Musser on Porter[24] and Alison McMahan on Alice Guy Blaché[25]), which diminishes and compromises the concept's predictive power.

In a long endnote, Bordwell also responds to Gunning's claim that he does not see attractions as a causal consequence of modernity[26]; instead, he simply identifies a rich "congruence" (Gunning's word) between modernity and early cinema. Gunning is again choosing his words carefully, because "congruence" simply suggests "similarity," or "analogy" between early films and modernity, rather than causality. Gunning is trying to avoid theorizing early films as a mere effect of a more general cause (modernity) while still attempting to articulate the relationship between early films and their cultural-historical context.

In relation to issue (1), Gunning argues that "recent spectacle cinema has re-affirmed its roots in stimulus and carnival rides, in what might be called the Spielberg-Lucas-Coppola cinema of [special] effects" (70/61) – or "tamed attractions," as he writes in the next sentence. The attractions are tamed because they have lost their political shock value, leaving only an aesthetic shock. If the attraction loses its political shock value, can it still be considered an attraction? The link between attraction and political shock value remains indeterminate in Gunning's essay. We do not discover if the political shock value is a necessary condition for the definition of an attraction. Moreover, can we really claim that special effects in contemporary cinema are non-illusionistic, that they are not co-opted into the ideology of realism and credibility?

In sum, Gunning's first problematic, his re-exploration of early cinema's inspiration for the avant-garde, is formulated in tentative language ("inspire," "congruence"), is based on indeterminate assumptions (especially the indeterminacy of the link between early cinema and modernity and the link between an attraction and political shock value), and is therefore not solved in a clear-cut manner. Nonetheless it is generally recognized as an original idea that had a significant impact on the reconceptualization and reperiodization of early cinema.

Problematics 2 and 3. In his second and third problematic states of affairs, Gunning examines the same data already classified by other film historians, and offers a different classification. The second and third problematics are conceptual, not empirical, involving the re-classification of familiar data. These problematics, while grounded in empirical data (over 500 films), are nonetheless conceptual, because the data (the films) equally support both Gunning's claims and the contrary claims of both standard film historians and Gunning's critics. Gunning is therefore using theory (theoretical concepts) to revise film history.

To give just one concrete example: the close-up in The Gay Shoe Clerk (Porter, 1903). For standard film historians, the close up signifies Porter's proto-narrative tendencies. Gunning puts this data (the close-up) under a different classification and argues that it is an attraction because its function is to display a woman's ankle.

In his turn, Gunning has been criticized for mis-classifying the data. According to Charles Musser, for example, Gunning mis-labels the close up in The Gay Shoe Clerk wholly as an attraction. Musser argues that the close-up is an attraction integrated into "a quite complex narrative unfolding" because it maintains the illusion of the fourth wall, and sets up different spaces of awareness between the lovers and the chaperone.[27] While clearly formulated, Gunning's second and third problematics are not based on uncontested assumptions, and is therefore not clearly solvable, because the theory is under-determined by the data.

In conclusion, a rational reconstruction "may be invaluable in suggesting directions in which the theory might be modified, changed, or generalized in order to deal with such difficulties as empirical anomalies, conceptual coherences, or failures of appropriate generality."[28] In this chapter I have only begun to reformulate and reorganize Gunning's rich and insightful essay in an attempt to recast its problematics and address its empirical anomalies, as well as its conceptual coherences and incoherences.

Notes

1. Lawrence Sklar, *Theory and Truth: Philosophical Critique within Foundational Science* (Oxford: Oxford UP, 2000) 107.
2. Rudolf Botha, *The Conduct of Linguistic Inquiry: A Systematic Introduction to the Methodology of Generative Grammar* (The Hague: Mouton, 1981). I have previously used Botha's work to analyze the formation of problems in film theory; see Warren Buckland, "Film Semiotics," *A Companion to Film Theory*, ed. Toby Miller and Robert Stam (Oxford: Blackwell, 1999) 84-104; "The Last Word on Filmic Enunciation?," *Semiotica* 135.3-4 (2001): 211-26; "Zwischen Shakespeare und Sirk: Eine rationale Rekonstruktion von *Tales of Sound and Fury*," trans. Michael Wedel, *Die Spur durch den Spiegel: Der Film in der Kultur der Moderne*, ed. Malte Hagener, Johann N. Schmidt and Michael Wedel (Berlin: Bertz, 2004) 387-95.
3. Tom Gunning, "The Non-Continuous Style of Early Film (1900-1906)," *Cinema 1900-1906: An Analytical Study*, ed. Roger Holman (Bruxelles: FIAF, 1982) 219-30.
4. Gunning, "The Non-Continuous Style" 220.

5.   These seven characteristics are: a) the actor's engagement with the audience; b) el-
      lipsis in the two-shot film; c) repeated action edits; d) the anthology format; e)
      abrupt transitions from documentary to staged shots; f) tableaux format; g) the in-
      troductory shot. Gunning, "The Non-Continuous Style" 222-28.

6.   In a paper published in French in 1980 and translated into English in 1982, André
      Gaudreault, who also began developing a theory of early film form and later be-
      came Gunning's collaborator in formulating the cinema of attractions, cautioned
      against the negativity of the concept of non-continuity: "our purpose is not to con-
      trast what is narrative and what is not, but rather to compare two narrative forms
      which do not deny one another, even though the later one became institutionalized
      at some point." André Gaudreault, "Temporality and Narrativity in Early Cinema
      (1895-1908)," *Cinema 1900-1906: An Analytical Study* 202. Although he goes on to
      quote Gunning's concept of "non-continuity" to characterize the earlier mode of
      filmmaking, Gaudreault is clearly unhappy with the concept.

7.   Tom Gunning, "Non-Continuity, Continuity, Discontinuity: A Theory of Genres in
      Early Films," *Iris* 2.1 (1984): 101-12.

8.   A.J. Greimas, *Structural Semantics: An Attempt at a Method* (Lincoln: U of Nebraska P,
      1983).

9.   Jonathan Culler, *Structuralist Poetics: Structuralism, Linguistics, and the Study of Litera-
      ture* (London: Routledge and Kegan Paul, 1975) 92.

10.   Tom Gunning, "An Unseen Energy Swallows Space: The Space in Early Film and Its
      Relation to American Avant-Garde Film," *Film Before Griffith*, ed. John Fell (Berke-
      ley: U of California P, 1983) 355-66.

11.   André Gaudreault and Tom Gunning, "Le cinéma des premiers temps: un défi à
      l'histoire du cinéma?" *Histoire du cinéma. Nouvelles approches*, ed. Jacques Aumont,
      André Gaudreault and Michel Marie (Paris: Sorbonne, 1989) 49-63. This article ap-
      pears in English translation in the dossier of the present volume.

12.   Tom Gunning, "The Cinema of Attraction: Early Cinema, Its Spectator, and the
      Avant-Garde," *Wide Angle* 8.3-4 (1986): 63-70; "The Cinema of Attractions: Early
      Cinema, Its Spectator, and the Avant-Garde," *Early Cinema: Space Frame Narrative*,
      ed. Thomas Elsaesser (London: British Film Institute, 1990) 56-62. I shall reference
      the original essay (Gunning 1986) and its reprint (Gunning 1990). The reprint adds
      the s to the word "attraction" and also adds one summary paragraph in the middle
      of the essay (bottom p. 58; top p. 59). Reprinted in the dossier of this volume.

13.   More accurately, the theory can be tested via "post-dictions," which are "predictions
      about phenomena, events, states of affairs, and so on in a past reality" (Botha 45). To
      state that Gunning's theory has a predictive/post-dictive capacity means that, in
      discovering pre-1906 films after formulating his theory of attractions, Gunning and
      other scholars should be able to predict that these films will be dominated by the
      aesthetics of attractions rather than narrative. This empirical dimension of Gun-
      ning's theory has been tested and contested by a number of film scholars as we shall
      see ahead.

14.   The list is the most unstructured way to organize information. Other, more struc-
      tured patterns include: topical nets, hierarchies, matrixes, linear strings, falling
      dominoes, and branching trees. For definitions of these terms, see Marilyn J. Cham-
      bliss and Robert Calfee, *Textbooks for Learning: Nurturing Children's Minds* (Oxford:
      Blackwell, 1998) 32-37.

15. See Jaques (on the musical) and Tomasovic (on the blockbusters) in this volume.

16. See also the contribution by Paci in this volume.

17. Noël Carroll, *Philosophical Problems of Classical Film Theory* (Princeton: Princeton UP, 1988) 83.

18. André Gaudreault calls this the laws of "trickality," in "Theatricality, Narrativity, and Trickality: Reevaluating the Cinema of Georges Méliès," *Journal of Popular Film and Television* 15.3 (1987): 111-19. This essay was first published in French as "'Théâtralité' et 'narrativité' dans l'oeuvre de Georges Méliès," *Méliès et la naissance du spectacle cinématographique*, ed. Madeleine Malthête-Méliès (Paris: Klincksieck, 1984) 199-219.

19. Standish Lawder points out that Constructivist art "was not developed as an aesthetic experiment, but sprang from [the artists'] passionate desire to incite the spectator to action." Standish D. Lawder, "Eisenstein and Constructivism (*Strike, Potemkin*)," *The Essential Cinema*, ed. P. Adams Sitney (New York: Anthology Film Archives and New York UP, 1975) 65.

20. Gunning presents attractions as non-illusionist, non-deceptive, and non-voyeuristic; a technique aimed to astonish rather than deceive. Yet the magic trick aims to deceive, and does not involve the spectator in its achievement, according to Eisenstein: "In so far as the trick is absolute and complete within itself, it means the direct opposite of the attraction, which is based exclusively on something relative, the reactions of the audience." Sergei Eisenstein, "Montage of Attractions [1923]," *The Film Factory: Russian and Soviet Cinema in Documents 1896-1939*, ed. Richard Taylor and Ian Christie (Cambridge: Harvard UP, 1988) 88. The precise relation between the trick film and the cinema of attractions therefore requires further exploration. Whereas Eisenstein opposes the trick to the attraction, Gunning conflates them.

21. See Charles Musser, "Rethinking Early Cinema: Cinema of Attractions and Narrativity," *The Yale Journal of Criticism* 7.2 (1994): 203-32. Reprinted in the dossier of this volume.

22. David Bordwell, *On the History of Film Style* (Cambridge: Harvard UP, 1997) 144.

23. Bordwell.

24. Musser.

25. Alison McMahan, *Alice Guy Blaché: Lost Visionary of the Cinema* (New York: Continuum, 2002).

26. Bordwell 301-02 (note 100).

27. Musser 210.

28. Sklar 107.

The Cinema of Attractions as *Dispositif*

Frank Kessler

I.

Raymond Bellour once characterized Christian Metz's *Grande Syntagmatique* as an *"opérateur théorique,"* a theoretical operator, because to him this widely discussed model of a cinematic code actualized the possibility of a semiotics of cinema "by bringing its virtualness onto a material level."[1] In a similar, though obviously different manner, the concept of "cinema of attractions" has become such a theoretical operator by creating a framework thanks to which early cinema could be seen as an object different from classical narrative cinema, as something which was not just *early* cinema, that is an earlier form of what cinema was to become, a primitive forerunner of film as an art form, interesting only in the way it already "announced" the immense possibilities of the new medium.[2] By contributing to its constitution as an object *sui generis*, defined by a certain number of distinctive traits, the concept of "cinema of attractions" helped to profoundly change the study of the early years of cinematography.[3]

For whoever has followed the developments in research on early cinema since the late 1970s, this certainly is a fact that can hardly be denied. But it is a much more complex question to determine what exactly the theoretical status of this concept is. In the entry he wrote for the *Encyclopedia of Early Cinema*, Tom Gunning in fact stresses two different aspects of this term:

> The phrase "the cinema of attractions" [...] characterized the earliest phase of cinema as dedicated to presenting discontinuous visual attractions, moments of spectacle rather than narrative. This era of attractions was followed by a period, beginning around 1906, in which films increasingly *did* organize themselves around the tasks of narrative.[4]

According to this definition, "cinema of attractions" firstly refers to a certain period in the history of cinema, and secondly it describes a mode of (re)presentation where visual attractions and spectacular moments dominate, followed by another period centered on narrative. Thus it serves two purposes: it produces a periodization, and it defines a mode of representation by establishing an opposition between attraction and narrative. Both these points have been contested by Charles Musser, stating that the period of a genuine "cinema of attractions" should probably be limited to the so-called "novelty period," and that narrativity quite early on was a much more important aspect of cinema than Gunning admits.[5]

With regard to periodization, however, one has to be aware of the fact (here I am using the poignant remark made by Jonathan Crary about continuities and discontinuities[6]) that there are no such things as periods in history, only in historical explanation. Periodizations, in other words, are always the result of historiographical constructions, and thus it is much more their usefulness and productivity that is at stake than their "correctness." In any case, the *Ungleichzeitigkeit* (non-simultaneousness) that one can observe at all levels during the years up to the First World War (and even beyond that) make clear-cut distinctions between historical periods in cinema history a rather hazardous undertaking. As for the second issue, the opposition between attraction and narrative, I have argued elsewhere[7] that the way Tom Gunning (and André Gaudreault) use these two phrases ("cinema of attractions" and "cinema of narrative integration") strongly suggests that they should not be read at a narratological level – which distinguishes this pair quite radically from the narratological couple of concepts "monstration" and "narration" proposed by Gaudreault[8] – but rather as two different modes of spectatorial address. Then the issue of whether or not there is a *narrative* in films such as Méliès's VOYAGE À TRAVERS L'IMPOSSIBLE (1904) becomes rather less important than the question of the function the narrative fulfils in the overall structure of the film. In this specific case, for instance, the catalogue description quite systematically highlights the spectacular effects that the different *tableaux* present, and much less the unfolding of an engaging story line.[9]

> 21st *tableau* – A Bitter Pill
> The train arrives full-steam and runs into the sun's mouth. After a series of comic grimaces, the latter starts to fret and fume as a result of the indigestion caused by this unforeseen bitter pill.

> 22nd *tableau* – A Formidable Crash
> Fantastic solar landscape providing a most striking effect. The train falls on the sun. The locomotive, the tender, and the carriages pile up upon one another in an indescribable chaos. This catastrophe produces on the solar surface a volcanic outburst with blazing fire and the emission of sparks giving a superb decorative effect. (This trick is an absolute novelty.)[10]

Thus attraction and narration should not be seen as mutually exclusive terms, when used in terms of structural properties of the film text. For Gunning the opposition between them concerns the different modes of address which they imply. In that respect it might be preferable to rather conceive this conceptual couple in terms of a "cinema of narrative integration" *versus* a "cinema of *attractional display*."[11]

When considered in the first instance as a specific form of address, other characteristics of the cinema of attractions – the gaze and gestures of actors directed towards the camera, the temporality, the frontality[12] – appear to be directly linked to this general orientation towards the spectator. In a (neo-)formalist perspective, one could say that the "attractional" mode determines these formal features quite similarly to the way in which the classical mode of narration is built upon a system of narrative causality, time, and space.[13]

In an often quoted definition of the cinema of attractions he gave in 1986, Gunning quite clearly presents this mode in opposition to the cinema of narrative integration, referring explicitly to film theoretical concepts of the 1970s:

> What precisely is the cinema of attractions? [...] Contrasted to the voyeuristic aspect of narrative cinema analyzed by Christian Metz, this is an exhibitionist cinema. An aspect of early cinema [...] is emblematic of this different relationship the cinema of attractions constructs with its spectator: the recurring look at the camera by actors. This action, which is later perceived as spoiling the realistic illusion of the cinema, is here undertaken with brio, establishing contact with the audience. From comedians smirking at the camera to the constant bowing and gesturing of the conjurors in magic films, this is a cinema that displays its visibility, willing to rupture a self-enclosed fictional world for a chance to solicit the attention of the spectator.[14]

This somewhat incidental reference to what in the English speaking countries has become known as "apparatus theory" in fact opens up a possibility to consider the cinema of attractions not just as a period in film history, a mode of address, or a mode of representation, but as a *dispositif*. In the remaining part of this essay I develop some ideas on how the re-reading of the cinema of attractions as a *dispositif* can be of use for film historical (and even more generally media historical) research.[15]

II.

In the early 1970s, Jean-Louis Baudry published two seminal essays that often are seen as the founding texts of the so-called "apparatus theory": "Effets idéologiques produits par l'appareil de base" (1970) and "Le dispositif: approches métapsychologiques de l'impression de réalité" (1975).[16] The first of these two articles in fact does not yet use *dispositif* as a central concept; the term appears rather *en passant* when Baudry describes the effects produced by the "*disposition*" of the screening situation:

La disposition des différents éléments – projecteur, "salle obscure," écran – outre qu'ils reproduisent d'une façon assez frappante la mise en scène de la caverne, décor exemplaire de toute transcendance et modèle topologique de l'idéalisme, reconstruit le dispositif nécessaire au déclenchement de la phase du miroir découverte par Lacan.[17]

It is only in the second article that Baudry actually theorizes the screening situation in terms of a specific *dispositif*, but already in the passage quoted above there clearly is a reference to Plato's allegory of the cave. In "Le dispositif" Baudry elaborates this point and establishes an analogy between the film spectator and the prisoners in Plato's cave:

Le prisonnier de Platon est la victime d'une illusion de réalité, c'est-à-dire précisément ce qu'on appelle une hallucination à l'état de veille et un rêve dans le sommeil; il est la proie de *l'impression, d'une impression de réalité.*

[…] Platon […] imagine ou recourt à un dispositif qui fait plus qu'évoquer, qui décrit de manière fort précise dans son principe le dispositif du cinéma et la situation du spectateur.[18]

The usual English translation of *dispositif* by "apparatus" poses a twofold problem: first of all it does not render the idea of a specific arrangement or tendency (*disposition*), which the French term implies, and secondly, it makes distinguishing between two concepts in Baudry's theory difficult, namely the *"dispositif"* on the one hand, and the *"appareil de base"* on the other. In a footnote, Baudry gives the following definition of both terms:

D'une façon générale, nous distinguons *l'appareil de base*, qui concerne l'ensemble de l'appareillage et des opérations nécessaires à la production d'un film et à sa projection, du *dispositif*, qui concerne uniquement la projection et dans lequel le sujet à qui s'adresse la projection est inclus. Ainsi *l'appareil de base* comporte aussi bien la pellicule, la caméra, le développement, le montage envisagé dans son aspect technique, etc. que le dispositif de la projection. Il y a loin de l'appareil de base à la seule caméra à laquelle on a voulu (on se demande pourquoi, pour servir quel mauvais procès) que je le limite.[19]

Thus, the *dispositif* is but one aspect of the *appareil de base*, the latter term covering all of the machinery necessary to produce and to screen a film. *Dispositif* refers exclusively to the viewing situation, i.e. the situation which, according to Baudry, seems somehow prefigured in Plato's allegory of the cave. In order to avoid any confusion, and also to mark a difference of the position I would like to present here with the 1970s apparatus theory, I will continue to use the French term *dispositif*.

In a somewhat simplified form one could summarize the configuration that Baudry describes with the aid of the concept *dispositif* as follows:

1. a material technology producing conditions that help to shape
2. a certain viewing position that is based upon unconscious desires to which corresponds
3. an institutionalized film form implying a form of address trying to guarantee that this viewing position (often characterized as "voyeuristic") functions in an optimal way.

Given the central assumption in Baudry's theory, that the *appareil de base* (that is both the production and the reception side of the cinematic institution) is in fact the realization of an age-old desire, the apparatus theory quite generally has been criticized for presenting this *dispositif* as a transhistorical norm.

However, Gunning's definition of the *dispositif* of the cinema of attractions hints at the fact that this interrelationship between a technology, a specific film form with its mode of address, and a specific positioning of the spectator can and should be historicized. At different moments in history, a medium can produce a specific and (temporarily) dominating configuration of technology, text, and spectatorship. An analysis of these configurations could thus serve as a heuristic tool for the study of how the function and the functioning of media undergo historical changes. Presupposing, for instance, different intentionalities ("to display spectacular views" or "to absorb into a narrative") one could analyze film form and filmic devices with regard to their mode of address in a given historical context (a close-up fulfils a different function in an "attractional" film than in a "narrational" film). Similarly, technological choices could be analyzed in terms of different intentionalities with regard to spectator address and exhibition contexts.[20]

Pushing this idea a little further, a historical analysis based on the concept of *dispositif* re-interpreted in a pragmatic perspective could actually take into account different uses of one and the same text within different exhibition contexts, or different institutional framings.[21] As Roger Odin has argued in his semio-pragmatic approach, a fiction film will not be viewed (or read) in the same way when it is presented in a movie theater (where it will dominantly be read within a fictionalizing regime) and in a class-room situation in a film studies program (where it may be read within a documentarizing regime, i.e. as a document of a specific historical or national style or movement, as documenting a specific filmmaker's personal style, or as an example for the use of a specific filmic device, etc.). Similarly, in the 1910s a travelogue about Africa could function as an exotic attraction in a moving picture theater, and as colonial propaganda when screened by the Deutsche Kolonialgesellschaft.[22] A historical investigation of historical and present *dispositifs* would thus have to take into account the different viewing situations, institutional framings, the modes of address they imply, as well as the technological basis on which they rest. In a recent article, Gunning argues for such a view as well:

> Particularly realizing the protean, even elastic, nature of early cinema, film scholars had to admit that there was no single essential film text that underlay film history. Rather films must be approached as texts whose meaning derived through a complex process of making meaning in the interaction of films with viewers and institutions.[23]

Another implication of such an approach is that the notion of both textual and medial identity becomes problematic. On the one hand, any given text may trigger a number of different readings, depending on the context in which it is embedded, and on the other hand one can argue that in spite of a continuity in *naming* a given medium (cinema, television, telephone, etc.) its functions and its functioning can vary so much over time that it would be more accurate to describe the different *dispositifs* in which it takes shape, rather than to look for the "identity" or "specificity" of that medium.[24] The cinema of attractions may thus use a technology quite similar to the one used by the cinema of narrative integration, but as the mode of address and the textual forms are in fact quite different, one should, as André Gaudreault argues, avoid thinking about both in terms of a continuity, or identity.[25]

III.

Among the textual forms that can be considered as emblematic for the cinema of attractions, the different types of trick films undoubtedly take a prominent position. Here one finds quite regularly various forms of the direct address to the audience which Gunning, in his first definition of the cinema of attractions, sees as one of the main features of this "exhibitionist" cinema.[26] Furthermore, Gunning also has shown that the stop trick requires a frontal and fixed framing for the illusion of a single shot to function.[27] The trick films, and especially those by Georges Méliès when considered within the context of his own theater, could, in other words, serve as an almost obvious illustration of the claim that the institutional framing, the viewing context, and the textual form, come together in an attractional *dispositif*, which indeed can be seen as being in an almost diametrical opposition to the *dispositif* of classical narrative cinema. There are, however, much more complicated cases such as the one that I would like to discuss in the third section of this article, where the idea of a "cinema of attractions" (or "attractional display") can serve as a useful heuristic tool in order to understand the strange combination of elements in the surviving print of a Gaumont film from 1910 about a fire which destroyed a large part of the World Fair held in Brussels that year.

The print of Incendie de l'exposition de Bruxelles (Gaumont, 1910) held by the Netherlands Filmmuseum in Amsterdam quite curiously appears to be an "extended" version of the film originally released by the French firm.[28] It contains a number of shots that visibly "do not belong here," that have been inserted by someone at a later stage, presumably by an exhibitor at the time the film was shown as a topical news film. The fire at the Brussels exhibition occurred on 14 August 1910, around 9 pm, which indicates that the actuality film made for and distributed by Gaumont had to be shot after the facts and essentially depicts the smoldering ruins of several pavilions which had fallen victim to the flames.[29] The Amsterdam print, however, also shows, among others, scenes of firemen rushing out of their quarters, the fire brigade riding in the streets, a rescue action, the latter being clearly staged, as well as numerous shots of actuality footage of a burning furniture factory, possibly taken from a Scandinavian film, since the word "Møbel" (furniture) can be distinguished on the façade of a wooden building.

The additional scenes are inserted right after the opening shot of the film and are preceded and followed by views of the parts of the exhibition affected by the fire. The heterogeneity of this material, even at the level of its visual qualities, is quite obvious, and one can safely assume that not even a naive spectator could have failed to notice the differences within the texture, the style and the thematic content. These additions to the Gaumont print appear to be elements inserted in order to "spice up" the comparatively less spectacular views obtained by the firm's cameramen after the actual fire had occurred – and this is indeed a quite valid explanation. At first glance, this material seems to have been selected more or less at random, on the sole basis that these scenes depict burning buildings and firemen at work. Nevertheless, a closer look at the events of the evening of August 14th shows that there are reasons to believe that the choices made here were in fact rather less arbitrary. According to several newspaper reports the fire actually also touched some residential areas bordering the terrain where the exhibition was held,[30] thus the scenes showing a fireman rescuing a child and a woman jumping out of a window into a safety net can be seen as referring to this aspect of the events. Also, a Dutch paper reports that a lot of valuable furniture was destroyed when the English pavilion went up in flames.[31] The images of a burning Scandinavian furniture warehouse or factory may have served to illustrate this fact. There is, however, no indication that this footage was chosen for precisely that reason, so rather than seeing here a direct reference to the actual events this should be regarded as being a sheer coincidence. In any event, and most likely so, these images could serve to show the effects of the flames, with the building's final collapsing functioning as a climactic attraction.

My hypothesis here, in the light of a contextualization on the basis of contemporary newspaper reports, is that a local exhibitor put this additional material into the Gaumont print in order to offer his audience a more adequate version of the events.[32] The scenes that were added can function, on the one hand, as attractions, showing images that are much more spectacular than the ones taken by the Gaumont cameramen. On the other hand, they help in creating a stronger narrative, since they can be referred to events, which had taken place that night and which were potentially known by the audience through the newspaper reports.

Consequently, an approach establishing a simple dichotomy between attraction and narration fails to grasp the complex functioning of a print such as this one: the strengthening of a narrative line with the help of additional footage does not necessarily modify its predominantly attractional character, since the heterogeneity of the material rather blocks the effect of narrative integration that the classical narrational mode tries to achieve. So if the original Gaumont version informs the viewer about the terrible devastation caused by the fire, showing the ruins of, respectively, the pavilions of Belgium and England as well as the Alimentation Française, all three clearly identified by intertitles, and (possibly, since there is no confirmation by an intertitle) the Bruxelles Kermesse, it presents a formal structure based on a juxtaposition of views relating the disastrous effects of the flames, thus conforming to the representational mode which Gunning has called "aesthetics of the view" and which can be considered the non-fictional equivalent of the cinema of attractions as it addresses the viewer by displaying the views, rather than structuring them in a rhetorical mode.[33] This is in fact one of the reasons why Bill Nichols claims that in early non-fiction films "the voice of the filmmaker was [...] noticeably silent"[34] (neglecting, however, the fact that even such a seemingly "neutral" juxtaposition of shots still does result in a particular structuring effect, and that, in addition, a screening could be accompanied by the actual voice of a lecturer).[35]

The *dispositif* within which the Amsterdam print (presumably) functioned is a slightly more complex one. Here, according to my hypothesis at least, by inserting this additional material an exhibitor addresses an audience he or she is quite probably familiar with, and which is either familiar with the details of the events, having read the newspaper reports, or is given additional information by, for instance, a lecturer anchoring the heterogeneous visual material in a narrative framework provided by those newspaper reports.

The question now is how to conceptualize the obvious differences between the prints and thus the way they may have functioned historically. How can the pragmatic difference, which I postulate, be described? For this I shall turn to a couple of concepts proposed by the art historian Michael Baxandall. In his analyses aiming at the historical explanation of paintings, he distinguishes between what he calls the "charge" and the "brief," both concepts referring to what one might call the "intentionalities" that literally shape the formal aspects of an art work. These concepts may be helpful also to clarify the functional difference between the Gaumont print and the "extended" version. Baxandall's overall goal is to show how "historical objects may be explained by treating them as solutions to problems in situations, and by constructing a rational relationship between the three."[36] In this perspective, the "charge" can be described as the general problem or the "generic and institutional intentionality" (building a bridge, painting a portrait), while the "brief" concerns the ever changing and historically specific determinations under which the charge is to be fulfilled.[37]

When looking at Incendie de l'exposition de Bruxelles by using Baxandall's terms, the original Gaumont version gives a description of the consequences of the a-filmic event, corresponding to the charge of a topical film (an *actualité* in the original French meaning of the word), while the brief here concerns the specific circumstances under which the film could be shot (after the facts, because of the impossibility to film at night during the actual fire). Gaumont could also have produced an *actualité reconstituée*, but in that case the film form would doubtlessly have respected the norms of an internal coherence, which the Amsterdam print so obviously lacks. Another aspect of the brief here concerns the fact that Gaumont wanted to sell, or rent, the film to the largest possible number of exhibitors, providing them with a product fulfilling the quality standards of the firm. For Gaumont, the *dispositif* within which the films are going to function is determined mainly by the general parameters characterizing non-fiction cinema at that time: the display of a series of views depicting phenomena of interest without constructing an internally structured rhetorical or narrative discourse.

For the anonymous exhibitor, the charge is indeed the same: screening a film referring to an a-filmic event, while his brief appears to be (to have been) somewhat different. Having control over the situation (the *dispositif*) within which the film (this specific print) will be screened, he can actually insert the heterogeneous material implying not only a reference to the a-filmic events, but also to some extent an account of them.[38] Aiming at a specific thrill he wants to provide his audience with, he inserts among others the rescue scene that bears a generic resemblance to films such as Williamson's Fire! (1901) or Porter's Life of an American Fireman (1903).

As this case study tried to show, individual films – or rather: prints – may be difficult to place within a binary opposition between attraction and narration. By trying to reconstruct the specific *dispositif* within which this print may have functioned, one can, however, arrive at hypotheses helping to explain its particular form, using the general idea of a "cinema of attractional display" as a guideline. Without any doubt, thus, the concept of the "cinema of attractions" can continue to function as a powerful theoretical operator, but it will be increasingly important to specify the theoretical status it has in the film historian's argument. Looking at it as a *dispositif* may prove to be a fruitful way to do this.

Notes

This article has been written as part of the Utrecht Media Research Project (UMR). I would like to thank the members of the Utrecht Media Seminar for their comments and suggestions.

1. Raymond Bellour, *L'Analyse du film* (Paris: Albatros, 1979) 248.
2. Two key publications here are André Gaudreault and Tom Gunning, "Le cinéma des premiers temps: un défi à l'histoire du cinéma?," *Histoire du cinéma. Nouvelles approches*, ed. Jacques Aumont, André Gaudreault and Michel Marie (Paris: Sorbonne, 1989) 49-63, based on their 1985 lecture at the Colloque de Cerisy; and Tom Gunning, "The Cinema of Attractions: Early Film, Its Spectator and the Avant-Garde [1986]," *Early Cinema: Space Frame Narrative*, ed. Thomas Elsaesser (London: British Film Institute, 1990) 56-62. Both articles are reprinted in the dossier of this volume.
3. One might ask why Noël Burch's distinction between PMR ("Primitive Mode of Representation") and IMR ("Institutional Mode of Representation") did not turn out to be as successful as the terminological couple "cinema of attractions"/"cinema of narrative integration." Noël Burch, *Light to those Shadows* (Berkeley/Los Angeles: U of California P, 1990) (Burch in fact started working on early cinema already in the late 1970s.) One explanation might be that the phrase "cinema of attractions" stresses more intensely the "otherness" of early cinema, and that the use of the word "primitive" still seems to suggest a teleological argument (see also the contributions by Gaudreault and Strauven in this volume). However, the importance of Noël Burch's work for the exploration of early cinema after the Brighton FIAF conference of 1978 cannot be underestimated. See also the homage to Noël Burch in *KINtop* 12 (2003), particularly the contributions by Thomas Elsaesser and Charles Musser.
4. Tom Gunning, "Cinema of Attractions," *Encyclopedia of Early Cinema*, ed. Richard Abel (London/New York: Routledge, 2005) 124.
5. Charles Musser presented his criticism of Gunning's ideas in 1993 at two conferences: "The Movies Begin: Film/History/Culture" at Yale University, and "Les vingt premières années du cinéma français" at Sorbonne University. These papers were published as "Rethinking Early Cinema: Cinema of Attractions and Narrativity," *Yale Journal of Criticism* 7.1 (1994): 203-32 (reprinted in the dossier of this volume) and "Pour une nouvelle approche du cinéma des premiers temps: le cinéma d'attractions et la narrativité," *Les vingt premières années du cinéma français*, ed. Jean A.

Gili, Michèle Lagny, Michel Marie and Vincent Pinel (Paris: Sorbonne Nouvelle/ AFRHC, 1995) 147-75.

6. Jonathan Crary, *Techniques of the Observer* (Cambridge/London: MIT P, 1990) 7.
7. Frank Kessler, "In the Realm of the Fairies: Early Cinema between Attraction and Narration," *Iconics. International Studies of the Modern Image* 5 (2000): 7-26.
8. André Gaudreault, *Du littéraire au filmique. Système du récit* (Paris: Méridiens Klinck-sieck, 1988).
9. The catalogue description is reproduced in Jacques Malthête, *Méliès. Images et Illu-sions* (Paris: Exporégie, 1996) 226-29. See also Gunning, "Cinema of Attractions" 124, where he remarks: "Furthermore, some films could use a story as an excuse to present attractions."
10. Malthête 228.
11. I would like to thank Britta Hartmann for her suggestion to reformulate the concep-tual couple in such a way.
12. Gunning, "Cinema of Attractions" 124-25.
13. See David Bordwell, *Narration in the Fiction Film* (London: Routledge, 1985) 156-204.
14. Gunning, "The Cinema of Attractions" 57.
15. See also my "La cinématographie comme dispositif (du) spectaculaire," *CiNéMAS* 14.1 (2003): 21-34.
16. "Effets idéologiques produits par l'appareil de base" was published in *Cinéthique* 7-8 (1970) and "Le dispositif: approches métapsychologiques de l'impression de réa-lité" in *Communications* 23 (1975). Together with another article and several inter-views with filmmakers, these two articles were subsequently turned into a book with the title *L'Effet cinéma* (Paris: Albatros, 1978).
17. Baudry, *L'Effet cinéma* 23 ["The arrangement of the different elements – projector, darkened hall, screen – in addition from reproducing in a striking way the mise-en-scène of Plato's cave (prototypical set for all transcendence and the topological model of idealism), reconstructs the situation necessary to the release of the 'mirror stage' discovered by Lacan." Jean-Louis Baudry, "Ideological Effects of the Basic Cinematographic Apparatus," *Narrative, Apparatus, Ideology*, ed. Philip Rosen (New York: Columbia UP, 1986) 294.]
18. Baudry, *L'Effet cinéma* 30-31. ["Plato's prisoner is the victim of an illusion of reality, that is, of precisely what we know as a hallucination, if one is awake, as a dream, if asleep; he is the prey of an impression, of *an impression of reality*. [...] Plato [...] would imagine or resort to an apparatus that doesn't merely evoke but precisely describes in its mode of operation the cinematographic apparatus and the specta-tor's place in relation to it." Jean-Louis Baudry, "The Apparatus: Metapsychological Approaches to the Impression of Reality in the Cinema," *Narrative, Apparatus, Ideol-ogy* 302.]
19. Baudry, *L'Effet cinéma* 31. ["In a general way we distinguish the *basic cinematographic apparatus* (*l'appareil de base*), which concerns the ensemble of the equipment and op-erations necessary to the production of a film and its projection, from the apparatus (*le dispositif*) discussed in this article, which solely concerns projection and which includes the subject to whom the projection is addressed. Thus the *basic cinemato-graphic apparatus* involves the film stock, the camera, developing, montage consid-ered in its technical aspects, etc., as well as the apparatus (*dispositif*) of projection. The basic cinematographic apparatus is a long way from being the camera itself to

which some have wanted to say I limited it (one wonders what bad arguments this can serve)." Baudry, "The Apparatus" 317.]

20. This is what I attempted in "La cinématographie comme dispositif (du) spectaculaire," see in particular 26-31.

21. See Roger Odin, "Pour une sémio-pragmatique du cinéma," *Iris* 1.1 (1983): 76-82, and "A Semio-Pragmatic Approach to the Documentary Film," *The Film Spectator. From Sign to Mind*, ed. Warren Buckland (Amsterdam: Amsterdam UP, 1995) 227-35. See also my "Historische Pragmatik," *Montage/AV* 11.2 (2002): 104-12. Odin in fact uses the term "institution" in a relatively broad sense and does not limit it to social institutions.

22. See Wolfgang Fuhrmann, "Locating Early Film Audiences: Voluntary Associations and Colonial Film," *Historical Journal of Film, Radio and Television* 22.3 (2002): 291-304.

23. Tom Gunning, "A Quarter of a Century Later. Is Early Cinema Still Early," *KINtop* 12 (2003): 17-31.

24. See my *Het idee van vooruitgang in de mediageschiedschrijving* (Utrecht: Universiteit Utrecht, 2002).

25. André Gaudreault, "Das Erscheinen des Kinematographen," *KINtop* 12 (2003): 33-48.

26. Gunning, "The Cinema of Attractions." These forms of address are particularly frequent in the films by Méliès; for a more detailed analysis, see Frank Kessler and Sabine Lenk, "L'adresse-Méliès," *Georges Méliès, l'illusionniste fin de siècle?*, ed. Jacques Malthête and Michel Marie (Paris: Sorbonne Nouvelle, 1997) 183-99.

27. Tom Gunning, "'Primitive' Cinema. A Frame-up? Or The Trick's on Us," *Early Cinema: Space Frame Narrative* 95-103.

28. According to a presentation of this film on http://gaumontpathearchives.com it consisted of nine views showing indeed only the consequences of the fire. The length of the print is given here as 6' 15" (not specifiying at what projection speed), the video copy of the Amsterdam print runs about 12'.

29. *The Times* 16 August 1910. The documentation that I use for this section partly comes from a seminar paper written by Sonya Baalti, Ingrid Hoofd and Susanne van Kooij for a course on early non-fiction cinema which I taught during the academic year 1998-99. I also would like to thank my research assistant Eva Baaren for tracing other contemporary press reports.

30. According to the *Nieuwe Rotterdamsche Courant* 15 March 1910, late ed., more than forty buildings in a residential area next to the exhibition were affected by the fire.

31. *Nieuwe Rotterdamsche Courant* 17 March 1910, late ed.

32. The nitrate material held by the Netherlands Filmmuseum does indeed appear to have been spliced together from different sources and thus seems to be a unique print. This is why I presume that the material was edited together by an exhibitor rather than a distributor, even though the latter hypothesis cannot be excluded, especially since this title can be found in numerous ads for second-hand films. I would like to thank Nico de Klerk for providing me with information about the nitrate print.

33. Tom Gunning, "Before Documentary: Early nonfiction films and the 'view' aesthetic," *Uncharted Territory. Essays on early nonfiction film*, ed. Daan Hertogs and Nico de Klerk (Amsterdam: Stichting Nederlands Filmmuseum, 1997) 9-24.

34. Bill Nichols, *Introduction to Documentary* (Bloomington: Indiana UP, 2001) 86.
35. Obviously, such a lecturer could have narrated also the dramatic events the Amsterdam print is referring to, the difference being, however, that there would have been no visual equivalent of this on the screen, whereas the Amsterdam print does show images which can be read as illustrating these events, though not as depicting them, given their textual heterogeneity with regard to the other images.
36. Michael Baxandall, *Patterns of Intention: On the Historical Explanation of Pictures* (New Haven/London: Yale UP, 1985) 35.
37. Baxandall 25-36. The reformulations of Baxandall's definitions are mine, see my "Regards en creux. Le cinéma des premiers temps et la construction des faits spectatoriels," *Réseaux* 99 (2000): 73-98.
38. In this respect the Amsterdam print cannot be considered a fake, unless the exhibitor actually claimed that the images were taken during, and at the site of the fire.

Spectacle, Attractions and Visual Pleasure

Scott Bukatman

The impact of Laura Mulvey's "Visual Pleasure and Narrative Cinema" continues to be widely felt, well beyond the parameters of film studies. Debates around its premises and methods continue; and it remains a fundament of film theory. Since it appeared in 1975,[1] the only essay that has come to rival it in the breadth and depth of its influence, has been Tom Gunning's "The Cinema of Attraction(s): Early Film, Its Spectator and the Avant-Garde."[2] The rise to prominence of Gunning's essay mirrored (and helped instigate) the shift in film studies away from a theoretical model grounded in the analysis of ideological effects and away from its close alignment with feminist studies and politics. It also signaled the movement of the field towards a greater emphasis on a multi-determinant historiography, with a significant importance placed on early cinema. Gunning's exploration of the cinema of attractions has proven immensely important to the study of visual culture as well as the cultures of sensation and sensationalism. In some ways, the model that Gunning elaborated in this and related essays has, if not replaced, then somewhat displaced the prominence of Mulvey's model.

Each essay is paradigmatic of its respective historical moment (not surprisingly, since they helped establish those very paradigms). Their differences are pronounced, and in some measure deliberate. Where Mulvey concentrated on Hollywood narrative film, Gunning emphasized pre-narrative and experimental cinemas. Mulvey stressed spectatorial passivity; Gunning described sophisticated participants existing as a social aggregate. Mulvey stressed the spectator's voyeuristic isolation; Gunning mapped the contours of an "exhibitionistic cinema." The abstraction of Mulvey's model was countered by Gunning's use of contemporaneous reports. And, of course, "Visual Pleasure and Narrative Cinema" was explicitly ideological in ways that "The Cinema of Attractions" was not.

Despite their evident differences, however, "The Cinema of Attractions" moves across some of the same ground as "Visual Pleasure." If we temporarily bracket gender out of Mulvey's argument – a perverse idea, I'll grant you – then what remains is an intriguing theory of spectacle, produced at a moment when film studies still operated in the shadow of narrative theory. Gunning briefly mentions Mulvey's treatment of the dialectic between narrative and spectacle in his essay, noting that her analysis operates "in a very different context."[3]

Mulvey treats spectacle as an aberration within a primarily narrative system, while Gunning's "attraction" precedes and subtends the system itself.

Mulvey: The Iconoclast

Even as theorists acknowledged the fundamental differences between film and literature at the time that Mulvey's essay appeared in 1975, the serious study of film in academia and journalism was largely organized around issues of narrative and methods derived from narrative theory. Raymond Bellour contended that film represented an "unattainable text"; in literary analysis one finds an "undivided conformity of the object of study and the means of study, in the absolute material coincidence between language and language," whereas written film analysis exists only in the rupture between the modes of representation. "Thus [filmic analysis] constantly mimics, evokes, describes; in a kind of principled despair it can but try frantically to compete with the object it is attempting to understand. By dint of seeking to capture it and recapture it, it ends up always occupying a point at which its object is perpetually out of reach."[4] Bellour emphasized that film's immutability distinguished it from the performative modes of theater or musical concerts: "film exhibits the peculiarity, remarkable for a spectacle, of being a fixed work."[5] Film studies found it easier to consider film texts as immutable (as *texts*) rather than something more performative or reader-centric. Semiotic-structural analysis privileged units of meaning understood by methods that downplayed, if not ignored, the experience of film viewing other than as an abstract act of perfect interpellation. Certainly psychoanalytic and Marxist schools of interpretation were already familiar to literary theory before they were systematically applied to cinema.

Structural/semiotic analysis had a complex relationship to the privileging of the auteur that had dominated and guided film appreciation and analysis from the late 1950s to the 1970s. On the one hand it tried to break with the image of the omnipotent director, locked in heroic struggle against the corporatism of the Hollywood factory/studio system. On the other it retained precisely that image, while shifting the emphasis from John Ford the man to "John Ford," the set of recognizable structures. It should be remembered that despite its celebration of the film director over the film writer, auteurist concerns owed much to traditional literary values. Coherent thematics, authorial consistency, and a command of the language were praised, along with maverick intensity and a primal toughness, which often revealed itself in masculine genres such as gangster films and westerns. Authorship and genre studies were productively combined through the 1970s; nevertheless, they remained, by and large, beholden to models of analysis developed for the study of literature. As Paul Willeman writes, "In the late sixties, film-theory was a theory of narrative cinema and was argued in relation to the productivity of a structuralist approach to the work of authors and to genres."[6]

Mulvey's essay is worth situating in the contexts of poststructuralism as well as auteurism. Her theory took the logical next step after Baudry and Metz had mapped the "ideological effects" of the "basic" apparatus by considering the content of the images and scenarios in Hollywood's "classic" period, from the 1930s to the 1960s (when the hegemony of the studio system broke down). What she described was an oppressive misogyny that was inexorably but invisibly reinforced by the conditions of film viewership. It is hardly coincidental that her target also happened to be the territory of film history especially beloved of auteurist critics – the heyday of Ford, Hitchcock, and Fuller. (I suspect that it was the auteurist concentration on westerns and gangster films ["gun films"[7]] that led Mulvey to initially underestimate melodrama). Willeman writes that *Screen* was "never a magazine where the murkier and more sustaining aspects of cinephilia had been particularly appreciated."[8]

In Mulvey's model, Hollywood narrative cinema of the "classic" period (a problematic term[9]) was organized around an active male presence whose actions gave the film spatio-temporal coherence – their actions took them to new places, the narrative called for them to effect changes on the environment, their gaze linked one shot to the next and inscribed them into a position of mastery. The represented woman interrupted the smooth coherence of this system, by serving as spectacular objects of the male gaze that provided a competing locus of fascination. The woman, defined in psychoanalytic theory as a site of unbearable lack, was fetishistically associated with a compensatory abundance and plenitude; *absence* was deflected into an excess of *presence* (the Bugs-Bunny-in-drag phenomenon).[10] The woman as iconic spectacle disrupted the forward progress of the narrative in any number of ways, but often in an initial cut to a vivid *close-up* – Gilda's "Who, me?" for example – the close-up, as Jean Epstein wrote, constituting the point of maximal tension and abstraction within a scene. The woman had to be demystified and naturalized (visually), and within the narrative, which reasserted its prerogatives, had to be either punished (often by being gunned down like Jane Greer in Out of the Past [1947]), repentant (Lana Turner in The Postman Always Rings Twice [1946]), or "solved" (as in Marnie (1964), problematic as that solution was).

"The magic of the Hollywood style at its best (and of all the cinema which fell within its sphere of influence) arose, not exclusively, but in one important aspect, from its skilled and satisfying manipulation of visual pleasure."[11] "Going far beyond highlighting a woman's to-be-looked-at-ness, cinema builds the way she is to be looked at into the spectacle itself."[12] Within the discourse of patriarchal power that Mulvey describes, a feminist "vision" of the cinema must resist the structures of cinematic pleasure that ultimately depend upon this notion of the woman as threat – these seductive visual pleasures must be refused:

> It is said that analyzing pleasure, or beauty, destroys it. That is the intention of this article. The satisfaction and reinforcement of the ego that represent the high point of film history hitherto must be attacked. [...] The alternative is the thrill that comes from leaving the past behind without rejecting it, transcending outworn or oppressive forms, or daring to break with normal pleasurable expectations in order to conceive a new language of desire.[13]

The "spell" of the image must be broken, its palpable pleasures refused. In a very literal way, Mulvey takes on the role of iconoclast. This is evident in her analysis of Sternberg's films with Dietrich; Dietrich's image is given such strong fetishistic power (it becomes "the ultimate fetish") that it even circumvents the "power" of the male protagonist's gaze. Here, fetishistic disavowal replaces the narrative of investigation, creating a sense of direct "erotic rapport" between image and audience. "At the end of DISHONORED," she writes, "the erotic impact" of the image of Dietrich's sacrifice, "sanctified by death, is displayed as a spectacle for the audience."[14] The sacred image has too much power; these idols must be smashed.

The terms of Mulvey's analysis would have been, in part, very familiar to readers of *Screen*. Not only was the journal reprinting texts on estrangement by such Russian Formalists as Osip Brik, two issues concentrated on Brecht: essays by Colin MacCabe, Stephen Heath, and Ben Brewster accompanied translations of two pieces by Roland Barthes and an excerpt from Brecht's writing.[15] There are some notable similarities between Brecht's calls for what he termed epic theater and Mulvey's polemic against the terms of cinematic pleasure operating in Hollywood cinema. Both demand the disruption of common modes of illusionism and narrative presentation in order to establish some critical distance between text and spectator. For Brecht, identification is a passive process (he writes that theatrical patrons "look at the stage as if in a trance"[16]). In Peter Wollen's elaboration of counter-cinema, Brechtian *estrangement* is explicitly opposed to dramatic theater's *identification*. Brecht calls for a new mode of theatrical production, however, while Mulvey proposes intervening at the level of *spectatorship*. Only a few years later, Mulvey, collaborating with Wollen, would turn to alternative film practice but here she emphasizes the critical intervention of "alienation effects" that should be performed by film *viewers*.

Against Narration

By bracketing off the issue of gender (a kind of "ideological reduction"), one can see how Mulvey's model recalls the more pervasive suspicion of excess which has suffused the critique of spectacle throughout its history. Aristotle famously dismissed staged spectacle as a cheap substitute for the true art of the poet, supplying effects that were unnecessary to effective drama. This line of critique continues through to the present dismissal of Hollywood blockbusters as empty spectacles (or attractions), nothing more than special effects, etcetera etcetera. Mulvey goes further than Aristotle, however; in her model, spectacle ("visual pleasure") becomes more than an unnecessary *supplement* to narrative ("the poet's art"). Because it is precisely *not narrative*, it therefore lies beyond a narratively-grounded conceptual schema, and that "beyond" threatens the totalizing coherence of the narrative system. Spectacle, by actively *disrupting* narrative coherence, *threatens* the stability of the narrative system. Mulvey's essay emphasizes the ways that narrative contains spectacle by the film's end, re-asserting the status quo. One consequence of Mulvey's emphasis on narrative closure is that the priority of narrative *over* spectacle remains an unchallenged assumption.

Mulvey, in this essay, certainly seems over-invested in the power of narrative, and particularly in the power of closure. The disruptive spectacle is built into cinema; it is allowed to enter only insofar as it is to be recontained. She outlines no less than three powerful means by which narrative closure recontains erotic spectacle. Yet even within the terms of the psychoanalytic model Mulvey privileges, repression can never be complete; the fetishist may operate under the sign of, "*I know very well, but,*" but nevertheless, discomforting knowledge can never be entirely disavowed. (Miriam Hansen argues that these frantic attempts to re-contain the unleashed power of women can be seen as patriarchy's fumbling – even ineffective – attempts to assert control in the face of women's expanding mobility and power in the early twentieth century.)

Molly Haskell, in *From Reverence to Rape*, takes a different approach that refuses an over-valuation of narrative: essentially, she argues that 5 minutes of "good" behavior by Hepburn or Stanwyck hardly obviates or obliterates the previous 85 minutes of their wreaking madcap havoc.

> Sure, they had to be punished every so often, particularly as women's real-life power in society and in the job market increased. [...] As women represented real threats to male economic supremacy, movie heroines had to be brought down to fictional size, domesticated or defanged. But even so, and in the midst of mediocre material, [these stars] rose to the surface and projected, through sheer will and talent and charisma, images of emotional and intellectual power.[17]

Haskell's model allows for the power and relative autonomy of *performance*, while Mulvey really only considers the actress as *image*. It is possible that narrative, with its concomitant gesture towards closure, represents only one system competing for the viewer's attention, and thus the ending may not be as deterministic as Mulvey would have it. Granted, Mulvey does not argue that narrative operates alone: its ideological operations are reinforced by composition, lighting, editing, and other aspects of cinematic signification. I would still argue that her essay tends to exaggerate both the centrality and the efficacy of narrative *telos*.

Endings are obviously privileged moments of narrative structure (as Kermode demonstrates in *A Sense of an Ending*[18]), but exaggerating its power requires both theorist and viewer to deny the *pleasure of disruption* – not simply as a trigger for its recontainment, but as something pleasurable in itself. Stanwyck's disruption of the encyclopedists' home in Ball of Fire (1941) is pleasurable for all kinds of reasons, the "visual" among them, and it is fun for female and male viewers alike. Disruption in Hollywood cinema is often the pie thrown in the face of dominant ideology and authority: not only Dietrich's cross-dressing in Morocco (1930), but Tony Camonte's ecstatic pleasure at the destructive power of his machine gun, Laurel and Hardy's measured destruction of James Finlayson's house, or the smoky "horse race" banter between Bogart and Bacall in The Big Sleep (1946) (and remember that this last was added *in place of* narrative coherence). Disruption is the flamboyance that exists for its own sake, the empty calories that just taste so good – there is a potential elision of structures, signs, and meanings that can never be fully contained by gestures toward narrative closure. "I Want To Be Bad," Helen Kane sang in 1929, and while female desire could only exist within certain limits, it constantly signals a chafing against those limits. The resistance to control, the disruption of structure, can be posited as a *good* thing.

I am no more arguing that Mulvey needs to lighten up and have fun with it than I am suggesting that Gilda needs to be Mother Courage. I am only pointing to the firmness of her position within theories of narrative. However, by emphasizing the disruptive power of spectacle, Mulvey's essay could also be understood as marking the beginning of a recognition of the limits of narrative theory in explicating cinematic form. It recognizes *something else*, but still sees that *something else* as a threat. It does not yet know how to fully theorize that excess. In other words, "Visual Pleasure and Narrative Cinema" signals the limits of understanding narrative cinema strictly in narratological terms. Gender difference can only be articulated within the singular master-narrative on which Mulvey relies, and so (gendered) spectacle can only exist when recontained by that system. Two problems here: this isn't the only possible narrative of gender difference (even within psychoanalysis), and this isn't the only way of understanding spectacle in relation to narrative. This is where Mulvey's schema is overdetermined: a limited theory of the articulation of gender difference neatly coincides with a limited theory of narrative and narrative closure.

Despite this overdetermined (albeit deeply creative) reliance on a particular psychoanalytic model, it is possible to read Mulvey's essay in retrospect as an early acknowledgment of the limitations of narrative theory, through its emphasis upon the presence of *something else* that exists in cinematic form. The filmic text is posited as a site of abundance, of multiple semiotic systems that only reinforce one another to *a degree*. The texts are fissured in ways that threaten their very coherence. "Visual Pleasure and Narrative Cinema," then, draws attention to the precariousness of stable meaning in the face of spectacle.

The Energy of Attractions

The hegemony of the semiotic-structural critical model within academia began to wane in the later 1980s as the field of film studies began to broaden its methodological base. Reader-response theory, theories of spectatorship, the rise of new technologies, attention to the politics of cultural identity, more detailed research into the history of cinema, and a certain exhaustion around the paradigm of psychoanalytic feminist film theory all contributed to this shift. In his introduction to *Early Cinema: Space Frame Narrative*, Thomas Elsaesser wrote that "The media-intertext of early cinema, the industrialization of entertainment and leisure turned out to be a rich source of insight,"[19] especially one should add,[20] at a moment when new technologies such as IMAX and early experiments with virtual reality emphasized the experiential, rather than the narrational, pleasures of the text. The result was a newly sophisticated approach to the archive, a reassessment as to what constituted the proper primary text for the field of film "and media" studies, and "a thorough re-examination" of earlier accounts of film history, with their emphasis on "fearless pioneers" and singular determinants.[21] "If much of the new film history has focused on early cinema," Elsaesser argued, it was "because here the claim was strongest that the models for understanding the cinema as a whole were inadequate, contradictory or based on unsound scholarship."[22] Certainly the assumption that narrative was not just *a*, but *the* fundament of cinema merited scholarly intervention.

Gunning had already made a significant contribution to the debate in 1984 with his essay, "An Unseen Energy Swallows Space,"[23] in which he argued that certain films and figures of The New American Cinema had reclaimed some of the cinematic territory that seemed to have gone into abeyance with the rise of the powerful model of "classical" narrative film. Gunning demonstrated the existence of a powerful counter-history in which spatial, temporal, and perceptual explorations were the film's clearest reason for being, rather than serving as more or less formally complex vessels for narrative content. In some ways, "Unseen Energy" is a proudly a-historical essay by an established historian: the task of the essay was less to explicate the connection between these disparate cinematic moments than to demonstrate – or, better, *proclaim* – their affinity.

"The Cinema of Attractions" follows quite logically from "Unseen Energy." Here, Gunning sets out to place early cinema in the context of the plethora of non-narrative entertainments familiar to the general public in the early 20th century. The attraction was characterized by a direct address to the spectator, novelty, a presentational (as opposed to representational) set of codes. The attraction constituted a form of spectacle that did not disappear after the emergence of dominating narrative structures, but which went famously "underground" into such Hollywood genres as musicals and science fiction films (genres that once segregated spectacle and narrative), or into the alternative practice of various cinematic avant-gardes.

Gunning was out to reclaim more than the complexity of early cinema and its modes of address; by continually signaling the vital function of the avant-garde, Gunning was standing against the tide of academic film studies, which had moved from its initial considerations of European art cinema and experimental film to the expanded notion of the film artist offered through auteurism, and finally to an almost monolithic attention to the ideological effects of dominant Hollywood practice. "The history of early cinema," he writes, "like the history of cinema generally, has been written and theorized under the hegemony of narrative films."[24] Gunning's work, among other things, intended to remind the academy of the history – the continuing history – of alternative practice. Hence his essay does not begin with a citation from the period preceding the emergence of narrative film, but rather with a quote from Fernand Léger about the cinema's remarkable power to harness visibility: "What precisely is the cinema of attractions? First, it is a cinema that bases itself on the quality that Léger celebrated: its ability to *show* something."[25] Modernist Parisian cinephilia throughout the 1920s was obsessed with the ecstatic possibilities of "pure" cinema. The textual prologue added to later prints of Ballet Mécanique (1924) is obviously wrong in calling it the first film with no scenario, but this error highlights ways in which French cinema was tapping into pre-narrative stores of energy and excess.

Noting, as we saw, that early cinema and cinema in general had been theorized under the hegemony of narrative would seem to tell us two things. First, the study of film has occurred within the historical framework of narrative film's dominance. Its methods, including its reliance on interpretive models, and the questions it poses are circumscribed by the pervasiveness of the paradigm of narrative cinema. But Gunning is also arguing that narrative theory has itself constituted a hegemonic structure that has limited our understanding of the medium, in part by effacing the long history of counter-traditions that underlies narrative cinema itself. This is why Gunning is particularly insistent on the "exhibitionistic" nature of the cinema of attractions: cinematic spectatorship can only be aligned with voyeurism when the figures onscreen no longer seem to return the spectator's gaze, when the structures of invisible storytelling preclude an acknowledgment of the presence of the camera. Miriam Hansen argues that the more univocal system of narration that was in place around 1907-08 introduced "the segregation of the fictional space-time on the screen from the actual one of the theater or, rather, the subordination of the latter under the spell of the former."[26] By contrast, the cinema of attractions is presentational, and is therefore more accurately described as exhibitionistic. Gunning returns to this point several times: even when discussing early peeping tom films, he notes that "its principal motive is again *pure* exhibitionism," and he also contrasts "exhibitionist confrontation" with "diegetic absorption."[27]

But there is actually little contradiction between Gunning's model of film history and Mulvey's paradigm. If Mulvey pointed to the *something else* in the film text, Gunning suggests that it was there from the outset: cinematic spectacle preceded and subtended the emergence of a stable (and stabilizing) set of narrative structures. "The Hollywood advertising policy of enumerating the features of a film, each emblazoned with the command, 'See!' shows this primal power of the attraction running beneath the armature of narrative regulation."[28] It is easy to forget that Mulvey recognized that equating the film spectator with the voyeur was, in a certain sense, manifestly absurd, because "what is seen on the screen is so manifestly *shown*,"[29] a statement easily aligned with Gunning's notion of an "exhibitionistic" cinema.

Untaming the Attraction

If Gunning will argue that attractions will continue to exist within narrative cinema in a "tamed" form, then Mulvey provides a gloss on how, in the case of the spectacular attraction of female sexuality, that taming has occurred. What Noël Burch has called the emblematic shot emerged around 1903; it usually involved a portrait of a character from the film, often making eye contact with the spectator.[30] Such a shot did not properly belong to the relating of the narrative, which is why it, in Burch's charming phrase, "wanders about the margins of the diegesis, with no fixed abode."[31] After 1906, Burch notes, the emblematic shot often presented "the smiling face of the heroine, at last seen from close to."[32] Thus the emblematic shot of early cinema quickly becomes gendered, presenting the spectacle of the woman existing apart from the diegesis. It would be anachronistic to state that the emblematic shot disrupted a system of narration that had not yet fully stabilized, but it is fair to say that women coexisted as both attraction and character within the heterogeneity of early cinematic narrative. The problem for narrative, once a self-contained, self-explaining, stable system of narration had emerged, was to find ways in which the woman could continue to function as a spectacle. Hence the woman of mystery, the showgirl, and the star system: all of these legitimated, without stigmatizing, the act of looking at the represented female.

In his later essay on the temporality of the cinema of attractions, Gunning emphasizes the present-time aspect of early cinema.[33] While cinema is frequently discussed as existing in an unfolding moment that is experienced as the present for the film spectator, narrative film involves an aspect of temporal *development* that is less present in the cinema of attractions. The time of early cinema, with one single-shot view (each with its own thick sense of flowing time), following one another in fairly rapid succession, is a temporality of *irruption*. The spectacle is a spectacle of the instant (and if this isn't too oxymoronic, an instant with duration). So, too, the spectacle of the woman is presented as an irruption in Mulvey's analysis, often again in the form of a close-up (*"Who, me?"*), an irruptive presentation that, like Burch's emblematic shot, does not quite properly belong to either the space or the time of the developing narrative.

The strength of Mulvey's essay in the context of "The Cinema of Attractions," then, lies in its early insistence upon the disruptive power of cinematic spectacle. Rather than dismissing it as extraneous because of its non-narrative aspect, Mulvey posited that spectacle was fundamental to the construction of cinematic meaning, so fundamental that within the particular system of Classical Hollywood Cinema, its dangerous potential needed to be tamed and contained. Yet the repetition-compulsion of the visual tropes and narrative structures which she identified also points to the forever unfinished work of containment, a labor that must be staged and restaged. Perhaps "Visual Pleasure and Narrative Cinema" demonstrates that the power of the attraction is not so easily or fully tamed, after all. (Mary Ann Doane has argued that the emergent structures of narrative cinema exist to contain the dangerous contingency of the cinematic attraction but also to allow it.[34])

I have pointed to the iconoclastic, Brechtian aspect of Mulvey's project, and it is worth remembering that Brecht had suggested adopting rhetorical strategies from earlier forms of narration – the epic was antithetical to psychologism and naturalism. Gunning's theorizing of an earlier mode of cinematic representation did not have the same polemical focus; he did not, for example, advocate a *re-*

turn to the mode of attractions. And yet he knew full well that this was precisely what Eisenstein was advocating when he wrote of "the montage of attractions" in 1924. Eisenstein's attraction was an attention-grabber, something that could not be naturalized through the terms of a psychologized narrative. The attraction thus had something of the Brechtian alienation effect about it, it returned the filmic spectator to the role of spectator or, perhaps even better, the role of witness. This is after all, the definition of spectacle itself: an impressive, unusual, or disturbing phenomenon or event that is seen or witnessed. The attraction was an early step for Eisenstein along the road toward an intellectual cinema that would teach the worker to think dialectically.[35] While Gunning's reintroduction of the term "attraction" twenty years ago first gestured toward the "non-narrative variety"[36] offered by fairground, circus, or vaudeville show, Eisenstein's use of the term also, explicitly, informed his choice of term. Gunning indicates ways that early cinema served as the "inspiration" for the avant-gardes of the 1920s (and later). The attraction is an important element of avant-garde film practice – as demonstrated by Eisenstein, Léger, Godard, Warhol, and others – in ways commensurate with Brecht's interest in epic modes of narration. Here, then, spectacle can be harnessed to serve the interests of ideological resistance – the attraction can return as an untamed form.

Notes

1. Laura Mulvey, "Visual Pleasure and Narrative Cinema," *Screen* 16.3 (1975): 6-18.
2. Tom Gunning, "The Cinema of Attractions: Early Film, Its Spectator and the Avant-Garde," *Early Cinema: Space Frame Narrative*, ed. Thomas Elsaesser (London: British Film Institute, 1990) 56-62.
3. Gunning, "The Cinema of Attractions" 61.
4. Raymond Bellour, "The Unattainable Text," *The Analysis of Film*, ed. Constance Penley (Bloomington/Indianapolis: Indiana UP, 2000) 22, 26.
5. Bellour 24.
6. Paul Willeman, "Introduction to Framework" at http://www.frameworkonline.com/about2.htm.
7. Manny Farber, "Underground Films," *Negative Space: Manny Farber on the Movies*, expanded ed. (New York: Da Capo, 1998) 20.
8. Willeman.
9. See Miriam Hansen, "The Mass Production of the Senses: Classical Cinema as Vernacular Modernism," *Reinventing Film Studies*, ed. Christine Gledhill and Linda Williams (London: Arnold, 2000) 332-50.
10. Fetishism was already rampant in the earlier cinema of attractions, as in the Edison Company's THE GAY SHOE CLERK, but it was not consistently connected to a male spectator within the diegesis.
11. Mulvey 8.

12. Mulvey 17.

13. Mulvey 8.

14. Mulvey 15.

15. *Screen* 15.2 (1974) and 16.4 (1975).

16. Bertolt Brecht, "Short Organum" (1948), quoted in John Willett, *The Theatre of Bertolt Brecht* (1959; London: Methuen, 1967) 166.

17. Molly Haskell, *From Reverence to Rape: The Treatment of Women in the Movies* (New York: Penguin, 1974) 8, see also 126. Haskell, as the title of her study implies, saw the concerted backlash against feminism in contemporary American cinema as far more insidiously misogynist. This moment of film history undoubtedly also fuelled Mulvey's polemic.

18. Frank Kermode, *The Sense of an Ending: Studies in the Theory of Fiction*, 2nd ed. (New York/Oxford: Oxford UP, 2000).

19. Thomas Elsaesser, "Early Cinema: From Linear History to Mass Media Archaeology," *Early Cinema: Space Frame Narrative* 3.

20. As Elsaesser does himself in later publications. See also his contribution in the present volume.

21. Elsaesser, "Early Cinema" 3.

22. Elsaesser, "Early Cinema" 3.

23. Tom Gunning, "An Unseen Energy Swallows Space: Early Film and the Avant-Garde," *Film Before Griffith*, ed. John Fell (Berkeley: U of California P, 1984) 355-66.

24. Gunning, "The Cinema of Attractions" 56

25. Gunning, "The Cinema of Attractions" 57.

26. Miriam Hansen, *Babel & Babylon: Spectatorship in American Silent Film* (Cambridge: Harvard UP, 1991) 83.

27. Gunning, "The Cinema of Attractions" 58, 59.

28. Gunning, "The Cinema of Attractions" 61.

29. Emphasis added.

30. Noël Burch, "A Primitive Mode of Representation?," *Early Cinema: Space Frame Narrative*, 223.

31. Burch 224.

32. Burch 223.

33. Tom Gunning, "'Now You See it, Now You Don't': The Temporality of the Cinema of Attractions," *Silent Film*, ed. Richard Abel (New Brunswick: Rutgers UP, 1996) 71-84.

34. Mary Ann Doane, *The Emergence of Cinematic Time: Modernity, Contingency, The Archive* (Cambridge: Harvard UP 2002) 32

35. Sergei Eisenstein, "Notes for a Film of Capital," trans. Maciej Sliwowski, Jay Leyda and Annette Michelson, *October* 2 (Summer 1976): 10.

36. Gunning, "The Cinema of Attractions" 60.

Attraction Theories and Terminologies

["Early Film"]

From "Primitive Cinema" to "Kine-Attractography"

André Gaudreault

In the late 1970s, a new generation of film scholars set themselves the task of re-examining from top to bottom the period of cinema's emergence. This did not fail to provoke major upheavals within the – quite young – discipline of "cinema studies," which had only recently been admitted to university and was still far from having acquired complete legitimacy. What is more, the forceful arrival of this enquiry into the "source" most certainly contributed to the remarkable reversal witnessed within the discipline in the 1980s, when questions of film *history* took their place alongside questions of film *theory*. For film theory had been the only field of interest to the leading academics of the 1960s and 1970s. We might even say that research into cinema's emergence has been the principal cause of this transformation, a transformation that has gone so far as to promote, for the first time in the field, a true complicity between theory and history. This first serious on-the-ground encounter between the synchronic and the diachronic, moreover, has had a lasting impact on the discipline, the effects of which are still being felt today. Indeed it would be impossible for such a demonstration, through years of practice, of the "organic" link between theory and history not to leave its mark on each of these two fields.

The starting gun of this movement to rediscover so-called "early cinema" was probably fired at the "Cinema 1900-1906" conference in Brighton in 1978, in which the present author was fortunate enough to participate.[1] There, our examination of "early cinema" privileged, and this was novel for the time, a highly *documented* approach: more than five hundred films of the period were brought together,[2] loaned for the occasion by some fifteen film archives around the world. The screening of these films to a small group of international specialists (many of them recent young graduates keen on developing a new approach to the field) was a true revelation. Film after film we witnessed vast sections of the existing "Histories of the Cinema" crumble before our eyes. Contrary to what all these books had told us, tracking shots, close-ups, parallel editing and other fundamental devices of film language had not waited for David Wark Griffith to make their appearance.

These intensive screenings of views which had not been seen for decades shook up the conception one might have had at the time of the early years of cinema. True, the specialists invited to Brighton were already relatively prepared for the change: most of them, in the months leading up to the conference, had written an article on the subject,[3] as a way of proposing their ideas to the international community of film archivists present at Brighton, and had thus viewed a certain number of films from the period.[4]

Identifying Points of Rupture

The reader will have noticed the scare quotes I have been placing around the expression "early cinema." Why such caution? Because, as far as historical method is concerned, it seems clear to me that the label we choose to identify our subject is already indicative of the attitude we have towards that subject. In my view, the label used already determines the *issues* at stake in the work of the person examining that subject. What's more, this label frames the subject and divides it up; in a sense it suggests a scenario, necessarily oriented in a certain direction, of the *historical material* itself. In other words, to paraphrase a common expression, you can know someone by the scenarios their labels call to mind.

Using the expression "early cinema" (or, in French, the expressions "le cinéma des premiers temps" ["the cinema of early times" or what we might even go so far as to translate as "the first cinema"] or "le cinéma des origines" ["cinema at its source"]), *directs* the historian's gaze, *determines* his or her approach and *inflects* his or her discourse. Indeed to speak of the *beginnings* of a socio-cultural phenomenon as being the *source* of that phenomenon is necessarily, and spontaneously, to put oneself in the service of a fundamentally evolutionary conception of history. Consciously or not, it is to pass over without comment the ruptures and continuities which make up history. It is also to subscribe to a somewhat idealist conception of history, in which what comes before explains, almost of necessity, what comes after.

In another sense, to speak of "early cinema" is to submit the object of study to an axiology which privileges the historical succession of determined periods, of which one, the *earliest*, is that of *"early"* cinema. A similar succession is postulated in the case of "supposed" moments of rupture ("supposed" in quotation marks because it sometimes proves to be the case that these moments of rupture are, in the end, nothing of the sort). Take for example the traditional distinction between "pre-cinema" and "early cinema." Such a distinction supposes that between these two periods there was a point of rupture. For the "Edisonians" (who date the birth of cinema to the invention of the Edison Kinetoscope), this rupture occurred around 1891-93, while for the "Lumièrists" (who date the birth of cinema to the invention of the Lumière Cinématographe), it occurred around 1894-95. The moment when the "basic device" was invented was certainly a turning point in the evolution of moving picture camera technology, but we have to ask ourselves if the emergence of that technology was accompanied by the passage to a new *paradigm*, to a new *order*. We must also ask if the invention of the Kinetoscope and/or the Cinématographe was a true point of rupture. Moments of rupture and changes of paradigm are not necessarily in synch with the invention of new procedures (of which the Cinématographe was one), nor even with the refinement of new techniques (such as editing).

The question we must ask in this respect is whether the relatively sudden availability of a new technology revolutionizes behaviour, transforms the cultural landscape, sets significant mutations in motion and makes it possible to pass on to a new cultural, artistic and media order. Nothing could be less certain. It is well known that nascent media take their "first steps" by reproducing, in a quite servile manner, other media from which they are derived. And the cinema does not appear to depart from this model.

By establishing, probably mistakenly, a point of rupture in the final decade of the nineteenth century, between the period of so-called pre-cinema and that of so-called early cinema, historians have literally cut cinema off from its deepest roots. These roots, of course, extend into the most remote lands of so-called "pre-cinema." What is more, this posture reinforces the historian's *teleological* reflex, leading him or her to analyze the place of early cinema from a strict "what does the future hold?" perspective and to view early or "first" cinema above all as an antechamber to a *later* or *second* cinema (or cinema's "second era"[5]), the logical and natural continuation of the *zero era* represented by "pre-cinema" and the *early* or *first era* represented by "early" or "first" cinema...

We should also ask the same kind of question about the relationship between so-called *early cinema* and *institutional cinema*. Not only was early cinema, as a rule, unaccompanied by recorded sounds; in addition, its viewers were not always seated in straight rows or subject to a strict code of silence. This "cinema" not only featured unknown actors; its black-and-white images also cast a grey pallor on the room (unless it was exploding with colors hand-painted directly onto the film). This "cinema" not only achieved its ends with quite brief screenings (much shorter, in any event, than the two hours generally privileged by the institution); the screenings in question were also made up of a dozen or more individual views. Etc.

Hence this question, which is essential to any historical thinking about film practices: can "early cinema" (or, to translate from the French, "the cinema of early times," "the first cinema," "cinema at its source," etc.) rightly be considered *cinema*? Wouldn't it be sound to establish a clear distinction between film practices from *before* cinema's *institutionalization* and those that came *with* (and *after*) it? Wouldn't we have good reason to postulate the existence of a clear break, a radical rupture, between so-called early "cinema" and institutional cinema? This is where the possible contradiction in terms found in an expression such as early *cinema* arises, if indeed what the era's cinematographists (a term used in both English and French at the time to describe the camera operator or filmmaker) were producing was not "cinema."

A "Primitive" Cinema?

Every generation of film historians, moreover, in French at least, has had a different way of describing the period when the cinema emerged.[6] The various names which followed one upon the other are, moreover, particularly representative of these historians' changing attitudes. In France, the first expression to take root for describing the period following the invention of the cinematograph was the controversial "primitive cinema," which caused a lot of ink to be spilled. This was a very loaded expression, and in French circles it dominated the scene for a good thirty or forty years. So wide is its appeal that it stuck to the skin of many French film historians and theorists to the extent that some of them are still incapable of shedding it to this day. Recently, Jacques Aumont wrote "Why replace a word [primitive], whose history after all is interesting, with the awkward and outrageously inelegant expression 'the cinema of early times' ('cinéma des premiers temps')?"[7]

There is no doubt about it, the expression "primitive cinema" has its appeal, and we might suppose that one day it will resurface, which would be completely legitimate. But, in my view at least, it would have been capital, over the past twenty or thirty years, to have criticized it severely and then be done with it for a time. Instead, as it was used from the 1940s to the 1960s in particular, the expression "primitive cinema" prevented, in my view, *historical thinking* about the cinema. In the end, this expression's supremacy in French film studies circles appears to have caused more harm than good.

One might retort that the word "primitive" does not always have negative connotations. As an adjective, according to the *Oxford English Dictionary*, the word has no fewer than twelve accepted meanings, of which only two are clearly pejorative. The first and thereby principal meaning given by the *OED* is "of or belonging to the first age, period, or stage; pertaining to early times; earliest, original; early, ancient" (note here the use of the adjectives "first" and "early").

But we must not forget that "primitive" also refers to "a group, or to persons comprising such a group, whose culture, through isolation, has remained at a simple level" and to art "[e]xecuted by one who has not been trained in a formal manner." In the context of our new approaches to the history of the cinematograph's early years, what do we have to gain by adopting a label for our object of study which might equate the earliest animated views with crude and simple objects, the product of an undeveloped culture and founded on ignorance?

Whatever one says, the word "primitive" always leaves a bad taste in the mouth. This is not new, if we are to believe one of the historical actors whose wide-ranging influence we study: Georges Méliès himself. In 1926, when the earliest French cinematographists (beginning with Méliès himself) had become fashionable in certain French intellectual circles, Méliès wrote:

> A true injustice is committed when certain columnists write such things as "these earliest cinematographists were 'primitives' [...]." Do they really believe that we were still primitives after twenty years of sustained work and constant perfecting of our craft? [...] why call us "primitives" with such an air of contempt?[8]

It is thus clear that, by the late 1920s, the use of the expression "primitive" to describe cinematographists could imply something negative.

But this is not all. Even in one of the non-pejorative noun forms of the word (the *OED* recognizes nine all told), "primitive" misses the mark when it comes to describing the cinematographists. In artistic usage, for the *OED*, a primitive is "A painter of the early period, i.e. before the Renaissance." The French-language *Robert* dictionary goes a step further in this direction; for this dictionary, a "primitive" is "an artist from a period *prior* to that in which the art form in question attained its maturity" (my emphasis). There are thus primitive Greek sculptors and primitive Dutch and Italian painters. But Georges Méliès, Edwin Porter and Louis Lumière can not be described as "primitive" in this sense! Rather, we should think of Charles Chaplin, Thos. Ince, Louis Feuillade, Abel Gance and D.W. Griffith as primitive, because these were the artists of the period prior to their art form's *maturity*. An art cannot be mature the moment it is born; as François Jost has effectively demonstrated,[9] film art was not born until the 1910s. And it would not reach so-called maturity until at least the 1920s.

Early Cinema?

Beginning in the 1960s, in French, the expression "le cinéma des premiers temps" gradually began to take the place of "primitive cinema." As I mentioned above, we might translate this expression as "the cinema of early times" or "the first cinema," while the expression that has been adopted in English is, of course, "early cinema"; we will return to all three of these expressions below. Contrary to what Michel Marie believed at the time of the conference on Méliès at Cerisy in 1996,[10] the present author was not the first person to use the French expression, in 1979 in the title of the French version of the Brighton proceedings which I edited.[11] The expression can be found here and there before that date, particularly in the work of Christian Metz,[12] without any special note concerning its use, which would tend to demonstrate that the expression was already accepted as early as the 1960s.

This expression beguiles us with illusions and is unsuited to the reality it pretends to describe. Beginning, as we have seen, with the use of the very word "cinema" to describe this period in which the *production of animated views* reigned; to describe these views as "cinema" seems to usurp the term. According to the position I am arguing here, the cinema as such did not yet exist in the period of so-called "early cinema."

Early *cinema*? Exit, therefore, "cinema"!

Each of the other two components of the expression "the cinema of early times" is worthy of suspicion. Let's look, for example, at the determinative complement "early times." Here is a determination whose first shortcoming is the way it implies a completely Western sense of historical time, as Silvestra Mariniello has described.[13] As Mariniello suggests, we should instead be addressing an *issue*. The expression "early times" gives off a whiff of ethnocentrism. It is not clear that early cinema in the United States, for example, has anything whatsoever in common with the early cinema of a country which had been unexposed to the new medium before the 1930s.

Some might say that this objection, although undeniable, is not a major one, because it is always possible to contextualize our use of this expression. Be that as it may, the shoe also pinches elsewhere, and in a way that is clearly beyond remedy. To use "early" to speak of practices around the cinematograph, in the sense understood here, supposes that the question of the path taken when the cinematograph became the cinema and the objective of that passage has already been settled.

To speak of "early cinema" or "the cinema of early times" is to adopt a position which, at bottom, is completely opposed to my position here. To speak of "early cinema" is to decide in advance to put on teleological glasses which oblige the observer to conclude that the phenomenon under observation is just beginning (this is what early means), that it isn't doing too badly for a youngster, and that it will surely make progress as the years go by…

In the end, however, the cinema's "early times" are also, and perhaps most of all, the "late times" of certain other phenomena. Let me make myself clear: I am not saying that the cinematograph cannot be seen as being at the early times of such and such a phenomenon. Of course it can. But to label our object of study "early cinema" is to give an advantage to one aspect that an enquiry such as ours has no interest in privileging, if indeed that enquiry is fully to grasp the subject's contours. Because the time of so-called early cinema is in fact a time bordering on two worlds: the time when the cinematograph *did not yet exist* (say before 1895) and the time when early cinema, having yielded its place to cinema – to institutional cinema – *no longer existed* (say around 1915).

When we give our allegiance to what is presupposed by the expression "early cinema" we find ourselves saying, for example, that Méliès *introduced* this or that *into* the cinema. If it is the least bit true that Méliès introduced the theater *into* the cinema, the contrary, which is always left unsaid, is a hundred times truer! Méliès did not just *introduce the theater into the cinema*, he also, and quite effectively, *introduced the cinematograph into the theater*, if only into the Robert Houdin theater! And this inversion of things makes all the difference. Because the arrival of the cinematograph in Méliès's world extended a firmly established practice. And, by situating this arrival in the extension of this previous practice, it becomes possible for us better to grasp its profound significance. Not by saying that something started with the introduction of this new technology and by making the past a blank slate. Nor, likewise, by consecrating Méliès as a "filmmaker" while not mentioning his "true nature" (here I should say his true *culture*) as a man of the theater.

Jacques Deslandes understood this perfectly when he wrote that "Méliès was not a pioneer of the cinema, he was the last man to work in fairy theater."[14] Méliès himself had no illusions about this true vocation when he declared that "My film career is so tied to my career at the Robert Houdin theater that it is impossible to separate them."[15] Or, once again, when he said about his film studio, "In sum, it was a quite faithful image, in miniature, of my fairy theater."[16]

There may not thus have been, as Méliès himself said, a clear break between his theatrical career and his film career. In the same way that there is no clear distinction either between the titles of his stage performances and the titles of his films. Indeed it would be impossible, without consulting the documentation, to discern which of Méliès's works were films and which were stage acts. This is true of the following list, which gives the impression of being a list of films, if it weren't for their production dates (given in parentheses), which confirm that they were all well and truly stage acts: *La Fée des fleurs ou le Miroir de Cagliostro* (The Flower Fairy or Cagliostro's Mirror, 1889), *L'Enchanteur Alcofrisbas* (Alcofrisbas the Enchanter, 1889), *Le Manoir du Diable* (The Devil's Manor, 1890), *Les Farces de la Lune ou les Mésaventures de Nostradamus* (The Moon's Pranks or the Misadventures of Nostradamus, 1891), *Le Charlatan fin de Siècle* (The Turn of the Century Charlatan, 1892) and *L'Auberge du Diable* (The Devil's Inn, 1894).[17]

Even if it applies almost absolutely to Méliès, the issue I am raising here remains of value, with a minimal degree of adaptation, for all "producers of animated views" in so-called early so-called cinema. What the Lumière brothers created, and this has often been acknowledged without all the repercussions being fully understood, was moving *photographs*, and their work must necessarily be seen as part of the history of photography. Lumière views belong as much if not more to the history of photographic views than to the history of cinema.[18] It would be more productive to write the history of this work by comparing it *synchronically* with other work from the cultural practice from which it is derived than to study it *diachronically* as part of film history. Because Lumière views did not take the place of the other work in the cultural practice from which they are derived; in a sense, what they did was amalgamate themselves with this work: naturally, still photography continued to exist in 1895, 1896 and 1897, and it would be highly profitable to study a synchronic slice of the diverse work within the cultural practice known as "photography," which includes, according to my proposal here, the work of the first people to turn the handle of moving picture cameras.

It is thus clear that the first experiments to which the introduction of the cinematograph gave rise belonged to practices which in no way whatsoever were in their "early" periods.

Early cinema? Exit, therefore, "early"!

What remains of this famous expression? Of "early cinema," nothing. But if we return to the French expression "le cinéma des premiers temps" and our translation of it as "the cinema of early times" or "the first cinema," we find a singular article, "the" – and a very curious one at that! And so we must also critique this word which, despite its relatively small size, beguiles us with illusions just as much as the other two terms of the equation. Because this "the," at bottom, is an attempt to join what can't be joined. The cultural practice "fairy play," even in its film version, had little in common with the cultural practice "magic act," even in its film version, and even when both were united somewhat artificially in a Méliès catalogue. The views screened at the Maison Dufayel cinema in Paris for children and their nannies surely had little in common with the exhibition in a travelling country fair of a film like Méliès's LA TENTATION DE SAINT-ANTOINE (The Temptation of St. Anthony, 1898). The screening in Paris of Méliès's RAID PARIS-MONTE CARLO (Paris-Monte Carlo Rally, 1905) had little in common either with the conditions in which Henry de Grandsaignes d'Hauterives screened views in Quebec.[19] And a Pathé film's gay tale of a rake screened in New York's Lower East Side had little in common with a view screened to complement a magic lantern show organized by *La Bonne Presse* in Paris. Before institutionalization, the various practices around the cinematograph had little in common with each other; it is film historians and theorists who have united them, artificially and idealistically, in their discourse: "the" first cinema, "the" cinema of early times. But there was not just *one* cinema before 1910, there were dozens, and none was truly dominant, because the cinema, precisely, had not yet been institutionalized.

The cinema of early times? Exit, therefore, "the"!

A Terminological Problem

How then are we to name our object of study without getting everything askew? How, on the basis of the criticisms I have just formulated, to avoid exposing myself to criticism in turn? What might I propose to take the place of the consecrated – and inadequate – expression "early cinema"? We might, for example, get around the problem by resorting, as I have been doing for several years, to the expression "animated pictures" ("vues animées") to speak of the films themselves. This was one of the terms used at the time of their production, but it is not suitable for describing a period or a paradigm. We might also, following the previous generation of scholars (Edgar Morin and Jacques Deslandes in particular), use the term "cinematograph" ("cinématographe") to identify "early cinematography" ("cinématographie des premiers temps") and contrast it with the "cinema," which would then be used for institutional cinema alone. Although this is a subtle and quite useful distinction, it is not enough, in my view, to enable us to distinguish clearly and unmistakably between the two entities. What we need for designating so-called "early cinema" is a general and all-encompassing term that ties everything together and subsumes the entire phenomenon we are attempting to put our fingers on.

Initially, I thought of returning to the expression "the cinema of attractions," which has the advantage of taking into account that fundamental category, the attraction. Tom Gunning and I introduced this expression into the field of "early cinema" studies in 1985.[20] But the thorny contradiction of the use of the word "cinema" remained. Then I thought of proposing the expression "early cinematography" (which I used a few lines back), but, as we have seen, the determinative complement "early" gives me cause for concern (although these concerns are fewer and less serious, because I refer to "cinematography" and not "cinema," but still…). I would very much have liked to have had a flash of genius and been able to blend these two expressions to come up with something like "cinématographie-attraction," but I found that I had been beaten to the punch: in consulting Jean Giraud's indispensable *Le Lexique français du cinéma des origines à 1930* I discovered that the term, in French, already existed.[21] For the moment, its only known occurrence is in the writings of one of the first film historians: not just anybody because, some twenty years before publishing his history of the cinema, he had been not only a contemporary of cinématographie-attraction but also one of its major figures.

This early (!) historian was G.-Michel Coissac, the author in 1906 of the imposing *Manuel pratique du conférencier-projectionniste*, published by La Bonne Presse.[22] In his *Histoire du Cinématographe* (1925), he wrote that, around 1907-08, "the large boulevards in Paris quickly became the center of cinématographie-attraction."[23]

Cinématographie-attraction... or, as I will henceforth describe it in English, *kine-attractography*[24]: this expression, in my view, has the quality of dynamically "problematizing" our object of study. It is an expression which, at the same time as it befits the gaze cast in the 1920s by a participant in the period, corresponds to the idea we have come to have of the early years of cinematography in the past few years, at the turn of the twenty-first century. That is, at the end of the twentieth century, which can pretty much be divided up evenly when it comes to the way it designated (in French at least) the period under observation: from the 1930s to the 1960s, the expression "cinéma primitif" held sway, while from the 1960s on "le cinéma des premiers temps" started to take its place.

The Attraction of the Cinematograph

We might suppose that Jacques Aumont would approve of the term "kine-attractography," if only because it incorporates one of the key themes – attraction – in the ideas of Sergei Eisenstein, of which Aumont is one of the most accomplished heralds. There is in fact a lot to be said about the convergence of Eisensteinian attraction and the attractions of the cinematograph's early times,[25] as well as about the importance of attraction throughout the twentieth century in the cultural sphere in general.[26]

We should not be surprised, however, at the convergence of the attraction of early times and Eisensteinian attraction. Because the latter, quite simply, has the former as its "source." Or rather, to put it more correctly, because they share a common source. The attractional quality of kine-attractography is not merely an intellectual category devised by contemporary scholars in need of interpretive models. Attraction was a fact of life that the various protagonists of the kine-attractography had to face in their daily activities, fully aware of the fact. When, in the early 1920s, Eisenstein seized on the concept of attraction and gave it a place in his theory (and thus in film theory as a whole), the word "attraction" had been on everyone's lips, or almost, *for nigh on thirty years already*. And all that time it had the same meaning as it had from the start for Eisenstein. In fact, *Eisensteinian attraction and the attraction of early times both derived directly from a common source, the culture of popular stage entertainments dating from the turn of the century*. Thus, in the same year that Eisenstein published his first article on attraction, in 1923,[27] the popular French magazine *Ciné pour tous* published an anonymously authored two-page article entitled "Attraction in Films,"[28] which basically set out how films of the day were constructed around brief moments of attraction such as storms, explosions and other sudden occurrences. The article praises chase films in particular for being able to exploit all the possibilities of movement. The author mentions the climactic rescue scenes in Griffith's films and does not hesitate to criticize the films of his own day (the early 1920s) for indiscriminately employing a wide range of catastrophes as climaxes (fires, cyclones, explosions, earthquakes, etc.): "We have quickly reached the point where the attraction reigns in a sensational manner and is incorporated into films with or without cause in order to heighten their appeal." The author even asks if so many "high points" are necessary when these so often seem to be "perfectly useless to the logical development of the action."

The word "attraction," as I remarked above, was on everyone's lips, and I would add that it was at the tip of everyone's pen. We find it in journalism as early as 1896: "With the arrival of the warm weather, attractions in Paris are more numerous and varied every day at the cinematograph."[29] Or, as another commentator wrote about a 1906 Pathé view, "LE TOUR DU MONDE D'UN POLICIER [A Policeman's World Tour] is a magnificent cinematographic attraction."[30] We also find the term in more theoretical or at any rate more reflexive texts. This is true of the following particularly penetrating judgment by Louis Delluc in 1917: "Viewers could care less about attractions. They prefer a story, a good story, vivid and well told."[31] The prize for lucidity, nevertheless, goes to E.-L. Fouquet, writing in 1912:

> The cinematograph was long seen as an "attraction." It was used in café-concert, music hall and vaudeville programs, just like a singer or an acrobat. [...] Today, this is no longer the case: cinematograph shows generally last the whole evening and the audience does not tire of them. The cinema is no longer an attraction but a standard form of entertainment.
>
> Unlike what was previously the case, now the cinematograph calls on certain attractions.
>
> [...] Moreover, what is seen as an attraction in music halls, vaudeville theaters and circuses (tests of strength, balancing acts, magic shows, comic scenes, dances) can be cinematographed and in this way become an entertainment just as interesting as it would be in reality.[32]

But what exactly is an attraction? Giraud describes it as the "captivating and sensational element of the program."[33] Or, as Gunning remarks, it is a moment of pure "exhibitionism"[34] characterized by an implicit acknowledgment of the viewer's presence, a viewer who is directly confronted in an exhibitionist manner. The attraction is there, before the viewer, *in order to be seen*. Strictly speaking, it exists only in order to *display its visibility*.[35] As a rule, attractions are momentary, if not instantaneous; Gunning says that "they can be defined as an immediate presence."[36] In other words, he comments elsewhere, an attraction is "an element which surges up, attracts our attention, and then disappears without developing a narrative trajectory or a coherent diegetic universe."[37]

The attractions of the kine-attractography are thus the peak moments of the show, the aggressive moments punctuating animated views. They are scattered throughout their discourse and even form the kernel of most views. This is the case of the uni-punctual view (a view made up of a single "shot," a single tableau) How it Feels to Be Run over (Hepworth, 1900), in which an automobile advances towards the camera and knocks it over, causing a sudden and unexpected interruption in the filming. It is also true of L'Arrivée d'un train en gare de La Ciotat (Lumière, 1897), at the spectacular moment when the locomotive seems like it is about to run the viewer over. And it is true, finally, of that moment of sudden action in L'Arroseur arrosé (Lumière, 1895) when the stream of water, suddenly unblocked, sprays the poor gardener in the face.

Attraction vs. Narration

Attractions are not just the dominant principle of kine-attractography. They are also in contradiction with the dominant principle of institutional cinema (and the cinema of institutionalization): *narration*. Nevertheless, it is true that attraction and narration can work well together: the attractions found in kine-attractography often even form part of a narrative infrastructure. This is what Méliès himself remarked when he wrote the following:

> We might say that in this case the script is nothing more than the thread for tying together the "effects," which are not closely connected, the way the announcer in a variety performance is there to link scenes which have nothing in common with each other.[38]

Conversely, narrative cinema is often riddled with attractions. Indeed these are present, often on a massive scale, in popular entertainment films, even the most recent; this is especially true of adventure films, musical comedies, suspense films, science fiction films, etc. What is a James Bond or Star Wars movie if not, at bottom, a series of "effects" without much to connect them? Doesn't the *tour de force* of the scriptwriter of such films consist precisely in tying these scenes together in not too slack a manner? Indeed this is one of the institution's principles: to dissolve the attractions scattered throughout the film's discourse into a narrative structure, to integrate them in the most organic manner possible.

After all, the apparent contradiction between attraction and narration is only the resurgence of what we might think of as the *essential contradiction of the cin-*

ema as a system, the ineluctable contradiction that weighs on the cinematograph, constantly torn between the *momentary* and *linear progression*.

The momentary is the attraction, which is inevitably and constantly called
into question by the contamination of narrative progression, by the folding of
the momentary into progression. By definition, the cinematograph supposes a
discourse that unfolds in time and is experienced in its *duration*. What this
means is that any film, and any view as well, no matter how short, is made up
of a *chain* of signifiers lined up one after the other: momentary signifiers subjected to progression (subjected to the process of creating progression involved
in the unspooling of the film strip).

This tension between the momentary and linear progression, moreover, can
be found everywhere in the categories we use to think about the cinema. Think
in particular of the opposition, with which I have elsewhere feathered my
nest,[39] between monstration and narration. Think too of the opposition between
spectacular effects and *narrative* effects, between the photogram and the shot,
framing and editing, etc. In the end, the problem of the cinema is always the
same: to create linear progression out of the momentary. On a strictly technological level, this is even the very definition of cinema: with one photogram, we
are in the realm of the momentary (this is the *thesis*); while with a second photogram, and those that follow on, we enter the realm of linear progression (this is
the *antithesis*). Thus we could probably put forward the idea that narration, by
virtue of this very dynamic, is a sort of antithesis of attraction.

Monstrative Attractions vs. Narrative Integration

An examination of these sorts of questions led Tom Gunning and me, some
twenty years ago now, to propose that this period from the invention of the
cinematograph to the institutionalization of cinema should be seen as a series
of "overarching systems," as we called them at the time. We set out to identify
and define these systems in order to be able to understand individual films in a
way that made it possible, as we remarked at the time, "to better discern, within
each of them, which elements conform to the system and which diverge from
it."[40] We thus had to bring to light the various systems of *rules* and *norms* which
contributed to establishing a coherent series of expectations around the way a
view or film should function in any given era. The stylistic choices of camera
operators and, later, film directors were made on the basis of these expectations.

Within the period leading up to the cinema's institutionalization, we identified two successive "modes of film practice."[41] The first of these modes dominated the very earliest period of film history, until about 1908, while the second

extended its dominion until about 1914. We called the former the "system of monstrative attractions" and the latter the "system of narrative integration." Within the system of monstrative attractions, film narration was of course completely secondary. In this system, rather, filmic monstration and the attraction reigned. The various cinematic devices we have come to call, perhaps with exaggeration, *film language* first made their appearance during this period (close-ups, high-angle shots, tracking shots, etc.). In the system of monstrative attractions, however, these devices did not necessarily have the same functions as they would have in the system that followed, that of narrative integration. Thus the close-up, for example, might in the former have a "magnifying glass" function (the filmic monstrator's close-ups enable us to see "swollen heads," an attractional element if ever there was one). In the system of narrative integration, however, the close-up had a more indexical and indicative function (the film narrator's close-up became this agent's principal means for indicating a detail and bringing it to the fore without using a magnifying glass effect, thereby highlighting the device's narrative function). In the first case, the object depicted is artificially brought closer to the viewer's eye through a kind of blowing up of the image. Our vision is stimulated by such an attraction, as for example by the highly attractional close-up showing the leader of the gang of robbers shooting at the camera in THE GREAT TRAIN ROBBERY (Edison, 1903). In the second case, through some mysterious, unknown process, the viewer comes closer to the object being observed and not the other way around (and herein lies the "magic" of narrative cinema). An example of such a highly narrative close-up is that of the medicine bottle in Griffith's film THE MEDICINE BOTTLE (Biograph, 1909).

Within the system of monstrative attractions, then, close-ups, high-angle shots and tracking shots do not have the same functions as they do in the system of narrative integration. The reason for this, in particular, is that in the former they are not strictly subjected to "narrativization." As Tom Gunning and I defined it, the system of narrative integration appears to be a system through which the cinema followed an integrated process of narrativization.[42] During this period, cinematic discourse was put *in the service* of the story being told. The various components of cinematic expression were thus mobilized around, and subjected to, strict narrative ends:

> The dominant feature of the system of narrative integration is that an element of cinematic signification is chosen and given an integrational role: that of telling the story. The narrator chooses the various elements of discourse as a function of the story, and it is also through the story that the viewer is led to interpret the various forms of cinematic discourse. The suturing of the film narrator and the viewer is guaranteed by the coherence of the process of narrativization. When the system of narrative integration was taking shape, a being was born whose existence is only theoretical but whose task is to modulate and direct cinematic discourse: the narrator, whose "voice"

is heard from the beginning of the film to the end, by means of the way it structures, at one and the same time, the profilmic, the camera work and editing.[43]

Institutional cinema is a narrative cinema, and thus requires a narrator. The "cinema" of attractions needs no such narrator. It prefers the fairground crier, the music hall, vaudeville theater or café-concert master of ceremonies, the storefront cinema barker, who add the attraction of their own performance to the attractions of kine-attractography.

By Way of Conclusion

To postulate a break between so-called early cinema and institutional cinema is to bring a radical change of attitude to the worthy subject that early cinema generally is for the film scholar. It is also to finally stop trying to see what remains of one (early cinema) in the other (institutional cinema). On the contrary, to postulate a break between early cinema and institutional cinema is to bring out the differences between these two entities and reveal the "organic" quality of these differences. This organic quality derives from the fact that, at the time, nothing was yet set in stone concerning cinematographic practices or habitus. Between the moment of the invention of the cinematograph (say, 1895) and the moment of cinema's institutionalization (say, 1915), the world of the cinematograph was an open field of enquiry and experimentation. Our task is to convince ourselves that the fundamental point of rupture in film history was not the invention of the moving picture camera in the 1890s (the Kinetograph, the Cinématographe) but rather the constitution of the institution "cinema" in the 1910s, an institution whose first principle was a systematic rejection of the ways and customs of early cinema, of a past to which the institution no longer owed a thing (which, moreover, is not entirely untrue). From this perspective, we must insist upon what I have called elsewhere[44] early cinema's *alien* quality, a properly irreducible alien quality which traditional film historians have always tried to paper over.

Translated by Timothy Barnard

Notes

This article was written under the aegis of GRAFICS (Groupe de recherche sur l'avène-ment et la formation des instititions cinématographique et scénique) at the Université de Montréal, which is funded by the Social Sciences and Humanities Research Council of Canada (SSHRC) and the Fonds québécois de recherche sur la société et la culture. GRA-FICS is a member of the Centre de recherche sur l'intermédialité (CRI) at the Université de Montréal. The present article is a revised version of part of a book previously pub-lished in Italian, *Cinema delle origini. O della "cinematografia-attrazione"* (Milano: Il Castoro, 2004).

1. This symposium was held as part of the 34th congress of the International Federa-tion of Film Archives (FIAF), organized by David Francis (at the time an archivist of the National Film Archive in London) in collaboration with Eileen Bowser (at the time an archivist in the Film Department of the Museum of Modern Art in New York).

2. For a compilation of these films, see *Cinema 1900-1906: An Analytical Study, Volume 2: Filmographie/Filmography,* ed. André Gaudreault (Bruxelles: FIAF, 1982).

3. These articles were published in the conference proceedings: *Cinema 1900-1906: An Analytical Study,* vol. 1, ed. Roger Holman (Bruxelles: FIAF, 1982). Most of the pa-pers presented at Brighton were also published in French in *Les Cahiers de la Ciné-mathèque* 29 (1979).

4. This is true in particular of the "Team U.S.A." which, under the leadership of Eileen Bowser, took very seriously their mission to choose which films found in US ar-chives were to be shown at Brighton. The members of this team screened several hundred films at the time, a good many of which were not shown at Brighton.

5. This is the expression used by Eric de Kuyper in "Le cinéma de la seconde époque: le muet des années 10," *Cinémathèque* 1 (1992): 28-35.

6. I will leave it to English-language scholars to trace the history of these terms in English. A brief and far from conclusive survey by me and the translator of these lines, however, has turned up the following: it would appear that the term "primi-tive cinema" came to English from the French, and at a much later date, possibly as late as Noël Burch's work (largely published in translation from French) in the early 1980s. "Early cinema" too seems to have appeared in English much later than the French "cinéma des premiers temps." Its first use as a historical category may date from a 1979 article by Charles Musser, immediately following the 1978 Brighton conference ("The Early Cinema of Edwin Porter," *Cinema Journal* 19.1 [Fall 1979]). A few years later, in the first published anthologies of the work of many of the "Brighton generation" historians, the term still had not taken root: in the Brighton proceedings edited by Roger Holman in 1982, some authors employed "early film" (or "early films," with less claim to describing a historical category), while others used "early cinema" (*Cinema 1900-1906,* vol. 1). The following year, in a book edited by John Fell, an article by Tom Gunning, whose name would later become synon-ymous with "early cinema" studies in the US, still employed the expression "early film" ("An Unseen Energy Swallows Space: The Space in Early Film and Its Relation to American Avant-Garde Film," *Film Before Griffith,* ed. John Fell [Berkeley: U of

California P, 1983]). In that same volume, "early cinema" is the term used in an article by André Gaudreault, in a translation by John Fell that was perhaps influenced by the presence of the word "cinema" in the French expression "cinéma des premiers temps" ("Temporality and Narrativity in Early Cinema, 1895-1908"). Finally, one might even argue that "early film" was the more natural choice in English and enjoyed the advantage of a certain distance from the institution "cinema"; it may be that "early cinema" prevailed because of the pervasive French influence in the field – in which case I assume my share of the blame, in light of my "early" translated article noted above! We have been able to trace the systematic use of "early film" as far back as Rachael Low's (in collaboration with Roger Manvell for the first volume) multi-volume history of early British cinema (we refer to the three volumes covering 1896-1918) published immediately after the Second World War, *The History of the British Film* (London: Unwin, 1948-50) – A.G. and T.B.

7. Jacques Aumont, "Quand y a-t-il cinéma primitif? ou Plaidoyer pour le primitif," *Le Cinéma au tournant du siècle/Cinema at the Turn of the Century*, ed. Claire Dupré la Tour, André Gaudreault and Roberta Pearson (Quebec City/Lausanne: Nuit Blanche/Payot-Lausanne, 1999) 17-32.

8. Georges Méliès, "En marge de l'histoire du cinématographe," *Propos sur les vues animées*, ed. André Gaudreault, Jacques Malthête and Madeleine Malthête-Méliès, spec. issue of *Les dossiers de la Cinémathèque* 10 (1982): 29.

9. François Jost, "L'invention du cinéaste," *Before the Author*, ed. Anja Franceschetti and Leonardo Quaresima (Udine: Forum, 1997) 53-62.

10. See in particular note 12 of my article "Les *vues cinématographiques* selon Georges Méliès, ou: comment Mitry et Sadoul avaient peut-être raison d'avoir tort (même si c'est surtout Deslandes qu'il faut lire et relire)," *Georges Méliès, l'illusionniste fin de siècle?*, ed. Jacques Malthête and Michel Marie (Paris: Sorbonne Nouvelle/Colloque de Cerisy, 1997) 111-31.

11. *Le cinéma des premiers temps 1900-1906*, ed. André Gaudreault, spec. issue of *Les Cahiers de la Cinémathèque* 29 (Winter 1979). This anecdote may interest the reader: my initial idea, before changing my mind at the last moment (but without much awareness of the important difference between the two expressions), was to entitle the issue of this journal *Le cinéma primitif 1900-1906*.

12. My thanks to Jean-Pierre Sirois-Trahan for bringing this fact to my attention. For Metz's use of the term, see his article "Problèmes actuels de théorie du cinéma," *Essais sur la signification au cinéma*, vol. 2 (Paris: Klincksieck, 1972) 35-86 (page 35 for the use of the term). This article is a book review of the second volume of Jean Mitry's *Esthétique et psychologie du cinéma*. It was first published in 1967 in *Revue d'Esthétique* 20.2-3 (April-Sept. 1967): 180-221. Metz uses the expression "cinéma des premiers temps" on at least one other occasion in the same volume, in "Montage et discours dans le film" 89-96 (page 96 for the use of the term).

13. This observation was made by Silvestra Mariniello in a paper delivered at the conference *Le Cinéma, cent ans après* held in Montreal in November 1995. The paper was later published, but minus the passage to which I refer. See Silvestra Mariniello, "L'histoire du cinéma contre le cinéma dans l'histoire," *Le Cinéma en histoire. Institution cinématographique, réception filmique et reconstitution historique*, ed. André Gaudreault, Germain Lacasse and Isabelle Raynauld (Paris/Quebec City: Méridiens Klincksieck/Nota Bene, 1999) 13-27.

14. Jacques Deslandes, *Le Boulevard du cinéma à l'époque de Georges Méliès* (Paris: Cerf, 1963) 71.

15. Quoted without indication of the source by Jacques Deslandes in "Vieux papiers d'un cinéphile. Trucographie de Georges Méliès (1861-1938)," published as an annex to a book by Pierre Jenn, *Georges Méliès cinéaste* (Paris: Albatros, 1984) 142. In an e-mail dated 23 April 1997, Jacques Malthête wrote to me concerning this reference that "Jacques Deslandes (*Le Boulevard du cinéma à l'époque de Georges Méliès* 30-31) indicated just once (on page 31) the source of this quotation. It was a letter from Méliès (to whom?) published in *L'Escamoteur* 8 (January 1948)."

16. Georges Méliès, "Les vues cinématographiques," *Propos sur les vues animées* 11.

17. For an up to date and annotated list of Méliès's magic shows, see Jacques Malthête, *Méliès. Images et illusions* (Paris: Exporégie, 1996) 33-46.

18. As suggested by Marc-Emmanuel Mélon at a seminar I conducted in Liège in February 1996 (under the auspices of the Université de Liège and the Cinémathèque Royale de Belgique): "The logic of the Lumière catalogue is the logic of the series, which comes out of photography and was heavily used in photography throughout the 19th century."

19. To learn more about this colorful character in the history of the exhibition of animated views in Canada, see Serge Duigou and Germain Lacasse, *Marie de Kerstrat* (Rennes: Ouest-France, 2002).

20. We did so at the Cerisy conference "Nouvelles approches de l'histoire du cinéma" in the summer of 1985. See André Gaudreault and Tom Gunning, "Le cinéma des premiers temps: un défi à l'histoire du cinéma?" *Histoire du cinéma. Nouvelles approches*, ed. Jacques Aumont, André Gaudreault and Michel Marie (Paris: Sorbonne, 1989) 49-63. This article appears in English translation in the dossier of the present volume.

21. Jean Giraud, *Le Lexique français du cinéma des origines à 1930* (Paris: CNRS, 1958).

22. G.-Michel Coissac, *La Théorie et la pratique des projections* (Paris: Maison de la Bonne Presse, 1906). An abridged version of this book, entitled *Manuel pratique du conférencier-projectionniste*, was published by the same publisher in 1908.

23. G.-Michel Coissac, quoted in Giraud 91 (entry "cinématographie-attraction"). The complete reference for Coissac's book is as follows: *Histoire du Cinématographe. De ses origines à nos jours* (Paris: Cinéopse/Gauthier-Villars, 1925). Note Coissac's use of the word "cinématographe" in the title. His use of the expression "cinématographie-attraction" can be found on page 359.

24. After much debate, the editor of this volume, the author of the present text, and its translator (the author of this note) agreed upon the term "kine-attractography" to translate "cinématographie-attraction." "Attractography" fancifully extends the tradition of the multitude of "graphs" introduced to the market, or the language, at the turn of the past century (the kinetograph, cinematograph, vitagraph, biograph, motiograph, etc.) and even well beyond (at least until 1957, with the introduction of the Mutoscope Voice-o-Graph, the street-corner recording booth in which Jean-Pierre Léaud, for example, records a 45 rpm love song in Jean-Luc Godard's MASCULIN FÉMININ [1966]). "Attractography," however, is not merely yet another "graph," but the genus to which all these species belong: it is the cultural series created by mechanical devices which use celluloid film to produce attractions. At the same time, "attractography" was created by adopting the popular penchant for word play and

word creation using a common suffix and the connector "o," whose lasting appeal is attested to by the "voice-o-graph." Even before the early twentieth century's plethora of "graphs" came the early nineteenth century's "ramas": the 1820s saw, after the panorama, the diorama, cosmorama, georama, uranorama, neorama, etc. And the popular practice of creating even more fanciful words based on such attractions goes back at least as far as Balzac's *Le Père Goriot* (1834-35), in which it is related that "[t]he recent invention of the diorama, carrying optical illusion farther than in panoramas, had brought into some of the ateliers the jest of throwing superfluous 'ramas' into one's talk": "souporamas," "healthoramas," "cornoramas" and the like. (We hope, however, to have avoided Balzac's historical anachronism: his novel is set in 1819, three years before the introduction of the diorama.) Finally, "kine" identifies the cultural series for the reader (on its own, "attractography" could mean anything) at the same time as it refuses to identify it with the institution "cinema." Beginning with Edison in 1888 and extending right into the 1920s, "kine" was an accepted and common form in English; indeed it is the standard English phonetic transcription of the Greek – even the Lumière cinématographe was initially known in English as the kinematograph. Once again, English seems to have followed the French rather than its own rules and inclinations – T.B.

25. On this topic, see my article "Les *vues cinématographiques* selon Eisenstein, ou: que reste-t-il de l'*ancien* (le cinéma des premiers temps) dans le *nouveau* (les productions filmiques et scripturales d'Eisenstein)?," *Eisenstein: l'ancien et le nouveau*, ed. Dominique Chateau, François Jost and Martin Lefebvre (Paris: Sorbonne/Colloque de Cerisy, 2001) 23-43. Some of the ideas and passages in this text can be found in the present article.

26. On this topic, see in particular Tom Gunning, "Cinéma des attractions et modernité," *Cinémathèque* 5 (1994) 129-39. [English version: "The Whole Town's Gawking: Early Cinema and the Visual Experience of Modernity," *Yale Journal of Criticism* 7.2 (Fall 1994): 189-201].

27. Sergei Eisenstein, "The Montage of Attractions [1923]," *Selected Works. Volume 1: Writings, 1922-34*, ed. and trans. Richard Taylor (London: British Film Institute, 1988) 33-38.

28. *Ciné pour tous* 118 (Nov. 1923): 10-11.

29. *La Nature* 11 Jan. 1896 (quoted in Giraud 48 [entry "attraction"]).

30. *Le Progrès* (Lyon) 17 July 1906 (quoted in Giraud 48).

31. *Le Film* 9 July 1917 (quoted in Giraud 48).

32. E.-L. Fouquet, "L'Attraction," *L'Echo du Cinéma* 11 (28 June 1912): 1.

33. Giraud 48.

34. Tom Gunning, "The Cinema of Attractions: Early Film, its Spectator, and the Avant-Garde," *Early Cinema: Space Frame Narrative*, ed. Thomas Elsaesser (London: British Film Institute, 1990) 57. Reprinted in the dossier of this volume.

35. Gunning, "The Cinema of Attractions."

36. Tom Gunning, "Attractions, truquages et photogénie: l'explosion du présent dans les films à truc français produits entre 1896 et 1907," *Les vingt premières années du cinéma français*, ed. Jean A. Gili, Michèle Lagny, Michel Marie and Vincent Pinel (Paris: Sorbonne Nouvelle/AFRHC, 1995) 179.

37. Gunning, "Cinéma des attractions et modernité" 132.

38. Georges Méliès, "Importance du scénario," in Georges Sadoul, *Georges Méliès* (Paris: Seghers, 1961) 115.
39. André Gaudreault, *Du littéraire au filmique. Système du récit* (Paris/Quebec City: Armand Colin/Nota Bene, 1999 [1988]). Forthcoming from the University of Toronto Press in an English translation by Timothy Barnard under the title *From Plato to Lumière: Monstration and Narration in Literature and Cinema.*
40. Gaudreault and Gunning 56-57. See also the dossier of this volume (372).
41. This expression is David Bordwell's: "Textual Analysis, etc.," *Enclitic* (Fall 1981/ Spring 1982): 129.
42. For the development of the system of narrative integration, see Tom Gunning, *D.W. Griffith and the Origins of American Narrative Film: The Early Years at Biograph* (Urbana: U of Illinois P, 1991).
43. Gaudreault and Gunning 58. See also the dossier in this volume (374).
44. At a conference held in Paris in 1993. See André Gaudreault and Denis Simard, "L'extranéité du cinéma des premiers temps: bilan et perspectives de recherche," *Les vingt premières années du cinéma français* 15-28.

From "Primitive Cinema" to "Marvelous"

Wanda Strauven

> Film offers us the dance of an object that disintegrates and recomposes itself without human intervention. It offers us the backward sweep of a diver whose feet fly out of the sea and bounce violently back on the springboard. Finally, it offers us the sight of a man [racing] at 200 kilometers per hour. All these represent the movements of matter which are beyond the laws of human intelligence, and hence of an essence which is more significant.
> – F.T. Marinetti[1]

In 1912, three years after the foundation of the Futurist movement, F.T. Marinetti acknowledges in his literary program the wonderful mechanics of cinema and its possible inspiration for the new generation of Futurist poets. Marinetti seems to be intrigued by the mechanical writing of the new medium, or rather by the transformation it induces from human to non-human, from man to matter. On screen, human movements are turned into "movements of matter which are beyond the laws of human intelligence, and hence of an essence which is more significant." In the Futurist poetics, theorized by Marinetti in three successive manifestos,[2] the "literary I" is sentenced to death and replaced with matter: "We want literature to render the life of a motor, a new instinctive animal whose guiding principle we will recognize when we have come to know the instincts of the various forces that compose it."[3] Rendering the life of objects, however, does not mean "assign[ing] human sentiments"[4] to them. Matter must not be humanized, but rather explored in itself, in its unknown, invisible dimensions. And it is in this sense that cinema might help us, revealing by means of trickery dimensions imperceptible to the (imperfect) human eye.

The opening quote, taken from the "Technical Manifesto of Futurist Literature" (1912), implicitly refers to three basic film tricks: the stop trick (or "stop-camera effect"[5]), reverse motion and fast motion. According to Marinetti, these tricks somehow disclose the non-human nature of the human profilmic, which results in the production of very significant "movements of matter." We should bear in mind that this mechanical, non-humanizing writing process is cited as example in a literary manifesto that pleads for the abolition of traditional syntax and the introduction of words-in-freedom, anticipating by more than ten years the Surrealist *écriture automatique*.[6] And, incidentally, the three concrete examples of film trickery given by Marinetti also anticipate Surrealist applications. The "object that disintegrates and recomposes itself without human interven-

tion" prefigures the animated and dislocated figure of Chaplin in BALLET MÉCA-
NIQUE (Fernand Léger, 1924); the "backward sweep of a diver" appears in Man
Ray's LES MYSTÈRES DU CHÂTEAU DE DÉ (1929); and "a man racing at 200 kilo-
meters per hour" can join the fast-motion funeral procession of ENTR'ACTE
(René Clair, 1924). If one wishes to underscore Marinetti's prophetic qualities,
other avant-garde examples can be added, from Hans Richter's decapitated
man in VORMITTAGSSPUK (1927-28) to Dziga Vertov's backward diver in KINO-
GLAZ (1924) and fast-motion city traffic in CELOVEK S KINOAPPARATOM (1929).
But the real question, I believe, is to understand which films might have had
such an influence on the founder of Futurism that they made him recognize the
"potential of the new art" and its trickery.[7]

Homage to Early Trick Films?

The three tricks that Marinetti is referring to have all been "invented" in the
early years of cinema. Master of the stop trick was Georges Méliès, who not
only transformed humans into animals, men into women, etc., but also, repeatedly, "disintegrated," or dismembered, bodies as if they were mere objects.
After having been ripped apart, the body parts usually recompose "without human intervention," as happens in NOUVELLES LUTTES EXTRAVAGANTES (1900),
DISLOCATION MYSTÉRIEUSE (1901) and LE BOURREAU TURC (1904). It is worth
mentioning that André Deed, whose body is "dislocated" by Méliès in DISLO-
CATION MYSTÉRIEUSE, repeats this trick for the Italian production house Itala in
the early years of Futurism, more particularly at the closure of CRETINETTI CHE
BELLO! (aka CRETINETTI E LE DONNE, 1910). According to the legend, Méliès
would have "discovered" the stop trick (which is the basic trick for the dislocation genre) by accident, while filming a "documentary" view in Paris, Place de
l'Opéra.[8] The trick of reserve motion, on the contrary, has been "invented" during exhibition, more precisely – again as the legend tells us – during the (backward) projection of DÉMOLITION D'UN MUR (1896) by the Lumière brothers. In
1897-98 this trick was also "discovered" by the Italian variety artist Leopoldo
Fregoli who had started to integrate moving pictures in his quick-change
shows. One night, as a joke, he decided to play some films backwards and it
quickly became a featured attraction in his program.[9] It is not impossible that
Marinetti, who was an admirer of Fregoli, had been initiated to the trick of reverse motion by the Fregoligraph. As for the last trick, fast motion, Fregoli supposedly tried it out as well in one of his own films, SEGRETO PER VESTIRSI (ca.
1898), to demonstrate (and exaggerate) his talent as lightning change artist.[10]
Here, we should make a distinction between camera speed and projection

speed, and not take early cinema's jerky, artificially high-speed movements which are simply due to wrong projection speed for intentional effects of fast motion. According to Barry Salt, the "intentional departures from a standard camera speed for expressive purposes were extremely rare" in the early years of cinema, simply because the camera speed was not stabilized. However, Salt cites one (possible) early example of intentional undercranking, which is Robert W. Paul's ON A RUNAWAY MOTOR CAR THROUGH PICCADILLY CIRCUS (1899).[11]

In short, Marinetti refers in his 1912 literary manifesto to "primitive" tricks, used nationally and internationally at the turn of the century. It is plausible that he became acquainted with these effects, these "movements of matter," through the indigenous film production of Fregoli and Cretinetti. This quite positive evaluation of the (early) trick film, however, does not last long. In 1916, Marinetti launches, together with Bruno Corra, Emilio Settimelli, Arnaldo Ginna, Giacomo Balla and Remo Chiti, the manifesto of "The Futurist Cinema." Here, they declare that the cinema "up to now *has been and tends to remain profoundly passéist*," mostly because of its theatrical legacy: "as a *theater without words*, it has inherited all the most traditional rubbish of the literary theater."[12] And further they write:

> Except for interesting films of travel, hunting, wars, and so on, the filmmakers have inflicted on us only the most backward-looking dramas, great and small. Even the scenario, whose brevity and variety might appear advanced, is usually nothing but a trite and wretched *analysis*. Therefore all the immense *artistic* possibilities of the cinema still rest entirely in the future.[13]

Without going into details, I would like to adopt two statements of the Futurists. First, in 1916, both theatricality and narrativity, apparently (and, I should add, unfortunately), triumphed over "trickality."[14] Within the specific Italian context, the epic genre of the *kolossal* and the melodramatic genre of the diva film could surely be held responsible for such a "passéist" trend. Note however that the Futurists' evaluation of their contemporary film production is not entirely negative: exceptions to the rule are "films of travel, hunting, wars, and so on." Thus, Marinetti is no longer enthused by trick films, but rather – as it seems – by documentary views, supposedly made by Luca Comerio, Giovanni Vitrotti and other (Italian) pioneers in sport and war reportage.[15] Second, in 1916, cinema is not yet an art form. In other words, the Futurists would have disagreed with both Georges Sadoul and Jean Mitry who date the "birth" of cinema as art in the middle of the 1910s.[16] They seem to concur instead with two other French film historiographers, namely Maurice Bardèche and Robert Brasillach, who situate this "birth" after the First World War, beginning in 1919.[17]

The Futurists go on proclaiming that cinema, in order to be a (Futurist) art, must "become antigraceful, distorting, impressionistic, synthetic, dynamic, free-wording."[18] Several propositions that follow seem to echo trick films from the early years of cinema, in particular the animation of the non-human (for the so-called "dramas of objects") and the dislocation of the human (for "unreal reconstructions of the human body" and "dramas of disproportion"); these propositions, however, are presented as authentic Futurist inventions. In other words, we cannot speak of an open homage to early cinema in this 1916 manifesto, although it is not impossible that – at least unconsciously – the Futurists' main source of inspiration was indeed early cinema and in particular the early trick films. It should be stressed that this unconscious or intuitive recuperation (or promotion) of "primitive" tricks happens at a time in which the "institutional mode of representation" (IMR) is prevailing in Italy, as is shown by the above mentioned phenomena of the *kolossal* and the diva film.

If the Futurist film program remained for the most part a written project during the heydays of Futurism, some of its ideas were picked up, after the First World War, by the Dadaists and the Surrealists. Whether or not the Futurist manifesto played an effective role in the (re)discovery of "primitive" tricks, is difficult to say; but that effects of "trickality" re-emerged, quite systematically, in film experiments of the 1920s is a fact. Besides the complex issue of influence and inspiration, which I will not address here, what most of the film productions of the historical avant-garde have in common is their will to *épater les bourgeois*, to awaken those who have gradually been accustomed to the "institutional mode of representation." Avant-garde films from the 1920s, from ENTR'ACTE (1924) to UN CHIEN ANDALOU (1929), still today seem to express the desire to transgress the dominant film grammar, in short, to go against the norm. Their effects of "trickality" should therefore not simply be seen as a return to the origins, to the "early" (years of) cinema, but rather as a return to the "otherness" of that cinema, of the "primitive mode of representation" (PMR), as a reaction against the dominant mode of representation of their time.[19] It is rather a return to "primitive" cinema than to "early" cinema, in that it is not a temporal, but a stylistic (or grammatical) matter. In other words, a "primitive" trick is not necessarily a trick of early cinema, but a trick that marks the otherness or alterity, the deviation from the norm, exactly as it was promoted in the 1910s by the Futurists.

A New Plea for the Term "Primitive"

New Film History has taught us to use quotation marks – the "birth" of cinema, the "invention" of the stop trick, the "first" close-up, the years of "maturity," etc. – in order to avoid any possible accusation of teleological attitude. Thus, we use quotation marks out of caution, sometimes maybe excessively or unjustly. I would prefer to omit the quotation marks around the term "primitive," since I believe its connotation has wrongly become negative in the field of early cinema, or rather its negative connotation has wrongly got the better of its positive one. Following Jacques Aumont, I will propose a distinction between two types (or meanings) of primitive, the relative and the absolute, and advocate for an appropriate use of the latter.

My plea directly echoes Aumont's "Plaidoyer pour le primitif,"[20] which he pronounced at the opening of the third Domitor conference in June 1994, in New York, and to which I wish to add a postscript. I am also in agreement with Philippe Dubois who used the term "in an absolutely positive sense" – and without quotation marks – in his 1984 article "Le gros plan primitif."[21] Tom Gunning, on the contrary, feels the need of the quotation marks in his discussion of early trick films, and in particular of Méliès's substitution trick, which – as Gunning correctly points out – is based on continuity, not of narrating but of framing. He writes: "The framing of Méliès' composition, taken by historians as a sign of his 'primitive' theatricality, reveals itself as consciously constructed illusion designed to distract attention from the actual cinematic process at work."[22] In the same article, originally published in 1989, Gunning affirms that the term primitive endures "partly out of inertia, but also because it cradles a number of connotations which stand in need of further examination and critique. The most regrettable connotations are those of an elementary or even childish mastery of form in contrast to a later complexity (and need we add that this viewpoint often shelters its apparent reversal in the image of a cinema of a lost purity and innocence?)."[23] I will come back to these two viewpoints, which can indeed be considered as two sides of the same coin.

My plea also attempts a reply to André Gaudreault who in his contribution to the present volume writes:

> There is no doubt about it, the expression "primitive cinema" has its appeal, and we might suppose that one day it will resurface, which would be completely legitimate. But, in my view at least, it would have been capital, over the past twenty or thirty years, to have criticized it severely and then be done with it for a time. Instead, as it was used from the 1940s to the 1960s in particular, the expression "primitive cinema" prevented, in my view, *historical thinking* about the cinema.[24]

Gaudreault might be correct that the term has not been criticized rigorously enough, but New Film History certainly did its job in making the young generation of (early) film scholars aware of its pejorative uses. Today, the term primitive is usually avoided, and, when used, it is usually put between "…". What New Film History did not do or did not do enough, in my opinion at least, is pointing out the (possible) positive uses of the term. And, therefore, New Film

History is partly responsible for the "loss" of Noël Burch's pair PMR-IMR in the terminological contest.[25] Although Burch himself considers these notions as "totally discredited"[26] today, he was one of the first to draw the attention to the "otherness" of early cinema and to the necessity to study it for itself. Or, as Thomas Elsaesser formulates it, he was "the first to posit an epistemic break"[27] between early cinema and narrative cinema, that is, between PMR and IMR.

One of the appeals and at the same time "problems" of Burch's approach is the underlying paradox that the PMR is both less and more than the IMR. To let Burch speak for himself: "There really was, I believe, a *genuine* PMR, detectable in very many films in certain characteristic features, capable of a certain development but unquestionably semantically *poorer* than the IMR."[28] This would mean that cinema gradually got rid of the typical characteristics of the PMR (namely the "autarky" of the tableau, the "non-centered" quality of the image, the general effect of "exteriority," and the "non-closure") in order to become semantically richer. But, on the other hand, it lost some of its purity, of its authenticity, in its evolution to IMR. Most stimulating for my own research, however, I find Burch's "dialectical approach" in attempting to understand avant-garde cinema through primitive cinema.[29] Instead of giving here a value judgment of Burch's "primitive" reading of avant-garde films (below there will only be a brief mention of his analysis of LE SANG D'UN POÈTE), I argue that the term "primitive" is crucial to the full understanding of such an approach.

"Relative" Primitives vs. "Absolute" Primitives

In his "Plaidoyer pour le primitif" Aumont draws attention to the double meaning of primitive in art criticism – that is, its relative and absolute meaning – which he then, rather roughly yet instructively, applies to film studies. The relative meaning of the term primitive would reveal the typical evolutionist conception of art history, according to which the art form or style in question is still in its earliest stage and must make progress in order to "achieve maturity," evolving for instance from Pre-Renaissance to Renaissance. In the case of film, this maturation would have come about through an "economic and formal 'institutionalization' (in the sense of Noël Burch, for instance)." The absolute meaning, on the contrary, "avoids this dubious evolutionism, but at the price of other difficulties." Here the term primitive is defined in opposition to the norm, to the "non-primitive." Aumont gives the example of a Dogon mask, which is not seen as an infantile or pre-mature expression of an art form in maturation, but as deviant or diverging from the "dominant definition of art." From this point of view, namely the perspective of institutionalized art forms in the early 20th century, film stood for "non-art," which is comparable – as Aumont adds – to the position of (certain forms of) television today.[30]

One could simplify by saying that the use of primitive in its relative meaning belongs to the chronological historiography (who came first?) and, corresponding to the etymological sense of the term which derives from the Latin *primitivus* (who was the first or earliest of its kind?), it almost automatically implies a teleological attitude. The use of primitive in its absolute meaning, on the other hand, would rather call for ontological questions and attempts to define an art form by what it is not. Applied to cinema, it could be summarized as follows: the difference between the relative and absolute use of the term primitive reflects the difference between pre-institutional and non-institutional cinema or between pre-classical and non-classical cinema or, I am tempted to add, between "early cinema" and "exhibitionist cinema" (aka "cinema of attractions").

Méliès's indignation at those columnists who considered the first filmmakers as "primitives" is symptomatic of the first attitude, implied by the relative use of the term. In his biography, published as "En marge de l'histoire du cinématographe" (1926), Méliès writes:

> Do they really believe that we were still primitives after twenty years of sustained work and constant perfecting of our craft? Aren't we the authors of most improvements and inventions that our continuators use today? Doesn't one take advantage of our work by finding today the equipment "ready for use" (as they say in English) and the techniques all set?[31]

Implicitly, Méliès affirms here that he was indeed a *primitivus*, that is, one of the first "authors" of film history who helped to improve the basic techniques in order to establish a full-aged art which is now, in the 1920s, practiced by their "continuators." Paradoxically, Méliès does not want his pioneering work to be seen as "primitive" because, from the perspective of the 1920s, this means less developed, less ripened; but at the same time he claims that his work was pioneering at the turn of the century precisely because it was "primitive," because it signified one of the first (and necessary) steps toward the full development of this new art form.

Whereas Burch's distinction between the PMR and the IMR is an easy prey for the Inquisitors of Teleology – "pre-institutional" being substitutable for the P and thus suggesting a finality toward I; his dialectical approach aligns itself more with the Church of Ontology. Especially his discussion of Jean Cocteau's LE SANG D'UN POÈTE (1930) is revealing in this aspect. According to Burch, Cocteau might have been inspired for the conception of the Hôtel des Folies Dramatiques by the many keyhole films of early cinema as well as by the trick of the perpendicular camera as used for instance in LA SOUBRETTE INGÉNIEUSE (1903). The question is: why would Cocteau turn to primitive tricks in 1930? He obviously wanted to create something different, something contrasting with the dominant mode. As Cocteau himself explained in 1932: "I used to think that [...] films weary us with shots taken from below or above. I wanted to shoot my films from the front, *artlessly*."[32] Thus, at a time in which cinema had established itself as art, Cocteau chose to practice it as non-art. Hence his interest in primitive cinema or, in Burch's words, his interest in "primitive strategies as 'antidote' to those of the Institution."[33] Among these "primitive strategies," the non-narrative structure of LE SANG D'UN POÈTE should be mentioned as well, that is – to say it in Gunning's words – "its dream-like discontinuities and sense of wonder," which within the family of peeping tom films assures a lineal line rather with Pathé's UN COUP D'OEIL PAR ÉTAGE (1905) than with Hitchcock's REAR WINDOW (1954).[34]

When Burch stresses "that the otherness of preinstitutional cinema was a natural pole of attraction for [...] the earliest modernist contestations of the institution,"[35] I would like to emphasize that it was not so much about restoring or renewing *pre*-institutional cinema, but rather about being appealed by *non*-institutional cinema, that is, primitive cinema in the absolute sense of the term. It is in this view that one can (try to) understand Méliès's statement regarding the "[un]importance of the scenario" as a conscious appropriation of primitive strategies, especially when one keeps in mind that this statement was made in the early 1930s. As quoted and translated by Gunning, Méliès wrote:

> As for the scenario, the "fable" or "tale," I only consider it at the end. I can state that the scenario constructed in this manner has *no importance*, since I use it merely as a pretext for the "stage effects," the "tricks," or for a nicely arranged tableau.[36]

Méliès clearly wanted to position himself in the tradition of non-narrative cinema, which from the perspective of the (Surrealist) avant-garde was the only valid mode of representation.[37]

To push this reasoning a bit further, we might also consider a more recent example such as the bullet time technique, which technically (and teleologically) is an improvement of an 1880s experiment by Eadweard Muybridge.[38] But the technique is employed, at least in the first episode of THE MATRIX (1999), as an instance of non-institutional cinema with the obvious intention to astonish the (bourgeois) Hollywood spectator. The bullet time technique goes against "classical" narration: it slows down (or even stills) the natural speed, it transgresses the 180° rule; in short, it goes against the dominant film grammar. But it does so not because it wants to return to pre-classical cinema, but because it wants to enunciate itself as non-classical cinema, or even better as non-cinematic cinema. In that sense, THE MATRIX is absolutely primitive!

In other words, the revival of "some of the major gestures of the Primitive Mode"[39] (such as camera ubiquity, time reversal, frontality, theatricality, camera stare, etc.) in avant-garde or commercial cinema should not be seen as a return to the origins, a nostalgia of Paradise Lost and, therefore, a search for "purity" (which corresponds with the relative use of the term primitive), but rather as a subversion of the institutional mode of representation, a search for "alterity." Here we can learn from Marinetti whom I quoted at the beginning of this essay. In 1913 Marinetti praised the variety theater for its (absolute) primitiveness, for its deviation from the institutional (or academic) theater:

> The Variety Theater is naturally anti-academic, primitive, and ingenuous, and hence more significant for the improvised character of its experiments and the simplicity of its means. (Example: the systematic tour of the stage that the *chanteuses* make, like caged animals, at the end of every refrain.)[40]

For the founder of Futurism, the concept of primitive covers not only the idea of ingenuity or simplicity (similar to the concept of *naïf* in art criticism), but rather the notions of non-classical, non-serious, non-solemn. The variety theater is a primitive form of art in that it violates all the rules of the academic theater, in that it reveals itself as subversive. As primitive theater stands for variety theater, so primitive cinema stands in the 1910s for the negation of both the monumentality of the epic genre and the pathos of the diva film. Following this thought, primitive cinema is anti-passéist; primitive cinema is Futurist.[41]

The Futurist "Marvelous"

The celebration of non-institutionalized art forms, such as the variety theater and the circus, is commonplace within the context of the historical avant-garde. It constitutes one of the closest links between the Italian and the Russian Futurists, and between Marinetti and Eisenstein. It is not unlikely that Eisenstein has been inspired by Marinetti's manifesto of "The Variety Theater," at least indirectly, through the practice of the Factory of the Eccentric Actor (FEKS) in the 1920s.[42] And we know that Eisenstein refers to the music hall in his first manifesto, "Montage of Attractions" (1923), as one of the best schools for the *montageur* of theatrical plays.[43] What is probably less known is that Marinetti used the term attraction in "The Variety Theater," and precisely in relation to the subversion of the institutional Art "with a capital A."

> The Variety Theater is destroying the Solemn, the Sacred, the Serious, the Sublime of Art with a capital A. It is helping along the Futurist destruction of immortal masterpieces by plagiarizing and parodying them, by making them seem commonplace in stripping them of their solemnity and by presenting them as if they were just another turn or attraction.[44]

In the original – which reads "come un qualsiasi *numero d'attrazione*"[45] – it is one of the few expressions that are italicized. Depending on the translation[46] they used, the young founders of the FEKS, Leonid Trauberg and Grigori Kozintsev, could have picked up the term from Marinetti and passed it on to Eisenstein. However, the term attraction as used by Marinetti in "The Variety Theater" clearly differs from Eisenstein's attraction. Marinetti's attraction is less developed, or – following Aumont[47] – it only covers the first definition of Eisenstein's attraction, namely the attraction as music hall number, as "peak moment in the performance," and does not take in both its associational dimension (second definition) and its "efficacy" (third definition). According to Eisenstein, the effect of the attraction upon the spectator had to be calculated on the basis of certain psychological and political laws, respectively of Pavlov's reflexology and Marx's ideology. As Aumont stresses, "the essential feature of the idea of attraction might be missed if we were to neglect [...] its third definition (inseparable, of course, from the first two), namely, everything in this idea that implies an effort *to attract* the spectator's attention."[48] This is also why Eisenstein himself makes a clear distinction between the (acrobatic) trick and the attraction:

> The attraction has nothing in common with the trick. Tricks are accomplished and completed on a plane of pure craftsmanship (acrobatic tricks, for example) and include that kind of attraction linked to the process of giving (or in circus slang, "selling") one's self. As the circus term indicates, inasmuch as it is clearly from the viewpoint of the performer himself, it is absolutely opposite to the attraction – which is based exclusively on the reaction of the audience.[49]

What really matters in Eisenstein's theory of "montage of attractions" is the impact on the spectator, which is one of the most important (and, in my view, valid) reasons why Gunning borrows the term attraction from him:

> An attraction aggressively subjected the spectator to "sensual or psychological impact." According to Eisenstein, theater should consist of a montage of such attractions, creating a relation to the spectator entirely different from his absorption in "illusory depictions." I pick up this term partly to underscore the relation to the spectator that this later avant-garde practice shares with early cinema: that of exhibitionist confrontation rather than diegetic absorption.[50]

In this respect, Gunning – significantly enough – refers also to Marinetti, and more specifically to his manifesto of "The Variety Theater." Along with its "anti-academic," primitive dimension, this form of theater is characterized by its active involvement of the spectator. As Marinetti wrote: "The audience is not static like a stupid voyeur, but joins noisily in the actions, singing along with songs, accompanying the orchestra, communicating with the actors by speaking up at will or engaging in bizarre dialogues."[51] On the model of the variety theater, Marinetti pleaded for the creation of a new spectator and proposed to introduce surprise and agitation in the auditorium, for instance by selling the same seat to ten different people or by giving free tickets to half-mad men and women.

Not only the spectators needed to be renewed drastically, but also what they perceived on stage. For that reason, Marinetti introduced the concept of Futurist "marvelous," along with the stages tricks of reducing *Parsifal* to forty minutes, condensing all Shakespeare into one single act and executing Beethoven symphonies backwards. The concept of Futurist "marvelous" has nothing to do with the fantastic, the *féérique* or the (Surrealist) *merveilleux*.[52] Basically, it is a theatrical technique that Marinetti borrows from the music hall and subverts on the traditional stage. Being "a product of modern machinism," the Futurist marvelous could be defined as a montage (or cascade) of absurdities. It is a mixture of all kinds of bright ideas: "1. powerful caricatures; 2. abysses of the ridiculous; 3. improbable and delightful ironies; [...] 5. cascades of uncontrollable humor; 6. deep analogies between the human, animal, vegetable, and mechanical worlds; [...] 12. a mass of current events dispatched within two minutes ('and now, let's glance at the Balkans': King Nicholas, Enver-bey, Daneff, Venizelos, belly-slaps and fist-fights between Serbs and Bulgarians, a chorus number, and everything vanishes); [...] 14. caricatures of suffering and nostalgia, deeply impressed into the spectators' sensibility by means of gestures that exasperate with their spasmodic, hesitant, and weary slowness; weighty terms made ridiculous by comic gestures, bizarre disguises, mutilated words, smirks, pratfalls." With this montage of absurdities, Marinetti aims to produce not only general hilarity ("the entire gamut of laughter and smiles, to relax one's nerves"), but also an antirational hygiene of the human psyche ("the entire gamut of stupidity, imbecility, mindlessness, and absurdity, which imperceptibly push intelligence to the edge of insanity").[53]

Because of this specific goal, this preoccupation of provoking a sane shock among the audience, the Futurist marvelous might be associated with Eisenstein's montage of attractions. But in terms of screen space (or stage space) it reminds me above all of Yuri Tsivian's discussion of the involuntary Kuleshov-effect created by early cinema. Compare the above cited formula regarding the Balkans with the following testimony of an early Russian cinemagoer: "The Spanish monarch and the British king jumped out after each other on a piece of white sheet, a dozen Moroccan landscapes flashed past, followed by some marching Italian cuirassiers and a German dreadnought thundering into the water."[54] What happened was that "the impressions from one picture were involuntarily transferred to the next, to which it was connected only by its random adjacency in the program."[55] Tsivian refers to this as the origins of the effect used in Kuleshov's experiment. We could also call it the origins of the effect produced by the Futurist marvelous. Or, to state it more straightfor-wardly, the Futurist marvelous might be directly linked not only to the stage of the variety theater but also to the screen of early cinema.

Early cinema was not just an attraction, but also and above all a concatena-tion of attractions that, because of its narrative or lack of narrative, because of its (in)voluntary logic or illogic, must have caused some astonishment or "marvel" among the spectators. While above I proposed to reserve the term primitive to indicate the non-institutional (or non-classical) dimension of early cinema (from the perspective of the historical avant-garde), I now put forward the term "mar-velous" to seize both its aesthetics of astonishment and the principle behind its practice of serial programming, of concatenating attractions.

By way of conclusion I would like to suggest a new denomination for early cin-ema (in addition to "primitive cinema"), which is based on the notion of Futur-ist marvelous and inspired by the categorization of "Moving Pictures" made by Vachel Lindsay in 1915, that is, two years after the publication of Marinetti's "The Variety Theater."[56] In *The Art of the Moving Picture*, Lindsay distinguished three main categories: 1) the dramatic "Action Pictures," 2) the lyrical "Intimate Pictures," and 3) the epic "Splendor Pictures." These three types of cinema find their counterpart in the other arts, the first type corresponding to "sculpture-in-motion" (associated by Lindsay with the color RED), the second one to "paint-ing-in-motion" (BLUE) and the last one to "architecture-in-motion" (YELLOW). The scheme is actually a bit more complex, since Lindsay defines four subcate-gories in the third category of "Splendor Pictures." In one of these subcategories he puts the "Fairy Splendor Pictures," which are not epic and thus not classifi-able under the label of "architecture-in-motion." The moving pictures of "Fairy Splendor" could be seen as a relic of early cinema, and in particular of early trick films. Lindsay cites for example an "old Pathé Film from France," in which objects, furniture, books, cloths, etc. are animated. But this type of moving pic-ture is at the end of its existence in the mid-1910s. As Lindsay concludes: "Then, after the purely trick-picture is disciplined till it has fewer tricks, and those more human and yet more fanciful, the producer can move on up into the higher realism of the fairy-tale, carrying with him this riper workmanship."[57] This statement about the "discipline" of the tricks clearly contrasts with Marinetti's positive evaluation of these very same "Fairy Splendor Pictures," as discussed at the beginning of this essay. I believe this subcategory deserves to be consid-ered as an independent fourth category, next to Action Pictures, Intimate Pic-tures and Splendor Pictures. And this new category could simply be denomi-nated "Attraction Pictures," which are characterized by their marvelous dimension and find their counterpart in the art of photography. The Attraction

Pictures, thus, are "photography-in-motion," a denomination that has the advantage of covering both the English concept of *moving pictures* and the French notion of *photographie animée*.

Whereas "Primitive Cinema" allows one to capture the phenomenon of early cinema as a whole, the category of "Attraction Pictures" indicates the individual works that constitute such a phenomenon. Both terms can be used either as (non-teleological) time-specific labels or as generic categories to define "post-early" film practices and products – avant-garde and commercial alike. The first term underlines the non-institutional or subversive aspect of the practice or product in question, while the latter qualifies the marvelous dimension on the level of the text and its reception. To take again the case of THE MATRIX, we may claim that it is "primitive" in that it consciously uses strategies that go against the norm, by slowing down the motion of high-speed bullets and by "crossing the line." But we may also simply say that, instead of an "Action Picture," it is an "Attraction Picture," which offers us marvelous "movements of matter."

Notes

1. F.T. Marinetti, "Technical Manifesto of Futurist Literature [1912]," *Modernism. An Anthology*, ed. Lawrence Rainey (Oxford: Blackwell, 2005) 18.
2. "Technical Manifesto of Futurist Literature" (May 1912), followed by "A Response to Objections" (Aug. 1912); "Destruction of Syntax – Wireless Imagination – Words-in-Freedom" (May 1913); and "Geometrical and Mechanical Splendor and Numerical Sensitivity" (March 1914).
3. Marinetti, "Technical Manifesto of Futurist Literature" 18.
4. Marinetti, "Technical Manifesto of Futurist Literature" 18.
5. Barry Salt, *Film Style and Technology: History and Analysis* (1983; London: Starword, 1992) 329.
6. In his "Response to Objections," that followed the "Technical Manifesto of Futurist Literature," Marinetti states: "That hand that writes seems to separate from the body and freely leave far behind the brain, which, having itself in some way become detached from the body and airborne, looks down from on high with terrible lucidity upon the unforeseen phrases emitted by the pen." *Modernism. An Anthology* 20-21.
7. Needles to say, I follow here Tom Gunning's suggestion to re-explore the "inspiration for the avant-garde of the early decades of the [20th] century," as he formulates it in the opening paragraph of his seminal essay "The Cinema of Attractions: Early Cinema, Its Spectator, and the Avant-Garde," *Early Cinema: Space Frame Narrative*, ed. Thomas Elsaesser (London: British Film Institute, 1990) 56.
8. Méliès's "paternity" of the stop-camera technique can easily be questioned, since the trick was "first carried out in THE EXECUTION OF MARY, QUEEN OF SCOTS made

by the Edison company in 1895, and this film probably reached Europe with the Kinetoscope machines well before Méliès started to make films in 1896." Salt 35.

9. Leopoldo Fregoli, *Fregoli raccontato da Fregoli. Le memorie del mago del Trasformismo,* intro. Mario Corsi (Milano: Rizzoli, 1936) 217.

10. Aldo Bernardini, *Cinema muto italiano. Volume 1: Ambiente, spettacoli e spettatori 1896-1904* (Roma/Bari: Laterza, 1980) 103-04.

11. Salt 48. An earlier example, according to *All Movie Guide,* would have been Wallace McCutcheon's THE FASTEST WRECKING CREW IN THE WORLD (1897). See: http://www.allmovie.com/cg/avg.dll.

12. F.T. Marinetti, et al., "The Futurist Cinema," *Futurismo & Futurismi,* ed. Pontus Hulten (1986; London: Thames and Hudson, 1992) 451.

13. Marinetti, "The Futurist Cinema" 451.

14. According to André Gaudreault, these three modes were already competing in Méliès's oeuvre. See "Theatricality, Narrativity, and Trickality: Reevaluating the Cinema of Georges Méliès," *Journal of Popular Film and Television* 15.3 (1987): 111-19.

15. For a Futurist reading of this early Italian documentary school, see my book *Marinetti e il cinema: tra attrazione e sperimentazione* (Udine: Campanotto, 2006).

16. The third volume of Georges Sadoul's *Histoire générale du cinéma* is dedicated to the birth of the art of cinema: *1909-1920: Le cinéma devient un art* (Paris: Denoël, 1951). According to Sadoul, it all started with the Film d'Art series in 1908. Jean Mitry, on the other hand, claims that cinema as art made its appearance only in 1915. See *Histoire du cinéma,* vol. 2 (Paris: Editions universitaires, 1969) 12.

17. Maurice Bardèche and Robert Brasillach, *Histoire du Cinéma* (Paris: Denoël, 1935). See the fourth chapter, which is titled "Naissance du Cinéma comme Art (1919-1923)."

18. Marinetti, "The Futurist Cinema" 451.

19. Here I follow Tom Gunning who makes an analogous statement regarding the new (American) avant-garde: "The fact that this difference [i.e. the "otherness" of early cinema] has been an inspiration to a number of recent avant-garde films is a part of the history of this difference." Tom Gunning, "Non-Continuity, Continuity, Discontinuity. A Theory of Genres in Early Films," *Early Cinema: Space Frame Narrative* 93.

20. Jacques Aumont, "Quand y a-t-il cinéma primitif? ou Plaidoyer pour le primitif," *Le cinéma au tournant du siècle/Cinema at the Turn of the Century,* ed. Claire Dupré la Tour, André Gaudreault and Roberta Pearson (Québec/Lausanne: Nota Bene/Payot, 1999) 17-32.

21. Philippe Dubois, "Le gros plan primitif," *Revue belge du cinéma* 10 (Winter 1984-85): 11-34.

22. Tom Gunning, "'Primitive' Cinema: A Frame-up? Or The Trick's on Us," *Early Cinema: Space Frame Narrative* 100.

23. Tom Gunning, "'Primitive' Cinema" 96. Gunning notices that recently some scholars, as for instance Kristin Thompson in *The Classical Hollywood Cinema,* have started to employ the term "in a non-pejorative sense."

24. See page 88 in this volume.

25. Frank Kessler also speculates on the reasons behind Burch's "failure" in his contribution to this volume; see in particular note 3. See also André Gaudreault in this volume who somehow "blames" the translations of Burch's work for having introduced the term "primitive" in the English-language studies of early cinema. If this

hypothesis is correct, New Film History would have created its own "enemy," the concept of "primitive cinema" being introduced by one of New Film History first adherents.

26. E-mail to the author, dated 9 August 2005. Burch resolutely opposed my idea to reprint in the dossier of the present volume his article "Porter, ou l'ambivalence," which was originally published in English in *Screen* 19.4 (Winter 1978-79) and contains the first outline of the PMR.

27. See page 206 in this volume.

28. Noël Burch, "A Primitive Mode of Representation?," *Early Cinema: Space Frame Narrative* 220. Emphasis added.

29. Noël Burch, "Primitivism and the Avant-Gardes: A Dialectical Approach," *Narrative, Apparatus, Ideology. A Film Theory Reader*, ed. Philip Rosen (New York: Columbia UP, 1986) 483-506.

30. Aumont, "Quand y a-t-il cinéma primitif?" 24-25.

31. Georges Méliès, "En marge de l'histoire du cinématographe [1926]," *Propos sur les vues animées*, ed. André Gaudreault, Jacques Malthête and Madeleine Malthête-Méliès, *spec. issue of Les dossiers de la Cinémathèque* 10 (1982): 29. Also partly quoted by Gaudreault in his contribution in this volume.

32. Quoted in Burch, "Primitivism and the Avant-Gardes" 499. Emphasis added.

33. Burch, "Primitivism and the Avant-Gardes" 499.

34. Tom Gunning, "What I saw from the Rear Window of the Hôtel des Folies-Dramatiques," *Ce que je vois de mon ciné…*, ed. André Gaudreault (Paris: Méridiens-Klincksieck, 1988) 37. Aumont briefly refers to Gunning's comparison between UN COUP D'OEIL PAR ÉTAGE and LE SANG D'UN POÈTE to point out that the comparison does not hold on the figurative level. Aumont, "Quand y a-t-il cinéma primitif?" 27.

35. Burch, "Primitivism and the Avant-Gardes" 500.

36. Georges Méliès, "Importance du scénario," *Cinéa-Ciné pour tous* (April 1932); rpt. in Georges Sadoul, *Georges Méliès* (Paris: Seghers, 1961) 116. Emphasis in the original.

37. See also Charles Musser, "Rethinking Early Cinema: Cinema of Attractions and Narrativity," *The Yale Journal of Criticism* 7.2 (1994): 230, note 17. Reprinted in this volume.

38. See the contribution of Eivind Røssaak in this volume.

39. Burch, "Primitivism and the Avant-Gardes" 495.

40. F.T. Marinetti, "The Variety Theater [1913]," *Modernism. An Anthology* 36.

41. In order to avoid any equivoque, I should stress that Marinetti himself never applied the term primitive to cinema; I deduct this positive meaning from his application to theater. On the other hand, it must be said that the film VITA FUTURISTA (1916), in which Marinetti actively participated, is a good example of primitive cinema in that it is non-institutional. With its chain of short "attractions," the film clearly goes against the norm of narrative integration. – N.B.: The term primitive returns in other Futurist manifestos, now in its relative use, then again in its absolute use; now negatively connotated, then again positively connotated. See, for instance, the "Technical Manifesto of Futurist painting," launched in 1910 by Umberto Boccioni, Carlo Carrà, Luigi Russolo, Giacomo Balla and Gino Severini: "Our art will probably be accused of tormented and decadent cerebralism. But we shall merely answer that we are, on the contrary, the primitives of a new sensitiveness, multiplied hundredfold, and that our art is intoxicated with spontaneity and

power." Especially Boccioni reiterates this idea of primitivism in his writings on "Plastic Dynamism."

42. In September 1922, the FEKS transformed Gogol's play *The Wedding* into a real variety show, for which they were directly inspired by Marinetti's manifesto. Eisenstein, who was befriended with the founders of the FEKS, came over from Moscow to help them with the dress rehearsal. For more details on this play and its Futurist legacy, see Wanda Strauven, "Notes sur le 'grand talent futuriste' d'Eisenstein," *Eisenstein: l'ancien et le nouveau*, ed. Dominique Chateau, François Jost and Martin Lefebvre (Paris: Sorbonne, 2001) 48-49.

43. S.M. Eisenstein, "Montage of Attractions [1923]," *The Film Sense*, trans. and ed. Jay Leyda (1947; San Diego/New York: Harcourt Brace, 1975) 233.

44. Marinetti, "The Variety Theater" 37.

45. F.T. Marinetti, "Il Teatro di Varietà," *Lacerba* 1.19 (1 Oct. 1913): 210.

46. In 1914 two Russian translations of Marinetti's manifesto were published, first in the Saint-Petersburg journal *Teatr i iskusstvo* and subsequently in the anthology of Futurist manifestos, edited by Vadim Sersenevich: *Manifesty italianskago futurizma* (Mosca: Russkago Tov-va, 1914). Whereas *Teatr i iskusstvo* translated the expression "attraction" as "kak samouïou obydennouïou vesh" (just as an ordinary thing), in the volume of Sersenevich the original notion was preserved: "attraktsiona"! For a more detailed discussion of the various translations and versions of "The Variety Theater" manifesto, see Wanda Strauven, "The Meaning of the Music-Hall: From the Italian Futurism to the Soviet Avant-garde," *Cinéma et Cie* 4 (Spring 2004): 117-34.

47. Jacques Aumont, "Attraction/Stimulus/Influence," *Montage Eisenstein*, trans. Lee Mildreth, Constance Penley and Andrew Ross (London/Bloomington: British Film Institute/Indiana UP, 1987) 41-51.

48. Aumont, "Attraction/Stimulus/Influence" 44.

49. Eisenstein, "Montage of Attractions" 232.

50. Tom Gunning, "The Cinema of Attractions" 59.

51. Marinetti, "The Variety Theater" 35.

52. The Futurist marvelous does not share with its Surrealist twin-brother the dimensions of the oneiric, the psychoanalytic and the beautiful. The Futurist marvelous is not a concept of aesthetics, but rather a strategy of (theatrical) provocation. It is a pre-Dadaist notion in that it calls for absurdities and non-sense, for everything that desecrates. See also my chapter-long discussion of the Futurist marvelous in *Marinetti e il cinema*.

53. Marinetti, "The Variety Theater" 34-35.

54. Quoted in Yuri Tsivian, "Some Historical Footnotes to the Kuleshov Experiment," *Early Cinema: Space Frame Narrative* 248.

55. Tsivian 248.

56. This idea directly results from the discussions between André Gaudreault, Timothy Barnard and me during our search for an appropriate English translation of G.-Michel Coissac's term "cinématographie-attraction."

57. Vachel Lindsay, *The Art of the Moving Picture*, intro. Stanley Kauffmann (1915; New York, Random House, 2000) 40-41.

The Attraction of the Intelligent Eye: Obsessions with the Vision Machine in Early Film Theories

Viva Paci

que le cinématographe soit d'abord fait
pour penser
on l'oubliera tout de suite
– Jean-Luc Godard[1]

One of the key elements of the "new film history" which arose in the wake of the Brighton conference in 1978 was that it put forth a *model of attractions*, one both heuristic and quite real at the same time; the tenets of this model and where it has led us today are the subjects of the present volume. This simultaneously theoretical and archaeological concept has produced another way of thinking about the relationship between viewer and film, taking as its starting point precisely the web of relationships found in early cinema and its connection to the era's popular entertainments and expositions of technologies and curiosities. What this concept, at times elevated to the level of a category, has enabled us to see is that there was indeed once a cinema which offered viewers a specific pleasure, a pleasure that could not be reduced to the one later put in place by the dominant narrative system of institutional or classical cinema. Narrative cinema, by its very nature, relegates the viewer to the safe position of an observer-voyeur. A cinema of attractions, on the contrary, addresses viewers directly. They become the privileged recipients of the pleasures of the spectacle and an essential part of the show, whose moving images stimulate their senses and emotions.[2] This concept of attraction was developed, above all, out of the (more or less unified) body of early films. Trick effects, magic acts and startling views were the underlying elements and even the founding principles of this cinema. The film spectacle, an act of *showing*, can be summarized in the idea of sudden bursts of presentations, and thus of presence, which were created for the pleasure of a fleeting and immediate vision-apparition – we might even say for the pleasure of its epiphanies – which was eventually delayed in order to heighten the thrill of its sudden appearance. Attraction has a temporality of its own; it offers itself up in a tension of the present by erupting on a monstrative level, which is distinct from narrative development, and by alternating between revealing and concealing in a way that is not dependent on the objects or time that precede – or follow – it in a cause and effect relationship. Attraction, by and large, is self-sufficient. Narrative, on the other hand, creates a sequence of events in which what occurs is connected by a series of causes and effects which take place in the necessary order of a unique temporal trajectory.

Often, naming something enables us to shine light on it, to *see* features of it that had remained hidden. Once conceived of and named, the "cinema of attractions" made it possible to open a valuable path towards a more balanced reading of film history, one capable of sketching, not a linear and evolutionary trajectory, but rather a history dotted with moments where attraction reigns.[3] This kind of history is all the more necessary today in that it enables us to see films situated at the frontiers of the narrative model in a new light. High-tech special effects films and films composed largely of digital images undermine the homogeneity of the narrative by their proximity to ways of seeing closer to those introduced and developed by forms of popular entertainment. These films rely on the foregrounding of visual pleasure and the almost physical participation of the viewer, as if he or she were in an amusement park. These films do not seek the viewers' attention by means of plot development; they capture their gaze through a "shooting star" effect that grabs their attention – reaching out to them, so to speak, in their seats.[4] They thereby establish a preferential and privileged channel of communication with the viewer, provoking different sensorial pleasures than those created by narrative cinema. Within a *storytelling* institution there still exist today films which enthral the viewer by means which owe very little to the principle of causality, just like early cinema.

The "cinema of attractions" model was conceived of and formulated in order to provide an account of a cinema with ties to the range of popular entertainment at the turn of the 20th century, when cinema did not enjoy an autonomous position. If, a century after this period in which a "system of monstrative attractions"[5] reigned, the cinema still retains "attractional" features, it is because the very essence of the cinematic apparatus[6] contains something which makes attraction possible, which makes possible its existence and resistance after so many decades of institutional narrative practice.

In this article, I propose to examine how a number of aspects characteristic of the cinema of attractions can be found in the view of the cinematic apparatus advanced by the first theoretical discussions of the cinema in the 1910s and 1920s, even if this was not, properly speaking, their purpose. In a sense, the historiographic proposition underlying the "cinema of attractions," that of a "system of monstrative attractions," makes it possible to examine, as if through a magnifying glass, the attractional conception of the apparatus in these writings. This conception is founded upon the ability of the camera to see and conceive of the world differently. In return, the presence of the attractional in these writings corroborates the idea that, no matter in which decade we find ourselves, there exists a kind of obsession with the powers and perceptual qualities of the machinery of cinema (powers and qualities which make the cinema, above all else, an *attraction machine*). It also corroborates the idea, which I will outline below, that attraction is enduringly present in the heart of the cinema and in theories of it.

Today, historians of early cinema agree that, during the cinema's first decade, a spectatorial model was created that was direct and exhibitionist and founded upon temporally discontinuous bursts of presence. This period reminds us that there was a time when the cinema was, above all else, a "vision machine,"[7] offering up magic tricks and marvelous visions.

Gradually, in the second decade of its existence, the cinema began to produce longer and more interconnected sequences of images. Increasingly, films seemed to be pointing towards the development of a narrative line, seeking coherence in its sequence of actions. Nevertheless, thinking and writing about the cinema seemed to be attracted to other features of this new "storytelling machine," as if what was most fascinating about it was still the fact that it was, above all, a "vision machine." Emblematic in this respect is the definition by Fernand Léger concerning the "radical possibilities of the cinema."[8] As Tom Gunning puts it: "Writing in 1922, flushed with the excitement of seeing Abel Gance's LA ROUE, Fernand Léger tried to define something of the radical possibilities of the cinema. The potential of the new art did not lay in 'imitating the movements of nature' or in 'the mistaken path' of its resemblance to theater. Its unique power was a 'matter of *making images seen*.'"[9] While institutional cinema was constructed around essentially narrative forms and methods, within this institution, in this first period of this thing called *cinema* as we know it today, pockets of resistance within cinematic discourse insisted on seeing the cinema as something other than a storytelling machine. Beginning with this second decade of the 20th century, which film history today views as the time when the cinema was institutionalized through the gradual and irreversible narrativization of films, we can identify a number of writings which advance the idea that the cinema could, precisely, serve for *seeing something else*. And here is where a two-fold connection to the idea of attraction offers itself to us. Attraction, as Eisenstein conceived of it, grabs hold of viewers and pushes them towards reflection, preventing them above all from forgetting themselves in the *opium* of bourgeois narrative. It is a kind of privileged channel of communication between the film, its viewers, and the world (which viewers must understand and in which they must act). In the same way, the cinema as a whole, in the reading proposed by these first theorists, shatters all forms of automatic perception by enabling viewers *truly to see*.[10]

From Visual Spectacle to Knowledge

In the selection of writings I will present below, what becomes apparent is the centrality of optical perception for these early film theorists (note that when these texts were written, the cinema's *purely visual pleasures* had lost their autonomy and been suppressed by the organising structure and increasing linearity of film narrative). What is also apparent, by virtue of this very fact, is the idea that the cinema, through this visual spectacle, possessed an unrivalled power to mediate our knowledge of the world. By suggesting a connection between attraction, knowledge and the intellect, I should emphasize that I am proposing that there exists continuity between the texts discussed below and Eisenstein's articles on attraction, which date from 1923-24. When we isolate the major stages, at least, of his thought, we can see a parallel course between these texts and those discussed below (leaving aside the question of ideology). In Eisenstein's view of attraction, the goal is to mould viewers by predisposing their feelings in the desired manner. The central focus of his enquiry is the viewer. Theater, cinema and art in general can act upon viewers, stimulating reflection upon their own condition. Attraction was the privileged ideological means for shaking viewers up and, in this way, for forcing them to act.

Although they do not speak precisely of attraction, these classic texts in the history of film theory do enquire into what it is about cinema that *attracts* us. The main thread running through each of these texts is that of the discovery of the cinema as the creator of a unique and astonishing vision, a stirring and ephemeral vision which, without too much trouble, we might see from the perspective of attraction. On another level, this is tied to an idea that often emerges in the texts discussed below: that there exists a sort of virtual and automatic marriage between the camera's eye and the brain. In this way, the "vision machine," which sees more than the human eye, is an intelligent machine, and thus autonomous. The camera extends and surpasses our senses, to the benefit of viewers and the vision of the world that is offered to them.

In fact, a common root can be seen in these earliest theoretical writings on the cinema: an enthusiasm for the birth of a new, entirely visual and emotive knowledge which only cinema can create. This is by no means a view of the cinema from the perspective of the narrative forms it was capable at that time of taking on and representing. It is an idea found most significantly in the earliest French theorists of the cinema, in the work of some of the thinkers of the "*photogénie* school,"[11] in particular Jean Epstein, Germaine Dulac and Louis Delluc, but also Emile Vuillermoz (and, outside of this school and in other respects, in the work of Pirandello, Benjamin, Eisenstein and Vertov, as I will attempt to illustrate by means of quick forays into their work below).

For these early film theorists, the medium's striking feature was its ability to touch viewers, to shock them, through suddenness, attacks and assaults (all characteristic of attraction), which they viewed as unique moments of *photogénie*.[12] The relationship their writings establish with the cinema privileges a number of its intensive and emotive *"photogénique"* and "attractional" aspects which resist the film's narrative development.[13] Here, the cinema is never seen simply as a new way of *re-presenting* an already visible or already seen world; rather, it is viewed as an unprecedented *technology for observation*. The possibility of observing motion, of slowing it down or speeding it up, offered hitherto unseen ways of shaping time and especially of producing new models of thought. In the ideas of these early thinkers, cinema's *monstration* of moving images becomes a veritable instrument for understanding the world.

Where Do Attractions Come From?

Before discussing these texts directly, it is important that we identify the historical and theoretical landscape which has arisen in the wake of André Gaudreault and Tom Gunning's article on the "challenge" early cinema posed to film history and the work that came after it. The common denominator of all this work is the view that attraction, in a film, is a moment in which the development of the narrative utterance pauses – a "peak moment" whose function is to address viewers directly and present them with a moment of pure spectacle. Gaudreault and Gunning's article (and those that succeeded it) sought to establish a position from which we might study, from various perspectives, the way cinema was made and viewed in its early years. This new approach made it possible to re-evaluate early cinema and more generally all popular entertainment at the turn of the twentieth century. Suddenly, the cinema at the time of its birth no longer resembled a husk containing the seeds of the cinema of the future, seeds that were still insufficiently developed because of the medium's entirely technological limitations at the time.

The emergence of cinema was part of the euphoria of modernity. Exoticism (as found in the era's expositions and in the Paris arcades celebrated by Baudelaire and Benjamin), train journeys (and the new visions of the landscape in movement and the proliferation of perspectives they offered), advances in the faculty of sight (from the air, for example, or with microscopes) and the improvements to fantastic images had already fed the collective imaginative identity, extended new aesthetic habits and enhanced the possibilities of public reception at the turn of the century. Science, for its part, from the 18th to 20th centuries, had been constantly extending the realm of what could be seen and

understood by measuring, representing and revealing through the use of tele-
scopes, microscopes, thermometers, X-rays, etc. According to Gunning, it is
clear that, in the logic of the system of attractions, the film image was made to
flaunt itself.[14] In this sense, it was indisputably a product of modernity. The cinema seems in this context to belong entirely to a system of *monstration*, of *showing*: it shows images, it is shown as a novelty, and it appears to show itself
(through its technological capabilities, which surpass and are separate from the
abilities of the showman/artisan/handle turner). In short, the cinema creates
around itself a commercial dimension which *attracts* and compels us to con-
sume (its images). Its enunciatory system fully shares the features of some of
the other fetish phenomena typical of modernity, such as billboards, posters,
expositions and store shelves: it is merchandise that makes itself visible, turning
its presence into spectacle. We must nevertheless insist upon the fact that the
cinema became a part of this movement of modernity in a significantly different
manner and with a greater *force of attraction*.

The cinema, we might note, has a technological dimension that is not content
with creating an atmosphere mediated by the apparatus and in particular its
machinery (unlike the train, for example, which creates a *mechanical* mediation
between the passenger-viewer and the landscape it sets in motion). Beyond its
factual and sentient aspects (filming and projecting, soliciting the viewer's sense
of sight), the cinema possesses a properly intellectual dimension, especially in
the insightful vision of the writers discussed below. This intellectual dimension
is apparent above all in the way it *makes us see* differently than we do with our
(tired, habit-ridden, imprecise) eyes. The cinema attracts and astonishes the
viewer: its act of *seeing* and of *making seen* (of making itself seen) derives from
its perception of the world, its analysis of its surroundings, and its powerful
ability to reveal all this to the viewer.

The very earliest films showed attractions, whether these were in the form of
military parades or magic acts, and can very well be seen as an attraction of
modernity, just like those on display in fairs, as the new approaches to film history have shown us. We might also consider that, once this initial period had
passed, certain discussions of the cinema reveal another dimension of its participation in modernity: the way it contributes to the erosion of the boundary
between subject and object by using the senses to speak to the intellect of its
audience. Benjamin appears inclined to this view when he experiences the metaphysical power of cinema, whose "explosive" images depict the world in a
way that awakens us to its possibilities. The cinema casts a new gaze on the
world; because of its mechanical nature it is able to bring out the intelligence of
objects, as if it contained a force of perception intrinsic to the apparatus which,
by this very fact, becomes an attraction in itself.

Writing the Attraction of Seeing

Let us now try to see how this attraction of seeing can be found at the heart of the work of some thinkers who have written about the cinema in the 1910s and 1920s. And let us start with an Italian voice, before discussing the *photogénie* school.

The multi-faceted literary figure Luigi Pirandello examined the medium whose birth he witnessed in his 1915 book *Si gira. I Quaderni di Serafino Gubbio operatore* (hereafter referred to by its English title, *Shoot!*).[15] As is often the case in Pirandello's work, this novel contains philosophical reflections. In this case, the cinematic apparatus, comprising both the camera (the *machinetta*) and the institution around it, is at the center of his ideas. By adopting the point of view of a camera operator, Pirandello assumes a point of view internal, in a sense, to the camera. Through the character Serafino Gubbio, "the hand that turns the handle," Pirandello assumes the gaze of the (objective) camera lens[16] and describes for us the features of this objective lens: it "looks at the ordinary" but in particular "sees far" and "sees beyond." In short, it sees more. The camera and the entire cinematic system is a "superhuman" eye which destroys all subjectivity and personal engagement and which can thereby penetrate people and objects. The cinema offers an emotionless gaze which is, for that reason, situated on the side of objects. It is thus capable of touching their deepest essence, which is never visible on the surface because the surface shows only "the theater of representation, staged by someone's gaze." In this novel, Pirandello makes explicit the *paradox of the objective lens*, which, on the one hand, asserts a neutral gaze estranged from all subjectivity and intentionality, and on the other casts a keen look which penetrates and reveals the truth of what lies before it.[17] This was a perspicacious view, in that Pirandello, in this novel dating from 1915, inaugurated a discourse which recognizes the *centrality of the technological apparatus* as the means for constructing knowledge out of intense snatches of images. In this light, his views on the cinema clearly go far beyond the central debates around the medium in the 1910s, concerning its aesthetic legitimacy. Although Pirandello did not yet see in the cinema the intelligence that Epstein would later see in it, he nevertheless recognized the power of attraction it can exercise on the modern masses by virtue precisely of its ability to "see more." This kind of discourse and these kinds of concerns would be central, as we know, to discussions of the cinema in the 1920s. We might note in passing that in 1929, in the face of the spectre of sound film, Pirandello called for a *cinemelografia*, or a "visible language of music," which would transform images in motion and make visible the sounds and rhythms which make up music.[18] Pirandello thus advocated a non-narrative, purely (audio-)visual cinema that could attain the heart of our knowledge of music, in a manner like music, thereby extending the line of thought that joins technology, knowledge and the cinema.

With his comments on the *machinetta* in *Shoot!*, Pirandello was already seeking what later writers would also seek: the specificity of the cinema in its mechanical nature. He opened a path which would soon see the "vision machine" as also being an intelligent machine.

This kind of discourse, and its conclusion concerning the intelligence of the "vision machine," would take every possible form in the 1920s (and, of course, beyond, in a few specific cases[19]). Before then, discussion of the cinema was confined to quite different issues, revolving for the most part around arguments such as "science and industry," "education and morality," and "the cinema as idle spectacle" or "the cinema as prestigious art."[20] "Essentialist"[21] *par excellence*, these theories of the 1920s, beyond their different obsessions (*photogénie*, rhythm, montage, purity), advocated a separate and independent path for the cinema. Intelligence (the ability to think abstractly beyond an initial sentient impression) was the condition of the very possibility of this independence (as it is for humans, I am tempted to add).

Emile Vuillermoz stands out among the 1920s theorists who, in their discussions of cinema's general conditions, sketched the features that I propose here we view in terms of attraction. Of particular significance is his work *La Musique des images. L'art cinématographique*, written in 1927. There, Vuillermoz writes:

> The camera has gradually been so improved that today it possesses the constitution of a human brain. Its thousands of recording cells have the same sensitivity as our grey matter. *The most fleeting impressions engrave their path on it and leave a definite trace of their passage.* This valuable little box, this well-sealed case, is the cranium of an artificial being which fixes its cyclopean eye on people and objects. This eye, at will, leans forward or back, raises or lowers its gaze and turns its face towards every point on the horizon. [...] *Its talents for perception are greater and keener* than those of the humble assistant who keeps its eyelid open. [...] Humankind has thus created an organism more powerful and richer than itself and made of it an appendage to and improvement on its own brain. When human receptivity has reached its outer limit, we will be able, thanks to this instrument for seeing into the future, to *advance the conquest of reality* and enlarge the realm of dreams accordingly. With its thousand parts, its recording mobility, its power of associating ideas and images and its lightning-quick perception, the camera has *extended and enlarged the brains of artists seeking to define the world.*[22]

We might see in this idea the echo of a comment by Jean Epstein in his 1921 book *Bonjour Cinéma*:

> The Bell and Howell is a standardized metal brain, manufactured and sold in thousands of copies, which transforms the outside world into art. The Bell and Howell is

an artist and it is only behind it that there are other artists, the director and camera operator. Finally, sensibility can be bought; it can be found in shops and pays customs duties just like coffee or oriental carpets.[23]

Vuillermoz and Epstein's ideas suggest more than the image of the cinema as an "all-seeing eye." It is a vision of the cinema as a brain, as a living organism, while at the same time celebrating its mechanical nature. We might even say that it anticipates cyberpunk! The camera's abilities (and, metonymically, those of cinema as a whole) are seen as much greater than those of the people who use it. Audiences respond to the cinema with their senses and intellect and, thanks to the attraction of the images, are able to see the world differently.

In the same vein, in 1926 Epstein emphasized, in *Le Cinématographe vu de l'Etna*, that "the cinema's mission does not seem to me to have been correctly understood. The camera lens is [...] *an eye endowed with non-human analytic properties*. It is an eye without prejudices, without morals, and free of all influences; it sees in human motion and the human face features that we, burdened [...] by our habits and thoughts, are no longer able to see. [...] If our first reaction in the face of our own image on film is a kind of horror, it is because we, civilized people, lie on a daily basis without any longer realizing it. *Brusquely*, this glassy stare pierces us with its amperage light."[24]

In an adjacent passage, Epstein (probably stimulated by the Sicilian sun and in a state already favorable to receiving epiphanies) relates his visual experiences while descending a staircase surrounded by mirrors. He describes the unusual images, whose entirely new power of unexpected points of view and their fleeting quality touch him. These images live only for a moment, *just long enough to be perceived*, a well-known characteristic of attractions. These parallel perceptions, magnified by multiplication, reveal to Epstein the unknown, which the nature of the image, for him a metonym of the cinematic image, can suddenly bring forth and make visible.

Elsewhere, Epstein asserts that "Cinematic vision makes us see the unexpected magical depths in nature which, because we always see it with the same eye, we have exhausted, we have stopped seeing."[25] Epstein thinks of a "tired" viewer to whom the cinema does a great service by surpassing his or her run down consciousness and by communicating with them directly, aggressively, through the senses.

Germaine Dulac too insists on the fact that the cinema is capable of touching our sensibility and intellect, our intellectual comprehension.[26]

A horse, for example, leaps over a hurdle. With our eye we judge its effort synthetically. A kernel of wheat sprouts, and we judge its growth synthetically as well. The cinema, by breaking movement down, *makes us see* analytically the beauty of the jump through a series of little rhythms which make up the overall rhythm. Paying particular attention to the wheat's germination, thanks to the cinema we no longer have just the synthesis of its growth but the psychology of this movement. We feel visually the pain felt by a shoot when it breaks through the ground and flowers. The cinema makes us witness its reaching for the air and light by capturing its unconscious, instinctive and mechanical motion.

Movement, through its rhythms, straight lines and curves, brings us visually into the presence of complex life.

We have seen that every technological discovery in the cinema has a highly determined purpose: the amelioration of visual impressions. The cinema seeks to make us see this thing and that. Constantly, in its technological evolution, it addresses itself to our eye in order to touch our understanding and our sensibility.[27]

In this way the cinema becomes the source of a true revelation of the nature of the world, because it can isolate, detach and bring elements together. It puts an end to the debate in the history of ideas over the degree to which art is a copy of the world:

> The Cinema, through its mechanical action, reveals to us its true artistic expression, it records and re-establishes the exact shape and movement of everything in its essential and profound truth. To be logical, the natural and direct function of cinema is thus to capture life, in a general sense, and to give it vitality.
>
> All art takes its inspiration from nature. Some forms of art copy it, while others describe it, explain it, and construct their dreams on transposed material and emotional realities. They act, so to speak, only in the second degree, by reflection. They do not work with the stuff of life itself the way cinema does.
>
> A simple claw mechanism placed inside a camera obscura equipped with a lens, past which it drags a long strip of light-sensitive and perforated film, has fulfilled the miracle hoped for by artists everywhere: to create a work of art out of true and direct elements undiminished by copying or interpretation.
>
> In sum, until now the arts have tried to get closer to life. The Cinema tries with life to create a work of art made out of visual correspondences, attitudes, shifting lines and expressions which, when brought together and arranged, create drama.[28]

Thus while the other arts are *copies of copies*, the cinema is a living thing. And the way the cinema attempts to apprehend the world has the gift of *immediacy*. This is similar to the ideas found in Epstein, who shows how the cinema has an exponential relationship to ideas:

> To see is to idealize, to detach and extract, read and select, to transform. We see on the screen what the cinema has already seen: a two-fold transformation; or rather, because it is multiplied, a transformation to the power of two. A choice within a choice. [...] [The cinema] presents us with a quintessence, with a product distilled twice over.[29]

Once again, we should view this immediacy as an attraction, because it divides up an automated series of elements and presents us with discontinuous samples in order to create a direct and aggressive confrontation.

Walter Benjamin, for his part, finds in the cinema the possibility of an almost tactile apperception of things in a world – the modern world – in which experience has been devalued and evacuated from daily life. The modern subject has become anaesthetized, distracted, tired, and this state affects our perception. The cinema, as it did for Epstein, comes to our rescue. Benjamin uses the term *reproduction* (which is not found in the work of Epstein, Vuillermoz or Dulac). It would be worthwhile to take a moment to examine this word. Following Benjamin, it is generally used today, rather ambiguously, to describe such completely different operations as manually *copying* (the attempt to re-do a work of art), *photographing* (in particular a face or an image) or mechanically *multiplying* the number of copies of an initial image. Following Sylviane Agacinsky, we should perhaps distinguish, within so-called "multiple" art forms, original *production* technologies (filming, photographing, engraving, recording) from their associated *multiplication* (copying) technologies.[30]

Cinema's interest in this equation lies in the fact that the cinema does more than duplicate reality. In his thoughts on the cinematic image, Benjamin maintains that it can reveal certain aspects of the model in reality which are inaccessible to the naked eye and can only be seen with the help of an adjustable lens:

One the one hand, film furthers insight into the necessities governing our lives by its use of close-ups, by its accentuation of hidden details in familiar objects, and by its exploration of commonplace milieux through the ingenious guidance of the camera; on the other hand, it manages to assure us of a vast and unsuspected field of action.

Our bars and city streets, our offices and furnished rooms, our railroad stations and our factories seemed to close relentlessly around us. Then came film and exploded this prison-world with the *dynamite of a split-second*, so that now we can set off calmly on journeys of adventure among its far-flung debris. With the close-up, space expands; with slow motion, movement is extended. And just as enlargement not merely clarifies what we see indistinctly "in any case," but brings to light entirely new structures of matter, slow motion not only reveals familiar aspects of movements, but discloses quite unknown aspects within them – aspects "which do not appear as the retarding of natural movements but have a curious gliding, floating character of their own" [here Benjamin is quoting Rudolf Arnheim]. Clearly, it is another nature which speaks to the camera as compared to the eye. "Other" above all in the sense that a space informed by human consciousness gives way to a space informed by the unconscious. Whereas it is a commonplace that, for example, we have some idea of what is involved in the act of walking (if only in general terms), we have no idea at all what happens during the split second when a person actually takes a step. We are familiar with the movement of picking up a cigarette lighter or a spoon, but know almost nothing of what really goes on between hand and metal, and still less how this varies with different moods. This is where the camera comes into play, with all its resources for swooping and rising, disrupting and isolating, stretching or compressing a sequence, enlarging or reducing an object. It is through the camera that we first discover the optical unconscious, just as we discover the instinctual unconscious through psychoanalysis.[31]

This vision reminds us once again that the nature revealed to the viewer through the eye of the camera is a different nature, an *other* nature, than what the human eye can perceive. A similar line of thought can be found in Dziga Vertov's writings on the kino-eye. Indeed Benjamin's remarks can not help but call to mind Vertov's comments in 1923 in a manifesto on the kino-eye:

> I, a machine, show you the world as only I can see it. [...] I am in constant motion, I draw near, then away from objects, I crawl under, I climb onto them. [...] My path leads to the creation of a fresh perception of the world. I decipher in a new way a world unknown to you.[32]

Beyond Periodization

In proposing the similarities discussed above and by looking closely at a few texts, this brief excursion has sought to link some of the earliest attempts to write film theory with the idea of attraction. What emerges is that, at the same time that films were becoming essentially narrative, film theory remained fascinated with the cinema's intrinsic ability to create attraction. When the cinema has left behind the first stage of its life, in which through technology it created a striking atmosphere for the consumption of a product or an aesthetic experience within the paradigm of modernity, the first film theorists, still interested in attraction, formulated a set of ideas which took attraction as their starting point and which saw the cinema as soliciting viewers' senses in order to touch their intellect.

We can thus see a thread running through different moments in film theory, out of which comes the idea that the movie camera is capable of seeing *differently*. This ability is a product of the mechanical nature of cinema, of the cinematic apparatus itself. This ability is not abstract, because it takes concrete shape in the relationship with the viewer, in the way the camera's gaze addresses the audience through emotional shocks, and finally in intellectual cognition, which makes us see not only things but people differently. For these thinkers, the cinema thus played a unique role in using attraction to mediate the sensations and knowledge at play between the world and the audience.

Translated by Timothy Barnard

Notes

Part of the present article has been previously published in French as "La persistance des attractions" in *Cinéma et Cie* 3 (Spring 2003): 56-63. This article was written under the aegis of the Groupe de recherche sur l'avènement et la formation des institutions cinématographiques et scéniques (GRAFICS) at the Université de Montréal.

1. Jean-Luc Godard, *Histoire(s) du cinéma*, episode 3a.
2. The founding text in this respect is André Gaudreault and Tom Gunning's "Le cinéma des premiers temps: un défi à l'histore du cinéma," *Histoire du cinéma. Nouvelles approaches*, ed. Jacques Aumont, André Gaudreault and Michel Marie (Paris: Sorbonne, 1989) 49-63. Translated into English in the present volume.
3. Gunning suggests, without however pursuing the idea, that there is continuity between periods in film history when attraction had a complex relationship with narrative structure, such as musical comedy, burlesque, or horror and science fiction films in which special effects are employed. See Tom Gunning, "Attractions, Trucages et Photogénie: l'explosion du présent dans les films à truc français produits entre 1896 et 1907," *Les vingt premières années du cinéma français*, ed. Jean A. Gili, Michèle Lagny, Michel Marie and Vincent Pinel (Paris: Sorbonne Nouvelle/AFRHC, 1995) 183.
4. The idea of *reaching out to viewers in their seats* in order to create audience participation in the film that can be emotional, sensorial or intellectual, according to one's desired goal, has an illustrious father (and a motley crew of cousins). Enumerating the attractions found in the epilogue to the play *Enough Simplicity for Every Wise Man*, Sergei Eisenstein describes how at the end of the play "there was a pyrotechnical explosion beneath the seats of the auditorium." See Sergei Eisenstein, "The Montage of Attractions [1923]," *Selected Works. Volume 1: Writings, 1922-34*, ed. and trans. Richard Taylor (London: British Film Institute, 1988) 38. A more comic and lucrative example can be found in late 20th-century amusement parks whose cinemas created a direct relationship with the viewer through the use of "butt shaker" seats. See Michèle Lagny, "Tenir debout dans l'image," *The Five Senses of Cinema*, ed. Alice Autelitano, Veronica Innocenti and Valentina Re (Udine: Forum, 2005) 187-98; Bernard Perron, "Le cinéma interactif à portée de main," *The Five Senses of Cinema* 447-75; and Viva Paci, "I Have Seen the Future," *Cahiers du GERSE* 6 (2004): 131-44.
5. The expression "system of monstrative attractions" is used by Gaudreault and Gunning 57ff. In Gunning's work the term "attraction" alone takes precedence. In Gunning, the word "monstrative" tends to disappear and be replaced by a term with fewer narratological constraints (and which is also decidedly more pleasing to the ear) to describe the cinema of attractions and attraction itself, which openly re-

veals itself to the viewer: *exhibitionist*. An attraction shows us something and at the same time it emphasizes that it is in the process of showing it. Here I am adopting one of the definitions of *monstration* given by André Gardies and Jean Bessalel in *200 mots-clés de la théorie du cinéma* (Paris: Cerf, 1992).

6. By "apparatus" I mean both the equipment and surroundings of the film shoot and projection on the one hand and those of the work's conception and reception on the other. On this subject, see the papers presented at the 2002 Domitor conference on the apparatus, particularly those published in *Cinéma et Cie* 5 (Spring 2003) and *CiNéMAS* 14.1 (Fall 2003).

7. "Vision machine" is here the translation of the French expression "machine à voir," and not of "machine de vision." The latter is a central concept of Paul Virilio's theory, which will not be addressed in this article. For two fundamental reasons I am obliged to distinguish his idea of "vision machine" (*The Vision Machine* [London: British Film Institute, 1994]), from the idea that I propose. One concerns the relationship between humankind and the vision machine and the other the definition of intelligence for the machine. For Virilio, the industrialization of vision, which he also calls the "market in synthetic perception," creates a dual point of view, as if human and machine (a machine able to see, recognize and analyze) shared the environment. We *can see* certain things and the machine others. What is different about the theorists discussed here is that for them, the cinema does not share the field of vision with us but rather makes it possible for us to *see* (shattering automatic behaviour, playing with dimensions and speed, etc.). Also, Virilio's idea of intelligence for the machine, "artificial intelligence," is defined by the machine's ability to apprehend the world and appreciate the surrounding environment, but within a circuit closed in upon itself and for itself in order to enable it, by itself, to analyze and control (calculate) its environment without a "video outlet" for the viewer. For the theorists discussed here, however, the machine reveals the surrounding world to us.

8. Fernand Léger, "A critical essay on the plastic qualities of Abel Gance's film *The Wheel*," *Functions of Painting*, ed. Edward Fry (New York: Viking, 1973) 21, quoted by Tom Gunning in "The Cinema of Attractions: Early Film, Its Spectator and the Avant-Garde," *Early Cinema: Space Frame Narrative*, ed. Thomas Elsaesser (London: British Film Institute, 1990) 56.

9. Gunning, "The Cinema of Attractions" 56.

10. Here we find ourselves in a world similar to that described by Viktor Shklovsky in his famous article "Art as Technique" (1917), in which poetic language (as opposed to prose), through a process of *singularization*, enables words to accomplish their real task, that of communicating the world. See my discussion of Shklovsky's relationship to Eisenstein in "Certains paysages d'Herzog sous la loupe du système des attractions," *CiNéMAS* 12.1 (2001): 97-104.

11. The path to a consideration of the similarities between attraction and *photogénie* in the "history of attraction" was clearly opened by Gunning in his article "Attractions, Truquages et Photogénie."

12. The concept of *photogénie* was explored in a vast number of texts, in particular by Louis Delluc and Jean Epstein, beginning in the very early 1920s. English-language scholarship on the subject is extensive and widely cited. This work includes David Bordwell, *French Impressionist Cinema: Film Culture, Film Theory and Film Style* (New

York: Arno, 1980); Stuart Liebman, "Jean Epstein's Early Film Theory 1920-1922," diss., New York U, 1980; and Richard Abel, *The French Cinema: The First Wave 1915-1929* (Princeton: Princeton UP, 1984). Two valuable studies in Italian should also be noted: *Fotogenia. La bellezza del cinema*, ed. Guglielmo Pescatore (Bologna: Clueb, 1992) and Laura Vichi, *Jean Epstein* (Milano: Il Castoro, 2003). A thin line separates the conception of *photogénie* in the work of Delluc and Epstein throughout their work. For Delluc, the cinema exists in order to discover the world's beauty, while for Epstein the cinema, thanks to the mechanical vision of the camera lens (see my discussion below of Luigi Pirandello's position in *Shoot!*), is a true cognitive instrument which makes it possible to be aware of the constantly varying and elusive essence of the life of people and objects. For Delluc, *photogénie* is the magnification of the beauty already existing in the world (somewhat like our common use of the term when we say that someone is "photogenic"), while for Epstein *photogénie* is created out of the encounter between the cinema and the world. Only cinema can create it.

13. This is the case even when the film in question is resolutely narrative (as opposed to the theorist's description of it, which sees it as eluding narration and basing itself on sudden bursts of *photogénie*, brief moments of emotion and defamiliarized visions). On this subject, see my article *"Pas d'histoires, il faut que le cinéma vive.* L'attraction dans le récit du film par quelques cinéastes de la première avant-garde," *Narrating the Film. Novelization: From the Catalogue to the Trailer*, ed. Alice Autelitano and Valentina Re (Udine: Forum, 2006) 205-12.

14. I refer in particular here to Tom Gunning, "Cinéma des attractions et modernité," *Cinémathèque* 5 (1994): 129-39. [English version: "The Whole Town's Gawking: Early Cinema and the Visual Experience of Modernity," *Yale Journal of Criticism* 7.2 (Fall 1994): 189-201].

15. Published in English as *Shoot! The Notebooks of Serafino Gubbio, Cinematograph Operator* (New York: Dutton, 1926) and reprinted by Dedalus in 1990 and the University of Chicago Press in 2005.

16. The present article, originally written in French, here uses an untranslatable play on words with the French word *objectif*, which can mean both "objective" and "camera lens" – Trans.

17. In his famous "Artwork" essay, Benjamin refers to *Shoot!* in a way that reveals a parallel concern to Pirandello's here. Benjamin is struck by the new role of the actor in Pirandello's novel. The actor must now perform for the camera, rather than play a character for an audience. Benjamin believed that *alienation* was at work and extremely productive here: the actor is alienated from the audience, from the performance and from identification with the character. The actor's image, like a specular image, is detached, transportable, and exercises control over the masses who will later watch it. A filmed image thus has a force, a power, which would not exist without the eye of the *machinetta*. See Walter Benjamin, "The Work of Art in the Age of its Mechanical Reproducibility" (second version, 1936), *Walter Benjamin, Selected Writings. Volume 3: 1935-1938*, trans. Edmund Jephcott and Harry Zohn, ed. Howard Eiland and Michael W. Jennings (Cambridge: Harvard UP, 2002) 112.

18. See Pirandello's article "Se il film parlante abolirà il teatro" published in the newspaper *Il Corriere della Sera* in 1929 and reprinted in *Saggi poesie scritti vari* (Milano: Mondadori, 1965) 1030-36. For discussions of Pirandello as a "film theorist," see the

essays in *Pirandello e il cinema*, ed. Enzo Lauretta (Agrigento: Centro nazionale di studi pirandelliani, 1978) and especially the article by Franca Angelini, "Dal *Teatro muto* all'*Antiteatro*: le teorie del cinema all'epoca del *Si gira...*" 65-83.

19. See for example Charles Dekeukeleire's book *Le Cinéma et la pensée* (Bruxelles: Lumière, 1947) or Epstein's writings throughout his life; see in particular his book *L'intelligence d'une machine* (Paris: Jacques Melot, 1946).

20. Richard Abel discusses these discourses around the cinema in his edited volume *French Film Theory and Criticism: A History/Anthology 1907-1939. Volume 1: 1907-1929* (Princeton: Princeton UP, 1988) 23. I have also written on these discourses on the cinema and the timid appearance of the search for *specificity* before 1915 in "*Les films impossibles* ou les possibilités du cinéma," *Distribution*, ed. Frank Kessler (London: John Libbey, forthcoming).

21. The idea of viewing 1920s film theory as essentialist is Alberto Boschi's. See his book *Teorie del cinema. Il periodo classico 1915-1945* (Rome: Carocci, 1998) 22ff.

22. Emile Vuillermoz, *La Musique des images. L'art cinématographique* (Paris: Félix Alcan, 1927). This work has been reprinted in its entirety in *Musique d'écran. L'accompagnement musical du cinéma muet en France 1918-1995*, ed. Emmanuel Toulet and Christian Belaygue (Paris: Réunion des musées nationaux, 1994) 113. My emphasis. My thanks to Pierre-Emmanuel Jaques for bringing this text to my attention.

23. Jean Epstein, "Le sens 1bis [1921]," *Ecrits sur le cinéma. Volume 1: 1921-1947* (Paris: Seghers, 1974) 92. An alternative translation can be found in *French Film Theory and Criticism* 244-45.

24. Jean Epstein, *Le cinématographe vu de l'Etna* [1926], *Ecrits sur le cinéma. Volume 1* 136-37. My emphasis.

25. Jean Epstein, "La Féerie réelle [1947]," *Ecrits sur le cinéma. Volume 2: 1946-1953* (Paris: Seghers, 1975) 44-45.

26. Intellectual understanding is of course also an issue for Eisenstein. In his writings, understanding travels in the same direction, from the senses to the intellect (with, in his case, a well-defined ideological objective), but, as we know, it is conveyed by one procedure in particular: montage. "An [...] attraction is in our understanding any demonstrable fact (an action, an object, a phenomenon, a conscious combination, and so on) that is known and proven to exercise a definite affect on the attention and emotions of the audience and that, combined with others, possesses the characteristic of concentrating the audience's emotions in any direction dictated by the production's purpose. From this point of view a film cannot be a simple presentation or demonstration of events; rather it must be a tendentious selection of, and comparison between, events, free from narrowly plot-related plans and moulding the audience in accordance with its purpose." Eisenstein 40-41.

27. Germaine Dulac, "Films visuels et anti-visuels [1928]," *Ecrits sur le cinéma (1919-1937)* (Paris: Expérimental, 1994) 119.

28. Germaine Dulac, "L'action de l'avant-garde cinématographique [1931]," *Ecrits sur le cinéma* 157.

29. Epstein, "Le sens 1bis" 91. An alternative translation can be found in *French Film Theory and Criticism* 244.

30. In *Le Passeur de temps. Modernité et nostalgie* (Paris: Seuil, 2000), Sylviane Agacinsky suggests that, within the new mechanical procedures, it would be useful to distinguish between, on the one hand, a product's *original production technologies*, for ex-

ample photography, and on the other the *copying technologies* applied to these objects. Just because prints can be made does not make photography essentially a reproductive technology: it is an original way of producing images. Nevertheless, it is on the basis of this somewhat fuzzy idea of reproduction that Benjamin suggests that a work of art (painting or architecture) is "reproduced" by photography. In this way he considers the work of art being photographed as "original" with respect to its photographic "reproduction."

31. Benjamin 117. My emphasis.
32. Dziga Vertov, "Kinoks: A Revolution [1923]," *Kino-Eye: The Writings of Dziga Vertov,* trans. Kevin O'Brien, ed. Annette Michelson (Berkeley: U of California P, 1984) 17-18. Obviously the connection between Vertov and the issues raised in the present article must be dealt with in greater depth on another occasion. This already seemed necessary in 1925, when Eisenstein wrote "*Cine-Pravda* does not follow this path – its construction takes no account of attractions." Eisenstein 41.

Rhythmic Bodies/Movies: Dance as Attraction in Early Film Culture

Laurent Guido

At the turn of the 20th century, cinema emerged in a context marked by the vast expansion of interest in bodily movement, at the crossroads of aesthetic and scientific preoccupations. Already developed by Enlightenment philosophers and Romantic poets, the quest for the origins of nonverbal language and mime permeated the discussion of disciplines such as psychology or anthropology,[1] which were in the process of being institutionalized. Furthermore, new images of the body were created and distributed via experimental sciences, which considered the mechanism of physical movement as stemming from circulation and energy consumption. Therefore, the 1882 founding of the Station Physiologique de Paris and Etienne-Jules Marey's work revealed a focused desire to study human movement (already featured, in part, in *La machine animale*, 1873) as well as to depend on the systematic use of serial photography inaugurated in the United States by Eadweard Muybridge. The development of this analysis tool, which would include film at the end of the decade, shows a transformation in the series of inscription machines used in physiology to record measurable traces of movement. The improvement of devices linked to the *graphic method*, as François Albera reminds us, represents an important "moment" where a mechanical vision of the human being and a mechanical recording technique meet.[2] At first, the discontinuity achieved by the chronophotographic machine responded to a logic, which conceived the body in a dynamic series of rhythmic cuts. Founded above all on the idea of scientific knowledge, this understanding of human mobility created an element that contained not only an aesthetic, but also even a spectacular dimension. Dance, just as sports and gymnastics, imposed itself at the beginning of the 20th century as a harmonious way of organizing body movement. It was considered that the muscular mimicry put into motion by physical performance would position spectators under an irresistible rhythmic spell.[3] This article discusses the development of the attraction aspect in dance, from its first exploitation on chronophotographic plates, by Georges Demenÿ in particular, to its formation as an editing model for French 1920s film directors.

Between Scientific Modernity and Renewal of the Antique Gesture

As François Dagognet points out, Marey's intervention, "sometimes without his knowledge," contributed to the creation of a series of important alterations within the arts, communication, and culture. In the famous *épures de mouvement* which reduced the silhouettes of subjects, entirely dressed in black, to a scintillating trajectory of points and lines, Dagonet identifies an "elementary trick" that anticipates the human body's exploitation in cultural industry: "How can one not be struck by the man-athlete metamorphosed into a series of lines?"[4] Very implicitly, this gathering of elements takes on an even stronger meaning, in considering Georges Demenÿ's contribution as *"préparateur"* at the Station Physiologique. As an engineer and artist (designer, musician), Demenÿ (1850-1917) proposed above all to take on a methodically and rationally based physical education. His objectives were in line with the utilitarian goal assigned to the Station by its governmental subsidy – i.e. the study of walking, running, and jumping to improve soldiers' or workers' performances.[5] This gave him the opportunity to focus his shots on already trained sportsmen and in particular students from the Military School in Joinville. These images became for him a valuable model not only of efficiency, but also of aesthetic perfection. Considering that "both the artist's and physiologist's spirit, starting from different points, must meet in front of nature," he praised "rhythm" and "harmony," which allowed him to find the "perfect effort" and focus on the "beauty of movements." His discourse was in accordance with various hygienist movements and the "body culture," typical of the turn of the 20th century (*hébertisme* in France, *Lebensreform* in Germany). Concerned with stylized sketches ("the line and design must take over the profusion of details"), he argued, in fact, for the regeneration of the corporeal in accordance with the physical canons of the antique statuary, which was key for a new "gestural sobriety."[6] Determinedly, Demenÿ tied his work to the renovators of gesture expression (Delsartian gymnastics, Laban): his wish to explore movement "in all directions possible" aimed to "fill the enormous gap between the art of dance and mimic."[7]

This resulted in a series of images recorded by Demenÿ in 1892-93 of ballerinas from the Paris Opera. These shots were taken for Maurice Emmanuel, specialist in antique Greek *orchestique*, who wished to obtain instantaneous "representations of movements borrowed from figurative monuments."[8] From attitudes conserved on bas-reliefs and painted vases, Emmanuel reconstituted a succession of poses, which he then had the dancers reinterpret. The "chrono-photographic analysis" allowed him in some way to test the validity of choreographic sequences already identified during Antiquity.

Similarly, in the first years of the 20th century, dance experimentalists (Isadora Duncan, Nijinsky, Dalcroze at Hellerau) incessantly referred to frozen images of movement from Antiquity, to liberate ballet from the conventions and thus to allow for a return to supposed natural perfection of antique rules. This articulation between innovation and archaism was in no way original, as it echoed the general opinion of that time by which the most innovative aspects of modernization and technical improvements of social life were always perceived as an opportunity to bring back traditional values. It was not only a question of trying to cover new media's most original characteristics with familiar concepts – as though to compensate for the traumatic shock represented in industrialization and urbanization – but also of creating a mythology that fed the field of research and technical inventions. A number of aesthetic treaties associated for instance the effects of rhythmic automatism emitted from physiology, anthropometry, or Taylorism with practices of "primitive" peoples or antique civilizations that anthropologists and archeologists were rediscovering.

The classical vision of the *fruitful* instant emanating from sculpture (Lessing) was therefore not completely put into question, at the end of the 19th century, with the appearance of new mechanical techniques of movement decomposition. Certainly, these scientific machines only produced *ordinary* instances determined by an arbitrary rhythm. However, the chosen immobile images could be assimilated to codified poses inherited from ancient systems of representation. Therefore, in *L'Evolution créatrice* (1907), Henri Bergson recalls that despite their fundamental differences, both the *classical* and *modern* concepts of movement are based on frozen images. Rejecting both in the name of the indivisible nature of *durée*, the philosopher assimilates them to the process of scientific knowledge, which he sees contained in the illusion of movement produced by the cinematograph (here, the image of the military procession).[9]

Early Cinema and the Attraction of Physical Performance

In 1892-93, when the Opera's ballerinas were being recorded at the Station Physiologique, which Marey judged with detachment,[10] Demenÿ took a decisive step toward breaking with the great physiologist by founding the *Société du phonoscope*, where he openly expressed a commercial and spectacular aim. This approach resulted in a particular choice of subjects, recorded between 1893 and 1894 in Demenÿ's own laboratory. Besides prosaic acts taken from daily life, one finds the images of two French cancan dancers as well as a ballerina executing an *entrechat*. These strips, with their erotic content (the young ladies are fairly undressed), recall the female body's exploitation by Muybridge, as ana-

lyzed by Linda Williams and Marta Braun.[11] When Demenÿ re-used the previously mentioned *entrechat* for a phonoscope disk, his motivations echoed
Muybridge's who isolated the image of a woman doing a *Pirouette* (1884-85)
and fixed it on a plate destined for projection.[12] Along the same lines, in 1893,
Albert Londe recorded a charming acrobat's movements, which were very different from the pictures he took for the Hospital of Salpêtrière. From then on,
whether the image was animated or not, Londe's gesture showed a desire to
exhibit, similar to the *attraction* mode of early cinema.

Demenÿ's work seems to actualize the functions and multi-purpose uses of a
medium in constant technical evolution. Technology, although in principle
meant for the rational study of movement, could also take on an *attraction* value.
This term can be interpreted according to two complementary definitions. On
the one hand, it qualifies a type of show, an *act* whose autonomy is preserved
during its insertion into a program or piece (depending on the level of integration, we can also talk (in French) of a *"clou"*[13]). On the other hand, it refers to the
relationship with the spectator, that is either by means of the spectacularization
of the medium's own characteristics or the value of what is shown.[14]

Whether it concerned the showing of mechanisms invisible to the naked eye,
by presenting the decomposition of a gesture – as an isolated or sequenced
shape[15] – or the illusion of mobility, which thanks to optical machines resulted
from the animation of these same images, all public displays of chronophotographic images evidently had a spectacular dimension. This dimension relied
not only on the fascination for a new technology capable of revealing original
images, but also on sport, dance or acrobatic performances, recorded by the
camera, staged and framed in front of a black backdrop. The international success of *Schnellseher* by Ottomar Anschütz, developed in the middle of the 1880s,
gives evidence, better than Muybridge's zoopraxiscope and Demenÿ's apparatuses, of the attractive aspect of chronophotographic shows. An advertisement
for the automated version of the *Schnellseher*, presented at the *Crystal Palace* in
London in April 1893, shows the impact of this form of entertainment, categor-
ized as "Permanent attractions": "*The Electrical Wonder* combining the latest development in instantaneous photography with electrical automatic action. Skirt
dancing, Gymnastics, Boxing, Steeple-Chasing, Flat-Racing, Haute-Ecole Step-
ping Horses, Military Riding, Leaping Dogs, Camels, Elephants in motion, In-
dians on the war path, etc."[16] If "attraction" refers here to the entire program
including the exhibition of the technical process itself, the starring of dancers,
showing their legs and athletic prowess, signals the preeminence of physical
performances already organized into acts.

This specific feature of the *Electrical Wonder* program appeared again in the
first film reels of the *Edison Kinetoscope* filmed by Dickson in 1894 (re-filmed for
the Biograph in 1896), which included the presence of stars such as culturist

Eugene Sandow, dancers Carmencita and Annabelle as well as boxing champions. Various studies have already pointed out the frequency of dance and sports in early cinema,[17] which André Gaudreault and Philippe Marion regard as characterized by a form of *"spontaneous intermediality."*[18] Even without taking into account military parades or cavalry demonstrations, numerous shots were effectively focused on athletic and acrobatic prowess, as well as traditional or exotic dances. Furthermore, *féeries* in color, such as those by Georges Méliès or Segundo de Chomón, gave great importance to the procession of young women in tights inspired by ballet or music hall reviews.[19]

My purpose here is not to closely examine this important aspect of early cinema production, but to continue a reflection on the crossroads between cinema and the culture of body movement, by considering the theoretical discourses of the period of institutionalization and artistic legitimatization of film in France in the 1910s and 20s.

The Beauty of Slow Motion: Toward the Ideal Gesture

After the commercial failures of his projects, Demenÿ dedicated most of his activity to the rational study of human movement at the laboratory of experimental physiology at the Ecole Normale de Gymnastique et d'Escrime de Joinville (between 1903 and 1907). There, he jointly used the graphic, chronophotographic and cinematographic methods. In March 1913, the great sport magazine, *La Vie au grand air*, published a special issue with original images taken "with the *chronophotographeur* of professor Marey, installed at Joinville by M. Demenÿ."[20] At this time, sport magazines frequently resorted to photographic deconstructions of movement to illustrate the question of peculiar *styles* of different athletic disciplines. The detailed reproduction of specific phases of technical gestures was, in fact, meant to promote the ability to improve efficiency.[21] This use of cinematographic images pursued both scientific and biomechanical aims, not only – as officer Rocher observed – "to give an exact idea of the different phases in movement, phases that escape even the most trained eye," but also to allow "progress to those in training."[22] Rocher's rationalist discourse was in accordance with Demenÿ's ideals, in a context where the antique statuary model always guided aesthetic reflections on the benefits of physical education and on the necessity to forge a new corporeality with rhythmic and considered perfect proportions.

From the end of the Great War, the cinematographic press echoed similar ideas, as was notably demonstrated by the enthusiastic reception of the improvement of "ultra-rapid" cinematography – slow motion – presented publicly at the beginning of the 1920s by the Marey Institute. In spite of the utilitarianism professed by the creators (especially factory work's rationalization), film critics were especially interested in the aesthetic value of the process and its power to reveal the hidden gestures in movement's flow. In *Cinémagazine*, the series of gestures of an Opera ballerina were particularly remarked upon as a film giving rhythm to human movement harmoniously and was judged as a visual "masterpiece" that "one could watch […] ten times, without getting tired of it, as the poses of Miss Suzanne Lorcia, bent over at fifty centimeters off the ground, were so beautiful."[23] The desire to be able to view the same images again and again points to the fetishist dimension in the act of watching in a continuous loop, which was at the core of the phonoscope device, elaborated by Demenÿ thirty years before. According to Demenÿ, this device allowed to "review periodically the phases of closed movement and to slow it down according to our desire."[24]

The opinion of the *Cinémagazine* chronicler refers back to a discourse, which was largely renewed by slow motion, where one estimated that "certain visual movements, decomposed by this extraordinary process sometimes reach such a strength and beauty that they evoke the greatest masterpieces of sculptural art"[25] or proved to be "as beautiful as Greek tragedy."[26] For his part, Emile Vuillermoz estimated that it rendered "the fundamental rhythm of life 'readable,'" and similarly using the choreographic metaphor "all is dance in the universe. […] Dance of muscles, dance of vegetation life, dance of water and fire, dance of volumes and lines."[27] This intimate relationship between the tool of cinematographic vision and rhythmic ordnance of nature gave strength to Fernand Divoire's belief, as modern dance's principal promoter in France, that slow motion signified a "caricature of human movement" represented by the stereotypical ballet poses. By contrast, he found Joséphine Baker's movements perfectly natural.[28] According to Gilles Deleuze, cinema participated effectively in a process of mutation where the art of poses left its place to gesture "depending on space and time, constructed continuity at each instant which did only let itself be deconstructed into remarkable immanent elements, instead of returning to pre-existing shapes to incarnate."[29]

The ability to reveal fundamental gestures is therefore among the characteristics attributed to cinema in the early decades of 20th century. In accordance with the neo-platonic idealism of the era, the cinematographic device was thought of as a prosthetic means to decode the harmoniously rhythmic and universal language. Likewise, film was meant to test the validity of the new directions taken by gestural expression, starting from the quest for its essential foundations.

The Girls' Phenomenon

André Levinson, another commentator of choreographic art during the 1920s, highlighted the ambivalence of such endeavors. If Isadora Duncan truly tried to "revive the Greeks' *orchestique,* in which figurative monuments conserved the remains," it is only by reformulating it with the typically expressive "Anglo-Saxon athletic" power.[30] In the same way, he broached the girls' phenomenon: while associating it with the great development of female athletics in the United States, he linked the persistent cadence marking of the girls with the revitalization of collective choreographic traditions that had become obsolete since Egyptian or Greek antiquity. Contrarily to European dance, conscious of its history and its evolution, "the radiant youth of svelte Americans, a race without memories," seemed to him to have rediscovered antique gestures "beyond centuries and civilizations."[31]

Following the examples of athletic manuals and physical education methods, especially Demenÿ's *harmonious* gymnastics, fashion and cinema magazines opened their pages, near the end of World War I, to the formulation of beauty criteria depending on the acquisition of ideal proportions defined by both the study of antique sculptures and the golden rule theory.[32] I have shown elsewhere[33] how a particular definition of *photogénie,* seen as the visual quality of the new body molded by physical exercise, could have come out of that context. Consequently, the *bathing girl* from the films of Mack Sennett appeared to Louis Delluc, in 1918, as the "daring equivalent of Loïe Fuller and Isadora Duncan."[34] The claim of "purified gestures," on which critics such as Delluc, Moussinac or Canudo commented, moved forward in popular culture's development between the two world wars. During that time, the production of the human body's serialized representations intensified, and media echoed the scientific attempts from the end of the 19th century to rationalize corporeality. The procession of soldiers was followed by fashion models, and still even more emblematic by showgirls.

In 1920s Germany the *Girl-Kultur* was, actually, the object of philosophical and sociological observations by numerous intellectuals, who perceived in the gathered choreographies a rationalized and machine-like image of the fetish-body promoted by industrial modernity. One example is Siegfried Kracauer's famous analysis associating the development of the *tiller girls* with the brutally revolutionary process of the Taylorist depersonalization.[35] Similarly, others, such as Fritz Giese, seized the opportunity to proceed with a "comparison between American and European rhythms and ways of life," associating the music-halls' and cinema's dance groups to a social mechanization process very different from the pantheistic and neoclassical aspirations of the *Körperkultur.*[36] In

France, the film press highlighted, from the middle of the 1920s onwards, the "capital role" played by "photogenic girls" associated with an age of "jazz" and "mathematics."[37] A commentator of *L'Art cinématographique* (1927), for instance, presented athletic bodies as a phenomenon directly issued from American industrialization, from "beauty institutes and physical education courses": "One would take them for brilliant automates, such are their movements seemingly commanded by motorized systems."[38]

This rationalized and refined objectification of the human (essentially feminine) body was already being praised in artistic milieus, linked to the Futurist and Dadaist avant-garde. Closely related to the "new" body culture, Picabia, in 1915, produced *Portrait d'une jeune fille américaine dans l'état de nudité* in the shape of a spark-plug.[39] In an article on his film BALLET MÉCANIQUE (1924), Fernand Léger mentioned for his part the "plastic value" of the girls' phenomenon: "50 girls' thighs rolling with discipline, projected in close-up, this is beautiful, this is *objectivity*."[40] In preparatory notes for his film, Léger had planned to start with the sudden arrival of a "small dancer [...] absorbed by a mechanical element." While this figure was actually replaced by the Chaplin marionette, the artist respected another indication from the initial sketch, namely the desire to produce "a constant opposition of violent contrasts."[41] Recalling the shock of attractions, advocated at the same years by S.M. Eisenstein, the editing of BALLET MÉCANIQUE effectively resulted in the permanent confrontation of heterogeneous visual elements. Signaling a new show value of the human body, the mechanical rhythms of this film (automates, fairground games, swing...) echo the fast editing sequences of LA ROUE (Abel Gance, 1921-22) and CŒUR FIDÈLE (Jean Epstein, 1923), which are marked by the same mechanical spirit. Likewise, Germaine Dulac uses the choreographic metaphor several times to qualify her 1929 short avant-garde films DISQUE 957, ARABESQUE and THÈME ET VARIATION.[42] The latter was furthermore based on alternate shots of a ballerina and machine pieces. Thus, dance was not only a privileged figure in the show, but also a model for the movement's "choreography," led by the entire piece, via the montage. Emile Vuillermoz again formulated this idea at the beginning of the 1930s, when he associated the girls' shows – then proposed as intermissions in certain Parisian movie theaters – to an audiovisual synchronization process accomplished by sound film, meaning the possibility to "submit all images to the laws of a superior choreography":

> Despite their personal grace, these charming performers have become only anonymous cells in a fabulous animal body, a sort of gigantic centipede in raptures. One observes, with satisfaction, this precision machine, with levers, wheels, pistons and connecting rods, so perfectly regulated, with its so well oiled joints. It is transfigured, exalted, and idealized by the decor, costumes, light, music, and the hallucinating grey that emanates from certain machines in full action, from which it is impossible

to look away, when one has imprudently observed their delicate and precise gestures. Such is the superior discipline of lines, volumes, and sound that the film brings in all areas of show.[43]

"Impossible to look away": the spectacle of the cinematographic machine, having established a synchronism of aural and visual rhythms, provided a powerful attraction value – the new medium's technical properties causing an irresistible spell, that Vuillermoz metaphorically described as the submission of the girls' increased movements to the same musical rhythm.

Dance as Aesthetic Model: The Influence of Loïe Fuller

As Inge Baxmann showed, dance played a central role in the 1920s as rhythm's privileged way of expression in the framework of a general energizing of all the arts.[44] Inspired by Maurice Emmanuel's studies and Marey's *épures de mouvement*, Paul Valéry for instance saw the artist "using movement and measure" when he managed to show, in imitation of the female dancer, "the pure act of metamorphosis."[45] Choreographic art intervened equally in aesthetic debates on film. From the end of World War I, these two forms of expression were frequently associated since they were both based on the same principle of *"plastique en movement."* Therefore, Elie Faure considered that dance shared with cinema, or at least its future version having reached maturity (*"cinéplastique"*[46]), a combination of musical and visual dimensions. In 1911, Ricciotto Canudo expressed this as the ability to reunite the rhythms of time and space.[47] In "La danse et le cinéma," Faure believed that the "universal rhythmic movement will find geometry, the measure of space, in the order and movement of machines and in the order and movement of the universe itself."[48]

This esoteric meeting of scientific technique and aesthetic preoccupations was realized in the shows of the American dancer Loïe Fuller. Articulating body movement with electrical effects – constantly modified colored lighting, mirrors, and mobile magical lantern combinations – Fuller's performances, presented at the Folies Bergères from 1892 on, gained a very large public appreciation. Presenting a continuous metamorphosis, her art was emblematic of the renewed concept of movement that recalled the arabesques of Modern-Style as well as the electricity cult displayed at the 1900 *Exposition*, in which the dancer directly participated. Fuller's performances also attracted the fascination of Symbolist writers and critics, who were committed to formulate a new aesthetics, in which the female body represented the essence of a mobility beyond any precise reference in the world.[49] This concept, however, did not do away with the modern and popular dimension of Loïe Fuller's luminous apparitions, perceived by Mallarmé as an "exercise [which] contains art's drunkenness and, simultaneously industrial accomplishment" and addressed both "the poet's intelligence and the crowd's stupor."[50] According to the poet, Fuller's potentiality to reunite the most varied of publics expressed just as much antique culture's resurgence as the contemporary world's mechanic and industrialized power: "Nothing astonishes more than that this prodigy is born in America and at the same time it is a Greek classic."[51] Fuller's scenic evolutions could also be envisaged as a variant on the aesthetic discourse that permeated thoughts on cinema: forging the principles of a new synthetic art that is both complex and immediate, elitist and popular, archaic and technological.

While the multiple relations between Loïe Fuller and movement culture around 1900 have been the objects of several in-depth studies, in particular those of Tom Gunning and Elisabeth Coffmann,[52] Fuller's influence on French film directors and critics during the 1920s remains relatively unknown. In the eyes of Marcel L'Herbier, however, she appeared to be the "pre-existence" of a "technique made with suggestive lighting and unceasing mobility."[53] Louis Delluc, on the other hand, situated the origins of *photogénie* itself in "electricity's reign" deployed by the serpentine dance, a "goldmine from where theater, cinema and painting drew deliberately." This "enlightening algebra," this veritable "electricity poem" seemed to indicate to Delluc "the synthesis" close to the future, the "visual equilibrium of cinema,"[54] and that the music hall had a far reach when it managed to conjugate light and gesture to the point of making a *girl* appear "stylized by the electric lightening."[55] René Clair, for his part, started as an actor in Le Lys de la Vie (1921), a film co-produced by Fuller and that retained Léon Moussinac's attention for its recourse to various visual effects (such as iris, mask effects, chromatic coloring, Chinese shadows, slow motion and negative printing).[56] For Germaine Dulac, this film constituted a "drama in optic harmony more than in the performed expression," announcing a "superior form of cinema" based above all on "light and color play." She attributed to the feminine dancer the revelation of "visual harmony" and the creation of "first light harmonies at the time when the Lumières were giving us cinema." Dulac perceived a "strange coincidence at the eve of an era that is and will be that of visual music,"[57] a reference which pointed to the paradigm of the musical analogy that dominated French aesthetic discourses in the 1910s and 20s.

The Montage Piece as "Dance of Images"

It seems that the issue brought up by Fuller is not linked to the dancing body, but to a new "photogenic dance" (Juan Arroy on Lys de la Vie) that exploited to the fullest cinema's diverse abilities by using a full range of variations: the profilmic arrangement, lighting, the film's unwinding speed, development and color, etc. However, journalists from the specialized press in the 1920s noted the omnipresence of dance images in contemporary film production. Apart from films centered on stars such as Alla Nazimova or Maë Murray, whose choreographic "*clous*" appeared to integrate themselves into the continuity of the film narrative, journalists regretted that the cinematographic role of dance was reduced most often to what Jean Tédesco termed "more or less organized attraction" or, in the words of Juan Arroy, "attraction of staging."[58] At first sight, dance causes a distinction between two fundamental paradigms of representation. On the one hand, one sees that in film rhythm emanates above all from the actors' physical performances. Jean Renoir briefly suggested in 1926 that if "rhythm is king" at the cinema, it does not situate itself "in the montage of a film, but in its interpretation."[59] On the other hand, one finds the argument that the filmic development of corporeal rhythms largely proceeds from exterior factors to the interpreters themselves. In his article in homage to Etienne-Jules Marey, André Levinson notes the "*incompatibility* in the character of both arts of movement," which explains why cinema is incapable to capture and restitute the "human body's natural rhythm." Film should, therefore, try to "*suggest* the vertiginous whirling and ecstatic stamping of dance with the help of peculiar practices," that is "the illusion obtained by the frequent *shot alternation* and the eloquent enlarging of *big close-ups*."[60] This statement from Levinson, a Russian emigrant, followed consciously or not, the Soviet theorist Lev Kuleshov's conclusions from his experiments in dance filming and montage.[61] For Kuleshov, as for Levinson, these montage practices constitute the very film method that distinguishes it fundamentally from the other arts. The only dance possible in cinema, therefore, is one that results from assembled images.

In his analysis of choreographic art and cinema, Fernand Divoire emphasized that if the former proceeded already from the synthesis of rhythm and movement, the latter, already considered as movement, must still develop its rhythmic aspect.[62] He agreed, therefore, with Léon Moussinac's recriminations, highlighting in 1925 the necessity to develop, beyond *interior* rhythm produced in filmed movements, potentialities more specific to *exterior* rhythm and resulting in a succession of shots. Moussinac then recommends the systematic recourse to studies of "*mesures cinégraphiques*" following the fast editing sequencing style of LA ROUE, which Divoire evokes: "One could dance to certain pieces in [the extract of LA ROUE titled] *Rail*."[63] This idea would equally be mentioned by dancer Georges Pomiès, also an actor for Jean Renoir at the beginning of the 1930s: "The superior shape of cinema is not simply to make movement, but to make images dance. One sees what a lesson and efficient contours the dance of the human body could bring to realize this concept."[64]

This "dance of images" recalls the French "school" desire that Gilles Deleuze identifies as an almost "scientific" obsession to free a *"quantity of movement"* by the intervention of the "metric relations that allow defining it."[65] As Jean Epstein noted in 1923, *photogénie*, as condition of true specificity of cinema, narrowly depended on the film's capacity to develop its rhythmic variables in both *spatial* and *temporal* dimensions.[66] Léon Moussinac, Emile Vuillermoz or Paul Ramain thus dreamt of an art based on mastering the rhythm of movement, purified from the dramatic conventions, organized on the analogical model of the principles in musical composition, and including the development of narrative tensions. Except for a minority current lead by Germaine Dulac's discourses, the principal defenders of the "visual symphony" or "pure movement" in fact aimed to establish figurative cinema, using visual leitmotifs with narrative value set up on the explicit model of transmitting myths, such as Richard Wagner had wished to do in his operas.

This theoretical discourse was especially embodied in the anthology scenes based on accelerated montage and in certain scenes dedicated to dance, such as the Mozhukhin folk dance in KEAN (Alexandre Volkoff, 1925), farandole in MALDONE (Jean Grémillon, 1928) or flamenco in LA FEMME ET LE PANTIN (Jacques de Baroncelli, 1928).[67] However, one should not perceive a claim of hybrid art in this practice of "rhythmic" cuts that mark the montage methods' ability to attract. That is, one should not think of film as heterogeneous successions of potentially "detachable" pieces. On the contrary, as Abel Gance states in 1923, the aesthetic ideal remains that of a coherent cinematographic piece, where each part responds to a complete formal logic, a general equilibrium.[68] Actually, these passages serve as temporary experiments to set out perspectives, where, in the words of Jean Epstein, "style" would finally be "isolated from anecdote."[69]

One finds in Epstein a two-part reference to dance. On the one hand, dance functions as a general metaphor to describe the paradigm of mobility, such as in *Bonjour Cinéma* (1921), where Epstein qualified as "photogenic" the "landscape's dance" taken from the train or from the car in full speed.[70] On the other hand, it constitutes an object of phantasm, a facet of the new form of ultra-mobile body, which can be multiplied in strength by the new representational tools of the technological era. Still in *Bonjour Cinéma*, Epstein in fact expresses the wish to show "a dance taken successively in the four cardinal directions. Then, with panoramic shots [...] the theater as seen by the dancer couple. An intelligent editing will reconstitute [...] the life of dance, both according to the spectator and the dancer, objective and subjective."[71] Concerned as much with camera movements as editing, the energizing of dance aimed to deplete the possible representations of mobility by exploring all possible aspects (exterior, then interior). This logic referred back to Epstein's own definition of *photogénie* as the exploitation of all space-time variables. He would develop this further in 1925 in his allegorical story of a man descending a staircase, while facing a wall where mirrors send back mobile and reduced images of himself.[72] This mechanism obliges the viewer to consider the objectification of one's body in the kaleido-scopic alteration. The succession of fragmented views, mentioned by film theor-ists of the 1920s precisely looked to display the shattered character and discon-tinuity of mechanical perception. The kaleidoscope's movement produced a dispersion of the body's image, a dismemberment that signaled its fundamen-tally geometric nature as a product of constant calculation and uninterrupted generation of distorted images of oneself. Far from constituting an "objective" point of view, as would state André Bazin,[73] the mechanical perception referred to the actualization of a determined measurable spatio-temporal relationship, a function of the incessant and never ending variability of the subject's move-ment. The example given by Epstein is certainly extreme, as one not only sees the variety of successive points of view, depending on the body's movement, but also the reflection in different mirrors of those details. It seems as if Epstein is projecting himself into the subject's vision during an experiment of move-ment recording. This is a *dispositif* already identified by Jonathan Crary in the optical machines of the 19th century – in particular the phenakisticope – as "confounding of three modes: an individual body that is at once a spectator, a subject of empirical research and observation, and an element of machine pro-duction."[74]

The aesthetic of cinema developed during the 1920s echoes somewhat the understanding of human mobility exalted by the experimental sciences less than half a century before. Objectified by the scientific methods and techniques, the physical body is therefore situated at the heart of an infinite production of images reflecting diverse aspirations and social and aesthetical phantasms. Dance henceforth imposed itself both as an essential facet of a new type of show, which made the corporeality an emblematic form of expression in master-ing the rhythm of movement. From then on, an oscillation began between two paradigms of representation of the human body in movement (dance, but also sport and martial arts) that would traverse the history of cinema: on the one hand, the capture/restitution prized by the dancers themselves (such as Fred Astaire); on the other, the editing of the performance, theorized by Lev Kule-shov or Slavko Vorkapich and developed at different levels, from the 1920s avant-gardes to experimental dance video, from Busby Berkeley to MTV clips.

Translated by Naomi Middelmann

Notes

1. See for instance the research of Théodule Ribot, Pierre Janet and Pierre Levy-Bruhl, whose ideas were popularized in the 1920s by Marcel Jousse's theories on the rhythmical gesture (*geste rythmique*).

2. François Albera, "Pour une épistémographie du montage: le moment-Marey," *Arrêt sur image, fragmentation du temps*, ed. François Albera, Marta Braun and André Gaudreault (Lausanne: Payot, 2002) 33.

3. Regarding this point and others, see my *L'Age du rythme. Musicalisme et mouvement dans les théories cinématographiques françaises des années 1910-1930* (Lausanne: Payot, 2006).

4. François Dagognet, *Etienne-Jules Marey. La passion de la trace* (Paris: Hazan, 1987) 102.

5. That is, for the War ministry, "the length of the soldier's step, the pace, [...] the rhythm's speed, which regulates the pace, to use one's forces as well as possible." Laurent Mannoni, *Etienne-Jules Marey: la mémoire de l'œil* (Paris/Milano: French Cinémathèque/Mazzotta, 1999) 191.

6. Georges Demenÿ, *L'éducation de l'effort. Psychologie – physiologie* (Paris: Alcan, 1914) 129-32.

7. Georges Demenÿ, *Science et art du mouvement* (Paris: Alcan, 1920) 11-12.

8. Maurice Emmanuel, *La Danse grecque antique d'après les monuments figurés, analyses chronophotographiques obtenues avec les appareils de M. le Professeur Marey* (Paris: Slatkine Reprints, 1896).

9. Henri Bergson, *L'Evolution créatrice* (Paris: Quadrige/PUF, 2001) 304-07.

10. The only comment Marey made about the programmed presence of dancers at the Station was that it could possibly add "some gayety." Letter of 6 Dec. 1892 in *Lettres d'Etienne-Jules Marey à Georges Demenÿ 1880-1894*, ed. Thierry Lefebvre, Jacques Malthête and Laurent Mannoni (Paris: AFRHC, 1999) 422. A session was held in July 1893. See the letter of 14 July 1893 in *Lettres d'Etienne-Jules Marey* 442.

11. Linda Williams, *Hard Core: Power, Pleasure, and the "Frenzy and the Visible"* (Berkeley: U of California P, 1989) 34-57; Marta Braun, *Picturing Time* (London/Chicago: U of Chicago P, 1992) 247-54.

12. Paul Hill, *Eadweard Muybridge* (Paris: Phaidon, 2001) 118-19.

13. Regarding the insertion of LA BICHE AUX BOIS (Gaumont, 1896) into a scenic show, *Le Gaulois* describes it as its "clou." Quoted in Laurent Mannoni, Marc de Ferrière la Vayer and Paul Demenÿ, *Georges Demenÿ Pionnier du cinéma* (Paris: French Cinémathèque/Pagine, 1997) 103. The term can also be used inversely as a live performance inserted into a cinema evening (music, acrobatics, dance…). These situations refer to common practices at the turn of the century in cabarets and music halls. Louis Laloy, for instance, defined in 1913 "Attractions" as "interludes executed by special virtuosos that inserted themselves into the show thanks to the inexhaustible use of dialogue." Louis Laloy, "Cabarets et Music-Halls," *SIM* (July-Aug. 1913): 52.

14. This separation echoes the distinction made by Frank Kessler between "*la cinématographie comme dispositif spectaculaire*" and "*la cinématographie comme dispositif du spectaculaire*" in "La cinématographie comme dispositif (du) spectaculaire," *CiNéMAS* 14.1 (Fall 2003): 21.

15. This sequencing can be operated either by superimposed images of different phases of movement on the same plate of glass (Marey in the first years at the Station); or by juxtaposing isolated images (Muybridge in *Animal Locomotion*, 1887).

16. Image reproduced in Deac Rossell, "Breaking the Black Box: A Reassessment of Chronophotography," *Arrêt sur image* 136-37.

17. See Laurent Veray, "Aux origines du show télévisé: le cas des vues Lumière," *Montrer le sport: photographie, cinéma, télévision*, ed. Pierre Simonet and Laurent Veray (Paris: INSEP, 2001) 77-78 (list of about 50 sport film reels between 1896 and 1903); Frank Kessler and Sabine Lenk, "Cinéma d'attractions et gestualité," *Les vingt premières années du cinéma français*, ed. Jean A. Gili, Michèle Lagny, Michel Marie and Vincent Pinel (Paris: Sorbonne Nouvelle/AFRHC, 1995) 195-202; Laure Gaudenzi, "Une filmographie thématique: la danse au cinéma de 1894 à 1906," *Les vingt premières années du cinéma français* 361-64.

18. André Gaudreault and Philippe Marion, "Un média naît toujours deux fois…," *S. & R.* (April 2000): 21-36. See also André Gaudreault, *Cinema delle origini. O della "cinematografia-attrazione"* (Milano: Il Castoro, 2004) 47-49; and Rick Altman, "De l'intermédialité au multimédia: cinéma, médias, avènement du son," *CiNéMAS* 10.2-3 (Spring 2002): 37-38.

19. Due to lack of space, I will not develop here the relation between the attraction of color and that of the dancing body in numerous early cinema film reels that show the relationship between the attraction of the performance and that of the apparatus. Besides the *féerie* genre, it is sufficient to mention the serpentine dances by the imitators of Loïe Fuller (between 1894 and 1897 at Edison, Lumière, Skladanowsky) where the addition of color aims to recreate the effect of the original show; or THE GREAT TRAIN ROBBERY (Edison, 1903) where the movements of female dancers take on an attraction value comparable to those of colorful explosions.

20. *La Vie au Grand Air* 757 (22 March 1913): 213

21. *La Vie au Grand Air* 791 (15 Nov. 1913) (special issue on style).

22. Lieutenant Rocher, "Le laboratoire de l'Ecole de Joinville," *La Vie au Grand Air* 768 (7 June 1913): 423.

23. Pierre Desclaux, "L'Ultracinéma et son inventeur," *Cinémagazine* 37 (30 Sept. 1921): 9-12.

24. Georges Demenÿ, *Les bases scientifiques de l'éducation physique* (Paris: Félix Alcan, 1920) 274-75. The idea of the zoetrope as slow motion was at the heart of Marey's and Gaston Carlet's research for *La machine animale*, in order to better capture the details of movements. See *Lettres d'Etienne-Jules Marey* 95.

25. Pierre Desclaux, "Les idées de Jaque Catelain sur l'art muet," *Mon Ciné* 32 (28 Sept. 1922): 12.

26. Jean Tédesco, "Etudes de ralenti," *Cinéa-Ciné pour tous* 57 (15 March 1926): 11-12.

27. Emile Vuillermoz, "Devant l'écran. Mouvements," *L'Impartial français* 21 May 1926: 2.

28. Fernand Divoire, "De Tahiti au Mexique, l'écran recueille les danses de l'Univers," *Pour Vous* 38 (8 Aug. 1929): 8-9.

29. Gilles Deleuze, *Cinéma 1. L'image-mouvement* (Paris: Minuit, 1983) 16.

30. André Levinson, *La Danse d'Aujourd'hui* (Paris: Duchartre and Van Buggenhoudt, 1929) 147-48.

31. André Levinson, "Les girls," *L'Art Vivant* 10 (15 May 1925) 26-28.

32. For example, Matyla Ghyka, *L'Esthétique des proportions dans la nature et dans les arts* (Paris: NRF, 1927); *Le Nombre d'or* (Paris: Gallimard, 1931).

33. See my article "Le Rythme des corps. Théorie et critique de l'interprétation cinématographique à partir des arts musico-corporels (danse et gymnastique rythmique) dans la France des années 20," *The Visible Man*, ed. Laura Vichi (Udine: Forum, 2002) 229-53.

34. Louis Delluc, "La photoplastie à l'écran," *Paris-Midi* 6 July 1918. Rpt. in *Ecrits cinématographiques*, vol. 2 (Paris: Cinémathèque française/Edition de l'étoile, 1986) 210-13.

35. Siegfried Kracauer, "Das Ornament der Masse [1927]," *Le voyage et la danse* (Saint-Denis: Presses Universitaires de Vincennes, 1996) 70.

36. Fritz Giese, *Girl-Kultur* (München: Delphin, 1925).

37. J. C.-A., "Les girls photogéniques," *Cinémagazine* 36 (3 Sept. 1926): 424.

38. Albert Valentin, "Introduction à la magie blanche et noire," *AC* 4 (1927): 113.

39. See also *Voilà la femme* (1915), *Parade amoureuse* (1917), and *Portrait de Marie Laurencin* (1916-17) by Picabia.

40. Fernand Léger, "Autour du *Ballet mécanique*," *Fonctions de la peinture* (Paris: Gonthier, 1965) 167.

41. Annotated drawing by Léger published in Standish D. Lawder, *Le cinéma cubiste* (Paris: Expérimental, 1994) 106-07.

42. See Tami Williams, "Germaine Dulac: Du Figuratif à l'abstraction," *Jeune, dure et pure*, ed. Nicole Brenez and Christian Lebrat (Paris: Cinémathèque française, 2001) 78-82.

43. Emile Vuillermoz, "Le cinéma et la musique," *Le Temps* 27 May 1933. During the 1930s, this *girls* reception did not weaken. In 1932, Nino Frank assimilated them to the contemporary formulation of the Greek chorus; see Nino Frank, "Girls de cinéma," *Pour Vous* 199 (8 Sept. 1932): 8-9. As for Jean Vidal, he perceived the girls as "harmony" et "balance," "general rhythm," "mechanism of living form." Jean Vidal, "Géométrie du sex-appeal," *Pour Vous* 326 (14 Feb. 1935): 8-9.

44. Inge Baxmann, "'Die Gesinnung ins Schwingen bringen': Tanz als Metasprache und Gesellschaftutopie in der Kultur der zwanziger Jahre," *Materialität der Kommunikation*, ed. Hans Ulrich Gumbrecht and Ludwig Pfeiffer (Frankfurt am Main: Suhrkamp, 1988) 360-73.

45. Paul Valéry, *Eupalinos, L'Ame et la Danse, Dialogue de l'arbre* (Paris: Gallimard, 2002) 132, 134, 189.

46. Elie Faure, "La cinéplastique [1920]," *Fonction du cinéma* (Genève/Paris: Gonthier 1963) 25.

47. Ricciotto Canudo, "La naissance d'un sixième Art. Essai sur le cinématographe [1911]," *L'Usine aux images* (1927; Paris: Séguier-Arte, 1995) 32.

48. Elie Faure, "La danse et le cinéma [1927]," *Fonction du cinéma* 13.

49. See Guy Ducrey, *Corps et graphies. Poétique de la danseuse à la fin du XIXe siècle* (Paris: Honoré Champion, 1996) 431-530.

50. Stéphane Mallarmé, "Autre étude de danse [1897]," *Oeuvres complètes*, vol. 2 (Paris: Gallimard, 2003) 174.

51. Stéphane Mallarmé, "Considérations sur l'art du ballet et la Loïe Fuller [1896]," *Oeuvres complètes* 314.

52. Tom Gunning, "Loïe Fuller and the Art of Motion," *The Tenth Muse. Cinema and Other Arts,* ed. Leonardo Quaresima and Laura Vichi (Udine: Forum, 2001) 25-53. Elizabeth Coffman, "Women in Motion: Loïe Fuller and the 'Interpenetration' of Art and Science," *Camera Obscura* 17.1 (2002): 73-105.

53. *Jaque Catelain présente Marcel L'Herbier* (Paris: Jacques Vautrain, 1950) 14-15.

54. Louis Delluc, "Le Lys de la vie," *Paris-Midi* 8 March 1921. Rpt. in *Ecrits cinématographiques* 237.

55. Louis Delluc, "Photogénie," *Comoedia Illustré* (July-Aug. 1920). Rpt. in *Ecrits cinématographiques* 274.

56. Léon Moussinac, "La poésie à l'écran," *Cinémagazine* 17 (13 May 1921): 16. On the film, of which only the first part remains, see Giovanni Lista, *Loïe Fuller. Danseuse de l'Art Nouveau* (Paris: Réunion des Musées Nationaux, 2002) 71-81; and *Loïe Fuller. Danseuse de la Belle Epoque* (Paris: Somogy/Stock, 1994) 522-23, 530-40. See also *Comoedia* 23 Feb. 1921 and 18 March 1921, as well as *Cinéa* 19 (16 Sept. 1921): 4.

57. Germaine Dulac, "Trois rencontres avec Loïe Fuller," *Bulletin de l'Union des Artistes* 30 (Feb. 1928). Rpt. in *Ecrits sur le cinéma (1919-1937)* (Paris: Expérimental, 1994) 109-10.

58. Jean Tédesco, "La danse sur l'écran," *Cinéa-Ciné pour tous* 1 (15 Nov. 1923): 6. Juan Arroy, "Danses et danseurs de cinéma," *Cinémagazine* 48 (26 Nov. 1926): 428.

59. M. Zahar and D. Burret, "Les cinéastes. Une visite à Jean Renoir," *Cinéa-Ciné pour tous* 59 (15 April 1926): 14-15.

60. André Levinson, "A la mémoire de Jules Marey. Le Film et la danse," *Pour Vous* 8 (10 Jan. 1929): 11.

61. Lev Kuleshov, "La bannière du cinématographe [1920]," *Ecrits (1917-1934)* (Lausanne: L'Age d'homme, 1994) 38-39.

62. Fernand Divoire, "Danse et cinéma," *Schémas* 1 (Feb. 1927): 43. The same criticism is carried out by Roland Guerard, who regrets that the harmony between "gestures dancing on the screen" and the rhythmic understanding of spectators remains at the moment very little exploited by film directors. Roland Guerard, "Le geste et le rythme," *Cinéa-Ciné pour tous* 112 (1 July 1928): 9-10.

63. Divoire, "Danse et cinéma" 43.

64. Georges Pomiès, "Propos sur la danse," *Danser c'est vivre. Georges Pomiès* (Paris: Pierre Tisné, 1939) 85-95.

65. Deleuze 61-62.

66. "... an aspect is photogenic when it moves and varies simultaneously in space and time." Original conference fragment [1923] in Jean Epstein, *Ecrits sur le cinéma*, vol. 1 (Paris: Seghers, 1974) 120.

67. Regarding this subject, see my detailed analysis "Le corps et le regard: images rythmiques de la danse dans *La Femme et le pantin*," *Jacques de Baroncelli cinéaste*, ed. François de la Bretèque and Bernard Bastide (Paris: AFRHC, forthcoming).

68. Abel Gance, "Ma Roue est incomprise du public [1923]," *Un soleil dans chaque image* (Paris: CNRS/Cinémathèque française, 2002) 57.

69. Jean Epstein, *Le cinématographe vu de l'Etna* [1926], *Ecrits sur le cinéma* 145.

70. Epstein 94-95.

71. Epstein 95.

72. Epstein 135-36. On this passage, see also Paci in this volume.

73. André Bazin, "Ontologie de l'image photographique [1945]," *Qu'est-ce que le ciné-ma?* (Paris: Cerf, 1999) 13.

74. Jonathan Crary, *Techniques of the Observer* (1990; Cambridge: MIT P, 1992) 112.

Audiences and Attractions

["Its Spectator"]

A Cinema of Contemplation, A Cinema of Discernment: Spectatorship, Intertextuality and Attractions in the 1890s

Charles Musser

This present anthology confirms what has been obvious for some time: the turn of phrase "cinema of attractions" has captured the enthusiastic attention of the film studies community as well as a wide range of scholars working in visual culture. It has not only provided a powerful means of gaining insight into important aspects of early cinema but served as a gloss for those seeking a quick, up-to-date understanding of its cultural gestalt. In his many articles on the topic, Tom Gunning has counterposed the cinema of attractions to narrative, arguing that before 1903-04 or perhaps 1907-08, cinema has been primarily about these moments of visual eruption rather than sustained storytelling. In "Rethinking Early Cinema: Cinema of Attractions and Narrativity,"[1] which is being reprinted in the dossier of this volume, I engaged this assessment of narrative in early cinema on several levels.

First, I argued that *cinematic* form was often more concerned with communicating a narrative than Gunning's descriptive paradigm would suggest. I emphasize *cinematic* as opposed to *filmic* form as a reminder that individual films were merely raw material for the exhibitor's programs and were inevitably transformed in the course of their cinematic presentation (the making of cinema). Exhibitors often reconfigured non-narrative moments or brief, one-shot films into more sustained narratives or embedded short comic gags into a larger, more sustained fictional milieu. Second, I offered a series of contestatory interpretations of such films as THE GAY SHOE CLERK (1903) and LE VOYAGE DANS LA LUNE (1902). Certainly Gunning and I can find common ground in that we both acknowledge that these attractions and narrative frequently coexisted, though I see them not only as intertwined but am fascinated by the ways in which cinematic form often enhanced as well as generated narrative (rather than interrupt it) even in this early period. In short, cinematic form did shape subject matter and create meaning in the 1890s and early 1900s. It did so in a different way, and certainly other things of equal (and often, of course, of greater) importance were also being pursued. But my understanding involves a more dialectical and open approach to these dynamics.

Third, my article was also about our basic understanding of early cinema (however one might choose to define the period of "early cinema"). I see this history as an amazingly dynamic, rapidly changing phenomenon. How one characterizes the cinema of 1896 is not necessarily the same for cinema in 1898 (just two years later); and there is a sea change between the cinema of 1898 and 1903; then again American cinema in 1907 is very different from cinema in 1903. Over the first 15 to 20 years of film history, fundamental changes were taking place on many different levels – in terms of production and exhibition methods, technology, business, subject matter and representation. Because it is a dynamic system, I emphasized the changing relationship of attractions to narrative over this period while Gunning tends to treat it as a period of fundamental unity.[2]

Obviously, this present essay does not need to repeat my earlier intervention. Rather I want to tease out other dimensions of early cinema by focusing on that extended moment in the United States when projected motion pictures were considered a novelty, a period that roughly extended from the debut of the Vitascope at Koster & Bial's Music Hall on April 23, 1896 to the release of THE COR-BETT-FITZSIMMONS FIGHT (May 22, 1897) or THE HORITZ PASSION PLAY (November 1897). Over the last decade I have continued to investigate this period, in an effort to better document and understand it.[3] Although in some ways a development of my earlier work, the results have also constituted a sustained self-critique on this topic. Inevitably, this reassessment has at least implicitly engaged Gunning's work for it was precisely during this novelty period that I saw cinema's representational practices to be closely aligned with cinema of attractions.[4]

To Gunning's cinema of astonishment and the spectator as gawker, I would now counterpose a multifaceted system of representation and spectatorship that also includes 1) a cinema of contemplation; 2) a cinema of discernment in which spectators engage in intellectually active processes of comparison and judgment; and 3) finally a reaffirmation of the importance of narrative and more broadly the diachronic sequencing of shots or films. There are other dimensions of 1896-97 cinema that I am not addressing here – particularly aspects related to fiction and acted scenes. Nonetheless, this essay engages films and aspects of cinema that have generally been kept at the margins. Rather than seeing cinema of this novelty period as dominated by cinema of attractions, I would describe it as a diverse phenomenon that can be understood as a series of tensions between opposing representational tendencies. Cinema of attractions is one way to look at and describe some important aspects of early cinema. There are not only other perspectives, there are other aspects that need to be assessed and reassessed.

How should we understand a system of cinematic representation at a given moment in history? In "An Aesthetic of Astonishment," Gunning notes, "I have called the cinema that precedes the dominance of narrative (and this period lasts for nearly a decade, until 1903 or 1904) the cinema of attractions."[5] This is because, as Gunning argues, cinema of attractions is the dominant feature of cinema in this period.[6] But this can quickly become a problematic even dangerous tautology when it encourages us to overlook other aspects of cinematic representation then being practiced. In fact, this essay wants to suggest that this assertion, though based to a degree on established assumptions (assumptions we all more or less accept), needs to be challenged and resisted. There is always a fundamental problem with associating or *equating* a period (however brief) with a particular kind of cinema.[7] To label the cinema before 1907, 1903, 1901, or 1897 as "cinema of attractions" is to marginalize other features, which were at least as important (for instance, the role of the exhibitor as a crucial creative force before 1901 or 1903). Moreover, if cinema of attractions characterizes a period, almost by definition anything that does not conform to that paradigm is marginalized. One can claim that cinema of attractions describes the dominant form of cinema in a given period, and we may (or may not) wish to accept this statement as true. But by calling cinema of a given period by the name of a specific style, this conflation erects a barrier for engaging such assumptions. Film scholars can seek to characterize historical periods by examining their systems of representation and modes of production (not only film production but cinema production, which includes exhibition and spectatorship). Or they can identify a certain manifestation of cinema – expressionism, realism, slapstick comedy, and (perhaps) cinema of attractions – and explore how this style or form was manifested in one or more historical periods. But are we ready to place Cinerama under the Cinema of Attractions rubric? The reality here may be that Gunning has enmeshed or imbricated the two – style and period – in a way that for many has come to define a historical formation. This is the term's power but also its flaw.

Style is regularly defined through difference and even opposition. What can be counterposed to the cinema of attractions within the period 1896-97? Is it only a weak, underdeveloped form of narrative? Narrative may constitute one opposition (or one aspect of one opposition), but there are others as well. What would happen if we take a more dialectical approach to reading form and history? What kinds of tensions (creative, aesthetic, rhetorical) are revealed by such an approach? Not all instances of early cinema generated shocks and displayed qualities that were the antithesis of traditional artistic values. There was also ways in which cinema reaffirmed and even fulfilled the artistic agenda that had been a feature of art and painting since the mid-eighteenth century.

A Cinema of Contemplation

To examine the many connections between early film and painting enables us to explore the ways that cinema often times embraced the principles of detached contemplation. These affinities were foregrounded in the museum exhibition *Moving Pictures: American Art and Early Film, 1880-1910*, in which curator Nancy Mathews identified a wide variety of visual rhymes involving specific films and specific art works, suggesting that some early films were conceived as paintings that move (thus the title of her exhibition – "Moving Pictures").[8] Many early motion picture posters, for instance, depict a film (in color) being projected onto a canvas enclosed by an elaborate gold picture frame. This can be seen in an early 1896 Vitascope poster, but such frames continued to be a part of cinema's iconography into the early 1900s. One even appears in UNCLE JOSH AT THE MOVING PICTURE SHOW (Porter/Edison, 1902). Moreover, this use of a picture frame can be linked to a Vitascope Company catalog statement from early 1896, which suggested that "a subject can be shown for ten or 15 minutes although four or five minutes is better."[9] This extended playing time was possible because the short films used on the Vitascope (often lasting only 20 seconds) were regularly shown as loops in 1896-97. This did more than denarrativize individual films: such sustained presentations also encouraged spectators to contemplate and explore the image. As this evidence suggests, one way that early audiences were meant to look at films was not unrelated to the way they were meant to look at paintings.

Numerous films would seem to allow for, even encourage a state of contemplative absorption. Edison's film PATERSON FALLS (July 1896) was described as a "beautiful picture of the Paterson Falls on the Passaic River"[10] and encouraged the kind of sublime reverie that Diderot felt was appropriate to nature and landscape painting. Michael Fried, has remarked that

> Diderot seems to have held that an essential object of paintings belonging to those genres was to induce in the beholder a particular psycho-physical condition, equivalent in kind and intensity to a profound experience of nature, which for the sake of brevity might be characterized as one of existential reverie or *repos délicieux*. In that state of mind and body a wholly passive receptivity becomes a vehicle of an apprehension of the fundamental beneficence of the natural world; the subject's awareness of the passage of time and, on occasion, of his very surroundings may be abolished; and he comes to experience a pure and intense sensation of the sweetness and as it were the self-sufficiency of his own existence.[11]

Films such as AMERICAN FALLS FROM ABOVE, AMERICAN SIDE (Edison, December 1896), FALLS OF MINNEHAHA (Edison, June 1897) and WATERFALL IN THE

CATSKILLS (Edison, June 1897), with their "water effects against a dark background,"[12] likewise encouraged spectators to experience a mesmerizing absorption. WATERFALL IN THE CATSKILLS was taken at Haines Falls, "a picturesque and almost inaccessible mountain cataract in the Catskills."[13] This location was not selected by chance. According to one tourist guide, "This charming spot was visited years ago by Cole, Durand, Kensett, Casilear, and others, when ropes and ladders had to be used in descending and ascending the ledges at the cascades. The paths are now good, and none should fail to visit this favorite resort of the artists."[14] Such films evoked (when they did not actually quote) a long and rich genre of American painting and mobilized a new medium for a similar spectatorial response.[15] They escaped, in Diderot's terms, a mannered theatricality and provided a naive directness that is close to the sublime: "It is the thing, but the thing itself, without alteration. Art is no longer there."[16] And yet for Diderot this naiveté was, in the end, an essential quality of art. At least at certain moments, early cinema embraced and even realized the aspirations of eighteenth- and nineteenth-century art.

Certain films, particularly when exhibited using loops, challenge Gunning's assertion:

> [The aesthetic of early cinema] so contrasts with prevailing turn-of-the-century norms of artistic reception – the ideals of detached contemplation – that it nearly constitutes an anti-aesthetic. The cinema of attractions stands at the antipode to the experience Michael Fried, in his discussion of eighteenth-century painting, calls absorption. For Fried, the painting of Greuze and others created a new relation to the viewer through a self-contained hermetic world which makes no acknowledgment of the beholder's presence. Early cinema totally ignores this construction of the beholder. These early films explicitly acknowledge their spectator, seeming to reach outwards and confront. Contemplative absorption is impossible here. The viewer's curiosity is aroused and fulfilled through a marked encounter, a direct stimulus, a succession of shocks.[17]

Even in the novelty period, many films were shown in ways that called for sustained, attentive contemplation from their audiences. This might include, for instance, a looped version of a colored serpentine dance. While this form of spectatorship was particularly relevant for early Edison films as projected on various machines (not only the Vitascope but the Phantoscope, Projectograph, Edison's Projectoscope, Projecting Kinetoscope and Cineograph among others), the cinematic experience offered by the Lumière and Biograph companies, which did not (and could not) show their films as loops, was not always incompatible. Some of these early Biograph films possess a majestic grandeur while the Lumière films reveal a naiveté that is "true, but with a truth that is alluring, original and rare,"[18] aligning them with certain painting genres and experiences. Of course, many Biograph films fully embody Gunning's analysis: from

EMPIRE STATE EXPRESS (September 1896) – a view of an onrushing express train, to A MIGHTY TUMBLE (November 1901) – a 17-second view of a collapsing building.

Living Pictures/Moving Pictures

If the connection between cinema and painting in the 1890s was frequently direct and often evoked, how did this relationship come to be established so powerfully? Although a full explanation would necessarily consider many factors, it seems telling that the gold frame within which Raff & Gammon projected the first motion pictures at Koster & Bial's Music Hall in April-June 1896 was the same frame that Oscar Hammerstein used to exhibit his Living Pictures at that same theater in 1894-95 (or at the least, a similar type of frame). Perhaps the biggest craze in vaudeville during the mid-1890s, tableaux vivants or "living pictures" prepared theatergoers, particularly those who frequented vaudeville, to look at projected moving pictures in a particular way. Living pictures generally involved the restaging of well-known paintings and statuary as performers assumed frozen poses within an oversized picture frame. Tableaux vivants had been intermittently popular throughout much of the nineteenth century, often as a form of amateur entertainment.[19] They became an American fad during the spring of 1894, when Edouard von Kilanyi (1852-1895) staged his "living pictures" on March 21, 1894, as an addition to E.E. Rice's musical farce *1492* at the Garden Theater.[20] Kilanyi's initial set of living pictures staged more than a dozen art works, everything from the paintings *Le Passant* by Emile Antoine Bayard (1837-1891) and *Psyche at the Well* by German-born Friedrich Paul Thurmann (1834-1908, aka Paul Thurman), which became the basis for the White Rock (soda) fairy logo, to the sculpture *Hebe* (1796) by Antonio Canova (1757-1822). The living picture that was based on *Pharaoh's Daughter* (the painting better known as *Miriam and Moses*) by Paul Delaroche (1797-1856) showed Miriam "making her way through imitation bulrushes to a painted Moses."[21] Audiences were expected to evaluate the posed pictures in relationship to a repertoire of familiar art works that they were seeking to mime.

Living pictures were introduced into New York vaudeville by Oscar Hammerstein on May 10th, 1894, when they were staged at Koster & Bial's Music Hall, once again to an enthusiastic reception:

> The assurance of the pictures was enough to crowd the house. As the successive pictures were displayed the upper part of the house became more than pleased; it was excited. The tableaus were disclosed in a large gilt frame. Black curtains were draped in front of it, and were drawn aside at the proper time by pages. The pictures were for

the most part excellently posed and lighted and were shown with much artistic effect. The most of them were reproductions of paintings and a few were original arrangements.[22]

Among the painting that Hammerstein reproduced were *The Helping Hand* (1881), perhaps the best known subject of French painter Emile Renouf (1845-1894); a "delightfully artistic reproduction" of *Queen of the Flowers* by the Italian painter Francesco Vinea (1845-1902); *The Three Muses* by Italian-born, San Francisco-based Domenico Tojetti (1806-1892); and *Angelus* (1859), the painting by Jean-François Millet (1814-1875), which had been shown a few years earlier in the United States to popular acclaim.[23] Meanwhile on April 14th, less than a month before Hammerstein debuted his living pictures, Edison's motion pictures had their commercial debut in a kinetoscope parlor on Broadway. Many of the subjects for these films were headline attractions from near-by Koster & Bial's Music Hall. Edison's newest novelty was using performers to make pictures while Hammerstein and Kilanyi were using pictures to construct performances. Koster & Bial's was a pivotal site for both entertainment enterprises. When the Vitascope was shown at the music hall, it brought the two together.

In general Kilanyi and Hammerstein fostered a broad knowledge of the visual arts, perhaps by assuming that audiences already possessed such fluency in an age when inexpensive reproductions of paintings were appearing in newspapers, magazines and books. Their choice of paintings was consistent with an urban, cosmopolitan internationalism that reigned at Koster & Bial's Music Hall and was also evident in the Edison's films of the peep-hole kinetoscope era (1894-95). Both novelties – living pictures and Edison motion pictures – offered their respective spectators similar kinds of pleasure as each reproduced a cultural work (painting, sculpture or performance) in another media, encouraging comparison between "the original" and its reproduction. Besides quoting art works, Hammerstein's living pictures also often required a sustained, focused viewing experience from seated spectators.

Living pictures quickly moved outside New York and provided a significant framework for the early reception of motion pictures, when they were finally introduced into American vaudeville two years later. Keith's vaudeville theaters enthusiastically embraced living pictures as they would the cinema. Since early films generally involved a single camera set up, a single shot (occasionally consisting of sub-shots) or framing, the analogies between a motion picture and a painting as well as moving pictures and living pictures could be powerful ones. The fact that at least some early films were hand-tinted or "colored" only furthered such associations. As the *Boston Globe* remarked, "The Vitascope is decidedly the most interesting novelty that has been shown since the living pictures, and rivals them in interest"[24] – and, one might add, often in mode of representation. With the enthusiasm for living pictures beginning to wane by the time projected motion pictures were being shown, vaudeville goers experienced a dissolving view of sorts, from living pictures to moving pictures. Not surprisingly, living pictures not only provided a paradigm for the reception of projected motion pictures, they sometimes quite literally provided the cinema with subject matter.[25]

At the end of the nineteenth century, cinema was a form in which the fine arts, theater, and motion pictures could intersect in the most literal ways (as well as more oblique ones). When the Lumière Cinématographe showed films at Keith's Bijou in Philadelphia in early September 1896, a critic commented that THE HORSES AT THEIR MORNING DRINK, "resembles one of Rosa Bonheur's famous paintings brought to life."[26] Undoubtedly this film was L'ABREUVOIR (THE HORSE TROUGH), which a Lumière cameraman shot in Lyon, France, during April 1896.[27] The painting was Rosa Bonheur's *The Horse Fair* (1853). Bonheur's *The Horse Fair* was mentioned again in an Edison catalog description of 9TH U.S. CAVALRY WATERING HORSES (Edison, May 1898), which the writer felt "reminds one forcibly of Rosa Bonheur's celebrated 100,000 dollar painting, 'The Horse Fair.'"[28] Scenes of landscapes, city views, and any number of moving pictures showing domestic scenes were built on a variety of popular genres in painting. But they possessed more than the shared iconography. Their presentational gestalt involved important parallels. Consider the description for FEEDING THE DOVES (Edison, October 1896), which emulated an earlier Lumière film (a subject that was also remade by both Biograph and the International Film Company). This serene one-shot picture, in which the movement of the birds is the most dynamic element of the scene, was described as follows:

> A typical farm scene showing a beautiful girl and her baby sister dealing out the morning meal to the chickens and doves. The doves and chickens form a beautiful spectacle as they flutter and flock around the givers – a beautiful picture, which would appeal to the sentiments of any audience.[29]

Here again, a film calls for the spectator to view it with a degree of detached contemplation.

From Astonishment to Contemplation

The cinema of contemplation was not only a powerful counterpoint to the cinema of attractions, they frequently interrelated in complex ways. THE WAVE, as it was called when shown on the Vitascope's opening night at Koster & Bial's Music Hall, is a case in point. In contrast to the majestic if tranquil moving pictures of water falls, this film and others like it were shot so that they would confront the spectator. A line drawing that ran in the *New York Herald* of May 5, 1896 shows the film being projected onto a canvas that was enclosed by the elaborate (gold) picture frame. Actually Rough Sea at Dover (1895) taken by Birt Acres, The Wave was the most popular film screened on the Vitascope's first program, April 23, 1896. One reviewer described its presentation as follows:

> Then came the waves, showing a scene at Dover pier after a stiff blow. This was by far the best view shown, and had to be repeated many times. [...] One could look far out to sea and pick out a particular wave swelling and undulating and growing bigger and bigger until it struck the end of the pier. Its edge then would be fringed with foam, and finally, in a cloud of spray, the wave would dash upon the beach. One could imagine the people running away.[30]

It is often remarked that people in the front row seats had a strong visceral reaction to this film. Feeling assaulted by the cinematic wave, they instinctively feared that they would get wet, and involuntarily flinched as they started to leave their seats. Stephen Bottomore has written a prize-winning essay on this reaction from early film audiences, which he calls the train effect.[31] Although this is a quintessential embodiment of the cinema of attractions paradigm, we need to ask: What happened as The Wave was shown over and over again, as a loop? It would seem that this visceral reaction must have abated. The spectator would gain a sense of mastery of this new medium, settle back into his or her seat and enter a more detached and contemplative state. This is certainly signaled by the statement "One could imagine the people running away," which suggests a degree of distanced observation. The spectator became free to explore the recurrent imagery and savor the tumbling waters.

　　Rough Sea at Dover and similar films suggest that the cinema of attractions and the cinema of contemplation sometimes have much more in common than we might think. In this instance at least, cinema of attractions depends to a considerable degree on spectatorial absorption and the beholder metaphorically entering the picture. Cinema is remarkable in the rapidity with which this can happen. If this were not the case, the theatergoer would not viscerally react to the crashing wave. Is this film as antagonistic to principles of eighteenth-century painting as Gunning argues? For Diderot, the key to a successful painting involved the representation of actions rather than attitudes: "An attitude is one thing, an action another. Attitudes are false and petty, actions are all beautiful and true."[32] Theatricality for Diderot was the "false ideal of grace" and "the Academic principle of deliberately arranged contrast between figures in a painting."[33] Not only Rough Sea at Dover but many street scenes are the very opposite of this theatricality. Although we can often point to local views where children (and some adults) play to the camera, the goal of the cinematographer was often the reverse. Consider this description of HERALD SQUARE (Edison, May 1896):

> A scene covering Herald Square in New York, showing the noonday activity of Broadway at that point as clearly as if one were spectator of the original seems incredulous, nevertheless is presented life-like. The cable cars seem to move in opposite directions and look real enough to suggest a trip up and down that great thoroughfare, while at the same time the elevated trains are rushing overhead, pedestrians are seen moving along the sidewalks or crossing to opposite sides of the street, everything moving, or as it is seen in real life.[34]

Cinema in many respects fulfilled the long-standing effort in art to depict action; in part this depiction of action was done, as Diderot would suggest, to grab the attention of the beholder.

Clearly cinema of attractions describes an important phenomenon about which Gunning has provided tremendous insight into many of its manifestations. But to some degree these attractions are exceptional moments rather than typical ones. Or if they are typical and so central to our understanding of early cinema, it is only through being consistently exceptional. At any given moment in the history of early cinema, contrary examples abound – if we look for them. In this respect cinema thrived on diversity not only in its subject matter but in the ways that spectators looked at and responded to moving images on the screen. Variety was an overarching principal of vaudeville (and the newspaper); it should not surprise us that variety was also an overarching principle of early motion picture practice. A non-stop succession of shocks was virtually impossible but certainly it would have been bad showmanship. Perhaps we might find an occasional Biograph program that systematically alternated between title slides and attractions but even here the title slides provided crucial pauses. For an accomplished exhibitor these non-conforming scenes or moments would be more, perhaps much more, than mere pauses between shocks or attractions.

Some of the inherent contradictions associated with attractions become clearer if we consider THE BLACK DIAMOND EXPRESS (Edison, December 1896): it shows a rapidly approaching train seemingly destined to burst out of the picture frame before passing from view. Gunning examines a number of ways in which this film was shown to maximize its operation within a cinema of attractions paradigm. However, in 1896-97 other factors often curtailed "an emphasis on the thrill itself – the immediate reaction of the viewer."[35] Again, one was the prevalence of looping: as the train approaches and disappears only to reappear and repeat its journey, the sense of astonishment inevitably faded. Spectators quickly learn to integrate such cinematic effects into their response system. Even as "this confirms Gunning's theory of the spectator's willingness to participate in modernity,"[36] it enabled other mental processes to come to the fore.

This was part of a larger problem, however: once a spectator had experienced the train effect, its thrill rapidly abated, forcing producers and exhibitors to mobilize other methods of maintaining interest. With cinema in 1896-97 considered a technological novelty, exhibitors scrambled to be the first to show films in cities and towns across the country – to be the first to have this visceral impact on audiences. Yet increasingly, even within this time frame, many people were seeing moving pictures on the screen for a second or third time. In big cities, some patrons clearly became fans, returning again and again. So imbedded within the fact of novelty was that of its opposite – familiarity. Perhaps there was the pleasure of knowing what to expect and experiencing the reaction of others, but these innocents became fewer and fewer, and watching fellow spectators lose their cinematic virginity was itself a pleasure that must have faded with repeated exposure. An exhibitor's use of sound effects or the addition of color might have restored wonder. Or an exhibitor's spiel might have put the film in a new context. If some lectures sought to keep the sense of wonder alive, others undoubtedly provided information about the train (the speed records for the Black Diamond Express, where the film was taken and how). This informational or educational function could rekindle interest but not perhaps astonishment. It moved away from both astonishment and contemplation to what Neil Harris has called an "operational aesthetic"[37] and finally beyond to the world of practical affairs and the notion of an informed citizenry.

So far I have argued that cinema in 1896-97 was as much a cinema of contemplation as a cinema of astonishment, but also that these two were not necessarily stable or mutually exclusive. Interestingly the two spectatorial positions I have associated with PASSAIC FALLS and THE WAVE conform in interesting ways to two positions of art spectatorship that Michael Fried argues were being advocated by Diderot: positions he says may at first appear to be in some way mutually exclusive but are closely related. The first constructs the beholder as absent ("the fiction that no one is standing before the canvas"[38]), while in the second the beholder metaphorically enters the world of the painting ("the fiction of physically entering a painting"[39]), which is to say that the beholder crosses over from his/her space into the world of the painting (or the film). Other early films that seemed designed for the viewer to enter the world of the film would include phantom rides where the spectator is drawn into a space by the camera placed in a vehicle moving through or into space. The train effect is also based on this second presumption – the viewer enters the world only to be chased back out.

In Gunning's use of Diderot and Fried, he generally associates early cinema with a third spectatorial position – that in which the filmed subject plays to and acknowledges the beholder. This "theatricality" typically involves a presentationalism that was certainly common in early cinema, particularly with short comedies, early trick films, scenes of vaudeville performances, and facial expression films. J. Stuart Blackton sketches a portrait of Edison and then bows toward the audience in INVENTOR EDISON SKETCHED BY WORLD ARTIST (Edison, August 1896). The comedy is sketched so broadly in LOVE IN A SLEIGH (Edison, July 1896) that it is hard to disregard its staginess. Although Diderot presented this theatricality in a negative light (which Gunning then flips), the spectator maintains a kind of distance that we might associate with (among other things) slapstick comedy. It is with films like THE BLACK DIAMOND EXPRESS that Gunning shifts this theatricality from the profilmic to the process of exhibition itself: "it is the direct address of the audience in which an attraction is offered to the spectator by a cinema showman, that defines this approach to filmmaking."[40] Clearly such gestures can happen on a number of levels either alternately or simultaneously.[41] Or not. The view of an on-rushing express train could be dolled up by an exhibitor, or the exhibitor could withdraw and let the spectator enter into the image as if it were a painting. This suggests, at the very least, that even in the novelty era, cinema encompassed and mobilized a range of spectatorial positions. Linking cinema in the novelty era to a specific mode of spectatorship seems problematic.[42]

A Cinema of Discernment

Cinema of attractions, writes Gunning, is a cinema of astonishment that supplies "pleasure through an exciting spectacle – a unique event, whether fictional or documentary, that is of interest in itself."[43] A cinema of contemplation likewise involves scenes, each of which is "of interest in itself." Yet we should not minimize the extent to which these scenes were also *not* self-contained and self-sufficient. We must attend to other levels of cinema and spectatorship that happened along both synchronic and diachronic trajectories (to gesture towards Saussure). Early film spectators performed significant intellectual activity involving comparison, evaluation and judgment – as opposed to (or simultaneously with) either the enraptured spectator passively contemplating a beautiful picture or the "gawker [...] held for the moment by curiosity and amazement."[44] Spectators were not just given over to visceral states of astonishment or contemplation: they were critically active.

Here, as had been the case with living pictures and paintings, correspondences and intertextualities play an important role. Newspapers certainly offered guidance on how spectators might view films in relationship to "original scenes."[45] When the Vitascope at Keith's Theater in Boston presented CISSY FITZGERALD (Edison, May 1896), the *Boston Herald* suggested that "Those who were captivated with Cissy Fitzgerald's kick and wink during her engagement at a city theater the past season will have an opportunity of passing judgment on the Vitascope's reproduction of same; it is said to be capital."[46] The perfect spectator for this film was apparently the individual who could make the comparison between Fitzgerald on film and in the flesh – and come to some kind of critical judgment as a result. When looking at THE BLACK DIAMOND EXPRESS or some other train film, a spectator might ask if it adequately conveyed its power and speed. Comparisons were at the heart of late nineteenth-century theatrical spectatorship in which regular vaudeville goers compared one tramp comedy act to another or one animal show (whether dog, monkey, cat, pony, or elephant) to another. Newspaper critics routinely compared an actor either to a different actor in the same role or the same actor in a different role. Likewise, knowledgeable spectators might have readily compared THE BLACK DIAMOND EXPRESS to the film that it was made to challenge: THE EMPIRE STATE EXPRESS. The Biograph film had been taken earlier in the year and was likely to have been shown either in a rival theater – or on an earlier program at the same theater. How did these two competing train services stack up (they were competing against each other on the New York City-Buffalo route)? And how might the Biograph and Edison films stack up – which was clearer, with less flicker? (Here Biograph generally offered a better quality image, though Edison provided broader diffusion.) Which service gave a better show (film service but perhaps also train service)?

Any time a viewer saw a film program, s/he was likely to ask how successful it was in relationship to rival exhibitions. Returning to the theater to see films for a second time did not necessarily mean the theatergoer was seeking some vestige of astonishment. S/he was now becoming an authority, a sophisticate. How was the Lumière Cinématographe better (or worse) than the Edison Vitascope and how was it different? The discerning spectator might also compare a film such as SURF AT LONG BRANCH (Edison, October 1896) to the previously available ROUGH SEA AT DOVER. The former was said to be "an excellent subject for water effects, the glittering spray being distinctly reproduced."[47] Were its water effects superior to the earlier Acres's film? Then too, sophisticated viewers might have compared these films to efforts in other media: When watching ROUGH SEA AT DOVER, perhaps they recalled paintings such as *Waves Breaking on a Lee Shore* (Joseph Mallord William Turner, 1836) or photographs such as *Caswell Beach-Breaking Waves* (John Dillwyn Llewelyn, 1853).[48] This would shed a more positive light on the tendency for production companies to produce pictures with very similar subject matter. In this respect, a film was not merely of interest "in itself." It was an image that spectators were meant to enjoy in relationship to other films, other images (newspaper illustrations, comic postcards, paintings, photographs), other artifacts (songs, plays, news reports) and to the scene it actually represented (city streets, performers doing their specialty, well-known sites of nature).

Intertexuality also involves an inevitable looking backwards. The viewer remembered last year's performance by Cissy Fitzgerald – one that would never come again. Here we see another contrary feature of modernity – nostalgia, retrospection and melancholy.[49] While cinema of attractions provides a way to conceptualize cinema's links to modernity via novelty, one can also be struck by the ways in which cinema also resisted this: the way in which its earliest practitioners offered sustained views rather than the "wealth and colorfulness of overhastened impressions."[50] NEW BLACKSMITH SCENE (Edison, January 1895) appeared on a Vitascope program in Boston under the title THE VILLAGE BLACKSMITH SHOP. According to the *Boston Herald*, "'The Village Blacksmith Shop' will recall to many young men and women who have resided in the city for long periods familiar scenes of their early childhood; it is a work of art."[51] What is worth noting is the extent to which these early films were often seen not as something radically new – something astonishing – but as a distillation of something familiar, a realization of something that had long been sought.

A Cinema of Narratives

With these new categories in mind (cinema of contemplation, cinema of discernment), we can briefly return to the issue of narrative in the cinema of 1896-97. To the extent that narrative and attractions involve actions, they have something in common. One strategy that exhibitors pursued as films lost their initial appeal as pure attractions was to incorporate them into multi-shot narratives. When THE BLACK DIAMOND EXPRESS was incorporated into a travel lecture, the train was no longer hurdling toward the spectator but emerging from one space in a cinematic world and departing into another. Instead of entering the space, the spectator became an invisible beholder. One question we should ask: does this integration of an attraction into a narrative curtail the emphasis on the thrill or does it revive it? Does the narrative subordinate the attraction or provide merely a setting for its presentation? Are not the narratives of some early films (LIFE OF AN AMERICAN FIREMAN, 1902-03) literally constructed out of attractions? Lyman Howe integrated shots (scenes/films) of charging, horse-drawn fire engines into mini-narratives of heroic fire rescues as early as 1896. In fact, an interpretation of the Vitascope's opening night program at Koster & Bial's Music Hall suggests that narrative has been an element – even a compelling one – since cinema's very beginnings, at least in the United States. The notion that cinema went through some linear development from attractions to narrative (and that single-shot films were first shown as attractions and then later incorporated into narratives) needs to be rigorously questioned.

The order of the films for the Vitascope's opening night program was 1) UMBRELLA DANCE, 2) THE WAVE aka ROUGH SEA AT DOVER, 3) WALTON & SLAVIN, 4) BAND DRILL, 5) THE MONROE DOCTRINE, and 6) a Serpentine or Skirt Dance.[52] The program thus started off by showing two young female dancers (the Leigh Sisters), asserting a continuity between stage and screen. According to one critic, "It seemed as though they were actually on the stage, so natural was the dance, with its many and graceful motions."[53] And yet they were not on the stage and the absence of their presence, this displaced view (the spectator's position in relation to the dancers on the screen was not the same as the camera's position in relation to the dancers) was liberatory. The dancers did not dance for the theatergoers as they would have with a "normal," live performance. The spectator watched them dance for the camera. This triangularization opened up a wide range of responses as the looped film was shown again and again.

The proscenium arch established by this first film was then broken by THE WAVE. It is crucial that spectators know that this wave is British – at least if the narrative that I discern in this sequence of images is to be intelligible. (Reviews consistently indicate this to be the case.) This cut from dancers to wave is a crucial moment in early cinema: it is nothing less, I would suggest, than the first example of early cinema's distinctive form of spectatorial identification. Given who participated in this exhibition (Edwin Porter claimed to be assisting with the projection, James White was there and one suspects that the Lathams, William K.L. Dickson and others would have attended as well), its effect may have been broadly felt and noted. The British wave metaphorically washed away the stage and the Leigh Sisters even as it assaulted Koster & Bial's patrons, causing initial consternation and excitement (a shock that gradually receded as the film continued to loop through the projector). The spectators found themselves in the same position as the dancers from the previous shot. They became bound together and this shared identity was nothing less than a nationalistic one. Dancers and spectators, women and men (the audience was overwhelming male), were brought together as they were collectively attacked by this *British* wave. (As an aside, I would point out that this method of identification can be found in THE GREAT TRAIN ROBBERY [1903], where the bandit shoots at the audience and then later shoots and kills a passenger inside the narrative. Another variant of this can be found in DREAM OF A RAREBIT FIEND [1906], where we see the drunken partygoer and also simultaneously see the world swirling about as he experiences it. If one disputes the direct genealogy of this trope from the first Vitascope Program to DREAM OF A RAREBIT FIEND, it only makes these repeated manifestations that much more compelling. But I digress.)

If the wave's assault initially pushed the spectators out of the picture, WAL-
TON & SLAVIN provides them with a new surrogate. On behalf of the newly
constructed community of Americans (patrons and performers), Uncle Sam responds. That is, this wave was followed by a familiar subject: the burlesque
boxing bout between "the long and the short of it," featuring lanky Charles
Walton and the short, stout John Slavin. According to some sources, Walton
also appears in THE MONROE DOCTRINE (Edison, April 1896): he played Uncle
Sam while Slavin's replacement, John Mayon, was John Bull. In any case, Walton and Slavin visually evoked Uncle Sam and John Bull engaging in a fistic
encounter. It is worth noting that in this looped film, "the little fellow was
knocked down several times."[54] Uncle Sam was beating up John Bull for his
presumptuous wave. That is, the relationship between the second and third
film are one of cause and effect. The fourth film, BAND DRILL, shows a marching
band in uniform: suggesting a mobilization of the American military, it "elicited
loud cries of 'Bravo!'"[55] from the audience. Uncle Sam and John Bull of WALTON
& SLAVIN are only symbolic figures of the nation. This next scene (film 4) is less
symbolic in that it shows a group of soldiers – marching as if to war, as if in
response to the British assault. BAND DRILL thus prepared the way for THE
MONROE DOCTRINE, which "twins" ROUGH SEA AT DOVER even as it reworked
the fistic exchange in WALTON & SLAVIN. The British bombard the shoreline of
another American nation – with guns instead of cinematic waves. Uncle Sam
(Walton) forces John Bull (Mayon) to stop. According to one report, "This delighted the audience, and applause and cheers rang through the house, while
someone cried, 'Hurrah for Edison.'"[56] With this imaginary but much-wished-
for American victory, there was a return to the status quo as patrons once again
viewed a dance film that was similar in style and subject matter to the opening
selection. The program ended as it began, with a film of a woman that indulged
male voyeuristic pleasures but also remobilized the possibility of identification.
Might this dancer not evoke Columbia or Liberty (as in the statue of Liberty in
New York harbor)? A masculinist-nationalist (English-American) confrontation
thus forces these pleasures aside until an American triumph is achieved (on the
screen), and audiences are able to return to their sensual pleasures.

Hardly a miscellaneous collection of films, this opening night program was
an elaborate achievement indicating that Raff & Gammon had consciously chosen to fight the expected influx of international machines (English as well as
French) by appealing to American patriotism with American subject matter –
even though they (like Maguire & Baucus) had marketed the kinetoscope on
the basis of a cosmopolitan internationalism.[57] This opening night program offered a narrative of sorts that was not just an excuse for the display of visual
images. Its meaning was expressed in a remarkably creative manner. It carried
multiple messages and an ideology. How can we evaluate the importance of this

narrative in relation to its other components. Undoubtedly some theatergoers might have simply (or partially) viewed this program as a miscellaneous collection of views, or dismissed the narrative as of no consequence. To the extent that this was true, intertextuality, spectatorial comparison and judgment would have emerged. As Walton repeatedly pummeled Slavin, the theatergoer/spectator might well have thought back to *1492*, the musical farce from which the scene was extracted and filmed. Yet for someone interested in this moment of American cinema – and the rise of an American nationalistic ideology on the screen that helped to move the United States to war with Spain two years later – this narrative is telling. On the level of the shot, this program was often moving towards something less than or different from cinema of attractions (though the initial unfurling of THE WAVE doubtlessly conformed to this paradigm); but on the level of the program it offered something more. Although we can only speculate as to the ways that actual vaudeville patrons negotiated these potentially conflicting cues (the narrative progression of the films, the denarrativization as well as the de-astonishization of the image through looping), there are no easy answers.

This opening program seems to me to be remarkable and immensely significant. In general, scholars have assumed that very early motion pictures programs, such as the Vitascope program discussed above, were a miscellaneous collection of films that were selected to show off cinema's technological proficiency and to hint at its potential. Gunning's concept of cinema of attractions helped to put this (and much more) in a positive light. What this new reading suggests, beyond the ability of motion picture practitioners to build narratives from day one of commercially successful cinema in the Untied States, is a sensitivity to the diachronic. The sequencing of images – the diachronic – was everywhere in turn-of-the-century culture that was becoming more and more visual. Whether successive living pictures, lantern slides, comic strip images, waxworks scenes or films, the diachronic succession of images cannot be equated with narrative, though narrative is often its most pervasive manifestation. Early programs and somewhat later films, such as THE SEVEN AGES (Edison, 1905) or THE WHOLE DAM FAMILY AND THE DAM DOG (Edison, 1905), may be non-narrative in their editorial structures but they have a logical diachronic structure. In *Film Art* David Bordwell and Kristin Thompson offer an array of non-narrative ways of structuring images: rhetorical, associational, categorical, abstract. Most if not all of these were in use during the 1890s. This concern with diachronic organization was, I would suggest, powerful even as it was complemented by intertextual concerns.

A closer look at various exhibition strategies suggest ways that cinema in the novelty period could be less, more or different than cinema of attractions – and for that matter later Hollywood cinema.[58] Early films often elicited much more than astonishment – they mobilized the sophisticated viewing habits of spectators who already possessed a fluency in the realms of visual, literary and theatrical culture. Early cinema was not just the shock of the new, it was the reworking of the familiar – not only a reworking of old subjects in a new register but of established methods of seeing and reception. If early cinema before 1903 was often a cinema of attractions, it could also be a cinema of contemplation and discernment and certainly also a cinema of shot sequencing (including but not only narrative). It was all of these, sometimes within a single program – as Raff & Gammon so clearly demonstrated with the Vitascope's opening night at Koster & Bial's Music Hall.

Notes

1. *Yale Journal of Criticism* 7.2 (1994): 203-32. This was part of a cluster of papers delivered at the conference "The Movies Begin: History/Film/Culture" on 7-9 May 1993 at the Whitney Humanities Center, Yale University. It honored the 100th anniversary of the first public presentation of modern day motion pictures. Other relevant papers published in this cluster include Yuri Tsivian, "The Rorschach Test of Cultures: On Some Parallels between Early Film Reception in Russia and the United States" (177-88) and Tom Gunning, "The Whole Town's Gawking: Early Cinema and the Visual Experience of Modernity" (189-201).
2. More implicitly, my article was about the writing of film history of this period. Gunning has certainly penned two rigorous, outstanding book-length historical treatments of the cinema, but they have not been on the pre-Griffith period (what I once used to call "early cinema"). If Tom and I often find ourselves on opposite sides of this friendly (if serious) debate about the nature of early cinema, it may be in part because Tom has written a brilliant array of discrete, self-contained articles on the topic, while my writings in this area has been dominated by much longer sustained narratives about the nature and substance of historical change. Our respective formats indeed reflect our perceptions of this period. I would urge Gunning to pursue the same kind of detailed look at pre-Griffith cinema as he gave to the first years of D.W. Griffith's work at Biograph (*D.W. Griffith and the Origins of American Narrative Film: The Early Years at Biograph*). My conviction is that this would bring his position much closer to my own. It would require, however, an acknowledgment that Edwin S. Porter (for example) already had a narrator system in place, just one that was quite different from Griffith (as well as not as elaborate). Moreover, as this essay would emphasize, the origins of American narrative film began in a significant way with the beginnings of American cinema.
3. Charles Musser, *Edison Motion Pictures, 1890-1900: An Annotated Filmography* (Friuli, Italy: Giornate del Cinema Muto and Smithsonian Institution, 1997); Nancy Mathews with Charles Musser, et al., *Moving Pictures: American Art and Film, 1880-1910* (Manchester: Hudson Hill Press and Williams College Museum of Art, 2005). Most

recently I have been pursuing a book project on THE JOHN C. RICE-MAY IRWIN KISS (April 1896).

4. Musser, "Rethinking Early Cinema" 216, 228.

5. Tom Gunning, "An Aesthetic of Astonishment," *Viewing Positions*, ed. Linda Williams (New Brunswick: Rutgers UP, 1994) 121.

6. Gunning, "The Whole Town is Gawking" 191.

7. For example, we might think of Soviet cinema of the 1920s as a cinema of montage, but any systematic review of this cinema shows so many exceptions that it is wrong to see montage as the dominant feature of Soviet Silent Film. It is perhaps the dominant feature of an important strand of Soviet Cinema (the one we find most interesting and accomplished). However, it would be wrong to see montage as the dominant quality of all Soviet film from this period.

8. Nancy Mathews, "Art and Film: Interactions," *Moving Pictures: American Art and Film* 146-48.

9. Raff & Gammon, *The Vitascope* (1896): 8.

10. F.Z. Maguire & Co., *Catalogue* [March 1898]: 30. These and other catalog descriptions in this essay can all be found in Musser, *Edison Motion Pictures*.

11. Michael Fried, *Absorption and Theatricality: Painting and the Beholder in the Age of Diderot* (Berkeley: U of California P, 1980) 130-31.

12. Maguire 44.

13. Maguire 44.

14. *Van Loan's Catskill Mountain Guide with Bird's-Eye View, Maps and Choice Illustrations* [New York: Rogers & Sherwood, 1890] 22-24.

15. Katherine Manthorne, "Experiencing Nature in Early Film: Dialogues with Church's *Niagara* and Homer's Seascapes," *Moving Pictures: American Art and Film* 55-60.

16. Diderot, *Pensées détachées*, quoted in Fried 100.

17. Gunning, "An Aesthetic of Astonishment" 123-24.

18. Diderot, *Pensées détachées*, quoted in Fried 101.

19. Robert C. Allen, "'A Decided Sensation': Cinema, Vaudeville and Burlesque," *On the Edge of Your Seat: Popular Theater and Film in Early Twentieth-Century American Art*, ed. Patricia McDonnell (New Haven: Yale UP, 2002) 75-76.

20. "Living Pictures a Great Success," *New York Herald* 22 March 1894: 16. For more on the introduction of Living Pictures in New York City in 1894 see Musser, "A Cornucopia of Images: Comparison and Judgment across Theater, Film and the Visual Arts during the Late Nineteenth Century," *Moving Pictures: American Art and Film* 7-8.

21. *New York Herald* 22 March 1894: 16.

22. "A New Set of 'Living Pictures,'" *New York Daily Tribune* 11 May 1894: 7.

23. See for instance, "Gallery and Studio," *Brooklyn Eagle* 26 January 1890: 10.

24. "Keith's New Theater," *Boston Globe* 26 May 1896: 5.

25. The American Mutoscope & Biograph Company produced more than a dozen motion pictures that were also living pictures in 1899 and 1900. See Musser, "A Cornucopia of Images."

26. "Vaudeville-The Bijou," *Philadelphia Record* 6 Sept. 1896: 10.

27. Michelle Aubert and Jean-Claude Seguin, *La Production cinématographique des Frères Lumière* (Paris: Mémoires de cinéma, 1996) 251.

28. Edison Manufacturing Company, *War Extra: Edison Films* 20 May 1898: 3.

29. *The Phonoscope* Dec. 1896: 16.

30. *New York Mail and Express* 24 April 1896: 12.

31. Stephen Bottomore, "The Panicking Audience?: Early Cinema and the 'Train Effect,'" *Historical Journal of Film, Radio and Television* 19.2 (1999): 177-216.

32. Diderot, *Pensées detachées*, quoted in Fried 101.

33. Fried 101-102. One can link Diderot's conception of theatricality to the presentational acting style of many early films as well as the syncretic representational evident in comedies and dramas, particularly before 1908-09.

34. *Buffalo Courier* 7 June 1896: 10.

35. *Buffalo Courier* 7 June 1896: 122.

36. Wanda Strauven to Charles Musser, 10 May 2006.

37. Neil Harris, *Humbug: The Art of P. T. Barnum* (Boston: Little, Brown, 1973) 72-89.

38. Fried 108.

39. Fried 118.

40. Tom Gunning, "Cinema of Attractions: Early Film, Its Spectator and the Avant-Garde," *Early Cinema; Space Frame Narrative*, ed. Thomas Elsaesser (London: British Film Institute, 1990) 58-59.

41. One crucial problem here is that early cinema goes about constructing the beholder on three or four levels: the profilmic, the filmic, the level of exhibition, and spectatorship.

42. Part of the issue here is the benchmark for sustained absorption. Is it the standard of the present-day feature film? Or that of a painting? By evoking Diderot and Fried, Gunning gestures toward a comparison with painting, which Mathews has shown to be both appropriate and compelling.

43. Gunning, "Cinema of Attractions" 58-59.

44. Gunning, "The Whole Town is Gawking" 190.

45. Gunning, "The Whole Town is Gawking" 195.

46. "Keith's New Theater," *Boston Herald* 24 May 1896: 10.

47. Maguire & Baucus, *Edison Films* 20 Jan. 1897: 5.

48. A reproduction of *Caswell Beach-Breaking Waves* (John Dillwyn Llewelyn, 1853) can be found in Phillip Prodger, *Muybridge and the Instantaneous Photography Movement* (New York: Oxford UP, 1995) 79.

49. Many of these issues are explored from the perspective of art history in Michael Ann Holly, "Mourning and Method," *Art Bulletin* 84.4 (Dec. 2002): 660-69.

50. Gunning, "The Whole Town is Gawking" 195.

51. "Keith's New Theater," *Boston Herald* 24 May 1896: 10.

52. For newspaper accounts of this screening see Musser, *The Emergence of Cinema* (New York: Scribner's, 1990) 116. I misidentified BAND DRILL as FINALE OF 1ST ACT OF HOYT'S "MILK WHITE FLAG" in *Before the Nickelodeon: The Early Cinema of Edwin S. Porter* (Berkeley: U of California P, 1991) 62.

53. "Wonderful is the Vitascope," *New York Herald* 24 April 1896: 11, in Musser, *Edison Motion Pictures* 200-01.

54. *New York Daily News* 24 April 1896, clipping, Raff & Gammon Collection, Harvard Business School, Baker Library, Boston.

55. "Wonderful is the Vitascope."

56. "Wonderful is the Vitascope."

57. Reports of the cinématographe reached Raff & Gammon from England. London screenings destroyed their hope for a significant foreign sale of Vitascope rights. Also British systems as well as the Lumière cinématographe were in use by this period. It this respect Great Britain was an appropriate if somewhat misplaced object of Raff & Gammon's barbs. I examine this rivalry in "Nationalism and the Beginnings of Cinema: The Lumière Cinématographe in the United States, 1896-1897," *Historical Journal of Film, Radio and Television* 19.2 (June 1999): 149-76.

58. Thanks to Jane Gaines for suggesting the first part of this formulation.

The Lecturer and the Attraction

Germain Lacasse

"Come here! Come here! Ladies and gentlemen, come to see the most surprising and exciting fairground attraction, the cinematograph." Such was the commentary of dozens, if not of hundreds of barkers (*bonisseurs*[1]) in front of theaters where the first "animated photographs" were presented all over the globe circa 1895. They invited passers-by to come to experience a "state of shock." This expression is appropriate to portray the first film spectator because the views represented the quintessence of what art historians have named the distraction, which characterized modernity, and that cinema historians have named "cinema of attractions."

Still, the ambivalence of the "cinema of attractions" notion has to be stressed: narratives and shows have always consisted of attractions, surprises, which had been invented by the circus well before cinema. The cinematograph, unlike a sword swallower or a gladiator, was a technological attraction. The cinematograph is in itself an attraction, a characteristic that is later transferred to films, which will progressively become more narrative than "attractive." The views then became an attraction, but the cinematograph had been mediated, that is presented, introduced, announced, and familiarized by the speakers and the lecturers who had played, in fact, the narration's role before its integration into films.

Beyond this encounter, the lecturer was also the encounter's mediator between tradition and modernity, between the traditional arts and the cinematographic technique. He softens the shock of the attraction and the modern, and at the same time accustoms the audience to this state of shock, that the movie about to be presented will cause, and that facilitates technical and cultural hegemony of some nations. So the lecturer is the "proof of attraction," but also the "voice of attraction": by the lecturer's mouth the cinematograph speaks; this new and virtual world attracts the spectator in itself for the duration of a program. It is a hypnotic trance, like those presided over by a priest or a shaman, but this time the catalyst is a machine to which a person's voice is given. The question of the lecturer's commentary will be discussed here as a proof, then as a mediator of the attraction, and finally as a witness of the transition between a world of human attraction to the mechanized attraction, and of the conceptual implications of this transformation.

The Commentary as a Proof of the Attraction

In this discussion, I will speak about the cinema of attractions as it has been defined by Tom Gunning in 1998 in "Early American Film," in which he comes back to this very notion and its appositeness by bringing together insights from a number of works on early cinema.[2] Gunning reminds us in this article that his notion is based on Eisenstein's concept, which he considers equivalent to the sensible experience of modernity as described by early 20th-century art historians Siegfried Kracauer and Walter Benjamin: an experience made of shocks, surprises, encounters with new and disparate things, fragmented, an experience that Benjamin referred to by the word "distraction."[3] The cinema of attractions relates to this experience by its aggressive address to the spectator and its content made of elements of shock and surprise: trick films, train travels, novelties, and exoticism. Furthermore, these elements are presented in accordance with the same mode of experience as that of urban life: surprise, discontinuity, and rapidity.

In a manner of speaking, the lecturer is the proof of the attraction, and consequently of the relevance of the "cinema of attractions" as a concept. How and why can one consider this role as a proof? The first screenings are performed by lecturers, or at least by lecturers who introduce the show (and by journal entries that prepare what is coming next). The barker calls upon spectators to see the novelty, the surprise, and the lecturer presents, explains, and comments on the attraction. He is there both to amplify the shock and to attenuate: he informs the spectator that he will see something unexpected, which will be surprising, disturbing, even frightening. So this predictable shock is anticipated, expected, but less surprising than if the spectator were not prepared at all.

The lecturer stimulates and praises the entertainment and the attraction by introducing them to soften the shock, but then he amplifies the surprise. So, the lecturer can be considered as an entry-exit process. Besides, the lecturer was generally situated at the theater's entrance, telling what would be experienced inside as well as what had been experienced by spectators who were leaving the place. However, if the movie was the main attraction, it had to be emphasized, and for this reason the lecturer was indispensable. For the spectator unfamiliar with the story, it was impossible to understand Uncle Tom's Cabin (Edwin Porter, 1903), and the lecturer's commentary was almost essential to indicate and to accentuate the attractions: who is the character on the left, why does he move forward, what does he want?

The history of the lecturer asserts the assumption of the commentary as a proof of the attraction. The speech function presents, explains, and connects. Its presence corresponds to that of the cinema of attractions. Its decline then coincides with the development of narrative processes (script, editing, insert titles) that will replace the attractions' presenter and announcer. Suspense, one of D.W. Griffith's favorite figures, is in fact based on a speech substitution: while he previously could create expectations by asking questions or pointing out details, knowing what is happening next, the editing and shot size now fulfill this function by cutting the narrative into details and presenting elements that before were provided by the verbal commentary, which prepared and linked the attractions.

In many contexts, like those of colonies and countries that import cinema, or of the national minorities within countries that produce films, the use of the lecturer lasted longer. Closer research would reveal that in these specific situations there is still a relation to the attraction. For a long time the lecturer's function consisted in translating insert titles, so to speak to introduce the attractions, to prepare the spectator to understand the narrative's meaning that otherwise would be drifting away from him. The narration as well as the attraction would escape from the spectator under such circumstances. This situation mattered for countries that were importing movies before the insert titles or soundtracks had been translated, and in a number of countries they have not yet been translated...

The technical "failures" of the inventors had been successful for the owners: the first pictures were animated, but they did not have a soundtrack, although many producers would have wanted to add one. This silence augments the strangeness of the experience that most of the time was perceived as such in spite of frequent projections that were completely silent. In a way, the attraction was counting on this very muteness, and the lecturer's voice that filled in the "blanks." These blanks were the awareness of silence, an anticipation of this strangeness, a rational explanation that reassured the viewer by restoring the connection between his understanding and this strange and amusing as well as disturbing experience.

When speaking about the lecturer's speech as a proof of the attraction, it is also important to discuss the development recently theorized by another disseminator of the attraction notion, André Gaudreault. Gaudreault now speaks of "cinématographie-attraction" (Kine-Attractography), an expression borrowed from the historian G.-Michel Coissac. He proposes this loanword to refer to an historical experience with a corresponding historical vocabulary.[4] The bulk of his demonstration especially insists on assimilating the attraction to a phenomenon of discontinuity. In an article written with Nicolas Dulac, he believes that "animated views" are a cultural series based on the attraction, which appeared with the first optical devices and ended with the first movies, which would take it from approximately 1830 to 1900.[5]

This theoretical development, although defined and historicized, still fails to take account of one element: the commentary (and possibly the subject's innermost speech?). Of course the optical devices could be manipulated only by a single person who, excited as well as surprised by the simulation of movement, understood the movement because it was assimilated to a prior experience: the figures of the optical toys, as well as those of the first movies, were assimilated to the movement because their spectators could assume that there was movement when there was none according to the "phi effect" (that has supplanted the theory of "retinal persistence" as an explanation of the views).

The optical devices were different from the magic lantern because of their "in-loop" attractions without narration, but the lantern's shows had already consisted of attractions as tricks that produce the illusion of movement (for example rotating mobile pieces in metal and glass plates). The attraction of optical devices was not only owing to the surprise caused by movement, but also to the observation of unanimated and separate drawings that can create the illusion of movement. However, this surprise was perhaps less important than one thinks (or than Gaudreault and Dulac think), because it was expected by the spectators who had experienced the lantern shows.

The film lecturer or the speaker was part of the experience of the magic lantern show since its appearance a few centuries earlier. This show was generally educational or narrative, but it often consisted of attractions such as Robertson's shows, which are the most eloquent and well-known example. The verbal narration of these shows was used to introduce the show, but also to prepare the attractions; it puts the spectator in a state of concentration, and often attempts to amplify his reactions the way a good storyteller or script writer usually does.

In the same way the optical devices were announced in newspapers, on posters, and by word-of-mouth. Their "spectator" had expectations, or at least was curious. The spectator's experience consisted of a surprise, which was organized, expected and prepared by the individual who presented, sold, or made use of it. Hence, the following proposal: this definition of the attraction as a discontinued experience has to be tempered; it is perhaps more appropriate to consider the attraction as a new experience in which narration is minor and attraction is major, but in which the spectator is not a clone fresh out of his box without any previous experience, and above all cut off from contextual discourses, spoken or written, of his period.

The attraction is a surprise that disturbs social or individual experience. The uniqueness of the attraction even stands out as an almost autonomous show that is rapidly caught by the stream of discourses, of which the spoken discourse that circulates, among its users and those who offer them attractions, is the smoothest and most enticing one. The commentary is the proof of the attraction because it tends to master it; it is the first narrative device by which there is an attempt to examine and control the attraction, to demonstrate the existence and strength of the attraction, but also to present its discursive and narrative strength.

The Commentary as a Mediator of the Attraction

If by his presence and intervention he demonstrates the existence of the attraction, the lecturer can also be portrayed as a mediator of the attraction, that is, the person who is able to disseminate this unusual form, to arouse and maintain the interest in its favor, and to prepare and negotiate its encounter with the audience. The word mediator has to be understood as an ambiguous position where the subject can make choices, indicate directions, and activate operations. The mediator lecturer can "manipulate" the audience because it is often "his own" audience. He recognizes the spectators and knows what they can appreciate as an effect (surprise, shock, discovery) or affect (fear, worry, anxiety).[6] If he does not always recognize the audience, at least he knows his art, he knows what he can do and what he can experiment with as effect or affect. He can sometimes be unaware of the precise outcome of the experience, but he knows its possibilities and can expect what happens next. He is a showman, and his art consists of preparing and amplifying the spectacular, and to ritualize it as a particular effect.

He was first the mediator of the transition between the magic lantern and the cinematograph: the lantern was an attraction that sometimes stimulated movement. The attractive characteristic of the cinematograph consists in a more sophisticated simulation of the movement, the "animated photography" meaning photography with movement added. The lantern's speaker who acquired a cinematograph certainly changed his commentary: whereas before his commentary consisted of still images, he will now probably announce the images' movement, and change his explanation according to this new characteristic. Richard Crangle supports a different opinion according to which the commentary of the lanterns and that of the animated views were quite different practices, educational versus recreational.[7] Although this observation is accurate in general, it neglects the numerous attractions used by the lanternists, many of whom became projectionists. Some will even become theorists of projection and eventually emphasizes the projector's abilities as attraction. Cecil Hepworth in England and G.-Michel Coissac in France are two notable examples.[8]

For that matter, the lecturer's history is the history of this mediation, or of the emergence of cinema that gradually becomes "auto-mediated": the lecturer first presents the invention and attraction; he then uses the views as attractions in his magic lantern animated show; finally, he is "thrown" out by the movie he "swallowed."[9] Although Gunning has questioned the generalization of this three-phase story, the lecturer's existence can appropriately be assimilated to the history of mediation of animated views.[10] Besides, this story softens the strength of attraction and theory based on it, since the lecturer's role was to prepare the surprise and distraction. However, as said earlier, the organized lecture confirms that it took place, and therefore that it happened.

Yet Gunning was the first to notice this important relation between the film lecturer and the attraction. In his well-known article "An Aesthetic of Astonishment," he insists on the fact that "[l]ike a fairground barker, [the film lecturer] builds an atmosphere of expectation, a pronounced curiosity leavened with anxiety as he stresses the novelty and astonishing properties which the attraction about to be revealed will possess."[11] Gunning gives as examples the projections presented by Albert E. Smith that were introduced and provided by a commentary during which Stuart Blackton was doing everything he could to dramatize the projection and film's effect. Gunning goes beyond this description to explain that "it expresses an attitude in which astonishment and knowledge perform a vertiginous dance"[12] in accordance with the aesthetic of distraction theorized by Benjamin.

Thus, the notion of attraction is related to a cognitive operation and corresponds to another interesting theoretical development, "l'image-attraction" (the attraction image), proposed by Livio Belloï. Belloï considers his designation more accurate than previous theories of attraction because it makes the notion of attraction more specified and therefore less general as well as more relevant.[13] Indeed, the notion of attraction image corresponds better to the transition of magic lantern to cinematograph because it shows what is most distinctively attractive and what constitutes the spectacular element in films. Belloï cites different examples, such as the "vue attentatoire" (assailing view).[14] The Lumière's and Biograph's trains are as many projectiles launched towards the target-spectators that are used to flabbergast them with disappearing rather than appearing locomotives, thus showing the assailing view as a fiction that reveals the reality of the image as an interlocutor.[15]

These attraction images are often accompanied by a spoken commentary, a prime example being the "Hale's Tours," of which the lecturer's interpretation is a fact that is often and even now ignored.[16] If one believes in the effect of attraction (the spectator's interest in a maximal distractive experience), how to explain the presence of this "he who explains" here? Without a doubt it is useful to go back to what has been previously considered: he softens the effect of the shock by introducing it, but he then amplifies it while integrating it in a performance that focuses on the exacerbation of the spectacular and distractive. Here the train operator with an abundant speech echoes the mediator discussed before: he invites the travelers to board, to take their seats, and announces the tour's stops. But when travelers approach a destination, they hear declarations and exclamations that arouse and stimulate their reactions.

The lecturer's role ends and is even disqualified from the moment the movie and the cinema become phenomena that are known, accepted, and legitimized. Indeed, the critical or aesthetic discourses attack the lecturer, and successfully eject him from the institution in many countries. In a way, the mediating role of the lecturer served the transition from the pre-industrial stage as a crisis to the institutional stage where cinema has become an accepted and normalized practice, as Denis Simard defines it in "De la nouveauté du cinéma des premiers temps."[17] The lecturer has been somewhat useful for the spoken institution, unfixed, and unregulated by written rules; he was the first practitioner who served to fasten the attraction to existent practices. After his disappearance, the attraction remains, but is now integrated into familiar practices whose device is assimilated to the point that it has become unconscious and implicit. The attraction is now included in a narrative, it is inscribed in a temporal and spatial development, it is an element of an expansion, it expresses modernity, but a modernity actually mastered as an experience where the surprise has become the usual instead of the unusual.

The Commentary as a Mediator of Modernity

Beyond his mediating role of the attraction, the lecturer has been the mediator of the transition between tradition and modernity. As demonstrated by Gunning, the notion of attraction refers very well to modernity as portrayed by historians mentioned earlier (Benjamin, Kracauer) and others like Georg Simmel. Mediator of this (violent) transition, the lecturer is therefore both proof and witness of the attraction: a proof, because his presence shows the necessity of an introducing and negotiating authority, that comes to attenuate the violence of the shock, and at the same time causes this shock and in a way justifies it; a witness, because his profession sees the rapid development between the surprise caused by the cinematograph and the posterior interest for narrative cinema including the attractions.

The cinematograph served the consolidation of scientific and materialist knowledge of the world, offering the spectator a narrative build-up by the reproduction of the real. Cinematograph images are the product of a knowledge that is not metaphysical nor empirical, but physical and objective. A train can be called to mind by speech and text, but thanks to the camera and the projector it can be copied and shown. The showing has become a technical operation achievable by machines. Ontotheology of images has become completely discredited, and historians have also located the sources of this "crisis." In *Une invention du diable*, a book-length study that pays tribute to the first Domitor congress, many historians examine the important conflicts opposing religious authorities of the period and the growing of cinematographic industry.[18] In most catholic countries, these authorities not only opposed the moral contained in films that was considered as scandalous, but they also attacked the very nature of the machine, proclaiming that it aggressed human nature, and moreover the supernatural order of the world. The cinema was an important part of the modern way of life as it upset traditions, laws, and beliefs; there is every reason to believe that if the lecturer had sometimes been the accelerator of this disruption, he also and at times decelerated it, to be more precise he had been the mediator, the one who knew how to adapt the show to the audience. Film lecturers were criticized for their outrageousness; but in general they could also do the exact opposite, and make what was not acceptable nonetheless acceptable to the public.

The lecturer was the mediator of another singular experience of modernity. The silent cinema has often been presented as a symbol of modernity because it was considered as a "universal language."[19] It enabled the spreading of foreign cultures and the consolidation of some hegemony, those of nations able to make films. But as I stressed in my book *Le bonimenteur de vues animées*, the lecturer was still the mediator here and the one who resisted hegemony. He commented on narratives from foreign countries in the local language, could give well-known names to the characters, create convenient explanations to the audience, and establish a distance between the foreign texts rather than strengthen its power. He provided the experience of the attraction image in the local language, so here again he softened the foreign origin of this experience, but could also amplify some of its effects by astonishing explanations.

Could we not consider the film lecturers as mediators of modernity as it is presented and spread by a hegemonic foreign cinema? What has been said about their commentary implies not only that they explain the films, but also that their explanation is an introduction to modernity and values proposed by the film narratives. This assumption would turn the lecture into a colonialist practice. In reality, however, the commentary was mostly an anti-colonialist practice, at least in colonial territories. The attraction often was a characteristic of dominant countries (machines, urban modernity), which by means of the lecture could become a simple surprise rather than a technological superiority.

The expression "vernacular modernism,"[20] used by Natasha Durovicova, seems appropriate to define the film lecturer's work. The lecturer effectively was the voice of modernity in show-business: he announced the new machines, prepared the surprise and its effect, and, in a way, "performed" modernity. He introduced technology while combining local cultural elements: language, accent, practices, and context. Durovicova believes that movies with multiple versions, like dubbed movies later on, had to preserve the local elements (the "vernacular modernism") from the hegemonic and inclusive tendency of modernity. The commentary of early cinema can certainly be associated or compared with these practices.

The Voice of Attraction

The lecturer tends to legitimize the relevance of the expression "cinema of attractions" when speaking of early cinema. The movement of the images and their muteness were essentially "strange attractors" whose foreign origin called for a safe haven, a reassuring space, an educational commentary that prepared and attenuated the strangeness of the experience. The film lecturer in a way softened the power of the attraction by supplying a soundtrack that could "unravel" the surprise. He softened the surprise of muted images and the strangeness of the experience, but he anticipated the soundtrack, which inventors would have wanted to join to the film at the very moment of its distribution.

He was therefore a voice of the attraction since he prepared and stressed it, but he also was the voice of modernity. This undeniably constituted a radically new experience of human evolution, and the cognition was confronted with sensations and questions that were often unexpected.[21] In this respect, the cinematograph was one of the most striking inventions, and that is the reason why it has become one of the most popular practices of the 20th century. However, its sudden and rapid development goes against the individual as well as collective knowledge, which explains the different means developed to control its appearance and diffusion.

This experience is still alive today in a postmodern context where the scientific attraction (such as landing on Mars or looking at neutrons) is the expectation of citizens and subjects, and where the number and the intensity of attractions begin to be a problem. Whereas the consumer of 1900 looked for modern surprise occasions, in 2000 he often looks for the occasion to run away from them, or to escape from their rhythm. His time experience is radically different. Twentieth-century man was fascinated by the speed, and acclaimed with enthusiasm each announcement of acceleration: steam, gas, turbine, car, plane, and rocket. His grandson is confronted to the effects of this velocity and often finds it less amusing. When he wants to live an experience less rapid, he turns off projectors and listens to the voices.

Translated by Julie Beaulieu (with Frank Runcie)

Notes

1. The words used to refer to the film lecturer can be confusing. In French, *bonisseur* (barker) generally refers to the person advertising in front of theaters, *bonimenteur* (film lecturer) refers to the person commenting on the screenings, improvising film commentary, and *conférencier* (speaker) refers to the person giving a well-prepared lecture with scholarly explanations.
2. Tom Gunning, "Early American Film," *The Oxford Guide to Film Studies*, ed. John Hill and Pamela Church Gibson (Oxford: Oxford UP, 1998) 255-71. This article constitutes one of the most complete and brilliant synthesis published on the cinema of attractions.
3. Gunning, "Early American Film" 266.
4. André Gaudreault, *Cinema delle origini. O della "cinematografia-attrazione"* (Milano: Il Castoro, 2003). See also his contribution in this volume.
5. André Gaudreault and Nicolas Dulac, "Head or Tails: The Emergence of a New Cultural Series, from the Phenakisticope to the Cinematograph," *Invisible Culture. An Electronic Journal for Visual Culture* (2004) http://www.rochester.edu/in_visible_culture/Issue_8/dulac_gaudreault.html. See also their contribution in this volume which is a revised version of "Head or Tails."
6. Here I use *effect* to indicate the cognitive aspect of the impression produced and *affect* to point out the emotive or physiological aspects.
7. Richard Crangle, "Next Slide Please: The Lantern Lecture in Britain 1890-1910," *The Sounds of Early Cinema*, ed. Richard Abel and Rick Altman (Bloomington: Indiana UP, 2001) 39-47.
8. Cecil M. Hepworth, *Came the Dawn. Memories of a Film Pioneer* (London: Phoenix House, 1951); G.-Michel Coissac, *Manuel pratique du conférencier-projectionniste* (Paris: La Bonne Presse, 1908).
9. On these three stages, see my book *Le bonimenteur de vues animées. Le cinéma muet entre tradition et modernité* (Québec/Paris: Nota Bene/Méridiens-Klincksieck, 2000).
10. Tom Gunning, "The Scene of Speaking Two Decades of Discovering the Film Lecturer," *Iris* 27 (Spring 1999): 67-79. Gunning challenges my conclusions on the lecturer as a means of resistance for local cultures.
11. Tom Gunning, "An Aesthetic of Astonishment. Early Film and the (In)Credulous Spectator," *Art and Text* 34 (Spring 1989): 36.
12. Gunning, "An Aesthetic of Astonishment" 42.
13. Livio Belloï, *Le regard retourné. Aspects du cinéma des premiers temps* (Québec/Paris: Nota Bene/Méridiens Klincksieck, 2001) 86.

14. The "assailing view" refers to the movie that seems to stress and threaten the spectator: the train rushing in the audience, the cowboy who is shooting at him, or any form of "attack."

15. Belloï 154.

16. Charles Berg, "The Human Voice and the Silent Cinema," *Journal of Popular Film* 4.2 (1975): 168.

17. Denis Simard, "De la nouveauté du cinéma des premiers temps," *Le cinéma en histoire. Institutions cinématographiques, réception filmique et reconstitution historique*, ed. André Gaudreault, Germain Lacasse and Isabelle Raynauld (Paris/Québec: Méridiens Klincksieck/Nota Bene, 1999) 30-56. In this article Simard depicts GRAFICS works.

18. Roland Cosandey, André Gaudreault and Tom Gunning, eds., *Une invention du diable. Cinéma des premiers temps et religion, Actes du 1er congrès de Domitor* (Sainte-Foy/Lausanne: Presses de l'Université Laval/Payot, 1992).

19. Lillian Gish, *Dorothy and Lillian Gish* (New York: Scribner's, 1973) 60. Gish attributes this discourse to D.W. Griffith, but it was announced by many other silent cinema propagandists.

20. Natasha Durovicova, "Introduction," *Cinéma et Cie* 4 (Spring 2004): 13.

21. Based on Jonathan Crary's work, Gunning in "Early American Film" reasserts this observation, criticizing Bordwell's opinion that wants to soften the novelty of the modern experience.

Integrated Attractions: Style and Spectatorship in Transitional Cinema

Charlie Keil

> The often free-floating filmic attractions of early film became part of a narrative system as film unambiguously defined its primary role as a teller of tales, a constructor of narratives.
> – Tom Gunning[1]

> The very transformation of film form occurring at this moment [1908-1909] involved, on one hand, the curtailment of a particular system of representation utilizing certain kinds of attractions (and a way of presenting them) and, on the other, the emergence of a new and different system of representation mobilizing other kinds of attractions and another way of presenting them.
> – Charles Musser[2]

In the twenty years since "the cinema of attractions" introduced a compelling periodization schema predicated on an attentiveness to early cinema's formal norms, the exact nature of the attraction's relationship to narrative remains open to debate. Linda Williams has suggested that "[Tom] Gunning's notions of attraction and astonishment have caught on [...] because, in addition to being apt descriptions of early cinema, they describe aspects of all cinema that have also been undervalued in the classical paradigm"[3]; according to this account, attractions stand as a refutation of classicism's reliance on causality and its appeal to a viewer's problem-solving capabilities. But others have argued that attractions and narrative "are effectively imbricated, even integrated" much earlier than Gunning's model allows, and continue to be so in Hollywood films where "attractions tend to be fully integrated with the story."[4] On different occasions, Gunning himself has pointed to the inevitable "synthesis of attractions and narrative [...] already underway" by "the end of the [attractions] period (basically from 1903 to 1906)."[5] Can attractions contest narrative at the same time that they aid in its execution? If so, how would we describe their function?

Privileged within appropriations of the attractions model which challenge classicism's tenets is its emphasis on shock, itself understood as a response to the enveloping cultural experience of modernity. I have expressed my reservations elsewhere about the tendency to overvalue the influence of modernity on early cinema's operations, not least because our ability to explain changes to film style become compromised in the process.[6] Undue emphasis on attractions' link to modernity tends to obscure how attractions play a role in the increased narrativity of subsequent periods, particularly the years 1907-1913, the era I have labeled transitional. For this reason, I propose reconsidering the model of spectatorial relations developed in versions of the attractions model indebted to the sway of modernity. At the same time, we need to remember that the cinema of attractions was envisioned as only one phase in a series of linked stages of formal developments preceding the emergence of the classical cinema by the late 1910s. By recognizing the sustained appeal of visual novelty without insisting that it retain its oppositional quality in the face of narrativization, I believe we can respect the unique attributes of transitional era cinema, one of whose characteristics is to internalize and eventually transform the attraction itself.

A Shockingly Confusing/Confused Spectator

When first devised, the cinema of attractions model derived from the observation of a set of interrelated formal features, designed to address spectators in a particular fashion, their distinctiveness attributable to clearly circumscribed proximate factors. The legacy of vaudeville, the underdeveloped nature of early film production, the viewing conditions within early exhibition sites – one could list all of these to explain the pervasiveness of an aesthetic predicated on near-autonomous moments of display. Similarly, as established narrative forms exerted influence on filmmakers, and both production and exhibition became increasingly subject to the forces of regulation and standardization, one could well understand the lessened role of attractions. But when the argument shifts so as to assert that attractions' mode of address, predicated on a principle of shock, finds its rationale in the experiential degradation common to modern life, one can no longer supply reasons for any alterations to the formal system as readily. The pervasiveness of shock as a condition of modern life militates against any identifiable change to the cinema of attractions' operations unless the contours of modernity undergo a similar shift.

Defined this way, the cinema of attractions sees itself boxed into a conceptual corner; it is now tied to an all-encompassing conception of modernity which scarcely permits one to imagine an aesthetic compatible with immediate post-attractions developments. In its current formulation, the cinema of attractions' features have become exemplary of a condition which supposedly defines the surrounding culture and in ways considerably more far-reaching than Gunning's model was designed to accommodate initially. Collectively, these features portray a spectator bombarded by shocks and accustomed to brief bursts of sensorial pleasure; the viewing experience has become synonymous with disruption and incoherence. If the cinema of attractions had continued to sustain itself in a heightened fashion in concert with those strains of modern life to which it responds, perhaps this portrait of spectatorial relations would prove persuasive. But as we know, the cinema of attractions gives way to a transitional period, wherein the tendency toward narrativization becomes more pronounced, and the prominence of shocks and visual display diminishes. Supposedly, the perpetually distracted urban dweller, buffeted by the dislocating transformations of modern life, would have become well-schooled in responding to such an aesthetic as the cinema of attractions developed. If constantly in a state of fragmentation, confirmed and reflected by the cinematic experience, why would the spectator see any reason to abandon it?

In particular what would such a spectator make of the transitional film, which retains remnants of the attractions phase, while gradually and inconsistently adopting methods and devices which promote continuity? The eventual displacement of the cinema of attractions seems nonsensical in the face of modernity's unabated power during the period in question. A problem emerges no matter which way one frames the question: if the cinema of attractions actively appealed to the spectator conditioned by modernity, specifically because its aesthetic was tailor-made for the time, the decision to abandon an attractions mode seems ill-advised; if, on the other hand, cinema, much like any other cultural form at the turn-of-the-century, merely reflected the social experience of modernity, what would explain cinema's shift away from this prevailing aesthetic in mid-decade?

Modernity has proven less help than hindrance in explaining the kinds of spectatorial shifts which would attend the changes represented by the transitional years. Being yoked in this way to the modernity thesis, the cinema of attractions model finds itself disengaged from the diachronic dimensions the concept possesses when understood in productive relation to subsequent periods. Ironically, the very formal specificity of the attractions model, which presupposes a distinctive spectatorial response, becomes subsumed within the broader sweep of modernity's claims. This, in turn, diminishes the relevance of changes to those formal features – chief among them, stylistic elements – as the transitional period emerges.

In other words, either the formal properties of early cinema are essential to understanding spectatorial response, or they are not. If they are, the modern spectator derived from "the aesthetic of astonishment" must undergo some substantial changes, even as the contextualizing force of his social environment remains unchanged. The danger with the modernity thesis lies precisely in its explanatory schema being so all-encompassing: when modernity becomes invoked as the rationale for attractions, one is hard-pressed to account for any finer-grained changes. No matter how one construes the modernity argument, one's notion of the spectator becomes considerably complicated when confronted with the changes the transitional era entails. If changed formal features do involve some type of shift in spectatorial relations, the modernity thesis has failed to explain what kinds of changed experiential factors have given rise to the mode of perception which emerges with the transitional period. Conversely, if modernity's influence on the spectator remains intact, the negotiation of transitional cinema must entail considerable disorientation, as the erratic process of devising effective storytelling devices often results in an aesthetic beholden to neither the attractions nor the classical phase. Given the modernity thesis, one would have difficulty understanding or explaining why transitional cinema occurs when and how it does; an equally challenging prospect is to imagine a spectator, her mode of perception already conditioned by modernity, who would or could accommodate the changes involved. Does the transitional cinema produce an impossibly conflicted spectator, one torn between a spectatorial stance shaped by modernity on the one hand and fumbling toward what will eventually become classical cinema on the other? Or must we subscribe to the notion that transitional cinema pulls the spectator away from any aesthetic based in the conditions of (modern) experience, in an admittedly clumsy effort, to impose the comforting nostalgia of more coherent (proto-classical) forms?[7]

Of course, the more detailed we become in our attempts at periodization based on formal change, the more conflicted our positing of a spectator derived from such features becomes. In light of this, it makes sense to devise alternative ways of understanding the hypothetical spectator's relation to such changes. Given the uneven and heterogeneous nature of development during the transitional era, we must think in terms other than those provided by the version of the attractions model indebted to the modernity thesis, or the spectator in question will be incoherent indeed, both inexplicably deprived of her shocks and stymied by a series of inconsistently articulated attempts at narrative integration.

Altered Attractions: Style during the Transitional Era

Assuming that the period of attractions does possess a relatively stable set of distinctive features and a concomitant mode of address, one could reasonably posit that the spectator would require some preparation for the changes increased narrativization entails. This occurs from approximately 1903 onward, as attractions cease to be the dominant but attempts at narrativization remain minimal. During this period, the influence of narrative begins to manifest itself more strongly, evident in the gradually diminishing attention given to display. In other words, narrative presentation begins to displace the largely non-narrative demonstrational tendencies of the attractions phase, though the efforts at integration evident by 1908 and later are still not in place. Moreover, the striking emphasis on POV trick effects, closer shot scale, etc. often evident in the earlier period is gradually abandoned. Replacing it is scarcely more than the existence of narrative itself, often told through multiple shots, but otherwise underarticulated; the devices popularized during the attractions era are not enlisted for the purposes of storytelling.[8] It is as though, to paraphrase Ben Brewster, these devices have to be stripped of their previous function and neutralized before they can be reintroduced within a narrativizing context.[9] By extension, the same process is occurring in relation to the spectator, as her understanding of the assumed address within the cinema of attractions is redrawn by the temporary retirement of these devices before they slowly reappear for altered purposes.

Throughout the extended post-attractions period, then, the spectator undergoes a process of learning how to comprehend cinema's narrational logic, at the same time filmmakers are developing suitable methods for storytelling themselves. This process, I would argue, is of considerable interest, both for the formal inconsistencies it produces, and the challenges it poses to conceiving of a spectator of uniformly predictable characteristics. A specific example from late in the transitional period can indicate the particular stylistic idiosyncracies involved during this era and the varied spectatorial relations they invite. A 1913 Selig film, BELLE BOYD, A CONFEDERATE SPY, embodies the kind of uneasy accommodation of increased narrativization one finds throughout this period. The film's story revolves around the act of spying: when a careless Union soldier creates a hole in the ground floor ceiling, the eponymous heroine uses the opportunity to view surreptitiously the army's plans from the vantage point of her bedroom floor, which is positioned directly above. Once she becomes aware of their plans, Belle proves her heroism by switching the documents and taking the originals to the Confederate forces. The first half of the film, wherein Belle's home is occupied by the Union soldiers, and she views the plans, seems designed to foreground the striking shot involving overhead POV. However, unlike a shot in the cinema of attractions phase, this one's motivation derives primarily from the story's demands. The film's awareness of the distinctiveness of its reliance on this shot is signaled by the elaborate lead-up to its use. The protracted preparation for and repeated use of the POV shot rehearses the act of narratively-aware looking the film's scenario provides for its viewer. The self-consciousness of the device's deployment, unlike its use in an earlier era, seems designed to train the spectator, to emphatically point to the narrative value of the information the POV shot frames.

But even as it stresses the narrational usefulness of analyzing space through a diegetically-motivated view, and buttresses that strategy with dissection of the spaces which surround Belle's bedroom, the film reverts to a tableau style in its second half. As Belle rushes to bring the plans to the Confederate forces, the film retains a consistent long shot scale which provides scant cues for understanding the relevant narrative action. Moreover, the film introduces no other strategies which might promote viewer comprehension, such as increased emphasis on staging in depth or the introduction of cross-cutting. As much as the film seems to train viewer awareness of narratively relevant material through the employment of a privileged device in the first half, it abandons this attempt in the second. Such is the manner of transitional cinema, though its manifestation is rarely as schematic as in this film.

As we learn more about the unique features of the transitional years, we will need to refine our notions of what manner of spectatorship it invites. Relying on overly broad designations such as the modernity-influenced attractions model entails can only impoverish our appreciation of the shifts occurring throughout the transitional period of early cinema. If we do not need to abandon the attractions model altogether, we certainly do need to free it of some of the highly determinant cultural baggage it has acquired along the way. The cinema of attractions should not epitomize a condition of viewing applicable to all of early cinema, in a way which reduces responses to the diverse patterns of change to a singular recognition of shock. Invoking metaphors of dislocation and fragmentation to convey the experience of viewing the cinema of attractions (or for that matter, post-classical or postmodern cinema) risks producing a distracted scholar who will fail to notice there is more to early cinema than encounters with a broad force named modernity.

Rethinking Attractions as a Function of Style

How might we advance another way of thinking about attractions, wherein their relationship to subsequent stylistic developments would allow us to see the relevance of attractions to narrative? Gunning himself has provided a starting point, when he allows that the "desire to display may interact with the desire to tell a story, and part of the challenge of early film analysis lies in tracing the interaction of attractions and narrative organization."[10] But this might still imply that attractions and narrativization exist in some kind of oppositional – or at least separable – relationship. And it does not move us beyond the situation where style works to promote aggressive display for the attractions period and yet operates as a systematized deployment of devices geared toward narrativization for the later years. Put another way, one could argue that within the attractions period, style is only novelty designed to shock, while later it becomes subsumed within the drive to create a diegetic world. The transformation of style becomes difficult to understand, however, when it is tied so completely to a rather binaristic model of spectatorial address, wherein the attractions-era spectator delights in shock and confrontation and the classical viewer basks in the comfort of covert and complicitous pleasures.

Despite the emphasis on spectatorial address within the attractions model, suggestions of why said address should shift are in short supply. If we look for the reasons for this shift elsewhere, our sense of developments within the period becomes clearer. In particular, we need to reintroduce a conception of style as a product of filmmakers' experiments with their material. The film industry's drive for increased length forced filmmakers to adopt more narratively developed material, which occasioned a re-evaluation of the function of various formal features, but scarcely eliminated their potential as exploitable visual sensations. For that reason, I would not abandon the notion of novelty the term attractions implies when discussing style in the transitional years.

The example of Belle Boyd has already demonstrated how a POV shot could function as both a kind of attraction and a narrative expedient. The level of overt display (or "confrontation") strikes me as no less pronounced in a film such as this than in one from the turn of the century, but now such a device is also being enlisted to abet narrative development. Eventually, the novelty aspect of these devices dissipates, particularly if they are adopted by other filmmakers as a conventionalized means of filmic storytelling. The eventual crystallizing of the classical style doubtless occurs at the point where novelty ceases to figure as prominently as presumed diegetic expediency. But in the intervening years, transitional style entails both flaunting the exoticism of attractions and aiding in the comprehension of narrative. The transitional spectator is both impressed by the visually novel and schooled in possible ways to understand potentially confusing plot points. Those ways which are adopted for widespread use are probably the formal features whose distinctiveness does not outweigh their narrational effectiveness.

Attractions are an integral part of later stylistic developments, but eventually they must prove their effectiveness as solutions to the problems filmmakers confront in shaping longer narratives. The classical style is a "new" style insofar as its aims differ substantially from those evident during the attractions era. What James Ackerman has said of style in art history – "A style, then, may be thought of as a class of related solutions to a problem – or responses to a challenge – that may be said to begin whenever artists begin to pursue a problem or react to a challenge which differs significantly from those posed by the prevailing style or styles"[11] – applies equally well to stylistic change within early cinema. As we can scarcely expect filmmakers to have arrived at workable solutions to the problem of increased narrative length without considerable experimentation, we should view the transitional period (and its stylistic tendencies) as producing hybrid works, wherein the nature of style fuses attraction-based novelty and classically-oriented narrative economy.

One such example occurs in another 1913 film, THE TRAIL OF CARDS, a telling demonstration of the difficulty one encounters separating the concepts of attraction and narrativization. The film's fairly simple plot hinges on a woman leaving a trail of playing cards as a clue when she is abducted by a jilted lover. The playing cards function as a privileged object, established early in the narrative in order to naturalize their employment later; their centrality to the film is registered by the title, a tactic of some typicality by 1913. Novelty resides in the stylistic means chosen to convey the dropping of the cards: the film employs extensive tracking shots to depict the abduction on horseback, during which the cards as clues are planted. Employing a mobile camera to capture movement occurs infrequently in the early 1910s; accordingly, the several instances of tracking in THE TRAIL OF CARDS would have appealed as a type of visual stunt. The self-conscious virtuosity involved in using a tracking shot to capture moving action is signaled by the substantial duration of the shot where a track first occurs. (The track's final appearance, as a backward traveling movement depicting the reunited couple's ride back to her ranch in the last shot of the film, similarly announces its privileged status.) As is the case with BELLE BOYD's striking overhead POV shot, the tracking shots are prepared for by an elaborate narrative lead-up, which points to the specialized nature of their deployment. But, at the same time, they also function as solutions to particular problems posed by narratives involving potentially illegible action. It is not impossible, in fact, that a narrative such as that found in THE TRAIL OF CARDS might have been constructed precisely to test out a stylistically adventurous kind of problem-solving.[12] If a solution of this kind proved both acceptable to audiences (as an aid to comprehension) and filmmakers (as a manageable form of stylistic expression), it would be adopted repeatedly, and eventually become a standardized figure of style.

Understanding the development of style as a series of experimental solutions to narrative-based problems does not eliminate the usefulness of the concept of attractions, nor does it deny the ongoing appeal of attractions themselves as a series of self-conscious effects, deliberately cultivating visceral viewer reactions. But the dominant aesthetic has moved beyond that of pure sensation and decontextualized effect. The residual appeal of the attraction in such films as BELLE BOYD and TRAIL OF CARDS speaks to the perceived value of the self-conscious display of style at this time, but the overall impetus seems to be only to highlight the attraction so as to rationalize it.

"The Cinema of Attractions" and Histories of Film Style

In *On the History of Film Style*, David Bordwell identifies the respective stylistic histories of André Bazin and Noël Burch as representing two distinct types of research programs: the dialectical and the oppositional. Bordwell's survey of recent research programs singles out Gunning's account of early cinema style for extended consideration, arguing that such revisionist work builds on the insights of Bazin and Burch while moving beyond the earlier writers' limitations.[13] As way of conclusion, I would like to consider anew how the cinema of attractions operates in the broad tradition of these previous models while suggesting a salient difference, one that may well ensure the lasting significance of the attractions model for future generations of scholars studying film style.

Much like Gunning's work on attractions, Bazin's "Evolution of the Language of Cinema" and Burch's *To the Distant Observer* exemplify how theoretically informed historical accounts of stylistic change typically assume a corresponding spectatorial response. Bazin and Burch launch their periodized studies of style by (implicitly) asking two related questions: what features constitute the system of devices being examined? (a question of description) and how can one account for the changes governing the emergence of this system so constituted? (a question of explanation). For Bazin, the anti-decoupage tendencies of 1940s cinema emerge as a function of the medium evolving toward its ontological basis in realist reproduction; Burch understands Japanese film of the 1930s as a refutation of Western codes of representation precisely because of the largely unfettered influence of indigenous theatrical practice. But the two authors also investigate stylistic change in terms of its bearing on the viewing practices of the spectator. Hence, the paired effect of deeper focus and longer takes in the work of Wyler and Welles promotes what Bazin labels a "more active mental attitude on the part of the spectator and a more positive contribution on his part to the action in progress,"[14] while Burch sees in Ozu's editing patterns the need for the spectator "to rectify with each new shot-change his mental position with respect to the players, [so that] the trap of participation no longer functions in quite the same way."[15]

If, in the examples of Bazin and Burch, explanation of spectatorial activity derives from observation of distinct stylistic operations, history demands that such explanations be subject to the change of style over time: just as the democratic staging of a figure like Welles marks an advance over the more controlling decoupage evident in the classical studio films of the 1930s, so, too do the idiosyncratic cutting patterns of Ozu constitute a direct challenge to the prevailing convention of directional matching. We find something quite different in the model offered up by the concept of attractions: here the stylistic anomalies arise not out of a spirit of opposition, but as a function of cinema's origins in a turn-of-the-century culture defined by display and sensation. Rather than presenting a challenge to established norms, as do the privileged stylistic systems analyzed by Bazin and Burch, Gunning's attractions-era cinema reverses the equation: it is a distinctly non-normative set of representational practices which gradually gives way to a more conventional mode. So, when change occurs, as it does with greater regularity from 1907 onward, it involves the lessening of the charge of novelty we attribute to attractions, supplanted by the narrativizing tendencies which begin to coalesce within the so-called transitional period. In other words, Gunning's work – when the notion of attractions remains productively aligned to that of narrative integration – indicates how the implementation of norms is the most complex of processes, modeled neither on notions of simple resistance nor smooth progress, but rather messy coexistence. In his recent analysis of an exemplary transitional-era Griffith one-reeler, THE LONEDALE OPERATOR (1911), Gunning demonstrates how the film retains the shocks of the attractions era, while harnessing them to a program of systematic repetition and alternation. By arguing in convincing fashion why formal issues remain essential in any discussion of how attractions operate beyond 1907, Gunning affirms the continuing centrality of his ideas to an ever-developing history of film style. My own contribution to this ongoing project, while suggesting modifications to some of the premises which have come to animate Gunning's work, still recognizes that centrality, and salutes its vitality and capacity for intellectual regeneration.

Notes

Acknowledgments: Special thanks to Ben Singer for helpful and perceptive last-minute advice, to Wanda Strauven for her editorial guidance and her patience, and to Tom Gunning for leading by example.

1. Tom Gunning, *D.W. Griffith and the Origins of American Narrative Film: The Early Years at Biograph* (Urbana: U of Illinois P, 1991) 43.
2. Charles Musser, "Rethinking Early Cinema: Cinema of Attractions and Narrativity," *The Yale Journal of Criticism* 7.2 (1994) 228. Reprinted in the dossier of this volume.
3. Linda Williams, "Introduction," *Viewing Positions: Ways of Seeing Film* (New Brunswick: Rutgers UP, 1995) 12.
4. Musser 211, 227.

5. Tom Gunning, "The Cinema of Attractions: Early Film, Its Spectator and the Avant-Garde," *Early Cinema: Space Frame Narrative*, ed. Thomas Elsaesser (London: British Film Institute, 1990) 60.

6. See, in particular, Charlie Keil, "'Visualised Narratives,' Transitional Cinema, and the Modernity Thesis," *Le Cinéma au tournant de siècle/Cinema at the Turn of the Century*, ed. Claire Dupré la Tour, André Gaudreault and Roberta Pearson (Lausanne/Québec: Payot/Nota Bene, 1998) 123-37; and "'To Here From Modernity': Style, Historiography, and Transitional Cinema," *American Cinema's Transitional Era: Audiences, Institutions, Practices*, ed. Charlie Keil and Shelley Stamp (Berkeley: U of California P, 2004) 51-65.

7. For a response to these arguments, please see Tom Gunning, "Systematizing the Electric Message: Narrative Form, Gender, and Modernity in *The Lonedale Operator*," *American Cinema's Transitional Era* 15-50, especially 44-45.

8. Charles Musser concurs, though he places the time when "American narrative cinema [...] is notable for its relative lack of attractions" somewhat later, in the years 1908-1909. Musser 228.

9. Ben Brewster, "A Bunch of Violets." Unpublished paper, 1991.

10. Tom Gunning, "'Now You See It, Now You Don't': The Temporality of the Cinema of Attractions," *The Velvet Light Trap* 32 (Fall 1993): 4.

11. James Ackerman, "A Theory of Style," *The Journal of Aesthetics and Art Criticism* 20.3 (Spring 1962): 236.

12. This differs in kind from attractions-era stories which are designed to highlight their series of tricks (as in the case of Méliès), because now the novelty aids in the viewer's discernment of diegetically-motivated narrative information. The military plans in BELLE BOYD and the heroine's whereabouts in THE TRAIL OF CARDS exert primary interest as narratively salient plot points.

13. See David Bordwell, *On the History of Film Style* (Cambridge: Harvard UP, 1997); in particular 125-28 and 139.

14. André Bazin, "The Evolution of the Language of Cinema," *What is Cinema?*, vol. 1 (Berkeley: U of California P, 1967) 35-36.

15. Noël Burch, *To the Distant Observer: Form and Meaning in the Japanese Cinema* (Berkeley: U of California P, 1979) 159-60.

Discipline through Diegesis: The Rube Film between "Attractions" and "Narrative Integration"

Thomas Elsaesser

"Life imitates the movies" is a phrase that nowadays only raises eyebrows because it is so clichéd. But one of the conclusions one can draw from this truism is that if we are in some sense already "in" the cinema with what we can say "about" it, then the cinema needs a *theory* that can account for the historical processes that put us "inside," and a *history* that takes account of the ontological anxieties to which this interchangeability of inside and outside gives rise.

In what follows I want to treat this sense of "life" imitating "the cinema" rather than the cinema "representing" life as a moment of rupture in our understanding of the cinema. But this rupture, which some associate with the change from analogue to digital imaging, need not be thought of as primarily technological, ethical or even aesthetic. Besides providing a new standard or medium of inscription, storage and circulation of sensory data and intelligible information, "the digital" can also serve as a metaphor: a metaphor for the discursive space of rupture itself. In other words, I would like to imagine that the paradigm change of analogue/digital – and the media convergence that digitization is said to imply – provides a chance to rethink the idea of cinema and historical change itself: what do we mean by "epistemic break" and "radical rupture," the buzzwords of the 1970s? Or by "emergence," "remediation," "appropriation" and "convergence," the buzzwords of the 1990s: terms that signify the opposite of rupture, namely gradual transition, imperceptible transformation, and what I would call "soft" history? And how does this change relate to the "cinema of attractions," itself a buzzword that has straddled the decades just mentioned, having been coined in the mid-1980s? Placing the cinema of attractions strategically in-between permits me to query a related piece of received wisdom: the denunciation of cinema's teleology, its inevitable turn to narrative. In other words, might it be time to give cinema of attractions' subordinate binary twin – "narrative integration" – another, less dismissive look?

Secondly, what about the cinema's social – or should I say, ethnographic-anthropological – function within the history of modernity and its multitudes? In the 1970s, the cinema's reality effect had to be deconstructed. The movies' purported imitation of life was a sham, a deception, from which the spectator had to be rescued. By the 1990s, this second nature, this naturalization of cinematic illusionism through narrative and the single diegesis (i.e. the coherent space-time continuum) had become first nature: life imitates the movies, precisely. What had happened? Did the cinema play a reactionary role in the 1970s and a progressive role by the 1990s? One could argue the case from both ends: reading Louis Althusser and Michel Foucault, the cinema's effects of interpellation and subjectification made it an ideal apparatus of the disciplinary society. Reading Walter Benjamin and Siegfried Kracauer (after Althusser and Foucault...) the cinema imposed a mode of *distraction* as well as *attention* and thus exposed the contradictions between *Erfahrung* (narratively integrated, authentic experience) and *Erlebnis* (unmediated, traumatic shock-experience). Rehearsing this tension between shock experience and narrative, did the cinema become, in Benjamin's words, modernity's optical unconscious?[1] By conflating the two (because claiming a progressive, modernizing role for distraction/attention), does the cinema of attractions function as a therapeutic or compensatory, and thus *disciplining* apparatus of integration, even though it is opposed to "narrative integration," or does it maintain a moment of irrecoverable rupture? Is it rupture itself – in the trauma-producing form of the contemporary cinema of attractions – which now has a disciplining function, readying the laboring body under the sign of *flexibilization* for its daily adaptation to the machines of surveillance, by a new kind of "linearized" attention to sensory stimulus and a distracted focalization on ocular detail, at the expense of (narrative, but also bodily) integration?[2]

Continuity and Rupture in Pre- and Post-Classical Cinema

For an answer to these questions, one might have to re-examine not only the idea of continuity and rupture in the fabric of the experience of cinema, but also the dynamics of convergence and divergence, of self-reference and self-differentiation, in short the idea of periodization, in the history of cinema. What arose in the 1980s in the wake of "new" or "revisionist film history" was a discussion about the radical otherness of the cinema of the first two decades. Noël Burch was the first to posit an epistemic break between "primitive cinema" (the cinema up to 1917) and the classical narrative cinema under Hollywood hegemony.[3] It is this "primitive cinema" that was re-baptized "early cinema" but eventually came to be known more widely as "cinema of attractions." Compared to the mode of representation that replaced it – the cinema of narrative integration – the cinema of attractions was the more authentic, the more interesting and even the more sophisticated of the two modes. This ran counter to accepted belief, according to which early cinema was unpolished, infantile, insecure – and above all, unable to tell stories, which was up to then believed to be the manifest destiny of the cinema as both an art form and an entertainment medium. In good Foucauldian fashion, emphasizing the differences separating early from classical cinema was to rid film history of its teleological assumptions.

Tom Gunning and André Gaudreault had launched the binary pair ("system of monstrative attractions"/"system of narrative integration") in 1985,[4] in a sense summarizing the debates between Noël Burch, Charles Musser, Barry Salt over the kinds of otherness and degrees of autonomy manifested by the cinema up to the First World War.[5] At times standing by itself, at others contrasted to the "cinema of narrative integration," the "cinema of attractions" named the different features of the early cinema's distinctive mode, quickly displacing not only Burch's "primitive mode of representation," but also Musser's "exhibition-led editorial control," as well as Gaudreault's "monstration" and the other, similarly aimed locutions. Not the least of the reasons why Gunning's formulation won the day and has become so extraordinary successful was that at the end of his article, he speculated that the cinema of attractions offered surprising parallels with contemporary filmmaking, where physical spectacle seems once more to gain in importance over carefully motivated and plotted narrative. Action-oriented heroes predominated over psychologically rounded characters, heralding a performative style, again similar to early cinema practice, where spectacular set pieces were responsible for a discontinuous rather than a smooth visual experience. More generally, it could be argued that the psychological realism of classical cinema had, in the blockbuster become subordinated to differently motivated types of fantasy and excess, again not unlike the rough-and-tumble of early chase films, the comic farces and slapstick routines. What the frantic pursuit or the graphic humour was in early film genres, became the roller coaster rides, the horror, slasher, splatter, or kung-fu scenes of contemporary cinema: skillfully mounted scenes of mayhem and destruction. These do not have to build up the classical arch of suspense, but aim for thrills and surprise, which in the action genres are delivered at close range and with maximum bodily impact. As in early cinema, audiences expect such set pieces, which suspend or interrupt the narrative flow, and in this sense externalize the action. The cinema of attractions, by focusing less on linear narrative progression, manages to draw the spectator's attention to a unique form of display, and thus a special economy of attention and sensory involvement.

Following these thoughts further and extending them to the realm of the digital, other writers have argued that the electronic media also fall under the heading of the cinema of attractions.[6] By encouraging viewers or users to immerse themselves in the image stream or data flow as total environment rather than to relate to the screen or monitor as a framed view or window on the world, both interactive and on-line forms of entertainment seemed to foster tactile, haptic modes of engagement. "Attraction" also seemed an apposite term to describe the thrills of video games, because they, too, created a different contact space between player and the screen as interface. Finally, parallels could be drawn between today's Hollywood big budget feature films as multi-functional, multi-purpose, multi-platform audiovisual products for the entertainment market (merchandising, music, fashion) and the surprisingly multi-medial context of early cinema. For the event-driven appeal of the modern blockbuster, with its ability to colonize social and media space with advertising and promotional "happenings" also has its predecessors from the 1910s onwards. For instance, we see the same kind of thinking behind the very successful Passion films of Pathé, the elaborate publicity around films specially produced for Christmas, or the large-scale disaster films that Italian producers first specialized in.[7] Everywhere, references back to early cinema practice seemed to offer themselves, which in turn made these nearly forgotten films appear strangely familiar and once more even popular in retrospectives and at festivals.[8]

Thus, Gunning's initial reflections on the relation between pre-1917 cinema and the avant-garde have been used for a much broader hypothesis, suggesting that early cinema, understood as a cinema of attractions, can encourage us to think of film history generally as a series of parallel (or "parallax"[9]) histories, organized around a number of shifting parameters which tend to repeat themselves periodically, often signifying also the subversion of a previously existing standard. Coming exactly ten years after Laura Mulvey's "Visual Pleasure and Narrative Cinema," which established a gendered opposition between spectacle and narrative and between two different modes of display (voyeurism and fetishism),[10] the "cinema of attractions" took over from Mulvey (whom Gunning cites in his essay)[11] as an almost magic formula for film studies, the Sesame opening new doors of perception and of classification.

Yet when applying this template to other moments of rupture, such as the opposition between the old Hollywood studio-system and the "New Hollywood" of the 1970s, and subsequently, the morphing of "New Hollywood" into "New New" or postmodern Hollywood, it became clear that revisionist historiography had to learn to accommodate also the continuities and mutual interferences between these periods rather than insist only on epistemic breaks (similar work has now been done on the 1910s, where several scholars have mitigated the rupture thesis by showing the different ways in which the years between 1909 and 1917 were a period of more fluid "transition").[12]

Paradoxes of Attention and Attraction

I want to argue that this fate of the "cinema of attractions" is symptomatic of an initial dilemma, already contained in the pairing that opposed it to a "cinema of narrative integration," but aggravated when the term is transferred to other periods, styles or modes. It is true that "cinema of attractions" perfectly fits many of our current preoccupations, including our present interest in bodily sensation, the history of perception and the "attention economy."[13] But the very smoothness of the tool it hands us comes at a cost, both historically and conceptually. Historically, it does not allow us to understand how and why the one-and-a-half to two-hour feature film has proved to be the standard product of the film industry. Nor can it account for cross-media configurations (adapting or re-purposing the same "content" or stories in different periods or for different media: the "postmodern" side of early cinema, if you like), or explain the coexistence, the overlap and sometimes interference among historically successive or wholly different technologies. For instance, early cinema did not relate to the magic lantern in strictly causal terms nor did it "respond" to it, by solving problems that had arisen in the practice of magic lantern shows. Cinema re-purposed aspects of magic lantern technology and parasitically occupied part of its public sphere. Television has not "evolved" out of cinema nor did it replace it. Digital images were not something the film industry was waiting for, in order to overcome any felt "deficiencies" in its production of special effects. Likewise, the history of sound in the late 1920s and throughout the 1930s still poses major problems of how to factor in the "media-interference" from radio and the co-presence or competition of the gramophone industry. The same goes for the history of television in the 1950s and its relation to radio, to canned theater or to the more avant-garde or experimental uses of video. Or how can we fit in the more recent migration of the moving image into the museum and the rise of installation art? This points to another paradox, namely that the immersive and transparent experience of the contemporary multiplex screen exists side by side with its apparent opposite: the multi-screen hyper-mediated experience of television and the billboard-and-poster cityscape.[14] On the one hand the IMAX screen and "virtual reality," on the other, the website, the computer's "windows" environment or the liquid crystal display on our mobile phone. Can we explain all of them as versions of the "cinema of attractions," without evacuating the concept of all meaning and reference?

In other words, once one takes such a longer view, it becomes obvious that a distinction such as "cinema of attractions" versus "cinema of narrative integration" is a binary opposition in which one term has become the dominant, and yet where the historical priority of one term (cinema of attractions) nonetheless seems to validate the conceptual priority of the other (cinema of narrative inte-gration), against which the first one appears to stage a resistance and a revolt. The provisional and variable nature of pre-, para- or post-cinematic pleasures and attractions (dioramas and panoramas, Hale's Tours and phantom rides, haptic-tactile images and bodily sensations in early cinema, as well as the con-temporary configuration of sound and image around portable devices such as MP3 players and mobile phones) make it evident how much the cinema, even after more than a hundred years, is still in permanent flux and becoming. Or, again put differently: given the cinema's opportunistic adaptation to all manner of adjacent or related media, it has always been fully "grown up" and complete in itself. At the same time, it still has yet to be "invented," if one is looking for a single ancestor or wonders about its purpose in human "evolution" – as André Bazin, who left us with the question "what is cinema" and who himself specu-lated on its "ontology," knew only too well.[15] The "unfinished" nature of both the cinema and the efforts to write its histories in the context of other media practices help to highlight several of the drawbacks of the seminal concept of the "cinema of attractions" beyond the problematic trope of the cyclical "re-turn."

For instance, there is the contested status, which the cinema of attractions occupies on its own terrain, the field of early cinema. Several other, competing explanations for the historical phenomena which the cinema of attractions so elegantly assembles under a single denominator have been offered by historians such as Charles Musser in the US, Laurent Mannoni in France or Corinna Mül-ler in Germany.[16] They are among the historians who have provided counter-evidence, by arguing, among other things, that the life-cycle of short films and the performative "numbers" principle as a programming and exhibition prac-tice in early cinema can best be understood in terms of a set of economic para-meters obtaining in the late 1900s. The disappearance of these features around 1909-12 in favor of the longer film would then have to be directly correlated to the conditions necessary to establish the film business as an industry. As a con-sequence, "narrative integration" turns out to be a much more contradictory process than Gunning's binary opposition (but also, of course, the old linear history of narrative as the cinema's natural destiny) suggests. In Musser and Müller, it is the struggle over control between the exhibitor and the producer, the shift from buying to renting films, the imposition of zoning agreements and exclusive rights (monopoly) for first-run theatrical exhibition, the difficulties of agreeing on norms of what constitutes a "film" which takes center stage. The "cinema of attractions" formula, strictly applied would elide these industrial-institutional contexts that give Gunning's formal distinctions their ultimate rea-lity and historical ground.

Likewise, there are other models of how to explain post-classical cinema. For instance, the revival of a numbers principle of staged combats alternating with seemingly self-contained narrative episodes in modern action-adventure films has more to do with the fact that a feature film is made today with a view to its secondary uses on television. Television, at least in the US context (but increasingly also in the rest of the world) means commercial breaks during the broadcast of a feature film. The "return of the numbers principle" is thus a direct consequence of the cinema adapting to its television uses, as well as the increasing need for individual chapter breaks on a DVD release, rather than any inherent affinity with early cinema. In other words, too easy an analogy between "early" and "post-classical" cinema sacrifices historical distinctions in favor of polemical intent, too keen perhaps to squeeze the hegemony of the classical cinema in a sort of pincer movement at either end of a hundred year continuum.

The Rube Films: Toward a Theory of Embedded Attention

And yet, there is no doubt that the "cinema of attractions" names an important part of the paradigm shift represented by the transition from early to classical cinema. If Burch was the one who "knew" that something had changed, Gunning was the first to name it and explain it in ways that made sense not only to professional film historians, but – at an intuitive, experiential level – also to many students not only of early film but of the contemporary media. So how can we accommodate the insights of the cinema of attractions while beginning to cautiously revise the historical pedigrees it presumes to have established, and to displace the terminological binaries on which it has built its formal and conceptual foundations? I want to sketch briefly such a possible revision by taking one particular type of film practice associated with early cinema, and repeatedly revived in subsequent decades. It concerns an aspect of reflexivity and self-reference, display and performativity that we have come to associate with the "cinema of attractions" but whose implications for both narrative and for the civilizing-modernizing-disciplining functions of cinema exceed the brief that the cinema of attractions gives itself, especially when it sets itself off against the implied norm of "narrative integration."

This type of film was originally referred to as "Uncle Josh" films, but has survived as "Rube" films. They emerged with the origins of the cinema itself, at the turn of the century, first in Great Britain and the US, but similar films were also produced in other countries.[17] They often presented a film-within-a-film, that is, they showed a member of the cinema audience, who does not seem to know that film images are representations to be looked at rather than objects to be touched and handled or scenes to be entered and immersed in. These so-called "rubes" or simpleton spectators usually climb up to the stage and either attempt to grasp the images on the screen, or want to join the characters on the screen, in order to interfere with an ongoing action or look behind the image to discover what is hidden or kept out of sight. The best-known example of this genre is UNCLE JOSH AT THE MOVING PICTURE SHOW, made by Edwin S. Porter for the Edison Company in 1902:

> Here we present a side-splitter. Uncle Josh occupies a box at a vaudeville theater, and a moving picture show is going on. First there appears upon the screen a dancer. Uncle Josh jumps to the stage and endeavors to make love to her, but she flits away, and immediately there appears upon the screen the picture of an express train running at sixty miles an hour. Uncle Josh here becomes panic stricken and fearing to be struck by the train, makes a dash for his box. He is no sooner seated than a country couple appears upon the screen at a well. Before they pump the pail full of water they indulge in a love-making scene. Uncle Josh evidently thinks he recognizes his own daughter, and jumping again upon the stage he removes his coat and prepares to chastise the lover, and grabbing the moving picture screen he hauls it down, and to his great surprise finds a Kinetoscope operator in the rear. The operator is made furious by Uncle Josh interrupting his show, and grappling with him they roll over and over upon the stage in an exciting encounter.[18]

UNCLE JOSH AT THE MOVING PICTURE SHOW was a remake of a British prototype, Robert Paul's THE COUNTRYMAN'S FIRST SIGHT OF THE ANIMATED PICTURES (1901). The differences, however, are telling. Porter, for instance, substituted for the films-within-a-film his own company's films PARISIAN DANCE (copyrighted 15 January 1897) and THE BLACK DIAMOND EXPRESS (copyrighted 27 April 1897) thus taking reflexivity from the realm of illusionism and trickery into that of product promotion and self-advertising.

These Uncle Josh films pose a twofold question. Are they intended, as is often claimed, as didactic parables to teach a rural or immigrant audience how not to behave in the cinema, by putting up to ridicule someone like themselves?[19] Yet was there ever such an audience, or a moment of "infancy" and simplicity in the history of the movies, where such an ontological confusion with regards to objects and persons might have existed? What comes to mind are the reports that at the first Lumière showings of L'ARRIVÉE D'UN TRAIN (1895), viewers fled from the theater by the oncoming train – a situation explicitly cited in Paul's and Porter's countrymen films. There is, as historians have pointed out, no documentary evidence that such panics ever occurred.[20] In other words, they belong to the folklore and urban mythology that early cinema generated about itself, realizing that stories of the spectatorial effects of moving images do make good publicity for the cinema as an "attraction." In relation to this first level of self-reference, the Uncle Josh films present a second level of self-reference, citing the first, and thus they stage a cinema of attractions, by promoting a form of spectatorship where the spectator watches, reacts to, and interacts with a motion picture, while remaining seated and still, retaining all affect resolutely within him/herself.

This, then, would raise the further question: Do these films construct their meta-level of self-reference, in order to "discipline" their audience? Not by showing them how not to behave, i.e. by way of negative example, shaming and proscription, but rather, by a more subtle process of internalized self-censorship? Do the Rube films not discipline their audience by allowing them to enjoy their own superior form of spectatorship, even if that superiority is achieved at the price of self-censorship and self-restraint? The audience laughs at a simpleton and village idiot, who is kept at a distance and ridiculed, and thereby it can flatter itself with a self-image of urban sophistication. The punishment meted out to Uncle Josh by the projectionist is both allegorized as the reverse side of cinematic pleasure (watch out, "behind" the screen, there is the figure of the "master") and internalized as self-control: in the cinema – as elsewhere in the new world of display and self-display – the rule is "you may look but don't touch."[21] This makes possible an additional dimension of the genre, in which the cinema colludes with the civilization process as conceived by Norbert Elias (or Pierre Bourdieu)[22] according to whom the shift of bodily orientation from the proximity sense of touch to the distance-and-proximity regulating sense of sight constitutes a quantum leap in human evolution. What, however, characterizes the cinema would be that it supports but also exacerbates this quantum leap, by "performing" the kind of cognitive-sensory double-bind which is usually associated with the commodity fetishism inculcated by the shop window display, that also says: "look, don't touch," in order to resolve the conflict by relieving the eye with the promise of possession (the plenitude of touch) through purchase. In the cinema, by contrast, the same scene of desire and discipline is staged as a form of traumatization of both touch and sight, both senses at once over-stimulated and censored, seduced and chastised, obsessively and systematically tied to the kinds of delays and deferrals we associate with narrative.

Two scenes from films of the mid-1920s exemplify and allegorize these dilemmas, by precisely citing the Rube film genre, while allegorizing it in different modalities. I am thinking of the scene of the dreaming projectionist in Buster Keaton's SHERLOCK JR. (1924) and in Fritz Lang's SIEGFRIEDS TOD (also 1924) the scene of the hero's encounter with Alberich and his first sight of the Nibelungen treasure. In both cases, the film spectator's implicit contract with the (barred) haptic palpability of the moving image and the perversity of that contract are made explicit. In the first one, we see the veritable ontological groundlessness that underlies cinematic representation (the master-projectionist behind the screen has disappeared, to become the perilous void within the image – note that now it is the projectionist himself who is the "Rube," confirming that already in Uncle Josh we are dealing with a philosophical-ontological dilemma and not with an issue of sociological maladjustment). In the second example from SIEGFRIEDS TOD, the allegorical import with respect to commodity fetishism is made further explicit, but rendered no less vertiginous in its implications.

After having defeated Alberich, the guardian of the Nibelungen treasure, by wresting from him his helmet of invisibility, Siegfried is shown by him the treasure, but conjured up in the tense of anticipation and in the form of a moving image projection on a rock. Stunned by its splendor, Siegfried wants to grasp the image, upon which it disappears like a mirage, pushing and sucking him forward into penetrating further into the world of Alberich. At one level, Siegfried shows himself to be the cinematic simpleton, the *Thumbe Thor*, in the Rube tradition. Ironically inverted in the rock is the notion of the shop window as display case. At another level, Siegfried is the hero as conqueror, lording it over a subservient and servile Alberich whose image is made the more troubling, especially for our sensibilities, by his stereotypical representation as a Jewish merchant and department store owner. However, at the meta-meta-level of Weimar cinema's predilection for sorcerers, puppet-masters and their nemeses, the unruly slave or apprentice, Alberich and Siegfried belong in the same tradition that connects the carnival stall owner, Caligari to his medium Cesare, or Mephisto to Faust in Murnau's film of that title. The treasure dangling before Siegfried's eyes acts as a visualization or allegory of the cinema itself as a machine that plants the never-to-be-satisfied desire for palpability in the viewer, and thus makes the cinema itself into an obsessive wish-generating but fulfillment deferring machine, as if to already indicate – by the enthronement of the eye over hand and touch – the eye's eventual ruin.

The theorist of this promise of proximity enshrined in the cinema, and also elegiac allegorist of its traumatic deferral is of course Walter Benjamin. One recalls the famous passage from the "Artwork" essay, in which he outlines the cultural-political significance of tactile proximity and haptic perception as it takes shape around the moving image and its contact with the masses:

> The desire of contemporary masses to bring things "closer" spatially and humanly, which is just as ardent as their bent toward overcoming the uniqueness of everyday reality by accepting its reproduction. Every day the urge grows stronger to get hold of an object at very close range by way of its likeness, its reproduction.[23]

What here is hinted at through the act of substitution – likeness – and mechanical duplication – reproduction – is the ontological gap that opens up in the trade-off between the one sense of proximity and the other of distance-and-proximity, and also the irreversible nature of the deferral which pushes haptic perception into the realm of the optical (unconscious), and ownership into the realm of obsessive and phantasmagoric possession. The appropriate cinematic illustration of Benjamin might be a scene from Jean-Luc Godard's LES CARABI-NIERS (1963) – a film precisely about the category mistake of thinking that the civilizational "quantum leap" from hand to eye is reversible, when the two country bumpkins go to war in order to rape, plunder and possess, and happily return with a suitcase full of postcards of the sights, monuments and women they believe they have conquered and taken possession of from the enemy. As will be recalled, LES CARABINIERS also features a famous re-creation of the "Rube" film, whose own complex double frame of reference cleverly comments on the second level of self-reference of the original via the inscription of the camera.[24]

The Performativity of Narrative: Diegesis De- and Re-constructed

What I am trying to suggest by this reference to the genre of the Rube film, in relation to attraction and attention, are some of the conceptual traps and dialectical turns that seem hidden in the notion of a "cinema of attractions" when juxtaposed with a cinema of narrative integration. The Rube films indicate to me at least that performativity and display, the existence of a scene or action in the cinema for the sheer pleasure of its "to-be-looked-at-ness" perhaps needs to be passed through the allegorical filter of Benjamin's meditations on modernity, proximity and the optical unconscious. But the oppositional term – narrative integration – may also have to be opened up, seeing how many diegetic-ontological layers these Rube films put into play, in their insistence on "attraction," distraction and selective attention. In other words, in the way it is presently employed, the notion of a recurrent, cyclical and in some sense, oppositional "cinema of attractions" is perhaps both too polemical and yet not radical enough, if we really want to break with the dominance of what we think we understand by "narrative integration." Or rather, if we seriously want to think not only about a post-classical, but also about a post-narrative cinema. A more thoroughgoing revisionism would have as its aim to once more re-assess the enunciative, performative status of the cinema in relation to the concept of diegesis, that is, the temporal, spatial and linguistic sited- and situated-ness of the cinematic event and its experience by a body and subject.

In all the cases of early cinema practice, which the cinema of attraction has tried to identify as typical for its mode, the cinematic event is precisely a process, taking place between the screen and the audience. As literalized in the Rube films, these interact at all times and cannot be rigorously separated from each other, as is the case, if the oppositional pair of cinema of attractions versus cinema of narrative integration is to be believed. I have written elsewhere[25] about the peculiar acts of transformation that turn an audience imagined to be physically present into individualized spectators, and which turn a stage imagined to be physically present into a screen, and thus an imaginary space. It is a process that lies at the very heart of narrative, which is why the Rube films finally signal to me the very impossibility of separating "attraction" from "narrative." And just as the dynamics which at every point in the cinema's history play between screen space and audience space, help to define the kinds of diegetic worlds possible in a given film or genre, so parameters like fixed spectator/ mobile view, mobile spectator/fixed view (and their permutations) are important clues to the embodied or site-specific "diegetic reality" of post-narrative modes of the moving image, as in video-installations or the emergent digital art.

The question, then, is not so much: on one side spectacle, on the other narrative. Rather: we need to ask how the cinema manages the event character of the film performance (one meaning of the "cinema of attractions") in such a way as to enter into a seemingly natural union with linear, causally motivated, character centered narrative. This would allow one to raise the follow-up question, from the perspective of a generalized "cinema of attractions," i.e. a cinema as event and experience. Under what conditions is it conceivable that the moving image no longer requires as its main support the particular form of time/space/ agency we know as classical narrative, and still establish a viable "diegesis," understood as the regulated interaction between place, space, time and subject? What forms of indexicality or iconicity are necessary, to accept other combinations of sounds and images as relating to a "me" – as subject, observer, spectator, user? The answers often given today are "virtual reality," "interactivity," "immersivity." But are these not mere attempts at re-labeling without confronting the question of what is a cinematic diegesis – with the possible disadvantage of being too focused on the subject without specifying a temporal (virtual reality) or spatial (interactivity) parameter, and giving priority to only one of the cinema's (weaker) effects, that of "presence," if understood as "real-time"?

Space, Time and Performative Agency in Contemporary Forms of Spectatorship

The media worlds we inhabit today are clearly not those of the single diegesis of classical cinema. They are ones that permit different spaces to coexist and different time frames to overlap. To that extent, they seem to be non-narrative in the classical sense, but that does not mean we need to file them under "attraction." They are diegetic, in that they address us, within the enunciative frames, constituted by the deictic marks of "I" and "you," and of the "here" and "now" of discourse. Discourse is here understood in Emile Benveniste's sense of being crucially constituted by these shifters and deictic marks just mentioned, whose characteristic it is to be at once universal in their use and unique in their reference, but in each case requiring additional specifications of time, place and self, provided by the speaker's presence.[26] The enunciative act, in other words, is always a function of making explicit the implicit reference points, the self-reference (deictics), the data or evidence, on which the speaking position, and thus the meaning of an utterance depend.[27] It is within such a redefinition of diegesis and enunciation that the embodied nature of perception can once more be thought, beyond any hasty opposition between hand and eye, touch and sight.

But such a "shifter" position within discourse identifies an empty place, activated only when filled by a presence. It is in order to resolve this issue, or at least to specify its conditions of possibility that a second step is required: what in the introduction I called "ontological," regarding both the spectators' particular "being-in-the-world," and the status of the moving images as "world-making," i.e. "life imitating the movies." Discussing this "cliché" with which I started under the heading of "diegesis," as a form of space/time/agency/subject articulation, has the advantage that the flow of images – irrespective of genre (thriller/musical), style (montage/continuity editing) or mode (documentary/fiction) – can be understood as not necessarily "real," but nevertheless as constituting a "world." In this respect, the concept of diegesis is meant to overcome several kinds of dichotomies: not only that between documentary and fantasy, or the opposition realism versus illusionism, but also the one between the "cinema of attractions" and the "cinema of narrative integration." These seem to me to stand in the way, rather than help when "revising" film historiography in light of the modernity thesis, when determining the place of cinema in the contemporary multi-media landscape, or when speculating, Deleuze-fashion, about the modern cinema's time-image ontologies. Focusing on one of early cinema's most crucial variables, namely the relation between screen space and auditorium space, I have argued that both spaces, taken together in their mutual interdependence, made up early cinema's unique diegetic space. Each viewing was a distinct performance, where spectators felt themselves directly addressed by the on-screen performer, and where the audience was assumed by the film to be present as a collectivity, rather than envisaged as individuals, interpellated through imaginary subject positions.[28]

If I am here arguing for reinstating the concept of diegesis, it is because I not only want early cinema studies to be able to provide the paradigms for studying the cinema as a whole. I also think these paradigms can become productive for understanding the kinds of interactions (converging or self-differentiating) between old and new media, which digitization may not have initiated, but certainly accelerated. In other words, in order to make headway with the idea of "cinema as event and experience" (next to, and following on from "films as artworks and texts"), we need to find a term that allows for the conjunction of the variables of time/space/place/agency that are explicit in the term diegesis and for the deictic markers that are implicit in the term discourse, as defined above, and yet not exclusive to cinema. In *The Language of New Media*, Lev Manovich put forward a different contender for the same role, using the term "interface" to designate the meta-space that enables and regulates the kinds of contact that can be made between audience space and screen space, but also between computer user and software.[29] I have chosen "diegesis" because, unlike Manovich, who looks at the cinema from the perspective of digital media, I come to contemporary media practice from the study of cinema, and also because, as I hope to show, the ontological, world-making associations of the term diegesis are relevant to my overall argument – extending to that part of new media now referred to as "augmented reality." The kinds of changes – architectural, social, economic – that eventually led to the separation of the two types of spaces in early cinema, making screen space autonomous, and dividing the audience into individual spectators would thus be the conditions of possibility of the emergence of classical cinema. In their totality they establish a new diegetic space, with formal, pictorial and narratological consequences, and it is this totality I would want to call classical cinema's specific "ontology." My argument would be that with augmented reality and similar concepts, this classical cinema's ontology is both preserved and overcome, giving the terms diegesis (formerly narrative integration) and discipline (formerly distraction/attention through subjectification) a new valency.

The Return of the Rube

How much of a learning process this separating/re-aligning of spaces and subjects involves, can be gauged by precisely the Rube films discussed earlier, which as we saw, show a character, repeatedly making category mistakes about the respective ontology of the cinematic, filmic and profilmic spaces he finds himself in. By referring to our present complex media spaces as in some sense a "return of the Rube" (the "return" being in honor of the "return to a cinema of attractions"), one can, however, also argue that early cinema's diegetic space was a complex, but comprehensible arrangement of time, space, place and diec-

tic markers. Fixed or mobile spectator, continuous or single shot, edited sequence or tableau, the look into the camera or off-frame: all of these parameters
are staged in early cinema as relevant variables in their different permutations.
The conclusion I would draw is that the successive phases of the cinema, but
also the cinema's relation to other media forms, such as television, video art
and digital media, can be mapped by analyzing their different and distinct diegetic worlds, comprising the technical apparatus and mental dispositifs, but
also depend on the temporal, spatial and enunciative locators/activators that
together constitute their particular "diegesis." For instance, the viewer who has
the set on all day, to accompany his or her daily routine has activated a different
diegesis of television than the viewer who sits down to watch a particular program, lights dimmed and remote control safely out of reach.[30] But feature films,
too, confront us with characters who "engage" with different diegeses, defined
by their temporal and spatial co-presence, activated by a performative or enunciative gesture. One could name THE MATRIX trilogy (1999-2003), but a possibly
more interesting example, because of its indirect reference to the Rube complex
of "acting as-if" would be Steven Spielberg's MINORITY REPORT (2002) where
the character of Tom Cruise tries to "touch" his missing son, whose (moving)
image he projects in his living room by means of a hologram screening system.
Cruise acts like a Rube: (he knows) his son is not there, and the hologram is a
mere image, yet nevertheless he wants to touch it/him.

  Thus, early cinema, classical cinema and digital cinema (to name only these)
could be mapped on the matrix of particular processes of "ontologization."
Each mode would be defined by the spatio-temporal and enunciative relation
that an actual spectator constructs for the images and the apparatus, and the
degree to which the images are separated from/indexed for not only their material referents, but also their individual recipients. In this I follow Francesco
Casetti who in *Inside the Gaze/Dentro lo sguardo* sets up a comparable typology
of variables, correlating types of shots with enunciative positions on the part of
the spectator.[31] Just as in painting one can describe the relation between frescos
and easel painting as a correlation of site, size and spectator, where ease of access, transportability and spectatorial freedom of movement compensate for the
reduction in size and the loss of site-specific markers of meaning when comparing the easel painting to the fresco, so in the history of cinema and in the interaction between the media, a similar set of variables could be established, whose
default values are the narrational and spatio-temporal parameters of spectators
imagined as physically present/invisibly present, directly addressed/sutured
into the fiction, and the other markers already named under the heading of
"diegesis." As we know, the cinema stabilized as an industry around aligning
the moving image with the special logic of linear narrative and multi-level embedded narration. But the histories of television or of video installations indicate

that there are other options. For instance, the genres of news, talk-shows or talent contests suggest that television has developed its own forms of diegesis (transferential as opposed to closed around a self-contained fiction), just as a video installation draws its place, time and subject-effect from the "world" of the museum, and brings this diegetic space into crisis (see the recurring debates around the "white cube" threatened by the "black box").[32]

Independently from the arrival of digital images, the particular temporal and discursive logic we call narrative may turn out to have been only one type of syntax (among others) that naturalizes these processes of separation and enunciative indexing, of mobility and circulation. In other words, it is now possible to envisage the historical conditions, where other forms of aligning or "knitting" sounds and images, with other architectures of space and other grammatologies of time, take over the tasks so far fulfilled by narrative: to create the diegetic effect that can open a space for the discursive effect of a subject-shifter. The moving image would thus "emancipate" itself from narrative, as it has been claimed by the avant-gardes in the 1960s and 70s and by the digital media in the 1980s and 90s (as "interactivity" and "virtual reality"). It would do so, though, in relation to establishing particular forms of time/space/subject: worlds, in which the parameters of narrative may well continue to play a (possibly subordinate) part.

If in the transition from early to classical cinema, it was narrative and the logic of implication and inference that "liberated" the image from its "here" and "now" (though not the spectator), then the move from the photographic to the post-photographic or digital mode could entail another "liberation," but it might just as well amount to an adjustment of diegetic spaces.[33] Certainly, when watching the video and installation work (from the 1960s and 70s, i.e. prior to digital images) of Andy Warhol, Dan Graham, Andrew McCall or Malcolm LeGrice, I am reminded of my Rube films, seeing how these artists manage to trap spectators in time-delay mirror mazes and have them catch themselves in cognitive loops. Could it be, then, that "interface" and "installation" are merely the shorthand terms for subsuming the diegetic space we call narrative under some other form of time/space (dis-)continuum, which spectators encounter or inhabit, while "learning" afresh different roles and forms of spectatorship: as viewers, users, visitors, witnesses, players and, I would add, especially as Rubes?

Notes

Material in this essay has previously been published as "Film History as Media Archaeology" in *CiNéMAS* 14.2-3 (2005): 75-117.

1. Walter Benjamin, *Reflections: Essays, Aphorisms, Autobiographical Writings*, trans. Edmund Jephcott, ed. Peter Demetz (New York: Schocken, 1978).

2. The term "linearized" was introduced into film studies by Noël Burch, "Passion, poursuite: la linearisation," *Communications* 38 (1983): 30-50.

3. One is reminded of the Pre-Raphaelites, their preference for Giotto's complexly spatialized narratives in his frescos at the Scrovegni Chapel in Padua. Coinciding with the rise of photography and antedating Cubism, they used Giotto in order to declare war on the perspectival, theatrical, illusionistic pictorial space of the Renaissance and Baroque.

4. At the Cerisy conference "Nouvelles approches de l'histoire du cinéma" in the summer of 1985. See André Gaudreault and Tom Gunning, "Le cinéma des premiers temps: un défi à l'histoire du cinéma?" *Histoire du cinéma. Nouvelles approches*, ed. Jacques Aumont, André Gaudreault and Michel Marie (Paris: Sorbonne, 1989) 49-63. This article appears in English translation in the dossier of the present volume.

5. Noël Burch, *Life to these Shadows* (London: Scolar, 1990); Charles Musser, *Before the Nickelodeon* (Berkeley: U of California P, 1991); and Barry Salt, *Film Style and Technology: History and Analysis*, 2nd ed. (London: Starword, 1992).

6. For the treatment of special effects as "attractions," see Vivian Sobchack, *Screening Space. The American Science Fiction Film*, 2nd ed. (New York: Ungar, 1987); Scott Bukatman, *Terminal Identity. The Virtual Subject in Postmodern Science Fiction* (Durham: Duke UP, 1993); Miriam Hansen, "Early cinema, late cinema: permutations of the public sphere," *Screen* 34.3 (1993): 197-210. See also the contributions by Sobchack, Tomasovic and Røssaak in this volume.

7. For an analysis of early disaster films, see Michael Wedel, "Schiffbruch mit Zuschauer. Das Ereigniskino des Mime Misu," *Kino der Kaiserzeit*, ed. Thomas Elsaesser and Michael Wedel (Munich: Edition text + kritik, 2002) 197-252.

8. The best-known and most established festivals of early cinema are the *Giornate del cinema muto* at Pordenone/Sacile, and the *Cinema ritrovato* festival at Bologna, annually since the mid-1980s and 1990s, but there are many other regular or irregular venues now celebrating early or silent cinema.

9. The term "parallax historiography" was coined by Catherine Russell, "Parallax Historiography and the Flâneur: Intermediality in Pre- and Post-Classical Cinema," *Scope* (July 2000): http://www.nottingham.ac.uk/film/journal/articles/parallax historiography.htm. Published in French: "L'historiographie parallaxiale et la flâneuse: le cinéma pré- et postclassique," trans. François Primeau and Denis Simard, *CiNéMAS* 10.2-3 (2000): 151-68.

10. Laura Mulvey, *Visual and Other Pleasures* (Bloomington: Indiana UP, 1989).

11. See also the contributions by Bukatman and Gunning in this volume.

12. See essays by Yuri Tsivian, Kristin Thompson, Elena Dagrada and myself on different films and directors from the 1910s in *A Second Life: German Cinema's First Decade*, ed. Thomas Elsaesser (Amsterdam: Amsterdam UP, 1996); and Ben Brewster, "Traffic in Souls: An Experiment in Feature-Length Narrative Construction," *Cinema Journal* 31.1 (1991): 38-39.

13. See among others the books of Jonathan Crary, *Techniques of the Observer* (Cambridge: MIT P, 1992) and *Suspensions of Perception* (Cambridge: MIT P, 1999); and Thomas H. Davenport and John C. Beck, *The Attention Economy* (Cambridge: Harvard Business School P, 2001).

14. See the distinctions made by Jay David Bolter and Richard Grusin in *Remediation: Understanding New Media* (Cambridge: MIT P, 1999).

15. André Bazin, after reading Georges Sadoul's *Histoire du cinéma*, was much impressed by the evidence that early cinema was often combined with sound, had used stereoscopic devices and featured mostly color: "The nostalgia that some still feel for the silent screen does not go far enough back into the childhood of the seventh art. [...] Every new development added to the cinema today [i.e. in the 1950s: color, wide-screen, 3D] must, paradoxically, take it nearer and nearer to its origins. In short, cinema has not yet been invented!" André Bazin, "The Myth of Total Cinema," *What is Cinema?*, vol. 1 (Berkeley: U of California P, 1969) 21.

16. Charles Musser, *The Emergence of Cinema* (Berkeley: U of California P, 1994); Laurent Mannoni, *The Great Art of Light and Shadow: Archaeology of the Cinema*, trans. and ed. Richard Crangle (Exeter: U of Exeter P, 2000); and Corinna Müller, "Anfänge der Filmgeschichte. Produktion, Foren und Rezeption," *Die Mobilisierung des Sehens. Zur Vor- und Frühgeschichte des Films in Literatur und Kunst*, ed. Harro Segeberg (München: Fink, 1996) 293-324.

17. For an extensive discussion of Rube films in American cinema, see Miriam Hansen, *Babel & Babylon: Spectatorship in American Silent Film* (Cambridge: Harvard UP, 1997) 25-30.

18. *Edison catalogue* 1902, online at: http://www.us.imdb.com/title/tt0000414/plotsummary

19. See for instance Isabelle Morissette, "Reflexivity in Spectatorship: The Didactic Nature of Early Silent Films," *Offscreen* (July 2002): http://www.horschamp.qc.ca/new_offscreen/reflexivity.html. "The spectator [in the film] is a country bumpkin and, in this case, someone that more sophisticated city people would laugh at for his display of naiveté. It functions on two levels even for contemporary audiences. Initially, the countryman seems to play the role of an entertainer, providing emphasis to the action happening on the screen, by imitating the woman dancing on the movie screen that the bumpkin sees. But the countryman's happy moment is suddenly interrupted by the arrival of a train, a very popular cinematic theme at the end of the 19th century, made famous by the fact that the historically significant ARRIVAL OF A TRAIN AT LA CIOTAT (Lumière Brothers) had a surprise effect on its audience similar to the reaction of the countryman's experiences."

19. Stephen Bottomore, "The Coming of the Cinema," *History Today* 46.3 (1996): 14-20.

20. For an inverse reading of the relation between looking and touching, see Wanda Strauven, "Touch, Don't Look," *The Five Senses of Cinema*, ed. Alice Autelitano, Veronica Innocenti and Valentina Re (Udine: Forum, 2005) 283-91.

21. Norbert Elias, *The Civilising Process* (Oxford: Blackwell, 2000); Pierre Bourdieu, *Language and Symbolic Power* (Cambridge: Polity, 1991).

22. Walter Benjamin, "The Work of Art in the Age of Mechanical Reproduction," *Illuminations*, trans. Harry Zohn (London: Fontana, 1992) 211-44.

23. See Wanda Strauven, "Re-disciplining the Audience: Godard's Rube-Carabinier," *Cinephilia: Movies, Love and Memory*, ed. Marijke de Valck and Malte Hagener (Amsterdam: Amsterdam UP, 2005) 125-33.

24. Thomas Elsaesser, "Introduction: Once More Narrative," *Early Cinema: Space Frame Narrative* (London: British Film Institute, 1990) 153-54.

25. Emile Benveniste, et al., *Problèmes du langage* (Paris: Gallimard, 1966).

26. The contrasting and complementary possibilities of linking narration, enunciation and diegetic spaces are already envisaged by André Gaudreault, in his different essays on "monstration," as well as by Francesco Casetti in *Inside the Gaze: The Fiction Film and Its Spectator* (Bloomington: Indiana UP, 1998).

27. See also Kessler in this volume.

28. Lev Manovich, *The Language of New Media* (Cambridge: MIT P, 2001).

29. An attempt to rethink "diegesis" in relation to both early cinema and television is made in Noël Burch, "Narrative/Diegesis – Thresholds, Limits," *Screen* 23.2 (1982): 16-33.

30. Casetti.

31. An overview of the challenge posed by the moving image in the museum space can be found in *White Cube/Black Box*, ed. Sabine Breitwieser (Vienna: EA-Generali Foundation, 1996).

32. Equally plausible, is not my avatar in *Grand Theft Auto* or *World of Warcraft* also another version of the Rube, learning from his category mistakes to deal more efficiently with his environment?

Attraction Practices through History

["The Avant-Garde": section 1]

Circularity and Repetition at the Heart of the Attraction: Optical Toys and the Emergence of a New Cultural Series

Nicolas Dulac and André Gaudreault

For nearly 200 years the term "attraction" has seen a host of semantic and theoretical shifts, becoming today one of the key concepts in cinema studies. According to the *Oxford English Dictionary*, the meaning of "attraction" as a "thing or feature which draws people by appealing to their desires, tastes, etc., *esp.* any interesting or amusing exhibition which 'draws' crowds" dates from as early as 1829 ("These performances, although possessing much novelty, did not prove sterling attractions"). This sense of attraction as something which "draws crowds" had by the 1860s come to mean both an "interesting and amusing exhibition" and a "ride" in what would become the amusement park – or what is known in French as the "parc d'attractions." Popular entertainment was the setting for the connection which would soon arise between the cinema and attraction. Not only were animated views, by virtue of their content and their mode of exhibition, a part of the variety show, but the new apparatus, the technological novelty known by various names and which we call today the cinematograph, did not waste time drawing and fascinating its own share of astounded spectators. As early as 1912 a particularly perceptive commentator distinguished between the "old-style" cinema, a cinema that was "seen as an attraction," and "today's" cinema, the cinema of 1912, "which suffices unto itself."[1] It was on the basis of this distinction, between an older cinema belonging to the fairground and amusement park and a later and more "autonomous" cinema separate from this earlier tradition that the concept of a "cinema of attractions" developed in the 1980s.

The "attraction" thus quickly earned a place in theoretical discourse, where it still enjoys a privileged place.[2] This discourse insisted on the way the cinematograph was part of a tradition of discontinuity, shock and confrontation. A tradition whose principles were diametrically opposed to those found in narrative cinema. The expression won favor, as we know, and carved out an existence well beyond the borders of early cinema alone.[3] Nevertheless, despite the abundance of texts which make use of the concept to study cinema other than early cinema, attraction remains, more often than not, rooted in a fairground tradition, the tradition of variety shows, vaudeville, music hall and "caf'conc" entertainment. This is true to such an extent that often we are inclined to forget the expression's theoretical breadth. We believe there would be something to be gained by examining the concept of attraction in the light of other "cultural series" which do not necessarily pertain to live entertainment alone.

The concept of attraction might prove to be entirely relevant to the study of that vast range of elements underlying the cinematograph which are known as the cultural series of *animated pictures*.[4] In this article, we propose to begin to examine the different forms of attraction in this cultural series, whose numerous visual apparatuses includes optical toys (the phenakisticope, zoetrope, praxinoscope, etc.). Our objective is two-fold. On the one hand, we want to better understand how the concept of attraction takes shape and is expressed within a group of media which predate the cinema and to demonstrate the ways in which it might be useful to address the question of attraction by resituating it before the fetish date of 28 December 1895, when tradition tells us it was born. On the other hand, we want to know how optical toys enable us today to bring to light certain features inherent in the very notion of attraction – in other words, to understand how the "attractional" dimension of optical toys, properly speaking, enables us to shed new light on the cinematograph. The advantage of such an approach is that attraction, here, is no longer seen as a stage phenomenon but rather as a structuring principle upon which the entire visual experience and very functioning of the apparatus rests.

Between 1830 and 1900, numerous scientific experiments, whose goal was to explain how the human eye functions and to better understand the nature of various visual phenomena, made it possible to devise a number of optical instruments which wasted no time in making the leap to popular entertainment. Throughout this period, during which optical toys inaugurated, in a manner of speaking, the cultural series of *animated pictures*, the attraction was the primary structuring principle. Indeed, the workings of the phenakisticope and the zoetrope established a form of attraction, based essentially on *rotation*, *repetition*, and *brevity*, which was to dominate throughout the period.

If, as Paul Ricoeur remarks, "time becomes human to the extent that it is articulated through a narrative mode,"[5] the temporality of optical toys is closer to that of the machine; it is more mechanical than anything else. The attraction of optical toys is a part, above all else, of that shapeless, a-narrative and even non-human temporality which, as Tom Gunning has remarked, is similar to a kind of "irruption": "[t]he temporality of the attraction itself [...] is limited to the pure present tense of its appearance."[6] Its manifestations know only the present tense. The visual experience which the optical toy provides thus rests not only on the illusion of movement it itself has created, but also on this repetitive temporality which determines the attractional forms specific to it. While socio-cultural factors, above all, determined that the earliest animated views would place attraction center stage, the role played here by the constraints of the apparatus need to be acknowledged. One of the earliest major constraints that made it possible for attraction to dominate within the cultural series of *animated pictures* was the medium used to convey these images.

n° 652

Fig. 1. Phenakisticope disc, 1833, manufactured by Ackermann & Co., London, after Joseph Plateau. Cinémathèque française, collection des appareils.

The Phenakisticope: Rotating Disk, Circular Repetition

The phenakisticope was a cardboard disk upon which a dozen figures were arranged in a circle around its edge (Fig. 1). Note in passing the extremely limited number of figures and the overweening simplicity of the series of images: here, a dancer turning on himself; in other models, a woman sewing, a jumping dog, a parading horseman, etc. The number of figures was of course limited by the way the drawings were arranged radially, on the axis of the imaginary rays emitted by this wheel, the phenakisticope disk. The very nature of the apparatus thus condemned it to an inalterable demonstration of a series of figures forming a loop. In a sense, the fundamental forms of attraction are reflected in the inherent characteristics of how the device functions: the absence of any temporal configuration (that is, the impossibility of identifying the beginning or the end of the action), the brevity of the series of images and its *ad nauseam* repetition, its purely monstrative value, etc. The phenakisticope, like the great majority of optical toys, is by definition resolutely a-narrative. In fact the very idea of its developing anything more than the sketch of a "story" is not even suggested; such an idea is completely alien to it. Because the elaboration of any narrative sequence requires, hypothetically, a linear progression, as minimal as this may be, which itself supposes at the very least a beginning and an end. The phenakisticope's very design, however, meant that its series of images was hostage to both circularity and repetition and that the thresholds of beginning and end were absent from it (because the virtual head and tail had to join up and match).

This at least is the impression phenakisticope designers strived to impart. With a few rare exceptions, the intervals between the phenakisticope's figures were measured to give the impression of a gradual moving forward of the "action," making it impossible to identify which of these figures was the very first in the series. The phenakisticope's figures made up a series with neither head nor tail. Set in motion by the rapid turning of the disk, which brought about an inalterable flow of images, the succession of figures was thus free of any disjunction or aberration. There was no breach in the rigid continuity of the figures, which would have allowed a glimpse of narrative. Narrative had no place in such an apparatus, because of the programmatic limitation of the dozen images engraved on the disk, images condemned to turn endlessly, to perpetual movement, to the eternal return of the same.

Here and there we can find a few examples of disks which transgressed this rule of the endless loop. In order to escape this atemporal loop, however, something must necessarily "happen" in the series of images: the action depicted on these disks must defy the constraints of the apparatus and in this way violate the structuring principle which governs the functioning of the optical toy. Indeed the perfect circularity of the phenakisticope is imperilled when the series of images develops a minimal narrative sequence, or rather a mere anecdote – when it introduces an initial premise followed by a modification. However, the attempt to develop a minimal narrative sequence does not go without provoking aberrations in the continuity of the action each time the initial image reappears: this minimal narrative sequence is necessarily a repetitive one. This was the case with the disk distributed by Pellerin & Cie (Fig. 2) showing two fishermen harpooning a whale. Here the head and the tail of the strip are easily identifiable. In the first image, the whale is rising to the surface. The two men throw their harpoon at it, and it will remain lodged in the whale's body until the end of the series of figures. When the disk is rotated, the final figure is necessarily followed by a recurrence of the first, in which the whale recovers its initial integrity in a truly "regressive" manner.

Fig. 2. Phenakisticope disc, c. 1890, manufactured by Pellerin & Cie, Epinal. Cinémathèque française, collection des appareils.

Examples of this kind of disk reveal one of the peculiarities of the phenakisticope. If a designer did not consent to submitting his figures to the strict continuity/circularity of the apparatus, he had to accept the fact that each revolution of the disk would create a visual interruption – unless a clever and ingenious narrative pretext was employed, as was the case with the disk manufactured by Thomas MacLean (Fig. 3). Here the character's nose, which is cut off with an axe, returns with each rotation. In this way the interruption, by means of the "narrativization" of which it is the subject, was in some way effaced. This is a good example, if ever there was one, of how the topic of the disk, or its "story," was subjected to the way the apparatus functioned.

Fig. 3. Phenakisticope disc, The Polypus, 1833-1834, manufactured by Thomas MacLean, London. Cinémathèque française, collection des appareils.

However there are few known examples of this kind of disk. Was it that the disruption, at the time, was noticeable enough to induce designers of disks to stick almost uniformly to a model of continuity? And yet, despite the break in the movement's continuity with each passing of the final image, producing a spasmodic effect, the element of attraction was just as present here (if not more so, in some respects, given the repetition of the visual shock produced by the interruption).

It would appear that the scarcity of disruptive subjects was a result of the constraints that the apparatus imposed on designers of phenakisticope disks. Don't all apparatuses impose a way of conceiving the subject they depict? In fact, can't something proper to the mechanics of the apparatus itself be seen in the bodies depicted on the disk? The phenakisticope's format and the way it functioned suggest a "world" in which everything was governed by circularity and repetition, a world which annihilated any hint of temporal progression. The subjects are like Sisyphus, condemned *ad infinitum* to turn about, jump, and dance. In another sense, the figures are machine-like: untiring and unalterable, they are "acted-upon subjects" rather than "acting-out subjects." The lack of interruption in the sequence of images was essential to the creation of this effect of uninterrupted and perpetual movement, this a-historical temporality within which beings and things could turn about for ever, without any threshold marking the beginning or end of their wild journey. Many disks depicting machinery, gears, and levers (Fig. 4) emphasize this aspect; as eternal and unbreakable machines, are they emblematic of the wildest dreams of modernity?

Fig. 4. Phenakisticope disc, c. 1834, manufactured by Charles Tilt, London. Cinémathèque française, collection des appareils.

The Zoetrope: Horizontal Circularity

The experiments of optical toy designers brought about a series of modifications to the apparatus which, eventually, made it possible to place the subject in a historical temporality, thereby making it pass to the level of "acting-out subject." Let's turn to the zoetrope, which arrived on the scene about the same time as the phenakisticope. With the zoetrope, the principle underlying the illusion of movement remained gyration, and as long as its drum remained of modest size, the number of images was as limited as the phenakisticope's. With the zoetrope, however, *the images and the apparatus are no longer joined as one*. When a user picked up the phenakisticope's disk of images, he or she was also picking up the apparatus itself. With the zoetrope, the apparatus is on one side and the strip of images on the other.

Note here the importance of this simple gesture, which consists in inserting the strip oneself and manually activating the device. Here, in fact, is the primary reason why these devices were true toys: people manipulated them, altered their speed, changed the strips, etc. This "interactive" aspect is central to the attractional quality of optical toys. The pleasure they provided had as much to do with manipulating the toy as it did with the illusion of movement. The device obligatorily supposed that its "user" would become part of its very functioning, not merely a viewer watching from a distance. In this sense so-called "pre-cinema" could be seen, in a decidedly inadequate way, from our perspective, as a "pre-computer game."

The zoetrope, for its part, demonstrates the tension between two paradigms found within the attractional way in which optical toys function. Here the separation between the material base and the device already indicates, albeit in a very subtle manner, the movement towards a "viewer mode of attraction" as opposed to what we might describe as a "player mode of attraction."[7] With the apparatus on one side and the strip of images on the other, the user of the zoetrope thus felt the presence of the apparatus a little less during the viewing. Moreover, the longitudinal rather than radial arrangement of the figures made possible a major transformation in the conception of animated pictures. While the zoetrope also appears to have been inexorably condemned to the return of the same, the transformation it introduced by separating the images from the apparatus, substituting a flexible strip for the disk, made possible minor innovations in the medium's "language," as we shall see later on.

What exactly was involved, then, in the move from a rotating disk to a flexible strip? With its rectangular shape, the zoetrope strip necessarily came with a head and a tail. In order to put the figures into motion, the user had to place the flexible strip inside the drum and create a loop, an endless loop. However, like the phenakisticope, every time the user placed the strip in the drum, the head and the tail had to match, thereby voiding the beginning/end distinction proper to the strip. Circularity thus remained at the heart of the apparatus.

Fig. 5. Phenakisticope disc, 1833, manufactured by Gillard, London. Cinémathèque française, collection des appareils.

With the zoetrope, the horizontal quality of the strip imposed limits of another sort on the series of figures: longitudinal limits (at the upper and lower limits of the strip). While the circular arrangement of figures in the phenakisticope some-times pushed them to go beyond the very border of the disk (as seen in T.M. Baynes' disk [Fig. 5], which gives the illusion that the rats are literally fleeing off the surface of the disk), the zoetrope's horizontal nature encouraged instead the "linear" development of the images. The action was conceived of in a slightly more "historical" manner. Since it did not always succeed in containing the ebullience of the images, the edge of the phenakisticope was not always an inviolate threshold. In addition, on a symbolic level, its circularity limited the action depicted to an absurd length of time, in which closure was impossible. The radial arrangement of the images ensured that they were invariably orga-nized in relation both to the center and to the edge of the disk. Centrifugal and centripetal force reigned there equally, along with a sense of movement beyond the confines of the disk. The phenakisticope functioned according to both *explo*-sion and *im*plosion (even if it was possible, on occasion, to depict the tranquil movements of a dancer turning about). Like the kaleidoscope, the phenakisti-cope belonged more on the side of the cosmic, of the big bang, and of the expan-sion and contraction of the universe (Fig. 6).

Fig. 6. Phenakisticope disc, 1834, manufactured by Alphonse Giroux, Paris. Cinémathèque française, collection des appareils.

On the other hand, the horizontal arrangement of the figures on the zoetrope strip encouraged a linearization of the action performed by the subjects depicted. Despite the repetitiveness of the figures and, in the end, their evident attractional quality, the zoetrope infused them with, we might say, a hint of self-realization. A yet-to-come phenomenon which would of course never materialize, because everything simply turned in circles. Because of the nature of its construction, however, the apparatus allows us to catch a glimpse of this. So too, the zoetrope was much closer to the terrestrial. Here animated pictures lost a large part of their propensity to fly off in all directions, of their whirlwind and high-riding quality. With the zoetrope we are still in the realm of attraction, but its "horizontalization" of the figures, their linearization, made it possible for narrative elements to seep into the series of images. Here, the figures were inscribed in a more matter-of-fact manner: they were brought back, neither more nor less, to terra firma, where they moved *laterally*, a common enough kind of movement for terrestrial animals (perhaps it was not without cause that the zoetrope's original German name was the *zoo*-trope). Moreover, in these scenes the ground was often depicted as part of the "decor," at the bottom of the strip, where it should be, without the troubling curvature it had in the phenakisticope. In addition, the zoetrope drum was itself equipped with a floor, on which the strip rested when the user put it into place.

The use of a flexible strip opened up new possibilities for presenting the figures. The zoetrope made it possible to exhibit images from two distinct strips at the same time. This was far from a negligible innovation, especially if we consider how this kind of manipulation bears a strange similarity to editing.[8] Here are some of the "combinations" a major distributor of zoetrope strips was advertising as early as 1870:

> Very effective and humorous Combinations can frequently be made by overlapping one strip of Figures with the half of another strip. Amongst some of the most effective of these combinations, the following numbers will give very amusing results: 4 & 5, 7 & 10, 3 & 13 [etc.].[9]

Note the effect, for the zoetrope user, of these "syntactical" combinations: a systematic alternation between two figures in movement was established, in an A-B-A-B pattern. Here the imperturbable filing by of the zoetrope's endless loop was called into question. And yet the basic quality of the images had not changed: "zoetropic editing" was more attraction than narration. We are not invited to follow, narratively speaking, the vicissitudes of this or that zoetropic figure from one time, space, or situation to another. Rather, we are invited to take delight in the transformation-substitution relationship the images are subjected to and which they illustrate. This is a *recurring metamorphosis* of the figure, not a *reiterated following* of the action.

Such a combination of strips made it possible, all the same, to transgress the canonical rule of the zoetrope, its homogeneous parade of images, a rule it shared with the phenakisticope. Here, however, the series of images contained thresholds, in the form of interruptions, which broke the rigid framework of figural unicity and opened the door to bifidity. Yet this form of editing remained a prisoner of the drum's circularity, which was clearly a coercive structure. The turning wheel continued to turn, indefinitely. Thresholds rose up, making it possible to pass, first, from the *end* of series A to the *beginning* of series B, and then from the *end* of series B to the *beginning* of series A (*ad nauseam*), but these thresholds were repetitive: we always come back to the same end, we always return to the same beginning. The alternation did not allow the action to start up again *narratively*, nor to start a new "chapter": it only allowed it to start up again *attractionally*. The "befores" and "afters" were not, to borrow Umberto Eco's expression,[10] essential "befores" and "afters," capable of containing the action effectively and of allowing it to aspire to the status of an embryonic minimal narrative sequence.

The Praxinoscope: Separation/Isolation of the Figures

Emile Reynaud's transformation of the zoetrope put this attraction/narration tension into play in a particularly apparent manner, as seen in his praxinoscope (1876), praxinoscope theater (1879), and praxinoscope projector (1882). In the end, in his optical theater (*Théâtre optique*, 1892), narration came to the fore as the primary structuring principle.

The three varieties of praxinoscope functioned in roughly the same way and according to the same basic principles as the zoetrope (rotating drum, flexible strip, etc.). The invention's originality lay in its prism of mirrors which, located at the center of the apparatus, replaced the zoetrope's cut-out slits. The introduction of this prism made it possible to get around the serious problem of reduced luminosity, which obliged the designers of previous optical toys to opt for simple figures with strong outlines, to neglect the background almost entirely, and to limit the scene to a repetition of a minimal sequence of events. The praxinoscope introduced a new approach to the figures by emphasizing the precision of the drawing and by exploiting the subtlety of the colors.

Fig. 7. Praxinoscope strip, c. 1877, Le repas des poulets, Emile Reynaud. Cinémathèque française, collection des appareils.

This new way of conceiving the figures was strengthened by a constant tendency on Reynaud's part to isolate the figures and to make them conspicuous. This tendency was seen, first of all, in the large black lines separating each figure on the praxinoscope strips, and then by the separation of figure and background in Reynaud's three other inventions, including the optical theater. When we examine a stationary praxinoscope strip, the black lines visibly isolate the figures from each other (Fig. 7), but what is of greatest importance is that these bars played the *same role* when the images were set in motion. With Reynaud's praxinoscope's strips,[11] the image seen in the show had become a *framed image*. With Reynaud, the moving figure was in fact delineated on all four sides: by the vertical bars to the left and right, and by the upper and lower edges of the mirror on the top and bottom.[12] Needless to say, this isolation of the figure was not complete; normally, the viewer of the praxinoscope would see three images at a time in his or her field of vision. The presence of the vertical bars on the strip, in conjunction with the play of mirrors, nevertheless made it possible to set one of these (the one most closely facing the viewer) off from the others and to detach it from the whole. Previous optical toys had not sought to isolate the image in this way. They invited the viewer, rather, to a "group performance." The absence of borders between the figures prevented any of them from standing out, and the two or three figures in the viewer's field of vision presented themselves to view simultaneously and more or less equally.

The isolation and conspicuousness of the image was amplified by Reynaud in the second and third versions of his apparatus – the praxinoscope theater and the praxinoscope projector – in which the number of figures presented to the viewer's gaze was generally even more limited. These apparatuses sometimes allowed only a sole figure in motion to filter through to the viewer. To obtain this result, Reynaud placed a mask between the images and the viewer which functioned as a passe-partout and cast the figures onto a black background. This allowed for the superimposition of a decor, which was painted on another material and remained immobile. Reynaud thus brought about a radical separation between figure and background, a procedure he retained right through to the optical theater.

The Optical Theater: Linearity and Narrativity

Nevertheless, the optical theater broke with the model of the toys which preceded it. In the different versions of the praxinoscope, the image remained a prisoner to the drum and, as in the phenakisticope and the zoetrope, the action formed an endless loop. With the optical theater, Reynaud repudiated the model of the endless loop. He broke the intrinsic circularity of the apparatus and turned his back on the canonical tradition of optical toys. Moreover, the optical theater was not, properly speaking, a "toy": the viewer no longer manipulated the apparatus directly, which was now hidden from sight; he or she simply watched the images file past.

Unlike earlier apparatuses and all other optical toys, the head and the tail of the strip used in the optical theater were not designed to meet. Here we find thresholds of the first degree, literally a physical, empirical beginning and end. The principle of *circularity* was dethroned in favor of *linearity*. For the drum, a closed receptacle which kept the strip of images prisoner, Reynaud substituted two reels – one dispensing the strip, the other taking it up – which made it possible to view the strip, which now wound onto itself, from head to tail. Also, not only was the image seen as a *framed* image, but it was also a *unique* and *singular* image. The strip was composed of a series of distinct frames. The isolation of the figure within the apparatus corresponded to the isolation of the figure on the screen; henceforth there was only one image, the changes to which the viewer followed.

Reynaud's apparatus thus went beyond mere gyration, beyond the mere thrill of seeing the strip repeat itself, beyond pure agitation. Here, even if attraction was still welcome, narrative had taken over from it as the *primary structuring principle*. A strip such as AUTOUR D'UNE CABINE ("Around a Cabin," c. 1895) was in fact part of a new paradigm, within which narration would play a decisive role. The story told in this strip (as well as in PAUVRE PIERROT ["Poor Pierrot," c. 1892]) eloquently went beyond the threshold of minimal narrativity. In AUTOUR D'UNE CABINE we see an initial title card, followed by an establishing "shot" and a conflict and its resolution, before finishing with a *finale:* on the sail of a small boat in the center of the image, we read "The Show is Over" ("La représentation est terminée"). The narrativity this strip demonstrates was possible because Reynaud was able to give his series of images the development required for any narrative to occur.

The optical theater thus transformed the apparatus in a way which was both quantitative and qualitative. It had *more* images, many more even, but at the same time, and paradoxically, for the viewer there was now *only one image*, magnified a hundred times to boot. In addition, this image was external to the viewer. In the case of optical toys, the viewer became one with the apparatus; he or she was in the apparatus, became the apparatus. In the optical theater, the image put into motion was, on the contrary, completely independent of the viewer. The viewer was cast beyond the limits of the apparatus and was kept at a distance from it, no longer having anything to manipulate. The optical theater thus relentlessly favored the "viewer mode of attraction" over the "player mode of attraction." Reynaud's device represents not only a turning point in the history of the series "animated pictures" because of this new autonomy of the image depicted – which derived from the conspicuousness of the image and the configuration of the new apparatus – but also because it effected a crucial change in the position of the "consumer" of the images, who went from the status of a "player" to that of a "viewer." If all the classical historians of the cinema see in Reynaud the decisive figure of what they call "pre-cinema," it is because the optical theater resolutely kept its distance from the paradigm of the "pre-computer game." Here the game player's gyration, repetition and participation give way to linearity, narrative development and the viewer's self-effacement. Reynaud's project, which led him to create narratives using animated pictures, certainly motivated this paradigm shift, precisely because a goal such as this forced him to rethink the fundamental properties of the optical toy and, in so doing, to rethink the role of the "recipient" within the functioning of the apparatus.

The Kinetoscope: Return to the Circularity of the Optical Toy?

From this we might conclude that attraction, which is based above all on repetition and circularity, is "more at home" in an open system than in a closed one. It would also appear that its model par excellence is the endless loop. These two features were present in the first apparatus for viewing animated photographic views to arrive on the world market, the Edison Kinetoscope.

This device, invented in the early 1890s, took up a number of procedures which were in the air at the time, particularly in the work of Reynaud. First of all, there was the flexible, perforated strip divided into distinct frames. However, with his animated photographs, Edison remained in the bosom of attraction, thereby exploiting the immense potential for the marvelous that animated views first possessed. The kinetoscope views, indeed, did not engage the resolutely narrative model Reynaud privileged with his animated drawings. Moreover, it is significant that the kinetoscope and the strips designed for it shared many features with optical toys, which were also in the camp of attraction. Its subjects were shown against a plain background, usually without any decor whatsoever. Thus, despite its indexical nature, the image nevertheless retained a certain degree of "abstraction" which, by distancing it from a strict depiction of reality and of a configured temporality, brought it closer to the drawn image.

With the kinetoscope, viewers themselves operated the mechanism, this time by inserting a nickel. The strip had no apparent head or tail and was arranged to form an endless loop through the device's system of pulleys. The kinetoscope mechanism, moreover, was designed so that the viewer could begin watching the strip of film at any point without concern for the effective beginning or end of the action depicted.[13] The device thus functioned along the lines of the endless loop found in the phenakisticope and the zoetrope. Naturally, animated photographs did not make it possible to create a perfect match between beginning and end, as these devices using drawings were able to do. With the kinetoscope, because of the very subjects depicted and the way they were staged, continuity was rarely broken in a decisive manner. The bodybuilder Sandow's series of poses, for example, was sufficiently repetitive for the transition from the last to the first of these poses (the transition from the end to the beginning of the film strip) for a minimal sense of continuity to be produced (since the interruption remained relatively discreet). In this way a sense of circularity was created in a relatively synthetic manner. In the same way, for example, as the above-mentioned phenakisticope disk showing two fishermen harpooning a whale, those kinetoscope views which contravened the principle of the endless loop ran the risk of provoking an "aberration" in the unfolding of the action.[14]

Moreover, in the kinetoscope, the action depicted was most often extremely simple and relied heavily on the agitation of the figures and repetitive outbursts of movement. We might thus describe the kinetoscope's subjects as acted upon rather than acting out, as seen in SANDOW (1894), [ATHLETE WITH WAND] (1894) and AMY MULLER (1896), for example. Naturally, there are limits to the analogy between optical toys and the kinetoscope. After all, the short strips it showed were not originally meant to be presented over and over, as was the case with optical toys.[15] The apparatus designed by Edison and Dickson imposed without fail initial thresholds, pre-determined limits; it was necessary that the show have a starting point and that it end by stopping at another point, even if these points did not correspond to the head or tail of the strip or to the beginning or end of the action. And yet these thresholds were not first-degree thresholds, which truly delineate the action and what it depicts. Rather, they were abrupt and unpredictable: the action began *in medias res* and it ended *in medias res*. Despite the realism of the images and the pre-determined length of the film, kinetoscope strips fell fundamentally and resolutely into the camp of attraction. Thus at the very moment when the cultural series of *animated drawings* (optical toys) was abandoning its sole recourse to attraction in order, with the "Pantomimes Lumineuses" (c. 1890-93), to explore the animated picture's narrative potential, which until then had been used very little, the cultural series of *animated photographs* appeared and, with the kinetoscope (an exact contemporary of Reynaud's device), updated a certain number of purely attractional strategies which had been the cause of the optical toy's success.

Attraction's Dual Nature

Naturally, we have not attempted here to describe the numerous and subtle technological, cultural and economic factors underlying the process whereby the view became autonomous. Suffice it to suggest that this delineation of the head and the tail was carried out parallel to the development of a certain cinematic narrativization process. The question of thresholds was thus very profitable for arriving at an understanding of the development of the series "animated pictures." It also makes it possible to better understand the movement from *attraction* to *narration*. Finally, we could mention here that this movement is closely connected to the apparatus – both in a technological sense (the device) and a social one (its mode of reception) – thanks to which these images are animated *and* "consumed." Each of the apparatuses fashions the way the animated pictures are conceived. The phenakisticope disk, the zoetrope's paper strip or kinetoscope's celluloid one, because of their very material, determine the way in which the systems of attraction and narration hold sway over the other and give form to the uncertain "desires" of the figures which move about upon them in their respective ways, as we saw with the examples of the optical theater and the kinetoscope. We can thus see how the appearance of a new apparatus or a technological innovation within the cultural series of *animated pictures* reaffirms the images' potential for attraction. This is why there is no real historical "transition" from attraction to narration but rather a fluid and constant coexistence between these two paradigms, in keeping with the evolutionary course of the apparatus.

In this respect, it is interesting to examine recent developments in the use of digital animated pictures. As Lev Manovich has remarked,[16] the sequential images which abound on the Internet (such as Flash and QuickTime) share a number of features with the earliest animated pictures. This form of animation, which has inaugurated a new paradigm in the cultural series of *animated pictures*, bears a strange resemblance to the images we have been discussing in this article: its images are of reduced size and short duration, they are shown in a loop, etc. It is significant that these same forms, whose primary interest rests almost entirely on their power of attraction, have resurfaced with these new media. However, as we might have guessed, it is now possible to see on the Internet various examples of short narrative films created with the help of animation software. This use of the apparatus for narrative ends is just one of many possible avenues that could be taken. Since digital images modify considerably the relationship with the reality they depict – and this was the case of the earliest cinematic images – it is easier for them to find their way into the camp of attraction. We also must not forget that the history of cinema, or rather the history of the cultural series of *animated pictures* in general, was not a gradual and direct march towards narration. The question of crossing thresholds (and of becoming free of them) illustrates one of the possibilities in the growth of a medium (the possibility, it must be said, whose central role in the process of cinema's institutionalization has to do with external factors unrelated to the medium alone).

Indeed it is impossible to confine attraction to a strictly historical paradigm (one which would encompass "pre-cinema" and early cinema) or for that matter to a purely technological paradigm (having to do with the technological dimension of the apparatus). Attraction has a dual personality, so to speak: it is a function of both technological prerogatives *and* historically precise socio-cultural factors. This is why attraction "survived" and lived on even after the emergence of narrative cinema, despite the configuration of the apparatus used to animate the images. Animated digital sequences, avant-garde films, American blockbusters or giant-screen technology such as IMAX are proof of this,[17] if proof were needed. Given its own power to fascinate, even if this appears, in the case of optical toys, determined above all by the limitations of the device (repetition, circularity, etc.), attraction can also appear for its own sake in any apparatus. While the concept of the "cinema of attractions" was initially used to distinguish early films from the later products of institutional cinema, we must nevertheless acknowledge that the very idea of attraction cannot be limited to a question of periodization alone. It is a structuring principle, resurfacing with every new phase in the diachronic development of the cultural series of *animated images* (as Edison's "move backwards" proves, but also Lumière's and Méliès's). As a system, attraction is fully assumed, so much so that it has never ceased to be present, sometimes to a considerable extent, in cinema. Film narration does not eclipse attraction completely. The system in question owes its name to the simple fact that narration is its *primary structuring principle*. Beyond the primary principle lay many other things, in particular attraction.

Translated by Timothy Barnard

Notes

This article was written under the aegis of GRAFICS (Groupe de recherche sur l'avènement et la formation des institutions cinématographique et scénique) at the Université de Montréal, which is funded by the Social Sciences and Humanities Research Council of Canada (SSHRC) and the Fonds québécois de recherche sur la société et la culture. GRAFICS is a member of the Centre de recherche sur l'intermédialité (CRI) at the Université de Montréal. The authors would like to thank Laurent Mannoni for granting them access to the collections of the Cinémathèque française. This text is a revised version of a previously published article, first in Italian ("Il *principio* e la *fine…* Tra fenachistoscopio e cinematografo: l'emergere di una nuova serie culturale," *Limina. Film's Thresholds*, ed. Verinoca Innocenti and Valentina Re [Udine: Forum, 2004] 185-201) and later in English ("Heads or Tails: The Emergence of a New Cultural Series, from the Phenakisticope to the Cinematograph," *Invisible Culture* 8 [Fall 2004]:http://www.rochester.edu/in_visible_-culture/Issue_8/dulac_gaudreault.html).

1. E.-L. Fouquet, "L'Attraction," *L'Echo du Cinéma* 11 (28 June 1912): 1.
2. On this question see in particular André Gaudreault, "From 'Primitive Cinema' to 'Kine-Attractography,'" in the present volume.
3. The concept of attraction has been used in studies of avant-garde cinema, the new Hollywood cinema, interactive cinema, etc.
4. We fully intend here to say "animated pictures," not "moving images," "moving pictures" or "animated views," which are distinct from the cultural series under discussion here.
5. Paul Ricoeur, *Time and Narrative*, vol. 1, trans. Kathleen McLaughlin and David Pellauer (Chicago: U of Chicago P, 1985) 52.

6. Tom Gunning, "'Now You See It, Now You Don't': The Temporality of the Cinema of Attractions," *Silent Film*, ed. Richard Abel (London: Athlone, 1996) 77.
7. The authors thank Wanda Strauven for suggesting this distinction.
8. On this topic, see André Gaudreault, "Fragmentation and assemblage in the Lumière animated pictures," *Film History* 13.1 (2001): 76-88.
9. Catalogue of the London Stereoscopic & Photographic Company. Rpt. in David Robinson, "Masterpieces of Animation 1833-1908," *Griffithiana* 43 (December 1991), ill. 31. The catalogue appears to date from the 1870s.
10. Umberto Eco, *The Open Work*, trans. Anna Cancogni (Cambridge: Harvard UP, 1989) 112-13.
11. In our research we discovered praxinoscope strips from other manufacturers with no such vertical line.
12. Of the strips by Reynaud we are familiar with, one (*L'Amazone*, a series of figures showing a woman riding a horse) actually transforms these black lines from thresholds which cannot be crossed into "obstacles" to be hurdled by the subject of the strip.
13. See Ray Phillips, *Edison's Kinetoscope and Its Films: A History to 1896* (Trowbridge: Flicks Books, 1997) 30.
14. Indeed we might well imagine the surprise of a patron of a Kinetoscope parlour beginning to view Mary, Queen of Scots at some point after the queen had been decapitated.
15. See also in this volume Musser on the looping practice "updated" by the Vitascope and other early projection machines, and Blümlinger on the looping practice re-enacted by contemporary avant-garde filmmakers.
16. In *The Language of New Media* (Cambridge: MIT P, 2001), Manovich writes, on page 316: "Early digital movies shared the same limitations of storage as nineteenth-century pre-cinema devices." The authors thank Bernard Perron of the Université de Montréal for drawing this quotation to their attention.
17. On the relation between attraction and avant-garde cinema, see Tom Gunning "The Cinema of Attractions: Early Film, Its Spectator and the Avant-Garde," *Early Cinema: Space Frame Narrative*, ed. Thomas Elsaesser (London: British Film Institue, 1990) 56-62; on the subject of American blockbusters, see Geoff King, *Spectacular Narratives: Hollywood in the Age of the Blockbuster* (London/New York: I.B. Tauris, 2000); and on giant-screen technology such as IMAX see Alison Griffiths, "'The Largest Picture Ever Executed by Man': Panoramas and the Emergence of Large-Screen and 360-Degree Technologies," *Screen Culture: History and Textuality*, ed. John Fullerton (Eastleigh: John Libbey, 2004) 199-220.

Lumière, the Train and the Avant-Garde

Christa Blümlinger

The history of cinema began with a train, and it is as if this train has been driving into film history every since; as if destined to return unendingly, it crisscrosses the Lumière films and their ghost train journeys, it drives the phantom rides of early cinema and is then embraced with open arms by the avant-garde as one of the primary motifs of the *cinématographe*, a motif which, more than almost any other, allows us to engage with the modern experience of visuality. Thus it is no coincidence that the development of an independent language of film can be traced through the railway sequences of early cinema and also those of the avant-garde cinema of the 1920s (one might think of Dziga Vertov, Abel Gance or Henri Chomette). Even Jean Renoir underlined, in the context of LA BÊTE HUMAINE (1938) – the beginning of which itself constitutes a small study in motion, through which the figure of the locomotive is introduced – that the fascination emanating from the railways and the films of the Lumière brothers extended into the 1930s.[1] And when Maurice Pialat begins his film VAN GOGH (1991) with the arrival of a steam train in a French station – almost one hundred years after L'ARRIVÉE D'UN TRAIN EN GARE DE LA CIOTAT and forty years after Renoir decided not to take on a similar project – it is not so much a postmodern flourish as a cinephile gesture from a filmmaker who has even claimed that cinema's first film remains the greatest.[2] At the same time he introduces an emblem of late nineteenth-century perceptual thinking into his reflection on painting, an emblem which perhaps more than any other stands for the transformation of the visual.

This revisiting of historical contexts finds its equivalent in the experimental practice of found footage. For instance, in the archival art film DAL POLO ALL'E-QUATORE (1986) by Yervant Gianikian and Angela Ricci Lucchi a train arrives from early cinema. This train recurs in the manner of a leitmotif, as if leading us through this avant-garde film – itself probing to the center of the individual frame – structuring through lengthy expeditions and conquests[3] the individual chapters set out in the original compilation film of the same title. In the figure of the locomotive, an aspect of the formal process of film is represented metaphorically – slowing down, bringing to a halt and winding up again. Both machines, the steam locomotive and the projector, incorporate the principle of repetition and availability: they are switched on, set into motion, pause and begin to rotate once more.

Railway trains, undergrounds and trams are inscribed into early cinema as signs of modernization in the sense of an ostensible shift in the subjective nature of experience or, more generally, in wholesale social, economic and cultural changes. This has been characterized in numerous studies of the cultural history of the telegraph and telephone, of railways and automobiles, of photography and cinematography. Leo Charney and Vanessa Schwartz for example argue that of all these emblems of modernity, none characterized and simultaneously transcended the age of its inception more successfully than cinema.[4]

The railway stands for the loss of the experience of travel as a spatial continuum, insofar as a train passes over or travels through an interstitial space. Thus the train, like cinema itself, functions both as a machine to organize the gaze and as a generator of linearity and movement. There is therefore a technical affinity between cinema and the railway, or rather between the machines that comprise them: the locomotive, the wagon and the projector. Like the railway, cinema constitutes a new temporality which is not only dependent on the destruction of traditional temporalities, but also bound up with a new value system, the enjoyment of speed, the discovery of foreign places and the loss of roots. The panoramic gaze of the train traveler, as described by Wolfgang Schivelbusch in a pioneering study, lives on in the cinema as what Jacques Aumont, in his history of the relationship between painting and film, terms the "variable eye."[5] As an immobile traveler watching the passage of a framed spectacle – the landscape traveled through – the train passenger of the nineteenth century prefigures the mass audiences of the cinema. This traveler, confronted with dynamic, moving, panoramic views must accept the loss of foreground on account of the speed.[6] The railway appears as a force eradicating space and time.

The introduction of the railway into film allows the perception of two forms of filmic movement: on the one hand towards or past the viewer, i.e. movement within the image; and, on the other, movement from the point of view of the locomotive or the traveler in the train compartment – the movement of the image. This second figure is encoded into the travel films of early cinema in the form of so-called phantom rides. Tom Gunning has described the films produced in the wake of those of Lumière and Edison as "views." They straightforwardly reproduce the *sights* of nature or culture "as found," and persist relatively unchanged in format between 1906 and 1916. These films belong to the category of the "cinema of attractions" because they invariably choose a particular viewpoint or serve as an eye-catcher in which display and the satisfaction of visual curiosity are pre-eminent. The enormous fascination of these views lies, according to Gunning, in the constant, often highly complex exploration of the gaze outside dramatic structures, an exploration which also reveals the paradoxical voyeurism of the viewer, tourist, colonialist and filmmaker.[7]

The kinship between the *panoramic* view out of the compartment window and cinema has been explored by Lynne Kirby.[8] It becomes particularly apparent in an account of a journey quoted by Schivelbusch, and compiled by Benjamin Gastineau in 1861 under the title *La vie en chemin de fer*:

> Devouring distance at the rate of fifteen leagues an hour, the steam engine, that powerful stage manager, throws the switches, changes the decor, and shifts the point of view every moment; in quick succession it presents the astonished traveler with happy scenes, sad scenes, burlesque interludes, brilliant fireworks, all visions that disappear as soon as they are seen [...].[9]

This description of a structure of visual presentation would seem to encapsulate precisely the heterogeneous conceptions of early cinema. It also highlights the panorama as forerunner of many developments in the history of the media. Tellingly, the railway and panorama are encoded into the titles of many Lumière films as a pointer to the pre-history of the cinematographic way of seeing: "Panorama, pris d'un train..." ("Panorama, taken from a train...").

The railway train doubtless prefigured cinema as a *dispositif* of perception more than any other machine. In the early years of the twentieth century the means of attraction and the means of transport develop within the same social and cultural fields of technology, tourism, public spectacle and photography, and both are grounded in an institutionalization of standardized time. As Kirby sets out, early cinema develops its power of attraction in tandem with the railway, not only in relation to its exhibition practice but also in relation to its topoi, modes of representation and narrative patterns.[10] According to Kirby, railway and cinema converge most precisely in the modes of perception of spectator and traveler: both create a tourist, a visual consumer, a panoramic observer, a deeply unstable subject. Discontinuity, shock and suggestibility characterize this experience. The constant withdrawal of the seen led to uncertainty regarding visual representation. This uncertainty is communicated in the cinema by means of high speed, the resulting increase in the number of impressions, disorientation and the unceasing changes of position. In this context one should not underestimate the significance of the fact that the new means of transport and the new media brought with them a disturbing increase in physical danger and nervous stimulation.[11] Georg Simmel characterizes this modern perception in the case of the city as an *"escalation of nervous activity* which results from the rapid and continuous alternation of outer and inner experience."[12]

Avant-garde Film and Early Cinema: The Paradigm of Repetition

The shift in experience described by Simmel is demonstrated in Ernie Gehr's now classic found-footage film Eureka (1974) which uses a three-minute film of a tram journey through San Francisco, shot at the beginning of the 20th century and slowed down eight times by Gehr. The complexity of a modern cityscape is revealed to the contemporary spectator by means of a purposeful temporal intervention on the part of the avant-garde filmmaker. This archaeological work shows time "as an unseen energy devouring space," to quote Tom Gunning's succinct phrase.[13] Gehr's gesture does not come out of the blue. Besides Gunning, William Wees and Bart Testa have also indicated the extent to which recent avant-garde film turns to early cinema in exploring the fundamental questions of cinema.[14] In what follows, this concurrence will be discussed in relation to a symptomatic structuring principle.

The analytical and aesthetic potential of contemporary found-footage film can be demonstrated in relation to repetition as a formal principle of avant-garde film which is intensified by gestures of re-filming and quotation. If one looks at this question historically, the structure can be traced back to the beginnings of cinema. Thus, according to Thomas Elsaesser, the one-minute Lumière films already display a closed structure because they were intended to be repeatable, given that in line with contemporary screening practice they were often shown a number of times in a row.[15] Repetition, I suggest, is also a figure that is reinforced by the *dispositif* of the railway.

On the basis of a selection of found-footage films from the end of the 20th century which engage with the motif of the train as it emerged from the end of the 19th century,[16] I intend to distinguish between three kinds of repetition:

1. Repetition as a structural attribute of cinematographic projection (Ken Jacobs).
2. Figurative repetition and narrativization of the *dispositif* of the railway as part of the history of cinema (Bill Morrison).
3. The iconographic afterlife of the first arrival of a train on film (Al Razutis and Peter Tscherkassky).

Contemporary avant-garde film's reliance on early cinema, and in particular the films of the Lumière brothers, will be discussed in relation to these three forms of repetition as demonstrated in the found footage films of these particular filmmakers. One can see that across a span of almost a hundred years, these avant-garde retrospections on very early films produce a new contextual understanding of film history.

First Variant: The Real and the Reel (Ken Jacobs)

Ken Jacobs was one of the first artists of the second generation of avant-garde filmmakers to rediscover and re-evaluate early cinema, and as such accompanied artistically what could be described as a paradigmatic shift in film historiography. Since the 1960s he has been working with found material from the Paper Print Collection of the US Library of Congress, where numerous American films were deposited by producers prior to 1912 in the form of single frame reproductions on paper for the preservation of copyright, and which have consequently survived up to the present day. TOM, TOM, THE PIPER'S SON (1969), Jacobs's monumental study of an early chase film by Billy Bitzer, is now seen as a classic of found-footage film and one of the greatest detailed studies of early mise-en-scène.[17] This film already worked with the principle of repetition: at the beginning and end the original film is shown in its entirety, and in-between is broken down repeatedly into individual scenes and spatial details, slowed down and enlarged in a series of figurative variations culminating in a high-speed chase which suddenly remodels the representational, dramatic performance as abstraction.

Within the framework of his 1990s project *The Nervous System* – which attempts to expand conventional cinematic perception three-dimensionally by means of various optical apparatuses, manipulations of the film and effects of projection – Jacobs produced a series of films which are constructed using early views of train journeys and which are shown in sequence as a performance under the title FROM MUYBRIDGE TO BROOKLYN BRIDGE (1996). Here Jacobs does not probe to the center of the individual frame, nor does he slow down or speed up the footage as in TOM, TOM, THE PIPER'S SON or indeed some of the earlier Nervous System performances. He also does not content himself with a ready-made of the kind he found in a rubbish bin and then presented, *tel quel*, as the (art) film PERFECT FILM (1985). Instead he creates a system of visual permutations using the principle of varied repetition, doubling and mirroring. Although the body of the initial film is not changed or cut we still have a restructuring. The original film can be seen afresh in its entirety by reason of the complexity resulting from the reversal and repetition of its material.

As presented within his Nervous System performances, Jacobs's reconfigured travel films correspond to modern modes of perception from the turn of the last century as described by Walter Benjamin: replete with fortuitous juxtapositions, chance encounters, diverse sensory impressions and unexpected meanings. Jacobs's approach is also modern in its correspondence to the working method of Benjamin, who described his unfinished *Passages* as a "literary montage": "I have nothing to say. Only to show," wrote Benjamin, whose aim in his montages was to take odds and ends and "let them come into their own in the only way possible: by using them."[18] Entirely in the spirit of Benjamin, Jacobs takes these early, long-forgotten and marginalized films and enables them to be exhibited and seen anew. This occurs in Jacobs's case through the reproducibility and associated three-fold variability of film: first in relation to the copying process, second in relation to the projection apparatus, and thirdly in relation to the way the film is reeled through the projector. A film can be played repeatedly and in reverse, a print can be inverted in various ways relative to its negative.

A kind of pre-study for the railway films of the Nervous System cycle had previously demonstrated the diversity inherent in this procedure. Ken Jacobs's OPENING THE NINETEENTH CENTURY: 1896 (1990) is based on those Lumière films that demonstrate the first traveling shots in film history: films shot around 1895 by the cameramen Promio, Mesguich and Doublier in Paris, Cairo, Venice and elsewhere from trams, trains and ships.[19] The application of the 3D Pulfrich Effect makes it possible to view the material in an enhanced, three dimensional form.

Jacobs's film is mirrored along its central axis, a principle already present in his early films[20] and rooted in the reversibility of the Lumière *cinématographe*, which functioned both as the recording and projecting apparatus. This mirroring is not only spatial but also has, as the title implies, a temporal dimension, denoting a "look back" at the nineteenth century. OPENING THE NINETEENTH CENTURY is exactly symmetrical in structure: first nine film fragments run from right to left, alternating between "normal" and "backwards"; then – during a blackout in a tunnel – a red light alerts the spectator to change the 3D filter from one eye to the other. From that point the entire montage is repeated in reverse in a movement from left to right, and what was originally perceived as strong contrasts now takes on the appearance of a relief. It is not by chance that Jacobs places the reversal in a tunnel: as a symmetrical motif within a train journey (entry/exit and light/dark/light) it in effect affirms the reversibility. Moreover, the railway tunnel stands for the vertigo of modern perception, it virtually prefigures the progressive formation of the cinematic close-up[21] as a widening black hole which races towards us and engulfs us.

The reverse movement in OPENING THE NINETEENTH CENTURY does not only generate a simple repetition and mirroring, but also allows the spectator to see some of the journeys which initially appeared in mirror image or upside as realistic illusions. Or, to put it another way: what originally was indecipherable can now be read, and what was previously legible is no longer readily identifiable. The film is much more than just a structurally through-composed and precisely thought-through montage of "found" Lumière journeys. OPENING THE NINETEENTH CENTURY makes it possible to feel something of the shock of perception experienced at the turn of the century. In the combination of mirrored repetition, spatial permutation and the 3D process, Jacobs underscores the modern loss of distance mapped out by the media, oversized billboards and the *dispositif* of the railway, where speed makes it impossible to perceive the foreground. In one of the Lumière cityscapes re-read here by Jacobs, giant posters suddenly spring up in front of the spectator, whose eyes are unable to grasp them on such a fleetingly appearance. The arrival of the train in the Lumière view PA-NORAMA DE L'ARRIVÉE EN GARE DE PERRACHE PRIS DU TRAIN (1896), which first appears in Jacobs's reworking as a departure from Lyon, demonstrates in a particularly plastic way this fleetingness of the railway and the city, together with the rapid alternation of images in the travel panorama. What appear at the outset of the film to be figurative puzzles and hieroglyphs – upside down locomotives and carriages resembling film strips and reversed, mirrored advertising which is indecipherable despite filling out the frame – finally become recognizable thanks to repetition; they can be identified as the origin of the *dispositif* of the panorama (a carriage with windows in its compartments which affords the panoramic view) and as an emblem of the city in the form of advertising text – we read "Lingerie," "Habillement," "Maison." The reprise of this arrival, which now forms the end of the film, reminds us once again of the affinity of the railway and filmic projection. We don't only see an enormous black locomotive as a metaphorical counterpart to the film projector (an iron machine which translates the rotations of its wheels into linear movement and throws a cone of light into dark spaces) but have also already seen its product, namely small clouds of steam which generate flat areas in the image. Steam,[22] like smoke, is an iconographic motif of early cinema, which with its light effects, textures, transparencies and lifting veils is part of the traveler's *dispositif* of perception, and also related to the white screen in the cinema.

A remark of Ken Jacobs about TOM, TOM, THE PIPER'S SON seems to pre-empt in an almost programmatic way his choice of an early phantom ride for a found-footage film of the 1990s: "Every film is a loop, endlessly repeatable, everything shown is wound on a spool."[23] THE GEORGETOWN LOOP (1903, newly rearranged by Ken Jacobs in 1996) is literally a loop – the famous, recently reconstructed railway loop built in 1884 between the city of Georgetown (Colorado) and the silver mines in the mountains. This loop had to overcome a substantial difference in altitude across a few kilometers. The spectacular view from the Devil's Gate viaduct affords a prospect of the track below and was already considered an attraction at the turn of the century. The mutual advertising of railway and film was already widespread in America, especially at Biograph, as Billy Bitzer reports in his autobiography.[24] The railway advertising films, which were not in fact marketed as such by the people who made them, supplemented the extensive travel literature produced by the railway companies right through to the 1920s.[25] Like many other contemporary films of the American Biograph studio,[26] the circa two-minute long train journey round the Georgetown Loop was probably filmed by an operator who either fixed his heavy camera to the side of the locomotive and then to the front, or possibly placed it in a wagon provided specially for this purpose. The people in the four-carriage train in front wave with dozens of white handkerchiefs out of the windows facing left whenever it becomes clearly visible round a bend. At the outset, as we look up at the railway loop from below, another train crosses the viaduct. Thus three trains are choreographed and synchronized: two which are filmed, and one from which the recordings are made. When the railway is out of sight the camera frames a panoramic journey through the mountainous snowy landscape and populated areas.

Jacobs enacts a complex repetition in four stages. First the film is seen on half of the wide screen projection. Then the film is reflected and projected twin-screen as a mirrored journey, on the left the original version, on the right the mirror, so that movements away from the central axis appear to separate from one another. In the second repetition Jacobs has the original version screened on the right and the mirror on the left, so that movements towards the central axis appear to flow into one another. In a third version the film and its mirror-image are switched again and also inverted. The sequence is repeated a final time, whereby left and right are again switched which results in further perspectives and streams of movement. In the framework of this particular increase in perceptual complexity, repetition no longer serves to help identify details previously unrecognized, but instead confronts the viewer with illusory, symmetrically dislocated spaces. The viewer knows that these spaces derive from a referential representation, but their coordinates can now only be pinpointed with reference to remembered details rather than a realistic, perspectival space. Through the mirroring an illusion of depth is repeatedly conjured up, a fissure into which the landscapes and trains vanish or out of which they emerge.

Jacobs's "nervous system" tries to activate a mode of perception which Simmel, as already mentioned, characterized in 1903 (the year in which the original film of THE GEORGETOWN LOOP was made) as an *"escalation of nervous activity* which results from the rapid and continuous alternation of outer and inner experience."[27] In THE GEORGETOWN LOOP we find everything that, according to Simmel, defines the modern experience of the city (and thus also of the railway and the cinema): the "rapid concentration of alternating images," the "abrupt intervals between things seen in a single gaze" and finally, and most importantly, "the unexpected nature of the impressions that force themselves upon you."

Alongside the effects of discontinuity and shock already alluded to, Jacobs's GEORGETOWN LOOP reinforces another affinity between the railway and film, that of suggestibility. At the point in Jacobs's film where two different viewpoints dissolve, where the middle axis becomes a rapid and all-consuming fissure, and where an abstraction is derived from the inversion – turning the image into a kind of mobile Rorschach Test – the spectator is disrupted from the realistic illusion of the moving image and thrown back on his imaginative inner world. Jacobs's claim that his GEORGETOWN LOOP is not suitable for children ("This landscape film deserves an X-rating!") doesn't simply refer to a possible lesson on sexual symbolism in the figurations of the newly composed image, but also to a perceptual potential which underpins the original film. What Tom Gunning has said about Jacobs's re-montage of a TV movie, A DOCTOR'S DREAM, can also be said of THE GEORGETOWN LOOP in relation to the analysis of perception in an early railway film: "Jacobs' relation to the original film, then, is one that takes up the burden of its original [...] cultural meanings."[28] The difference between these two film "traumas" analyzed by Jacobs (THE DOCTOR'S DREAM and THE GEORGETOWN LOOP) could thus be characterized, to use Freud's terminology, as the difference between sexually provoked psychoneuroses and actual neuroses. What becomes manifest in the dizzying, monstrous maws and the constantly mutating chasms is an aesthetic which characterized early cinema. The aggression and excessive discontinuity of this aesthetic has been defined by Tom Gunning elsewhere as an "aesthetic of astonishment."[29] By way of the "nervous system" (a customary psychological designation in nineteenth-century medicine) this modern shock-like destabilization affects the sexuality of the spectator of early cinema, particularly when one considers that male hysteria was studied by Charcot and others using the example of the male victims of railway accidents.[30]

The idea of the loop is thus taken up by Jacobs in a double sense: his reconfiguration does not simply show the railway loop, as was the case in the original film; just as the train coming repeatedly into view becomes something *different* in the inversion, so too does the film. Not unlike the Lumière mountainscapes, the *dispositif* of the journey round the Georgetown Loop maps out the notion of repeatability. The journey can be undertaken again and again and experienced in stages, an ideal arrangement for a film shot or, in the case of THE GEORGETOWN LOOP, two shots. In what amounts to an anticipation of montage, the Lumière brothers themselves, for example, suggest in their catalogue that three journeys, probably shot in 1898 along the Côte d'Azur between Beaulieu and Monaco, could be shown "one after the other."[31] Of the films 1230, 1231 and 1232 they write, "these three views, which follow on from one another, can be joined together. They were shot in one of the most picturesque spots on the Côte d'Azur."[32]

Finally, the depth of field generated technologically by Jacobs relates back to another aspect of doubling as employed by the Lumière brothers, and which has its origins in another piece of apparatus – the twin images of the stereoscope. With the 3D vision of Opening the Nineteenth Century and the bifocalism of double projection in The Georgetown Loop Jacobs takes the early cinematic views back to one of the most important spectacles of the nineteenth century, and one which was dearer to the hearts of the Lumière brothers than the *Cinématographe*: the stereoscope. It is not by chance that the Lumière films differ aesthetically from later views, as Thomas Elsaesser has noted:

> Instead of constructing the image according to the laws of perspective and the single vanishing point (the markers of the classical image), Lumière seems to have chosen a different logic, one that splits perception, utilizes parallax vision, and one that presses the eye to see the image as a bi-level or even tri-level representation, at once flat and in depth, at once unified and divided, at once anamorphic and centered.[33]

Second Variant: The *Dispositif* (Bill Morrison)

There are some striking parallels between Jacobs's Nervous System performances of the 1990s and Bill Morrison's The Death Train (1993) which was produced a little earlier: for his found-footage film Bill Morrison used not only an educational film from the 1950s about how "moving images" function, titled How Motion Pictures Move and Talk,[34] and various other material, but also the two phantom rides The Georgetown Loop and A Trip Down Mount Tamalpais, which Jacobs reworks in Disorient Express (1996) in a way comparable to The Georgetown Loop. In their films of the 1990s both Jacobs and Morrison relate the principles of Eadweard Muybridge's chronophotography to the train: Jacobs in Muybridge On Wheels (1996), part of the Nervous System performance From Muybridge to Brooklyn Bridge (1996), and Morrison in some studies in movement which are animated in The Death Train with the help of a zoetrope.

In Morrison's film the railway stands emblematically for the *dispositif* of pre-cinematographic perception. In this assemblage of found (not only early) films and pre-cinematographic visual material we are initially confronted with a technological parallel between two machines which translate circular motion into linear motion: the locomotive and the projector. As demonstrated by the digits, both systems are related to the standardization of time, they also introduce the "countdown structure" well known in narrative cinema. In Morrison's montage the transport technology of these two machines is figuratively presented as parallel: the perforated film strip consisting of identically-sized individual frames is prefigured in the zoetrope strips and the individual images in the phenakisti-cope; in the case of the train the rows of windows figuratively match the film frames and the rows of wheels correspond to the perforations. In both cases the individual pictorial space can only be perceived in stasis.

Muybridge's chronophotography can be associated culturally and economically with both the railway and the cinema thanks to its synchronizing of time. The recourse to the animation of real images by Muybridge – whose studies of movement, *animal locomotion*, astonished the world – in contrast to the drawn animation of the zoetrope shows the ambiguity of the "living" in film. In Morrison's film the possibility of arresting movement is consistently seen as the uncanny dimension of film, with its unexpected apparitions waiting to leap out at the seated spectator, only to turn out to be lifeless and immaterial once the projector's lamp is extinguished.

By means of a kind of technical comparison, Morrison also draws a parallel between the modern, panoramic gaze in the railway train and the optical effects generated by the viewing slits in the rotating zoetrope. The columns that adorn city buildings flit past the sluggish eye of the traveler – as the Biograph film INTERIOR NY SUBWAY, 14TH ST. TO 42ND ST. (1905, and probably shot by Billy Bitzer) had already demonstrated – and function like a Light-Space-Modulator, reminding one of László Moholy-Nagy's "Apparatus for demonstrating phenomena of light and movement." Moreover, they also generate unexpected stroboscopic effects and divide the continuum of the cityscape into a rapid sequence of discrete single images.

In his film, Morrison takes a series of proto-cinematographic motifs of the railway journey which all have the principle of symmetry in common. These include passing through a tunnel with the camera at the front of the train, where the tunnel races towards the immobile traveler like a black hole and swallows him up before opening up a view of the world again in the form of a bright spot rapidly increasing in size.

In THE DEATH TRAIN the principle of repetition is introduced, first, by the circular movements and sounds of motors and toys on the screen, together with loops composed of the early travel film material which stand for the cinematic illusion of reality – films which "film life." A film can be spooled endlessly and, as was the case with pre-cinematographic optical toys (the praxinoscope and mutoscope), allows repetition and endless loops to generate rhythmic and kinetic optical stimuli.[35] Second, the principle of repetition is also evident in the admittedly minimal difference between the individual frames of a single shot, something that Morrison draws attention to with temporal leaps and intervals. Two adjoining frames in a sequence of movement, seen side by side, are an almost identical repetition. The change only becomes apparent in the temporal interval between two motionless images in a series.[36]

THE DEATH TRAIN was originally designed to provide structure for the production of John Moran's *The Death Train of Baron von Frankenstein* at the Ridge

Theater in New York. In his accompanying film, Morrison displaces the condition of the railway as ghost train and automaton onto the "living images" of cinematography; at the turn of the century the arrival of a train at a station, accompanied by smoke and dust, was, after all, always seen as an "apparition,"[37] and the journey through a tunnel invariably had something frightening about it. The undead of film history are reawakened again and again, remain forever young and thereby suspend time. According to Jean-Louis Schefer this is why it is the films are looking at *us*. In the figure of the phantom, the ghost and the revenant, according to Schefer, cinema incarnates itself as the "eternal and immaterial zone of virtual human beings."[38] THE DEATH TRAIN reveals its own spectral quality by fostering moments of cinematographic *suspension*, those moments which derive from the relationship between movement and stasis and also from the clouding-over of the visible. It happens that this duplicates the experience of the train traveler transported from station to station by a steam-spitting locomotive.

Third Variant: Lumière's Afterlife (Razutis and Tscherkassky)

The third form of repetition as a central figure of the concurrence of the railway, early cinema and contemporary avant-garde film is to be found in revisiting the material of the first film as a cinematic archetype, in regarding its afterlife as an iconographic continuum and in a self-referential reconnection of the process of repetition with the reworking of found material.

Al Razutis's film LUMIÈRE'S TRAIN (1979) can be classified as a structural film on the basis of its formal structures and the materiality of its reworking of found footage, but it is also much more than that. What the filmmaker has termed the "plot" of the film – the arrival of the train culminating in a "catastrophe" and the play on the title of the Lumière film L'ARRIVÉE D'UN TRAIN EN GARE DE LA CIOTAT – is only *one* key to discovering why and how one of the first publicly screened films in film history has been appropriated here. Razutis's found-footage film is constructed using three different film fragments (from L'ARRIVÉE D'UN TRAIN by Lumière, Abel Gance's LA ROUE and the Warner feature film SPILLS FOR THRILLS). What is striking about it, is the degree of variation in the repeated reworking of the same material – namely the Lumière *arrival* – corresponding to variations in the intertitles, which recombine in three different ways Razutis's film title LUMIÈRE'S TRAIN with a fragment of the Lumière title ARRIVING AT THE STATION. The result can be read so that "Lumière's train arriving at the station (of La Ciotat)" is abridged into "Lumière's train," that train which has fundamental, mythological connotations in relation to cinema.

Razutis begins his four-part film with two alternating motifs: first, parts of a machine – initially the wheels of a locomotive – and second, the railway tracks which constantly change speed. This passage relates to the experience of the nineteenth-century traveler who felt like a projectile. As Schivelbusch puts it: "the rails, cuttings, and tunnels appear as the barrel through which the projectile of the train passes."[39] A rhythmic sound evokes regular mechanical movement and the image-montage evokes the mechanical ensemble of wheel and track. The optical reworking of the material (shots from LA ROUE and SPILLS FOR THRILLS), which in pulsating positive-negative alternations underlines the intermittent nature of movement, and the kinetic effects of close-ups of the track during the journey point to the theoretical loop with which Razutis translates railway technology into the technology of projection. This becomes explicit at the end of the film: here the track no longer flits across the image and instead we see filmstrips, the individual frames of which can no more be seen in projection than the sleepers during the train journey.

At the end of the first part of LUMIÈRE'S TRAIN a shock is in the offing, but the image itself is faded out, only to be shown in the repetition. A circular fade which punctuates each part of the film serves as a kind of tunnel through which the film is pulled again and again. The figurative insistence on *interval* generated by the flicker effect (in the alternation of positive and negative) and the variations in the speed at which the material is run, has its corollary in the history of technology: the electric telegraph system used first in tunnels, and later along the entire railway track, is known as the "space interval system" and works by dividing the track up into individual sections: initially one telegraph was responsible for each of the sections in order to communicate to the next when the track became free (in the fourth part of the film corresponding signals for the driver can be seen).[40]

In the second part of LUMIÈRE'S TRAIN, bearing the intertitle *Lumière's Train (Arriving* – the brackets remain open – repetition becomes manifest as a figure of staging in narrative film: the train races towards a level crossing and only just misses a car crossing the track; a second car, however, does not escape the collision. The suddenness of the collision can only be shown by a series of shots which successively show the same moment from different perspectives. In Razutis's film these conventions are decomposed into a breathtaking kinetic spectacle which is repeated with numerous variations. Accompanied by a consistently ghostly flickering, the scene is deconstructed as the sound of the accident becomes asynchronous and the shots are intercut with others, including the speeding tracks seen in the first section. The clouding-over of the image after the crash with smoke, dust and steam alludes to the texture of the film as a whole, which in contrast to a narrative film *visibly* operates with effects of light, transparencies and veils, beams and frames.

In the third part of the film, *Lumière's Train Arriving (at the Station* – again the brackets remain open – the first film finally appears, having already been iconographically foreshadowed. It consists of a single shot, not this time with its general principle explosively amplified, as in the SPILLS FOR THRILLS scene, but instead remodeled by Razutis to form the core of his film by means of an excessively repetitive loop. He only takes a fragment of L'ARRIVÉE D'UN TRAIN EN GARE DE LA CIOTAT, the movement of the train as it arrives, and through positive-negative alternation turns it into a chronophotographic spectacle. In the last repetition the alternation is also slowed down and the interval becomes manifest as a temporal difference between two single frames, with the result that the asynchronous sound of an approaching steam train off-screen no longer serves as a means for achieving realism, but instead points to both the mechanical principle of repetition itself and to the virtual nature of the train's appearance. LUMIÈRE'S TRAIN thus touches on the issue of the repetition of individual frames of a filmstrip, which can be identical, minimally different or substantially so. This repetition is normally masked by the speed of projection. It becomes apparent that the film is propelled forward by this principle of "photogrammatical" repetition.[41]

Razutis closes his film with scenes from the Warner compilation film SPILLS FOR THRILLS,[42] this time showing a train crash in a station, which he transforms into hallucinogenic spaces by again reworking individual frames and using positive-negative-effects; it ends with the title *at the Station)* and this time the brackets are closed. This part of the film has a good deal in common with Peter Tscherkassky's L'ARRIVÉE (1998), a miniature lasting three minutes which reworks footage from MAYERLING (1968) by Terence Young, and which also concentrates on a scene in a railway station. In Tscherkassky's case the "arrival" is as uncertain as it was with Razutis. Initially the image appears to be searching for its rightful place in the field of projection – it moves cautiously from the right into the empty field, unstable, mirrored or doubled it displaces the frame line before finally finding its rightful place and locating a representative space for the event itself, the arrival of the train. As with Razutis, Tscherkassky's "arrival of a train in the station" culminates in a chaotic torrent of images stripped of their materiality. In both films the perforated filmstrip surfaces at this point as a visible image support which goes through a process not dissimilar to that turmoil experienced by the wagons, buildings and people caught up in a crash. But why does the replication (Razutis) or the refiguration (Tscherkassky) of Lumière's L'ARRIVÉE D'UN TRAIN generate such violent action in the realm of image and structure? One explanation may lie in the attempts by the filmmakers to investigate the different ways in which found images can be repeated. This is particularly evident in both the countless effects achieved by copying and also in those techniques which target the materiality of the original. Unlike Jacobs, whose work still speaks of cinema's paradoxical position between referentiality and the illusion of the real, Razutis and Tscherkassky are no longer concerned with the idea of the imprint of reality but rather the imprint of film. A film print serves as material, as primary and original imagery, and no longer as the trace of light from a profilmic reality. A second reason for the dissolution of images may well lie in an archaeological break within the history of visual representation which cinema as a visual phenomenon brings with it.[43] Finally, a third reason may rest in a reflection on the iconographic legacy, the afterlife of this first film.

Film history tends to extol the well-chosen construction of the Lumière film L'ARRIVÉE D'UN TRAIN, its dynamic composition, the invention of the planned sequence, of optical contrasts and of shot selection which enhances spatial depth.[44] Henri Langlois for example highlighted the slightly slanted framing with its perspectival alignment, the diagonal movement, the triangular structure (no principle action in the center of the frame), actions occurring in different directions which enhance one another visually or do not "cancel each other out."[45]

It would perhaps be too simple to claim that the myth of the audience's reaction at the first film screening is what led Razutis and Tscherkassky to show the dissolution of images and the point at which they begin to be obliterated. The legend of the panic at the Lumière screening in the Grand Café in Paris can, after all, not be authenticated historically, as recent studies of Lumière have shown.[46] It is more likely that both Tscherkassky and Razutis are exploring the emotional response of subsequent audiences of the film and attempting to read these responses – which become increasingly conventional and one-dimensional across the course of film history – into what was one of the most sensational film of early cinema: for example the somatic reaction of the audience confronted by the spectacular movements of an action film (in the case of Razutis) or the use of the most emotionally charged image of all, the close-up (in the case of Tscherkassky). Both are there in L'ARRIVÉE D'UN TRAIN: the headlong, dizzying spectacle and the loss of a sense of distance within the frame on account of movement directly towards the spectator.

In line with Gunning's theory, it could be argued that the myth of the horrified audience at that first screening can be related back to bewilderment at the power of the cinematic *dispositif* rather than the speed of the actual train: "It is not credibility that counts, but rather the incredible nature of the illusion itself which renders the viewer speechless."[47] The fear aroused by L'ARRIVÉE D'UN TRAIN can also be analyzed, as does Philippe Dubois, as a consequence of the loss of distance, the unsettling proximity of the image to the viewer. Because already with the "arrival of the train" he is gradually introduced to the close-up which "threatens to exit the frame in order the tear the screen and enter the auditorium."[48] Already in the case of Lumière, the approaching locomotive and the approaching figures establish an immeasurable closeness. It is perhaps in this context that the end of Tscherkassky's film should be read: having opened up the seams in the material, expanded the visual field beyond the frame, and attacked the perforations and emulsion to the point of distortion in order to generate a vertiginous sensation of pulsating diagonals, he finally has another train emerge from the catastrophic torrent of images and a woman climb out of it. Seen mythologically, the woman in Tscherkassky's reworked scene from Terence Young's iconographic reiteration of Lumière is, of course, not a descendant of Mme Lumière herself but rather a female star, Catherine Deneuve. And whilst in Lumière's case two vanishing points or actions can be registered in the visual field, we have in the classic narrative film a single focus of attention placed at its center. The shocking phenomenon from the turn of the century has become the anticipation of a star, the close-up is no longer of the locomotive but of the female face which has become the image.

To conclude, we could say that the Lumière "arrival of the train" and, in particular, the numerous (train) journeys produced by the Lumière operatives mark the beginning of an aesthetic and cultural concurrence of railway and film which was emotionally prefigured much earlier. Contemporary avant-garde film has reflected on the technical and mythological history of this connection and also on the kinship between the two *dispositifs* of perception. As well as highlighting two fundamental components of the cinematographic aesthetic – movement and the interval – the diverse reworkings of found material I have analyzed also lead us back to a particular type of repetition which could be termed complex insofar as it makes technical requirements manifest, but is not itself reducible to mechanical or material repetition.

Translated by Martin Brady

Notes

This text is a revised version of a lecture given on March 9, 2002 as part of the conference "Early Cinema and the Avant-garde" organized by *Sixpack* and held in the Vienna Stadtkino. For their valuable suggestions and help I would like to thank Peter Tscherkassky, Gabriele Jutz, Brigitta Burger-Utzer and Jan-Christopher Horak. The text was first published in German, under the title "Lumière, der Zug und die Avantgarde," *Die Spur durch den Spiegel. Der Film in der Kultur der Moderne,* ed. Malte Hagener, Johann N. Schmidt and Michael Wedel (Berlin: Bertz, 2004) 27-41.

1. Michel Ciment, "Entretien avec Jean Renoir (sur LA BÊTE HUMAINE)," *Positif* 173 (1973): 16.
2. Maurice Pialat, quoted in Raymond Bellour, *L'entre-image 2* (Paris: POL, 1999) 172.
3. Here an aesthetic principle of reordering is combined with the figure of the *dispositif.* The motif of the train thus acquires a different function from that in classic, narrative films, where the figure of the railway is also present as a structuring device. An example is Chaplin's MONSIEUR VERDOUX (1947) where the murders are intercut with close-ups of rotating wheels.
4. Leo Charney and Vanessa Schwartz, "Introduction," *Cinema and the Invention of Modern Life,* ed. Leo Charney and Vanessa Schwartz (Berkeley/Los Angeles: U of California P, 1995) 1.
5. Jacques Aumont, "The Variable Eye, or the Mobilization of the Gaze," *The Image in Dispute. Art and Cinema in the Age of Photography,* ed. Dudley Andrew (Austin: U of Texas P, 1997) 231-58.
6. The perception of the foreground was a fundamental experience of pre-industrial travel. See Wolfgang Schivelbusch, *The Railway Journey. The Industrialization of Time and Space in the 19th Century,* trans. Anselm Hollo (Oxford: Blackwell, 1980) 65.
7. Tom Gunning, "Before Documentary: Early Non-Fiction Films and the 'View' Aesthetic," *Uncharted Territory: Essays on Early Non Fiction Film,* ed. Daan Hertogs and Nico de Klerk (Amsterdam: Nederlands Filmmuseum, 1997) 9-24.
8. Lynne Kirby, *Parallel Tracks. The Railroad and Silent Cinema* (London: Durham, 1997).
9. Benjamin Gastineau quoted in Schivelbusch 63.
10. Kirby describes in particular the exhibition practices of Hale's Tours; as examples of topoi and stories she refers to ARRIVÉES..., A RAILWAY TRAGEDY, THE HOLD-UP OF THE ROCKY MOUNTAINS EXPRESS and LE TUNNEL SOUS LA MANCHE. Suspense and attraction were guaranteed equally in both chase and travel films. Kirby 250.
11. This is often understood by contemporary theorists as a signal of modernity. See for example Ben Singer, "Modernity, Hyperstimulus, and the Rise of Popular Sensationalism," *Cinema and the Invention of Modern Life* 72-102.
12. Cosmopolitan perception is characterized by Georg Simmel in "Die Großstädte und das Geistesleben" (1903) as "the rapid crowding of changing images, the sharp discontinuity in the grasp of a single glance and the unexpectedness of onrushing impressions" (quoted in Schivelbusch 60).
13. Tom Gunning, "An Unseen Energy Swallows Space: The Space in Early Film and Its Relation to American Avant-Garde Film," *Film Before Griffith,* ed. John L. Fell (Berkeley: U of California P, 1983) 355-66.
14. William Wees, *Recycled Images. The Art and Politics of Found Footage Films* (New York: Anthology Film Archives, 1993); Bart Testa, *Back and Forth. Early Cinema and the Avant-Garde* (Ontario: Art Gallery of Ontario, 1992).
15. Thomas Elsaesser, "Louis Lumière – the Cinema's First Virtualist?," *Cinema Futures: Cain, Abel or Cable?,* ed. Thomas Elsaesser and Kay Hoffman (Amsterdam: Amsterdam UP, 1997) 57-58.
16. Along with the films I analyze here there are, of course, other examples of contemporary found-footage films that have the railway as their theme. William Wees

notes the following examples of films that deal with trains: Bruce Baillie's CASTRO
STREET, Stan Brakhage's SONG XIII, Bruce Conner's VALSE TRISTE, Ken Jacobs's
GEORGETOWN LOOP and DISORIENT EXPRESS, Jean Mitry's PACIFIC 231, Bill Morrison's THE DEATH TRAIN, Marta Nielson's TRAINS OF THOUGHT, Al Razutis's LUMI-
ÈRE'S TRAIN (ARRIVING AT THE STATION), David Rimmer's CANADA PACIFIC I & II,
Kim Thompson's THIS IS THE END OF ME and Steven Topping's reading Canada
backwards. Wees has pointed out that there is concentration of these films in Canada, where the development of the railway played a decisive role in the constitution
of geographical identity. See William Wees, *Proposal 'Trains and Experimental Film'*
(unpublished manuscript, 1999). It should also be noted that in Canada multi-media
artists have also turned to early views of the railways: Stan Douglas, for example,
uses a phantom ride for his installation OVERTURE which he couples with a reading
from Proust's *À la recherche du temps perdu*.

17. See the detailed study by Tom Gunning, "Doctor Jacobs' Dream Work," *Millennium
Film Journal* 10-11 (Fall-Winter 1981-82): 210-18; and the special issue of *Exploding
Cinema*, Oct. 2000, which is dedicated to the French video edition of TOM, TOM, THE
PIPER'S SON.

18. Walter Benjamin, *Das Passagen-Werk*, vol. 1 (Frankfurt/Main: Suhrkamp 1981) 574.
[English translation: *The Arcades Project* (Cambridge/London: Belkrap Press of Harvard UP, 1999).]

19. On the origin of the film see Philippe-Alain Michaud, "La terre est plate," *1895*,
spec. issue *Exotica* (1996): 7.

20. For example, THE DOCTOR'S DREAM (1978) begins with a shot which is, numerically,
at the center of the original film – Jacobs here places side by side two sequences of
shots which head towards the end and the beginning of the original film.

21. See Philippe Dubois, "Le gros plan primitif," *Revue belge du cinéma* 10 (Winter 1984-
85): 24.

22. Dubois.

23. Ken Jacobs, "Kommentierte Filmographie," compiled by Birgit and Wilhelm Hein,
Kinemathek 70 (Nov. 1986): 62.

24. Bitzer writes: "We were invited to avail ourselves of special engines, or cars, for the
purpose of taking movies of the scenery along the way. [...] The advertising was
then put on a commercial basis – first by the Union Pacific, whose crack train, the
Overland Limited, we photographed. [...] Next came the Canadian Pacific, contract-
ing with us for movies." (quoted in Kirby 22-23). See also Charles Musser, *The Emergence of Cinema* (New York: Scribner's 1990) 150.

25. See Kirby 23.

26. See Jacques Deslandes and Jacques Richard, *Histoire Comparée du Cinéma. Volume 2:
Du cinématographe au cinéma 1896-1906* (Tournai: Casterman, 1968) 286 (quoted in
Dubois 24).

27. See note 13.

28. Gunning, "Doctor Jacobs' Dream Work" 217.

29. Tom Gunning, "An Aesthetic of Astonishment. Early Film and the (In)Credulous
Spectator," *Art and Text* 34 (Spring 1989): 42.

30. Lynne Kirby and Miriam Hansen relate this paradoxical crisis of white, male, technological culture, within which the railway neurotic is reduced to the status of a

female, to the position of the spectator in the early cinema of attractions, which, unlike narrative film, was not yet coded as specifically male. See Kirby 67.

31. André Gaudreault calls this practice in "texto assemblage" to differentiate it, for example, from "in situ editing." André Gaudreault, "Fragmentation and assemblage in the Lumière animated pictures," *Film History* 13.1 (2001): 81.

32. At the time the films were sold singly, shot by shot; the sequencing of them was up to the projectionists.

33. Elsaesser 60.

34. Information to the author from Bill Morrison.

35. See Elsaesser 57-58. See also the contribution by Dulac and Gaudreault in this volume.

36. The term "interval" refers generally to the jump between two shots. In relation to cinema this jump is usually understood as a temporal one. This is defined by a change of shot in which the viewpoint remains unchanged whilst a temporal cut is made (for example by a jump cut). Jacques Aumont therefore suggests that one should refer to this as a (temporal) interval between two immobile images in a series or sequence. This is why the single, instantaneous shot, and in particular the photograph, is best suited to creating sequences which mark out time. On the aesthetic level, according to Aumont, the effect of the interval is in inverse proportion to the degree of narrative content in the images either side of the interval. See Jacques Aumont, *L'Image* (Paris: Nathan, 1990) 185. [English translation: *The Image*, trans. Claire Pajackowska (London: British Film Institute, 1997).]

37. On the ghostlike quality of locomotives in film, see Dubois 24.

38. Jean-Louis Schefer, *Du monde et du mouvement des images* (Paris: Cahiers du cinéma, 1997) 18. When making his Frankenstein-Film Morrison may have had in mind Dreyer's Vampyr (1932), in which the vampire dies as a motoric effect of various temporal images.

39. Schivelbusch 58.

40. Schivelbusch 38.

41. On the "internal repetition" of film see Raymond Bellour, "Ciné-répétitions," *Recherches poïetiques IV. Créations et repetition*, ed. René Passeron (Paris: Klincksieck, 1982) 138.

42. Spills for Thirills is probably a compilation of material from various decades. I am grateful to Jan-Christopher Horak for this suggestion.

43. For a discussion of the archaeological break, see Gunning, "An Aesthetic of Astonishment." Nicole Brenez suggests that Razutis is read in this archaeological sense. Nicole Brenez, *De la figure en général et du corps en particulier. L'invention figurative au cinema* (Bruxelles: De Boeck, 1998) 316.

44. See Barthélémy Amengual, "Lumière, c'est le réalisme...," *Lumière, le cinéma* (Lyon: Institut Lumière, 1992) 60.

45. Henri Langlois, quoted Amengual 60.

46. In his critical study of sources, Martin Loiperdinger investigates the extent to which L'Arrivée d'un Train can be seen as an icon for the beginning of film, and also as a striking example of the manipulatory power that cinema has seemingly had since its inception. Martin Loiperdinger, "Lumières Ankunft des Zuges. Gründungsmythos eines neuen Mediums," *Kintop* 5 (1996): 40. See also on this subject Stephen Botto-

more, "The Panicking Audience? Early Cinema and the 'Train Effect,'" *Historical Journal of Film, Radio and Television* 19.2 (1999): 177-216.

47. Gunning, "An Aesthetic of Astonishment" 42.

48. Dubois 22.

Programming Attractions: Avant-Garde Exhibition Practice in the 1920s and 1930s

Malte Hagener

The cinema program – the sequence of films and numbers within a circum-scribed performance space and time – has recently become a focus of film his-torical research, mostly in relation to early cinema.[1] The program, at least until the 1960s, was an integral and vital part of film exhibition and therefore of the reality of cinema-going. Most often, the implicit (or explicit) imperative of cin-ema programs was to create a harmonious and well-rounded whole in which the constituent elements (entire films and live addresses, outtakes and excerpts, musical interludes and stage spectacles) would blend into one another in order to provide the audience with an integrated unity. Yet, there are exceptions to this rule, one of which will be the focus of this essay: the screening practice of avant-garde clubs and emergent art cinemas in the 1920s and early 1930s in major European cities. So far, the avant-garde has mostly been researched in terms of high modernism, i.e. by focusing on formal-aesthetic composition and by abstracting the work of art from their context of production and reception. A look at the exhibition practices of the Dutch *Filmliga*, the German *Volksfilmver-band*, the London *Film Society*, and some Parisian ciné-clubs and cinemas can open up the avant-garde towards a contextual history in which the practice be-comes a constituent part of its history and theory.[2]

Integrating Attractions

Like any successful concept that transcends the scope of its first application and becomes a catch-phrase, Tom Gunning's idea of "the cinema of attractions" as the paradigm for pre-1906 cinema, has been systematically misunderstood and misapplied. In its current usage the term is most often used as the opposite to "narrative integration" in a simplistic binary schema.[3] In fact, re-reading Gun-ning's canonized 1986 article,[4] one notices that he introduces the two terms as dialectical recto-and-verso which coexisted (and continue to do so) ever since the first films encountered an audience as "it is important for the radical hetero-geneity which I find in early cinema not to be conceived as a truly oppositional program, one irreconcilable with the growth of narrative cinema."[5] The change around 1906 – the alleged shift from attraction to narrative integration – should not be conceptualized as a jerky and mutually exclusive switch from one position to another, but rather as a slow, but constant sliding on a continuum in which the dominance of one term over the other imperceptibly gave way; what has remained stable in this transition is the mutual dependency and coexistence of both extremes. Where one can find attractions, one can find also integration on another level – and the other way around. Despite the term's excessive use leading to the over-stretching and wearing out of the original ideas, I still believe that the concepts can be useful if applied in their original dialectic form. The coexistence of contemplation and distraction in the reception process, of psychology and stimulation in the filmic text, of depth and surface in the audience address, of harmony and shock in narrative strategies is a crucial and basic feature of the cinema. Gunning locates these two specific modes in the uniquely cinematographic relation that couples the (imaginary) filmic space of the screen to the (real) auditorium space of the spectator. Any far-reaching change in the cinema as an institution and as a set of practices is bound up with this relation – here lies the fundamental value of Gunning's conceptual advance. The term, as I understand it, is thus not a purely formalist description of textual features, but aims at the dynamic interchange between spectator and screen.

True to his original dialectical conception, Gunning concedes that "the cinema of attractions does not disappear with the dominance of narrative, but rather goes underground both into certain avant-garde practices and as a component of narrative films."[6] Not coincidentally, Gunning had borrowed his term from Sergei Eisenstein's conception of "montage of attractions," a notion in turn developed by Eisenstein first in relation to his theater work. Tellingly, Gunning opens his article with Léger's reaction to seeing Abel Gance's LA ROUE in 1922. It is the avant-garde of the 1920s that provides the entry point as well as the conceptual framework for the dialectics of attraction and narrative integration. Tracing back this genealogy one becomes aware that exhibition and stage practice in the avant-garde provides indeed the origin of the term "attractions" as used by Gunning (by way of Eisenstein's theorization) and at the same time the point of departure for his argument (by way of Léger's commentary). My essay can thus also be seen as a gesture of circling or a return to an origin (of the concept and the term), yet with a somewhat different agenda in mind.

Alternative Screening Institutions and the Historical Avant-Garde

The historical – or canonical – avant-garde that thrived in major (European) centers[7] from the turn-of-the-century until the mid-1930s is today mainly re-membered for two dozen films exhibiting formal and aesthetic innovations that proved to be influential. While the relatively small numbers of (surviving) films might reflect the dire production circumstances for the film avant-garde in gen-eral, its wing in exhibition was much more accommodating, inclusive and argu-ably also much more active. Focusing solely on the (small) output of a couple of canonized artists is in fact a severely limiting view of the actual (screening and viewing) practice of the avant-garde. One does more justice to the film avant-garde if one considers it to be a wide-ranging initiative with the aim of trans-forming cinema culture as a whole, including production and exhibition, but also the discourse surrounding the cinema and, ultimately, the relationship of the spectator to the screen.

Before turning to concrete examples, let me give a brief overview of the most important avant-garde screening institutions: The *Film Society* in London, most probably the longest-living audience organization in interwar Europe, was ac-tive for 14 seasons (1925-39) with normally eight events per year (only six per-formances during the last two seasons), showing approximately 500 short and feature-length films in a total of 108 programs.[8] On average close to five films were presented in a single event. Of the films screened by the *Film Society* 23% were of British origin, 20% came from France and from Germany respectively, 15% were American, and 7.5% Soviet. A bit more than half of the presented films were silents (263 films), the other half consisted of sound films (237 films); the majority of films had not been shown before in England (312 films), while many shorts (137) were revivals, mostly comedy classics (Chaplin, slapstick). The *Film Society* was ultimately a bourgeois club as the membership fee (twenty-five shillings per season) was too high for workers.[9] Already this statis-tical overview illustrates that the purity and rhetorical militancy to be found in avant-garde manifestoes was basically a publicity stunt and that in (screening) practice the avant-garde was much more diverse than in a limited high modern-ist perspective.

In Germany the most active alternative screening organization was the *Volks-filmverband für Filmkunst* (VFV),[10] a left-wing institution that was initially based on a popular front of communists, socialists and liberal democrats, but that in-creasingly followed the orthodox views issued by the international division of the communist party (ComIntern). Nevertheless, during its short life from early 1928 to mid-1931 it had an impressive track record. In the end of 1929, it peaked with numbers: the VFV had evolved into 14 groups in Berlin (with 62 payment offices) and 33 in other cities. 6000 members were listed for the capital, 1500 in Hamburg, 3000 in Breslau (today: Wrocław) with chapters operating in Chemnitz, Dresden, Erfurt, Frankfurt, Leipzig, Munich, Nuremberg, Offenbach, and other cities.[11] In November 1929 a report stated that the VFV had organized 730 film evenings during the year in different parts of the country and that 32 film programs were at that moment on tour through different cities and regions of Germany. In fact, the organization had become so powerful that it was perceived to be a threat by the nationwide organization of cinema owners (*Reichsverband der Kinobesitzer*) which repeatedly refused to rent space to the organization for fear of nurturing a rival.

The Dutch *Filmliga* was a highly efficient, nationwide association that was active from September 1927 until July 1933 with chapters in more than half a dozen Dutch cities. It emerged from artistically and intellectually minded circles; it had little of the popular front sentiment that characterized the German VFV in its early stages or some later French institutions such as Léon Moussinac's immensely successful, but ultimately short-lived *Les amis de Spartacus*. Besides touring film programs that would be screened in the major cities, the *Filmliga* could boast of visits of international celebrities such as Eisenstein, Vertov, Ruttmann or Moholy-Nagy while also publishing a monthly magazine.[12] The range of activities covered by virtually all film societies and ciné-clubs testifies to the far-reaching and Utopian nature of these avant-garde clubs: the ultimate goal was a transformation of the cinema as institution, art form, industry and *dispositif*. Within the framework of the avant-garde the relationship of the spectator to the screen was a central element – and, as stated above, this is exactly where the concept of attractions becomes useful.

The most important center for alternative activities in the cinema sector in the interwar period was probably France, Paris to be exact, which has been the capital of cinephilia ever since the 1920s when the first screening organizations were started by Louis Delluc, the *Club Français du Cinéma*, and Ricciotto Canudo, the *Club des Amis du Septième Art* (CASA). In the mid-1920s, the mushrooming ciné-clubs were joined by movie theaters specializing in avant-garde and film art while also constructing a repertory of classics.[13] Three places deserve mention as the most legendary permanent screening spaces: the *Théâtre du Vieux Colombier*, run by Jean Tédesco who had taken over the editorship of the cinephile magazine *Cinéa* in 1924 after Louis Delluc had died, opened on 14 November 1924, the *Studio des Ursulines*, directed by Armand Tallier, opened on 21 January 1926 in Montparnasse and the *Studio 28*, under the directorship of Jean Mauclair was active from 10 February 1928 onwards.

Already these overviews of different countries raise questions as to the status of these screening organizations. If we consider the film avant-garde as a small task force of elitist conviction then the relatively broad appeal of these screening organizations contradict the traditional idea of the avant-garde. Yet again, a certain opposition to commercial cinema was necessary as a shared enemy proved to be productive for the internal cohesion of the avant-garde groups.

Screening Practice: Programming Attractions

The first program of the London *Film Society* in October 1925 demonstrates quite well the variety of interests as the mix of films presented was to become typical for the audience organizations of these years, ranging from commercial art cinema[14] with Paul Leni's WACHSFIGURENKABINETT (1923) – often presented as revivals months or years after the première, thus pointing forward to the construction of a canon of classical works and the repertory cinema movement – to abstract films with Walter Ruttmann's LICHTSPIELOPUS 2, 3, 4 (1919-25), from the ever-popular Chaplin (CHAMPION CHARLIE, 1916) and local heroes (Adrian Brunel's TYPICAL BUDGET, 1925) to pre-war Westerns (HOW BRONCHO BILLY LEFT BEAR COUNTRY, 1912). Whereas some of the radical manifestoes of the avant-garde read as if purely abstract, "absolute" films were the sole diet, in fact the programs were very much a composition of divergent styles in order to cater to the audience that was similarly diversified. The combination of commercial art cinema, avant-garde in the narrow sense and older films foregrounded the contrast between different filmmaking styles, a built-in reflexivity that encouraged the spectator to reflect on the medium as such.

A typical feature of avant-garde screening practice all through the 1920s and 1930s was the inclusion of revivals. A typical program of the avant-garde screening organizations combined new material with older films, articulating a sense of history by the contrast between films from different eras. Aside from the avant-garde's successful establishment of film as art, the screening practice also put the idea on the map that film was a medium with its own history.[15] Moreover, seeing Ruttmann's "absolute" animations alongside a Chaplin-short foregrounds self-reflexively the medium that encompasses such diverse examples. Since the avant-garde as a movement was searching for the essence of film – concepts that had been nominated include the French *photogénie*, Eisenstein's *montage of attractions*, the *absoluter Film*, but also Balász' *Geist des Films* or Menno ter Braak's dialectical pair of rhythm and form – the pure variety of different film formats posed the question of what constitutes cinema. Even though an art film such as Leni's WACHSFIGURENKABINETT might provide a closed narrative universe, the inclusion of such a film within a varied program directly works against a purely contemplative stance. The screening situation, often with lectures and guests, and the gathering of films from diverse styles into one program highlights the sheer diversity of the films screened within the avant-garde and thus confronts the spectator with the question of what constitutes the common denominator if such diverse examples can be combined in a program. As a result, the question of the essence of film was high on the agenda of the avant-garde screening organizations. Thus, the confrontational nature of the avant-garde attractions was less an effect of the single film than of the confrontation between different films, an external montage instead of an internal one. Effectively, the exhibition wing of the avant-garde advanced – implicitly in the programs – its own idea of what was specific about the medium: a syncretist form as exemplified by the attractionist combination of films.

The German context was characterized by political fights, but also by frictions with the commercial film industry. Already the first event organized by the *Volksfilmverband* ran into difficulties when the film industry attempted to block the renting of the Berlin movie theater Capitol in order to stop the VFV from their first public outing.[16] This event on 26 February 1928 boasted two programmatic addresses by Heinrich Mann and Béla Balász,[17] a montage of snippets from newsreels and features entitled WAS WIR WOLLEN – WAS WIR NICHT WOLLEN (Béla Balász, Albrecht Viktor Blum, 1928), while the main feature of the evening was Vsevolod Pudovkin's KONEC SANKT-PETERBURGA (1926).[18] Blum, today a largely forgotten filmmaker, was a specialist of the so-called cross-section films that addressed social, cultural and economic issues.[19] Already the title of the film, "What we want, what we don't want," appears to illustrate the dialectical approach of the avant-garde – showing that which is wanted alongside that which is unwanted. Images and scenes from different sources are not blended into a coherent whole, but put into a free play of contrast between positive and negative elements. Motivating the spectator to actively evaluate the fragments on the screen demands a very different conception of spectatorship, one less based on an enveloping and immersive story world that smoothly and snugly tucks in the spectator, but rather an assaulting and aggressive environment with which the visitor has to cope. Moreover, the isolation of fragments fits Gunning's description of the early cinema of attractions as it "directly solicits spectator's attention, inciting visual curiosity, and supplying pleasure through an exciting spectacle."[20] The montage from different sources obliged the spectator to stay alert since the film took turns with every new fragment, even though one could argue that the pleasure lies rather in the spectator's activity of creating an ordered universe (based on politics) out of a chaotic jumble.

Distributors, producers and cinema owners alike attempted to block activities of the VFV: the society publicly complained about (politically motivated) unfair prices and behavior by various cinema owners in medium-sized German cities which forced the institution to switch to multi-purpose spaces in pubs, restaurants or union halls – an environment not well-suited for either the contemplative self-absorption of high modernism or the cozy and self-forgotten classical diegetic universe.[21] Already the spatial surroundings created a situation more akin to the early cinema of the fairground and variety than to the alternative film theaters of the 1920s. A typical program took this environment into account and looked like this: "Gut gewählte und geschnittene Teile" (Well-selected and edited pieces) from three films directed by Vsevolod Pudovkin, MATJ (1926), KONEC SANKT-PETERSBURGA (1926), POTOMOK CINGIS-HANA (1928), and parts of ZEMLJA W PLENU (Fedor Ozep, 1928). Not only Pudovkin attended the screening, but also Ozep, MATJ-actress Vera Baranovskaia and cameraman Anatoli Golownja.[22] Contrary to later belief, also fostered in cinémathèques and film museums, the organic unity of the artwork played only a subordinate role in avant-garde screening practice. Penetrating excerpts with speeches meant downplaying the integration of the filmic text at the expense of highlighting isolated parts which could count as attractions in their confrontational value and their nature of pure visibility, two factors important in Gunning's theorization of the cinema of attractions.

Less than three weeks later, the same organization presented a program of educational and scientific films (*Kulturfilme*), selected and introduced by Dr. Edgar Beyfuß working for the German major Ufa at the time. According to contemporary sources the program attempted to give the audience an insight into the many-sided matter of film production.[23] The main feature, DIE WUNDER DES FILMS (Edgar Beyfuß, 1928), consists of three parts: the first part shows how travelogues are being made followed by a presentation of the problems faced when making animal documentaries while the third part deals with trick technique within educational cinema. Aesthetic appreciation and artistic innovation take second position behind the educational impetus of the film programs. Especially the politically motivated institutions, often aimed at a working class audience, gravitated towards a didactic and educational approach. Moreover, Beyfuß's film is a lesson in how cinematic illusion is constructed as it constantly discloses and uncovers the fabricated nature of the cinema, similar to the self-referential logic of early cinema: "this is a cinema that displays its visibility, willing to rupture a self-enclosed fictional world for a chance to solicit the attention of the spectator."[24] Indeed, rupturing a fictional world was seen as a radical weapon in itself, be it via abstraction, Surrealist juxtaposition or political agitation – a key feature of the avant-garde (and maybe its lowest common denominator) is its opposition to the stable and self-enclosed diegetic universe that was commercial narrative cinema's mainstay.

The screening practice at the Parisian ciné-clubs and specialized theaters were initially rather inspired by notions of film history and classics than animated by ideas of abstract or experimental work. On the one hand very few avant-garde films existed in the first half of the 1920s (the first wave of films now canonized as part of the classical avant-garde was made around 1924), on the other the notion of film art had to be worked through and established. For that reason the early programs of the French outlets for alternative cinema consisted of Chaplin and Griffith, Feuillade and Sjöström, Stiller and Lang – it was first of all a historical orientation that contributed to the emergence of alternative screening outlets.[25]

A brief look at the opening programs of the major avant-garde cinemas in Paris should give a rough idea of what was current practice at the time. The *Théâtre du Vieux Colombier* opened on 14 November 1924 with a program of André Sauvage's mountain-climbing documentary LA TRAVERSÉE DU GRÉPON/ L'ASCENSION DU GRÉPON (1923), Marcel Silver's experimental L'HORLOGE (1924) and Charlie Chaplin's short SUNNYSIDE (1921). This mixture of repertory classics (Chaplin), non-fiction (GRÉPON) and experimental work in a stricter sense (L'HORLOGE) was typical for avant-garde clubs as well as specialized movie theaters in the 1920s (we have seen a similar program in London). The mixed interests combining scientific, educational and aesthetic streaks were much broader than retrospective considerations of the avant-garde focused on formal innovations in a handful of classics would have it. Likewise, the initial program of the *Studio des Ursulines*, that opened on 21 January 1926 in Montparnasse, consisted of a mixture of repertory, experiment, and accessible art cinema: MIMOSA LA DERNIÈRE GRISETTE (Léonce Perret, 1906), a re-edited version of ENTR'ACTE (René Clair and Francis Picabia, 1924) and FREUDLOSE GASSE (G.W. Pabst, 1925). The French film clubs leaned towards debate and were more communicative than their British pendants. Film societies in Britain were far more frontal with introductions to the films, whereas in France it was more common to have discussion afterwards. The inaugural program of the *Studio 28* in February 1928 consisted of a documentary on the making of Abel Gance's NAPOLÉON (1925-1927) and of Abram Room's TRET'JA MESCANSKAJA (1927), a Soviet comedy about the perils and pleasures of the lack of living space in the big cities. Again, Gunning's thought on pre-1906 cinema fits this practice as well: "Making use of both fictional and non-fictional attractions, its energy moves outward towards an acknowledged spectator rather than inward towards the character-based situations essential to classical narrative."[26] The energy flowed outward in the avant-garde screening practice as it opposed the closed forms that classical cinema had established in the 1920s.

The same centrifugal flow of energy can also be found in the Netherlands. The Dutch *Filmliga* presented many films that are by now classics of art cinema: F.W. Murnau's NOSFERATU (1921), C.T. Dreyer's LA PASSION DE JEANNE D'ARC (1928), and Russian montage films. Besides, it had perhaps one of the most regulatory boards of directors of international film societies: Older, pre-war films were combined with avant-garde classics, but also with quality art films to prove the superiority of abstract film art. The main proponent of this educational programming policy seems to have been Menno ter Braak who put his theoretical convictions down in a book of film theory entitled consequently *Cinema Militans* and published in 1929.[27] The main asset of the *Filmliga* was the sheer variety of different films. The aim of this policy was manifold: On the one hand, spectators should learn to recognize the "superior quality" of avant-garde cinema; for that reason sometimes sequences from commercial feature films were presented, discussed and commented upon. On the other hand, any new development in the cinema that could possibly be a subject for further research should be explored. Out of these ideas evolved a screening and programming practice that saw comparing and contrasting as the key ingredients of the *Filmliga*.[28] The *Filmliga* was against mixing different forms of entertainment (film with musical numbers etc.), yet it also rejected the superficial unity of the commercial cinema that aimed at a creating an impenetrable illusion for the spectator – often, excerpt and scenes were screened or very diverse films came together in a single program.

The Birth of Film History from the Spirit of Attractionist Avant-Garde

As should have become obvious from this brief overview of the screening practice, it is only retrospectively that the film societies and the avant-garde have been purified and reduced to a handful of formal experiments. Whereas today's list of avant-garde classics is short and could be squeezed into 3 or 4 evenings of film presentation (and indeed often is at cinémathèques and film museums), the film societies organized screenings on a regular basis (normally once every month) and were often active over a period of years. Thus, it was a necessity to resort to "commercial art cinema," older slapstick (often Chaplin or Keaton), documentary, scientific or educational film. And indeed, even the canonized classics clearly show these influences: ENTR'ACTE and VORMITTAGSSPUK pay homage to slapstick, L'AGE D'OR and LAS HURDAS poke fun at scientific filmmaking, Adrian Brunel made a whole series of parodies (TYPICAL BUDGET, CROSSING THE GREAT SAGRADA) while educational films were made by figure heads such as Joris Ivens or Hans Richter.

Film societies had basically three options for putting a program together. Either they could only meet at irregular intervals (whenever new films were available) or they had to resort to older films which had been shown before. While the first option led almost invariably to a process of disintegration, the second was the most common option, yet it had the side effect of blurring the initial opposition to ordinary cinema culture. This tendency led to an overlap with commercial cinemas and finally to art cinemas which took away the more lucrative films from the screening clubs. A third option was the programming policy of the Dutch *Filmliga* which had a didactic approach to programming with screening bits and pieces from older films in order to demonstrate specific points. The choice of the *Filmliga* was only possible with a strong board pushing through their agenda.

The French context of the 1920s is full of examples in which earlier film styles were rediscovered; the crucial revival of Gance's La Roue which provides Gunning's point of entry into his argument has already been mentioned in the beginning. Suffice it to point out two other instances here linked in a peculiar way to the emergence of film historiography, the archive movement, and a general sense of film as a medium with a history. The first is the (re)discovery of Georges Méliès in the late 1920s which has been documented thoroughly by Roland Cosandey.[29] The revival of one of early cinema's masters peaked in a gala evening on 16 December 1929, an event in which both Jean Mauclaire and Armand Tallier (directors of, respectively, the avant-garde cinemas *Studio 28* and *Studio des Ursulines*), the high-brow modernist magazine *Revue du cinéma* (edited by Jean-George Auriol, published by Gallimard) as well as more nationalist circles took part in. What strikes me in this context is how issues of early cinema (the fascination for attractions), modernism (the films provided the avant-garde with an alternative model of how conventional narrative could be resisted) and nationalism (the re-discovery was partly motivated by claiming the cinema's pedigree as French) intersected in public screening practice related to the avant-garde. These concerns materialized around the idea of (film) history, a notion that presupposes a contrasting approach and a sense of change because historiography is based upon the concept of transformation over time. Contrasting as a strategy of screening thus not only adhered to the underlying philosophy of the cinema of attractions, but also gave rise to film historiography.

That this strategy was not limited to avant-garde circles – at least at a crucial moment when many people believed that the avant-garde would truly become a mass movement – can be illustrated quite well by the program accompanying Berlin, die Sinfonie der Grossstadt on its première and also in subsequent screenings in major cities across Germany on the "first run-circuit." Ruttmann's film was preceded by a program of short films from the years 1905 to 1910 entitled *Kintopp vor 20 Jahren* and described as a "hilarious retrospective to the time when the cinema was young."[30] These films were aimed to demonstrate the "progress" that the cinema had made in the intervening twenty years, the development in the meantime and the achievements of film culture. This act of framing an avant-garde film with short films of a bygone era only makes sense when thinking about the cinema in historical terms and the avant-garde in its rhetoric of advance towards a brighter future surely had a sense of historical calling. Of course, the films were meant to be laughed at and ridiculed as specimen of a primitive age that the present day has left behind, but as critic Willy Haas, lucid as ever, remarked, this was not without its imminent dangers:

> To start with, short films, about twenty years old. Including the narrator as it used to be. "From step to step"; "Mother, your child is calling!"; "Parisian fashion show"; "Piquanterie with lady's panties and bathing suit." Around the year 1910. The audience squealed with delight.
>
> Big fun – but mean fun. Plebeian fun. The mocking laughter about yesterday; the triumphant laughter: how far we have gotten... And a dangerous fun.
>
> Tomorrow – in twenty years time – one will laugh even more about the film BERLIN, SYMPHONY OF A BIG CITY. One will have gotten even further. The pompous title will be met with derision. "The minuet of a small town" – some film critic will say ironically twenty years from now.[31]

More than the amused spectators Haas is highly aware of his own historical situatedness. Especially the avant-garde which, in its choice of name, had projected the spatial metaphor of the military into the temporal realm should have been wary of the a-historical arrogance implicit in the opening program for BERLIN. The avant-garde by conception needed the mainstream to follow, yet by becoming popular with the masses the avant-garde had to find a new path to pursue. Thus, a cycle of innovation and proliferation of certain features is characteristic of the avant-garde and its becoming out-of-date is to be expected as Willy Haas clearly saw.

Let me now turn to a final example, one not taken from avant-garde screening practice, but exemplifying the spectatorship that relates early cinema and the avant-garde. The accentuation of the isolated attraction, "this harnessing of visibility, this act of showing and exhibition"[32] as Gunning claimed, with the simultaneous downplaying of narrative integration was neither limited to film production nor to exhibition, but it can also be found in the act of cinema going and in the reception posture. The doyen of the Surrealist movement André Breton has remembered his habits of cinema-going in his late 1910s in Nantes as a playful zapping activity:

> ...appreciating nothing as much as dropping into the cinema when whatever was playing was playing, at any point in the show, and leaving at the first hint of boredom – of surfeit – to rush off to another cinema where we behaved in the same way, and so on [...]. I have never known anything *more magnetizing*: [...] the important thing is that one came out "charged" for a few days...[33]

Although Breton did not visit here avant-garde screening houses, what he describes is a spectator position similar both to the early cinema of attractions as well as to avant-garde strategies described above. Breton is proposing a truly deconstructionist operation; instead of following closely the cues provided by the film's audiovisual structure as purported in neo-formalist doctrine,[34] the Surrealists sought the impact of (random) fragments where continuity is created arbitrarily through a loose series of confrontation with isolated parts. Following a preordained logic is replaced by an *ad hoc* logic, the tightly-knit causality gives way to a loose succession and the coherent time-space continuum (of classical cinema as well as of a standard show at a movie theater) is transformed at the expense of an a-logical, disparate mixture of shards of time and space. This radical act of self-confrontation with moments removed from a closed diegetic universe creates the same relationship between screen and spectator as that of the cinema of attractions and as that of avant-garde screening clubs.

Conclusion

The specific contribution of the avant-garde to the film culture of the 1920s and 1930s was its constant attention to the tensions and contradictions haunting the cinema as an economic enterprise, a social force, a cultural power, and, last but not least, an art form. The "great unresolved equation between art and business"[35] was foregrounded on different levels by avant-garde activities. Whereas commercial cinema attempted to conceal and cover the inherent strains, fissures, cracks and fault lines of the cinema, the avant-garde exposed and allegorized these aporias on different levels. Thus, while the pair of attractions and narrative integration went "underground" within commercial cinema, the avant-garde acknowledged and actively engaged with these factors: yet, this dialectical relation is not limited to the films as formal-aesthetic objects, but also to be found, as I have hoped to illustrate, in the screening practices of the avant-garde organizations where not only a limited number of avant-garde films were screened, but a diverse mixture of styles and genres confronted the spectator in this "harnessing of visibility, this act of showing and exhibition."

Notes

1.   See for example Frank Kessler, Sabine Lenk and Martin Loiperdinger, eds., *Kinematographen-Programme*, spec. issue of *KINtop* 11 (2002).

2. See my *Moving Forward, Looking Back. The European Avant-garde and the Invention of Film Culture, 1919-1936* (Amsterdam: Amsterdam UP, forthcoming).
3. These terms were first introduced by André Gaudreault and Tom Gunning in their 1985 paper at Cerisy. See also the dossier of this volume.
4. Tom Gunning, "The Cinema of Attractions: Early Film, Its Spectators and the Avant-Garde," *Early Cinema: Space Frame Narrative*, ed. Thomas Elsaesser (London: British Film Institute, 1990) 56-62.
5. Gunning, "The Cinema of Attractions" 61.
6. Gunning, "The Cinema of Attractions" 57.
7. On the significance of cosmopolitan centers such as Paris, Berlin, Vienna, Prague, London, Amsterdam/Rotterdam for modernist art and culture see Malcolm Bradbury, "The Cities of Modernism," *Modernism 1890-1930*, ed. Malcolm Bradbury and James McFarlane (Harmondsworth: Penguin, 1976) 96-103.
8. For memories and eyewitness accounts of the British Film Society, see Jen Samson, "The Film Society, 1925-1939," *All Our Yesterdays. 90 Years of British Cinema*, ed. Charles Barr (London: British Film Institute, 1986) 306-13; Peter Wollen, Alan Lovell, Sam Rohdie, "Interview with Ivor Montagu," *Screen* 13.3 (Fall 1972): 71-113; Ivor Montagu, "Old Man's Mumble. Reflections on a Semi-Centenary," *Sight & Sound* (Fall 1975): 222. For an unauthorized reprint of the programs accompanying the screenings, see *The Film Society Programmes, 1925-1939* (New York: Arno, 1972). For a thorough historiographic overview of this period in Great Britain, see Jamie Sexton, *The Emergence of an Alternative Film Culture in Inter-War Britain*, diss., University of East Anglia, 2001; and his article "The Film Society and the creation of an alternative film culture in Britain in the 1920s," *Young and Innocent? The Cinema in Britain, 1896-1930*, ed. Andrew Higson (Exeter: U of Exeter P, 2002) 291-320.
9. It was this economic threshold built into the Film Society membership fee that contributed to the foundation of workers' film clubs around 1929. See Bert Hogenkamp, *Deadly Parallels. Film and the Left in Britain, 1929-1939* (London: Lawrence & Wishart, 1986).
10. For film activities in Germany on the left of the political spectrum, see Willi Lüdecke, *Der Film in Agitation und Propaganda der revolutionären deutschen Arbeiterbewegung (1919-1933)* (Berlin: Oberbaumverlag, 1973); Gertraude Kühn, Karl Tümmler and Walter Wimmer, eds., *Film und revolutionäre Arbeiterbewegung in Deutschland 1918-1932* (Berlin/DDR: Henschel, 1975); Jürgen Berger, et al., eds., *Erobert den Film! Proletariat und Film in der Weimarer Republik* (Berlin: Neue Gesellschaft für Bildende Künste, 1977); David Welsh, "The Proletarian Cinema and the Weimar Republic," *Historical Journal of Film, Radio and Television* 1.1 (1981): 3-18; Bruce Murray, *Film and the German Left in the Weimar Republic. From "Caligari" to "Kuhle Wampe"* (Austin: U of Texas P, 1990); Stattkino Berlin, et al., *Revolutionärer Film in Deutschland (1918-1933)* (Berlin: Stattarchiv, 1996).
11. See Rudolf Schwarzkopf, "Unser Ziel und unser Weg," *Film und Volk* 1.1 (March 1929): 5.
12. On the history of the Filmliga, see Nico de Klerk and Ruud Visschedijk, eds., *Het gaat om de film! Een nieuwe geschiedenis van de Nederlandsche Filmliga 1927-1933* (Amsterdam: Bas Lubberhuizen/Filmmuseum, 1999). For a complete reprint of their magazine, see Jan Heijs, ed., *Filmliga 1927-1931* (Nijmegen: SUN, 1982).

13. For an overview of the Parisian avant-garde context of the 1920s, see Christophe Gauthier, *La Passion du cinéma. Cinéphiles, ciné-clubs et salles spécialisées à Paris de 1920 à 1929* (Paris: AFRHC/Ecole des Chartres, 1999); and Noureddine Ghali, *L'avant-garde* cinématographique en France dans les années vingt. Idées, conceptions, théories (Paris: Expérimental, 1995). For an English-language overview, see Richard Abel, *French Cinema: The First Wave 1915–1929* (Princeton: Princeton UP, 1984).

14. I am aware that "commercial art cinema" is a term that is not contemporary to the interwar period, but a concept that emerged in the 1960s. I am using the expression in the sense that has been suggested by Thomas Elsaesser, *Weimar Cinema and After. Germany's Historical Imaginary* (London/New York: Routledge, 2000).

15. A thorough discussion of the emergence of film historiography (and of the archive movement) would lead me too far astray here; suffice it to point out that Paul Rotha, Georges Sadoul, Henri Langlois, Iris Barry, Jerzy Toeplitz and virtually all film historians and archivists of the first generation were educated in ciné-clubs and film societies of the 1920s and 1930s.

16. See *Berliner Volkszeitung* 22 Feb. 1928, quoted in Karl Tümmler: "Zur Geschichte des Volksfilmverbandes," *Filmwissenschaftliche Mitteilungen* 5 (1964): 1229.

17. Both speeches were reprinted in the magazine of the society. See Béla Balász, "Der Film arbeitet für uns!," *Film und Volk* 1 (March 1928): 6-8; Heinrich Mann, "Film und Volk," *Film und Volk* 2 (April 1928): 4-6.

18. See for a review of the event Bernard von Brentano, "Volksverband für Filmkunst," *Frankfurter Zeitung* 28 Feb. 1928.

19. See Thomas Tode, "Albrecht Viktor Blum," *CineGraph – Lexikon zum deutschsprachigen Film*, ed. Hans-Michael Bock (München: edition text + kritik, 1984ff).

20. Gunning, "The Cinema of Attractions" 58.

21. See the open letter by the *Volksfilmverband*, "Der Verband will ins Kino," *Film-Kurier* 13 Dec. 1928.

22. See –e–, "Russische Film-Matinee. Die Künstler sprechen," *Lichtbild-Bühne* 14 Jan. 1929.

23. "Die Wunder des Films. Sondervorstellung des Volks-Film-Verbandes im Tauentzienpalast," *Lichtbild-Bühne* 4 Feb. 1929.

24. Gunning, "The Cinema of Attractions" 57.

25. For an account of the birth of film history and of the creation of a canon of classical films, see Gauthier 81-102.

26. Gunning, "The Cinema of Attractions" 59.

27. Menno ter Braak, *Cinema Militans* (Utrecht: De Gemeenschap, 1929).

28. See Tom Gunning, "Ontmoetingen in verduisterde ruimten. De alternatieve programmering van de Nederlandsche Filmliga," *Het gaat om de film!* 242-46.

29. See Roland Cosandey, "Georges Méliès as l'inescamotable Escamoteur. A Study in Recognition," *A Trip to the Movies. Georges Méliès, Filmmaker and Magician (1861-1938)*, ed. Paolo Cherchi Usai (Pordenone: Giornate del cinema muto, 1991) 56-111.

30. See for example *Film-Kurier* 29 Sept. 1927.

31. Willy Haas, "Film-Kritik. Berlin, die Symphonie der Großstadt," *Film-Kurier* 24 Sept. 1927. My translation.

32. Gunning, "The Cinema of Attractions" 56.

33. André Breton, "As in a Wood" (first published in 1951); rpt. in translation in *The Shadow and Its Shadow. Surrealist Writing on the Cinema*, ed. Paul Hammond (Edinburgh: Polygon, 1991) 80-85, here 81.

34. See the work of David Bordwell and Kristin Thompson, especially Thompson, Bordwell, *Film Art. An Introduction* (New York: McGraw, 1993); Bordwell, *Narration in the Fiction Film* (London: Routledge, 1985); Thompson, *Breaking the Glass Armor. Neoformalist Film Analysis* (Princeton: Princeton UP, 1988).

35. Paul Rotha quoted in Geoffrey Nowell-Smith, *The Oxford History of World Cinema* (Oxford: Oxford UP, 1998) xix.

The Associational Attractions of the Musical

Pierre-Emmanuel Jaques

In use again in the 1980s, the concept of attraction first provided a way to analyze the discourse features of early cinema. However, since his first article on this concept, Tom Gunning has not failed to note that attractions, far from disappearing with the development of integrated narrative cinema, continue to exist within certain genres: "In fact the cinema of attraction does not disappear with the dominance of narrative, but rather goes underground, both into certain avant-garde practices and as a component of narrative films, more evident in some genres (e.g. the musical) than in others."[1] In the same article, he did not hesitate to see in the "Spielberg-Lucas-Coppola cinema of effects"[2] a certain heritage, "ambiguous" to be sure, of this early cinema.

More recently, the notion of attraction has extended so far as to include the cinematic apparatus itself, in particular when technical aspects are involved. The promotion of MOULIN ROUGE! (Baz Luhrmann, 2001) has largely insisted on the new technologies allowing for an integral show.[3] Reviving a genre almost gone, MOULIN ROUGE! is said to reach the peak of it because of its camera: ubiquitous (and digital), it can join in dancing like a proper character. It is actually worth asking if the unbroken pace of the film does not tend to obliterate the dancing bits – what we would call the attractions – to make of the whole film a unique attraction. Edouard Arnoldy regards this particular film as willing to "exhibit the outstanding command of the techniques at its disposal."[4]

Rather than going into the question of new technical developments, I would like to examine the notion of attractions in the specific case of their surviving within the musical of the 1930s.[5] How to define attractions and how far do they integrate into films are indeed still central questions since the period of early cinema. The point is not only to investigate the analytical and heuristic power of this concept, but also to see whether it does not activate some other elements of definition, in particular with special reference to Eisenstein's original definition. To do so, I have felt it judicious to use as evidence two classics of the musical – 42ND STREET (Lloyd Bacon) and GOLD DIGGERS OF 1933 (Mervin LeRoy), both of 1933. The more so as in these two particular cases we find very different readings of how the singing and dancing are integrated. Alain Masson for instance views the numbers as working in a purely metonymic way to the whole film: for him the two films are, like encyclopedias, enumerations of spectacular

figures.[6] Likewise, Tino Balio, regarding each final numbers as having no relation to the narrative, writes: "The screenplays contained nothing to suggest the
song or how they might be staged."[7] On the contrary, Rick Altman's analysis
suggests a strong tie between numbers and plot, the former being part of the
filmic structure.[8] Along with the musicals comes naturally the question of how
to integrate numbers or attractions within the rest of the film.

It is necessary, then, to go briefly over Tom Gunning's definition of attractions
again. Certain parameters are central here: the first one concerns the limited
aspect of attraction. If the analysis of attractions has mainly been carried out on
"single-shot" films made of a unique attraction, like THE BIG SWALLOW (James
Williamson, 1901), Tom Gunning has also often included films in which the
attraction occupies a definite moment, like some Méliès films. Within a rather
long narrative film, the attraction characteristically and literally "bursts in."
Hence, attraction is quite similar to pure show. Secondly, attraction affects the
time construction of film by breaking into the process of storytelling. Attraction
is therefore seen as a potential danger to textual cohesion. Thirdly, attraction
establishes a very special relationship to its spectator. Far from denying its presence, it seeks confrontation. By pointing at us, attraction tries to unsettle, surprise, provoke and even assault us.

Location and Delimitation of Numbers

As compared to early cinema, musical attractions are blocks you can easily spot
and delimit within a larger unit characterized by principles of coherency and
fluidity. These blocks of pure show make themselves known as such. A few
numbers, for instance "Young and Healthy" in 42ND STREET, "The Shadow
Waltz" in GOLD DIGGERS OF 1933, begin with a character singing on a stage.
The camera is on the spectator's side or backstage, making the theatrical location of these singing and dancing numbers quite clear. Having made us aware
of this spatial demarcation, the camera makes its way into the space of the number itself, literally breaking apart the diegetic universe. The number area is specially organized and built for the film spectators only. No one assisting at the
show in the diegetic music hall would have such a viewpoint. The stage works
therefore as a threshold between the spectators' world and the universe of the
show itself. The spectators' look converges on the stage and makes of it a place
of voyeurism which invites in turn the film spectators to look as well. The sequence forms a sort of *mise en abyme*: the film spectators can see the audience
assisting at the show, when simultaneously watching the show themselves with
the extra capacity to see what goes on backstage. The omniscient look permits

to pass the usual limits: the number and its whereabouts becomes a space which grows almost infinitely, far from the laws of the "real" world. In the same way, bodies are transformed and multiplied under the camera omniscient look. As for the progress of the plot, the few numbers scattered along the film work as some sort of pauses. But following Rick Altman's semantic-syntactic approach, these numbers appear to be actually part of the story development. According to Altman, the narrative outline at hand in every musical is the constitution of one or several couples of lovers, as in 42ND STREET and GOLD DIGGERS OF 1933. Always present in every *backstage* musical is also the putting on of a singing and dancing show. But if the numbers have so often been considered as outsiders in these films, it is, among other things, because they are usually to be found at the very end of famous titles like FOOTLIGHT PARADE (Lloyd Bacon, 1933) or DAMES (Ray Enright, 1934). In 42ND STREET, the first steps in dancing occur in the middle of the film and are part of the action: one dances to put on the show. But these moments are usually brief. In this respect, the beginning of GOLD DIGGERS OF 1933 is a notable exception: it opens with a number which is however soon interrupted, as if letting the whole number happen would prevent the diegetic world from developing, and the spectator from penetrating it.[9] The other musicals rely more on the fact that spectators are waiting for the dancing and singing which are the highlight of the film, as prove their minute preparation, high costs and a specially designated director like Busby Berkeley. This particular situation has led to the shrinking of the rest of the film, often been considered as pure filling.

Two things do contradict this view without however obliterating the actual outstanding dimension of numbers, be it from a sound, visual or plastic standpoint. The film, as it develops, makes sure that its spectator impatiently waits about, by giving him/her bits of the final show. 42ND STREET is full of short moments proclaiming the numbers still to come: the images immediately following the opening credits form a dancing kaleidoscope. In the same way, the camera, while filming the dancing rehearsals, moves in a much more complex way as in the rest of the sequences, which are only based on the classical continuity principle of the shot/reverse shot. Indeed, a long camera movement starts on the *girls* to stop at an exceptional height. Further on during a tap dance rehearsal, the dancers' legs form a spinning figure that works as a sort of prolepsis: the numbers to come actually base themselves on proliferating and transforming bodies into plastic figures (in particular in "Young and Healthy" where the girls' legs form an arch under which the camera flows).[10] Even more, as mentioned, GOLD DIGGERS OF 1933 at its very beginning rouses us to intense wait, since the film opens with a number that ushers brutally interrupt to seize pieces of scenery and costumes. After one third of the film, a number which proclaims the achieving of the show goes uninterrupted: "Pettin' in the Park." Having been prepared by these few singing and dancing all along the film, the spectator now waits for a grand finale.

This bursting of the spatial limits between stage and viewer goes along with a change in the enunciation system. While enunciation is not obvious and rubs any trace of its construction during most of the film, its character of address becomes on the contrary quite clear during the musical numbers. Actors and actresses turn towards and look at the camera when singing, aiming directly at the film viewers. This ubiquitous approach permits to go beyond the passive nature of recording by adopting unexpected points of view. Thanks to the two-dimensional and monocular nature of the camera, film images can play with flat surfaces or can give, on the other hand, a great depth impression. Every shot then relies on the composition possibilities of the camera and its infinite and unusual positions. The marked enunciative quality of these elements goes along with a pause within the narration level: they stop being active agents of the narrative to become pure visual pleasure. As Rick Altman has pointed out,[11] the singing and dancing imply a generalized inversion that puts music at the top of hierarchy: tempo and melody lead the dancers' movements as well as the editing pace. In the same way, it is a purely aesthetic function that starts to rule all that goes with narration. These are moments of pure show given as such. Bodies become figures that very elaborate camera movements keep rear-ranging; or being shot from unusual places, they become moving abstract pic-tures.

Back to Eisenstein

The musical numbers considered as such relate quite closely to the early cinema attractions. They precisely refer to what Jacques Aumont, as quoted by Gau-dreault and Gunning, designates as "peak moment[s] in the show, relatively autonomous, and calling upon techniques of representation which are not those of dramatic illusion, drawing upon more aggressive forms of the performing arts (the circus, the music hall, the sideshow)."[12] But this reading of Eisenstein may have obliterated certain aspects of the question. Indeed, when looking in particular at the "intellectual attraction"[13] variant of 1928, one term keeps ap-pearing under the Soviet director's pen, the word "association." Its complex meaning, which has to be understood here as metaphorical process, shall lead to the idea of intellectual editing, of *concepts producer*. To take into account this aspect allows for detailing several central practices within musical numbers.

The association phenomenon occurs at different levels. First, as already men-tioned, the narrative lines keep mingling until merging eventually: to put on a show means to create a theatrical moment, but also to form couples and fight the economic crisis. Narratively speaking, 42ND STREET and GOLD DIGGERS OF 1933 insist on the severe financial conditions of the time. In both films, the crisis subject is central. While less obvious in 42ND STREET, it nonetheless explains the director Julian Marsh (Warner Baxter)'s obstinate resistance. His final speech to Peggy Sawyer (Ruby Keeler) who is unexpectedly about to take the leading role: "Two hundred people – two hundred jobs – two hundred dollars – five weeks of grind – and blood and sweat – depend upon you." In the same way, as already said, the opening number of GOLD DIGGERS OF 1933 is cut short by crisis; theaters shut down and chorus girls get unemployed. The film precisely ends with "My Forgotten Man," a number that is generally considered as socially very explicit. A woman, prostitute as it seems, sings "A Woman's Got to Have a Man" that several other women take up as well. It then goes on to describe the particularly dark social conditions by evoking American history since the country went to war. Soldiers set off for the front to the cheering of the people, women particularly. The description of their return is, in contrast, very gloomy. As rain is pouring, the wounded are carrying those unable to go on on their own. Men then are queuing up for soup. The final shot shows the female character singing the refrain while men praised by the crowd are surrounding her. The fact that this dark conclusion – a lonely woman encircled by unemployed men – is precisely part of the spectacular finale compensates for its pessimism. Even war and crisis are pretexts for dancing and singing, hence generously helping the industry of entertainment. The same goes with 42ND STREET in which putting on a show implies the pairing of several couples while giving at the same time employment to a whole company. The same function of *mise en abyme* characterizes both films: by offering a show that brings together in communion characters *and* spectators, the musical provides a way to beat the crisis. It is then easier to understand the usual focus on the rehearsal scenes since only hard work can give results.

Beyond the plot level, the association phenomenon is quite central in the development and meaning of numbers themselves. But, if, according to Altman, the musical only defined itself by the unusual subordination of images to sound and music, musical numbers would be nothing but an outpouring of pure and useless visual plasticity. "Shadow Waltz," on the contrary, best exemplifies how the metaphoric association mode works. The number opens with Brad (Dick Powell) and Polly (Ruby Keeler) on a stage. The young man is courting his beloved with a song ("Let me bring a song to you" are the first words). The following images can be seen as a visualization of it. A series of oppositions organize the whole number (shadow, blackness – lightness, whiteness, male – female, desiring object – desired object) to lead in the final shot to the union of the couple. Brad's song celebrates his darling in the first place, but goes on to

praise women in general. As the music notes multiply (the orchestral accompaniment grows more and more; the chorus is joined by more voices), the female
figures multiply as well. From one, they become ten, twenty and more copies of
the model (Polly). Now they are visual motifs that vary according to an associative system which identifies woman to flower and violin. Dancers shape the
object that makes them move. To my mind, these motifs do imply sexual allu-
sions. Indeed, how is it possible not to see behind flowers the idea of deflower-
ing, and behind a violin sexual intercourse?[14] Following the same sexual meta-
phors, some commentators have seen in the chorus girl circles symbols of the
female sex.[15] There is no denying the fact that these motifs continuously play
on associations that make of the female body an object of sex and desire. This is
what the act "Young and Healthy" exemplifies particularly well: women's legs
are arranged in a triangle that the camera literally penetrates.[16] The dancing and
singing choreographies that Berkeley has designed are therefore as much transforming plastic figures as the love parade of a sexual symbol. Patricia Mellencamp suggests a similar reading of the motifs in GOLD DIGGERS OF 1933. Their
transformation into abstract elements appears to her as the respectable make-
over of female sexuality. She writes:

> The film shifts from an emphasis on the women's genitals, the strategic coin place-
> ments of "We're in the Money," to the abstract shape of the female body as a neon
> violin, collectively bowed in "Shadow Waltz." The process of the film legitimizes, as
> art, a sublimation, making respectable what was illegal, uncivilized (at least for Freud
> and Berkeley) – women, female sexuality.[17]

Ploughing Brains

Attraction as associational process fits in well with Eisenstein's definition. But
the Soviet cinematographer adds up another dimension to it, the effect aspect.
Indeed, for Eisenstein the central role of attractions is "to plough up the spectators consciousness," to lead them to a better revolutionary understanding of
political and historical developments. The Busby Berkeley numbers, which
magnify entertainment and women bodies, have no relationship to Soviet ideology, even if it sometimes do come to cheer up a country struck down by crisis.
Besides, far from breaking the filmic illusion, they mainly contribute to dazzle
and fascinate us, in just the same way as when we look through a kaleidoscope.

But even outside Soviet ideology, Eisenstein's method of the attractions can
be very effective as political instrument. As demonstrated by Alain Labelle,
ROCKY IV (Sylvester Stallone, 1985) comprises a "montage of attractions."[18] The

binary structure that opposes the American boxer with the Russian one serves to prove how superior American values (such as family, free undertaking, citizen's unity and equality, etc.) are: the attractional editing of the final fight gives justifications for the characters' actions. Using such formal constructions also tends to "shape the spectator" ideologically. According to Labelle, the very foundation of attraction is ideological. And we have to admit that as the musical numbers combine singing, dancing and refined editing with all sorts of other impressive means, they are part of an aestheticism of shock. Even if they do rely on contemporary elements like the crisis in GOLD DIGGERS OF 1933, numbers serve an illusive project based on pure spectacular impressiveness, which deprives partly performance of reality.

The coming of sound made the integration of dancing and singing possible, and with it opened a large semantic and syntactic field. This renewal happened within a highly rationalized and regulated industry. The question is to know whether such attractions in musicals are not to be related to the sound technological deep mutations and to the following new configuration of genres. Attractions are visual moments that the consumption society fully integrates, in a way that Kracauer has analyzed within his famous essays of the 1920s, in particular in "Das Ornament der Masse" (1927).[19] He perceives a new trend in physical culture towards mass movement and abstraction, corresponding to deep social changes such as the new work organization implied by mechanization and Taylorism.

The Berkeley musical attractions, far from being as brutal as in early cinema, do work in a way that tends to decorativeness and sexual fetishism mainly because of their capacity of association, their metaphoric dimension so to speak, that Eisenstein has duly pointed up. But their position in a codified genre, while allowing them visual excess and great innovation, confines them to spectacle illusion. The aestheticism and the emotion of modernity that Gunning has described as a shock are here used in a polished way to serve the prevailing ideology (as in ROCKY IV). The final numbers of GOLD DIGGERS OF 1933 are designed to cheer up a country struck by crisis. In the same way, the entertainment industry of today makes use of attraction features in a film like MOULIN ROUGE! to revive its past successes. But to do so it gambles on old recipes (the dancing and singing acts) that are made fashionable (through digital images), and relies on a more adequate spreading means: the DVD and its numerous bonuses.[20]

Translated by Marthe Porret

Notes

1. Tom Gunning, "The Cinema of Attractions: Early Film, Its Spectator and the Avant-Garde," *Early Cinema: Space Frame Narrative,* ed. Thomas Elsaesser (London: British Film Institute, 1990) 57.
2. Gunning 58.
3. See Edouard Arnoldy, *À perte de vues. Images et "nouvelles technologies" d'hier et aujourd'hui* (Bruxelles: Labor, 2005).
4. Arnoldy 27.
5. I thank Viva Paci for her insightful comments and for sharing her ideas on the importance of the attractions in film history.
6. Alain Masson, "Le style de Busby Berkeley," *Positif* 173 (Sept. 1975): 41-48.
7. Tino Balio, *Grand Design. Hollywood as a Modern Business Enterprise, 1930-1939* (Berkeley: U of California P, 1992) 214. That a designated director is specially charged with the numbers strengthens the idea of a gap between the general plot and the numbers for one thing, and of a stylistic difference between the narrative parts and the singing and dancing for the other.
8. Rick Altman, *The American Film Musical* (1987; Bloomington/London: Indiana UP/British Film Institute, 1989).
9. Here is the assumption that in "classical" fiction film the spectator is expected to enter the diegesis. See Roger Odin, "L'entrée du spectateur dans la fiction," *Théorie du film,* ed. Jacques Aumont and Jean-Louis Leutrat (Paris: Albatros, 1980) 198-213.
10. Lucy Fischer, "The Image of Woman as Image: The Optical Politics of *Dames* [1976]," *Genre: The Musical,* ed. Rick Altman (London: British Film Institute, 1981) 70-84. About the same tracking shot, in a later film (DAMES), Fischer insists on the phallic dimension of the camera approaching the female legs as if to penetrate them.
11. Altman 70-74.
12. Jacques Aumont, *Montage Eisenstein,* trans. Lee Mildreth, Constance Penley and Andrew Ross (London/Bloomington: British Film Institute/Indiana UP, 1987) 42.
13. S.M. Eisenstein, "Inédit: A.I. 1928 [Attraction intellectuelle]," *CiNéMAS* 11.2-3 (Spring 2001): 147-60.
14. It is indeed a quite frequently used metaphor to figure the sexual act. See also Fisher 75.
15. Jerome Delamater, "Busby Berkeley: An American Surrealist," *Wide Angle* 1 (1979): 24-29. Delamater explicitly links the round shape to the vagina.
16. See note 10.
17. Patricia Mellencamp, "Sexual Economics. *Gold Diggers of 1933*," *The Hollywood Musicals. The Film Reader,* ed. Steven Cohan (London/New York: Routledge, 2002) 72.
18. Alain Labelle, "L'utilisation du montage des attractions de S.M. Eisenstein dans *Rocky IV*," *Etudes littéraires* 20.3 (Winter 1987-88): 111-12.
19. Translated as "The Mass Ornament" by Barbara Correll and Jack Zipes, *New German Critique* 5 (Spring 1975): 667-76.
20. The DVD sales have largely been responsible for the film success.

Digital Media and (Un)Tamed Attractions

["The Avant-Garde": section 2]

Chez le Photographe c'est chez moi: Relationship of Actor and Filmed Subject to Camera in Early Film and Virtual Reality Spaces

Alison McMahan

In the original formulation of the cinema of attractions theory, Tom Gunning and André Gaudreault conceived of the attractions phase as a mode of film practice discernible before the development of classical cinematic editing and narration. In *Alice Guy Blaché, Lost Visionary of the Cinema* I argued, building on work by Charles Musser,[1] that attractions represent only one possible approach to filmmaking in the earliest phase of cinema. Another approach, characterized by a sophisticated use of on- and off-screen space, was in full use at the same time – most notably in some of the earliest one-shot films produced at Gaumont and directed by Alice Guy.[2] In this paper I explore another approach quite common in early cinema, whose sophistication we can appreciate retrospectively in the context of today's digital interactive narratives, where we see it re-emerging. I am referring to early films that consciously combine diegetic immersion with non-diegetic engagement in their audience address, much as virtual reality environments and computer games with first person and over-the-shoulder perspectives in three-dimensional spaces do today. To give these films a short-hand name I will call them "homunculus films."

The Homunculus

Various meanings of the word "homunculus" (Latin for "little man," sometimes spelled "homonculus") exist, and several of them are relevant here. Most sources attribute the earliest use of the term to the fifteenth-century physician (pioneer in toxicology, among other things) and alchemist Paracelsus. Paracelsus claimed that he had created a kind of golem (though only 12 inches tall) that performed physical work for its creator until it got fed up and ran away. These creatures originated from human bones, sperm, and skin fragments and hair from animals, which were fermented in dung for forty days. In the late 17th century "spermists" would argue that individual sperm contained tiny "little men" that, when placed inside a woman, would grow into a child. Derivatives of this argument included mandrake roots that germinated in the ground under gallows, and were stimulated to grow into homunculi from a hanged man's spurt of semen emitted during his death throes. Impregnating a prostitute with a hanged man's sperm produced a woman devoid of morals or conscience.

Today the word homunculus refers less often to a real little man and more often to illustrate the functioning of a system thought to be run by a "little man" inside. Such a system includes human beings, as some inner entity or agent is somehow assumed to be inside our brains, making things run. One example of this was Descartes's use of the homunculus to resolve his theory of dualism, that the soul and the body are two completely separate entities. He posited a "little man" behind the eye to process visual stimuli. Of course, this immediately raises the question of who is behind the "little man's" eyes – another little man? And so on, ad infinitum.

In philosophy, homunculus arguments are used as yardsticks for determining where a theory is failing. For example, in theories of vision:

> Homunculus arguments are common in the theory of vision. Imagine a person watching a movie. They see the images as something separate from them, projected on the screen. How is this done? A simple theory might propose that the light from the screen forms an image on the retinas in the eyes and something in the brain looks at these as if they are the screen. The Homunculus Argument shows this is not a full explanation because all that has been done is to place an entire person, or homunculus, behind the eye who gazes at the retinas. A more sophisticated argument might propose that the images on the retinas are transferred to the visual cortex where it is scanned. Again this cannot be a full explanation because all that has been done is to place a little person in the brain behind the cortex. In the theory of vision the Homunculus Argument invalidates theories that do not explain "projection," the experience that the viewing point is separate from the things that are seen.[3]

A more modern use of the terms is "the sensory homunculus":

> the term used to describe the distorted human figure drawn to reflect the relative sensory space our body parts represent on the cerebral cortex. The lips, hands, feet and sex organs are considerably more sensitive than other parts of the body, so the homunculus has grossly large lips, hands and genitals. Well known in the field of neurology, this is also commonly called "the little man inside the brain."[4]

The Homunculus as Cameraman

We can see Descartes's theory of the homunculus reflected in early cinema. As if to answer the question "Who is behind the camera?" a series of early films "stepped back" and depicted within the film's story world, or diegesis, the camera and the person operating the camera. Although a cameraman [with camera] was depicted within the diegesis, he was often at right angles to the action as it was actually filmed, creating a triangulated relationship: at one apex was the subject being filmed; at the another, the cameraman character; and at the third (and non-diegetic) apex the camera which was actually filming at what would become the spectator's viewing position.

Though in the "wrong" position, the cameraman character (the camera in the diegesis) is often an emotional stand-in, or homunculus, for the spectator. That is, the homunculus occupies the narratee position that the film has carved out for the viewer.

Let us look at some examples of early films where the homunculus is depicted as a still photographer. One of the earliest is the Lumière film PHOTO-GRAPHE (1895), quickly remade as CHEZ LE PHOTOGRAPHE (1900), for Gaumont by Alice Guy. PHOTOGRAPHE is a one-shot film, and shows two men outside, one about to take a still photograph of the other. We see their activity in profile.

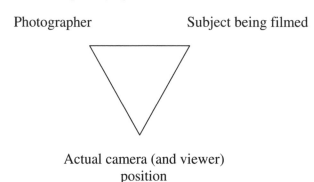

Fig. 1. Setup for PHOTOGRAPHE (Lumière, 1895)

The photographer sits his subject in a chair, encourages him to comb his hair, positions his body at the correct angle for the camera (that is, slightly facing the movie camera), then walks behind the still camera and bends over to take the picture. (However he has no darkening cloth so it seems clear that the camera is only a prop.) His subject, not aware that the photographic exposure has already begun, takes a handkerchief out of his pocket and begins to blow his nose. This makes the photographer irate, and he jumps forward to take the handkerchief away. In the process he knocks over his tripod and the camera falls to the ground. He argues with the photographic subject, who has also jumped up. Both argue for a couple of beats, and then the man playing the photographic subject clearly checks in with the film director, "have we done this long enough yet?" They are encouraged to go on so they continue to argue while the man playing the photographer picks up his camera and gesticulates that it is broken. The man playing the photographic subject goes out of character again, pausing to look at the real camera, apparently taking direction.

The film is clearly making fun of the photographic subject's vanity, his lack of knowledge of how the photographic process works and his resistance to it. Then there is the humor in seeing the two men argue and nearly come to blows, the action that takes up more than half the film.

PHOTOGRAPHE is an early example of the multiple complexities of the homunculus film. The viewer's identification with the photographer is complicated when the other character addresses the film camera directly. This unwitting gesture calls attention to the fact that the action is being filmed by a second camera.

CHEZ LE PHOTOGRAPHE is clearly a remake of Louis Lumière's PHOTO-GRAPHE.[5] Guy's version of the story is psychologically more complex. First, the setup is not an outdoor path, but a photographic studio; in addition to the still camera, we see a larger camera set in the background. The photographer is at work arranging things when a man arrives carrying a potted plant and asks to have his picture taken. After some discussion (haggling over price?), the photographer encourages the man to sit down in a chair facing the camera, takes his potted plant and sets it aside. The subject removes his hat and smoothes his hair, then replaces his hat. When all seems ready the photographer goes behind the camera and drapes himself with the darkening drape. The exposure has clearly begun. The subject seems unaware of this and is still trying to decide how best he wants to be photographed; he picks up the potted plant and holds it close to his face. The photographer comes out from under the drape and explains that he cannot move during the exposure. The subject puts the potted plant down, but now he is aware that the source of control is in the camera lens and peers directly into it. This makes the cameraman lose his temper, who yells at him to sit down and maintain his pose. Inexplicably, given that the man came in for his photograph in the first place, he returns to his chair but turns his back on the camera and bends over, so that all the camera can see is a nice view of his rear. Now the cameraman is really angry and they argue; the camera is knocked over; and the cameraman hands the client his plant and makes it clear that he must leave.

Fig. 2. Still from CHEZ LE PHOTOGRAPHE (Alice Guy, 1900)

As in the Lumière film, the cameraman is posited as a source of institutional control. Although the client seems willing to submit himself to this control, in fact he is resistant: he doesn't want to pose the way the photographer tells him, wants to be photographed with his cherished plant, and once he understands that the source of control is centered in the camera lens he interrogates it and then flouts its authority by turning around and bending over for the lens. This leads to his eviction from the institutional space, plant and all.

Alice Guy clearly understood the complexities of the original Lumière film and has expanded on its theme while modifying its practice in one important regard.

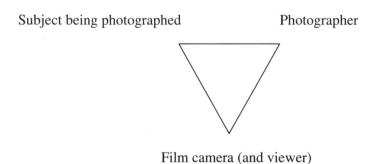

Fig. 3. Setup for CHEZ LE PHOTOGRAPHE (Alice Guy, 1900)

As in the Lumière film, the photographer is the controlling force, the subject resists; and there is a homunculus feeding us the picture stream. The triangulation is almost identical to that of PHOTOGRAPHE, except the photographer character is screen right whereas in the original he was screen left. The film camera (the homunculus) is located at a ninety-degree angle to the staged action. The film cameraman is represented indirectly by the character of the still photographer in the film. In the Lumière film we were made aware of the homunculus position accidentally, because the actor playing the client consults with the film director about his performance. In Guy's film, though there is no direct address, we are reminded that the photographer character is only our emotional stand-in because he gets a full view of the subject's buttocks, while we, visually positioned at a ninety-degree angle, do not. Bending over is the subject's last act of resistance to being photographed. It is a diegetic act that invites the viewer to reflect on the power of the camera… when they are done laughing.

Compare Guy's satire of resistance to the Edison slapstick comedy, OLD MAID HAVING HER PICTURE TAKEN (Edwin S. Porter & George S. Fleming, 1901).[6] This one-minute film has two parts. First, an "old maid" (a man in drag), enters a photographer's studio to have her portrait taken. Discussion between maid and photographer. The photographer exits the frame. While she waits for him the old maid looks first at samples of the photographer's work, but something about her presence makes the poster fall to the floor. She then looks at the clock. The clock hands whirr around faster and faster and drop to the floor. Finally she preens in front of a full-length mirror, turning around to admire herself from all angles, and to her horror the mirror cracks. It is hard to escape the meaning of this: she is so ugly that even the objects in the room cannot stand the sight of her without breaking. Finally the photographer comes in, expresses chagrin at the cracked mirror and broken clock, then sits her down in the chair to pose her for the photograph. The two are now in profile to the film camera, the same setup as in Guy's film. The photographer pushes the woman's face so that the film spectator gets a full view of her hooked nose, pronounced chin, and vacant expression. At that angle, it is impossible for the photographer to get a good portrait of her, which seems to be the point. He goes behind his camera to take the picture, and when he does the camera explodes. The old maid jumps in her chair, kicking up her skirt and revealing her bloomers.

By 1901 the hegemony of the still camera, as well as the film camera, was clearly established. The man behind the camera would decide who was worthy of being photographed, in what pose, and where. The subject, now a female who can only react to this process without taking control of it, can only hope to fit the photographer's requirements; the relationship between the two has moved from bawdy resistance to a sexualized dominator-dominated relationship. The humor in this film comes from the woman's blissful lack of awareness of her unsuitability as a camera subject due to her lack of sex appeal. This movie is of particular interest because the spectator is aligned with the photographer only for the second half of the film; for the first half the photographer is mostly absent, and the woman's preening and encounters with various reactive objects is staged directly for the film camera in an attractions mode.

The Homunculus as Ocularizer

In other early films, instead of a photographer standing in for the viewer, there is simply a character, often a voyeuristic one. Gunning argues that, in the cinema of attractions paradigm, such sequences are governed by *ocularization* rather than *focalization*, that is, these films put something on display for a spectator rather than construct a character within a narrative. Gunning particularly focuses on films that "share a common pattern of alternation, cutting from a curious character who uses some sort of looking device (reading glass, microscope, keyhole, telescope, transom window, or [...] a deck of magically suggestive playing cards)."[7]

Richard Abel refers to these "ocularized" films as "looking" films, and points out that they usually show someone looking at a woman in a risqué position, but the view is staged to satisfy the voyeurism of the film spectator and not the character in the film. Here the off-screen space is indicated or marked within the framing of the film.[8] Of course, not all films of this type are erotic and not all of them use "looking devices." For example, in Pathé's THE ARTIST (1900) a client walks into an artist's atelier. He examines a painting in profile – the painting is turned so we can see it but we don't see it from his point of view – and leans over so far to look into it that he falls and damages the painting, which he now has to buy. Compare this to Emile Cohl's PEINTRE NÉO-IMPRESSIONNISTE (1910) in which an artist shows a client of series of images; for each image there is a close-up of the painting which ends up showing an animated sequence (red lobsters swimming in the red sea for the red canvas, and so on). Elena Dagrada explains the mechanism at work here: the close-up of the painting, which enables the spectator to enjoy the animated sequence, is less a point of view shot for the character than it is a re-staging of the action for the film viewer's maximum enjoyment, and the figure of the art-purchaser in the film is a stand-in for the viewer:

> In the future [that is, in narrative films that create a diegesis], however, the POV shot would presuppose a diegetic conception of camera position. During a POV shot, in fact, the camera symbolically assumes the role of a fictional character, thus projecting a diegetic look onto the screen. But in early cinema, the diegetic conception of camera

position did not exist, and in fact this position was presumed to be occupied by the spectator's look. For this reason, and despite appearances, keyhole films do not represent at this stage a fictional character's viewpoint, as one would be led to believe today; rather, they represent the spectator's look.

If we observe these films carefully, we realize that they restructure more or less explicitly the spectator's experience as an onlooker who, outside the cinema, at fairs, or at home, was accustomed to looking *through* something, whether through mutoscopes and kinetoscopes at peep shows [...].[9]

Dagrada goes on to describe the spectator as "autonomous in relation to the syntagmatic continuity of the films in which they are set."[10]

The same mechanism is at work in THE GAY SHOE CLERK (Porter, 1903). The action is staged in much the same way as in PHOTOGRAPHE, with the lady, the subject being viewed, screen right, the shoe clerk who enjoys the privileged view of her ankle screen left. The film camera is positioned at a ninety-degree angle to this action, but at the crucial moment cuts in, so that the spectator gets a nice close-up of the lady's ankle and calf as well; this close-up is not from the clerk's point of view, but from the spectator's.

Though films like THE GAY SHOE CLERK have been discussed often, scholars have rarely given extended attention to the films I have labeled homunculus films. Gunning, however, does note them: "Point of view operates in these films independently of a diegetic character. In its outward trajectory the cinema of attractions addresses a viewpoint from which both the look of the camera and the look of the spectator originates [...] it is precisely this subordination [typical of classical film narrative] of the gaze to a diegetic character that the cinema of attraction avoids."[11] In a footnote, Gunning takes issue with Noël Burch who sees THE BIG SWALLOW (James Williamson, 1901) as "basically in concert with later classical style. Burch, I believe, underestimates the importance of the narrativization of the identification."[12]

THE BIG SWALLOW is harder to recognize as a homunculus film precisely because the spectator and camera are aligned and the camera shows the spectator's point of view – which is also a diegetic point of view for most of the film. The film begins with a man in medium-long shot walking towards the camera; from the description in Williamson's 1901 catalogue[13] we know that he is resisting being photographed. He comes closer and closer until all we can see is his mouth; his mouth opens and becomes a huge, dark cavern; and then we see first, a camera falling into the dark depth, followed by the photographer himself, who falls in head over heels. However, that is not the end of *us*, the real camera temporarily aligned with the cameraman character, because we continue to watch as the resistant subject backs up, mouth now closed, munching contentedly. In other words, the three apexes of the triangle are still there, but two of them are intermingled for the first part of the film and then separated:

Subject being photographed

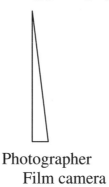

Photographer
Film camera

Fig. 4. Setup for THE BIG SWALLOW (James Williamson, 1901)

Immersiveness and engagement are therefore invoked by the same point of view shot. At first we see the photographic subject from the cameraman's point of view, but once he is swallowed we occupy an imaginary position. This makes it hard to separate the two at first: the homunculus camera position is easier to identify when the camera/spectator perspective and the diegetic perspective (of a spectator played by a character in the film) are separated; Christian Metz referred to this as "the empty placement for the spectator-subject."[14] This setup is characteristic of numerous early erotic films.

The Erotic Homunculus Film

When the object on view is a woman's objectified body, then the stand-in for the viewer incorporates a level of commentary on the film spectator, for the film spectator's benefit as well. For example, in [FIVE LADIES] (Pathé, 1900) a series of five short films of one shot each are joined together, each featuring a different lady. In the first, a rather teasing one, a woman is standing with her backside to the camera, while a painter, profile to camera, paints her image on a canvas we cannot see. However, a black woman, also in a state of undress, is seated on the floor and can see the woman's frontal nudity. The film spectator is left to enjoy the first model's lovely backside, the second model's frontal nudity, and her reactions, as well as the painter's, to the view of the first model, which are our only indicator for what we cannot see.

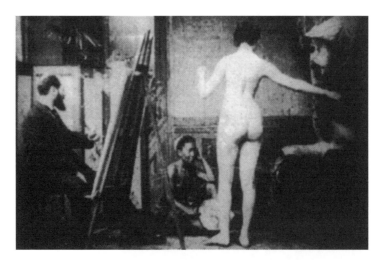

Fig. 5. Still from [FIVE LADIES] (Pathé, 1900), first film in series

In the fourth film in the series a man, fully dressed, sits behind a curtain screen right, but positioned to face the camera. He observes a woman screen left, ostensibly positioned for the benefit of the hidden gentleman but in fact angled ideally for the camera, dressed only in a towel, who washes, powders, perfumes, and puts lotion on herself with no apparent awareness of her observer, who gets progressively more excited and makes asides to the camera.

Fig. 6. Still from [FIVE LADIES] (Pathé, 1900), fourth film in series

In a variation of this positioning, [WIFE SURPRISED WITH LOVER] (Pathé, 1900) begins with the wife sitting on the sofa with her lover, both facing the camera.

They hear the husband returning unexpectedly and the lover hides behind the sofa. The wife then greets her husband and sits on the sofa lavishing attention on him while the lover peers out and makes faces at the camera, to communicate his anxiety and discomfort.

Fig. 7. Still from [WIFE SURPRISED WITH LOVER] (Pathé, 1900)

The Edison Co. released a similar film in 1896, entitled INTERRUPTED LOVERS (William Heise and James White). In a mere 150ft a couple, consisting of an urban-style swell and a country girl, sit on a park bench. The man takes his cigarette out of his mouth and kisses the girl, while a young country man approaches the couple from the back. He runs to get the girl's father, who comes running in screen left and drags her away, while the young man deals with his suave rival. As in [WIFE SURPRISED WITH LOVER], the action of the lovers is

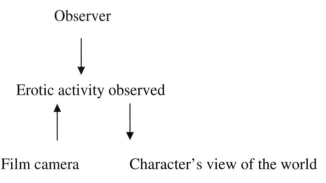

Fig. 8. Setup for [WIFE SURPRISED WITH LOVER] (Pathé, 1900)

staged for the camera, while the people who are reacting to them come up from behind, and their reactions are also played frontally. In both of these films the three apexes are in a straight line:

What each of these films has in common is that someone (usually a man) is looking at something (a painting, a naked woman), but what he is looking at is staged so that the film spectator, who is positioned usually at a ninety-degree angle to the action (but in any case not in the viewing character's line of sight, or anything remotely like it), gets the maximum benefit out of the spectacle. The viewing character has exaggerated emotional reactions to the view, apparently the reactions the film attributes to its ideal spectator, although a level of non-diegetic comment on the viewing character's reactions is present as well (humor at the art buyer being duped, for example, or empathy with the hidden lover's chagrin).

The Virtual Homunculus

This triangulated relationship is essentially the same as the player's or immersant's (to use Espen Aarseth's term for the person willfully experiencing an interactive environment) positioning in contemporary immersive interactive environments. It is interesting to examine this relationship now in relation to two new technologies at the turn of another century: first, webcams, and second, the positioning of subject, actor, and spectator in first person perspective 3D environments, such as virtual reality environments and certain types of computer games. In webcams, the subjects of the camera's eye not only initiate but control the discourse. 24 hour webcams like the "jennicam" keep watch over private spaces; the subject who is seen and filmed not only invites but installs the camera eye onto a stationary island to record life as it streams by. Real life or "meatspace" is now what is off-screen, and not what is self-consciously and often even habitually performed for the web-eye. By considering the early "chez le photographe" films in relation to interactive and streaming media we can trace a development in the way we have perceived on-screen and off-screen space, public and private, dominant and powerless. Likewise, early erotic films with their complex triangulations of viewing spaces and the separation of identification between the gazing character on-screen and the spectator have much in common with current conventions for interaction design of 3D spaces.

Espen Aarseth identifies these three positions as *intriguee*, the target of the game's intrigue (whom he also calls the "victim"), *narratee*, for the textual space outlined for the player, and *puppet* (or avatar), the graphic character which is partially controlled by the player. To explain the difference between these three functions, he gives the example of character death: "the main character [the avatar or puppet] is simply dead, erased, and must begin again. The narratee, on the other hand, is explicitly told what happened, usually in a sarcastic manner, and offered the chance to start anew. The user, aware of all this in a way denied to the narratee, learns from the mistakes and previous experience and is able to play a different game."[15] In other words, the avatar is at a level of focalization, the narratee is at the level of non-diegesis, and the intriguee or user is at the level of extra-diegesis.

The issue of focalization brings us back to the sensory homunculus described at the beginning of this paper. Focalization in interactive fiction works precisely in this way: we experience our bodies as having centers (the trunk and internal organs) and peripheries (limbs, hands and feet, hair). We view our centers as more important than our peripheries, so that someone who has lost a limb is still seen as the same person. This schema has three important elements: an entity, a center, and a periphery.[16] Focalized levels of narration emphasize the character's direct experience of events. This is an egocentric narrative, comparable to that of internal focalization (surface) narrative of film; the player sees directly through her avatar's eyes. Depending on the immersiveness of the virtual environment and the sensitivity of the interface, virtual reality can come very close to completely overlapping two of the apexes of the triangle: the view of the homunculus (in this case, the avatar) and the view of the user/player. However, the overlap will never be complete. To begin with, the user will always remain in meatspace, in the real world; his body can never be completely absorbed into the diegetic cyberspace. And the virtual environment has some degree of "intelligence"; some of this intelligence has been programmed into the player's avatar, so that the avatar will be able to do, or refuse to do, certain actions regardless of the desires of the player.

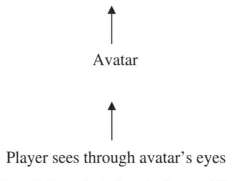

View of the virtual world

↑

Avatar

↑

Player sees through avatar's eyes

Fig. 9. The Egocentric Perspective in Computer Games and Virtual Reality

Although the player cannot see her avatar, the avatar has been programmed to have a certain size – the default "height" for CAVEs (computer automated virtual environments) is six feet and the default width of the head is two feet, for example – which means that the player cannot walk through an arch that is scaled to five feet, among other things. The avatar is usually invisible, represented on occasion by a hand that helps the user accomplish tasks in the virtual space. Some VR environments, though always egocentric, allow the user to get a glimpse of their avatar at certain moments, such as when the user looks at their reflection in a pond.[17] This perspective is reminiscent of point of view shots and subjective films like LADY IN THE LAKE (Montgomery, 1947).

The exocentric perspective of VR is analogous to what we mean by external focalization in film. Typically this results in a visible avatar that the user relates to exocentrically (as in all those over-the-shoulder games such as the *Tombraider* series where the user is always one step behind their avatar). This perspective is closer to that of the homunculus films of early cinema, because the homunculus (the avatar), though now "truly" under the control of the user, also is programmed, to an extent, to "have a mind of its own." The avatar, such as Lara Croft in *Tombraider* or Aladdin in the 3D version of *Prince of Persia*, is our homunculus, a stand-in for us in the diegesis that we identify with but whose perspective we do not always share:

View of the virtual world

Avatar
Player sees over the avatar's (homunculus') shoulder

Fig. 10. Perspective of over-the-shoulder games; compare to Fig. 4.

In most games the two perspectives are interchangeable. Even when they are not, such as in the early first person shooter games where the player always saw through his avatar's eyes, an image of his avatar's face would be placed in the tool bar at the bottom of the screen; this face reacted as the game progressed, grimacing when the avatar took a hit or cheering when he made a successful strike in games like *Quake*.

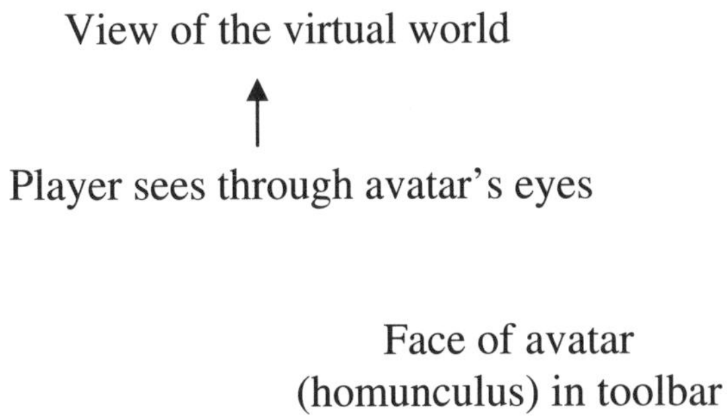

View of the virtual world

Player sees through avatar's eyes

Face of avatar
(homunculus) in toolbar

Fig. 11. The homunculus displaced to the toolbar.

And what about internal focalization (depth), the more complex experiences of thinking, remembering, interpreting, wondering, fearing, believing, desiring, understanding, feeling guilt, that is so well depicted in film? This is where software programming can really add something to the avatar. Leon Hunt gives the example of martial arts games, such as the *Tekken* series, which enables the user to "know Kung Fu." These games allow your avatar to incorporate the martial arts moves of various martial artists, as well as the signature gestures of various film stars playing martial artists.[18] As a result the internal depth focalization of this avatar – it knows Kung Fu, even if its user does not – is given authenticity by extra-diegetic signs: the signature moves of well-known martial artists and the gestures of movie stars. So an avatar's skills, whether it be rogue, wizard or warrior, and any back story they care to share with their user, can all be described as internal focalization depth.

Transferring the Homunculus Function to the Player

There are computer games and virtual reality environments where the user has no avatar at all. In tabletop VR, or god point of view games (such as most strategy games with isometric design like *Simcity* or *Civilization*) the user has a lot of control over events but no digital representation. This does not mean that there is no narratee position for the user. In games like *Creatures* or *Black and White*, for instance, users care for the little creatures or select which of the game's denizens will evolve and which will not. The range of possible choices and the specific choices made become the user's narratee position in the text, a position of focalization without direct representation.[19] In games like *Jedi Knight* the player's choices add up until the player is defined as knight on the "dark side" or the "light side" of the force.

Sequential narrative, which assumes a causal connection between a sequence of events and is seen most frequently in films and literature, does not work very well in interactive fiction. This means that the narratee position is weaker in interactive fiction than in sequential fiction. The user is also limited in how much control she has over the avatar; she can dictate most of its moves, depending on her skill level, but not too much of its basic programming (its internal focalization), except by choosing which game to play. In computer games, total immersion in the story world is not the goal, as it is in classical cinematic narration. The aim is a combination of immersion (involvement with the story at the diegetic level) and engagement (involvement with the game at a strategic, or non-diegetic level).[20]

I am not arguing that the relationship between player and avatar is the same as that between early film spectator and homunculus (the figure often found at a right angle to the "empty placement of the spectator-subject"). But a careful analysis of the complexities of these early homunculus films gives us insight into the relationships between avatar, player, and player perspective in virtual space. What we learn from early cinema is that the homunculus function is a moveable one. Once we know this we can trace its displacement from avatar to player and sometimes back to avatar (depending on the way the game is programmed). The key is to accept the homunculus analogy as simply that, an analogy that helps us understand what we are seeing.

In early cinema the spectators had no control over their homunculus; they could only enjoy their privileged view, and the photographer character in the film had all the capability for action. In virtual reality environments the reverse is true: Aarseth calls the avatar a "puppet" for a reason, because the player is the source of its movement and most of its choices. Armed with this understanding we can now trace hierarchical relationships between homunculi in film or in 3D game, and the spectator or player, based on the degree of agency claimed by the latter. For example, in *The Sims*, players can direct their Sim characters to eat dinner, go to bed, or put out a fire; but even if hungry the Sim characters can resist food or choose to paint a painting while their house burns down around them.

Rather than accept Gunning and Gaudreault's term "cinema of attractions" as a definition of a period in film history (usually defined as 1896 to 1904), we need to see attractions as only one aesthetic possibility chosen by filmmakers of the time. In this paper I have identified another possibility that was quite common in early cinema, which I call "homunculus films," and whose sophistication we can only appreciate now that we see it re-emerging in interactive narratives. This is an approach that *combines* the creation of a diegetic universe through narrative with an extra-diegetic engagement for the spectator by aligning the spectator with the camera position but separate from the characters in the diegesis. After a century of near-domination of "seamless" classical cinematic narrative, we are seeing a revival of other early cinematic approaches in interactive art forms, with their attendant complexities, specificities, and promise for the future.

Notes

1. Charles Musser, "Rethinking Early Cinema: Cinema of Attractions and Narrativity," *The Yale Journal of Criticism* 7.2 (1994). Reprinted in the dossier of this volume.
2. Alison McMahan, *Alice Guy Blaché, Lost Visionary of the Cinema* (New York: Continuum, 2002) 32-36.
3. http://en.wikipedia.org/wiki/Homunculus referring to Richard L. Gregory, *Eye and Brain: The Psychology of Seeing* (Oxford: Oxford UP, 1990) and *The Oxford Companion to Mind* (Oxford: Oxford UP, 1987).
4. http://en.wikipedia.org/wiki/Homunculus.
5. Gaumont no. 120, Lumière no. 118. The Lumière film can be seen on the Kino Video Series, *The Movies Begin*, vol. 1. For a detailed comparison of Alice Guy's remakes of Lumière films, see McMahan 23-30.
6. All of the Edison films described in this paper can be seen on the Kino DVD, *Edison: The Invention of the Movies*, disc 1.
7. Tom Gunning, "What I saw from the Rear Window of the Hôtel des Folies-Dramatiques," *Ce que je vois de mon ciné…*, ed. André Gaudreault (Paris: Méridiens-Klincksieck, 1988) 37. Gunning takes over this distinction between *ocularization* and *focalization*, with some modification, from François Jost, *L'oeil-caméra: Entre film et roman* (Lyon: Presses Universitaires de Lyon, 1987).
8. Richard Abel, *The Ciné goes to Town: French Cinema 1896-1914* (Berkeley: U of California P, 1994) 117-21.
9. Elena Dagrada, "Through the Keyhole: Spectators and Matte Shots in Early Cinema," *Iris* 11 (Summer 1990): 99.
10. Dagrada 100.
11. Gunning 35.
12. Gunning 42, note 19.
13. "I won't! I won't! I'll eat the camera first." Gentleman reading, finds a camera fiend with his head under a cloth, focusing him up. He orders him off, approaching nearer and nearer, gesticulating and ordering the photographer off, until his head fills the picture, and finally his mouth only occupies the screen. He opens it, and first the camera, and then the operator disappear inside. He retires munching him up and expressing his great satisfaction. – Liner notes for *The Movies Begin*, vol. 2: *The European Pioneers*, Kino Video, 1994.
14. Christian Metz, *The Imaginary Signifier: Psychoanalysis and the Cinema* (Bloomington: Indiana UP, 1982) 55.
15. Espen J. Aarseth, *Cybertext: Perspectives on Ergodic Literature* (Baltimore: John Hopkins UP, 1997) 113; quoting Espen J. Aarseth, "Nonlinearity and Literary Theory," *Hyper/Text/Theory*, ed. George P. Landow (Baltimore: John Hopkins UP, 1994) 73-74.

16. George Lakoff, *Women, Fire and Dangerous Things: What Categories Reveal About the Mind* (Chicago: U of Chicago P, 1987) 274.

17. William R. Sherman and Alain B. Craig, *Understanding Virtual Reality: Interface, Application and Design* (Amsterdam: Morgan Kaufman, 2003) 466.

18. Leon Hunt, "'I know Kung Fu!' The martial Arts in the Age of Digital Reproduction," *ScreenPlay: cinema/videogames/interfaces*, ed. Geoff King and Taynya Krzywinska (London/New York: Wallflower, 2002) 194-205.

19. Alison McMahan, "Immersion, Engagement and Presence: A Method for Analyzing 3-D Video Games," *The Video Game Theory Reader*, ed. Mark Wolf and Bernard Perron (New York/London: Routledge, 2003) 67-86.

20. Alison McMahan and Warren Buckland, "The Cognitive Semiotics of Virtual Reality," Virtual Reality International, an affiliated Conference of the Human Computer Interaction (HCI) International Conference, Las Vegas, July 2005.

The Hollywood Cobweb: New Laws of Attraction

(The Spectacular Mechanics of Blockbusters)

Dick Tomasovic

The metaphor is not new: the cinema, like a cobweb, traps the spectator's gaze. This quasi-hypnotic preoccupation of the image rules nowadays contemporary Hollywood production, and more specifically what forms today a type of film as precise as large, the blockbuster. If the analysis of these extremely popular, very big budget entertainment films, produced in the heart of new intermediality, can be based mainly on questions of intertextuality,[1] it can also, far from any definitive definition, be fuelled by a rich and complex network of notions which carries along in its modern rush the term of attraction.

The Spider Spins Its Web

During the 1980s, while the concept of the "cinema of attractions" entered the academic world to redefine early cinema, a series of young contemporary film directors forgot about film history and created their own style of visually aggressive films, eager to quickly surpass their models, Steven Spielberg and George Lucas, godfathers of new Hollywood, and to propose a purely playful, almost fairground cinema, entirely devoted to the only pleasure of the shocking images.

Twenty years later, three of them established themselves as new kings of Hollywood, and some film critics, at times poorly informed about film theory,[2] inscribed them in a long cinema of attractions history: James Cameron, Peter Jackson and Sam Raimi. In spite of the obvious differences of their cinematic writing and their sensibility, these three film directors share numerous common points. All three began in the 1980s with small and limited budget genre films, in a parodic, nonconformist, and school kid spirit (Cameron signed[3] Piranha 2 in 1981, Sam Raimi realized his first Evil Dead in 1981 as well, and Peter Jackson finished his good named Bad Taste in 1987). These works, overtly intended for a teenager public, suffer a lack of scenario, and turn out to be only fed by some insults to the good taste and, especially, a crafty profusion of funny visual tricks.

These small productions allowed them to play a "one-man band" and sharpen their sense of the spectacular. The creation of funny images and breathtaking sequences – to borrow the vocabulary from the circus which suits them well – will determine just as much their trademark as their business. In this way, they are the heirs, distant but real, of Georges Méliès's cinema. They will sign several gigantic hits during the 1990s and 2000s, joining Lucas and Spielberg in the little circle of American Top Ten box-office.[4]

Each one of them achieves such an exploit by importing into cinema a marginal universe he knows well (the catastrophic imagination of romanticism, mixed with anticipation for Cameron,[5] heroic fantasy for Peter Jackson[6] and comic-books for Sam Raimi[7]). Above all, these three filmmakers, unlike Jan de Bont or Michael Bay for example, abandoned the cinema of permanent spectacular, of all attraction, in order to find, in the style of Spielberg and Lucas, some attachment to the narrative, the characters, and the serial writing. But despite of what has often been written, the exhibition (or *monstration*) does no longer help revitalize the narration as it was the case with Spielberg and Lucas, on the contrary it uses the story as a springboard allowing to spring at the right time, strengthening its brilliant power. Consequently, the history of cinema and particularly the concept of the "cinema of the attractions" can help enlighten certain characteristics of this new type of blockbuster.

The success of the "cinema of attractions" concept, notably among the new generation of young researchers, could probably be explained by its paradoxical qualities: it seems precise and misty at the same time. Coined with rigor on the basis of a clearly defined historical corpus of film practices until 1908, identifying a *dispositif* that is radically different from, or even opposite to,[8] the well known one of classical narrative cinema (mainly in its mode of address to the spectator), the concept very quickly knew uncountable changes, deformations and corruptions, offering a new tool of approach, sometimes a little bit hazy, that allowed to simply evoke the superiority of exhibition over narration in the most various film practices. These exercises of distortion reached such proportions that some people ended up writing that there simply never existed a cinema of attractions, or, at least, not as a homogeneous, historically bounded, object.[9] The expression itself knows, at least in French, different appearances, such as "cinéma-attraction,"[10] "cinématographie-attraction,"[11] "image-attraction,"[12] or simply "attraction."

In brief, the concept seems to have something malleable, which makes it extremely problematic. This particular nature invites, of course, film theorists and historians to seize the concept and enlarge its definition, corrupt it in other corpuses and widen its field of application. The cinema of attractions becomes itself an attraction, whose swallowing power has nothing to envy to the character of Williamson's famous THE BIG SWALLOW (1901). It is not necessary to remind that Tom Gunning himself, ventured to widen the concept's reach by asserting that the attractions constitute a visual mode of address to the spectator not only in early cinema but also in other periods of film history. Gunning quotes pornography, the musical, newsreels, and even, in a more general way, classical cinema in which attractions would survive, allowing interaction between spectacle and narration.[13] Since then, similar propositions, by different scholars, grew in numbers.[14]

Using the case study of SPIDER-MAN, this article will also contribute to widen a little more the notion of attraction. The two episodes of this film, recently realized by Sam Raimi for Sony Pictures and dedicated to the adventures of the popular hero of the comics firm Marvel, update very literally the analogy of attraction force between cinema and cobweb, captivating and capturing millions of spectators throughout the world. The analysis of SPIDER-MAN 1 (SM1, 2002) and SPIDER-MAN 2 (SM2, 2004) will allow understanding how the history of concepts can make a return and how early films can help us to watch contemporary Hollywood cinema...[15]

The Spectacular in Question

"Spectacular" was surely the adjective most used not only by film critics but also by the studio to qualify the two episodes of SPIDER-MAN. The film is in line with the profound definition of Hollywood cinema.

As everyone knows, the consumption culture took a decisive turn at the end of the 1970s to triumph in the 1980s. It came along with a visual aggressiveness carried out by a new generation of filmmakers, heirs of a long lineage of American directors that possibly goes back to Cecil B. de Mille. These filmmakers rediscovered the taste of the spectacular, which was somewhat forgotten by Hollywood. If we look into the etymology of the French word *spectaculaire*, we find an ancestor less neutral, coined around 1770 in the field of the theater: *spectaculeux*. This term indicates a surplus of spectacle, an excess, an ostentatious sign of spectacle as machine, as apparatus.[16] And, indeed, it is this exhibitionist and megalomaniac determination that characterized, about two centuries later, the films of Steven Spielberg and George Lucas, unbeatable filmmakers of the spectacular.

If JAWS (1975) and STAR WARS (1977) signal the return of great narration in Hollywood,[17] they also aspire to visual shocks that unmistakably produce grandiloquent images in a story full of new developments and repetitions (the serial mode favoring, in fact, the prominence of attractions). The most exemplary sequence of this cinema remains, for a whole generation, the attack of the Death

Star by the small star fighters of the Rebel Alliance in STAR WARS, a sequence of pure demonstration of the subjective camera's power and fast forward tracking, indefatigably repeated since in Hollywood as a magic formula which allows to fasten the spectator in his seat and hypnotize him by reproducing visual sensations very close to those offered by spectacles of pyrotechnics and speed.[18]

Lucas himself declared that his films are more closely related to amusement park rides than a play or a novel.[19] In the 1980s, the link between Hollywood and amusement parks became more and more vivid. In the line of the Disney project, films provided inspiration for fairground attractions (a tendency that today seems to be reversed[20]), and the first interactions between cinema and video games began to take shape (see, for example, the physical treatment of the main character or the astonishing narration in DIE HARD [John McTiernan, 1988]) before becoming a rule these days (the *Matrix* project incorporates the plot of a video game into the story of the brothers Wachowski's trilogy, the numberless licenses of the *Star Wars* games, the attempts to impose on movies characters from games such as Lara Croft, etc.). The teenage audience becomes gradually the main target of an entertainment which wants to dazzle the gaze, with an audiovisual inflation as working principle. The audience wants to get his money's worth. The art of screenwriting loses its rights to the advantage of the creation of stunning images...

"Striking," "surprising," "stunning," "awesome" were some of the epithets given to Raimi's films whose hero is generally qualified this way (the most popular comics series dedicated to his adventures is entitled "Amazing Spider-Man"). It is true that SM1 and SM2 can be seen as results of the new Hollywood policy, devoted to the project of the ultimate blockbuster. The attraction is the golden rule. It concerns the gaze (vertiginous effects, shocks of colors, speed of camera movements and editing, grandiloquence of special effects) and the body in exhibition (after all the film is about a boy and a girl and maybe, more exactly, about what happens to the body of a young boy when he is attracted by another body[21]).

Besides, the crowd scenes (the parade of Thanksgiving Day in Time Square in SM1, the permanent heavy traffic in the main avenues, the swarming streets of hurried pedestrians, etc.), the aerial shots of an excessive metropolis (New York City, idealized, is reconstructed using its most famous administrative centers, but also other city fragments, real[22] or imaginary), the images of acrobatic exploits between vertiginous buildings and gigantic billboards, the apocalyptic battles scenes in the subway, cafés or banks, insist on the modern experience of urban life, its unpredictable irruption of aggressiveness, which distracts the *flâneur*, and which attractions have to compete with, as we know.[23]

Moreover and, in a certain way, like the films of Georges Méliès, the surprise is the operating mode of the film (when Peter and his aunt ask for a loan to the bank, Octopus brutally appears to rob it; when Peter reconciles with M.J. in a café, the promise of a kiss is pulverized by a car thrown in the window of the building, etc.). The film's nervous rhythm and its scopic impulses (in particular the gripping editing effects, such as the stunning cross-cutting, seen through the eye of the protagonists, between the birth of the Green Goblin and the waking up of the teenager) are other syndromes of a certain conception of the spectacular here envisaged.

The Mechanics of Attraction

But what is really amazing in SM1 and SM2, is the presence of some notions inherited from the historiography of early cinema, or the theory of its history, and comes under the concept of the cinema of attractions. Far from willing to make up an exhaustive list of inherited elements, I suggest here some possible connections between early cinema and contemporary blockbusters.

1. Moving Image Machine. SPIDER-MAN, like all films recently adapted from Marvel comics, begins with the logo of the film production company of the famous publishing house. We see a lightning-fast succession of drawings, often in extreme close-up, that come from the adapted comic book. The tonality of the images and the set of colors refer to the film hero's outfit (red in SPIDER-MAN, green in THE HULK [Ang Lee, 2003], black in THE PUNISHER [Jonathan Heinsleigh, 2004], etc.). The sequence of the images is so fast that it is practically impossible to recognize the drawings. Like a disordered flipbook, the sequence shows an order of pages completely mixed up, preventing any animation of the superheroes. Inevitably, the gaze gets lost: the saturation of images is so intense, the effect of explosion and fragmentation so powerful, the graphics and the colors so lightning that the spectator is condemned to run after these images without being able to catch up with them. There is only the continuity of strong, dynamic and colorful images, really attractive images,[24] shown without any concern of narrative or chronological organization. These images tell nothing, their dazzling flashes bewilder the eye. Before finding the way of the early cinema (or maybe in order to find it), these sequences replay the attractions of the pre-cinema optical amusements.

Furthermore, in SPIDER-MAN, very strange title credits follow, in a 3D movement simulation, recalling the thrill ride of amusement parks[25] and announcing clearly its belonging to the cinema of attractions. The spectator is taken through cobwebs, rising scenery and the letters of the credits. The ride will be repeated right in the heart of the film, during the mutation of Parker in Spider-Man, and will show obvious disruptions of his DNA. Ride sequences, like new impressive and autonomous visual prostheses, use effects of acceleration and losses of spatial marks. Their real purpose is to disturb the spectator's perceptions, to give him the sensation of a vertiginous mobility. Their sole legitimacy in the film is to impress the spectator, sometimes to his discomfort.[26] The sequence gives the tone: the gaze is not allowed to linger: it is excited, provoked, exhausted even before the beginning of the film.

2. *Exhibitionism.* Raimi's mise-en-scène seems to alternate spectacular actions sequences of titanic fights and stunning acrobatics (the Spider-Man aspect) with a love intrigue complicated by the agonies and vicissitudes of adolescent age (the Peter Parker aspect). Nevertheless, we must note that the opposition between the "system of monstrative attractions" and the "system of narrative integration" is not valid any longer here. According to the tradition of comics, the supernatural is attached to the character ("The Amazing Spider-Man"). Without the character, there is no attraction. The dichotomy narration/attraction becomes actually the condition of the attraction.

SM1 stages the transition from narration to attraction (the progressive discovery by the teenager of his power goes hand in hand with the progressive capacity of the cinema to dazzle in a long crescendo), whereas SM2 stages the crisis of the spectacular (the first scene, showing Peter Parker who delivers pizzas, is a parody of the spectacular moments of the first episode; later, the character doubts and loses his power: spectacular announced scenes lose then their magnificence for instance when Parker falls pitifully in an alley). The spectacular becomes then the catalyst of the emotion. As a matter of fact, the attraction becomes itself a suspense issue, and subject of this new cinema of attractions. The repetition of sequences from one film to the other (a building on fire, for example) and the serial aspect of all these new Hollywood films, telling incessantly the same history (the various versions of Terminator, the numberless wars in the LORD OF THE RINGS trilogy, etc.), fully participate in the expectation of the attraction sequence, as if it were some kind of a ritual.

Like early films, SPIDER-MAN proposes hence a profoundly exhibitionist system of the *image-attraction*,[27] because, after all, it is always a question of giving to see rather than of telling; moreover, the stories do not have much to tell (the story of Spider-Man has been told thousand times in the comics, just like everybody knows the history of TITANIC). Thus, these films appear as challenges to Hollywood who must manage to make spectacular and credible a young man walking on the wall in a ridiculous leotard. All in all, that's what it is about: giving a demonstration of know-how, while succeeding in amazing the public with visual spectacle.

This kind of cinema attracts the spectator to the spectacle of its technology, but, at the same time, aims at the fantastic element and transfers the attraction of the technology toward the diegetic. This is particularly evident in the sequences shot with the so-called "spider-cam"[28] which is constantly showing its own virtuosity while being completely subjected to the recording of the extraordinary acrobatics of the hero. The technological device exhibits itself while highlighting, above all, the extraordinary action of the diegesis offering throughout these bewildering moments a double attraction (the attraction of the film and the attraction of the *dispositif*).

3. *Phantom Rides.* The first films by Lumière, Gaumont, Edison or Biograph subjected the spectators of the turn of the century to a series of unusual visual experiments by taking as main topic and shooting device the railway vehicles, the trains or the subways. Early cinema fascination for fast space and vision modifications which shooting aboard allowed, powerful sensations of movement and speed, constructions of viewpoints which intensify the impressions of the locomotives' impetuosity, and exasperated visual pleasure of the *mobile* are well known today. In his work on early cinema, Livio Belloï lists under the term of "vues attentatoires"[29] (assailing views) attacks on the spectator: machines, locomotives, characters, landscapes charge at them. It is a cinema of effect and reaction.

In SM2, it seems that Raimi wants to re-conquer the fetish of these assailing views by proposing a complete catalogue of extreme visual possibilities provided by an elevated railway. The long scene is a fight between the hero and Octopus in and around the subway. To the mobility of the vehicle and the camera, Raimi adds the mobility of the protagonists who spin around the railway, and exploits all the places and available viewpoints (the roof of the subway, the inside, the left side, the right side, the head of the locomotive, etc.). Everything is in perpetual motion, until Spider-Man succeeds in slowing down the crazy race of the vehicle by stopping it with his own body in front of the train. This sequence presents some striking subjective viewpoints which show the end of the railway getting closer at full speed.

More generally, Raimi exaggerates the visual power of the assailing views by massively using the subjective camera and fast forward tracking, or amazing computer-generated rides which plunge the spectator into the meanders of improbable images. The *image-projectile* is a permanent feature of his cinema.

4. *The Emblematic Shot.* By the notion of "emblematic shot," of which the most known is still today the scene with the outlaw leader firing at the spectator in THE GREAT TRAIN ROBBERY (Edwin S. Porter, 1903), Noël Burch intended to define a sort of portrait appearing most of the times at the extremities of the film

(beginning or end) and whose semantic function consists in introducing or summarizing the chief element of the film.[30] The presentational function of the emblematic shot was frequent between, roughly speaking, 1903 and 1910.

I am tempted to write that SM1 and SM2 re-use a certain conception of the emblematic shot. It is a strong attraction, a limited moment of visual fascination, appearing at the extreme end of both films, and transforming the spectator into a distanced observer. It is an autonomous sequence that constitutes itself as a pure moment of visual happiness, unmotivated, dedicated to the acrobatics of Spider-Man. A very mobile camera hesitates between long shot, medium shot and big close-up of the hero's face, making of its mask the main motif.[31] Autonomous, placed at the end of the film, like the emblematic shot in early films, this scene acts as last scopic bait, a last attraction. This very strong visual sequence is offered in a variety of forms, such as trailers, posters and animations on the DVD, becoming the emblem of the film.[32]

5. *Addressing/Assailing the Spectator.* As a devil brutally taken out of its bag of tricks, Spider-Man appears towards the spectator, and stares him in the face. We cannot keep count of the shots where the characters, heroes or bad guys, are suddenly grimacing, in close-up towards the camera, even if this means going off screen rushing into the camera (the motif of the eye, the one of Green Goblin or Spider-man, swallowing the spectator is recurrent). Neither can we keep count of the sequences where projectiles (cobwebs, tentacles, explosive grenades, cornice fragments, cars, gorgeous young girls or defenseless old ladies) are thrown at top speed to the head of the spectator.

The screen seems to be ready to burst permanently in the direction of the spectator, as in the sequence of the missed fusion experiment in SM2: all the metallic elements of Dr. Octavius's laboratory are attracted by an unstable mass energy; screws are extracted of the walls, steel sheets snatch away from the ceiling, and windows blow up. A myriad of glass fragments assaults Octavius's wife, whose viewpoint the spectator takes up for some time. In slow motion, the woman's screaming face is reflected in the flying windows which get ready to slash her lethally. This reflection could be that of the frightened – or at least fascinated – spectator, who is directly aimed at by these threatening glass fragments. Unsurprisingly, the visual aggression comes along with a thundering soundtrack which participates in this particular mode of addressing the spectator. The camera's movements, moreover, contribute to interrupt the process of identification of classical narration. In SM2, strangely furious and vertiginous tracking shots (the director's specialty) go through buildings and window to be reflected, eventually, in the glasses of Octopus before bouncing all the more…

If the address of the spectator uses little the look at camera by actors, the narrative break and the reminder of the spectator's status is revealed by the hyperbolic camera's movements, but also, among other things, by a series of referential shots (the surgical scene of Octopus's tentacles amputation, a wink at Raimi's faithful spectators in the direction of his previous films), and the recourse to the burlesque close-up (the insert of the spider which bites Peter into SM1, a real visual moment, autonomous, striking and comic).

We also notice the hilarious intensification of the soundtrack which drags, at times, the film towards the side of animated cartoons. A series of sounds effects reminds the practices of figuralism and Mickey-Mousing rather than classic sound effects, as is shown by the curious noise of strong lashes that grotesquely emphasizes the camera's fast movements, or the way the heavy and threatening steps of Dr. Octopus organize the rhythm of the editing (a series of close-ups on the frightened faces of his next victims).

Caught in the Cobweb

In the continuation of the early cinema of attractions, Raimi's films take part in a vast culture of the consumer society. The gaze is even more fragmented than at the beginning of the last century, and the interactions between the different types of entertainment have multiplied. SPIDER-MAN incorporates some entertaining media and perpetually refers to them: comics (not only the story and the characters, but also the quotation of famous covers, striking drawings or logos of the publishing house[33]), movies (quotations and different borrowings, such as the scene where the hero runs and opens his shirt to uncover his costume, a tribute to another adaptation of superhero: SUPERMAN [Richard Donner, 1978]), video games (the setup of cameras on moving bodies, alternating between the establishment shot from the ceiling and the subjective view of the characters; the unusual animations of the bodies of hero and villains), music videos (the fragmentation of editing, the concert of pop singer Macy Gray in SM1), licensed products (the stereotyped positions of the characters for T-shirts and action figures, the reification of the bodies), etc. The film integrates them into its writing by referring to them. It is a perfect object of consumption because it creates the appeal of other products while synthesizing them. As we can see, SPIDER-MAN inherits and fully claims the tradition of spectacular entertainment, born with modernity and unmistakably connected to the urban mode of consumption. SPIDER-MAN, following the example of other recent big Hollywood successes, appropriates a series of elements enlightened by the concept of cinema of attractions. It builds itself in an effective perceptive trap and tries by all possible means to suspend the gaze, and maintain it in a perpetual state of fascination and subjugation.

In the center of the complex phenomena of intermediality and intertextuality, the blockbuster, as integral part of an economic and ideological system of extreme consumption of possessions and signs, has to reinvent its relation to the spectator. It is probably mostly in this sense that it re-encounters and renews the cinema of attractions. However, at the same time, the blockbuster, by integrating such a huge economic system, participates in replacing the spectator in a consumer, distancing itself, in such a degree that it would be useful to study, from the cinema of attractions such as it was defined for early cinema. Hollywood production, being too referential, does not propose a real break in terms of attraction and replays with enjoyment numerous artifices of the cinema of attractions. Nevertheless, it constitutes itself, blockbuster after blockbuster, in an aesthetics differentiated from the early cinema of attractions: its current mode of functioning is an overstatement with which it sentences itself to a logic of self-consuming and incessant hybridization, to a perpetual crisis of aesthetics.

Until Hollywood frees itself from this crisis, popular cinema, never forgetting its fairground origins, continues to appear as a gigantic cobweb which keeps the captive spectator in its center, eyes wide open.

Notes

1. See my work on the connections between contemporary blockbuster, film noir and gothic novel: *Le Palimpseste Noir. Notes sur l'impétigo, la terreur et le cinéma américain contemporain* (Crisnée: Yellow Now, 2002).
2. See, for example, the use of the term in José Arroyo, ed., *Action/Spectacle Cinema* (London: British Film Institute, 2000).
3. If James Cameron is credited, the producer Ovidio G. Assonitis edited the film without the director. Cameron will assume all the responsibilities on his following film: THE TERMINATOR (1984).
4. At the moment of writing this article, the films of the American top ten box-office are, in decreasing order: TITANIC (1997), STAR WARS (1977), SHREK 2 (2004), E.T. THE EXTRA-TERRESTRIAL (1982), STAR WARS I: THE PHANTOM MENACE (1999), SPIDER-MAN (2002), STAR WARS III: REVENGE OF THE SITH (2005), THE LORD OF THE RINGS: THE RETURN OF THE KING (2003), SPIDER-MAN 2 (2004), THE PASSION OF THE CHRIST (2004) (source IMDb).
5. TITANIC (1997) and TERMINATOR 2: JUDGMENT DAY (1991). TERMINATOR 3: RISE OF THE MACHINES (2003) was directed by Jonathan Mostow but produced by Cameron.
6. The trilogy of THE LORD OF THE RINGS (2001, 2002 and 2003).
7. DARKMAN (1990) allowed Raimi to work on SPIDER-MAN 1 (2002) and, then, on SPIDER-MAN 2 (2004). As for Cameron and Jackson, the critics and the audience approved by a large majority the "fidelity" to the original subject.

8.   See Frank Kessler, "La cinématographie comme dispositif (du) spectaculaire," *CiNéMAS* 14.1 (Fall 2003): 21-34.

9.   See Livio Belloï, *Le Regard retourné. Aspects du cinéma des premiers temps* (Québec/ Paris: Nota Bene/Méridiens Klincksieck, 2001) 85.

10. Common in French newspapers and film reviews.

11. "Cinématographie-attraction" was first used by G.-Michel Coissac in 1925 (*Histoire du Cinématographe. De ses origines à nos jours* [Paris: Editions du Cinéopse/Librairie Gauthier-Villars, 1925] 359) and adopted by André Gaudreault in the 1990s. See André Gaudrault, "Les *vues cinématographiques* selon Georges Méliès, ou: comment Mitry et Sadoul avaient peut-être raison d'avoir tort (même si c'est surtout Deslandes qu'il faut lire et relire)," *Georges Méliès, l'illusionniste du fin de siècle?*, ed. Jacques Malthête and Michel Marie (Paris: Sorbonne Nouvelle/Colloque de Cerisy, 1997) 111-31. See also André Gaudreault, "From 'Primitive Cinema' to 'Kine-Attractography,'" in the present volume.

12. According to Belloï, the *image-attraction* is a double exhibition: it says at the same time "Here I am" and "This is what I show." Belloï 84.

13. Tom Gunning, "Cinéma des attractions et modernité," *Cinémathèque* 5 (Spring 1994): 131. [English version: "The Whole Town's Gawking: Early Cinema and the Visual Experience of Modernity," *Yale Journal of Criticism* 7.2 (Fall 1994): 189-201.]

14. Questions often come from the development of the digital technology (digital special effects and new possibilities of interaction between film and spectator). See, for example, Bruno Cornellier, "Le sublime technologique et son spectateur dans le parc d'attraction. Nouvelles technologies et artefacts numériques dans JURASSIC PARK," *Cadrage* (2001): http://www.cadrage.net/films/jurassik/jurassik.html; or Viva Paci, "Cinéma de synthèse et cinéma des premiers temps: des correspondances examinées à la loupe du système des attractions," *Cinéma et Cie* 5 (Fall 2004): 112-14.

15. If we only use the example here of Raimi's SPIDER-MAN, a similar work could be done for the films by Cameron and Jackson, among others.

16. Philippe Roger, "Spectaculaire, histoire d'un mot," *Le Spectaculaire*, ed. Christine Hamon-Sirejols and André Gardies (Lyon: Aléas, 1997) 9-10. The term *spectaculaire* that replaces *spectaculeux* at the beginning of the 20th century means a weakening of its meaning. I will retain the idea of excess of the term *spectaculeux*.

17. See Pierre Berthomieu, *Le Cinéma Hollywoodien. Le temps du renouveau* (Paris: Nathan, 2003) 29.

18. Lucas will frequently reproduce this type of sequence, sometimes until the exhaustion of the gaze. See for example the endless sequence of the pod race on Tatooine in THE PHANTOM MENACE (1999).

19. *Time* 15 June 15 1981. Quoted by Laurent Jullier in *L'Ecran post-moderne. Un cinéma de l'allusion et du feu d'artifice* (Paris: L'Harmattan, 1997) 37.

20. See, for instance, THE HAUNTED MANSION (Rob Minkoff, 2003) or PIRATES OF THE CARIBBEAN (Gore Verbinsky, 2003).

21. It is difficult to make a distinction between the syndromes of the mutation of the superhero and those of a teenager (new muscle structure, uncontrollable organic jets, etc.).

22. San Francisco or Chicago, particularly for the elevated railway, which is non-existent in New York and nevertheless in the center of a spectacular scene in SM2.

23. Gunning 133.

24. Their function is also advertising: it is the illustration of the trademark of the firm.

25. One of the most famous rides is probably the "Star Tour" in the various Disney-land's. The simulator proposes to relive again the attack of the Death Star in STAR WARS from an unexpected angle.

26. Recently, rides became frequent in the credits of blockbusters. See, for example, David Fincher's FIGHT CLUB (1999) or Bryan Singer's X-MEN (2000) and X2 (2003), other comics adaptations. In THE LORD OF THE RINGS, they appear within the story, transforming an establishment shot in a moment of attraction (see for example the discovery of the Saruman's army in THE FELLOWSHIP OF THE RING).

27. See note 12.

28. Finalized by Earl Wiggins and John Dykstra, this computer-controlled camera, suspended on a cable from a height of thirty floors, risks some extreme movements of pendulum between buildings and above the streets.

29. Belloï 77-159.

30. Noël Burch, *La lucarne de l'infini* (Paris: Nathan, 1990) 186-88.

31. Spider-Man's face has often been used as logo by Marvel. Besides, we recall the mediatization of the images of the film's mask that reflected the Twin Towers.

32. However, in SM2, the last shot of the film is dedicated to Mary-Jane Watson, the girl-friend of the hero, who is watching him leaving through a window. The anxiety can be read on her face. It promises the beginnings of a new story...

33. We can also mention the references to comics in the story. In SM1, Peter sketches the costume that he is going to make, trying to find the postures and drawings of famous artists who followed one another in the comic strip. In SM2, after the title sequence which summarizes the intrigue of the first episode by means of the drawings by celebrated artist Alex Ross, Peter Parker worries about the disappearance of his comic books during the move of his aunt.

Figures of Sensation: Between Still and Moving Images

Eivind Røssaak

It was Alexander Gottlieb Baumgarten's *Aesthetica* (1750), which gave the new discipline of aesthetics its name. Aesthetics was concerned with a special faculty of perception that Baumgarten titled "sensuous knowledge" (*cognitio sensitiva*). In contrast to clear and distinct conceptual knowledge, sensuous knowledge is a *cognitio confusa*, a confused knowledge form. "It is not aimed at distinctions; it pursues an animated intertwinement of aspects even when it is a matter of a stationary object. It lingers at a process of appearing," Martin Seel remarks.[1] These processes of aesthetic appearing involve compounds of sensation or what I will call figures of sensation. Gilles Deleuze would call them "sensory becomings […] caught in a matter of expression."[2] But I will focus on the way figures of sensation may *happen* in the process of appearing between still and moving images. Aesthetically speaking these modes of appearing can be said to be cinematic events before cinema and precinematic events within cinema. They disrupt the eye and seem to pull the spectator into a zone of confusion of appearances, between media, between art forms, between forms of mobility and immobility.

Tom Gunning's conceptions of the "cinema of attractions" and "aesthetic of astonishment" explain fundamental aspects of the figure of sensation. Gunning highlights the important connection between media, motion and sensation. In this article, I will first look at one of the examples of early cinema he discusses and then see how the processes of appearing are refigured and extended in THE MATRIX (Andy and Larry Wachowski, 1999). I will then widen my scope and explore related issues in the works of Gilles Deleuze and Sergei Eisenstein.

The Sudden Transformation

With the introduction of cinema in 1895, new energies of appearing entered our visual culture. The Lumière screenings in Paris enacted on a small scale, at every show, the rupture cinema enacts in our visual regimes of representation. The relationship between the still and the moving in cinema was not simply a play with forms, but a way of demonstrating the abilities of a new medium. At this specific moment in history, the rupture of the eye coincided with the rupture of art history itself.

> [I]n the earliest Lumière exhibitions the films were initially presented as frozen unmoving images, projections of still photographs. Then [...] the projector began cranking and the image moved. Or as Gorky described it, "suddenly a strange flicker passes through the screen and the picture stirs to life." [...] [T]he sudden transformation from still image to moving illusion, startled audiences...[3]

This transformation event is complex. The audience is placed in between conflicting modes of appearing, transported from the qualities of photography to that of cinematography. Initially, in front of the stilled image, the audience felt a stroke of disappointment. "They got us all stirred up for projections like this? I've been doing them for over ten years," says Georges Méliès. Gunning spends some time on the interstice between the initial disappointment and the upcoming amazement: "I have frozen the image of crowds [at this point]," he writes.[4] This interstice is a composite one. It is the space between two qualities of media or between two modes of presentation, the way of the old medium of the stilled image, photography, and the way of the new medium of film, where the stilled image takes on motion. It is also an emotional space, a space where the audience is transported from the familiar to the unfamiliar, from the canny to the uncanny. The emotions are specifically linked to the appearance of motion, which transforms the emotion into a state of shock. It is this magical metamorphosis that so astounds the audience. Méliès says: "Before this spectacle we sat with gaping mouths, struck with amazement, astonished beyond all expression." Gunning also stresses the importance of suspension here, of "withholding briefly the illusion of motion which is the apparatus's raison d'être [...]. By delaying its appearance, the Lumière's exhibitor not only highlights the device but signals its allegiance to an aesthetic of astonishment which goes beyond a scientific interest in the reproduction of motion."[5] They were concerned with the logics of sensations.

The Bullet Time Effect

Gunning's concept of attraction liberates the analysis of film from the hegemony of narratology, which is dominated by its focus on genre, character, and the structural development of a story. The concept of attraction enables us to focus, rather, on *the* event of appearing as itself a legitimate aesthetic category. The deepest pleasure and *jouissance* of cinema may reside in such attractions, rather than in the way the film is narrated. This was my feeling after having seen THE MATRIX, approximately 100 years after the Lumière exhibitions. When I experienced the fabulous bullet time or frozen time shots I didn't believe my own eyes. The strange way the special effects of this movie manipulate time and movement had never been seen before. "Movies as we knew them changed," art and film critic David Edelstein reported in the *New York Times*.[6] It seems that both the beginning of cinema with the Lumière brothers and the end of cinema as we have known it, that is, an end marked by the use of new phases of digital cinema, with the Wachowski brothers, flaunt their mastery of showmanship by playing on the passage between the still and the moving. But the bullet time effect seems to recreate this attraction of the first cinema exhibitions by reversing the order of the process of appearing. The famous bullet time attraction does not pull us from a sensation of the still to the moving as described in the Lumière screenings, but rather takes us onto an uncanny ride from an illusion of movement to one of sculptural freeze and back again.

Let us detail some of the negotiations between media technology and art forms at play in the bullet time effect. I believe the sudden impact of this figure of sensation is to be found in the way it recreates and extends energies and affects belonging to several media techniques and art forms, new and old. First of all, it remediates older techniques of photography developed by Eadweard Muybridge, before cinema as we know it. In an experiment in the 1880s Muybridge rigged six super fast cameras in an arch around the naked body of a man while he jumped into the air.[7] The six cameras were triggered at the same time and give us six exact images of a man at one single moment of time from six different angles. This so called Muybridge effect was not used extensively in film before the experiments of artist-scientist Tim Macmillan in 1980, when he started experimenting with the relationship between new technology and the theory of Cubism.[8] During the 1990s director Michel Gondry used the technique in commercials such as Smirnoff's "Smarienberg," Polaroid's "Live for the moment," and Virgin Records's music video "Like a Rolling Stone" by the Rolling Stones.[9] But the effect was not widely known to the cinema audiences before 1999, when the special effect team of THE MATRIX refashioned and refined the technique into what they called the bullet time effect.

The bullet time effect explores and challenges certain logics of media by exploring alternative processes of appearing. The accelerations or decelerations of the effect also enact a kind of sliding into strange and unexpected negotiations with other art forms and modes of aesthetic appearance. The principal of this effect is to make a strip of film by using a series of still cameras instead of an ordinary movie camera. The complex mode of production also demonstrates the aesthetic negotiations at play. The effect mixes analogue camera techniques (Muybridge style) with digital interpolation and virtual camera techniques.[10] The still cameras take multiple images within a fraction of a second from several perspectives of a body as it jumps. The trick is to show the images of *frozen time* sequentially, as film. Space and time seem to switch places. A slice of time is extended spatially *and* space (a body) is explored temporally. Time is opened up and explored spatially outside time. This creates fabulous 3D images. Both visually and technically it forces us to reevaluate some of the essential characteristics of cinema. Photography stills time or "embalms time," according to André Bazin. "The photographic image is the object itself, the object freed from the conditions of time and space that govern it. [...] the cinema is objectivity in time," he argues.[11] The primary task of cinema was to produce mechanical recordings of movement *in time,* not outside time – the other arts could do that. The bullet time *derealizes* some of these characteristics by recording an event both inside and outside of time *at the same time.*[12]

The play of time and space in the bullet time effects works beautifully with the characteristic in-between-ness of the whole film. We follow a group of hackers into cyberspace, the matrix. We are in a world that obeys laws and speeds of a different order. We are in a way both inside and outside time or in the interstice between our communications and representations, inside the networks that condition what we see and what we can say. The film needed a new kind of special effects to mark this space. Visual effect designer John Gaeta and his team ended up using up to 122 digital still cameras rigged in a circle around the actors. At both ends of the arc Gaeta placed high-speed photosonic motion-picture cameras, which can take more than a thousand frames per second. These were used to create a smooth transition from bullet time speed, frozen time, and back into normal time. The effect is used in scenes where the action is fast, extreme and involves life-threatening interactions between the characters.

Freeze!

Approximately two minutes into THE MATRIX, we encounter the first use of the bullet time effect. Cyberpunk rebel Trinity (Carrie-Ann Moss) hides in an abandoned downtown hotel trying to hack into *the system.* She is interrupted by a group of policemen breaking into the apartment. A policeman screams "Freeze!" and it looks like she surrenders, but as the policeman is about to handcuff her, she turns around and swiftly breaks his arm. She runs towards the next policeman and jumps up in the air. As a master in martial arts she prepares to strike a blow to his face. Suddenly she appears to freeze in mid-air while a camera seems to truck 180 degree around her. A violent sound evaporates into a calm silence. Trinity appears to float like a ballet dancer in thin air, or rather, she is frozen and the camera dances around her as if it were on ice. It is as if we enter a limbo between the movements of film and the otherworldly contemplation of a sculptural freeze. The aesthetic negotiation with a sculptural mode of appearance is significant. Sculpture is in many ways the most immobile and the most auratic of the arts, the cinema the most mobile and the least auratic of the arts, according to Walter Benjamin.[13] But the appearance is not simply sculptural. Due to high-speed camera technology, we have paradoxically moved from slow mo to no mo within a mobile frame.

The effect may remind us of the magical last moment of LES QUATRE CENTS COUPS (1959) by François Truffaut. When the boy turns around and looks at the audience, the frame is stilled on a medium shot of the boy, but the camera uncannily continues to zoom in to a close-up on the still. In THE MATRIX the effect is of a different order: a large number of stills taken by a large number of still cameras and a series of digitally interpolated images are connected in a sequence that simulates an *impossible* camera movement. We still lack good names for this kind of virtual camera movement. It looks like a sequence of ordinary slow motion produced by a single high-speed camera, but technically it is the result of a large number of still cameras simulating the slow movement of a motion-picture camera, a kind of dolly shot, a swish pan of paradoxically crisp images slowed down. Is it possible? The clue is: the camera seems to move, but time stands still. Trinity floats, freezes. The two high-speed photosonic movie cameras at the head and tail of the rig of still cameras make sure the transition is smooth from *the slow sequence of stills*, the Zen Buddhist moment of stillness, and back into the next joint of the sequence, the super fast kick at the jaw of the policeman. There the out-of-joint-ness of time is restored. The film accelerates smoothly from freeze to normal speed and into high speed and back again. The malleability of the virtual body and the film edit enter into a sublime cooperation. The poor policeman should never have said the word "Freeze." The ease and flexibility of the bullet time effect in the treatment of any bodily movement and configuration of body and space astound the audience. We enter new bodily sensations as Trinity enters new time-space dimensions. Gaeta concludes as much: "All of these techniques and alterations in time created new physiological and psychological moments for the audience."[14]

Cinematography liberates the arts from their "convulsive catalepsy,"[15] Bazin argued. The bullet time effect extends the language of cinema and renews its relationship to what Bazin called "the tortured immobility"[16] of sculpture and painting. The effect explores sensations and becomings in the passage in between the still and the moving. Cinema thus renegotiates its relationship to other media and art forms. Cinematography has finally, or yet again, managed to turn itself into the other of cinema while at the same time retaining the appearance of cinema. In the bullet time effect, the audience is moved from a portrayal of the living as animate to a moving portrayal of the living as inanimate, or sculptural. The mobile frame of the freeze-time shot keeps the imagery within the medium of film, in the sense of film as living pictures, but the way it refigures the relationship between the still and the moving, the animate and the inanimate, translates the logic of the aesthetic experience from the medium of film to the medium of the sculpture. The sensation is no longer simply of the cinematic, but also of the sculptural.

The Logic of Sensation

Figures of sensation seem to depend on conflicts of some sort. In his book *Francis Bacon: The Logics of Sensation*, Gilles Deleuze discusses the logic of sensations as a result of a series of more or less traceable clashes between media forms, techniques, cultural clichés, modes of visibility and invisibility, and last but not least, clashes between modes of mobility and immobility.[17] He develops his conceptual framework in an intimate dialogue with the painter Francis Bacon. *Francis Bacon: The Logics of Sensation* appeared in 1981, when David Sylvester had just published a book of several in-depth interviews with Bacon.[18] Here Bacon talks about sensation in a manner reminiscent of Cézanne and his enigmatic idea of *painting sensations*. The great majority of Bacon's paintings are of people. Many of his so-called *Figure in Movement* paintings are based on the time-lapse photography of Eadweard Muybridge. But unlike most figure or portrait painters, Bacon did not want to create close physical likeness. Bacon does not copy Muybridge; instead, he uses radical distortion to convey a sense of the person as a living energy or, as he puts it, "to trap this living fact alive."

The logic of sensation is intimately connected to the Deleuzian term "Figure," but the term is tricky. First of all, it refers to what Bacon himself calls "Figure." Almost all his paintings have the word "Figure" in their titles, even if the painted figure is rather unreadable or undecipherable. Secondly, it refers to Jean-François Lyotard's concept of the *figural*, but without the strong bias towards the Freudian unconscious, which dominates Lyotard's elaborations of the term in his book *Discours, figure*.[19] Lyotard wanted to develop a kind of energetics of sensations, not dissimilar to the later Deleuze. The figural became a key term in this approach. Lyotard opposed the figural to discourse. Discourse is an order of meaning. It is a spatial and conceptual grid that controls and guides a logical process. It reduces the sayable and the visible to the representable. The figural interrupts this logic. It is resistant to the rule of signification. "The figural opens discourse to a radical heterogeneity, a singularity, a difference, which cannot be rationalized or subsumed within the rule of representation."[20] Deleuze refashions the figural into both a more concrete issue, that is, in the workings of the Figures of Bacon, and a more general issue, its relationship to the event and bodily sensations. According to Deleuze, the Figure *is* sensation.[21] The crucial point here is the way he links the logic of sensation to a conflict between media and motion. He actually analyzes Bacon as a kind of special effects painter. Consequently, his book on Bacon is more of a primer on special effects than his cinema books. Bacon's cinematic special effects and painterly attractions were actually one of the reasons many of his contemporaries, many Abstract Expressionists among others, distanced themselves from him. In contrast, Deleuze thinks that Bacon's line of flight between the figurative and the abstract is exactly what makes him so interesting. It seems to be one of Deleuze's many polemical gestures in this book to maintain that both figurative and abstract art are cerebral practices, and that only the in-between art of the Figure is of the body and of so-called pure sensations.

Bacon established this in-between zone by creating Figures through a process of isolation. He sometimes stages his painting like a circus ring. These and similar techniques of isolation trap the energy at play. "The important point is that they [Bacon's techniques] do not consign the Figure to immobility but, on the contrary, render sensible a kind of progression, an exploration of the Figure within a place, or upon itself."[22] A quick look at the film studio designs of the bullet time effect – easily accessible in the special feature section of the DVD releases of THE MATRIX – likewise demonstrates the way the special effect team isolates its figure. The actors are placed in what looks like a boxing ring of cameras and the images taken of this scene are worked over and over in almost the same way a painter would rework a canvas, using many layers of virtual paint, that is, computer grafted imagery, virtual cinematography processes such as photogrammetry techniques for building backgrounds, and systems of digital interpolations between image frames, to build a special sensation on the screen in the final result. The almost analytical mode of presentation of this scene, the freeze and slow motion effects I discussed above, renders sensible an unusual process of appearing, a kind of latent energy becoming manifest. This process of appearing not only carries the figure onto the screen and into another plane of existence, beyond the laws of gravity where the protagonist, Trinity, floats between heaven and hell, both within and outside time, it even manipulates the flesh of Trinity/Carrie-Ann Moss by occasionally rendering it virtual, by digital interpolations. This strong and paradoxical cinematographic figure of sensation transports the spectator into a process of appearances which involves the body in both an existential and phenomenological way. Deleuze's argument can be applied to both Bacon and the bullet time effect:

> The Figure is the sensible form related to a sensation; it acts immediately upon the nervous system, which is of the flesh, whereas abstract form is addressed to the head, and acts through the intermediary of the brain, which is closer to the bone [...] at one

and the same time I *become* in the sensation and something *happens* in the sensation
[…] As a spectator, I experience the sensation only by entering the painting, by reaching the unity of the sensing and the sensed […] sensation is not in the "free" or disembodied play of light and color; on the contrary, it is in the body, even the body of
an apple.[23]

For a phenomenologist of the flesh like Deleuze, the sensation event obliterates
the difference between the flesh of the subject and the object. We end up in a
strange "Fleshism,"[24] a flesh-like unity of the sensing and the sensed. This is
energetics, not hermeneutics.[25] The process does not reveal an intentional structure, as if the spectator senses the true meaning of the work, nor a mimetic
structure in any sense, where the bodily sensation of the represented equals the
bodily sensation of the spectator. No, sensations for Deleuze are planes of existence, or rather planes of immanence, where the sensational being enters a zone
of an other-awareness and a zone of art, which are zones of a certain *becoming*.

Both the logic of sensation and attraction disrupt narrative. Deleuze expresses
it thus: "As Valéry put it, sensation is that which is transmitted directly, and
avoids the detour and boredom of conveying a story."[26] The rupture of sensation renders visible a clash of different media and materials. Bacon deforms
flesh and figure by physically working on the limits of color, brush, oil paint
and canvas. Looking at his paintings in a museum, the speed of his strokes in
the way he lets the canvas itself shine through arbitrarily here and there can
often be sensed, as in the fabulous *Figure in Movement* (1985) at Tate Britain.[27]
The contorted body walks hastily but awkwardly towards the viewer. His
rather impossible movements seem to deform his appearance as if the body
experiences the tortured immobility of the support, the canvas. As part of the
process of isolation the support is doubled and relocated through a series of
reframings. The floor seems to float and to partly rise above the ground, while
the figure struggles somewhere in between two rooms and several arrangements of *framing*. All the elements in conflict here create an intense energy of
movement and counter-movement. Deleuze states in one of his many apt
phrases that what "fascinates Bacon is not movement, but its effect on an immobile body."[28] This sentence is both simple and complex – Deleuze says here that
invisible forces are rendered visible through the working deformations (and re-
locations and isolations on the canvas) of the figurative, the body. The painted
figure is transformed into shivering flesh. This transgressive act or movement
takes on the appearance of what Deleuze likes to call "pure sensation." The
painting is the vacillating clash between movement and immobility. It is also in
this sense that Bacon – as he deforms, doubles and multiplies the appearances
of the stills of Muybridge – believes he is painting sensation, the fact of sensation, rather than just documenting an externality, as he believes photography
does.

Some of the same logics of sensation are at work in the bullet time effect, but in a strange way the relationship between movement and immobility seems to switch places. We could say that, and here I am reversing the Deleuzian phrase, in using the bullet time effect, the Wachowski brothers are fascinated not by immobility, but by its effect on a moving body, and this effect is explored through a process of isolation, both technically and aesthetically, to achieve the most intense figure of sensation. Here again, "immobility" and "moving body" need to be understood in both wide and precise terms. Instead of repeating the explication of the bullet time effect from above, I will simply refer to the intricate way this effect plays upon the aforementioned multiple uses and combinations of the still and the moving.

An objection to this comparison between Bacon and the bullet time effect could refer to the treatment of the body in each case. Bacon deforms the body; the bullet time reframes and suspends the body in the air and so the body is not deformed as in Bacon's paintings. Yet simply referring to these processes on the level of representation misses the point. The question is not whether the body is deformed or not, but concerns the process or the logic, as Deleuze calls it, of the appearance of the Figure, of the ways it is isolated and suspended in an unfamiliar way between media, art forms, and logics of representation. This kind of suspended isolation creates the kind of sensation at issue here. It is not simply an issue of deformation in the simple sense of torturing a body or anything of that sort. This becomes clearer in another example Deleuze uses, the religious paintings of the Renaissance. The floating figures of saints, peasants, angels and nudes on large canvases are also a way of artistically liberating what Deleuze calls Figure. Christian painting was not simply narrative painting or figurative tableaux sanctified by faith.

> The Figures [of Christian painting] are lifted up and elaborated, refined without measure, outside all restraint. Despite appearances there is no longer any story to tell; the Figures are relieved from their representative role, [...] they no longer have to do with anything but "sensations" – celestial, infernal, or terrestrial sensations. [...] One must not say, "If God does not exist, everything is permitted." It is just the opposite. For with God, everything is permitted [...] because the divine Figures are wrought by a free creative work, by a fantasy in which everything is permitted.[29]

The point here is not the similarities between Christian painting and THE MA-TRIX, but rather the open manner in which Deleuze sees possibilities for liberating Figure in many settings, arenas and ages – even, I would like to add, in the age of digital reproduction.

Cinematics before Cinema

It is well known that both Tom Gunning and Gilles Deleuze are keen readers of
Sergei Eisenstein. Gunning adopts his term "attraction" from Eisenstein, and
Deleuze picks up his idea of cinema's ability to produce "a shock to thought"
from him. But they rarely pay much attention to the fact that Eisenstein's idea of
the cinematic to a large extent was based on the art of painting, or rather, that he
meant that the art of painting was already cinematic, at least since the Renaissance. This is fundamental for understanding his idea of montage, which was a
kind of art of painting applied to the filmstrip. To Eisenstein, simply recording
the movement of living bodies did not create a strong sensation of movement;
you need montage, you need painting, so to speak.

Montage, according to Eisenstein, connects disparate images and creates a
shock of thought. Eisenstein had a strong sense for the creative energies hidden
in juxtapositions of different kinds. His early writings on the montage of attractions were primarily related to the theater. Juxtaposing different media and
modes of presentation such as live acting, posters, and sequences of projected
film on the theater stage constituted elements of this early montage of attractions. For the theater production of *The Mexican* in Moscow in 1920, he even
converted the theater space into a boxing ring. Strong emotions are created in
the interstice between media and different forms of representation. It is as if art
works or, rather, installations create strange emotions when they move beyond
the logic of one medium and towards another.

In the history of art, the tension between the materiality of a medium and its
potential level of kinesis, for example, using the "immobile" marble or bronze
to depict a strong sense of movement, has been important at least since the Ancient Greeks. Art historians have often treated the presence of the play between
actual immobility and virtual mobility as a sign of quality. Today it is a commonplace to view the history of art, that is, the transition from the archaic to
the classical and the Renaissance, as fundamentally a history in which the representation of motion is transformed from being indicated by simple signs or graphic poses, as in Egyptian art, to the representation of motion, as in the art of
illusionism in the Renaissance and the Baroque. The dialectic between stasis and
kinesis is striking in the works of the art historian Gombrich. His comment on
the famous *Statue of Bartolomeo Colleoni* (1479) by Andrea del Verrocchio, Leonardo da Vinci's teacher, is typical. This bronze is great, according to Gombrich,
because it looks like General Colleoni is "riding ahead of his troops with an
expression of bold defiance."[30] Gombrich cannot explain in any simple way
why it looks as if the statue moves. He simply talks of a certain "energy": "the
greatness and simplicity of Verrocchio's work [...] lies in the clear outline which

his group presents from nearly all aspects, and in the concentrated energy which seems to animate the man in armour and his mount."[31]

There is a certain energy that animates the inanimate; it is an energy that imbues the immobile with movement of some sort. How does this happen? How can the immobile appear to some of our senses, but not intellectually perhaps, as moving? Sergei Eisenstein has written several articles on this issue and among the richest is his long essay entitled "Laocoön," which is a comment to Gotthold Ephraim Lessing's *Laocoön: An Essay on the Limits of Painting and Poetry* (1766).[32] Lessing is well known for dividing the arts into temporal arts (poetry, music, etc.) and spatial arts (painting, sculpture, etc.). The value of each artwork, he says, lies in the way it observes the limitations of the medium.

> It remains true that the succession of time remains the province of the poet just as space is that of the painter. It is an intrusion of the painter into the domain of the poet, which good taste can never sanction, when the painter combines in one and the same picture two points necessarily separated in time, as does Fra Mazzuoli when he introduces the rape of the Sabine women and the reconciliation effected by them between their husbands and relations, or as Titian does when he presents the entire history of the prodigal son, his dissolute life, his misery, and his repentance.[33]

Eisenstein disagrees with Lessing's normative approach, but, nevertheless, Lessing is looked upon as a transitional figure. Eisenstein quotes from the preface of the Russian translation of Lessing's *Laocoön*. Here Lessing becomes the hero of a struggle "between two diametrically opposed views on art: the aristocratic courtly attitude" and "the bourgeois-democratic attitude."[34] In this scenario, Eisenstein puts himself in "a further, third stage": the synthesis. According to Eisenstein, Lessing's aristocratic opponents defended and extended the primacy of static pictoriality "even into the dynamic art forms (that is, poetry)."[35] Lessing criticized this attitude and removed from the art of poetry, as Eisenstein observes, "the enslaving function of depiction." Lessing, Eisenstein continues, "stresses the principle of dynamic coming-into-being, [but] without admitting it beyond the confines of poetry."[36] Eisenstein believes that Lessing was not able to see that this latter principle is pregnant with the future of all the arts, as they are realized in cinema: "in Lessing's day neither Edison nor Lumière had yet supplied him with that most perfect apparatus for research and assessment of the aesthetic principle of art: the cinematograph."[37]

Eisenstein re-reads the history of art according to the gradually emerging aesthetic principle dominating the, to him, most technically advanced art form, the cinema. According to Lessing, only poets, not painters, ought to challenge the primacy of static pictoriality. But to Eisenstein, it was importunate to celebrate the tendency towards dynamism, the principle of the future, wherever it props up, such as in the drawings and paintings by Daumier and Tintoretto. "The 'trick' of the unusual mobility of their figures is purely cinematic," he says.[38] He analyses at length some of the characteristics at work in paintings by these two artists and it is the montage principle he is looking for. It is not clear which Tintoretto painting Eisenstein is referring to, but *St. George and the Dragon* (1560) is a good suggestion. Here Tintoretto destroys, barely visible, the integrity of form and literal reality by using what Eisenstein calls the "chopped-up"[39] method. That is, he juxtaposes spatially three scenes (the heroic deed of St. George, the divine revelation and the escape of Princess Sabra), which originally were separated in time. This creates an enormous tension and drama in the image. Additionally, the movement of each image group is given force, direction and energy by being guided by what Eisenstein calls "the law of *pars pro toto*,"[40] that is, the depiction of parts substitutes for the whole. Each limb of the body indicates metonymically the phase of the movement of the whole body. We experience a strange co-presence of temporally conflicting gestures, all of which animate the image with movement, particularly the figure of Sabra. Eisenstein's ability to explain emotional phenomena with scientific precision is exquisite.

> Unlike the miniatures of the Middle Ages, however, they [Daumier and Tintoretto] do not give the temporally sequential phases of the movement to one limb [of the body] depicted several times but spread these phases consecutively over different parts of the body. Thus the foot is in position A, the knee already in stage A + a, the torso in stage A + 2a [...] and so on.[41]

This is a very apt description of Princess Sabra's dramatic body. She is animated by a series of almost impossible gestures. Her left hand and upper parts of the body are moving away from her right hand, which seems to already be in a future present. Her head and parts of her lower body and feet seem to belong to an earlier phase of the movement. Perhaps her thigh and knee are already placed in a future phase. Is she running, walking, kneeling or even falling? It is hard to tell. The drapery blowing violently in the wind further dramatizes the heterogeneity of the movement. In addition, there is an optical illusion that further enhances the *cinematics* of the attraction here. When anyone moves in front of the image, Sabra's outstretched hand seem to poke right through the canvas and reach out after the viewer, no matter what angle she is seen from. The effect works in the same way as the cinematic images of early cinema: "[it] displays its visibility, willing to rupture a self-enclosed fictional world for a chance to solicit the attention of the spectator," Gunning says.[42]

Jean-François Lyotard's theory of the figure is based on interruptions of this sort, on disruptions that have a strange way of breaking out of the medium to interrupt the eye. In *The Ambassadors* (1533) by Hans Holbein, also on display in the National Gallery in London, not far from Tintoretto's *St. George and the Dragon*, Lyotard locates a paradigmatic instance of the figural in the optical illusion of an anamorphosis, the hidden skull in the picture. The way the skull is painted means the eye is in the "wrong" position: the eye has to move to truly see. As Lyotard says: "The simple rotation of ninety degrees on the axis is enough to dissipate the representation. [...] To carry out this rotation is thus an ontological act that reverses the relationship between the visible and the invisible, between the signifier and the signified."[43] The "stain" that disrupts the frame of representation reveals the superimposition of two different (spectatorial) spaces. The number of possible spaces, of possible phases of movement and imagery, deconstructs the pictorial realism of these early modern paintings. The way these images appear as a multiple and heterogeneous play of appearances of different orders, even between various phases of a single movement creates figures of sensation that belie the tortured immobility of the media. They open up an interstice of sensations. According to Lyotard, the figural reveals "la mobilité immobile," the moving immobility and the immobilized movement.[44]

Coda

For me, the play upon movement and immobility is more than just a category for understanding aesthetic forces through the ages. In the case of cinema, it becomes a way of surviving as a medium of attraction. The way both the princess Sabra and Trinity appear creates figures of sensation by undermining the habitual mode of appearance within their respective media. The aesthetic force of their appearances follows what the Russian Formalist Viktor Shklovsky calls "the general laws of perception," based on the fact "that as perception becomes habitual, it becomes automatic."[45] According to Shklovsky, "art exists that one may recover the sensation of life." A successful figure of sensation in the arts depends on an insight into clichés or into the ecology of images and energies of the age. At times when actual movement in the pictorial arts was only a dream, simulating movement where there was none created awe-inspiring sensations. For example, during the Renaissance the vitality and dynamism of the images in works by painters such as Tintoretto shocked and bewildered their audiences, and during the early days of cinema, at the time when movement became the immediate given of the image itself, the newness of the moving image was in itself an attraction. Today, contemporary cinema needs to rethink this history. Moving images have become "automatic" in Shklovsky's derogative sense. Movement is no longer an attraction in itself as it was during the days of the first Lumière screenings in Paris. This is a great challenge for what has been called the most mobile of art forms. How can it renegotiate its basic parameters? The new fluid image-forms of digital cinema have become an important way of renegotiating the place of cinema today. These images transcend *and* extend the scope and potential of moving images by playing on new and unthinkable, that is, unseen, nuances in the passage between still and moving images. They renegotiate the ecology of images and energies in the history of art to make us feel things and see things anew. With its new digital technology, cinema can with greater ease than before pick up energies in the margins of the medium of every thinkable art form. As we have seen above, cinema has created new attractions and vital figures of sensation by borrowing the appearance of sculpture, painting and still photography, while at the same time retaining the appearance of cinema. This is the new cinema of attractions. It does not try to observe the *limitation* of a given medium in the way Lessing demanded. Rather, it lures to temporarily put cinema under erasure, that is, to completely arrest movement, so as to kick us even harder the next time. Just like Trinity.

Notes

1.   Martin Seel, *Aesthetics of Appearing* (Stanford: Stanford UP, 2005) 29.
2.   Gilles Deleuze and Félix Guattari, *What is Philosophy?* (London: Verso, 1994) 177.
3.   Tom Gunning, "An Aesthetic of Astonishment: Early Film and the (In)Credulous Spectator [1989]," *Film Theory and Criticism*, ed. Leo Braudy and M. Cohen (Oxford: Oxford UP, 1999) 822-23.
4.   Gunning 832.
5.   Gunning 832.
6.   David Edelstein, "Bullet Time Again: The Wachowskis Reload," *The New York Times* 11 May 2003, section 2A, 1, column 1.
7.   See Plate 522 in Eadweard Muybridge, *Complete Human and Animal Locomotion* (New York: Dover, 1979).
8.   On Tim Macmillan's experiments see: http://www.timeslicefilms.com/.
9.   Richard Linnett, "The Gondry Effect: the mastery of the frozen moment incites multi-camera mania – director Michel Gondry – Special Report: Visual Effects/Spring Edition," *Shoot* 8 May 1998.
10.   The film also engages in several cultural negotiations: East meets West not only thematically (kung fu fights robots), but also on the level of production (Woo-ping Yuen's wire fu techniques marry Californian new digital fluidity techniques).
11.   André Bazin, "The Ontology of the Photographic Image [1945]," *What is Cinema?* (Berkeley: U of California P, 1967) 14.
12.   Additionally, the bullet time effect challenges "realist" film theories such as Bazin's to the extent that what looks most real, the hyperreal image clarity of the bullet time effect, is unthinkable without digital interpolations. The way the reality of digital film production paradoxically challenges the ends or the basic plot of this film, the heroic struggle against simulations, is discussed in Eivind Røssaak, "The Unseen of the Real: Or, Evidential Efficacy from Muybridge to *The Matrix*," *Witness: Memory,*

Representation, and the Media in Question, ed. Ulrik Ekman (Copenhagen: Museum Tusculanum Press, forthcoming).

13. Walter Benjamin, "The Work of Art in the Age of Mechanical Reproduction," *Illuminations* (London: Fontana, 1973) 211-44.

14. This quotation and information on technical features of the bullet time effect are taken from Kevin H. Martin, "Jacking into the Matrix," *Cinefex* 79 (1999): 66-89.

15. Bazin 15.

16. Bazin 11.

17. Gilles Deleuze, *Francis Bacon: Figures of Sensation* (London: Continuum, 2003).

18. David Sylvester, *Interviews with Francis Bacon 1962-1979* (London: Thames and Hudson, 1980).

19. Jean-François Lyotard, *Discours, figure* (Paris: Klincksieck, 1971).

20. Bill Readings, *Introducing Lyotard: Art and Politics* (London: Routledge, 1991) 4.

21. I use the capital F in Figure in accordance with Deleuze. While Deleuze emphasizes the aesthetic figure has nothing to do with rhetoric, Lyotard has another approach. One of the critical functions of his concept of the figural seems to be to create a new kind of rhetoric. Bill Readings places Lyotard's concept of the figural within a deconstructive account of rhetoric: "The crucial distinction is between an instrumentalist conception of rhetoric and a deconstructive account of rhetoric as a displacement or suspension of meaning. For the traditionalists as well as many devotees of 'cultural studies,' rhetoric is understood as the instrument by which significations are ordered and disposed. Rhetoric is thus a modification of a signification by means of a second-order signification. The analysis of rhetoric is a matter of setting signs in contexts that will allow us to determine their true signification. On the other hand, deconstruction thinks of rhetoric as *figure* rather than *instrument*. Rather than being a modification of meaning, figurality is necessarily present to signification whilst radically heterogeneous from it. Figure thus evokes a difference which cannot be regulated." Readings 29.

22. Deleuze 2.

23. Deleuze 34-35.

24. Deleuze and Guattari 178.

25. Here the term hermeneutics is understood in a narrow sense as a method of interpretation where a disembodied observer penetrates the surface of the world to extract its underlying meaning. See Hans Ulrich Gumbrecht, *The Production of Presence: What Meaning Cannot Convey* (Stanford, CA: Stanford UP, 2004) 16ff.

26. Gumbrecht 36.

27. Available online: http://www.francis-bacon.cx/figures/movement_85.html.

28. Gumbrecht xi.

29. Gumbrecht 9-11.

30. E.H. Gombrich, *The Story of Art* (1950; Oxford: Phaidon, 1989) 221.

31. Gombrich 221.

32. Sergei Eisenstein, "Laocoön," *Selected Works. Volume 2: Towards a Theory of Montage,* ed. and trans. Richard Taylor (London: British Film Institute, 1991) 109-202.

33. Gotthold Ephraim Lessing, *Laocoön: An Essay on the Limits of Painting and Poetry* (1766; Baltimore/London: John Hopkins UP, 1962) 91.

34. Eisenstein 156

35. Eisenstein 157.

36. Eisenstein 157.

37. Eisenstein 154-55.

38. Eisenstein 111.

39. Eisenstein 110.

40. Eisenstein 111.

41. Eisenstein 111.

42. Tom Gunning, "The Cinema of Attractions: Early Film, Its Spectator and the Avant-Garde," *Early Cinema: Space Frame Narrative*, ed. Thomas Elsaesser (London: British Film Institute, 1990) 57.

43. Lyotard 377.

44. Lyotard 9.

45. Viktor Shklovsky, "Art as Technique," *Contemporary Literary Criticism. Literary and Cultural Studies*, ed. R.C. Davis and R. Schleifer, 3rd ed. (New York/London: Longman, 1989) 264.

"Cutting to the Quick": *Techne*, *Physis*, and *Poiesis* and the Attractions of Slow Motion

Vivian Sobchack

> [T]he coming to presence of technology harbors in itself what we least suspect, the possible upsurgence of the saving power. […] How can this happen? Above all through our catching sight of what comes to presence in technology, instead of merely gaping at the technological.
> – Martin Heideigger[1]

> The movement from still to moving images accented the unbelievable and extraordinary nature of the apparatus itself. But in doing so, it also undid any naïve belief in the reality of the image.
> – Tom Gunning[2]

In "Re-Newing Old Technologies: Astonishment, Second Nature, and the Uncanny in Technology from the Previous Turn-of-the-Century," a remarkable essay that furthers his investigation of "attraction" and "astonishment," Tom Gunning asks two related questions: first, "What happens in modernity to the initial wonder at a new technology or device when the novelty has faded into the banality of the everyday?"[3]; and second, "Once understood, does technology ever recover something of its original strangeness?"[4] Although it has attracted and astonished us since the beginnings of cinema, in what follows I want to explore the particular appeal of "slow motion" cinematography as it now appears against the naturalized ground of "the movement from still to moving images," first enabled by the once "extraordinary" nature of the cinematic apparatus. Reversing the trajectory of this "original" movement (although never achieving its anticipated end point in "stillness"), slow motion cinematography is in wide use today in live-action cinema, its recent variants assisted and enhanced by sophisticated computer technologies and effects. Although it has always seemed uncanny, slow motion has a particularly compelling quality in a contemporary "cinema of attractions" that is based primarily on intensely kinetic movement and speed. Paradoxically, it hyperbolizes movement by "forestalling" and "distilling" it to what seems its "essence."[5] Indeed, my title is meant to point to this paradox and what appears to be (but is not) a dialectical opposition between slowness and speed, forestalment and action. "Cutting to the quick" means moving "rapidly" to the "essentials": "getting to the heart of the matter" – only faster, and by inflicting a wound. This colloquial expression came spontaneously to mind as I was watching a thrillingly sublime (and autonomous) sequence of virtuoso cinematic swordplay between two characters in HERO (2002), Zhang Yimou's first venture into the extremely popular martial arts genre. It seemed a profound description – not only *literal* but also *metaphoric* – of the sequence's particularly hyperbolic use of slow motion cinematography.

As we all know, common usage of "quick" denotes "rapid movement" or, as the *Oxford English Dictionary* puts it, an "occurrence that is over or completed within a short span of time." But the *OED* also defines "quick" as "the central, vital or most sensitive part, the seat of feeling and emotion" and, more particularly, as "the tender or sensitive flesh in a part of the body" such as "under the nails or surrounding a sore or wound." It is this second meaning that is dominant in my titular expression and, in a strange reversal, it is the verb "cutting" that entails speed and action – this evoked by HERO not only in the paradoxical slow motion "thrust" of a sword meant to fatally wound an opponent but also in the abrupt cinematic operations of a rapid "cut" to action "slowed" and suddenly perceptible as the paradoxical "distillation" of something both vitally "quick" and elementally "essential." The expression thus presents a complex – and heuristic – invitation to meditate on the more languorous attractions of slow motion, particularly in relation to contemporary live-action cinema in which, as Linda Williams writes, "many films now set out, as a first order of business, to simulate the bodily thrills and visceral pleasures of attractions that [...] take us on a continuous ride punctuated by shocks and moments of speed-up and slow-down."[6]

In an extraordinary essay called "The Slow and the Blind" that addresses such moments of speed-up and slow-down, Ryan Bishop and John Phillips mark the particular "power of modernity" (which generated cinematic technology but was also co-constituted by it) as "the power to make qualitative distinctions between kinds of production that are in fact *dimensions of the same process.*" Thus, they argue, "slowness [...] should not be qualitatively opposed to speed, but rather the categories 'slow' and 'fast' should be regarded as relative powers of the single category 'speed.'"[7] Furthermore, "slow" and "fast" are not abstractions; as relative powers, they are always beholden for their specific ascription not only to each other but also to the embodied and situated subjects who *sense* them as such. Although the contrast between "slow" and "fast" may be sensed *universally* (transhistorically and transculturally), the limits, intensity, and significance of that contrast are experienced against the normative rhythms of a specific life-world and are *historical* and *cultural* phenomena.

I do not, however, want to speed ahead to particularize slow motion as it now compels and differentially "quickens" us from its earlier manifestations – for both that differential (which allows for a sense of the uncanny) and that quickening (which mobilizes and intensifies our attention) occur in the context of some widely-noted similarities between the present cinema of attractions and its historical antecedent. These are as significant as the differences between them. As Gunning himself has said, "the two ends of the Twentieth-Century hail each other like long lost twins."[8] Certainly, the "cinema of narrative integration" that superceded (by subtending and subordinating) the historical "cinema of attractions" has largely dis-integrated. The plots and stories of most popular feature films today have become pretexts or alibis for a series of autonomous and spectacularly kinetic "monstrations" of various kinds of thrilling sequences and apparatical special effects – elements that characterized the early cinema of attractions.[9] Indeed, many contemporary narratives are either so "underwhelmingly" simple and familiar or so overwhelmingly convoluted that, as one reviewer put it: "No single [plot] twist seems to wield more force than any other, and you soon slump back and submit to the wash and surge of the action, [or you] feel wiped and blinded by [kinetic and visual] ravishment."[10] The *raison d'être* of such films is to thrill, shock, stun, astonish, assault, or ravish an audience, now less interested in "developing situations" than in the "immediate" gratification offered by a series of momentous – and sensually experienced – "instants" to which narrative is subordinated: discrete shots and sequences that assert the primacy of their autonomous and extended "moment" through intense kinesis, spectacular and exhibitionist action and imagery, the "trickality" of special effects,[11] and a sensual saturation of motion, color, and sound. This immediate gratification, however, is – as today's audiences know – highly mediated through an increasingly sophisticated and enhanced apparatus that makes its own revelatory presence "felt" correlative with every thrilling attraction "seen."

Thus, much as Gunning has argued of cinema's first audiences, our keen awareness of the technology of images (whether its processes are understood or not) undoes any "naïve" belief in the "reality" of those images. From cinema's beginnings, Gunning suggests, our relation to cinema was complex, if not yet sophisticated. It was always already entailed with the recognition of *mediation and/as poiesis* – that is, of cinema's power to transform the world through the correlation, doubling, and movement of the radical and poetic "bringing-forth" from "concealment into unconcealment" that Martin Heidegger ascribes both to *techne* (the creative, rather than merely instrumental, "essence" of technology) and to *physis* (the inherent and self-generating energy of nature).[12] In an activity of *poiesis* that was experienced as uncanny, cinematic images "brought-forth" into visible "presencing" an unprecedented reversal (or *peripeteia*) of the "real" that, recognized by spectators as "being the same," nonetheless also "reveal[ed] itself to be different."[13] Thus, then as now, the significant question was less about our belief in the *reality* of the live-action image than about our wonderment at the profoundly *real grip* that image had on embodied consciousness.

In this regard, the astonishment generated by the historical "cinema of attractions" is an astonishment that has latently endured to re-emerge in full force today: an astonishment not at the cinema's seeming lack of mediation between ourselves and the world, but at the *reality of the image* that makes visible to us – in another mode and register that is as metaphysically inquisitive and illuminating as it is physically illusory – an *image of reality*. Given its doubled modality, however, this gripping sense of "reality" is as ambiguous now as it was then – and, indeed, has become even more so in today's live-action cinema which incorporates a third modality and register of digital simulation that yields only *real images* (these, whatever their delights, erasing the copula that allows for uncanny reversal, ambiguity, and metaphysical shock). Thus, now as then, this acute sense that we are watching an "image of reality" references a complex indexicality that has less to do with the *illusion of transparence* than with the *experience of revelation*. Through the cinematic apparatus, reality is "re-cognized" – and the thrilling shock and danger of existence we feel in astonished response, emerges, as Heidegger suggests, from "catching sight of what comes to presence *in* technology, instead of merely gaping *at* the technological."[14] Like the first spectators whom Gunning redeems from simple naiveté, our own gasps of awe, terror, and delight at this sudden "presencing" are not only respirational, but also inspirational – an intake of existential *breath* and an intake of existential *breadth*.[15] Indeed, such embodied responses are a profound recognition of, as Gunning writes, "the power of the apparatus to sweep away a prior and firmly entrenched sense of reality." And he continues: "This vertiginous experience of the frailty of our knowledge of the world before the power of the visual illusion produced the mixture of pleasure and anxiety which the purveyors of popular art had labeled sensations and thrills and on which they founded a new aesthetics of attractions."[16]

But, of course, this "new aesthetics of attractions" is no longer all that new, and we are not the first cinema spectators – despite the similarities between us. Indeed, the recognition that we are, today, somehow still "the same" as those first spectators "reveals itself to be different" – and this, too, in an uncanny and dramatic *peripeteia* or reversal of expectations and perspective. If, as Gunning suggests, the *movement from still to moving images* set the primal scene of "attraction" for cinema's early spectators, then, I would argue, the primal scene for today's spectacularly kinetic and high-tech cinema is dramatically *reversed*: what is particularly astonishing and metaphysically perturbing now is the *movement from moving to still images*. However, in order to appreciate this reversal, it is important to emphasize that what is "primal" in both scenes, what "attracts," is not simply "still to moving" or "moving to still" but, rather, the *movement from* one terminus to the other – indeed, the *movement of movement* itself, which, made visible in slow motion, occupies the uncanny space "between" these end points, and reveals them both to be merely different "dimensions of the same process."

This reversal in the trajectory of both movement and astonishment is not all that historically surprising. As Gunning emphasizes: "Astonishment is inherently an unstable and temporary experience. One finds it difficult to be continually astonished by the same thing. Astonishment gives way to familiarity."[17] Furthermore, always open to amendment and reversal, this shift is "triggered by changing relations to the world, guided or distracted by language, practice, representation and aesthetics."[18] At the turn of the 19th century, new technologies of speed (and its representation) astonished, shocked, disoriented, and delighted lived-bodies in the life-world – these phenomenological effects emerging from a radical sense of the sudden shift of movement from *slow to fast*. And, as Stephen Kern writes in *The Culture of Time and Space: 1880-1918*: "[O]f all the technology that affected the pace of life, the early cinema most heightened public consciousness of *differential* speeds."[19] Although slow motion was in use in early cinema (effected most often by differentials in hand-cranked cinematography and projection speeds, but also by the occasional "scientific" cinematography of natural phenomena),[20] early cinema was not historically compelled to use "slow motion" as a *specific tropological figure* to point to this new and uneven sense of acceleration. Rather, early cinema co-constituted "slow motion" as its *context*: the *residual premise* or *ground* not only of earlier forms of representation but also of a presently-vanishing life-world. Thus, emphasized by cinema, the over-arching impact of "new technology," as Kern writes, phenomenologically "speeded up the tempo of current existence and transformed the memory of years past, the stuff of everybody's identity, into something slow."[21] And he adds: "As quickly as people responded to the new technology, the pace of their former lives seemed like slow motion."[22] However, Kern also notes this "pace was unpredictable," and, "like the cinema, not always uniformly accelerated."[23]

At the turn of the 20th century, the fact and trajectory of acceleration are no longer unpredictable. Speed and the technologies that sustain and ever more rapidly accelerate it have been sufficiently familiarized so that differential shifts in accelerated movement are perceived phenomenologically as not from *slow to fast* but, rather, from *fast to faster*. This is a less differentially disjunctive and, indeed, less unpredictable movement than that foregrounded at the turn of the earlier century. So, to reverse another colloquial expression, the more things stay the same, the more they change. Amidst the sensuous plenitude and hyperbolic display of the movies "moving," and immersed in a world (not merely cinematic) marked by an accelerated sense of speed (and a correlatively-sensed

lack of time), we are now historically and culturally habituated to rapid movement even as we are utterly distracted by it – as well as by the various technologies that have accelerated it. Thus, it is not surprising that the *forestalment* and
slowing of movement strike us as strange and extraordinary today – this particularly (but not solely) when hyperbolic uses of slow motion cinematography
attract and astonish us in their uncanny reversal of both our – and the cinema's
– quotidian speed. However, as emphasized above, this forestalment and slowing of movement is not equivalent (either in effect or function) to movement's
cessation. Unlike the "freeze frame," and against the increasing accelerations of
cinematic and social life, the operations and effects of slow motion visibly and
sensually interrogate those accelerations in what seems a "revelation" – not of
immobility or stillness, but of the "essential" *movement of movement* itself.
Furthermore, this revelation of the essence of movement emerges correlatively
with an *extended sense of time* – precisely what, today, we feel we lack.

Consider the following sequence from HERO that generated this essay – one
among many in the film that both literally and metaphorically "cut to the
quick" of accelerated movement through a particularly hyperbolic use of slow
motion. The set-up for the sequence (itself an autonomous "set piece") is a beautiful but conventional combination of kinetic live-action and slow motion that
shows off skilled wire-work in concert with bravura physical performance.
Here, Nameless (one of the film's central characters) fights and defeats a group
of bodyguards so he can then engage a great swordsman, Sky, in ritualized
combat that will presumably end in the latter's death. The sequence in question
emerges in awesome visual symmetry – both of composition and movement.
The setting is the partially-covered courtyard of a chess house and rain leaks
through openings in the roof to fall upon the two men (and a blind musician
who plays to their battle). Despite their flurries of balletic live-action and kinetic
swordplay, the comportment of the two men is almost "stately" (here resonant
with its sense of the slow and static). Indeed, however rapidly cut, many shots
in the sequence function almost as *tableaux* and there is – in the midst of what
seems intense action – an over-arching sense of anticipatory stillness. (If there
were such a word, I would have used "stilled-ness" here.)

Throughout, as in the set piece that precedes it, the sequence relies on what
has become the conventional use of slow motion (particularly in the martial arts
genre) to punctuate and, by contrast, emphasize the force and speed of the live
action as well as to foreground and display, through its extension, the virtuosity
of physical bodies in the extremity of motion. Thus, we see slow motion shots
inserted in the action to emphasize a small detail or elongate a particularly
graceful trajectory of movement: the splash of a soft leather shoe on the rainy
cobblestones, the arc of a body as it inscribes its slowed fury in the air. The
sequence, however, also inserts close-ups of the still faces of the two men be-

tween bouts of action, their eyelids lowered in brief meditation that echoes and is echoed by the sequence's slowing of not only motion but also time. Indeed, describing the encounter in voice-over, Nameless says, "We stood facing each other for a long time. Neither of us made a move, while our combat unfolded in the depths of our minds."

But there is more "in stall" for us yet – and it is here that the function of slow motion yields more than diacritical punctuation, a lingering detail, or extended physical action, and becomes revelatory, uncanny, astonishing. The paradoxical nature of what seems a meditative space-time carved from brief flurries of quick action culminates in the rapid cutting of an extraordinary series of shots memorable for their statically-charged movement and micro-temporal speed – these marked and emphasized by the extreme slow motion of raindrops as their vertical fall is breathtakingly redirected by the weapons and bodies of the two combatants. One sees, in extreme close-up and from screen left, Nameless's sword lunging – in extreme slow motion – to smoothly cut through individual droplets as it moves toward the off-screen Sky. In the next shot, against a background of individual raindrops falling so slowly they seem almost suspended, in close-up Nameless rushes toward his off-screen opponent, his face in the rain causing droplets to cascade and scatter like jewels as he passes through them. A few shots later, the horsehair tassel on Sky's lance – pointed at Nameless and at us – forcefully inscribes in extreme slow motion a circular swirl of crystalline droplets in the near center of the screen. And, in the penultimate shot of the sequence, this circular swirl of droplets emerges again in a coupling rhyme as Nameless's sword – pointed at Sky and away from us – moves slowly through the rain toward the final and fatal cut.

What is so particularly astonishing here? As indicated, slow motion cinematography as a contemporary "attraction" has become a convention of action cinema – not only in the martial arts genre but also in many others that foreground and hyperbolize such accelerated movements as large explosions and bravura physical stunts, and that, by slowing these down, make their constitutive and elemental micro-rhythms viscerally visible.[24] Given its frequent and often (cognitively) banal use in today's cinema (what Gunning has called the "Spielberg-Lucas-Coppola cinema of effects"), one could argue (as Gunning does) that the slow motion cinematography I'm heralding as an "attraction" has by now been reduced to a mere "effect" – that is, an "attraction" effectively contained and "tamed" both by narrative and habit.[25]

Indeed, if we follow Gunning's argument, this historical "taming" or transformation of a discrete and powerful "attraction" into an integrated, if spectacular, technological "effect" seems to me a significant variant of what Heidegger characterized as modernity's technological transformation of "world" (as *physis*) into the reduced and managed care of "world picture." "World picture," he writes, "does not mean a picture of the world but the world conceived and grasped as picture."[26] "World picture" conceals *physis* by containing and "taming" it, so that "whatever *is* comes into being" and seems to appear only "*in* and *through* representedness."[27] Thus, the *poiesis* of *physis* (its uncanny power to generate movement from within itself) is obfuscated and reduced by the representational "enframing"[28] effected by the power of modern technology – a power made most literal and concrete (although Heidegger doesn't mention it) by the enframing operations of cinema. *Physis* becomes merely a "standing reserve": a "resource" for our illusory containment and mastery of the world. The consequence, as Heidegger writes, is that, "above all, enframing conceals that revealing which, in the sense of *poiesis*, lets what presences come forth into appearance."[29] *Poiesis* is reduced to calculation (surely, experiencing today's movies and their spectacular computer graphic "effects," we sense this reduction in the form of mere "delight"). Thus, "the Open becomes an object."[30]

Nonetheless, the world is not really mastered and not all attractions are easily tamed. Against the spectacular digital simulations that, in effect, now calculate and substitute for the world, these attractions remind us that the world cannot be really mastered or disavowed through technological substitution and simulation – or even by cinematic emulation. These are the attractions that endure and, to varying degree, overpower and break their "effective" narrative bonds. Thus, even in the most generically unsurprising of films, they may astonish us (if only for a shot or sequence) into dramatic and world-changing re-cognition of their uncanny *originality*. In this regard, Scott Bukatman writes: "It's possible to argue that attractions can take on a newly disruptive, interruptive function, [and] that narrative does not completely (or simply) contain (or tame) the energies characteristic of the attraction."[31]

This seems to me particularly apposite when the attraction in question – here, extreme slow motion applied to "live action" – not only abruptly cuts to the quick of the movement underlying the accelerated movements of contemporary existence but also cuts to the quick of a perceptual and metaphysical "sore spot." Through cinematic technology, the extremity of slow motion suddenly reveals to us not only the radical energies and micro-movements of movements we live yet cannot grasp but it also interrogates, reveals, and expands the extremely narrow compass of our anthropocentric orientation and habitual perceptions of "being in the world." Thus, cut to the quick, we are compelled to recognize that we are, at once, too temporally fast and too slow, too spatially large and too small, to apprehend the movements of movement – not merely our own but also, and more significantly, those of *physis*: the elemental micro- and macro-movements of the natural world. Confronted with the uncanny cinematic vision of forces and energies that intimately affect us but which, technologically unaided, we cannot see, with an alterior – and differential – time and space that we live but do not explicitly feel, we are wounded in our "sore spot" twice over: first, by an acute recognition of the gap in our perception that technology both reveals and fills; and second, by technology's sudden revelation (not "taming") of *physis* as the self-generating nature of "nature" that exceeds and escapes both our anthropological and technological grasp, even as its elemental *élan vital* in-forms them.

Certainly (and often) "wonder can be worn down into habit." However, when cinema cuts to the quick in hyperbolized slow motion images such as the ones I've described in HERO but which can be found as well in the slow motion explosions of myriad action films like DIE HARD 3 (1995) or in the more complex and composited "bullet time" of THE MATRIX (1999), its banal "effects" become re-energized as "attractions" – powerful and compelling in their "explosive, surprising, and even disorienting temporality."[32] Indeed, it is precisely when the attraction "surprises" and "disorients" us at the most profound levels of our perception and *habitus* that, as Gunning suggests, "habit can suddenly, even catastrophically, transform back into a shock of recognition."[33] Thus, watching HERO, while we may be somewhat "distractedly" attracted to the conventional slow motion detail or acrobatic movement, we give our full and intense attention to the extremity of the slow motion raindrops – astonished at their micro-movement and their micro-temporality in an uncanny space that is shared by the characters and yet not inhabited or lived by them (or by us, in the rain falling outside the theater). The slow motion cascades and swirls of raindrops are, in the moment, more significant and thrilling – more "palpable" if abstract, more ravishing if philosophically "dangerous" – than the man and his lance who, in the narrative, perturb their fall.[34] The raindrops and their micro-movements, the strange space they occupy, assert their temporal and spatial autonomy from the narrative and, indeed, overwhelm it – even as they lend it the "aura" of their metaphysical gravity.

We could say, in these circumstances, that narrative is "put in its place." That is, when foregrounded in its radical alterity, slow motion reduces the narrative's anthropocentric temporal importance by revealing a time-space of *physis* which is "beyond" and yet "beneath" all human perception and endeavor. Here, the extreme slow motion close-ups no longer merely function as smaller metonymic "details" of a larger comprehensible (and comprehended) action, but, rather, metaphorically inform and superimpose upon the narrative's temporal and spatial drama another more elemental and expansive one. HERO is paradigmatic of what occurs with frequency, if to lesser degree, in much of contemporary popular live-action cinema. It is filled with autonomous shots and sequences that, through foregrounding the slowed and distilled motion of *physis*, reveal its *poiesis* as a spatio-temporal "difference in sameness." We watch the characters' hair carve languorous arabesques in the wind; the sensuous undulations of silken clothing and billowing curtains stirred by air and movement; a slowed whirl-wind of reddening leaves in which two women fight each other with no care for gravity; the slowed ripples on a glassy lake made by men who seem like skim-ming dragonflies; and, of course, the raindrops. What the slow motion and "stilled-ness" foreground *within* but *against* the artifice of human drama (both reducing and making it mythic or epic) is the *elemental* movement of movement. In HERO, through the permutations of slow motion, the *poiesis* of cinematic *techne* reveals the *poiesis* of the world – *physis* here astonishing and uncanny, its "bringing-forth" of movement from within itself visibly grasped (and gripping) not as "a self contained state but rather closer to the unstable *aporia* of a unity so self-contained that it tends to dissolve before our very eyes."[35]

This is the autonomy of the "attraction" at its most physical – and metaphysi-cal. And this is an encounter with cinematic "realism" of a different order of magnitude from the ones to which we are accustomed. This encounter not only thrills and forestalls us with the revelatory power of cinematic technology but also shocks and installs within us a psychosomatic sense of the extraordinarily delimited extra-cinematic perspective we have on the physical world that we think we and our technology have mastered. Such revelation – "unconceal-ment" emergent from "world picture" – forces an astonished and awe-filled recognition that, although we are *of* and *in* that physical world, most of its movements are not "for us." Thus, the hyperbolically slowed raindrops that fall into the human space-time of HERO's dramatic action provoke a profound (even tragic) "re-cognition" that dramatically reverses our orientation – both in the world and toward our presumed dominion over it. This is *"anagnoresis as peri-peteia"* as Samuel Weber has described it: here, as with the ambiguous "reality" of the cinematic image, "a formula for the uncanny recognition of something that, in being the same, reveals itself to be different."[36] Furthermore, this uncan-ny difference in sameness is revealed as "nonexclusive and, indeed [...] conver-gent (although, again, not simply identical)," and is usually "exemplified in a certain kind of 'theatricality.'"[37]

But what kind of non-exclusive and theatrical convergence? In the first in-stance, and specific to today's digitally-enhanced cinema, the convergence of the alterior temporality of *physis* with the quotidian – and accelerated – tempor-ality of human "live-action" occurs not only in the latter's interruption and punctuation by slow motion or fast (the latter familiar, and thus often comic), but also – and most remarkably – by the *simultaneous compositing* of *differential temporalities* as *visibly relative*, each to the other. Hence, the incredibly suspended raindrops in HERO fall in a rhythm different than the ones that slowly cascade from Nameless's face or echo the quicker movement of Sky's lance. Hence, in THE MATRIX, the micro-movements of bullets can be dodged by the slower live-action human movements of Neo, who, different in his sameness and in an uncanny and confounding reversal, is now also "faster than a speeding bullet." Indeed, what digitally-enhanced slow motion imagery exhibits is the *essential relativity* of movement. "Fast" and "slow" are revealed not as opposites, but as "qualitative distinctions [...] that are in fact *dimensions of the same process.*" Thus, as Bishop and Phillips write: "The failure of the visual sense to apprehend nature in its full complexity [becomes] technology's opportunity [...]. To understand and represent the speed of nature (and speed *in* nature), it needed to be slowed down to a point of stasis."[38]

And this brings us to the second instance: the "theatricality" or exhibitionism of slow motion's essential "revelation" of technology's "sore spot" – namely, the non-exclusive convergence of its sameness and difference from *physis*. That is, "brought-forth" and revealed by *techne* in the slowest of motion, the primary "bringing-forth" of the elemental and self-generating power of *physis* is revealed as *trumping* technology's own secondary creative and revelatory power. What converges and is revealed through *techne* and "re-cognized" by the astonished spectator is the profound and uncanny exhibition of a sudden reversal of power in which "world picture" cedes its apparent precedence to "world." Although it is "brought-forth" for us to visibly see only through the creative power of *techne*, what the non-identical convergence of *techne* and *physis* exhibits is that *techne* is only an *emulation* of the inaugural and grounding power of *physis*: "the arising of something from out of itself."[39] (Computer graphics, when they are cinematically "constitutive," do not emulate but *simulate* this power and thus lack the non-identical convergence that would challenge "world picture.")

It is not surprising, then, that amazed as they were by the marvels of the cinematic apparatus, early spectators were especially attracted to and regularly commented upon "what would now be considered the incidentals of scenes: smoke from a forge, steam from a locomotive, brick-dust from a demolished wall,"[40] as well as "the wind blowing through the leaves of trees and the rhythmic motion of the waves of the sea."[41] As Vachel Lindsay wrote in 1915, "The shoddiest silent drama may contain noble views of the sea. This part is almost sure to be good. It is a fundamental resource."[42] Of course, in the midst of a Heideggerian discussion, Lindsay's articulation of the sea as "a fundamental resource" seems not only prescient but also ambiguous. It bears immediately – if unexpectedly – upon the philosopher's critique of modern technology as "enframing" the world as "world picture" and conceiving *physis* as merely the "fundamental resource" for modern humans, its real power contained and concealed. Nonetheless, clearly unimpressed with the world concealed by "shoddy drama," Lindsay uses the word "resource" to recognize the sea as a primary "attraction" – re-cognizing also (and without our contemporary need of slow motion) what cinematic *techne* has suddenly "unconcealed": the world, not technology, as "fundament." As Dai Vaughan notes, what really impressed early spectators was "the presence, *in some metaphysical sense*, of the sea itself: a sea liberated from the laboriousness of painted highlights and the drudgeries of metaphor."[43] Thus, whether then or now, "the coming to presence of technology harbors in itself what we least suspect, the possible upsurgence of the saving power." And Lindsay at the cinema, looking at the upsurging of the sea, caught "sight of what comes to presence in technology, instead of merely gaping at the technological."

Heidegger writes: "*Physis* is indeed *poiesis* in the highest sense." And he continues (in what, today, would "bring-forth" the hyperbolic emphasis of extreme slow motion): "For what presences by means of *physis* has the bursting open belonging to the bringing-forth, e.g., the bursting of a blossom into bloom, in itself."[44] Paradoxically concrete, as "brought-forth" through the creative power of cinematic *techne*, *physis* becomes a *literal meta-physics*: "an overwhelming power, a luminous eruption of living energy inexhaustibly appearing and bringing beings into the light."[45] The uncanny of live-action cinema thus emerges in this paradox of a literal meta-physics in which the *poiesis* of *techne* and *physis* are not only conjoined and doubled but inextricably and ambiguously convergent: the same but not identical.

Certainly, in the present day, unless it is foregrounded in the enhanced operations of slow motion cinematography, unless the contemporary spectator is forestalled in the meditative space-time it installs, astonishment at this *doubled poiesis* is generally taken for granted. Nonetheless, it retains a latent – and, indeed, grounding – power. As Gunning suggests, although "new technologies" such as the cinema evoke "a short-lived wonder based on unfamiliarity which greater and constant exposure will overcome," they also evoke "a possibly less dramatic but more enduring sense of the uncanny, a feeling that they involve magical operations which greater familiarity or habituation might cover over, but not totally destroy. It crouches there beneath a rational cover, ready to spring out again."[46] Heidegger, too, speaking of wonder and astonishment, agrees: "Yet we can be astounded. Before what? Before this other possibility: that the frenziedness of technology may entrench itself everywhere to such an extent that someday, throughout everything technological, the essence of technology may come to presence in the coming-to-pass of truth."[47]

For Heidegger, although "truth" (or *aletheia*) is essential, it is not absolute; it is not about "correctness" or an impression of something that "matches" an external reality for that would be "naïve" realism. Rather, it is the revelation of "inwardness" – of "the heart of the matter," the "vital" center and "essence" of things. The attraction of cinema is that, as Bishop and Phillips suggest, it is "a virtual encyclopedia of modernity's tropes: agency, control, technological prowess, speed, intelligence (both human and machine), the power to render the invisible visible, and the intimate connections between aesthetics and technology."[48] On the one hand, slow motion today foregrounds and glorifies these tropes. On the other, however, it reveals that they are based on a more powerful "truth" – a vital "essence" – that exceeds the cinema and modernity's grasp. Thus, and at once, slow motion serves as both the uncanny affirmation and *memento mori* of modernity. Interrogating the differential speed of modernity's earliest and latest phases, the essential revelations of slow motion are radical – potentially sublime and dangerous in their capacity to wound. Indeed, they "cut to the quick" not only of speed but also of the heart of our modern lives.

Notes

1. Martin Heidegger, "The Question Concerning Technology," *Martin Heidegger: Basic Writings,* trans. William Lovitt, ed. David Farrell Krell (New York: Harper & Row, 1977) 314.
2. Tom Gunning, "An Aesthetic of Astonishment: Early Film and the (In)Credulous Spectator," *Film Theory and Criticism: Introductory Readings,* ed. Leo Braudy and Marshall Cohen (New York: Oxford UP, 1999) 832.
3. Tom Gunning, "Re-Newing Old Technologies: Astonishment, Second Nature, and the Uncanny in Technology from the Previous Turn-of-the-Century," *Rethinking Media Change: The Aesthetics of Transition,* ed. David Thornburn and Henry Jenkins (Cambridge: MIT P, 2003) 42.
4. Gunning, "Re-Newing Old Technologies" 45.
5. I have chosen the words "forestalling" and "distilling" quite purposefully here, borrowing upon several of the *OED*'s definitions. "Forestall" means, among other things, "to hinder, obstruct, or prevent by anticipation." (My use of "forestalment" later in this essay refers to "the action of forstalling" and to "anticipation in general.") "Distill" plays on the word "still" but also signifies the extractive processes of "distilling" which render "the extract, abstract" and produce a "refined or concentrated essence" of a substance or thing.
6. Linda Williams, "Discipline and Fun: *Psycho* and Postmodern Cinema," *Reinventing Film Studies,* ed. Christine Gledhill and Linda Williams (London: Arnold, 2000) 357.
7. Ryan Bishop and John Phillips, "The Slow and the Blind," *Culture and Organization* 10.1 (March 2004): 62 (emphasis added).
8. Gunning, "Re-Newing Old Technologies" 51.
9. "Monstration" is a term coined by André Gaudreault for a mode of presentational narration characteristic of early cinema. See André Gaudreault, "Film, Narrative, Narration: The Cinema of the Lumière Brothers," *Early Cinema: Space Frame Narrative,* ed. Thomas Elsaesser (London: British Film Institute, 1990) 68-75.
10. Anthony Lane, "Partners," *New Yorker* 10 Dec. 2004: 109. It is not irrelevant here that Lane is reviewing Zhang Yimou's 2004 martial arts sequel to HERO, HOUSE OF FLYING DAGGERS (2004).

11. "Trickality," and its entailment of magical illusion with performance and exhibition, was a term coined by André Gaudreault. See André Gaudreault "Theatricality, Narrativity, and Trickality: Reevaluating the Cinema of Georges Méliès," trans. Paul Attallah, adapted and revised by Tom Gunning and Vivian Sobchack, *Journal of Popular Film and Television* 15.3 (Fall 1987): 110-19.

12. Heidegger, "The Question Concerning Technology" 293-95.

13. Samuel Weber quoted in Simon Morgan Wortham and Gary Hall, "Responding: A Discussion with Samuel Weber," *South Atlantic Quarterly* 101.3 (2002): 698.

14. Emphasis added.

15. Here it is worth noting that one definition of "attraction" in the *OED* is the "drawing in of the breath, inspiration, inhalation."

16. Gunning, "An Aesthetic of Astonishment" 825.

17. Gunning, "Re-Newing Old Technologies" 41.

18. Gunning, "Re-Newing Old Technologies" 46.

19. Stephen Kern, *The Culture of Time and Space: 1880-1918* (Cambridge: Harvard UP, 1983) 130.

20. There is some evidence that Jean Comandon used slow motion (along with time lapse cinematography) for a series of vernacular science films made for Pathé between 1910 and 1917. Nevil Maskeleyne (son of the magician and early filmmaker John Maskeleyne) experimented with slow motion and was asked to film artillery shells in flight for purposes of analysis by the British War Office some time around the first World War. For the most part, then, slow motion was appropriated by avant-garde filmmakers, primarily beginning in the 1920s – until it emerged in American mainstream cinema in the late 1960s and 70s as a major mode of detailing and inspecting violence (a major civil concern at the time). On the use of slow motion in the 1920s, see Guido in this volume.

21. Kern 129.

22. Kern 130.

23. Kern 130.

24. For an excellent essay on the "basic rhetoric of spectacular explosions," see Nick Browne, "The 'Big Bang': The Spectacular Explosion in Contemporary Hollywood Film," *Strobe* (April 2003): http://www.cinema.ucla.edu/strobe/bigbang/.

25. Tom Gunning, "The Cinema of Attractions: Early Film, Its Spectator and the Avant-Garde," *Early Cinema: Space Frame Narrative* 61.

26. Martin Heidegger, "The Age of the World Picture," *The Question Concerning Technology and Other Essays*, trans. William Lovitt (New York: Harper & Row, 1977) 129.

27. Heidegger, "The Age of the World Picture" 130 (emphasis added).

28. For a more elaborated discussion of "Enframing," see Heidegger, "The Question Concerning Technology" 301-314.

29. Heidegger, "The Question Concerning Technology" 309.

30. Martin Heidegger, "What Are Poets For?," *Poetry, Language, Thought*, trans. Albert Hofstadter (New York: Harper and Row, 1971) 110.

31. Scott Bukatman, *Matters of Gravity* (Durham: Duke UP, 2003) 120.

32. Tom Gunning, "'Now You See It, Now You Don't': The Temporality of the Cinema of Attractions," *Velvet Light Trap* 32 (Fall 1993): 4. It is worth noting here that one may well be aware cognitively of the re-energized attraction's banality and yet still be astonished and thrilled by it. Indeed, this is what is sometimes so irritating about

watching iterations of the spatio-temporal disruptions wrought by "morphing" or "bullet time" – we recognize that they are banal in the way they are used, and yet that recognition does not forestall our being, at some bodily level, still thrilled by them.

33. Gunning, "Re-Newing Old Technologies" 46.
34. Gunning, "An Aesthetic of Astonishment" 819. Here Gunning speaks to the spectator's physical apprehension of the cinematic image's palpable and dangerous nature.
35. Weber 670.
36. Weber 698.
37. Weber 699.
38. Bishop and Phillips 67.
39. Heidegger, "The Question Concerning Technology" 293.
40. Dai Vaughan, "Let There Be Lumière," *Early Cinema: Space Frame Narrative* 64. Vaughan cites Georges Sadoul's *Histoire générale du cinéma*, vol. 1-5 (Paris: Denoel, 1973ff).
41. Richard Grusin, "Premediation," *Criticism* 46.1 (Winter 2004): 35.
42. Vachel Lindsay, *The Art of the Moving Picture [Being the 1922 revision of the book first issued in 1915]* (New York: Liveright, 1970) 67.
43. Vaughan 65 (emphasis added).
44. Heidegger, "The Question Concerning Technology" 293. It is worth noting here that the blossoming of the blossom in itself is not all that different from "the bursting open belonging to the bringing-forth" of slow motion explosions (temporally extended even further by different views of its movement) in any number of recent action movies. (See Browne, "The 'Big Bang" noted above.) In this regard, I would also observe the overwhelming attraction of *implosions* – whether extra-cinematic, cinematic, or televisual. Even before September 11, 2001 and the terrifying implosion of the Twin Towers, spectators have been fascinated by implosions. Not only are they often uncannily visible in what seems super-slowed movement, but (and more significantly) implosions nihilistically *reverse* "the bursting open belonging to the bringing-forth"; that is, they reveal not an elemental and generative movement that emerges and *opens out from within* itself but, rather, an elemental and degenerative movement that *closes in upon* itself. The fascination of implosions is that they don't merely collapse in space, but seem to collapse space itself.
45. David Michael Levin, *The Opening of Vision: Nihilism and the Postmodern Situation* (New York: Routledge, 1988) 102.
46. Gunning, "Re-Newing Old Technologies" 47.
47. Heidegger, "The Question Concerning Technology" 316-17.
48. Bishop and Phillips 66.

Dossier

Pie and Chase: Gag, Spectacle and Narrative in Slapstick Comedy

Donald Crafton

Whether judged by production statistics, by contemporary critical acclaim, by audience popularity or by retrospective opinions, it is abundantly clear that the American silent film comedy (in its two-reel and its feature version) was flourishing in the mid-twenties, and that it rivaled the drama as the dominant form of cinematic expression. My aim is to rethink the function of the gag in relation to the comic film as a classical system – not to examine or catalogue all the possible variations of the gag (as joke, as articulation of cinematic space, or as thematic permutations[1]), but rather to examine its operation in the slapstick genre.

Let us introduce the subject by way of an amusing account of a screening of Charlie Chaplin films in Accra, Africa, reported in the *New York Times* in 1925:

> It was a film from the remote antiquity of filmdom; a film from the utter dark ages of the cinematograph, so patched and pieced and repieced that all continuity was gone; a piebald hash chosen from the remains of various comedies and stuck together with no plot. Just slapstick. But Charlie had survived even that, and how they did love it![2]

The anecdote provides several insights into the status of film comedy in its "Golden Age." Most important for us, it expresses the opinion that this assemblage of Chaplin shorts is primitive because it lacks continuity. The writer intuitively distinguishes between the linear aspects of film – plot, narrative, diegesis – and its non-linear components – spectacle and gags. Take away the story and what do you have left? "Just slapstick."

Much criticism of silent film comedy still hinges on the dichotomy between narrative and gag. When Gerald Mast remarks in *The Comic Mind*, that Max Linder's film SEVEN YEARS BAD LUCK "is interested in a gag, not a story to contain the gags or a character to perform them,"[3] or that the plots of Sennett's Keystone films "are merely apparent structures, collections of literary formulas and clichés to hang the gags on,"[4] there is, in such statements, an implicit valorization of narrative over gags. These films are flawed because the elements of slapstick are not "integrated" with other elements (character, structure, vision, cinematic style – Mast's criteria).

In this reading of film comedy, slapstick is the bad element, an excessive tendency that it is the task of the narrative to contain. Accordingly the history of the genre is usually teleological, written as though the eventual replacement of the gag by narrativized comedy was natural, ameliorative, or even predestined.

Viewing dozens of short comedies from the teens and twenties in preparation for the Slapstick Symposium, it became clear that there was no such selective process operating. On the contrary, slapstick cinema seems to be ruled by the principle of accretion: gags, situations, costumes, characters, camera techniques are rehearsed and recycled in film after film, as though the modernist emphasis on originality and the unique text was unheard of. Unlike "mainstream" dramatic cinema which progressed rapidly through styles, techniques and stories, in slapstick nothing is discarded. Camera tricks perfected by Méliès and Zecca are still in evidence a quarter-century later; music hall turns that were hoary when Chaplin, Linder and Keaton introduced them to cinema in the teens were still eliciting laughs by those clowns and others at the end or the silent period. We are forced to ask, if gags were so scorned, then why did the gag film linger on for so long, an important mode of cinematic discourse for at least forty years? And is there not something perverse about arguing that what is "wrong" with a film form is that which defines it to begin with?

The distinction between slapstick and narrative has been properly perceived, but incorrectly interpreted. I contend that it was never the aim of comic filmmakers to "integrate" the gag elements of their movies, or to subjugate them to narrative. In fact, it can be seen that the separation between the vertical, paradigmatic domain of slapstick – the arena of spectacle I will represent by the metaphor of the thrown pie – and the horizontal, syntagmatic domain of the story – the arena of the chase – was a calculated rupture, designed to keep the two elements antagonistically apart. In *Narration in the Fiction Film* David Bordwell asks, "Is there anything in narrative film that is not narrational?"[5] My answer is yes: the gag.

If we examine typical Hal Roach two-reel comedies from 1925-26, we find a microcosm of what some film analysts have described as the series of symmetries and blockages that define the systematicity of classical American cinema. To synthesize and paraphrase their theories (too grossly), every narrative begins by establishing a schema, or set of spectator expectations, then systematically disrupts this initial stasis. The remainder of the narrative is a series of lurches, waves, pendulum swings, reprises and reversals that all tend, in the end, to regain (however incompletely) the lost ideal equilibrium of the opening. In classical film especially, these "imbalances" or impediments to narrative resolution frequently take the form of an intrusive spectacle – the way the story in a musical film "stops" for a number (e. g., a Busby Berkeley routine or a Harpo Marx performance), or, perhaps an even better parallel, the way the flimsy story of a pornographic film stops for shots of sexual performance. Similarly, in a comedy, when the gag spectacle – the Pie – begins (the reel-long pie fight from Laurel and Hardy's THE BATTLE OF THE CENTURY is exemplary), the diegesis – the Chase – halts. One important difference between slapstick and the dramatic film is that these intrusions of spectacle are much more frequent in comedy, producing a kind of narrative lurching that often makes the plots of slapstick comedies quite incoherent (and delightfully so).

The Pie

Let us first look more closely at those non-narrative gag elements that the term slapstick usually encompasses. This usage is appropriate when we consider the origin of that word, referring to a circus prop consisting of two thin slats joined together so that a loud clack was made when one clown hit another on the behind. The violent aural effect, the "slap," may be thought of as having the same kind of disruptive impact on the audience as its visual equivalent in the silent cinema, the pie in the face. In fact, very few comedies of the twenties really used pies, but nevertheless their humor in a general sense frequently depended on the same kind of emphatic, violent, embarrassing gesture. The lack of linear integration that offends some slapstick commentators can also be traced back to its roots in popular spectacle. In his 1913 home correspondence manual, Brett Page advised would-be vaudeville comics that

> The purpose of the sketch is not to leave a single impression of a single story. It points no moral, draws no conclusion, and sometimes it might end quite as effectively anywhere before the place in the action at which it does terminate. It is built for entertainment purposes only and furthermore, for entertainment purposes that end the moment the sketch ends.[6]

Such an aesthetic of spectacle for its own sake is clearly inimical to the classical narrative feature, but not at all hostile to slapstick cinema of the teens and twenties.

However gag and slapstick are not synonymous. Slapstick is the generic term for these non-narrative intrusions, while gags are the specific forms of intrusions. Like verbal jokes, to which they are closely related, gags have their own structures, systems and logic that exist independently of cinema. The gag may also contain its own microscopic narrative system that may be irrelevant to the larger narrative, may mirror it, or may even work against it as parody. "Sight gags," those that depend primarily on visual exposition, still have characteristic logical structures, the same that one finds in multi-panel comic strips. Think for example of the gag in JUS' PASSIN' THRU, a Will Rogers film from 1923, produced by Hal Roach and directed by Charles Parrott (Charley Chase), where we see a hobo checking the gates of houses for the special chalk tramp sign that indicates whether there is a mean dog inside. One can easily see how the sequence could be presented effectively as a wordless comic strip: In the first two frames we would see "shots" of the tramp eschewing those yards with the mark on the gate (the exposition of the non-humorous part of the joke that vaudevillians would have called "the buildup"); in the penultimate panel we would see him fleeing a yard through an unmarked gate with a dog in hot pursuit; the final panel would show him adding his own beware-the-dog sign to the gate.

Other examples of "comic strip logic" might be mistaken identity gags (accomplished by fluid montage and parodic sight-line construction) such as the one that begins the Charley Chase film LOOKING FOR SALLY: The arriving hero waves from a ship at a girl on the dock that he incorrectly assumes to be his fiancée; she waves back, not at Charley (as he thinks) but at *her* friend on another deck. (See also Chaplin, A DOG'S LIFE, and dozens of other films which use the same gag.) Also commonplace are camera tricks, for instance double exposures and animation, that exploit the film medium's capability of disrupting the normal vision that the narrative depends on for its consistency and legibility. Manipulation of cause and effect – for example, when a little action produces a disproportionate reaction – is another form of cinematic excess characteristic of the sight gag. It is important to remember that the narrative content of the gag may be *nil* – for example, the jarring close-ups of Ben Turpin's eyes. Such cases are illustrations of what Eisenstein called "attractions," elements of pure spectacle.

Writing in 1923, Eisenstein defined the "attraction" as

> every aggressive moment in [the theater], ie. every element of it that brings to light in the spectator those senses or that psychology that influence his experience.[7]

Eisenstein also referred to those moments as "emotional shocks" and insisted that they are always psychologically disruptive (for example, the gouging out of an eye). He contrasted the attraction to the lyrical, meaning the part of the presentation readily assimilated by the spectator. Probably referring to THE KID, he notes that the lyrical may coexist with the disruptive attraction, for example, the "specific mechanics of [Chaplin's] movement." In slapstick comedy, I am claiming, there is a variant of this concept: the "lyrical" is the narrative, functioning as the regulating component; the "attraction" is the gag or, again in Eisenstein's words, the "brake" that has to be applied to sharpened dramatic moments.[8] In another context, Tom Gunning has described early cinema (pre-1906) as a "cinema of attraction":

> Whatever differences one might find between Lumière and Méliès, they should not represent the opposition between narrative and non-narrative filmmaking, at least as it is understood today. Rather, one can unite them in a conception that sees cinema

less as a way of telling stories than as a way of presenting a series of views to an audience [...] In other words, I believe that the relation to the spectator set up by the films of both Lumière and Méliès (and many other filmmakers before 1906) had a common basis, and one that differs from the primary spectator relations set up by narrative film after 1906 [...] Although different from the fascination in storytelling exploited by the cinema from the time of Griffith, it is not necessarily opposed to it. In fact the cinema of attraction does not disappear with the dominance of narrative, but rather goes underground, both into certain avant-garde practices and as a component of narrative films, more evident in some genres (eg, the musical) than in others.[9]

Gunning's observation is astute; the disruptive gags of slapstick can be regarded as an anachronistic "underground" manifestation of the cinema of attraction. I disagree though with his unwillingness to polarize the two components. While other genres work to contain their excesses, in slapstick (like avant-garde, a kind of limit-text), the opposition is fundamental. Furthermore, it is carefully constructed to remain an unbridgeable gap.

The Chase

We'll look more briefly at the other component, the Chase, or the narrative dimension of film comedy. Rather than examine specific narrative structures, it is enough to say for our purposes that the narrative is the propelling element, the fuel of the film that gives it its power to go from beginning to end. (To continue the automotive metaphor, one would say that the gags are the potholes, detours and flat tires encountered by the Tin Lizzie of the narrative on its way to the end of the film.) Film narrative has been the subject of considerable recent scholarly exposition, and rightly so. But its other, that is, those elements that block narrativity – the Pie – has been dismissed as textual excess, if it has been considered at all. Although I am using the term Chase to indicate the linear trajectory of the narrative in general, in fact actual chases are encountered more frequently than pie-throwings in the twenties. Pursuing a criminal, retrieving a lost abject, and – most importantly – reuniting a separated couple in marriage are the most important themes in twenties comedy. Not surprisingly, the same themes predominate in dramatic films as well and we should bear in mind that, as Tom Gunning, Eileen Bowser and others have noted, the line between comedy and melodrama can be very fine. One thinks, for example, of Anita Loos's claim that she tried to turn the screenplay of Griffith's THE STRUGGLE (essentially a remake of TEN NIGHTS IN A BARROOM) into a comic farce, while the film that Griffith directed turned out to be a "serious" temperance melodrama. The disruptive elements, the "attractions" concocted by Loos, were recuperated by Griffith's narrative priorities.

So much for theory. Let us look at His Wooden Wedding, produced in 1925 by Hal Roach, directed by Leo McCarey and starring Charley Chase.[10]

Rich playboy Charley is marrying Katherine (Katherine Grant) on Friday the 13th. The date is a portent of the loss of stasis that is about to occur, and an explanation, couched in the uncanny, of several aspects of bad luck that will inevitably mar the wedding: the best man (unknown to Charley) is Katherine's former suitor (now spiteful). He plants false knowledge in the form of a note to Charley informing him what his fiancée is not what she seems: "Beware! The girl you are about to marry has a wooden leg." By coincidence (extraordinary in life, but typical in fiction), Katherine sprains her ankle just before the wedding, causing her to limp down the aisle which appears to substantiate the rumor. Charley shouts "Stop! I've been engaged to a girl with a wooden leg – I must break it off."

Charley boards a cruise ship to escape his sorrow. On board he deduces the plot, recovers his diamond engagement ring from the best man and turns the boat around to find Katherine, who has independently learned of the hoax and is following the ship with her father on his yacht. She arrives just as Charley falls overboard, immediately strips down to her bathing suit and saves him. As a seeming closure, she displays her very real bare leg to the best man (and the audience) and uses it to kick him overboard, thus canceling the effects of his libelous false knowledge with this empirical demonstration of her corporeal integrity.

What is especially interesting, and also very typical of many films of the period, is the manner in which the apparent closure is not really final. Here it is the scene of reunion as they pose in an embrace that ends the film. It is inscribed outside the symmetry of the narrative as a formal tableau composition, as though the validity of the narrative must be confirmed by subsuming it into spectacle in order to confirm that the initial promise of order – the protagonists' marriage – will be fulfilled. To put it another way, the man and woman are rejoined (visually wed) at the moment that the division between narrative and spectacle is balanced, but not resolved, and the film must end.

Also typical, but, more so of melodrama, is the insistence on a woman's body as the site of the restoration of natural order. In this reading the latent narrative is essentially a castration nightmare; the revelation to the groom on his wedding day that his bride has a horrifying lack (a missing leg), followed – in a fantasy sequence showing his future children and the family dog all sporting wooden legs – by the fetishization of its prosthetic substitute. The woman is being projected as the scene of the man's fears and anxieties concerning familial responsibility and sexual performance. Only when the threat of the woman's repugnant phallic intrusion into their relationship, the despised wooden leg, is removed can the wedding – of flesh and not of wood – take place.

[Projection: His Wooden Wedding, 1925, produced by Hal Roach, directed by Leo McCarey. Cast: Charley Chase, Katherine Grant, Fred de Silva, John Cossar, Gale Henry.]

This film is an excellent example of the narrative complexity of all the McCarey-Charley Chase collaborations, as well as an illustration of how gag and narrative interact and regulate each other by means of a lively dialectic. One cannot help but compare the complex system of alternation of spectacle and diegesis to the same systems observable in Eisenstein's films of the same period. The opposition of Pie and Chase may be outlined in a chart: [11]

"Pie"	"Chase"
Gag Titles	Glance-object editing style
Inappropriate actions (Charley recognizes old friend)	Expected chain of events (wedding)
Fantasy insert	Triple pursuit:
	1) Katherine-Charley
	2) Rival-diamond;
	3) Charley-diamond, Katherine
Attenuated reaction (long glance at camera when manikin's leg falls)	Motivating action: duplicitous note to Charley
Drunken gags	Disruption of chain of events by fate (Katherine sprains ankle)
Running gag of hats (occurs several times with different hats, different characters)	Disruption of chain of events by mistaken perception (cane for leg, manikin leg for real)
Small action – large reaction (suitcase smashes car)	Parallel action in several spaces
Repeated action (car smashing)	Actions to restore order:
Inappropriate action (car pushed into water)	Rival retrieves diamond
	Charley gets drunk
	Diamond in hat
	Katherine's fathers' discovery
	K and father pursue
Truncated syllogism (throwing hat over rail into wind)	Charley pursues hat, finds girl
	Ch hides ring in boa
	Ch tricks rival (keyhole scene)
Sight gag (hat hanging by string)	Ch tries to recover ring
	K and father pursue
Spatial gags (girl's cabin door opens at top), boat tossing on waves	Diamond retrieved (1st closure)
	Ch dives in ocean
	Ch commandeers boat, turns it around
Semi-diegetic insert (dance scene)	(2nd closure)

Progression ad absurdem (dance scene)	Boat and yacht meet
	Ch and rival into ocean
Exaggerated reaction (boat turning at high speed, dancers falling)	Katherine undresses, reveals "real leg" (3rd closure)
	Katherine uses leg to kick rival (4th closure)
Revelation (Katherine's "real" leg displayed)	
Final tableau [apotheosis] (father turns away while couple kisses) (couple restored, final closure)	

Table 1. Pie versus Chase

In a response to this paper in its original version, Tom Gunning has made some valuable criticism that I should briefly address.[12] First, he draws attention to the two-dimensionality of my picture of "the forces that disrupt and the forces that contain" and insists on the complexity of the relationship. I agree. But I cannot follow the argument that the narrative is "a process of integration which smaller units are absorbed into a larger overarching pattern and process of containment" or that gags are "an excess that is necessary to the film's process of containment." This is probably an accurate description of other genres but slapstick seems to me to be defined by this failure of containment and resistance to bourgeois legibility. Gunning cites the dancing sequence as an example of the recovery of gags by narrativization. True, the purpose served by the scene is to retrieve the engagement ring from the "virgin wilderness of the old maid's underclothes," but at what lack of economy! The same point would have been served by Charley's finding the ring on the deck. Instead, he musters all his persuasive resources and incites the old maid to literally make a shimmying spectacle of herself. The abruptness of Charley's desertion after he gets the ring is funny in part because his off-hand gesture mimics the irrelevance of the ring to the narrative. The diegetic fact here becomes the excessive part of the elaborate joke.

Gunning also rightly notes that my chart contains several elements (such as truncated syllogisms) that are inversions of narrative logic. The point here is that such inversions are possible only through the gag's deceptive assimilation of narrative form. It is by seeming to resemble certain narrative situations that narrative anticipation is subverted. This is not simply an issue of two separate forms, but of a dialectical interrelation. It is in fact the process of parody, in which narrative logic is not so much ignored, as laid bare.

No one would argue that HIS WOODEN WEDDING is lacking in parody. Charley's "courting" of the old maid, for example, is a parody of his courtship with Katherine. But again, it seems to beg the question. I maintain that in these instances, the tail *really is* wagging the dog, and to say that the gags' assimilation of narrative structure is a laying bare of the illusionistic invisibility of the fictional mechanism is simply another way of saying that spectacle is here containing narrative, and not the other way around. The "message" of this and other slapstick films is that the seeming hegemony of narrative in the classical cinema is vulnerable to assault by the "underground" forces of spectacle. The film's multiple narrative closures are overly redundant even by classical standards (I count four). The obstacles mounted by *fate* are overcome, but not at the cost of annihilating the impact of the gags. It is the non sequitur components of the humor that we recall best. Like the wooden wedding of the title, the absorption of all the disruptive elements by the narrative never takes place.

One way to look at narrative is to see it as a system for providing the spectator with sufficient knowledge to make causal links between represented events.[13] According to this view, the gag's status as an irreconcilable difference becomes clear. Its purpose is to misdirect the viewer's attention, to obfuscate the linearity of cause-effect relations. Gags provide the opposite of epistemological comprehension by the spectator. They are atemporal bursts of violence and/or hedonism that are as ephemeral and as gratifying as the sight of someone's pie-smitten face.

Notes

First published in *The Slapstick Symposium*, ed. Eileen Bowser (Bruxelles: FIAF, 1987) 49-59; and subsequently, in a revised version, in *Classical Hollywood Comedy*, ed. Kristine Brunovska Karnick and Henry Jenkins (New York: Routledge, 1994) 106-19.

1. For example, as Dan Kamin does in his chapter on "The Magician" in *Charlie Chaplin's One-Man Show* (Metuchen: Scarecrow, 1984) 37-55.
2. "Chaplin's Gold Coast Triumph," *New York Times*, quoted in *Film Daily Yearbook* 1926: 15.
3. Gerald Mast, *The Comic Mind: Comedy and the Movies* (Indianapolis: Bobbs-Merrill, 1973) 39.
4. Mast 53.
5. David Bordwell, *Narration in the Fiction Film* (Madison: U of Wisconsin P, 1985) 53.
6. Brett Page, *Writing for Vaudeville* (Springfield: The Home Correspondence School, 1915) 98 fn. Thanks to Henry Jenkins for bringing this book to my attention.
7. Sergei Eisenstein, "Montage of Attractions," *Film Form and The Film Sense*, ed. Jay Leyda (New York: World, 1957) 230-31.
8. Eisenstein, "The Unexpected," *Film Form*, ed. Jay Leyda (New York: Harcourt, 1949) 23.
9. Tom Gunning, "The Cinema of Attraction: Early Film, Its Spectator and the Avant-Garde," *Wide Angle* 8.3-4 (1986): 64.

10. HIS WOODEN WEDDING is available in 16mm from Blackhawk Films, Davenport, Iowa. Other players are Gale Henry, Fred de Silva, John Cossar. Photographed by Glen R. Carrier. Edited by Richard Currier. Running time: 24 minutes.

11. I have omitted a discussion of the 1926 Hal Roach film DON KEY, SON OF BURRO that was part of my original presentation for reason of space. The film was projected at the time of my presentation and is available for viewing at The Museum of Modern Art.

12. I am grateful for Gunning's comments at the Slapstick Symposium presentation on May 3, 1985, and again at a Columbia Seminar meeting at The Museum of Modern Art a few weeks later.

13. "Narration refers not to what is told, but rather to the conditions of telling – to the overall regulation and distribution of knowledge in a text." Edward Branigan, "Diegesis and Authorship in Film," *Iris* 7 (1986): 38.

Early Cinema as a Challenge to Film History

André Gaudreault and Tom Gunning

> And the chronological question: "Who said it first?" is not essential.
> Juri Tynianov (1927)[1]

> The aim of this article is not polemical.
> Boris Eichenbaum (1925)[2]

In 1927, Boris Eichenbaum claimed for theory the right to become history.[3] In 1969, in this very same room here in Cerisy, Gérard Genette affirmed it was more a necessity than a right: "a necessity," he said, "that originates from the movement itself and from the needs of the theoretical work."[4] In his paper, Genette tried to explain why what he calls the "history of forms" took so long to establish itself. Along with a number of circumstantial factors, Genette stressed two causes that we would like to take into consideration. Let's let him speak: "The first of these causes is that even the objects of the history of forms have not yet sufficiently freed themselves from the 'theory' of literature [...] The lateness of history here reflects the lateness of theory, because, to a great extent and contrary to a stubborn prejudice, in this area at least theory must precede history because it is theory that frees its objects."[5] We will return to this below, but it is clear that this formulation can be equally applied to the field of cinema, especially if one considers the remarkable, historically determined delay that, until very recently, film theory had compared with literary theory. As a function of these considerations, let us take for our study the following formula: we have the (film) history that (film) theory affords us. But let us resume our reading of Genette: "A second cause [...] is that in the analysis of forms itself, [...] another prejudice dominates which is – in Saussurian terms – the opposition or rather the incompatibility of the study of synchrony and the study of diachrony, the notion that it is only possibly to theorize from within the synchronic moment [...]."[6]

Actually, the two causes cited by Genette belong to the same family. Both of them arise from the entirely 20th-century tension between synchrony and diachrony, structure and development, theory and history. Recently, this tension has had a tendency to dwindle, which is certainly linked to the return to power of history, at least in the area of cinema studies. However, since the 1920s, the

Russian Formalists have preached and practiced a politics of conciliation between the two terms of this tension.

The first step that now has to be taken to continue this work of reconciliation
between the two opposing terms is to question, following Siegfried Kracauer,
"the primacy of the diachronic perspective in historiography."[7] Likewise it is
urgent, we believe, to question the primacy of synchrony in theory analysis, as
David Bordwell also argues at the close of an important article published recently.[8] The barriers between the synchronic and diachronic study of phenomena have their origins, as we know, in the work of Ferdinand de Saussure, who
identified the axis of simultaneity from which the temporal vector is excluded
and the axis of succession for which, on the contrary, the analyst has to take into
consideration transformations of a temporal nature. For Saussure, the opposition between the two axes cannot be reduced: one cannot simultaneously analyze synchronic relationships that form a system as well as the course of their
evolution in time. Even if both approaches are essential, one must first outline a
synchronic description because transformations can only be understood once
one has described the static functioning of the system.

Furthermore, another factor, also inherited from the Saussurian tradition,
overdetermines and reinforces the barriers in question. It is this principle, so
essential to structuralism, that demands that we understand the text as a closed
system. This principle comes directly from the Saussurian concept of the linguistic sign. For Saussure, the linguistic sign joins, as we know, not an object
and a word but rather a concept and an acoustic image. Thus the signifier and
the signified comprise a closed system in which the signified cannot be assimilated to the object with which it may be associated. On the contrary the signifier
is a purely linguistic entity. When we apply these principles to literary or cinematic works, we necessarily assume that they are closed systems which cannot
be analyzed by mobilizing exterior social factors. Not, at least, if we want to
arrive at an explanation of the singular internal organization of these systems.
When one strictly adheres to a synchronic description, literary or cinematic texts
are understood as being incompatible with historical understanding because
they are apparently cut off from any consideration of systemic evolution, and
removed from social relationships by their very constitution as closed systems.

However, such a principle, which would dictate that only a-temporal and a-
social phenomena may be the objects of a structural approach, is not to be found
in Saussure. Synchronic description must precede diachronic description, but
does not exclude it. As Saussure himself wrote: "one truth does not exclude the
other."[9] Acknowledging this Todorov wrote: "at the same time, the artificial
opposition between 'structure' and 'history' disappears: it is only at the structural level that one can describe literary evolution; the knowledge of structure
does not only impede the knowledge of variability, but it also becomes the only

means that we have of approaching it."[10] Obviously one must not confuse system and evolution. Both imply totally different temporal principles. However, synchronic description does not eliminate the history of the evolution of system(s). Effectively it is nothing more than a precondition capable of providing the basis from which we may describe its/their evolution.

However, for a number of years now, theory and history seem to be compatible again within the domain of film studies. The recent publication of a special issue of *Iris* entitled "For a theory of film history"[11] and the organization of this conference[12] can be seen as the most recent symptoms of this new attitude. We are beginning to understand that theory is like oxygen which history needs, and that, on the other hand, history can serve to oxygenate the grey matter of theory. Today, there are countless calls for a reunion of the two disciplines, calls that repeat, like an echo, Jean-Louis Comolli's pioneering phrase, published in a series of articles to which we will have occasion to return. Notably, he wrote that: "Whatever may be the difficulties of this work (and they are considerable), it is no longer possible to maintain film history and theory as impervious to one another [...]."[13]

Today, in 1985, we do not do, we can no longer do, film history as it was done before 1970. Of course, this seems to be a truth, which – as well as being a truism – also appears to have universal applicability. But in the field of cinema studies, this simple truth takes on even greater urgency given that the period in question has seen film theory advance in giant steps. If a minority of the film historians of the previous generation were theorists (Jean Mitry was the most important figure among these exceptional cases), today the numbers are reversed. This, moreover, is one of the reasons that explain the relative success of New Film History. We believe effectively, following Ron Mottram, that all film historians should definitely also be theorists, if only for these (very simple, but so important) reasons which he invoked. In analyzing a cut within a medium shot in FOR LOVE OF GOLD (Griffith, 1908), which Lewis Jacobs claimed[14] was the first example of its kind, Mottram wrote: "Two things need to be said about this claim [...]. First, it is not true. The scene being referred to is done in one take; there is no cut within the scene. [...] Second, the question needs to be raised, why does the historian make this claim? Or rather, why is such a fact being affirmed? To point it out in the first place implies that a cut within a scene is significant. [...] Does not the historian who makes this point do so on the basis of a theoretical consideration? [...] Inevitably the historiographer is a theorist, perhaps not a good one, but some kind of theorist."[15]

We would like to take this opportunity to question the place of theory in film history, in light of the quantity of stimulating research, recently conducted by young scholars, addressing that which has come to be known as early cinema. We also take this opportunity to highlight the way we intend to go beyond the

historical conceptions of our predecessors, and in particular those of Jean Mitry[16] who often had occasion to refer to his work as an historian, to explain its
ins and outs and therefore, to "expose his [historical] methods," to use an expression coined by the Russian Formalists. It will then be desirable, once we
have digested the results of our critique, to highlight what seems to have become the main task today in film history by sketching a tentative program for
its application. Over the course of our discussion, one will notice (as one might
already have noticed) the insistent presence of references to the Russian Formalists. This is because, we believe, their heritage has not yet been sufficiently
assimilated by scholars in film history and it seems evident that we cannot
ignore their insights if we wish to see progress in the science of history.

Over the last few years we have witnessed the return to power of film history.
And, to give credit where credit is due, the "honor" of being the first object of
this re-examination (if one may refer to it as such) goes to those whom we mistakenly call "primitives." And for this, of course, there are many reasons. Following all of the studies undertaken between 1960 and 1980 that address that
which we have not yet agreed to call "film language," it is perhaps not surprising that young "post-structuralists" have strongly felt the desire to know more
about this Atlantis somewhat forgotten and, let us say, often mistreated (and ill-
treated) by historians of previous generations. There was also, surely, something of the attraction of the possible purity of origins, the Paradise Lost, before
the seeds of discontent had been sown (read: the foundation of the Motion Picture Patents Company and the subsequent birth of Hollywood). Those too
young or too far removed, who had to be content to watch May 1968 on TV,
must also have felt the appeal of a time at which a cinema reigned that, as one
of us has written, "feared neither God nor man."[17] Add to this the effects of the
recent arrival of cinema studies at the University and the obvious willingness of
certain film archives to open up to research, and there you have, its seems to us,
the principle ingredients likely to have created a situation for historical research
that Dana Polan has recently described as follows: "The attempt(s) to think
early cinema are certainly the dominant activity in current historical thought on
cinema. Above all, there is more than simply historical writing itself but also the
examination of what it means to do history."[18]

Originally, however, it was a series of articles published almost fifteen years
ago (in 1971-72), that dusted off the annals of official History. Of course, we
refer to Jean-Louis Comolli's "Technique et idéologie"[19] which, in spite of its
incompleteness and its errors, contained the blueprints for future scholars of
(rediscovered) early cinema. Comolli's acerbic critique of empirical historians
who, to quote Polan again, "continue to write texts where history is considered
to be an exact and transparent reflection of historical events"[20] or again, in the
very appropriate words of Pierre Sorlin, do not understand that, "even if they

are completely lost in the middle of their archives, even isolated in the second millennium before Jesus Christ, historians only answer the questions of their contemporaries,"[21] his acerbic critique, thus, commanded a great deal of attention and is generally celebrated today as an historical turning point. In an important article published in 1983, Kristin Thompson and David Bordwell summarized so well (even if very succinctly) the insights (and deficiencies) of Comolli's theses, that it does not bear rehearsing here.[22]

Let us recall, to refresh our memory, that in his articles Comolli opposed what he called the "conception established by the body of prevailing 'histories of cinema,'" veritable compendiums of obsolete theories and, to be frank, long since rejected by the most serious historians of literature and other forms of artistic expression. In the second batch of his series of articles, Comolli enumerated the principal mistakes of official History as follows: "causal linearity, the autonomy claim on the dual counts of the 'specificity' of cinema and of the model of idealist histories of 'art,' teleological concerns, the idea of 'progress' or 'improvement' not only of techniques but also of forms, in short, identification, recovery, submersion of cinematic practice to and under the mass of films produced, already existent, finished, considered as uniquely concrete, 'oeuvres' equal to the right to founding and writing this history, even if more or less 'elevated.'"[23] The results of such a trenchant analysis followed shortly. This is why, some years later, as a result of a resurgence of interest in early cinema, a number of studies appeared that, implicitly or explicitly, attempted to avoid the pitfalls pointed out in Comolli's analysis. Two aspects of this new attitude clearly emerged:

1. Early cinema presents discursive forms not inherent to institutionalized cinema after 1915 and its intrinsic values should be evaluated following the program that cinema had set for itself at that time. It is historically indefensible to measure early cinema by the yardstick of norms that had not yet appeared on the horizon of history.

2. The norms that were to be erected to give birth to that to which some refer as "film language" are not the last word in cinematic expression: in the final analysis they are nothing more than, in spite of their durability, an instance of code. These norms are certainly film specific but they could never, by themselves, entirely represent the specificity of cinematic expression.

Historians of previous generations contravened these two principles. They had the irritating habit of considering and judging early cinema on the basis of not yet extant norms, of the only kind of cinema worthy, in their eyes, of the label "specifically cinematic quality." It is precisely this vision that has been qualified as teleological because it has a tendency to privilege a logic of finality in the assessment of a reality, namely the cinema of 1895 to 1915 which, on the contrary, should be measured on the basis of its own successive finalities, year after year, or at least period after period.

New historians appropriated, consciously or not, the lessons of Tynianov who stated, at a time in which David Wark Griffith had not yet retired: "The study of the evolution of literary variability must break with the theories of naïve estimation resulting from the confounding of point of view: one follows the criteria of one system [...] to judge phenomena belonging to another system."[24]

Ignoring principles which today seem almost elementary, traditional historians, with their teleological vision and their evolutionist conceptions, implicitly arrived at three conclusions of which we recognize the programming function in all film histories published until very recently:

1. A language specific to cinema exists for which the code is relatively limited.
2. This specific language is that which must ultimately, necessarily, have ended up dominating film practice.
3. The period of early cinema is nothing but a crucible which should have allowed this form of specificity to reveal itself.

This, for example, is exactly what Jean Mitry does in entitling the fifth chapter of the first volume of his *Histoire du cinéma*[25] "Découverte du Cinéma (1908-1914)," thereby adapting, for the analysis of cinema that preceded the so-called "discovery," a theoretical frame and a limited point of view that can be compared, *mutatis mutandis*, with the "point of view of the orchestra conductor" that Georges Sadoul applied to the films of Méliès.

The same Mitry repents this gesture when he states, in an entirely "untimely"[26] fashion: "L'INCENDIAIRE (The Arsonist) [Pathé, 1905] [...] marks real progress. Firstly, because the news item that it illustrates is plausible, because the narration offers a certain credibility and because it is the first drama in the Pathé production that was filmed on location."[27] Or again: "Porter's film [THE GREAT TRAIN ROBBERY (Edison, 1903)] [...], although considerably outmoded, carries in it the seeds of cinematic expression and remains, in the face of history, the first film that was really cinema."[28]

The plausibility of a news item, the credibility of the narration and the recognition of the value of filming on location are criteria of another age, still to come, criteria that one can only take to be transcendent (as Mitry does) at the risk of historical truth. But given this, such conclusions are not surprising if one begins with premises that were intended to prove that "the generative principle behind the entire oeuvre of Méliès [...] had to be false,"[29] that the "birth of real cinema"[30] happened in 1914, or that "film language was still," at the time of Film d'Art, "ill-defined."[31] Nevertheless, it is clear that from Terry Ramsaye to Jean Mitry, film history made a great deal of progress: several myths were uncovered and destroyed, we were able to correct certain flagrant errors and the methods of verification were refined (although they cannot be considered as really scientific, in our opinion, till Jacques Deslandes[32]). *But we remained on the same* (mined) *terrain*. Of course, Mitry does not show the same verbal inflation as Ramsaye. The latter is among the first of those responsible for the myth created around the figure of Griffith. In his book published in 1926, he wrote: "Griffith began to work out a syntax of screen narration. He started to use the close-up for accents, and fade-outs for punctuation. With cutbacks and manipulations of sequence, he worked for new intensities of suspense. The motion picture spent the years up to 1908 learning its letters. Now, with Griffith, it was studying grammar and pictorial rhetoric."[33]

Mitry does not go that far, of course, but his summary of Griffith's contribution, although less bombastic, does not in our opinion engage a different dimension than that of Ramsaye. Let us judge for ourselves: "We shall see that, if he did not invent all the techniques he made use of, Griffith did at least use them for the first time in a systematic and concerted way, establishing in a few years the elementary syntax of an art that was still in its infancy."[34] Mitry, you see, follows the track of Ramsaye (that in the meantime will have been followed by Jacobs[35] and Sadoul[36]) while decanting it a little. It must be said, however, that Mitry, as well in part as Sadoul, shows a much greater theoretical and historical subtlety than Ramsaye or even Jacobs. We are indebted to him for a theory which saw the cinema between 1903 and 1911 as being divided into two major tendencies: theatricality and narrativity. Despite the theoretical and historical disagreements that we have with Mitry's hypotheses in this respect (and that one of us outlined four years ago, in this very place, at a conference dedicated to Méliès[37]), this appears to be a real effort of historical theorizing that partly corresponds with the solutions we envisage, as we will see below, in order to bring to light the specific features of each of the successive systems that were operating between 1895 and 1915.[38] And one starts to dream of what Mitry's *Histoire du cinéma* could have been if he had followed the quite "modern" principles he once formulated (without retrospective self-criticism) in an article published in 1973 in reply to, among other things, Comolli's criticism: "In truth the historian notices present facts exactly in the same way in which he may notice past facts. Then he looks, discovers and analyzes chains of cause and effect that formed, and that were in substance, the past. But these continuous chains do not lead to linear development which would unfold, deterministically and univocally, in a direction that goes necessarily from less perfect to more perfect. He does not postulate a finality that the retroactive effect gives him to understand as incessantly predictable, even if the present state is the outcome of a series of intentions more or less fortified, counteracted or diversified in the course of ages. There is progression, but not necessarily 'progress.' Progress is a value judgment applied to historical facts but not these historical facts themselves."[39]

Would Comolli's lesson have been fruitful for a Mitry who spoke of L'INCEN-DIAIRE as having marked "real progress" or who, in various passages which we have not cited, spoke of Film d'Art as manifesting a "step backwards" compared to the films of Smith, Williamson or Porter,[40] or Smith's two films as marking "a regression" from those of Méliès or Pathé?[41] Unfortunately not, because this is the same Mitry who, in the same article, a little earlier (just as in his "Propos intempestifs" published in *Cinématographe*), in spite of the long "lapse" that we just cited, re-claimed the victory of teleology and linearity: "I set out to follow the constant formation of the means of cinematic expression through manifestations which, however distinct they may be, progressively assure adjustments and improvements."[42]

Could one state it more clearly? Continuity, progression, improvement. What we are proposing, with the goal of advancing our historical comprehension of the immergence of cinema, is to retain a methodology, inherited from the Russian Formalists, that would itself illuminate both the practice of history and the period(s) examined. Indeed, Tynianov suggested the following: "If we agree that evolution amounts to a change in the relation of systemic terms, in other words a change in the formal functions and elements, evolution turns out to be a 'substitution' of systems. These substitutions, whose rhythm is, depending on the period, either slow or staccato, presuppose not the renewal and the sudden and total replacement of formal elements, but the creation of a new function for these formal elements."[43]

In examining this proposition, we would like to assert that the first task of the film historian consists in establishing the succession, the diachrony, of various systems that have been engendered over the course of film history. In this way we will be able to carry out to the program that Hans-Robert Jauss has recently defined for the history of literature. What Jauss has called the aesthetics of reception demands that we "insert the individual work into its 'literary series' to recognize its historical position and significance in the context of the experience of literature."[44] The construction of such a diachronic system should not however become an authoritative argument which is mobilized to define the style of cinema at a particular time. On the contrary, such a series should be conceived as a dynamic construction, much in the manner of Mukarovsky's concept of "aesthetic norms" or Tynianov's notion of "literary evolution." It is not about defining, through the construction of every system (the "literary series"), all of the individual works that constitute that system. What is more, the identification and definition of the system (and this is already a major step) facilitates the revelation of the contextual background against which these individual works can be understood, permitting us to better discern, within each of them, which elements conform to the system and which diverge from it.

The construction of diachronic series is not, however, a simple, non-theoretical chronology of various events that have marked film history. In doing so, one must take into account the organic interdependence of diachronic series and synchronic analysis. Here again Jauss provides us with, in his case for literature, an important reflection: "it must also be possible to take a synchronic cross-section of a moment in the development, to arrange the heterogeneous multiplicity of contemporaneous works in equivalent, opposing, and hierarchical structures, and thereby to discover an overarching system of relationships in the literature of a historical moment. From this the principle of representation of a new literary history could be developed, if further cross-sections diachronically before and after were so arranged as to articulate historically the change in literary structures in its epoch-making moments."[45] In order to identify "overarching systems of relationships" that were current at the time of early cinema, we will refer to the concept of "modes of film practice" put forward by David Bordwell in the previously cited article. Modes of film practice would constitute a system of rules and norms that lead to the establishment of a coherent series of expectations concerning the way films should function. These various expectations would be the primary determinant for stylistic decisions on the part of the filmmaker and for the spectator's understanding. In a text in which he emphasizes the interdependence of textual analysis and historical perspective engendered by that which he calls modes of film practice, Bordwell explains that these modes "would exist at a level of abstraction higher than that of the individual text; higher even than that of genres, schools, and oeuvres; but at a lower level of abstraction that the cinematic *langue* conceived as an a-temporal logical construct."[46] We have identified, for the period with which we are concerned (1895-1915), two modes of film practice for which we would like to provide a tentative definition. For the moment, these two successive modes cover the entire period but it is not unthinkable that a refinement of our hypotheses and a better understanding of the period would lead us to multiply this number. The first mode would cover the entire first period of film history until 1908, whereas the second mode would stretch to 1914. We have decided to call the first mode the "system of monstrative attractions" and the second the "system of narrative integration." For the purposes of our demonstration, we believe it is preferable to describe the second of these modes first.

The system of narrative integration, as we define it at this stage of our research, appears to be a system by which cinema has followed an integrated process of narrativization. It was at this time that cinematic discourse began to serve the purpose of storytelling. At every level, elements of cinematic expression were mobilized for narrative ends, be it profilmic elements, the composition of the frame, or editing. This system distinguishes itself, and quite radically, from the one which preceded it, namely the system of monstrative attractions in which, as we will see, narrativity did not yet dominate at the level of cinematic discourse. The distinction between the system of narrative integration and that which replaced it is, however, less clear-cut. One reason for this is because there is still a great deal of research to be done on the first feature films made from 1913-14 onwards. But this is also attributable to the fact that there is no strong solution of continuity between the two systems. Both are actually subordinate to the regime of narrativization. What primarily distinguishes the system of narrative integration from the system which it succeeded, is exactly that it marks the distinction between pre-Griffith monstrative cinema and so-called classical cinema for which narrativization is entirely dominant. It is also this aspect which marks the importance of the study of the system of narrative integration. This is to say that, in the system of narrative integration, the process of narrativization is at least visible. Here we see the immergence and the shaping of a fictional world. In the system of narrative integration, signs of enunciation have not yet been erased, as Jacques Aumont correctly pointed out in his analysis of ENOCH ARDEN made by Griffith in 1911: "Griffith does nothing to hide the white threads which sew the frames together: on the contrary, he makes much of them, flaunts them, puts a great deal of emphasis on them, marks them with a whole signifying apparatus."[47] Furthermore, the importance of the films made by Griffith for Biograph resides precisely in the fact that they reveal the process of narrativization. For spectators accustomed to classical cinema, which is the product of the invisibilization of narrative procedures, these films permit us to see the narrative functions of cinematic discourse in full operation. As we watch these films, we are able to perceive the capacity of cinema to transform its discourse into figures of narration.

The dominant feature of the system of narrative integration is that an element of cinematic signification is chosen and given an integrational role: that of telling the story. The narrator chooses the various elements of discourse as a function of the story, and it is also through the story that the viewer is led to interpret various forms of cinematic discourse. The suturing of the film narrator and the viewer is guaranteed by the coherence of the process of narrativization. When the system of narrative integration was taking shape, a being was born whose existence is only theoretical but whose task is to modulate and direct cinematic discourse: the narrator, whose "voice" is heard from the beginning of the film to the end, by means of the way it structures, at one and the same time, the profilmic, the camera work and editing.

On the contrary, in the system of monstrative attractions, the regime of cinematic narration is barely perceptible in the way in which one of us explained in a recent article.[48] Here, cinematic monstration reigns supreme, a system for which the privileged domain and the basic unity is the shot. The cinematic story, as it was constructed in the 1910s, was communicated at the level of both narration and monstration. Each shot was, therefore, understood as a microstory (sometimes quite laconic), communicated at the level of monstration, while the film in its entirety (at least after the system of narrative integration did its job) was communicated at the level of monstrative attractions, where each shot is implicitly understood as an autonomous and autarkic unity and the potential connection between shots, when there is more than one, is restricted to a minimum. Where there is pluri-punctuality,[49] the film resembles an "aggregate" of shots, where each in its turn sets off the system of monstration, without setting off the process of narration. If the film is uni-punctual,[50] all of the action is congregated around the same segment which has obvious monstrative qualities. But we would also like to suggest the use of the term attractions to refer to this period... It seems to us that monstration alone was not adequate as a means of characterizing the very essence of the mode of film practice that reigned at the turn of the century.[51] Early cinema shares many if not all of its characteristics with one of the definitions that Eisenstein attributed to the word attraction. Indeed, in reading Jacques Aumont's trenchant description of the system of attractions which was so dear to the Soviet filmmaker, its appropriateness is clear: "the attraction is originally the music hall number or sketch, a peak moment in the show, relatively autonomous, and calling upon techniques of representation which are not those of dramatic illusion, drawing upon more aggressive forms of the performing arts (the circus, the music hall, the sideshow)."[52] It's all there! Even the sideshow... What UNCLE TOM'S CABIN (Edison, 1903) offers, are peak moments of the spectacle from which it derived, what WHAT HAPPENED ON TWENTY-THIRD STREET, IN NEW YORK CITY (Edison, 1901) shows, after a wait even longer than the film's title, is the punctual moment when a woman walks over a vent which blows up her skirt. The moment privileged by L'ARRIVÉE D'UN TRAIN EN GARE DE LA CIOTAT (Lumière, 1895) is the moment at which the engine appears to charge at the spectator. Filmed stage numbers, circus and acrobatic acts number in the dozens and perhaps in the hundreds. Without knowing it Aumont made a place for Méliès and his imitators in his description of the attraction. He wrote: "the most fully developed example of [the attraction] is the 'trick,' that is, any kind of special performance."[53] Even the popular chase, despite the necessary link between shots, amounts to a collection of attractions. Shots that serve only to show the alternation between the chaser and the chased are rare. On the contrary, each shot is rather, generally speaking, a self-sufficient unit and constitutes an isolated attraction: those giving chase all run into the same obstacle and pile up on each other; another attraction comes in the form of women who raise their skirts in order to cross a fence; and yet elsewhere a body of water must be crossed over slippery stones, insuring that at least one of the protagonists stumbles into the water. This trend continues right up to THE GREAT TRAIN ROBBERY (Edison, 1903) in which many shots have obvious attractional qualities: the explosion in the freight car, the murder of the engine driver, the killing of the traveler who tries to escape, the dance scene in the saloon, the armed battle with its sensa-

tional clouds of smoke and, of course, the final (or initial) shot of the leader of
the bandits firing his gun at the spectator, this is an attraction par excellence if
ever there were one. In short, this is a cinema of monstration, a cinema of the
monstrator, in other words, this is a cinema of the showman.[54] The system of
monstrative attractions should be seen as a moment in film history, a time at
which filmmakers "discovered" (inevitably, we are tempted to add) most of the
elements which would soon form that to which we refer as "film language": the
close-up, the high-angle shot, the tracking shot and editing. But in order to write
the history of the close-up, the high-angle shot, the tracking shot or of this or
that editing technique, one must not forget that the function of these elements,
as they move from one "overarching" system to another, may have changed.
Often, the close-up used in the system of monstrative attractions does not have
the same function as a close-up used in the system of narrative integration. It
remains to be said, and one needn't be afraid of stating the obvious because it is
perhaps not obvious to everyone, that both are, despite all this, close-ups *at any
rate*. To cite but one example, even if Méliès used editing to achieve different
goals and functions than Griffith, it remains well and truly editing. This is why
we are opposed to the logic that subtends Mitry's thought when he claims that:
"Whether or not there is editing in Méliès's films is merely a question of terminology."[55] In our view it is rather a question of respect for historical truth. This
is why we have adapted Tynianov's old but not faded proposition, namely that:
"the confrontation of a given literary phenomenon with another should take
place at both the formal and the functional level. Phenomena that appear to be
totally different and belong to different functional systems may be analogous in
their function and vice-versa."[56] Close-ups, high-angle shots, tracking shots and
editing techniques do not have the same function in the system of monstrative
attractions as they have in the system of narrative integration, because in the
former they have not been strictly subordinated to narrativization.

These are our suggestions concerning the first task that needs to be faced by
the history of early cinema today.

But there is a constant danger that haunts the historian who undertakes such
a task. Film history is the history of an art, of a significant and particularly complex practice that cannot be the object of simple "decoding." On the contrary,
one must absolutely deploy a method of interpretation. This is the reason why
we believe, in spite of what has just been said, that the historical meaning of
these films cannot be limited to the relationship between them and their contemporary production modes. In our evaluation of these films, one must absolutely take into account the important factor which, in our opinion, is constituted by our own contemporary reception of them. We must not situate our
relationship to these films outside of history. To believe in the possibility of the
exact and "objective" renewal of past stylistic norms would be to fall into the

trap of historicism. As Hans-Georg Gadamer has shown: "This was […] the naive assumption of historicism, namely that we must transpose ourselves into the
spirit of the age, think with its ideas and its thoughts, not with our own, and
thus advance toward historical objectivity. In fact the important thing is to recognize temporal distance as a positive and productive condition enabling understanding."[57]

For Gadamer, as for Jauss, it is impossible to have "direct access to the historical object that would objectively reveal its historical value."[58] The historian
must, therefore, take into account the historicity of the gaze which he directs at
works of the past, while taking into consideration the temporal distance that
divides him from them. The task of the historian of a significant practice does
not only consist in the restitution of a past time. This restitution is always necessarily accompanied by some form of interpretation. Interpretation, which is always renewed, never the same, following the course of history, the course of its
own history. Gadamer concurs: "[The reader] can, indeed he must, accept the
fact that future generations will understand differently what he has read in the
text. And what is true of every reader is also true of the historian."[59]

If Gadamer is correct, all historians, Jean Mitry as well as we, must acknowledge that their reading is "mediate[d] with [their] own present existence,"[60]
even this reading. This is, according to Gadamer, the method available to the
historian in order to keep his interpretation "open for the future."[61]

Hence, our understanding of early cinema will remain incomplete if it is limited to a simple restitution of its historical context, both at the level of the modes
of film practice and at that of the conditions of production. As contemporary
spectators, we are directly interpellated by films arisen from the past; and the
relationship that we maintain with them has to be part of our historical understanding. The films that Griffith made for Biograph, for instance, were at the
origin of a particular historical tradition in cinema. The exact nature of this tradition has not yet served as the object of a serious study, neither for its partisans,
nor for its detractors. If one is to acknowledge the exact nature of this tradition,
one must understand it not only as a reified past, but also as a force which has
already exercised its influence on us. When we analyze these works, we do
more than merely discovering the past. This however, does not mean that this
past is completely inaccessible. The reconstitution of past horizons is necessary
if one wishes to arrive at a correct understanding of what has happened. But, at
the same time, this should not imprison us. Likewise, just as history is a succession of transformations, a series of changes, historical comprehension itself can
be a means of bringing about change.

Translated by Joyce Goggin and Wanda Strauven

Notes

Published in French as "Le cinéma des premiers temps: un défi à l'histoire du cinéma?" in *Histoire du cinéma. Nouvelles approches,* ed. Jacques Aumont, André Gaudreault and Michel Marie (Paris: Sorbonne, 1989) 49-63. Previously translated in Japanese: "Eigashi No Hohoron," *Gendai Shiso. Revue de la pensée d'aujourd'hui* 14.12 (Nov. 1986): 164-80.

1. Juri Tynianov, "De l'évolution littéraire," *Théorie de la littérature* (Paris: Seuil, 1965) 135.
2. Boris Eichenbaum, "La théorie de la 'méthode formelle,'" *Théorie de la littérature* 32.
3. Cited by Gérard Genette, "Poétique et histoire," *Figures III* (Paris: Seuil, 1972) 18.
4. Genette 18.
5. Genette 18.
6. Genette 18.
7. Hans-Robert Jauss, "Literary History as a Challenge to Literary Theory," *Toward an Aesthetic of Reception,* trans. Timothy Bahti, intro. Paul de Man (Brighton: Harvester, 1982) 36. Jauss refers to Kracauer's study "Time and History."
8. David Bordwell, "Textual Analysis, etc.," *Enclitic* 5-6 (Fall 1981/Spring 1982): 125-36.
9. Ferdinand de Saussure, *Cours de linguistique générale* (Paris: Payot, 1976) 135.
10. Tzvetan Todorov, *Qu'est-ce que le structuralisme?*, vol. 2, Poétique (Paris: Seuil, 1968) 95.
11. "Pour une théorie de l'histoire du cinéma," *Iris* 2.2 (1984).
12. Whose initial title, curiously enough, was also "Pour une théorie de l'histoire du cinéma"!
13. Jean-Louis Comolli, "Technique et idéologie (3). Caméra, perspective, profondeur de champ," *Cahiers du cinéma* 231 (Aug.-Sept. 1971): 44.
14. Lewis Jacobs, *The Rise of the American Film* (New York: Teachers College P, 1968) 102.
15. Ron Mottram, "Fact and Affirmation: Some Thoughts on the Methodology of Film History and the Relation of Theory to Historiography," *Quarterly Review of Film Studies* 5.3 (Summer 1980): 338-39.
16. By this means we shall answer to the pressing call that Mitry recently made to one of us in an open letter published in *Cinéma 85* 315 (March 1985): 3-4: "That I am sometimes wrong, there is no doubt. Everybody makes mistakes. But I don't think I made 'metholodogical' mistakes. [...] But since Gaudreault claims I did, let him tell us which ones. I have never pointed out other people's mistakes [...] without providing proof or explaining where or why. Let Gaudreault do the same, not for me but simply for this better historical knowledge that he claims and that he would wrongly keep for himself alone."
17. André Gaudreault, "Un cinéma sans foi ni loi," *Iris* 2.1 (1984): 2-4.
18. Dana Polan, "La poétique de l'Histoire: *Metahistory* de Hayden White," *Iris* 2.2 (1984): 35.
19. Jean-Louis Comolli, *Cahiers du cinéma* 229 (May 1971): 4-21; 230 (July 1971): 51-57; 231 (Aug.-Sept. 1971): 42-49; 233 (Nov. 1971): 39-45; 234-235 (Dec. 1971/Jan.-Feb. 1972): 94-100; 241 (Sept.-Oct. 1972): 20-24.
20. Polan 31.

21. Pierre Sorlin, "Promenade dans Rome," *Iris* 2.2 (1984): 7.
22. David Bordwell and Kristin Thompson, "Linearity, Materialism and the Study of Early American Cinema," *Wide Angle* 5.3 (1983): 4-15.
23. Comolli, *Cahiers du cinéma* 230 (July 1971): 55-56.
24. Tynianov 121.
25. Jean Mitry, *Histoire du cinéma* (Paris: Editions universitaires, 1967).
26. This is an illusion to a column titled "Propos intempestifs" (Untimely comments) that Jean Mitry regularly wrote for the journal *Cinématographique*.
27. Mitry, *Histoire du cinéma* 221.
28. Mitry, *Histoire du cinéma* 240.
29. Mitry, *Histoire du cinéma* 120.
30. Mitry, *Histoire du cinéma* 171.
31. Mitry, *Histoire du cinéma* 256.
32. Jacques Deslandes, *Histoire comparée du cinéma* (Tournai: Casterman, 1966-68).
33. Terry Ramsaye, *A Million and One Nights* (New York: Simon and Schuster, 1926) 508.
34. Mitry, *Histoire du cinéma* 270.
35. Jacobs.
36. Georges Sadoul, *Histoire générale du cinéma*, vol.1-6 (Paris: Denoël, 1948-75).
37. André Gaudreault, "'Théâtralité' et 'narrativité' dans l'oeuvre de Georges Méliès," *Méliès et la naissance du spectacle cinématographique*, ed. Madeleine Malthête-Méliès (Paris: Klincksieck, 1984) 199-219. [English trans. "Theatricality, Narrativity, and Trickality: Reevaluating the Cinema of Georges Méliès," *Journal of Popular Film and Television* 15.3 (1987): 111-19.]
38. One of us has written a detailed study of Mitry's hypotheses of theatricality and narrativity. See Tom Gunning, *Early Development of Film Narrative: D.W. Griffith's First Films at Biograph (1908-1909)*, diss., New York U, 1986. See also Tom Gunning, "Le récit filmé et l'idéal théâtral: Griffith et 'les films d'Art' français," *Les premiers ans du cinéma français*, ed. Pierre Guibbert (Perpignan: Institut Jean Vigo, 1985) 123-29.
39. Jean Mitry, "De quelques problèmes d'histoire et d'esthétique du cinéma," *Les Cahiers de la Cinémathèque* 10-11 (Summer-Fall 1973): 121.
40. Mitry, *Histoire du cinéma* 254.
41. Mitry, *Histoire du cinéma* 229.
42. Mitry, "De quelques problèmes" 116.
43. Tynianov 136.
44. Jauss 32.
45. Jauss 36.
46. Bordwell 129.
47. Jacques Aumont, "Griffith: the Frame, the Figure," *Early Cinema: Space Frame Narrative*, ed. Thomas Elsaesser (London: British Film Institute, 1990) 353. Originally published in French as "Griffith, le cadre, la figure," *Le cinéma américain*, ed. Raymond Bellour (Paris: Flammarion, 1980) 51-68.
48. André Gaudreault, "Narration et monstration au cinéma," *Hors Cadre* 2 (April 1984): 87-98. See also André Gaudreault, "Film, récit, narration; le cinéma des frères Lumière," *Iris* 2.1 (1984): 61-70. [English trans. "Film, Narrative, Narration: The Cinema of the Lumière Brothers," *Early Cinema: Space Frame Narrative* 68-75.]

49. That is, films composed of more than one shot.

50. That is, composed of one shot.

51. During a working session with Adam Simon the authors decided on this term, following a suggestion made by Don Crafton in his paper "Pie and Chase. The State of the Art of the Gag, 1925-26," at the Slapstick Symposium, 41st annual FIAF conference at the Museum of Modern Art of New York in May 1985. Speaking about shots in which Ben Turpin simply rolls his eyes facing the camera, he said: "Such cases are illustrations of what Eisenstein called 'attractions,' elements of pure spectacle." [Donald Crafton, "Pie and Chase: Gag, Spectacle and Narrative in Slapstick Comedy," *The Slapstick Symposium*, ed. Eileen Bowser (Bruxelles: FIAF, 1987) 52-53.]

52. Jacques Aumont, *Montage Eisenstein*, trans. Lee Mildreth, Constance Penley and Andrew Ross (London/Bloomington: British Film Institute/Indiana UP, 1987) 42.

53. Aumont 42.

54. In the US, the first cinema exhibitors were showmen that often combined multimedia films, magic lantern projections (sometimes accompanied by songs that the slides illustrated), sketches and other "curiosities" in the same spectacle.

55. Jean Mitry, letter published in *Cinéma 85*: 4.

56. Tynianov 136. Emphasis added.

57. Hans-Georg Gadamer, *Truth and Method*, trans. Joel Weinsheimer and Donald G. Marshall (London: Sheed & Ward, 1989) 297.

58. Gadamer 327.

59. Gadamer 340.

60. Gadamer 340.

61. Gadamer 340.

The Cinema of Attraction[s]: Early Film, Its Spectator and the Avant-Garde

Tom Gunning

Writing in 1922, flushed with the excitement of seeing Abel Gance's LA ROUE, Fernand Léger tried to define something of the radical possibilities of the cinema. The potential of the new art did not lie in "imitating the movements of nature" or in "the mistaken path" of its resemblance to theater. Its unique power was a "matter of *making images seen.*"[1] It is precisely this harnessing of visibility, this act of showing and exhibition, which I feel cinema before 1906 displays most intensely. [Its] inspiration for the avant-garde of the early decades of this century needs to be re-explored.

Writings by the early modernists (Futurists, Dadaists and Surrealists) on the cinema follow a pattern similar to Léger: enthusiasm for this new medium and its possibilities; and disappointment at the way it has already developed, its enslavement to traditional art forms, particularly theater and literature. This fascination with the *potential* of a medium (and the accompanying fantasy of rescuing the cinema from its enslavement to alien and passé forms) can be understood from a number of viewpoints. I want to use it to illuminate a topic I have [also] approached before [...], the strangely heterogeneous relation that film before 1906 (or so) bears to the films that follow, and the way a taking account of this heterogeneity signals a new conception of film history and film form. My work in this area has been pursued in collaboration with André Gaudreault.[2]

The history of early cinema, like the history of cinema generally, has been written and theorized under the hegemony of narrative films. Early filmmakers like Smith, Méliès and Porter have been studied primarily from the viewpoint of their contribution to film as a storytelling medium, particularly the evolution of narrative editing. Although such approaches are not totally misguided, they are one-sided and potentially distort both the work of these filmmakers and the actual forces shaping cinema before 1906. A few observations will indicate the way that early cinema was not dominated by the narrative impulse that later asserted its sway over the medium. First there is the extremely important role that actuality film plays in early film production. Investigation of the films copyrighted in the US shows that actuality films outnumbered fictional films until 1906.[3] The Lumière tradition of "placing the world within one's reach" through travel films and topicals did not disappear with the exit of the Cinématographe from film production.

But even within non-actuality filming – what has sometimes been referred to as the "Méliès tradition" – the role narrative plays is quite different than in traditional narrative film. Méliès himself declared in discussing his working method:

> As for the scenario, the "fable," or "tale," I only consider it at the end. I can state that the scenario constructed in this manner has *no importance*, since I use it merely as a pretext for the "stage effects," the "tricks," or for a nicely arranged tableau.[4]

Whatever differences one might find between Lumière and Méliès, they should not represent the opposition between narrative and non-narrative filmmaking, at least as it is understood today. Rather, one can unite them in a conception that sees cinema less as a way of telling stories than as a way of presenting a series of views to an audience, fascinating because of their illusory power (whether the realistic illusion of motion offered to the first audiences by Lumière, or the magical illusion concocted by Méliès), and exoticism. In other words, I believe that the relation to the spectator set up by the films of both Lumière and Méliès (and many other filmmakers before 1906) had a common basis, and one that differs from the primary spectator relations set up by narrative film after 1906. I will call this earlier conception of cinema, "the cinema of attractions." I believe that this conception dominates cinema until about 1906-1907. Although different from the fascination in storytelling exploited by the cinema from the time of Griffith, it is not necessarily opposed to it. In fact the cinema of attraction[s] does not disappear with the dominance of narrative, but rather goes underground, both into certain avant-garde practices and as a component of narrative films, more evident in some genres (e.g., the musical) than in others.

What precisely is the cinema of attraction[s]? First, it is a cinema that bases itself on the quality that Léger celebrated: its ability to *show* something. Contrasted to the voyeuristic aspect of narrative cinema analyzed by Christian Metz,[5] this is an exhibitionist cinema. An aspect of early cinema which I have written about in other articles is emblematic of this different relationship the cinema of attractions constructs with its spectator: the recurring look at the camera by actors. This action, which is later perceived as spoiling the realistic illusion of the cinema, is here undertaken with brio, establishing contact with the audience. From comedians smirking at the camera, to the constant bowing and gesturing of the conjurors in magic films, this is a cinema that displays its visibility, willing to rupture a self-enclosed fictional world for a chance to solicit the attention of the spectator.

Exhibitionism becomes literal in the series of erotic films which play an important role in early film production (the same Pathé catalogue would advertise the Passion Play along with "scènes griviosees d'un caractère piquant," erotic films often including full nudity), also driven underground in later years. As Noël Burch has shown in his film CORRECTION, PLEASE OR HOW WE GOT INTO PICTURES (1979), a film like THE BRIDE RETIRES (France, 1902) reveals a fundamental conflict between this exhibitionistic tendency of early film and the creation of a fictional diegesis. A woman undresses for bed while her new husband peers at her from behind a screen. However, it is to the camera and the audience that the bride addresses her erotic striptease, winking at us as she faces us, smiling in erotic display.

As the quote from Méliès points out, the trick film, perhaps the dominant non-actuality film genre before 1906, is itself a series of displays, of magical attractions, rather than a primitive sketch of narrative continuity. Many trick films are, in effect, plotless, a series of transformations strung together with little connection and certainly no characterization. But to approach even the plotted trick films, such as LE VOYAGE DANS LA LUNE (1902), simply as precursors of later narrative structures is to miss the point. The story simply provides a frame upon which to string a demonstration of the magical possibilities of the cinema.

Modes of exhibition in early cinema also reflect this lack of concern with creating a self-sufficient narrative world upon the screen. As Charles Musser has shown,[6] the early showmen exhibitors exerted a great deal of control over the shows they presented, actually re-editing the films they had purchased and supplying a series of offscreen supplements, such as sound effects and spoken commentary. Perhaps most extreme is the Hale's Tours, the largest chain of theaters exclusively showing films before 1906. Not only did the films consist of non-narrative sequences taken from moving vehicles (usually trains), but the theater itself was arranged as a train car with a conductor who took tickets, and sound effects simulating the click-clack of wheels and hiss of air brakes.[7] Such viewing experiences relate more to the attractions of the fairground than to the traditions of the legitimate theater. The relation between films and the emergence of the great amusement parks, such as Coney Island, at the turn of the century provides rich ground for rethinking the roots of early cinema.

Nor should we ever forget that in the earliest years of exhibition the cinema itself was an attraction. Early audiences went to exhibitions to see machines demonstrated (the newest technological wonder, following in the wake of such widely exhibited machines and marvels as X-rays or, earlier, the phonograph), rather than to view films. It was the Cinématographe, the Biograph or the Vitascope that were advertised on the variety bills in which they premièred, not [LE DÉJEUNER DE BÉBÉ] or THE BLACK DIAMOND EXPRESS. After the initial novelty period, this display of the possibilities of cinema continues, and not only in magic films. Many of the close-ups in early film differ from later uses of the technique precisely because they do not use enlargement for narrative punctuation, but as an attraction in its own right. The close-up cut into Porter's THE GAY SHOE CLERK (1903) may anticipate later continuity techniques, but its principal motive is again pure exhibitionism, as the lady lifts her skirt hem, exposing her ankle for all to see. Biograph films such as PHOTOGRAPHING A FEMALE CROOK (1904) and HOOLIGAN IN JAIL (1903) consist of a single shot in which the camera is brought close to the main character, until they are in mid-shot. The enlargement is not a device expressive of narrative tension; it is in itself an attraction and the point of the film.[8]

[To summarize, the cinema of attractions directly solicits spectator attention, inciting visual curiosity, and supplying pleasure through an exciting spectacle – a unique event, whether fictional or documentary, that is of interest in itself. The attraction to be displayed may also be of a cinematic nature, such as the early close-ups just described, or trick films in which a cinematic manipulation (slow motion, reverse motion, substitution, multiple exposure) provides the film's novelty. Fictional situations tend to be restricted to gags, vaudeville numbers or recreations of shocking or curious incidents (executions, current events). It is the direct address of the audience, in which an attraction is offered to the spectator by a cinema showman, that defines this approach to filmmaking. Theatrical display dominates over narrative absorption, emphasizing the direct stimulation of shock or surprise at the expense of unfolding a story or creating a diegetic universe. The cinema of attractions expends little energy creating characters with psychological motivations or individual personality. Making use of both fictional and non-fictional attractions, its energy moves outward an acknowledged spectator rather than inward towards the character-based situations essential to classical narrative.]

The term "attractions" comes, of course, from the young Sergei Mikhailovich Eisenstein and his attempt to find a new model and mode of analysis for the theater. In his search for the "unit of impression" of theatrical art, the foundation of an analysis which would undermine realistic representational theater, Eisenstein hit upon the term "attraction."[9] An attraction aggressively subjected the spectator to "sensual or psychological impact." According to Eisenstein, theater should consist of a montage of such attractions, creating a relation to the spectator entirely different from his absorption in "illusory [depictions]."[10] I pick up this term partly to [underscore] the relation to the spectator that this later avant-garde practice shares with early cinema: that of exhibitionist confrontation rather than diegetic absorption. Of course the "experimentally regulated and mathematically calculated" montage of attractions demanded by Eisenstein differs enormously from these early films (as any conscious and oppositional mode of practice will from a popular one).[11] However, it is important to realize the context from which Eisenstein selected the term. Then, as now, the "attraction" was a term of the fairground, and for Eisenstein and his friend Yutkevich it primarily represented their favorite fairground attraction, the roller coaster, or as it was known then in Russia, the American Mountains.[12]

The source is significant. The enthusiasm of the early avant-garde for film was at least partly an enthusiasm for a mass culture that was emerging at the beginning of the century, offering a new sort of stimulus for an audience not acculturated to the traditional arts. It is important to take this enthusiasm for popular art as something more than a simple gesture of *épater les bourgeois*. The enormous development of the entertainment industry since the 1910s and its growing acceptance by middle-class culture (and the accommodation that made this acceptance possible) have made it difficult to understand the liberation popular entertainment offered at the beginning of the century. I believe that it was precisely the exhibitionist quality of turn-of-the-century popular art that made it attractive to the avant-garde – its freedom from the creation of a diegesis, its accent on direct stimulation.

Writing of the variety theater, Marinetti not only praised its aesthetics of astonishment and stimulation, but particularly its creation of a new spectator who contrasts with the "static," "stupid voyeur" of traditional theater. The spectator at the variety theater feels directly addressed by the spectacle and joins in, singing along, heckling the comedians.[13] Dealing with early cinema within the context of archive and academy, we risk missing its vital relation to vaudeville, its primary place of exhibition until around 1905. Film appeared as one attraction on the vaudeville program, surrounded by a mass of unrelated acts in a nonnarrative and even nearly illogical succession of performances. Even when presented in the nickelodeons that were emerging at the end of this period, these short films always appeared in a variety format, trick films sandwiched in with farces, actualities, "illustrated songs," and, quite frequently, cheap vaudeville acts. It was precisely this non-narrative variety that placed this form of entertainment under attack by reform groups in the early 1910s. The Russell Sage Survey of popular entertainments found vaudeville "depends upon an artificial rather than a natural human and developing interest, these acts having no necessary, and as a rule, no actual connection."[14] In other words, no narrative. A night at the variety theater was like a ride on a streetcar or an active day in a crowded city, according to this middle-class reform group, stimulating an unhealthy nervousness. It was precisely such artificial stimulus that Marinetti and Eisenstein wished to borrow from the popular arts and inject into the theater, organizing popular energy for radical purpose.

What happened to the cinema of attraction[s]? The period from 1907 to about 1913 represents the true *narrativization* of the cinema, culminating in the appearance of feature films which radically revised the variety format. Film clearly took the legitimate theater as its model, producing famous players in famous plays. The transformation of filmic discourse that D.W. Griffith typifies bound cinematic signifiers to the narration of stories and the creation of a self-enclosed diegetic universe. The look at the camera becomes taboo and the devices of cinema are transformed from playful "tricks" – cinematic attractions (Méliès gesturing at us to watch the lady vanish) – to elements of dramatic expression, entries into the psychology of character and the world of fiction.

However, it would be too easy to see this as a Cain and Abel story, with narrative strangling the nascent possibilities of a young iconoclastic form of entertainment. Just as the variety format in some sense survived in the movie palaces of the 1920s (with newsreel, cartoon, sing-along, orchestra performance and sometimes vaudeville acts subordinated to, but still coexisting with, the narrative *feature* of the evening), the system of attraction remains an essential part of popular filmmaking.

The chase film shows how, towards the end of this period (basically from 1903 to 1906), a synthesis of attractions and narrative was already underway. The chase had been the original truly narrative genre of the cinema, providing a model for causality and linearity as well as a basic editing continuity. A film like Biograph's PERSONAL (1904, the model for the chase film in many ways) shows the creation of a narrative linearity, as the French nobleman runs for his life from the fiancées his personal column ad has unleashed. However, at the same time, as the group of young women pursue their prey towards the camera in each shot, they encounter some slight obstacle (a fence, a steep slope, a stream) that slows them down for the spectator, providing a mini-spectacle pause in the unfolding of narrative. The Edison Company seemed particularly aware of this, since they offered their plagiarized version of this Biograph film (HOW A FRENCH NOBLEMAN GOT A WIFE THROUGH THE NEW YORK HERALD PERSONAL COLUMNS) in two forms, as a complete film or as separate shots, so that any one image of the ladies chasing the man could be bought without the inciting incident or narrative closure.[15]

As Laura Mulvey has shown in a very different context, the dialectic between spectacle and narrative has fuelled much of the classical cinema.[16] Donald Crafton in his study of slapstick comedy, "The Pie and the Chase," has shown the way slapstick did a balancing act between the pure spectacle of gag and the development of narrative.[17] Likewise, the [traditional] spectacle film [...] proved true to its name by highlighting moments of pure visual stimulation along with narrative. The 1924 version of BEN HUR was in fact shown at a Boston theater with a timetable announcing the moment of its prime attractions:

8:35   The Star of Bethlehem
8:40   Jerusalem Restored
8:59   Fall of the House of Hur
10:29   The Last Supper
10:50   Reunion[18]

The Hollywood advertising policy of enumerating the features of a film, each emblazoned with the command, "See!" shows this primal power of the attraction running beneath the armature of narrative regulation.

We seem far from the avant-garde premises with which this discussion of early cinema began. But it is important that the radical heterogeneity which I find in early cinema not be conceived as a truly oppositional program, one irreconcilable with the growth of narrative cinema. This view is too sentimental and too a-historical. A film like THE GREAT TRAIN ROBBERY (1903) does point in both directions, toward a direct assault on the spectator (the spectacularly enlarged outlaw unloading his pistol in our faces), and towards a linear narrative continuity. This is early film's ambiguous heritage. Clearly in some sense recent spectacle cinema has reaffirmed its roots in stimulus and carnival rides, in what might be called the Spielberg-Lucas-Coppola cinema of effects.

But effects are tamed attractions. Marinetti and Eisenstein understood that they were tapping into a source of energy that would need focusing and intensification to fulfill its revolutionary possibilities. Both Eisenstein and Marinetti planned to exaggerate the impact on the spectator[s], Marinetti proposing to literally glue them to their seats (ruined garments paid for after the performance) and Eisenstein setting firecrackers off beneath them. Every change in film history implies a change in its address to the spectator, and each period constructs its spectator in a new way. Now in a period of American avant-garde cinema in which the tradition of contemplative subjectivity has perhaps run its (often glorious) course, it is possible that this earlier carnival of the cinema, and the methods of popular entertainment, still provide an unexhausted resource – a Coney Island of the avant-garde, whose never dominant but always sensed current can be traced from Méliès through Keaton, through UN CHIEN ANDALOU (1928), and Jack Smith.

Notes

First published in *Wide Angle* 8.3-4 (1986): 63-70; and subsequently, with some variations, in *Early Cinema: Space Frame Narrative*, ed. Thomas Elsaesser (London: British Film Institute, 1990) 56-62. The variations and additions to the original version are put between squared brackets.

1. Fernand Léger, "A Critical Essay on the Plastic Qualities of Abel Gance's Film *The Wheel*," *Functions of Painting*, ed. and intro. Edward Fry, trans. Alexandra Anderson (New York: Viking, 1973) 21.
2. See my articles "The Non-Continuous Style of Early Film," *Cinema 1900-1906*, ed. Roger Holman (Bruxelles: FIAF, 1982) and "An Unseen Energy Swallows Space: The Space in Early Film and its Relation to American Avant Garde Film," *Film Before*

Griffith, ed. John L. Fell (Berkeley: U of California P, 1983) 355-66, and our collaborative paper delivered by M. Gaudreault at the conference at Cerisy on Film History (August 1985) "Le cinéma des premiers temps: un défi à l'histoire du cinéma?" I would also like to note the importance of my discussions with Adam Simon and our hope to further investigate the history and the archaeology of the film spectator.

3. Robert C. Allen, *Vaudeville and Film: 1895-1915, A Study in Media Interaction* (New York: Arno, 1980) 159, 212-13.

4. Georges Méliès, "Importance du scénario," in Georges Sadoul, *Georges Méliès* (Paris: Seghers, 1961) 116 (my translation).

5. Christian Metz, *The Imaginary Signifier: Psychoanalysis and the Cinema*, trans. Celia Britton, Annwyl Williams, Ben Brewster and Alfred Guzzetti (Bloomington: Indiana UP, 1982), particularly 58-80, 91-97.

6. Charles Musser, "American Vitagraph 1897-1901," *Cinema Journal* 22.3 (Spring 1983): 10.

7. Raymond Fielding, "Hale's Tours: Ultrarealism in the Pre-1910 Motion Picture," *Film Before Griffith* 116-30.

8. I wish to thank Ben Brewster for his comments after the original delivery of this paper which pointed out the importance of including this aspect of the cinema of attractions here.

9. S.M. Eisenstein, "How I Became a Film Director," *Notes of a Film Director* (Moscow: Foreign Language Publishing House, n.d.) 16.

10. S.M. Eisenstein, "Montage of Attractions," trans. Daniel Gerould, *The Drama Review* 18.1 (March 1974): 78-79.

11. Eisenstein, "Montage of Attractions" 78-79.

12. Yon Barna, *Eisenstein* (Bloomington: Indiana UP, 1973) 59.

13. F.T. Marinetti, "The Variety Theater [1913]," *Futurist Manifestos*, ed. Umbro Apollonio (New York: Viking, 1973) 127.

14. Michael Davis, *The Exploitation of Pleasure* (New York: Russell Sage Foundation, Dept. of Child Hygiene, Pamphlet, 1911).

15. David Levy, "Edison Sales Policy and the Continuous Action Film 1904-1906," *Film Before Griffith* 207-22.

16. Laura Mulvey, "Visual Pleasure and Narrative Cinema," *Screen* 16.3 (Fall 1975): 6-18.

17. Paper delivered at the FIAF Conference on Slapstick, May 1985, New York City.

18. Nicholas Vardac, *From Stage to Screen: Theatrical Methods from Garrick to Griffith* (New York: Benjamin Blom, 1968) 232.

Rethinking Early Cinema: Cinema of Attractions and Narrativity

Charles Musser

We are in the midst of a multiyear centennial celebration of cinema's beginnings. Motion pictures had their first première just over one hundred years ago, on 9 May 1893, when George M. Hopkins gave a lecture on Thomas A. Edison's new motion picture system, the kinetoscope and kinetograph camera, at the Brooklyn Institute of Arts and Science. When the lecture concluded, at least two twenty-second films were shown: BLACKSMITHING SCENE and HORSE SHOEING. Four hundred people in attendance lined up in front of Edison's peep-hole kinetoscope and one by one looked into the viewer and saw one of these two films.[1] From this date until sometime in 1896, there were a series of moments in which motion pictures cumulatively entered the public sphere and had their initial impact on culture. If the Lumières represent a high point in this process, particularly from a European perspective, as historians we have learned – not only from research but from personal experience – that insights and achievements often occur more or less simultaneously and independently in different places.

Those who study early cinema are also celebrating another anniversary, that of the 1978 Brighton conference sponsored by FIAF (Fédération Internationale des Archives du Film). That conference was really the first time that film scholars from Europe and North America could look systematically at most of the surviving fiction films made between 1900 and 1906. It brought together scholars who had been working in relative isolation and created a critical mass for intellectual inquiry. Moreover, it helped to inaugurate a new relationship between the archives and the larger scholarly community (a relationship today's graduate students might easily take for granted).[2] In the years immediately after Brighton we shared photocopies of motion picture catalogues, letters, and court cases. We traded ideas and speculations, and undertook translations of each other's work. And we sometimes argued and disagreed. This group undertook to explore a history of early motion picture practices that was as yet unwritten, particularly for the United States. Crucially to our endeavor, we rejected the prevailing paradigm that viewed films of the pre-Griffith era as either simpler versions of later classical cinema or naive and often mistaken gropings toward a natural cinematic language. This new history considered these early films as cultural works on their own terms rather than as mere precursors to a subsequent canon of artistic masterpieces. But, and I find this quite fascinating, core differences of approach, understanding, and naming have been present from the outset – from the papers that Tom Gunning, André Gaudreault, Noël Burch and I presented at Brighton. These differences are suggested by the three terms commonly used to name motion picture practices from roughly 1895 to 1907-1908, what John Fell has called "film before Griffith."[3] These terms are early cinema, primitive cinema, and cinema of attractions.

At this moment in our study of the pre-Griffith (before 1908-1909) and pre-classical cinema (before 1920), it seems to me imperative to reflect upon these differences. Can apparent disagreements be clarified or resolved? What, in fact, is at stake? This is not an easy task, particularly since each of these terms is used by numerous scholars who frequently don't mean the same thing. Given the practical limits of this article, I want to focus on one of these terms, "cinema of attractions."

In 1986, my colleague Tom Gunning made an important and highly influential intervention in the film studies field with the publication of his article "The Cinema of Attractions: Early Cinema, Its Spectator and the Avant-Garde." Gunning, in conjunction with André Gaudreault, coined a phrase, the "cinema of attractions," that has enjoyed great popularity and provided important new insights. Until about 1906, Gunning argues, filmmakers used cinema less as a way to tell stories than as a way of presenting views to an audience.[4] In a paragraph added when the essay was republished in Thomas Elsaesser's anthology, Gunning wrote:

> To summarize, the cinema of attractions directly solicits spectator attention, inciting visual curiosity, and supplying pleasure through an exciting spectacle – a unique event, whether fictional or documentary, that is of interest in itself. The attraction to be displayed may also be of a cinematic nature, such as the early close-ups just described, or trick films in which a cinematic manipulation (slow motion, reverse motion, substitution, multiple exposure) provide the film's novelty. Fictional situations tend to be restricted to gags, vaudeville numbers or recreations of shocking or curious incidents (executions, current events). It is the direct address of the audience, in which an attraction is offered to the spectator by a cinema showman, that defines this approach to filmmaking. Theatrical display dominates over narrative absorption, emphasizing the direct stimulation of shock or surprise at the expense of unfolding a story or creating a diegetic universe.[5]

And he remarks in a subsequent article:

> If we consider the sorts of attractions I have examined here in order to investigate their temporality certain insights into the metapsychology of the spectator of early cinema suggest themselves. The sudden flash (or equal sudden curtailing) of an erotic spectacle, the burst into motion of a terroristic locomotive, or the rhythm of appearance, transformation and sudden appearance that rule a magic film, all invoke a spec-

tator whose delight comes from the unpredictability of the instant, a succession of excitements and frustrations whose order can not be predicated by narrative logic and whose pleasures are never sure of being prolonged.[6]

Gunning borrowed the term "attractions" from Soviet filmmaker Sergei Eisenstein, who proposed a kind of cinema based on the "montage of attractions," a juxtaposition or collision of facts or shocks (isolated as individual shots) that had a calculated effect on the audience.[7] Eisenstein had taken this term, in turn, from the fairground. Gunning thus utilized a term that reaffirmed early cinema's affinities with Coney Island and its rides that thrill, disorient, and shock those who visit these heterotopic spaces.[8]

In his several essays on this topic, Gunning examines an array of relevant single-shot films commonly found in the repertoire of pre-1903 cinema: onrushing trains, disrobing women, acrobatic feats, and so forth. I find Gunning's discussion illuminating and helpful when applied to this important strand of cinema, which flourished in vaudeville houses prior to the rise of the story film in 1903-1904; these pre-1903 films were brief and often non-narrative, emphasizing variety and display.[9] It is when he claims both that cinema of attractions characterizes all of pre-1903 cinema and continues to be a dominant feature of the post-1903 period, that I find myself in sharp disagreement. These disagreements have been implicitly acknowledged in Gunning's own work. In emphasizing cinema's non-narrative capacities, Gunning takes aim at a group of historians who examined early cinema from a different perspective.

> The history of early cinema, like the history of cinema generally, has been written and theorized under the hegemony of narrative films. Early filmmakers like Smith, Méliès and Porter have been studied primarily from the viewpoint of their contribution to film as a storytelling medium, particularly the evolution of narrative editing. Although such approaches are not totally misguided, they are one-sided and potentially distort both the work of these filmmakers and the actual forces shaping cinema before 1906.[10]

Although Gunning does not specify these historians, by the fall of 1986, I can only assume he was referring to the work of such scholars as Noël Burch, David Bordwell, Kristin Thompson, Janet Staiger, myself, Martin Sopocy, and even his collaborator André Gaudreault – in short to the wave of post-Brighton scholarship that was then coming out in article form. Gunning's statement reflects differences evident since those initial Brighton essays.

Although Gunning's characterization of my work is basically accurate, I do not want to accept it completely. Even before the publication of Gunning's Brighton essay on the non-continuous style of early film, I had published an article that explored the uses of variety programming for short films, though it also contrasted such practices with the grouping of films by genre or subject and emphasized the exhibitor's potential role in constructing narratives out of a succession of short films. In brief, I saw a range of possibilities for the organization of programs ranging from variety to unified narrative programs.[11] Much of my subsequent work did return to issues of narrative. At this time, many scholars were enamored with the work of Robert Allen, who argued (1) that the story film became a dominant genre as a result of the nickelodeon boom of 1906-1907 rather than acting as a precondition for it; (2) that non-fiction films remained generally popular but were more expensive to make than fiction films; and (3) that production of actualities thus fell off because of some conspiracy among production companies rather than because these films, with a few notable exceptions, no longer sold. Given Allen's influence, basic work in this area had to be done if so-called revisionist scholarship was not going to result in a major step backwards.[12] And to the extent that Gunning cited and used Allen and saw cinema of attractions as dominant until about 1906, his argument was premised on some of the very work against which I necessarily argued.

In Gunning's initial formulation, the relations between narrative and attractions in early cinema take three somewhat different forms:

A. Films that are essentially non-narrative. These lack a beginning, middle, and end, even as they provide moments of display, shock, or pleasure. Two potentially familiar examples suffice: first, the non-fiction actuality S.S. "COPTIC" RUNNING AGAINST THE STORM (1898) is a single-shot film taken from the deck of an ocean vessel as it plows into one billowing wave after another; second, in OLD MAID IN THE DRAWING ROOM (1901, copyrighted as OLD MAID IN A HORSE CAR), female impersonator Gilbert Sarony – dressed as a "the giddy girl" – talks directly to the camera in a medium close-up. In each film we can find no recognizable change or progression. The waves are no different at the end of S.S. "COPTIC" than at the beginning, and Sarony goes through a non-stop repertoire of gestures that seem to lead us nowhere. In the first film the audience is placed in a position of apparent danger as we vicariously experience the shot. There is a discrepancy between the position of the seated spectator seeking pleasure and amusement in a theater and the cameraman's "point of view" and experience. The spectator becomes a surrogate passenger who feels the tension between the safety and comfort of his or her seat and the dangers of the milieu in which he or she is transported as hypothetical traveler. Mobilizing this "absence of presence" is one way in which S.S. "COPTIC" RUNNING AGAINST THE STORM functions as an attraction.

B. Gags and one-shot mini narratives. According to Gunning, "Fictional situations tend to be restricted to gags, vaudeville numbers or recreations of shocking or curious incidents (executions, current events)."[13] One classic example of the gag film is L'ARROSEUR ARROSÉ (1895), the sprinkler sprinkled, or as it was commonly known in the United States, THE GARDENER AND THE BAD BOY. The bad boy blocks the water from going through the hose. When the gardener looks into the nozzle, the boy unblocks the hose and sprays him. Single-shot gag films remained common through 1903, after which even the shorts began to include more than one shot.[14]

C. Films in which display, exhibitionism and spectacle take precedence over narrative. Gunning proposes to unite the Lumières and Méliès "in a conception that sees cinema less as a way of telling stories than as a way of presenting a series of views to an audience."[15] For Gunning, Méliès's LE VOYAGE DANS LA LUNE (1902) exemplifies the kind of film for which "the story simply provides a frame upon which to string a demonstration of the magical possibilities of the cinema."[16] However, many other films might easily conform to this pattern, for instance LIFE OF AN AMERICAN FIREMAN (1903) and THE GAY SHOE CLERK (1903).

I. Attractions and the Story Film

Each of these three forms poses interesting problems that need to be explored in greater depth than I can do here, but I will at least begin the process by examining the last one first. What is the relationship between pure exhibitionism and storytelling in these films? Gunning turns to Georges Méliès, who wrote:

> As for the scenario, the "fable" or "tale," I only consider it at the end. I can state that the scenario constructed in this manner has *no importance*, since I use it merely as a pretext for the "stage effects," the "tricks," or for a nicely arranged tableau.[17]

For Méliès, the story of A TRIP TO THE MOON may have been only an excuse for his magical tricks, but for his audiences it was a crucial one. A simple review of Méliès's promotional material for these films shows that he emphasized *both* the story and the spectacular way in which the story was being presented. BLUE BEARD (1901) was described as "a great fairy drama, with spectacular tableaux"; the material for A TRIP TO THE MOON provides short descriptions for thirty scenes that cumulatively emphasize the story.[18] A comparison with today's special-effects artists might be helpful. They are often enthralled with pyrotechnics and completely uninterested in the larger story, but that does not mean audiences dismiss the stories of these science fiction films – though critics of JURASSIC PARK, for example, admittedly wish it were possible to do so. The compelling nature and realization of A TRIP TO THE MOON's story accounts to a significant degree for its international success, then and today. Comments from Keith vaudeville house managers support this view. When Vitagraph's exhibition service replaced Biograph's in the spring of 1903, the quality of the projected images declined; but in contrast to the previous programming of miscellaneous views, Vitagraph offered compelling story films. Méliès's A Trip to the Moon and other narrative films were clearly hits, and often made other programming choices appear weak.

> [Boston:] 19 min. Splendid lot of pictures, every one of the scenes being applauded, that portraying scene in Hans Christian Anderson's fairy story, "The Little Match Seller," making a particularly big hit. Great improvement on the biograph.[19]

> [New York:] They gave us two or three views this afternoon of rather mediocre quality, and then presented "The Trip to the Moon" which is really the best moving picture film which I have ever seen. It held the audience to the finish and was received with a hearty round of applause.[20]

> [Boston:] Another corking lot of motion pictures, every one of which were applauded. I retained "Jack and the Beanstalk" for the benefit of the children, and better value would be obtained in all houses of the circuit if this policy were pursued, as it only gives them time to be talked about during the first week.[21]

> [New York:] I do not think that the selection of views this week is hardly up to the standard. It consists of a series of pictures of the Swiss Alps, and naturally was a little monotonous.[22]

> [Philadelphia:] A fair selection of views. We miss "The Trip to the Moon."[23]

> [Boston:] 20 min. Excellent lot of pictures, the principal being a series illustrating "Little Red Riding Hood," which proved as interesting and amusing to older folks as it did to the children.[24]

These reports are symptomatic of the often-noted "rise of the story film," which reached a critical breakthrough point around 1903-1904. If this understanding of developments in early film practice is part of traditional historiography (written by Lewis Jacobs, Georges Sadoul, Jean Mitry) now in general disrepute, this particular piece of analysis nonetheless remains fundamentally valid.

Gunning ultimately sees spectacle/attractions and narrative operating quite independently in a wide range of films. Narrative may sometimes provide a kind of container for attractions but it is the attractions that ultimately provide the film's substance, its kick. Narrative traces can be discerned, for instance, in certain trick films, but Gunning contends that the unpredictable succession of transformations offers the genre's *raison d'être*. But when it comes to films such as A Trip to the Moon, is it the narrative that we enjoy or is it some visual pleasure independent of the story? Formulated in this way, the question is one of figure and ground. However, the question of pleasure might be reformulated so that attractions and narrative are effectively imbricated, even integrated: the *coups de théâtre* that Méliès loved are typically integral to the narrative, giving it substance.

Méliès's cinematic dexterity performs a narrative function. For instance, in the space scene, the camera dolly suggests that the rocket ship approaches the moon. The earthling scientists who swat the Selenites (i.e. the moon's inhabitants) out of existence do not do so in a way that defies narrative logic – or issues of power, race, and ideology. The Selenites strongly resemble the "primitive peoples" who were then being subjected to European imperialism. And if we accompany these scientists to the moon we do so not by rocket ship but via another technological wonder – the cinema. Scantily clad women do more than just display their sexuality. They load the huge gun and cheer as the space capsule is discharged into the sky, in a scene that begs for interrogation from feminist and psychoanalytic perspectives; moreover, the action in these scenes lampoons certain kinds of public rituals (such as ship launchings) in ways that cannot be fully appreciated if the intimate interrelationship between attraction and narrative action is not acknowledged. This is not the moment to offer an extensive analysis of A Trip to the Moon (something that still needs to be done). But if the tale was a pretext for Méliès as he began work on the film, it seems to me *integrally* important at the end.

There is a great deal at stake in our different approaches, and it becomes apparent in the contrast between Gunning's and my analyses of Edwin Porter's work, epitomized by three films: The Gay Shoe Clerk (1903), The Great Train Robbery (1903), and The Kleptomaniac (1905). Among other things, our contrasting interpretations of these films point to some of the failures of cinema of attractions as a concept for generalizing about early cinema as a whole. Porter certainly did not work in absolute opposition to cinema of attractions – he made plenty of short, essentially non-narrative films in his very first years as a filmmaker. However, we miss something essential if we do not explore his methods of storytelling, the way these narratives were articulated in early cinema's changing, never completely stable system of representation, and the meanings these films were likely to generate for audiences. As I understand it, Gunning argues not that we cannot locate a story in these films but that the representational techniques mobilized in these films evidence other concerns. The films lack any real interest in narrativity. For the moment I wish to turn to The Gay Shoe Clerk. Gunning has argued in several places that this is a film in which story plays little or no role – that the film, and the close-up of the woman's ankle, is about erotic display and revelation:

The close-up cut into Porter's THE GAY SHOE CLERK may anticipate later continuity techniques, but its principle motive is again pure exhibitionism, as the lady lifts her skirt hem, exposing her ankle for all to see.[25]

However in many of these films the cut-in functions as a scarcely narrativized attraction, an enlargement of a cute kitten (THE LITTLE DOCTOR) [...] an erotic glimpse of a lady's ankle (THE GAY SHOE CLERK) rather than a detail essential to the story.[26]

The contrast between these films [THE GAY SHOE CLERK is one of two mentioned] of erotic display in which story plays little or no role and the narrativization of eroticism in a melodrama like THE LONELY VILLA is significant.[27]

There is no doubt that we are dealing with an "attraction" here in some form – the presumably titillating view of the woman's ankle. Even here, however, it operates within a quite complex narrative unfolding as the shoe clerk – as well as the spectator – wonders how far up her calf the girl will pull her skirt. This tease thus has real narrative significance: it is a way for the young woman to signal her erotic interest to the salesman. And it is done ostensibly for his benefit alone (she does not acknowledge the camera or the spectator). As a result of this exchange of signals, the shoe clerk caresses her ankle and when this is permitted he leans over and they kiss. For narrative purposes, the raised skirt and the shoe clerk's caress are best done in close-up. At the same time, the erotic charge for the spectator is acknowledged and highlighted by setting the shot against a plain white background. Certainly, direct erotic display is an important factor in the film but nonetheless is grossly insufficient for explaining the complexity of even this single shot, never mind the larger three-shot comedy.

The comedy as a whole tells the story of the younger generation sneaking a mutual kiss right under the nose of the girl's chaperon. When that matron somewhat belatedly becomes aware of this transaction, she asserts her generational authority to chastise the lovers and censor our voyeuristic pleasure. On one hand, the close-up is strongly marked by the voyeurism of both cameraman and hypothetical male spectator – raising the kinds of issues articulated by Laura Mulvey regarding scopophilia and its uses in narrative film.[28] While the shoe clerk can touch and even kiss the girl (though he ultimately gets punished), the male viewer merely sees but runs no risk of chastisement. He can enjoy the shoe clerk's fate in contrast to his own safety. On the other hand, the close-up delimits a space which only the lovers (i.e. not the chaperon) share. There is a tension here between patriarchy (the shot as an explicit manifestation of male voyeurism) and sexual equality (a private space shared equally by the two lovers). We can only gain an adequate appreciation of this interplay if we recognize the important role of narrative and the way it operates throughout the film, including the close-up.[29] To summarize: story plays a central role in THE GAY SHOE CLERK rather than being of "little or no importance," as Gunning has asserted; the close-up enhances narrative clarity and in fact has expressive features; and in this instance, the girl does not raise her skirt "for all to see" since clearly the chaperon is not meant to see this gesture nor does the young woman in any way signal her awareness of the camera or a hypothetical audience. THE GAY SHOE CLERK participated in the story film's ascendancy in 1903. Although not the strongest example given its brevity, it certainly represents a sharp break from such erotic displays of female undress as TRAPEZE DISROBING ACT (Porter, 1902).[30]

II. Gags, Attractions, and Narrative

I wish to turn next to the problem of the short gag films. Rather than seeing gags as mini-narratives, Gunning opposes the two – the spectacle of gags and the story. This argument owes something to two sources, the first of which is an audacious paper by Donald Crafton on slapstick comedy that characterizes the pie (which he calls non-narrative gag) and the chase (or narrative). In Crafton's discussion of HIS WOODEN WEDDING, the gag is constantly interrupting the advance of narrative with moments of spectacle. Gags indeed may delay or disrupt narrative but these gags are typically micro-narratives coming from another trajectory or operating another level.[31] Another source for Gunning's argument seems to be André Gaudreault article "Film, Narrative, Narration," which argues that narrative operates on two levels, monstration (level one, involving showing) and narration (level two, involving telling). To the extent that cinema is a succession of film frames that show x as it changes in time, Gaudreault asserted in "Film, Narrative, Narration" that all films have narrative, whether they be LE DÉJEUNER DE BÉBÉ or L'ARROSEUR ARROSÉ. "Thus when cinema is said to have taken 'the narrative road' at a certain moment in its history," Gaudreault argued that "this is not the 'innate' kind of narrativity just described, but the second level."[32] In an argument that Eisenstein would certainly have appreciated, this second level is dependent on the sequencing of spatio-temporal fragments or shots. It is only on this second level that a film can be said to have narration and a narrator, that the story is told. From this observation Gaudreault concluded, "L'ARROSEUR ARROSÉ (and any other film made in one shot) comprises a single narrative layer; despite the symmetry in its action, it does not have a second level of narrativity. [...] The film shows no sign of any intervention by the narrator (whose discourse, or narration, comes from the articulation between shots)."[33]

Although juxtaposing shots is certainly an important way for a narrating presence to assert itself, such a narrational voice would seem to be at work even with one-shot actuality films. The choice of subject matter, camera position and the framing of the picture, the decision to show this moment and not some other – to start at moment x and stop at moment y – all imply the presence of a narrator who is telling us what to see, what to look for, and from what perspective. Bazin taught us this – so did Hitchcock's ROPE. But a gag is also a narrative that is constructed profilmicly. Noël Burch has responded to Gaudreault's position in *Life to Those Shadows* by arguing for the minimum conditions of narrative as defined by Propp: beginning-continuation-conclusion, "which can, of course, all be contained in a single shot, and are as in L'ARROSEUR ARROSÉ."[34] Again, if L'ARROSEUR ARROSÉ is cinema of attractions it is not because narrative plays a less important role in relationship to exhibitionism or display. In instances such as these, I support Miriam Hansen's "wish to de-emphasize the opposition between narrative and non-narrative film that sustains [Gunning's] argument."[35] Here the film's brevity and its place in a variety format are crucial to its function as an isolated attraction. When such a film is followed by another picture on an unrelated topic and made by a different company, the film's narrational presence is erased before it is effectively established, before the spectator becomes fully oriented. (The introduction of multi-shot films within a program forced a differentiation between editing on one hand – in which the coherence of filmic narration is assumed across the cut – and programming on the other, in which such coherence is assumed not to occur.) In this respect, one-shot gag films have much in common with other short non-narrative films of the 1890s.

III. Non-Narrative Films of the 1890s

Using Burch's evocation of certain minimum conditions of narrative, we can still see, however, that there are many, many early films that do not meet these conditions. Consider, for example, the numerous Edison films of the Spanish-American War (1898): actualities of American battleships in the Dry Tortugas off of Florida, of the sunken battleship "Maine" in Havana Harbor, or of U.S. troops feeding their horses or milling around in a train. These individual shots do not provide a beginning, middle, or end in the way that L'ARROSEUR ARROSÉ does. This also holds true for travel views showing street scenes or waterfalls, and for serpentine dances. An almost endless number of early films can be identified that are not under the sway of narrative. Do these films, which quite possibly dominated film production in the 1890s, constitute the basis for a cinema of attractions? Certainly they constitute one basis, but here again the situation is not so simple.

Grasping the nature of cinema's production methods in the late 1890s is crucial to understanding the possibilities both for cinema's use of attractions and for sustained narrative. In this period creative responsibilities were divided between motion picture producers and exhibitors. What we now call postproduction was almost completely in the hands of the exhibitors. Producers generally made and marketed one-shot films to exhibitors. These showmen selected their pictures from a vast array of possibilities, controlling the duration of a given film in many instances (not only through projection speed but in deciding the amount of film footage they would buy of a particular film – in this period films could often be purchased in several lengths). They would then organize these films into programs that could assume a wide range of forms. At one extreme was the variety format. Short films were shown in an order that was not so much random as would create maximum effect by juxtaposition. Inevitably certain non-narrative associations would be formed in the process.[36] In a Biograph program for October 1896, UPPER RAPIDS OF NIAGARA FALLS was shown, followed several films later by another shot of the American falls. The first Niagara Falls scene was juxtaposed to a fire scene, the second to a scene of a child being given a bath in a small tub. Each offers a different contrast. Biograph put two films of William McKinley at the end of this program, assigning special importance to the presidential candidate. Applause that Biograph could expect at the conclusion of its exhibition would double for the Republican candidate and vice versa. This program also contained several excellent examples of cinema of attractions: in one film, images of the Empire State Express train assault the spectator while in another, A HARD WASH, the action is in medias res and frontally arranged against a white background. Shock and disruption did not only depend on the individual images themselves but also on the way they were juxtaposed. The arrangement of shots, the program, maximized the possibilities of cinema of attractions that were inherent in the films.

Other, very different arrangements of films were possible. Consider a sequence of Spanish-American War pictures assembled by Lyman Howe. Here a series of a dozen films begins with troops parading through the streets prior to leaving for the front. The sequence of shots follows them to Tampa, Florida, then to Cuba, and finally culminates with "a thrilling war scene." Not insignificantly, this progression is interrupted by a group of lantern slides that provide desirable, related images unavailable on film: few film programs in this era presented only motion pictures. An exhibitor such as Dwight Elmendorf juxtaposed slides and films in an integrated manner for his evening-length, narratively structured program *The Santiago Campaign*. Both Elmendorf and Howe combined their images not only with music but with effects and a lecturer's live narration. If later films have what Gunning and others call a *filmic* narrator, these programs each have a *cinematic* narrator. The showman in his capacity as exhibitor provided a dominant narrating presence, shaping if not creating meaning even as he organized the diverse, perhaps miscellaneous elements of narration, already present in the individual shots, into a more or less coherent form.

With their quite elaborate narratives, these programs (particularly Elmendorf's) cannot be called cinema of attractions without broadening the term's meaning to the point where it has lost virtually all of its specificity. In terms of its representational effectiveness, Elmendorf's illustrated lecture bears many similarities with voice-over documentaries of the 1950s, though his program lacked standardization and its postproduction elements were recreated every night in the process of exhibition. This demonstrates the real limitations of looking at films from this period as autonomous or self-contained. Such films may appear to be non-narrative, but in the process of becoming cinema, that is, as part of a larger program of projected motion pictures for an audience, they often came to function in a radically different manner – as components of narrative. A film that acted as an isolated, discrete, non-narrative moment in one program was routinely integrated into a larger narrative in another.

IV. Periodization within Early Cinema

Although comparatively broad terms such as primitive cinema, early cinema, and cinema of attractions are useful in helping us make sense of cinema's one-hundred-year history, they can be deceptive in that they direct our attention toward a radical shift in production methods, representational practices, and the relationship between spectator and screen that occurred in roughly 1907-1908, obscuring early shifts in cinematic production and representation that need to be underscored. The Brighton conference of 1978 achieved much, but it also had a few notable shortcomings. It drew our attention away from the 1890s and encouraged us to think of the pre-Griffith cinema as a single period. It also kept our attention focused on fiction film when actualities were the dominant form until around 1903-1904. While many characteristics of early cinema allow us to see 1895 to 1907-1908 as a unified period – as I have argued elsewhere it was only in early 1908 that cinema met conventional criteria for mass communication – important changes in representation occurred at earlier points along the way.[37] In what follows, I sketch three periods or shifts.

One. The novelty period of cinema lasted a year or so, from late 1895 to early 1897 – one theatrical season. While the fit is not perfect, cinema as novelty and the cinema of attractions are very closely allied. Within this general framework, however, there was significant variation, for instance between the vitascope, which showed loops, and the cinématographe or biograph projectors, which did not. When film loops were shown on a vitascope, it often meant that a scene was shown at least six times (a film lasted twenty seconds, and it took two minutes to take a film off a projector and thread on a new one; to give a continuous show with two projectors thus required such repetition). Certainly the repetitious quality of film loops tended to obliterate narrative. Whatever nascent signs of narrativity one might find in THE MAY IRWIN KISS or CHINESE LAUNDRY SCENE were effectively squelched, even as the qualities of display and exhibitionism were further foregrounded. On the other hand, the gemlike brevity of the film tended to be weakened by this repetition. In the biograph, these tendencies were typically reversed since films could not be repeated (except the last one, which could be shown in reverse). The Lumière cinématographe did not utilize loops but because the exhibitor showed each film separately (the strands of film were allowed to fall into a basket rather than be wound up on a reel), the scene could be repeated if the audience so demanded.

This novelty period was extremely brief, like attractions themselves. A few days of screenings in smaller towns often sufficed. The decline of novelty meant the decline of loops. Although they continued in a kind of residual capacity into 1898, precocious if limited instances of sequencing images appeared as early as December 1896. By then Lyman Howe had acquired three different films which he ordered to tell the simple story of a fire rescue: (1) responding to the alarm of fire; (2) firemen at work, the rescue; (3) burning stables and rescue of horses. To keep novelty alive, some exhibitors moved beyond simple cinema of attractions quite quickly. Narrative sequencing became an "attraction" – though not strictly a cinema of attractions in that the succession of shots was determined by a narrative logic.[38] (In general filmmakers have constantly looked for novelty and an array of subjects, themes, and cinematic devices that will grab the spectators' attention.)

Two. A second period lasted from about 1897 until about 1901 or 1903. During this period creative responsibilities were shared by production company and exhibitor. As I have already noted, many aspects of the cinema of attractions continued in the variety format of exhibition. However, a second tendency emerged which reasserted certain established traditions within screen practice: exhibitors sequenced films into narrative-based programs of greater or lesser complexity or length. Here I would like to make a point of clarification and distinction in the way that Gunning appears to understand this. The selection and sequencing of subjects is not "re-editing."[39] Richard Koszarski has detailed the ways exhibitors re-edited their films in the 1920s. Rather, this sequencing into programs is "editing" at a point before that process came under the principal control of the production company. In the 1890s, the functions of programming (embodied by the variety form of exhibition) and of editing (the construction of narrative through the juxtaposition of shots and scenes) were not yet differentiated. The exhibitor played both roles. Narrative sequencing was one option and became increasingly common. Between about 1899 and 1903, editorial responsibilities were increasingly centralized in the production company, while programming remained in the hands of the exhibitor (though this responsibility was later shared with the film distributor).

In his essay, "Now You See It, Now You Don't," Gunning has implicitly retreated from some of the broader characterizations of the pre-Griffith cinema as cinema of attractions, treating it more as a strand or element of early cinema. There he acknowledges that cinema of attractions does "not build its incidents into the configuration with which a story makes its individual moments cohere. In effect, attractions have one basic temporality, that of the alteration of presence/absence which is embodied in the act of display."[40] Film programs based on variety, such an Eberhard Schneider vaudeville program that alternated war views with other scenes, acted in this manner. Schneider constructed attractions out of these short films while Lyman Howe constructed narratives. Here we see the rich diversity of early cinema exhibition, one that defies any simple categorization. Although cinema of attractions operated most effectively within a variety format and had obvious affinities with vaudeville, even in the 1890s vaudeville exhibition services certainly did not always construct their programs using variety principles and did not always produce programs that could be characterized as cinema of attractions.[41]

It is perhaps helpful to situate an understanding of these two ways of making cinema into the context of pre-Brighton historiography. Consider a statement by Lewis Jacobs from *The Rise of the American Film* (1939):

> By 1902 Porter had a long list of films to his credit. But neither he nor other American producers had yet learned to tell a story. They were busy with elementary, one-shot news events (PRESIDENT MCKINLEY'S INAUGURATION, MCKINLEY'S FUNERAL CORTEGE, THE COLUMBIA AND SHAMROCK YACHT RACES, THE JEFFRIES-RHULIN SPARRING CONTEST, THE GALVESTON CYCLONE), with humorous bits (GRANDMA AND GRANDPA series, HAPPY HOOLIGAN series, OLD MAID series), with vaudeville skits (cooch dancers, magicians, acrobats), scenic views (A TRIP THROUGH THE COLUMBIA EXPOSITION), and local topics (parades, fire departments in action, shoppers in the streets). None of these productions stood out from the general; literal and unimaginative, they are significant today mainly as social documents.[42]

Gunning has played a key role in articulating how the films in Jacobs's descriptive categories are full of imagination and surprise. He accounts for much of the pleasure in viewing them today as then. Yet in other respects, Gunning con-

forms to Jacobs's paradigm by emphasizing early cinema's non-narrative dimensions (in part by equating story films or sustained fictional narratives with
narrative itself). In the process, both have neglected the exhibitor's potential
role as editor, as constructor of narrative, as narrator and author of sustained
programs. One of my principal goals has been to show how exhibitors took
these short films and often transformed them into something that was more
complex and sophisticated than Jacobs ever imagined – to open up a dimension
of early cinema that has been not only neglected but virtually suppressed. My
goals potentially complement Gunning's, but to ignore one aspect of exhibitor-
dominated cinema at the expense of the other is to impoverish our understanding of 1890s cinema. For whatever reason, Gunning's evaluative inversion of
Jacobs has been easier for scholars to grasp – perhaps because they can simply
see it on the screen while the assessment I am making can only be established
through sustained historical examination of primary course materials.

When seeking to understand better the diversity and complexity of 1890s cinema, scholars should consider two important film genres that do not readily fit
into the cinema-of-attractions paradigm: Passion plays and fight films. These
genres are significant because they were very popular and involved the representation of sustained narratives. The impact of photography and motion pictures on the Passion play, which I have traced elsewhere through a series of
historical instances,[43] inevitably evokes the work of the Frankfurt School, particularly Walter Benjamin and his discussion of aura and authenticity in "The
Work of Art in the Age of Mechanical Reproduction." The work of art, Benjamin remarks, has its basis in ritual, the location of its original use value. For all
artwork, this ritual can be traced back to religious origins. The fight over the
Passion play in nineteenth-century America was precisely a fight over its ritual
significance; evangelical Protestants refused to accept the Passion as a suitable
subject for dramatic treatment on the stage. The weight of tradition had not yet
given way. Whether performed in Horitz or Oberammergau, the Passion play's
intimate relation to religious ritual and event made it much more than a work of
art. First photography and then cinematography extracted these presentations
from their religious setting and so "emancipate[d] the work of art from its para-
sitical dependence on ritual"; the cathartic effects produced by filmed images
results in the "liquidation of the traditional value of the cultural heritage."[44] As
reproductions of a religious-based ritual, these films freed the Passion play from
the weight of tradition and soon enabled it to function both in the artistic sphere
and beyond it. It allowed avatars of urban commercial popular culture to appropriate a subject that had previously resisted easy incorporation into a capi-
talist economy and modern culture.

Fight films evidence a similar trajectory. Prizefighting was illegal in every
state of union during the early 1890s, and in one instance a heavyweight cham-

pionship bout was staged just on the south side of the US-Mexican border. Because films of such events were only representations, their exhibition was considered legal. The legality of such films soon undermined the prohibition of live encounters. This legalization of boxing, in turn, enabled it to be incorporated into the entertainment industry with films of such events making boxing a profitable sport per se (before legalization, successful fighters made most of their money as actors on the stage). The kinds of disjunctions and slippages in the public sphere that Miriam Hansen has discussed from a Frankfurt School perspective are particularly evident in the cinematic exhibition and reception of Passion play and prize fights.[45] This phenomenon of liberation stands in distinct but dialectical relationship to many aspects of the cinema of attractions.

These two genres, like the illustrated lecture, generally involved a direct address of the audience as the showman typically stood by the screen and delivered a spoken commentary during the exhibition. Nevertheless, these extended programs often created a diegetic universe and encouraged narrative absorption on the part of the spectator. A reviewer for the *Boston Herald* described his gradual absorption into the world depicted in THE HORITZ PASSION PLAY:

> At first the spectator thinks of the pictures only as a representation of a representation – regards them in the light of an effort to show how the peasants at Horitz acted their "Passion Play." It therefore seems in order to attend to the way in which the effects are being produced to calculate the probable speed of the machine, and watch for the right focussing of the images. This one can do at one's ease while Prof. Lacy is sketching, in the style of a literary artist, the environs of Horitz, as such pictures as "The Village Street," "The Stone Cutters," "Peasants Working the Fields," and "The Passion-Spielhaus" fall upon the screen.
>
> But when the play begins there is a new mental attitude toward the representation. The thought that one is gazing at a mere pictorial representation seems to pass away, and in its place there comes, somehow or other, the notion that the people seen are real people, and that on the screen there are moving the very men and women who acted the "Passion Play" last summer in the Bohemian forest for the delight of thousands of foreigners.
>
> [...]
>
> Then the players begin to depict the birth and life of Christ, and with this change of subject there comes a new change of mental attitude. So absorbing becomes the interest of the pictures that the onlooker, from merely regarding the figures of the real, live people who acted the play in Bohemia, begins to forget all about what was done in Bohemia and henceforth is lost in the thought that the faces and forms before him are the real people who lived in Palestine 2000 years ago, and with their own eyes witnessed the crucifixion of Christ.[46]

When the Corbett-Fitzsimmons fight was shown in Boston six months before, a reviewer likewise remarked on "the intense interest of the story the pictures told," particularly as Corbett was being counted out by the refer. "The agony he suffered when [...] he found he had not the power to regain his feet, was so apparent that many men as well as women found this as dramatic a situation as they had ever experienced and as real."[47] This spectator's immersion into the diegetic world, of course, is in contrast to his/her response to a kaleidoscope of images offered by the variety format. Even in the 1890s there was a wide range of relationships between spectator and screened images. With the rise of the story film coinciding with the introduction of the three-blade shutter (1903), which reduced the flicker effect, the spectator potentially achieved a new level of sustained attention.

This is to argue that cinema served a wide range of functions, particularly in the 1890s; as Robert C. Allen has pointed out, cinema was often referred to as a visual newspaper.[48] The notion of a visual newspaper may favor a variety format but does not necessarily exclude narrative logic. In many instances, filmmakers seemed very concerned about the full reporting of a news story, coordinating several crews to cover the unfolding of important events such as New York's reception for Admiral George Dewey (1899) or the funeral of President William McKinley (1901). I have also suggested, following the work of Neil Harris, that Lyman Howe used elements of surprise and shock characteristic of cinema of attractions but then incorporated them into an overarching "cinema of reassurance."[49] Cinema of attractions was a prominent feature of American cinema of the 1890s but not necessarily the primary or dominant one (as was the case during the novelty period). To characterize American cinema of the 1890s as "cinema of attractions" is to move other equally essential aspects of early cinema to the periphery. My goal has been to understand the dialectics of film representation in a way that has something in common with André Bazin's look at feature films of the late 1940s. On one hand he celebrated the Italian Neo-Realism of Vittorio De Sica and Roberto Rossellini, while on the other he praised the cinematographic theater of Jean Cocteau, Lawrence Olivier, and Orson Welles with its faithfulness to theatrical stylization.

Three. A third period of early cinema emerged as editorial control gradually shifted from exhibitor to producer. This shift, which centralized basic kinds of narrative responsibility inside the production company, was protracted both because it met with some resistance by exhibitors who saw their prerogatives challenged and because it required conceptual rethinking on the part of producers. The entire process, which can be said to divide the larger history of screen practice into two parts, spanned roughly four years, from 1899 to 1903, though residual aspects of the old ways remained apparent for many years thereafter. The shift from filmmaking practices heavily inflected by actuality production to an emphasis on fiction contributed significantly to this achievement. Although this centralization of control allowed for greater efficiencies in production, it was most important in *allowing for a new kind of storytelling*, often involving the overlapping of actions from one scene to the next – that is, it made possible such films as A Trip to the Moon and Life of an American Fireman. Porter seems to have felt, and I concur, that this introduction of new levels of continuity was a revolution in cinematic storytelling. This is a period that could indeed be called a period of narrative integration, a period in which the filmmaker as creative artist became a reality. We can talk about Porter and Méliès as filmmakers in a way that is not really appropriate for cameramen of the 1890s such as James White or William Paley.[50] In short, I would argue that the process of narrative integration – which required the centralization of production and postproduction – was completed in most of its essential features by 1904-1905, rather than 1906-1909.

By 1904 multi-shot narrative filmmaking became the dominant type of film production for major companies – not of course within the representational framework of Griffith or classical Hollywood cinema but within a quite different representational system of its own. Some films from as early as 1899 – Love and War (Edison) or The Tramp's Dream (Lubin) – were harbingers of this system, and we can find many examples by 1901 or 1902, from Stop Thief! (Williamson, 1901) to Execution of Czologsz (Edison, 1901). Multi-shot narrative filmmaking continued until this system of early cinema went into crisis around 1907-1908. Here we need to focus on the range of possibilities within that system. Certainly there was a tension between spectacle or attractions on one hand and narrative on the other, but the result of this interplay was a kind of syncretic storytelling that utilized its own distinctive temporality and continuity which involved overlapping action and narrative repetition as well as ellipsis and occasional match cuts (as in The Escaped Lunatic). Such diversity need not imply incoherence; the existence of a range of techniques within early cinema's system of representation privileged a flexible temporality.

Because Gunning, at least in his book *D.W. Griffith and the Origins of the American Narrative Film,* is too eager to see the films from 1903 to 1907 as part of an era of cinema of attractions, he downplays the role of narrative, narration, and the filmic narrator in the films of that period, particularly in those of Edwin Porter. In the opening chapter of his book on Griffith, Gunning remarks:

> no narrative film can exist except through its narrative discourse. It logically follows that every narrative film has a filmic narrator embodied by this discourse. [...] Therefore the filmic narrator appears in a wide range of forms determined by specific choices.[51]

In the 1897-1901 period, the exhibitor acted as the principle *cinematic* narrator and his presence was strongly felt in the narratives that he constructed, not only through the selection and arrangement of films and slides but with a lecture and the introduction of music and effects. Even when confronted with elements of narration that were beyond his control, that were determined by the camera-man, the exhibitor structured them in such a way as to give them relative coherence and unity.

If the post-1901 period can be characterized as one of increasing narrative integration, when cinematic narration became filmic narration, and as one that culminated with a distinctive system of representation involving a *filmic* narrator, then these films will have a narrating presence or voice. To be sure, some aspects of narration were still delegated to the exhibitor – particularly music and effects. And some films, at least, were designed for verbal accompaniment – either for a lecture or for actors providing dialogue from behind the screen. Porter and other producers, however, typically signaled at least some of the verbal contributions they imagined might enhance the film exhibition through catalogue descriptions. To downplay the methods of narration and the presence of a cinematic/filmic narrator in Porter's pre-Griffith films (in terms of tense, mood, voice) is to minimize the importance of narrative in these films and stack the deck in Griffith's favor.[52] This is what Gunning does, not only with THE GAY SHOE CLERK but THE GREAT TRAIN ROBBERY and THE KLEPTOMANIAC.

Here Gunning, while seeming to acknowledge that these films may contain narratives, argues that the filmmaker is little concerned with storytelling per se and is much more interested in using these stories as opportunities to present attractions. The proof of this relative lack of narrativity is an underdeveloped narration, the effective lack of a sustained, coherent system of narration in the pre-Griffith period. For instance, about THE GREAT TRAIN ROBBERY, Gunning writes that it

> exemplifies the non-moralizing aspect of pre-Griffith cinema. At no point does the narrative discourse of the film create empathy for the characters or moral judgements about their actions. Porter filmed the violence of bandits and posse with equal detachment.[53]

About the famed close-up of the bandit chief Barnes firing his six-gun into the audience, Gunning asserts that

> Such introductory shots thus played no role in the temporal development of the story and simply introduce a major character outside of the action of the film.[54]

But within early cinema's system of representation, this close-up functions within the spectator-as-passenger convention of the railway subgenre of the travel film (which eventually culminated in Hale's Tours).[55] The train robber thus assaults the spectator in a quite brutal fashion, helping to ensure the spectator's strong identification with the passengers, everyday members of proper society. (This may not be identification within the framework of Hollywood moviemaking but it is within the well-established conventions of early cinema.) Such identifications resonate throughout the first part of the film, with its scenes occurring on or alongside the railway tracks. The bandits likewise brutally shoot a fleeing passenger in the back, an action that seems to condemn these callous murderers even as it evokes the introductory close-up (or anticipates the close-up if it is placed at the end). Thus spectators are assaulted by a bandit in a manner similar to the passengers inside the story world of the film – only cinema's absence of presence protects them. (That the "passengers" in the audience are shot in the face while the passenger in the diegetic world of the film is shot in the back plays with these antinomies.) At another point the telegraph operator, a victim of the bandits' machinations, is found by a young girl who is presumably his daughter, in a scene that associates him with the family. To say that Porter does not offer a moral stance in THE GREAT TRAIN ROBBERY leaves me puzzled. This does not mean that the close-up of the outlaw Barnes firing into the audience is not also an attraction, but as Eisenstein himself argued about American cinema more generally (Griffith, Chaplin), Porter incorporated attractions into his films.

Gunning's comments on THE KLEPTOMANIAC are even more pejorative and miss both the power this film would have had for 1905 audiences and its many parallels with Griffith. Gunning claims that the film fails to "us[e] editing for social criticism" and that Porter's "voice" is located primarily in the final tableau of justice weighing the scales in favor of wealth.[56] In almost every respect, I find myself at odds with this analysis.[57] This is a film that contrasts the fate of the rich kleptomaniac Mrs. Banker (shown in the first portion of the film) with the poor widowed mother who steals bread for her children (presented in the second portion of the film, with the penultimate shot bringing the two story lines together). While not made through parallel editing, the parallels and contrasts are nonetheless obvious to the spectator and are made through the selection of similar kinds of moments. For instance, Mrs. Banker and the poor mother are both led into the police station. The poor woman is forced to climb over a snowbank while Mrs. Banker is shown an easy pathway. The poor woman steals bread left unattended on the street while Mrs. Banker goes inside a department store (Macy's) to steal. The two characters are contrasted in terms of their motives and psychology (the film's title itself implies a psychological interest). The poor woman, shown with her hungry children, steals for her family: she has an economic motive. The wealthy woman, who shoplifts a bauble, steals for the thrill and perhaps because she is immune from any serious consequences. These parallels and oppositions are carefully worked out and suggest the firm presence of a narrator.

Gunning writes: "The cinema of narrative integration introduces not only characters whose desires and fears motivate plots, but also a new wholeness and integrity to the fictional world in which action takes place."[58] Certainly such comments are applicable to The Kleptomaniac. In fact as I try to show in my book, without the full benefit of several theoretical insights Gunning brings to the conceptualization of narrative, Porter not only offers a moralizing voice similar to Griffith's but they both seek to represent simultaneous actions in ways that are more extreme than their respective contemporaries – one through temporal repetition (these two stories obviously occurred more or less simultaneously) and the other through parallel editing.[59] Contra Gunning, both filmmakers are engaged in contrast editing and both use editing to express social criticism. Moreover, the use of tableau at the end is not something that divides Porter from Griffith but something that often unites them. We cannot say that the apotheosis at the end of Birth of a Nation retains a coherent fictional world, and it would not be hard to list many classical films that have some kind of extradiegetic conclusion (or beginning).

Films such as The Kleptomaniac also challenge the notion that frontality and a presentational style are characteristic of cinema of attractions per se. As Noël Burch and I have argued, a presentational style is broadly characteristic of the pre-Griffith cinema more generally. But it also continues in the post-1908 era as well: in Porter's The Prisoner of Zenda (1913) and Griffith's The Birth of a Nation (1915). Presentationalism may not be a characteristic that necessarily defines early or primitive cinema. Not only Charlie Chaplin in The Tramp (1915) but Cary Grant in His Girl Friday (1940) acknowledge the spectator with a glance at the camera. Nor do these presentational techniques necessarily undermine the diegetic absorption of the spectator. It is the frontality in conjunction with the relative brevity of the scene and the specific subject matter that defines the cinema of attractions.

I agree that there was a fundamental transformation in methods of representation (and production) that occurred in the 1907-1909 period, but it is significantly different than the one that Gunning describes to the extent that he has (1) neglected the formation of the filmmaker in this earlier period via the production company's assertion of unprecedented control over the processes of film production *and* postproduction and (2) failed to characterize fully a "pre-Griffith" form of storytelling. There is no doubt that the control of production and representation was further centralized in the 1907-1909 period when individual pictures achieved a more efficient, consistent and self-sufficient means of storytelling. The regular use of intertitles, the linear unfolding of narrative, and an increasingly seamless fictional world were some of the new rules of storytelling (effectively combining to reduce and eventually eliminate dependency on a lecture or the spectator's foreknowledge of the story).[60]

V. Cinema of Attractions/Hollywood Attractions

If THE GREAT TRAIN ROBBERY (1903) and THE KLEPTOMANIAC (1905) are strong examples of early cinema's capacity for storytelling, there are multi-shot films from this period in which narrative does not provide the organizing principle and in which cinema of attractions would, at first glance, seem to play an important role. THE WHOLE DAM FAMILY AND THE DAM DOG (Porter/Edison, 1905), which is based on a popular postcard, opens with a series of close-ups of Dam family members and concludes with a short one-shot scene in which the Dam dog pulls the tablecloth and the family's meal onto the floor. Certainly, as Gunning has pointed out, this film comically inverts the normal relationship between "introductory shots" and story. Many films (such as THE GREAT TRAIN ROBBERY or HOW A FRENCH NOBLEMAN...) begin with an introductory shot and then are followed by a multi-shot narrative. Here Porter reverses the relationship between introductory shots and story in a playful, self-reflexive manner; attractions would seem to wag the narrative tail. And yet this film, like THE SEVEN AGES (Porter/Edison, 1905), poses serious questions about cinema of attractions. The succession of shots does not privilege the unexpected or defy any kind of logical succession of scenes and images, but is rather based on what David Bordwell and Kristin Thompson call categorical editing.[61] A kind of logic, even if it is not narrative logic, is at work.

Longer films, even if they avoid narrative, generally rely on alternative kinds of logical structures. This is even true of some of Méliès's longer single-scene trick films, such as LE ROI DU MAQUILLAGE (THE UNTAMABLE WHISKERS, 1904): the succession of similar attractions (here lightning sketches that are brought to life) greatly reduce "the unpredictability of the instance." Rhetorical form is yet another way that filmmakers could organize film material in rational and predictable ways. I take it that films in which these forms of non-narrative organization predominate do not generally fall under the rubric of cinema of attractions. If they did, a wide range of non-fiction films – in *Film Art* Bordwell and Thompson see OLYMPIA, PART 2 and THE RIVER as exemplary of each organizational principle – would have greater affinity to cinema of attractions than they do.[62] Two other patterns of non-narrative editing, abstract and associational, are potentially less predictable in their juxtapositions: the two examples featured by Bordwell and Thompson in *Film Art* are avant-garde films, respectively BALLET MÉCANIQUE (Dudley Murphy and Fernand Léger, 1924) and A MOVIE (Bruce

Conner, 1958). Each offers the kind of freewheeling juxtapositions that have many affinities with variety programming of the 1890s. If we hesitate to call these later films examples of cinema of attractions, it is because they entail, as Gunning points out, a different kind of historical spectator.[63]

Gunning indicates that attractions have continued to appear, albeit in more muted form, in various Hollywood genres, for example as stage numbers in musicals. He also suggests that "recent spectacle cinema has reaffirmed its roots in stimulus and carnival rides, in what might be called the Spielberg-Lucas-Coppola cinema of effects."[64] Effects are tamed attractions. But a wealth of attractions arguably exists in most films, and as Eisenstein suggests, particularly those made in Hollywood. If we think of "attractions" as non-narrative aspects of cinema that create curiosity or supply pleasure, attractions of some kind can be found in virtually all narrative films (in fact in all cinema). More specifically, Hollywood cinema and its uses of cinematic form cannot be explained by its efforts simply to tell stories. The numerous "coming attractions" that are now reprised on American Movie Channel should remind us of this. Stars, the use of a pre-sold property (play, musical, or novel), suspense, sex, acting performances, dramatic situations, shocking revelations, spectacle and so on – all these are Hollywood attractions that trailers foreground to sell the movies without "giving away" their stories. In the films themselves, these attractions tend to be fully integrated with the story: a character performs a particular action and we see not only that character and the unfolding story but the star – an attraction – at the same time.

André Bazin remarked that "normal editing" (perhaps what we might call classical editing) "is a compromise between three ways of possibly analyzing reality": (1) a purely logical or descriptive analysis; (2) a psychological analysis from within the film; and (3) a psychological interest from the point of view of the spectator.[65] In many films, the use of close-ups does not simply allow us to better understand the story. Editing and close-ups are also used to give opportunity to look at stars. Certain moments and gestures are meaningful only in terms of a star's persona, not merely in terms of the story itself. In general, cinematic form can be said to play with both narrative and attractions. The nature of attractions has varied from cinema to cinema – unquestionably for pre-Griffith filmmakers it was different than for those working after the rise of the star system. In fact, American narrative cinema around 1908-1909 – the cinema that Gunning focuses on most intensely – is notable for its relative lack of attractions. (The rapid appearance of popular players such as the various "Biograph" girls was in this respect a surprise, and their value as attractions at first considered a mixed blessing.) The very transformation of film form occurring at this moment involved, on one hand, the curtailment of a particular system of representation utilizing certain kinds of attractions (and a way of presenting them) and, on the other, the emergence of a new and different system of representation mobilizing other kinds of attractions and another way of presenting them. There is no doubt that there are significant differences in pre-code (before 1935) and post-code Hollywood sound films, precisely in the area of attractions. Certain kinds of attractions were allowed only if they were required by the narrative. In the history of screen practice, there have been moments when attractions have all but obliterated narrative and there have been moments – such as 1907-1909 – when narrative concerns were center stage. In comparison to most films of 1908-1909, many cinemas appear closely allied to cinemas of attractions.

These historical considerations suggest a two-pronged approach to exploring the question of attractions, an approach that is at least implied in much of Gunning's work. First, there is the largely transhistorical, more theoretically oriented approach to attractions. Here the term "attractions" will either incorporate or compete with such important insights and discursive terms as Christian Metz's and Laura Mulvey's exploration of scopophilia and "visual pleasure." On the other hand, there is the way that these aspects of cinema are constructed in relation to an array of organizing structures of which narrative is easily the most important. In his essays, Gunning points to a number of ways that these attractions are constructed in the pre-Griffith period: attractions dominate narrative or operate independently of it altogether; effects are brief and powerful; and an array of presentational techniques are used. My goal has been (1) to define cinema of attractions more rigorously and with greater specificity, and (2) to argue that storytelling played a more important role in early cinema than Gunning has been willing to recognize. Gunning has argued that early cinema can be largely characterized as a cinema of attractions and that this cinema of attractions was dominant. I am arguing that this cinema of attractions (this way of presenting views) stands in dialectical relation to the numerous, sustained efforts at cinematic storytelling that were present from the 1890s onward. Only in cinema's initial novelty period (1895-1896, 1896-1897) was cinema of attractions dominant. After this initial display of cinema's unique potential, cinematic form found a wide range of expressions even as certain genres and types of exhibition sites favored one side of this dialectic or the other.

Notes

First published in *The Yale Journal of Criticism* 7.2 (1994): 203-32. An initial draft of this essay was presented at the conference "The Movies Begin: Film/History/Culture" at Yale University, 7-9 May 1993. I would like to thank Tom Gunning, Yuri Tsivian, and André Gaudreault for providing generous feedback.

1. "First Public Exhibition of Edison's Kinetograph," *Scientific American* 20 May 1893: 310; "Department of Physics," *Brooklyn Daily Eagle* 10 May 1893: 9. In the original version I only mentioned BLACKSMITHING SCENE, but in the meantime I have established two films were shown at the Brooklyn Institute of Arts and Science on 9 May 1893.

2. The Brighton conference, a follow-up screening of fiction films from 1907 and 1908 organized by Eileen Bowser, Jay Leyda's Griffith seminar at NYU, and the Columbia University Seminars in New York City hosted by Eileen Bowser for more than a dozen years, all ensured that our investigation of early cinema would be a joint project of a kind that was extremely rare, if not unprecedented.

3. John Fell, ed., *Film Before Griffith* (Berkeley: U of California P, 1983).

4. Tom Gunning, "The Cinema of Attraction[s]," *Wide Angle* 8.3-4 (1986): 64.

5. Tom Gunning, "Cinema of Attractions," *Early Cinema: Space Frame Narrative*, ed. Thomas Elsaesser (London: British Film Institute, 1990) 58-59. Unless otherwise noted, I will cite this version of Gunning's article.

6. Tom Gunning, "'Now You See It, Now You Don't': The Temporality of the Cinema of Attractions," *Velvet Light Trap* 32 (Fall 1993): 3-12.

7. Sergei Eisenstein, "The Montage of Film Attractions [1924]," *Selected Works*, vol. 1, ed. and trans. Richard Taylor (London: British Film Institute, 1988-91) 39-58.

8. Tom Gunning, "An Aesthetic of Astonishment: Early Film and the (In)Credulous Spectator," *Art and Text* 34 (Fall 1989): 31-45; Miriam Hansen, *Babel & Babylon: Spectatorship in American Silent Film* (Cambridge: Harvard UP, 1991) 108-10; John Kasson, *Amusing the Million: Coney Island at the Turn of the Century* (New York: Hill and Wang, 1978).

9. Tom Gunning, "Cinema of Attraction[s]," *Wide Angle* 63-70. For the importance of narrative in Passion play programs see Noël Burch, "A Primitive Mode of Representation?," *Early Cinema: Space Frame Narrative* 220-27.

10. Gunning, "Cinema of Attractions" 56.

11. Charles Musser, "The Eden Musée in 1898: Exhibitor as Creator," *Film and History* 5.4 (Dec. 1981): 73-83ff.

12. See Charles Musser, "Another Look at the 'Chaser Theory,'" *Studies in Visual Communication* 10.4 (Nov. 1984): 24-44ff.

13. Gunning, "The Cinema of Attractions" 58-59.

14. At the Edison Manufacturing Company, however, single-shot scenes from these comedies were sold individually – "Burglar and Bulldog" from THE BURGLAR'S SLIDE FOR LIFE, for example.

15. Gunning, "The Cinema of Attractions" 57.

16. Gunning, "The Cinema of Attractions" 58.

17. Georges Méliès, "Importance du scénario," in Georges Sadoul, *Georges Méliès* (Paris: Seghers, 1961) 116; cited in Gunning, "Cinema of Attractions" 57. This statement, however, must be understood within the context of its utterance. Méliès was addressing avant-garde, often Surrealist artists and patrons who had rescued him from obscurity and were interested in the irrational non-narrative elements of his films.

18. *Complete Catalog of Genuine and Original "Star" Films* (New York, 1903) 23, 25.

19. "Boston Show," week of 20 April 1903, M.J. Keating, *Keith Reports*, I: 248. The *Keith Reports* are in the Edward Albee Papers, Special Collections, University of Iowa.

20. "New York Show," week of 27 April 1903, S.K. Hodgdon, *Keith Reports*, I: 254.
21. "Boston Show," week of 4 May 1903, M.J. Keating, *Keith Reports*, I: 258.
22. "New York Show," week of 11 May 1903, S.K. Hodgdon, *Keith Reports*, I: 263.
23. "Philadelphia Show," week of 11 May 1903, H.A. Daniels, *Keith Reports*, I: 265.
24. "Boston Show," week of 18 May 1903, M.J. Keating, *Keith Reports*, I: 268.
25. Gunning, *D.W. Griffith and the Origins of the American Narrative Film: The Early Years at Biograph* (Urbana: U of Illinois P, 1991) 42.
26. Gunning, *D.W. Griffith* 78.
27. Gunning, *D.W. Griffith* 156.
28. Laura Mulvey, "Visual Pleasure and Narrative Cinema," *Visual and Other Pleasures* (Bloomington: Indiana UP, 1989).
29. The question of whether narrative is "dominant" may be inappropriate or it may depend upon the answer to such questions as for whom, for what spectator? Tom Gunning, who is interested in the affinities between early cinema and the avant-garde, may savor its "cinematic," non-narrative elements – one thinks of Canudo who, around 1910, urged his readers to go to the cinema, ignore the banal plots, and enjoy the play of light instead. In the context of a comparison with Griffith's driving narratives, the narratives of these earlier films seem weaker, somewhat favoring erotic display over story. Of course, I, who worked as a film editor in Hollywood, and made documentaries which tell stories, may be biased the other way. And if I choose to compare these early films to a Hollywood musical such as Stormy Weather, the equation is similarly weighted in the opposite direction. If we turn to historical evidence such as the catalogue description for The Gay Shoe Clerk, it becomes apparent that Porter and the Edison Manufacturing Company's Kinetograph Department promoted these films largely on the basis of their narrative.
30. Moreover, Gunning's comparison of The Gay Shoe Clerk to The Lonely Villa is inappropriate: an analogy with an early Mack Sennett film would underscore this film's affinity to later cinema.
31. Donald Crafton, "Pie and Chase: Gag, Spectacle and Narrative in Slapstick Comedy," *The Slapstick Symposium*, ed. Eileen Bowser (Bruxelles: FIAF, 1988), 49-60; Gunning cites this article in "The Cinema of Attractions" 60.
32. André Gaudreault, "Film, Narrative, Narration [1984]," *Early Cinema: Space Frame Narrative* 71.
33. Gaudreault, "Film, Narrative, Narration" 73. In his reprint of this article, André Gaudreault suggests that his thinking on this subject has changed: he, in fact, concludes that we should distinguish between "narrative fragments" on one hand and complete, if short, narratives (such as L'Arroseur arrosé) on the other (André Gaudreault, *Du Littéraire au filmique: système du récit* [Paris: Méridiens, 1988]).
34. Noël Burch, *Life to Those Shadows*, ed. and trans. Ben Brewster (London: British Film Institute, 1990) 159, n 1.
35. Hansen, *Babel & Babylon* 304.
36. See David Bordwell and Kristin Thompson, *Film Art: An Introduction*, 4th ed. (New York: McGraw, 1993) 102-40, for a discussion of non-narrative forms of organizing programs.
37. See Charles Musser, *Before the Nickelodeon* (Berkeley: U of California P, 1991) 372.
38. Narrative sequencing was not new to screen entertainment per se, and there was a certain logic to avoiding it – or being indifferent to it – in the initial stages of the

novelty period. Narrative tended to dominate screen practice before cinema and one might readily argue that it was unimportant if not counterproductive to the showing of new features that cinema brought to the screen.

39. Gunning, "The Cinema of Attractions" 58.

40. Gunning, "Now You See It, Now You Don't" 6.

41. One of my underlying problems with Gunning's argument about attractions is his avoidance of the use of programs. For illustration of some of these points I encourage readers to look at programs that I provide in Musser, *The Emergence of Cinema* (New York: Scribner's, 1990) 179, 180, 259, 273, 302, 312-13; and in Charles Musser with Carol Nelson, *High-Class Moving Pictures* (Princeton: Princeton UP, 1991) 53, 89, 105-06, 135-36, 168-70.

42. Lewis Jacobs, *The Rise of the American Film* (New York: Harcourt, 1939) 36.

43. Charles Musser, "Passions and the Passion Play: Theater, Film and Religion, 1880-1900," *Film History* 5.4 (1993): 419-56.

44. Walter Benjamin, "The Work of Art in the Age of Mechanical Reproduction," *Illuminations*, ed. Hannah Arendt, trans. Harry Zohn (New York: Schocken, 1969) 220, 221.

45. See Hansen, *Babel & Babylon*.

46. "'The Passion Play' Given Here in Boston," *Boston Herald* 4 Jan. 1898: 6.

47. "Does Its Work Well," *Boston Herald* 1 June 1897: 7.

48. Robert Allen, "Contra the Chaser Theory," *Film Before Griffith*, ed. John Fell (Berkeley: U of California P, 1983) 105-15.

49. See Gunning, "Now You See It, Now You Don't."

50. My book *Before the Nickelodeon* is precisely about the process of something like narrative integration – on the level of production as well as representation.

51. Gunning, *D.W. Griffith* 21.

52. See my discussion of Porter in *Before the Nickelodeon* 296-302.

53. Gunning, *D.W. Griffith* 165.

54. Gunning, *D.W. Griffith* 108.

55. Charles Musser, "The Travel Genre in 1903-4: The Move toward Fictional Narrative," *Iris* 2.1 (Spring 1984): 47-59; rpt. in *Early Cinema: Space Frame Narrative* 123-32.

56. Gunning, *D.W. Griffith* 137-38.

57. Gunning, incidentally, offers an incorrect shot-by-shot description of the film – after chastising Lewis Jacobs for doing so. Gunning, moreover, suggests that the tableau is the penultimate shot (*D.W. Griffith*, 138) – it is, in fact, the last or final one. Let me hasten to add that although I find Gunning's readings of Porter's work reductive and unsympathetic, I find his analyses of Griffith's films extremely perceptive.

58. Gunning, *D.W. Griffith* 138.

59. See Musser, *Before the Nickelodeon* 296-302, for my examination of THE KLEPTOMANIAC.

60. Here again the simple opposition between early cinema as involving spectatorship based on distraction versus one based on narrative absorption seems to me too simple. One can easily find reviews from the early period that indicate high levels of protracted absorption. Obviously, cinema of attractions as I have delimited it in this essay does inhibit narrative absorption as Gunning suggests. I do not feel, however, that this absence of narrative absorption applies to THE GREAT TRAIN ROBBERY or THE KLEPTOMANIAC.

61. See Bordwell and Thompson, *Film Art.*

62. Bordwell and Thompson, *Film Art* 102-41.

63. Gunning, "The Cinema of Attractions" 61.

64. Gunning, "The Cinema of Attractions" 61.

65. André Bazin, "Theater and Cinema – Part One," *What's Cinema?*, vol. 1 (Berkeley: U of California P, 1967) 91-92.

Notes on Contributors

Christa Blümlinger teaches film studies at Université de Paris 3. Writer and art critic, she has curated for Duisburger Filmwoche, Diagonale, Arsenal and other festivals and cinemas. She has published about documentary and avant-garde cinema, media art, film theory and aesthetics. Her most recent books as (co-)editor are: *Serge Daney – Von der Welt ins Bild. Augenzeugenberichte eines Cinephilen* (2000), *Das Gesicht im Zeitalter des bewegten Bildes* (2002) and *Harun Farocki – Reconnaître et poursuivre* (2002). The publication of her *habilitation* at Freie Universität Berlin about appropriation in film and media art is forthcoming.

Warren Buckland is author of *The Cognitive Semiotics of Film* (2000), *Studying Contemporary American Film* (2002, with Thomas Elsaesser), *Film Studies* (2003), *Directed by Steven Spielberg: Poetics of the Contemporary Hollywood Blockbuster* (2006), and editor of *The Film Spectator: From Sign to Mind* (1995). He is also the founding editor of the new paper-based journal, the *New Review of Film and Television Studies*.

Scott Bukatman is Associate Professor in the Film and Media Studies Program at Stanford University. He is the author of three books: *Terminal Identity: The Virtual Subject in Postmodern Science Fiction* (1993), the BFI monograph on *Blade Runner* (1997), and a collection of essays, *Matters of Gravity: Special Effects and Supermen in the 20th Century* (2003). He has published widely on issues of popular media, technology, and embodied experience, and is now working on a study of the early comics creator and animator, Winsor McCay.

Donald Crafton is Professor of Film and Culture in the Department of Film, Television, and Theater at the University of Notre Dame. His most recent publication is *The Talkies: American Cinema's Transition to Sound, 1926-1931* (1999). He was named Academy Film Scholar by the Academy of Motion Picture Arts and Sciences in 2001, and received a National Endowment for the Humanities Fellowship for 2003-2004. At the World Festival of Animation, Zagreb, Croatia, in 2004, he received the Award for Special Contribution to the Theory of Animation.

Nicolas Dulac is currently preparing a PhD dissertation about seriality in mass media and popular culture, at both Université de Montréal and Université de Paris 3. His other research areas are early cinema and optical toys. He taught several classes in film history at the Département d'histoire de l'art et d'études cinématographiques at Université de Montréal and acts as research assistant for GRAFICS (Groupe de recherche sur l'avènement et la formation des institutions cinématographique et scénique).

Thomas Elsaesser is Professor in the Department of Media and Culture and Director of Research Film and Television at Universiteit van Amsterdam. His most recent books as (co-)editor are: *Cinema Futures: Cain, Abel or Cable?* (1998), *The BFI Companion to German Cinema* (1999), *The Last Great American Picture Show: Hollywood films in the 1970s* (2004) and *Harun Farocki – Working on the Sightlines* (2004). Among his books as author are: *Fassbinder's Germany: History, Identity, Subject* (1996), *Weimar Cinema and After* (2000), *Studying Contemporary American Film* (2002, with Warren Buckland), *Filmgeschichte und Frühes Kino* (2002) and *European Cinema: Face to Face with Hollywood* (2005).

André Gaudreault is Professor in the Département d'histoire de l'art et d'études cinématographiques at Université de Montréal, where he directs GRAFICS (Groupe de recherche sur l'avènement et la formation des institutions cinématographique et scénique). He has (co-)edited several books, among which are *Pathé 1900. Fragments d'une filmographie analytique du cinéma des premiers temps* (1993) and *Au pays des ennemis du cinéma* (1996). His books as author include: *Du littéraire au filmique. Système du récit* (1988, revised edition 1999), *Le récit cinématographique* (1991, with François Jost) and *Cinema delle origini. O della "cinematografia-attrazione"* (2004). He is also editor-in-chief of the journal *CiNéMAS*.

Tom Gunning is Professor in the Art Department at the University of Chicago, where he is the Acting Chair of the Committee on Cinema and Media Studies. He is the author of *D.W. Griffith and the Origins of American Narrative Film* (1991) and *The Films of Fritz Lang: Modernity, Crime and Desire* (2000); and has co-edited *An Invention of the Devil? Religion and Early Cinema* (1992) and *Pathé 1900: Fragments d'une filmographie analytique du cinéma des premiers temps* (1993).

Laurent Guido currently teaches film and media at Université de Lausanne, where he received his PhD in Humanities in 2004. In 2002 and 2003, he was invited as a Swiss National Fund Researcher by the University of Chicago and Université de Paris 1. He has published and organized exhibitions on the relationships between cinema, music and dance, as well as film historiography. He is co-author of *La Mise en scène du corps sportif/Spotlighting the Sporting Body* (2003, with Gianni Haver) and editor of *Les Peurs de Hollywood* (2006). His most recent book is *L'Age du Rythme* (2006).

Malte Hagener teaches film and media in the Department of Media Studies at Friedrich-Schiller-Universität Jena. His research interests include European avant-garde cinema of the interwar period, popular cinema of the 1930s and German film history. He is (co-) editor of *Als die Filme singen lernten: Innovation und Tradition im Musikfilm 1928-38* (1999), *Geschlecht in Fesseln. Sexualität zwischen Aufklärung und Ausbeutung im Weimarer Kino* (2000), *Film: An International Bibliography* (2002), *Die Spur durch den Spiegel. Der Film in der Kultur der Moderne* (2004) and *Cinephilia. Movies, Love, and Memory* (2005).

Pierre-Emmanuel Jaques is currently involved in the research project "Views and Perspectives: Studies on the History of Non-Fiction Film in Switzerland" (funded by the Swiss National Science Foundation) in the Film Studies Department at Universität Zürich. He has been an assistant at Université de Lausanne where he is completing his PhD on the birth of film criticism in Geneva during the 1920s. He has published articles on the history of cinema in Switzerland and *Le spectacle cinématographique en Suisse 1895-1945* (2003, with Gianni Haver).

Charlie Keil is an Associate Professor in the History Department and director of the Cinema Studies Program at the University of Toronto. He is the author of *Early American Cinema in Transition: Story, Style and Filmmaking, 1907-1913* (2001) and co-editor, with Shelley Stamp, of *American Cinema's Transitional Era: Audiences, Institutions, Practices* (2004). Currently, he is preparing an anthology on American cinema of the 1910s with Ben Singer for the Screen Decades series.

Frank Kessler is Professor of Film and Television History at Universiteit Utrecht and currently the president of Domitor. He is co-founder and co-editor of *KINtop. Jahrbuch zur Erforschung des frühen Films*, and has published numerous articles in the field of early cinema, in particular on early non-fiction films, the genre of the *féerie*, and acting. As guest editor he compiled a special issue of the *Historical Journal of Film, Radio and Television*, "Visible Evidence – But of What? Reassessing Early Non-fiction" (2002).

Germain Lacasse teaches cinema studies at Université de Montréal. He has published papers and books about early cinema in Quebec (*Histoires de* scopes, 1988) and about film lecturers (*Le bonimenteur de vues* animées, 2000). Still interested in early cinema, he is now also doing research about later practices of lectured films or "aural cinema."

Alison McMahan, PhD, is a documentary filmmaker (see www.Homunculusprods. com). Her latest film was CAMBODIA: LIVING WITH LANDMINES (2004). From January 2002-December 2003 she held a Mellon Fellowship in Visual Culture at Vassar College where she built a virtual reality environment with a biofeedback interface for CAVEs. From 1997 to 2001 she taught early cinema and new media at Universiteit van Amsterdam. She is the author of the award-winning *Alice Guy Blaché, Lost Cinematic Visionary* (2002) and *The Films of Tim Burton: Animating Live Action in Hollywood* (2005).

Charles Musser is Professor of American Studies, Film Studies and Theater Studies at Yale University, where he co-chairs the Film Studies Program. He is the author of *The Emergence of Cinema* (1990), *Before the Nickelodeon* (1991), *High-Class Moving Pictures: Lyman H. Howe and the Forgotten Era of Traveling Exhibition, 1880-1920* (1991, with Carol Nelson) and *Edison Motion Pictures, 1890-1900: An Annotated Filmography* (1997). With Nancy Mathews, he co-authored the catalogue *Moving Pictures: American Art and Early Film, 1880-1910* (2005). He wrote his most recent essay while a residential fellow at the Clark Art Institute.

Viva Paci is a doctoral candidate, with a PhD dissertation on *De l'attraction au cinéma*, at Université de Montréal, where she is a member of GRAFICS (Groupe de recherche sur l'avènement et la formation du spectacle cinématographique et scénique) and CRI (Centre de recherche sur l'intermédialité). For her current research she compares computer animation to the beginnings of cinema. She has published in journals such as *Cinéma et Cie*, *CiNéMAS*, *Comunicazioni sociali*, *Sociétés et Représentations*, *Médiamorphoses et Intermédialités*. She is the author of *Il Cinema di Chris Marker* (2005) and co-editor of *L'Imprimerie du regard. Chris Marker et la technique* (forthcoming).

Eivind Røssaak is Associate Professor of Literature and Creative Writing, currently doing a PhD, preliminarily titled *Between still and moving images*, as part of the project

MediaEstetikk in the Department of Media and Communication at Universitetet i Oslo. He has published several articles and books on photography, film, theory and literature. Among his most recent books are: *Det postmoderne og De Intellektuelle* (1998), *Sic: Fra Litteraturens Randsone* (2001), *Kyssing og Slåssing: Fire Kapitler om Film* (2004, with Christian Refsum) and *Selviakttakelse: En Tendens i Kunst og Litteratur* (2005).

Vivian Sobchack is Professor of Critical Studies in the Department Film, Television and Digital Media at the UCLA School of Theater, Film and Television. Her books include *The Address of the Eye: A Phenomenology of Film Experience* (1992), *Screening Space: The American Science Fiction Film* (1997) and *Carnal Thoughts: Embodiment and Moving Image Culture* (2004). She has also edited two anthologies: *The Persistence of History: Cinema, Television and the Modern Event* (1996) and *Meta-Morphing: Visual Transformation and the Culture of Quick Change* (2000).

Wanda Strauven is an Assistant Professor and director of the Film Studies Program in the Department of Media and Culture at Universiteit van Amsterdam. She co-edited *Homo orthopedicus: le corps et ses prothèses à l'époque (post)moderniste* (2001), and published on early and avant-garde cinema in various international editions and journals. She is the author of *Marinetti e il cinema: tra attrazione e sperimentazione* (2006). At the Amsterdam School for Cultural Analysis (ASCA), she co-directs, with Thomas Elsaesser, the research project "Imagined Futures."

Dick Tomasovic is a Postdoctoral Researcher (FNRS, Belgium) in the history and aesthetics of cinema and performing arts. He teaches at Université de Liège. He makes music videos, writes fictional works and develops projects for the stage. He is the author of *Le Palimpseste noir, notes sur l'impétigo, la terreur et le cinéma américain contemporain* (2002), *Freaks, la monstrueuse parade de Tod Browning* (2006), and *Le Corps en abîme. Sur la figurine et le cinéma d'animation* (2006).

General Bibliography

This bibliography, compiled in collaboration with Viva Paci, is not exhaustive. It is general in the sense that it is not limited to studies on early cinema, bringing together references from various disciplines and research areas. Partly a selection of the references cited by the different contributors, it lists entries that specifically relate to the notion of "cinema of attractions" (or "attraction" in general) as well as those that are relevant for the contextualization and the theory formation of the concept.

Abel, Richard. "That Most American of Attractions, the Illustrated Song." *The Sounds of Early Cinema*. Ed. Richard Abel and Rick Altman. Bloomington: Indiana UP, 2001. 143-55.

—. *The Ciné goes to Town: French Cinema 1896-1914*. Berkeley: U of California P, 1994.

—. *The French Cinema: The First Wave 1915-1929*. Princeton: Princeton UP, 1984.

Albera, François. "Archéologie de l'intermédialité: SME/CD-ROM, l'apesanteur." *CiNéMAS* 10.2-3 (2000): 27-38.

Allen, Robert C. *Vaudeville and Film: 1895-1915, A Study in Media Interaction*. New York: Arno, 1980.

Altman, Rick. *Silent Film Sound*. New York: Columbia UP, 2004.

—. "De l'intermédialité au multimédia: cinéma, médias, avènement du son." *CiNéMAS* 10.1 (1999): 37-53.

—. "The Silence of the Silents." *The Musical Quarterly* 80.4 (Winter 1996): 648-718.

—. "Penser l'histoire (du cinéma) autrement: un modèle de crise." *Vingtième siècle* 46 (1995): 65-74.

—. *The American Film Musical*. 1987. Bloomington/London: Indiana UP/British Film Institute, 1989.

Amengual, Barthélemy. *Que viva Eisenstein!* Lausanne: L'Age d'Homme, 1980.

Arroyo, José, ed. *Action/Spectacle Cinema*. London: British Film Institute, 2000.

"Attraction in Films." *Ciné pour tous* 118 (Nov. 1923): 10-11.

Auerbach, Jonathan. "Chasing Film Narrative: Repetition, Recursion, and the Body in Early Cinema." *Critical Inquiry* 26.4 (Summer 2000): 798-820.

Aumont, Jacques. "Quand y a-t-il cinéma primitif? ou Plaidoyer pour le primitif." *Le Cinéma au tournant du siècle/Cinema at the Turn of the Century*. Ed. Claire Dupré la Tour, André Gaudreault and Roberta Pearson. Quebec City/Lausanne: Nuit Blanche/ Payot-Lausanne, 1999. 17-32.

—. "The Variable Eye, or the Mobilization of the Gaze." *The Image in Dispute. Art and Cinema in the Age of Photography*. Ed. Dudley Andrew. Austin: U of Texas P, 1997. 231-58.

—. *Montage Eisenstein*. Paris: Albatros, 1979. English trans. *Montage Eisenstein*. London/ Bloomington: British Film Institute/Indiana UP, 1987.

—. "Griffith, le cadre, la figure." *Le cinéma américain*. Ed. Raymond Bellour. Paris: Flammarion, 1980. 51-67. English trans. "Griffith: the Frame, the Figure." *Early Cinema:*

Space Frame Narrative. Ed. Thomas Elsaesser. London: British Film Institute, 1990. 348-59.

Balides, Constance. "Scenarios of Exposure in the Practice of Everyday Life: Women and the Cinema of Attractions." *Screen* 34.1 (Spring 1993): 19-37. Rpt. in *Screen Histories: A Screen Reader*. Ed. Annette Kuhn and Jackie Stacey. Oxford: Clarendon, 1998. 61-80.

Bazin, André. *Qu'est-ce que le cinéma?* 1958. Paris: Cerf, 1981. English trans. *What is Cinema?* Berkeley: U of California P, 1967.

Bean, Jennifer M. "Technologies of Early Stardom and the Extraordinary Body." *Camera Obscura* 16.3 (2001): 8-56.

Belloï, Livio. *Le regard retourné. Aspects du cinéma des premiers temps*. Québec/Paris: Nota Bene/Méridiens Klincksieck, 2001.

Benjamin, Walter. *Das Kunstwerk im Zeitalter seiner technischen Reproduzierbarkeit*. Frankfurt: Suhrkamp, 1936. English trans. "The Work of Art in the Age of Mechanical Reproduction." *Illuminations*. London: Fontana, 1973. 211-44.

Bertozzi, Marco. *L'Immaginario urbano nel cinema delle origini. La veduta Lumière*. Bologna: Clueb, 2001.

—. "Icaro, il paesaggio e l'occhio del cinematografo." *La Decima Musa. Il cinema e le altre arti*. Ed. Leonardo Quaresima and Laura Vichi. Udine: Forum, 2001. 115-21.

Blümlinger, Christa. "Lumière, der Zug und die Avantgarde." *Die Spur durch den Spiegel. Der Film in der Kultur der Moderne*. Ed. Malte Hagener, Johann N. Schmidt and Michael Wedel. Berlin: Bertz, 2004. 27-41.

Bordwell, David. *On the History of Film Style*. Cambridge: Harvard UP, 1997.

—. "Textual Analysis, etc." *Enclitic* 5-6 (Fall 1981/Spring 1982): 125-36.

Bottomore, Stephen. "The Panicking Audience? Early Cinema and the 'Train Effect.'" *Historical Journal of Film, Radio and Television* 19.2 (1999): 177-216.

—. "The Coming of the Cinema." *History Today* 46.3 (1996): 14-20.

Brent, Jessica. "Beyond the Gaze: Visual Fascination and the Feminine Image in Silent Hitchcock." *Camera Obscura* 19.1 (2004): 77-111.

Brewster, Ben. "Periodization of Early Cinema." *American Cinema's Transitional Era*. Ed. Charlie Keil and Shelley Stamp. Berkeley: UCP, 2004. 66-75.

—. (with Lea Jacobs). *Theatre to Cinema: Stage Pictorialism and the Early Feature Film*. New York: Oxford UP, 1997.

—. "A Scene at the 'Movies.'" *Screen* 23.2 (July-Aug. 1982): 4-15. Rpt. in *Early Cinema: Space Frame Narrative*. Ed. Thomas Elsaesser. London: British Film Institute, 1990. 318-25.

Browne, Nick. "The 'Big Bang': The Spectacular Explosion in Contemporary Hollywood Film." *Strobe* (April 2003): http://www.cinema.ucla.edu/strobe/bigbang/.

Bukatman, Scott. *Matters of Gravity*. Durham: Duke UP, 2003.

—. *Terminal Identity. The Virtual Subject in Postmodern Science Fiction*. Durham: Duke UP, 1993.

Burch, Noël. *Light to those Shadows*. Berkeley/Los Angeles: U of California P, 1990.

—. "Un mode de représentation primitif?" *Iris* 2.1 (1984): 113-23. English trans. "A Primitive Mode of Representation?" *Early Cinema: Space Frame Narrative*. Ed. Thomas Elsaesser. London: British Film Institute, 1990. 220-27.

—. "Primitivism and the Avant-Gardes: A Dialectical Approach." *Narrative, Apparatus, Ideology. A Film Theory Reader.* Ed. Philip Rosen. New York: Columbia UP, 1986. 483-506.

—. "Porter, or Ambivalence." *Screen* 19.4 (Winter 1978-79): 91-105. French version: "Porter ou l'ambivalence." *Le cinéma américain II.* Ed. Raymond Bellour. Paris: Flammarion, 1980. 31-44.

Callahan, Vicki. "Screening Musidora: Inscribing Indeterminacy in Film History." *Camera Obscura* 16.3 (2001): 58-81.

Carluccio, Giulia. *Verso il primo piano. Attrazioni e racconto nel cinema americano 1908-1909: il caso Griffith-Biograph.* Bologna: Clueb, 1999.

Casetti, Francesco. *L'Occhio del Novecento. Cinema, esperienza, modernità.* Milano: Bompiani, 2005.

Charney, Leo and Vanessa Schwartz, eds. *Cinema and the Invention of Modern Life.* Berkeley/Los Angeles: U of California P, 1995.

Coissac, G.-Michel. *Histoire du Cinématographe. De ses origines à nos jours.* Paris: Cinéopse/Gauthier-Villars, 1925.

Cornellier, Bruno. "Le sublime technologique et son spectateur dans le parc d'attraction. Nouvelles technologies et artefacts numériques dans JURASSIC PARK." *Cadrage* (2001): http://www.cadrage.net/films/jurassik/jurassik.html.

Cosandey, Roland. "Georges Méliès as l'inescamotable Escamoteur. A Study in Recognition." *A Trip to the Movies. Georges Méliès, Filmmaker and Magician (1861-1938).* Ed. Paolo Cherchi Usai. Pordenone: Giornate del cinema muto, 1991. 56-111.

Cosgrove, Peter. "The Cinema of Attractions and the Novel in Barry Lyndon and Tom Jones." *Eighteenth-Century Fiction on Screen.* Ed. Robert Mayer. Cambridge: Cambridge UP, 2002. 16-34.

Costa, Antonio. *La Morale del giocattolo. Saggio su Georges Méliès.* Bologna: Clueb, 1995.

Crafton, Donald. "Pie and Chase: Gag, Spectacle and Narrative in Slapstick Comedy." *The Slapstick Symposium.* Ed. Eileen Bowser. Bruxelles: FIAF, 1988. 49-59. Rpt. in *Classical Hollywood Comedy.* Ed. Kristine Brunovska Karnick and Henry Jenkins. New York: Routledge, 1995. 106-19.

Crary, Jonathan. *Techniques of the Observer.* 1990. Cambridge: MIT P, 1992.

Cubitt, Sean. *The Cinema Effect.* Cambridge: MIT P, 2004.

—. "Phalke, Méliès, and Special Effects Today." *Wide Angle* 21.1 (Jan. 1999): 114-30.

Dagrada, Elena. "Through the Keyhole: Spectators and Matte Shots in Early Cinema." *Iris* 11 (Summer 1990): 95-106.

—. *La Rappresentazione dello sguardo nel cinema delle origini in Europa. Nascita della soggettiva.* Bologna: Clueb, 1998.

De Bruyn, Eric. "The Museum of Attractions: Marcel Broodthaers and the section cinema." http://www.medienkunstnetz.de/themes/art_and_cinematography/broodthaers/1/.

Delamater, Jerome. "Busby Berkeley: An American Surrealist." *Wide Angle* 1 (1979): 24-29.

Deslandes, Jacques. *Le Boulevard du cinéma à l'époque de Georges Méliès.* Paris: Cerf, 1963.

Doane, Mary Ann. *The Emergence of Cinematic Time. Modernity, Contingency, The Archive.* Cambridge: Havard UP, 2002.

Dubois, Philippe. "Le gros plan primitif." *Revue belge du cinéma* 10 (Winter 1984-85): 11-34.

Dulac, Nicolas (with Pierre Chermantin). "La femme et le type: le stereotype comme vecteur narratif dans le cinéma des attractions." *CiNéMAS* 16.1 (Fall 2005): 139-61.
— (with André Gaudreault). "Il *principio* e la *fine*... Tra fenachistoscopio e cinematografo: l'emergere di una nuova serie culturale." *Limina. Film's Thresholds*. Ed. Veronica Innocenti and Valentina Re. Udine: Forum, 2004. 185-201. English trans. "Heads or Tails: The Emergence of a New Cultural Series, from the Phenakisticope to the Cinematograph." *Invisible Culture* 8 (Fall 2004): http://www.rochester.edu/in_visible_culture/Issue_8/dulac_gaudreault.html.
During, Simon. "Popular Culture on a Global Scale: A Challenge for Cultural Studies?" *Critical Inquiry* 23.4 (Summer 1997): 808-33.
Eisenstein, Sergei M. "Laocoön." *Selected Works. Volume 2: Towards a Theory of Montage*. London: British Film Institute, 1991. 109-202
—. "Inédit: A.I. 1928 [1928]." *CiNéMAS* 11.2-3 (Spring 2001): 147-60.
—. "The Unexpected [1928]." *Film Form*. Trans. Jay Leyda. New York: Harcourt, 1949. 18-27.
—. "The Montage of Film Attractions [1924]." *Selected Works. Volume 1: Writings, 1922-34*. London: British Film Institute, 1988. 39-58.
—. "Montage of Attractions [1923]." *The Film Sense*. New York: Harcourt, 1949. 230-33.
—. "How I Became a Film Director." *Notes of a Film Director*. Moscow: Foreign Language Publishing House, n.d.
Ekstrom, Mats. "Information, Storytelling and Attractions: TV Journalism in Three Modes of Communication." *Media, Culture & Society* 22.4 (2000): 465-92.
Eleftheriotis, Dimitris. "Early Cinema as Child: Historical Metaphor and European Cinephilia in *Lumière & Company*." *Screen* 46 (Fall 2005): 315-28.
Elsaesser, Thomas. "Early Film History and Multi-Media: An Archaeology of Possible Futures?" *New Media, Old Media: A History and Theory Reader*. Ed. Wendy Hui Kyong Chung and Thomas Keenan. New York: Routledge, 2005. 13-25.
—. "Film History as Media Archaeology." *CiNéMAS* 14.2-3 (2005): 75-117.
—. "Louis Lumière – the Cinema's First Virtualist?" *Cinema Futures: Cain, Abel or Cable?* Ed. Thomas Elsaesser and Kay Hoffman. Amsterdam: Amsterdam UP, 1998. 57-58.
—, ed. *Early Cinema: Space Frame Narrative*. London: British Film Institute, 1990.
—. "Early Cinema: From Linear History to Mass Media Archaeology." *Early Cinema: Space Frame Narrative*. Ed. Thomas Elsaesser. London: British Film Institute, 1990. 1-8.
—. "The New Film History." *Sight and Sound* (Fall 1986): 246-51.
Farquhar, Mary. "Shadow Opera: Towards a New Archaeology of the Chinese Cinema." *Post Script: Essays in Film and the Humanities* 20.2-3 (Winter-Summer 2001): 25-42.
Fell, John, ed. *Film Before Griffith*. Berkeley: U of California P, 1983.
Fouquet, E.-L. "L'Attraction." *L'Echo du Cinéma* 11 (28 June 1912): 1.
Fielding, Raymond. "Hale's Tours: Ultrarealism in the Pre-1910 Motion Picture." *Film Before Griffith*. Ed. John L. Fell. Berkeley: U of California P, 1983. 116-30.
Fischer, Lucy. "The Image of Woman as Image: The Optical Politics of *Dames* [1976]." *Genre: The Musical*. Ed. Rick Altman. London: British Film Institute, 1981. 70-84.
Friedberg, Ann. *Window Shopping: Cinema and Postmodern*. Berkeley: U of California P, 1993.
Gaines, Jane M. "First Fictions." *Signs: Journal of Women in Culture and Society* 30 (2004): 1293-317.

—. "Everyday Strangeness: Robert Ripley's International Oddities as Documentary Attractions." *New Literary History* 33 (2002): 781-801.

Gardies, André and Jean Bessalel. "Monstration." *200 mots-clés de la théorie du cinéma.* Paris: Les Editions du Cerf, 1992. 142-43.

Gaudenzi, Laure. "Une filmographie thématique: la danse au cinéma de 1894 à 1906." *Les vingt premières années du cinéma français.* Ed. Jean A. Gili, Michèle Lagny, Michel Marie and Vincent Pinel. Paris: Sorbonne Nouvelle/AFRHC, 1995. 361-64.

Gaudreault, André. *Au seuil de l'histoire du cinéma. La cinématographie-attraction.* Paris, CNRS: forthcoming in 2007.

— (with Philippe Marion). "Du filmique au littéraire: les textes des catalogues de la cinématographie-attraction." *CiNéMAS* 15.2-3 (Spring 2005): 121-45. Italian trans. "Dal filmico al letterario: i testi dei cataloghi della cinematografia-attrazione." *Narrating the Film. Novelization: From the Catalogue to the Trailer.* Ed. Alice Autelitano and Valentina Re. Udine: Forum, 2006. 25-35.

—. *Cinema delle origini. O della "cinematografia-attrazione."* Milano: Il Castoro, 2004.

—. "Cinématographie-attraction et attraction des lointains." *Imatge i viatge. De les vistes òptiques al cinema: la configuració de l'imaginari turístic.* Girona: Fundació Museu del Cinema-Col·lecció Tomàs Mallol/Ajuntament de Girona, 2004. 85-102.

— (with Philippe Marion). "Le cinéma naissant et ses dispositions narratives." *Cinéma et Cie* 1 (2001): 34-41.

—. "Les *vues cinématographiques* selon Eisenstein, ou: que reste-t-il de l'*ancien* (le cinéma des premiers temps) dans le *nouveau* (les productions filmiques et scripturales d'Eisenstein)?" *Eisenstein: l'ancien et le nouveau.* Ed. Dominique Chateau, François Jost and Martin Lefebvre. Paris: Sorbonne/Colloque de Cerisy, 2001. 23-43.

— (with Philippe Marion). "Un média naît toujours deux fois ..." *Sociétés et représentation* 9 (April 2000): 21-36. English trans. "A Medium is Always Born Twice." *Early Popular Visual Culture* 3.1 (May 2005): 3-15.

—. "Les genres vus à travers la loupe de l'intermédialité; ou, le cinéma des premiers temps: un bric-à-brac d'institutions." *La Nascita dei generi cinematografici.* Ed. Leonardo Quaresima, Alessandra Raengo and Laura Vichi. Udine: Forum, 1999. 87-97.

—. "Les *vues cinématographiques* selon Georges Méliès, ou: comment Mitry et Sadoul avaient peut-être raison d'avoir tort (même si c'est surtout Deslandes qu'il faut lire et relire)." *Georges Méliès, l'illusionniste fin de siècle?* Ed. Jacques Malthête and Michel Marie. Paris: Sorbonne Nouvelle/Colloque de Cerisy, 1997. 111-31.

— (with Denis Simard). "L'extranéité du cinéma des premiers temps: bilan et perspectives de recherche." *Les vingt premières années du cinéma français.* Ed. Jean A. Gili, Michèle Lagny, Michel Marie and Vincent Pinel. Paris: Sorbonne Nouvelle/AFRHC, 1995. 15-28.

— (with Tom Gunning). "Le cinéma des premiers temps: un défi à l'histoire du cinéma?" *Histoire du cinéma. Nouvelles approches.* Ed. Jacques Aumont, André Gaudreault and Michel Marie. Paris: Sorbonne/Colloque de Cerisy, 1989. 49-63. Japanese trans. "Eigashi No Hohoron." *Gendai Shiso. Revue de la pensée d'aujourd'hui* (Tokyo) 14.12 (Nov. 1986): 164-80.

—. *Du littéraire au filmique. Système du récit.* Paris: Méridiens Klincksieck, 1988.

—, ed. *Ce que je vois de mon ciné...* Paris: Méridiens Klincksieck, 1988.

—. "'Théâtralité' et 'narrativité' dans l'oeuvre de Georges Méliès." *Méliès et la naissance du spectacle cinématographique.* Ed. Madeleine Malthête-Méliès. Paris: Klincksieck,

1984. 199-219. English trans. "Theatricality, Narrativity, and Trickality: Reevaluating the Cinema of Georges Méliès." *Journal of Popular Film and Television* 15.3 (1987): 111-19.

—. "Film, récit, narration; le cinéma des frères Lumière." *Iris* 2.1 (1984): 61-70. English trans. "Film, Narrative, Narration: The Cinema of the Lumière Brothers." *Early Cinema: Space Frame Narrative.* Ed. Thomas Elsaesser. London: British Film Institute, 1990. 68-75.

—. "Temporality and Narrativity in Early Cinema, 1895-1908." *Film Before Griffith.* Ed. John Fell. Berkeley: U of California P, 1983. 311-29.

—, ed. "Filmographie analytique/Analytical Filmography." *Cinema 1900-1906: An Analytical Study.* Bruxelles: FIAF, 1982.

—, ed. *Le cinéma des premiers temps 1900-1906.* Spec. issue of *Les Cahiers de la Cinémathèque* 29 (Winter 1979).

Guerin, Frances. "Dazzled by the Light: Technological Entertainment and its Social Impact in *Varieté.*" *Cinema Journal* 42.4 (Summer 2003): 98-115.

Giraud, Jean. "Attraction," "Cinématographie-attraction." *Le Lexique français du cinéma des origines à 1930.* Paris: CNRS, 1958. 48, 91.

Gopalan, Lalitha. *Cinema of Interruptions: Action Genres in Contemporary Indian Cinema.* New Delhi: OUP, 2003.

Gordon, Rae Beth. "From Charcot to Charlot: Unconscious Imitation and Spectatorship in French Cabaret and Early Cinema." *Critical Inquiry* 27.3 (Spring 2001): 515-49.

Griffiths, Alison. "'Journeys for Those Who Can Not Travel': Promenade Cinema and the Museum Life Group." *Wide Angle* 18.3 (1996): 53-84.

Grusin, Richard. "Premediation." *Criticism* 46.1 (Winter 2004): 17-39.

Gunning, Tom. "Cinema of Attractions." *Encyclopedia of Early Cinema.* Ed. Richard Abel. London/New York: Routledge, 2005. 124-27.

—. "Systematizing the Electric Message: Narrative Form, Gender, and Modernity in *The Lonedale Operator.*" *American Cinema's Transitional Era: Audiences, Institutions, Practices.* Ed. Charlie Keil and Shelley Stamp. Berkeley: U of California P, 2004. 15-50.

—. "Re-Newing Old Technologies: Astonishment, Second Nature, and the Uncanny in Technology from the Previous Turn-of-the-Century." *Rethinking Media Change: The Aesthetics of Transition.* Ed. David Thorburn and Henry Jenkins. Cambridge: MIT P, 2003. 39-59.

—. "A Quarter of a Century Later. Is Early Cinema Still Early?" *KINtop* 12 (2003): 17-31.

—. "1903, Teetering between Stories and Attractions." *Cinegraphie* 16 (Summer 2003): 327-35.

—. "Loïe Fuller and the Art of Motion." *La Decima Musa. Il cinema e le altre arti.* Ed. Leonardo Quaresima and Laura Vichi. Udine: Forum, 2001. 25-35.

—. "The Scene of Speaking Two Decades of Discovering the Film Lecturer." *Iris* 27 (Spring 1999): 67-79.

—. "Early American Cinema." *The Oxford Guide to Film Studies.* Ed. John Hill and Pamela Church Gibson. Oxford: Oxford UP, 1998. 255-71.

—. "In Your Face: Physiognomy, Photography, and the Gnostic Mission of Early Film." *Modernism/Modernity* 4.1 (1997): 1-29.

—. "Before Documentary: Early nonfiction films and the 'view' aesthetic." *Uncharted Territory. Essays on early nonfiction film.* Ed. Daan Hertogs and Nico de Klerk. Amsterdam: Stichting Nederlands Filmmuseum, 1997. 9-24.

—. "Metafore colorate: l'attrazione del colore nel cinema delle origini."/"Colorful Meta-phors: The Attraction of Color in Early Silent Cinema." *Fotogenia* 1 (1995): 25-38.

—. "Response to 'Pie and Chase.'" *Classical Hollywood Comedy*. Ed. Kristine Brunovska Karnick and Henry Jenkins. New York: Routledge, 1995. 120-22.

—. "Attractions, trucages et photogénie: L'explosion du présent dans les films à truc fran-çais produit entre 1896 et 1907." *Les vingt premières années du cinéma français*. Ed. Jean A. Gili, Michèle Lagny, Michel Marie and Vincent Pinel. Paris: Sorbonne nouvelle/ AFRHC, 1995. 177-93.

—. "The World as Object Lesson: Cinema Audiences, Visual Culture and the St. Louis World's Fair, 1904." *Film History* (Winter 1995): 422-44. Abridged French version: "L'image du monde: cinéma et culture visuelle à l'Exposition internationale de Saint Louis (1904)." *Le Cinéma au tournant du siècle*. Ed. Claire Dupré la Tour, André Gau-dreault and Roberta Pearson. Québec/Lausanne: Nota Bene/Payot, 1999. 51-62.

—. "The Whole Town's Gawking: Early Cinema and the Visual Experience of Moder-nity." *Yale Journal of Criticism* 7.2 (Fall 1994): 189-201. French trans. "Cinéma des attractions et modernité." *Cinémathèque* 5 (Spring 1994): 129-39.

—. "'Now You See it, Now You Don't': The Temporality of the Cinema of Attractions." *Velvet Light Trap* 32 (Fall 1993): 3-12. Rpt. in *The Silent Cinema Reader*. Ed. Lee Grieve-son and Peter Kramer. London: Routledge, 2004. 41-50. *Silent Film*. Ed. Richard Abel. London: Atholone, 1996. 71-84.

—. "Attractions, Detection, Disguise: Zigomar, Jasset and the History of Genres in Early Film." *Griffithiana* 47 (May 1993): 111-35.

—. *D.W. Griffith and the Origins of American Narrative Film: The Early Years at Biograph*. Urbana: U of Illinois P, 1991.

—. "'Primitive' Cinema. A Frame-up? Or The Trick's on Us." *Cinema Journal* 28.2 (1989): 3-12. Rpt. in *Early Cinema: Space Frame Narrative*. Ed. Thomas Elsaesser. London: British Film Institute, 1990. 95-103.

—. "An Aesthetic of Astonishment: Early Film and the (In)Credulous Spectator." *Art and Text* 34 (Fall 1989): 31-45. Rpt. in *Film Theory and Criticism*. Ed. Leo Braudy and Mar-shall Cohen. Oxford: Oxford UP, 1999. 818-32. *Viewing Positions*. Ed. Linda Wil-liams. New Brunswick: Rutgers, 1995. 114-33. Czech trans. "Estetika uzasu: rany film a (ne)dureriivy divak." *Nová filmová historie*. Ed. Peter Szczepanik. Praha: Herr-mann & synové, 2004. 149-66. Finnish trans. "Hämmästyksen estetiikka. Varhainen elokuva ja (epä)uskoinen katsoja." *Varjojen valtakunta. Elokuvahistorian uusi lukukirja*. Ed. Anu Koivunen and Hannu Salmi. Turku: Turun yliopiston täydennyskoulutus-keskus, 1997. 18-35. Portugese trans. "Uma estética do espanto: o cinema das ori-gens e o espectador (in)crédulo." *Imagens* 5 (Aug.-Dec. 1995): 52-61.

—. "What I saw from the Rear Window of the Hôtel des Folies-Dramatiques, Or the Story Point of View Films Told." *Ce que je vois de mon ciné…* Ed. André Gaudreault. Paris: Méridiens-Klincksieck, 1988. 33-43.

—. "The Cinema of Attraction[s]: Early Film, Its Spectator and the Avant-Garde." *Wide Angle* 8.3-4 (Fall 1986): 63-70. Rpt. in *Theater and Film: A Comparative Anthology*. Ed. Robert Knopf. New Haven: Yale UP, 2005. *The Film Studies Reader*. Ed. Joanne Hol-lows, Peter Hutchings and Mark Jancovich. London: Arnold, 2000. 161-65. *Film and Theory: An Anthology*. Ed Robert Stam and Toby Miller. Oxford: Blackwell, 2000. 229-35. *Early Cinema: Space Frame Narrative*. Ed. Thomas Elsaesser. London: British Film Institute, 1990. 56-62. Hungarian trans. "Az attrakció mozija: a korai film, nézője és az avantgard." *A kortárs filmelmélet útjai*. Ed. Kovács András Bálint and Vajdovich Györgyi. Budapest: Palatinus, 2004. 292-302. Japanese trans. in *Cinema and Modernity*. Ed. Masato Hase and Hideyuki Nakamura. Tokyo: U of Tokyo P, 2003. 303-23. Finnish trans. "Attraktioiden elokuva – varhainen elokuva, katsoja ja avantgarde." *Lähikuva* 1 (2002): 7-13. German trans. "Das Kino der Attraktionen: Der frühe Film, seine Zuschauer und die Avantgarde." *Meteor* 4 (1996): 25-35. Danish trans. "Attraktionsfilmen – den tidlige film, den tilskuer og avantgarden." *Tryllelygten* 2.2 (1995): 47-56. Swedish trans. "Attraktionernas film. Tidig film, dess åskådare och avantgardet." *Modern filmteori* 1 (1995): 171-79.

—. "Non-Continuity, Continuity, Discontinuity: A Theory of Genres in Early Films." *Iris* 2.1 (1984): 101-12. Rpt. in *Early Cinema: Space Frame Narrative*. Ed. Thomas Elsaesser. London: British Film Institute, 1990. 86-94. Hungarian trans. "Non-kontinuitás, kontinuitás, diskontinuitás: a korai filmek müfajainak elmélete." *A kortárs filmelmélet útjai*. Ed. Kovács András Bálint and Vajdovich Györgyi. Budapest: Palatinus, 2004. 304-19.

—. "An Unseen Energy Swallows Space: The Space in Early Film and Its Relation to American Avant-Garde Film." *Film Before Griffith*. Ed. John Fell. Berkeley: U of California P, 1983. 355-66.

—. "The Non-Continuous Style of Early Film (1900-1906)." *Cinema 1900-1906: An Analytical Study*. Ed. Roger Holman. Bruxelles: FIAF, 1982. 219-30.

—. "Doctor Jacobs' Dream Work." *Millennium Film Journal* (Fall-Winter 1981-82): 210-18.

Hagener, Malte. *Moving Forward, Looking Back. The European Avant-garde and the Invention of Film Culture, 1919-1939*. Amsterdam: Amsterdam UP, forthcoming.

Hamus, Réjane. "Segundo de Chomón." *1895* 27 (1999): 49-60.

Hansen, Miriam. "Early Cinema, Late Cinema: Permutations of the Public Sphere." *Screen* 34.3 (1993): 197-210.

—. "'With Skin and Hair': Kracauer's Theory of Film, Marseille 1940." *Critical Inquiry* 19.3 (Spring 1993): 437-69.

—. *Babel & Babylon: Spectatorship in American Silent Film*. Cambridge: Harvard UP, 1991.

—. "Reinventing the Nickelodeon: Notes on Kluge and Early Cinema." *October* 46 (Fall 1988): 178-98.

—. "Benjamin, Cinema and Experience: 'The Blue Flower in the Land of Technology.'" *New German Critique* 40 (Winter 1987): 179-224.

Hediger, Vinzenz. *Verführung zum Film. Der amerikanische Kinotrailer seit 1912*. Marburg: Schüren, 2001.

Hozić, Aida. "Hollywood Goes on Sale; or, What Do the Violet Eyes of Elizabeth Taylor Have to Do with the 'Cinema of Attractions'"? *Hollywood Goes Shopping*. Ed. David Desser and Garth S. Jowett. Minneapolis: U of Minnesota P, 2000. 205-21.

Jayamanne, Laleen. "Sri Lankan Family Melodrama: A Cinema of Primitive Attractions." *Screen* 33.2 (Summer 1992): 145-53.

Jacobs, Lea and Richard DeCordova, "Spectacle and Narrative Theory." *Quarterly Review of Film and Video* 7.4 (1982): 293-307.

Jenkins, Henry. "Games, the New Lively Art." *Handbook for Video Game Studies*. Ed. Jeffrey Goldstein and Joost Raessens. Cambridge: MIT P, 2005. 175-89.

—. *What Made Pistachio Nuts?: Early Sound Comedy and the Vaudeville Aesthetic*. New York: Columbia UP, 1992.

Jullier, Laurent. *L'Ecran post-moderne. Un cinéma de l'allusion et du feu d'artifice*. Paris: L'Harmattan, 1997.

Kasson, John. *Amusing the Million: Coney Island at the Turn of the Century*. New York: Hill and Wang, 1978.

Keil, Charlie. "'To Here From Modernity': Style, Historiography, and Transitional Cinema." *American Cinema's Transitional Era: Audiences, Institutions, Practices*. Ed. Charlie Keil and Shelley Stamp. Berkeley: U of California P, 2004. 51-65.

—. "'Visualised Narratives,' Transitional Cinema, and the Modernity Thesis." *Le Cinéma au tournant du siècle / Cinema at the Turn of the Century*. Ed. Claire Dupré la Tour, André Gaudreault and Roberta Pearson. Lausanne/Québec: Payot/Nota Bene, 1998. 123-37.

Kember, Joe. "The Cinema of Affections: The Transformation of Authorship in British Cinema before 1907." *The Velvet Light Trap* 57 (2006): 3-16.

Kern, Stephen. *The Culture of Time and Space: 1880-1918*. Cambridge: Harvard UP, 1983.

Kernan, Lisa. *Coming Attractions. Reading American movie trailers*. Austin: U of Texas P, 2004.

Kessler, Frank. "La cinématographie comme dispositif (du) spectaculaire." *CiNéMAS* 14.1 (2003): 21-34.

—. "Cinématographe et arts de l'illusion." *La Decima Musa. Il cinema e le altre arti*. Ed. Leonardo Quaresima and Laura Vichi. Udine: Forum, 2001. 535-42.

—. "In the Realm of the Fairies: Early Cinema between Attraction and Narration." *Iconics. International Studies of the Modern Image* 5 (2000): 7-26.

— (with Sabine Lenk). "L'adresse-Méliès." *Georges Méliès, l'illusionniste fin de siècle?* Ed. Jacques Malthête and Michel Marie. Paris: Sorbonne Nouvelle/Colloque de Cerisy, 1997. 183-99.

— (with Sabine Lenk). "Cinéma d'attractions et gestualité." *Les vingt premières années du cinéma français*. Ed. Jean A. Gili, Michèle Lagny, Michel Marie and Vincent Pinel. Paris: Sorbonne Nouvelle/AFRHC, 1995. 195-202.

Kinder, Marsha. "Violence American Style: The Narrative Orchestration of Violent Attractions." *Violence and American Cinema*. New York: Routledge, 2001. 63-100.

King, Geoff, "Ride Films and Films as Rides in the Contemporary Hollywood Cinema of Attractions." *CineAction* 51 (Feb. 2000): 3-9.

—. *Spectacular Narratives. Hollywood in the Age of Blockbuster*. London/New York: Tauris, 2000.

Kirby, Lynne. *Parallel Tracks. The Railroad and Silent Cinema*. London: Durham, 1997.

Knopf, Robert. *The Theater and Cinema of Buster Keaton*. Princeton: Princeton UP. 1999.

Labelle, Alain. "L'utilisation du montage des attractions de S.M. Eisenstein dans *Rocky IV*." *Etudes littéraires* 20.3 (Winter 1987-88): 111-22.

Lacasse, Germain. *Le bonimenteur de vues animées. Le cinéma muet entre tradition et modernité*. Québec/Paris: Nota Bene/Méridiens-Klincksieck, 2000.

Laloy, Louis. "Cabarets et Music-Halls." *SIM* (July-Aug. 1913): 52.

Lant, Antonia. "Haptical Cinema." *October* 74 (1995): 45-73.

Larouche, Michel. "Les nouvelles technologies au cinéma: le retour du mode énergétique." *Cinéma: acte et présence*. Ed. Michel Bouvier, Michel Larouche and Lucie Roy. Québec/Lyon: Nota Bene/Centre Jacques Cartier, 1999. 99-110.

Léger, Fernand. "A Critical Essay on the Plastic Qualities of Abel Gance's Film *The Wheel*." *Functions of Painting*. Intro. Edward Fry. New York: Viking, 1973.

Lindsay, Vachel. *The Art of the Moving Picture*. Intro. Stanley Kauffmann. 1915. New York: Random House, 2000.

López, Ana M. "Early Cinema and Modernity in Latin America." *Cinema Journal* 40.1 (Fall 2000): 48-78.

Lungstrum, Janet Ward. "The Display Window: Designs and Desires of Weimar Consumerism." *New German Critique* 76 (Winter 1999): 115-60.

MacDonald, Scott. "The Attractions of Nature in Early Cinema." *Unseen Cinema: Early American Avant-Garde Film 1893-1941*. Ed. Bruce Posner. New York: Anthology Film Archives, 2005. 56-63.

Mannoni, Laurent. *The Great Art of Light and Shadow: Archaeology of the Cinema*. Trans. and ed. Richard Crangle. Exeter: U of Exeter P, 2000.

Marinetti, Filippo Tommaso. "Il Teatro di Varietà." *Lacerba* 1.1 (Oct. 1913): 209-11. English trans. "The Variety Theater." *Futurist Manifestos*. Ed. Umbro Apollonio. New York: Viking, 1973. 126-31.

Marsh, Tim. "Presence as Experience: Film Informing Ways of Staying There." *Presence: Teleoperators and Virtual Environments* 12.5 (Oct. 2003): 538-49.

Mathews, Nancy, et al. *Moving Pictures: American Art and Film, 1880-1910*. Manchester: Hudson Hill P and Williams College Museum of Art, 2005.

McMahan, Alison. *Alice Guy Blaché: Lost Visionary of the Cinema*. New York: Continuum, 2002.

Méliès, Georges. "En marge de l'histoire du cinématographe [1926]." *Propos sur les vues animées*. Ed. André Gaudreault, Jacques Malthête and Madeleine Malthête-Méliès. Spec. issue of *Les dossiers de la Cinémathèque* 10 (1982): 20-31.

—. "Importance du scénario." *Cinéa-Ciné pour tous* (April 1932). Rpt. in Georges Sadoul, *Georges Méliès*. Paris: Seghers, 1961. 113-16.

Miller, Angela. "The Panorama, the Cinema, and the Emergence of the Spectacular." *Wide Angle* 18.2 (1996): 34-69.

Minguet Batllori, J. *Segundo de Chomón, Beyond the Cinema of Attractions (1904-1912)*. Barcelona: Filmoteca de la Generalitat de Catalunya, 1999.

Moore, Rachel O. *Savage Theory. Cinema as Modern Magic*. Durham: Duke UP, 1999.

Mottram, Ron. "Fact and Affirmation: Some Thoughts on the Methodology of Film History and the Relation of Theory to Historiography." *Quarterly Review of Film Studies* 5.3 (Summer 1980): 335-47.

Müller, Corinna. "Anfänge der Filmgeschichte. Produktion, Foren und Rezeption." *Die Mobilisierung des Sehens. Zur Vor- und Frühgeschichte des Films in Literatur und Kunst*. Ed. Harro Segeberg. München: Fink, 1996. 293-324.

Mulvey, Laura. "Visual Pleasure and Narrative Cinema." *Screen* 16.3 (1975): 6-18. Rpt. in *Visual and Other Pleasures*. Bloomington: Indiana UP, 1989. 14-27.

Musser, Charles. "A Cornucopia of Images: Comparison and Judgment across Theater, Film and the Visual Arts during the Late Nineteenth Century." *Moving Pictures: American Art and Film, 1880-1910*. Manchester: Hudson Hill P and Williams College Museum of Art, 2005.

—. "Historiographic Method and the Study of Early Cinema." *Cinema Journal* 44.1 (Fall 2004): 101-07.

—. *Edison Motion Pictures, 1890-1900: An Annotated Filmography*. Washington: Smithsonian Institution P, 1997.

—. "Rethinking Early Cinema: Cinema of Attractions and Narrativity." *The Yale Journal of Criticism* 7.2 (1994): 203-32. French trans. "Pour une nouvelle approche du cinéma des premiers temps: le cinéma d'attractions et la narrativité." *Les vingt premières années du cinéma français*. Ed. Jean A. Gili, Michèle Lagny, Michel Marie and Vincent Pinel. Paris: Sorbonne Nouvelle/AFRHC, 1995. 147-75.

—. (with Carol Nelson). *High-Class Moving Pictures*. Princeton: Princeton UP, 1991.

—. *Before the Nickelodeon: The Early Cinema of Edwin S. Porter*. Berkeley: U of California P, 1991.

—. *The Emergence of Cinema*. New York: Scribner's, 1990.

—. "The Nickelodeon Era Begins: Establishing Hollywood's Mode of Representation." *Framework* 22-23 (Fall 1983): 4-11. Revised version in *Early Cinema: Space Frame Narrative*. Ed. Thomas Elsaesser. London: British Film Institute, 1990. 256-73.

—. "The Eden Musée in 1898: Exhibitor as Creator." *Film and History* (Dec. 1981): 73-83.

—. "The Early Cinema of Edwin S. Porter." *Cinema Journal* 19.1 (Fall 1979): 1-38.

Ndalianis, Angela. "Special Effects, Morphing Magic, and the 1990s Cinema of Attractions." *Meta-Morphing: Visual Transformation and the Culture of Quick Change*. Ed. Vivian Sobchack. Minneapolis: U of Minnesota P, 2000. 251-71.

Nichols, Bill. "Documentary Film and the Modernist Avant-Garde." *Critical Inquiry* 27.4 (Summer 2001): 580-610.

Noussinova, Natalia. "Eisenstein excentrique." *Eisenstein: l'ancien et le nouveau*. Ed. Dominique Chateau, François Jost and Martin Lefebvre. Paris: Sorbonne, 2001. 67-75.

—. *Leonid Trauberg et l'excentrisme*. Crisnée: Yellow Now, 1993.

Paci, Viva. "*Pas d'histoires, il faut que le cinéma vive*. L'attraction dans le récit du film par quelques cinéastes de la première avant-garde." *Narrating the Film. Novelization: From the Catalogue to the Trailer*. Ed. Alice Autelitano and Valentina Re. Udine: Forum, 2006. 205-12.

—. "Cinéma de synthèse et cinéma des premiers temps: des correspondances examinées à la loupe du système des attractions." *Cinéma et Cie* 5 (Fall 2004): 112-14.

—. "La persistance des attractions." *Cinéma et Cie* 3 (Spring 2003): 56-63.

—. "Certains paysages d'Herzog sous la loupe du système des attractions." *CiNéMAS* 12.1 (2001): 97-104.

Pang, Laikwan. "Walking Into and Out of the Spectacle: China's Earliest Film Scene." *Screen* 47 (Spring 2006): 66-80.

Pearson, Roberta E. "The Attractions of Cinema, or, How I Learned to Start Worrying About Loving Early Film." *Cinema: The Beginnings and the Future*. Ed. Christopher Williams. London: U of Westminster P, 1996. 150-57.

Petro, Patrice. "Nazi Cinema at the Intersection of the Classical and the Popular." *New German Critique* 74 (Spring-Summer 1998): 41-55.

Pierson, Michele. "Reinventing the Cinema of Attractions." *Special Effects Still in Search of Wonder*. New York: Columbia UP, 2002. 118-23.

—. "No Longer State-of-the-Art: Crafting a Future for CGI." *Wide Angle* 21.1 (Jan. 1999): 28-47.

Predal, René. "Le cinéma holographique: les expérimentations de Claudine Eizykman et Guy Fihman." *CiNéMAS* 1.3 (1991): 61-76.

Prokhorov, Aleksandr. "Cinema of Attractions versus Narrative Cinema: Leonid Gaidai's Comedies and El'dar Riazanov's Satires of the 1960s (in Soviet and Russian Blockbuster Films)." *Slavic Review: American Quarterly of Russian, Eurasian and East European Studies* 62.3 (Fall 2003): 455-72.

Rabinovitz, Lauren. "Traveling at the Limit: Spectatorship and Techno-Spectacles." *I Limiti della rappresentazione. Censura, visibile, modi di rappresentazione nel cinema.* Ed. Leonardo Quaresima, Alessandra Raengo and Laura Vichi. Udine: Forum, 2000. 46-69.

—. "From *Hale's Tours* to *Star Tours*: Virtual Voyages and the Delirium of the Hyper-Real." *Iris* 25 (Spring 1998): 133-52.

Rajadhyaksha, Ashish. "Strange attractions." *Sight and Sound* 6 (Aug. 1996): 28-31.

Roger, Philippe. "Spectaculaire, histoire d'un mot." *Le Spectaculaire.* Ed. Christine Hamon-Sirejols and André Gardies. Lyon: Aléas, 1997. 9-14.

Røssaak, Eivind. "The Unseen of the Real: Or, Evidential Efficacy from Muybridge to *The Matrix.*" *Witness: Memory, Representation, and the Media in Question.* Ed. Ulrik Ekman. Copenhagen: Museum Tusculanum P, forthcoming.

Russell, Catherine. "Parallax Historiography: The Flâneuse as Cyberfeminist." *A Feminist Reader in Early Cinema.* Ed. Jennifer M. Bean and Diane Negra. Durham: Duke UP, 2002. 552-70.

—. *Experimental Ethnography. The Work of Film in the Age of Video.* Durham: Duke UP, 1999.

Salt, Barry. *Film Style and Technology: History and Analysis, 1983.* London: Starword, 1992.

Schivelbusch, Wolfgang. *Geschichte der Eisenbahnreise.* Munich: Carl Hanser, 1977. English trans. *The Railway Journey. The Industrialization of Time and Space in the 19th Century.* New York: Urizen, 1979.

Singer, Ben. "Modernity, Hyperstimulus, and the Rise of Popular Sensationalism." *Cinema and the Invention of Modern Life.* Ed. Leo Charney and Vanessa Schwartz. Berkeley/Los Angeles: U of California P, 1995. 72-99.

Smith, Tom. *Industrial Light & Magic: The Art of Special Effects.* New York: Ballantine, 1986.

Sobchack, Vivian, ed. *Meta-Morphing: Visual Transformation and the Culture of Quick Change.* Minneapolis: U of Minnesota P, 2000.

—. *Screening Space. The American Science Fiction Film.* New York: Ungar, 1987.

Staiger, Janet. *Perverse Spectators: The Practices of Film Reception.* New York: New York UP, 2000.

Stewart, Jacqueline. "'Negroes Laughing at Themselves'? Black Spectatorship and the Performance of Urban Modernity." *Critical Inquiry* 29.4 (Summer 2003): 650-77.

Strauven, Wanda. *Marinetti e il cinema: tra attrazione e sperimentazione.* Udine: Campanotto, 2006.

—. "The Meaning of the Music-Hall: From the Italian Futurism to the Soviet Avant-garde." *Cinéma et Cie* 4 (Spring 2004): 117-34.

—. "Notes sur le 'grand talent futuriste' d'Eisenstein." *Eisenstein: l'ancien et le nouveau.* Ed. Dominique Chateau, François Jost and Martin Lefebvre. Paris: Sorbonne/Colloque de Cerisy, 2001. 45-65.

—. "L'art de Georges Méliès et le futurisme italien." *Georges Méliès, l'illusionniste fin de siècle?* Ed. Jacques Malthête and Michel Marie. Paris: Sorbonne Nouvelle/Colloque de Cerisy, 1997. 331-55.

Srinivas, Lakshmi. "The Active Audience: Spectatorship, Social Relations and the Experience of Cinema in India." *Media, Culture & Society* 24.2 (2002): 155-73.

Testa, Bart. *Back and Forth. Early Cinema and the Avant-Garde.* Ontario: Art Gallery of Ontario, 1992.

Toulet, Emmanuelle. "Cinema at the Universal Exhibition 1900." *Persistence of Vision* 9 (1991): 10-36.

—. *Cinématographe, invention du siècle.* Paris: Gallimard, 1998.

Tsivian, Yuri. *Early Cinema in Russia and its Cultural Reception.* New York: Routledge, 1994.

—. "Some Historical Footnotes to the Kuleshov Experiment." *Early Cinema: Space Frame Narrative.* Ed. Thomas Elsaesser. London: British Film Institue, 1990. 247-55.

Vaughan, Dai. "Let There Be Lumière." *Sight and Sound* 5.2 (1981): 127-27. Rpt. in *Early Cinema: Space Frame Narrative.* Ed. Thomas Elsaesser. London: British Film Institute, 1990. 63-67.

Vaz, Mark Cotta. *Industrial Light & Magic: Into the Digital Realm.* New York: Ballantine, 1996.

Waltz, Gwendolyn. "Embracing Technology: A Primer of Early Multi-Media Performane." *La Decima Musa. Il cinema e le altre arti.* Ed. Leonardo Quaresima and Laura Vichi. Udine: Forum, 2001. 543-53.

Wedel, Michael. "Schiffbruch mit Zuschauer. Das Ereigniskino des Mime Misu." *Kino der Kaiserzeit.* Ed. Thomas Elsaesser and Michael Wedel. Munich: Edition text + kritik, 2002. 197-252.

Wees, William. *Recycled Images. The Art and Politics of Found Footage Films.* New York: Anthology Film Archives, 1993.

White, Mimi. "The Attractions of Television." *Mediaspace. Place, Scale and Culture in the Media Age.* Ed. Nick Couldry and Anna McCarthy. London/New York: Routledge, 2004. 75-91.

Williams, Linda. "Discipline and Fun: *Psycho* and Postmodern Cinema." *Reinventing Film Studies.* Ed. Christine Gledhill and Linda Williams. London: Arnold, 2000. 351-80.

—, "Introduction." *Viewing Positions: Ways of Seeing Film.* New Brunswick: Rutgers UP, 1995. 1-20.

—. *Hard Core: Power, Pleasure, and the "Frenzy and the Visible."* Berkeley: U of California P, 1989.

Wood, Aylish. "Timespaces in Spectacular Cinema: Crossing the Great Divide of Spectacle Versus Narratives." *Screen* 43 (Winter 2002): 370-86.

Index of Names

Index of Film Titles

Index of Subjects

Film Culture in Transition

General Editor: *Thomas Elsaesser*

Thomas Elsaesser, Robert Kievit and Jan Simons (eds.)
Double Trouble: Chiem van Houweninge on Writing and Filming, 1994
ISBN paperback 978 90 5356 025 9

Thomas Elsaesser, Jan Simons and Lucette Bronk (eds.)
Writing for the Medium: Television in Transition, 1994
ISBN paperback 978 90 5356 054 9

Karel Dibbets and Bert Hogenkamp (eds.)
Film and the First World War, 1994
ISBN paperback 978 90 5356 064 8

Warren Buckland (ed.)
The Film Spectator: From Sign to Mind, 1995
ISBN paperback 978 90 5356 131 7; ISBN hardcover 978 90 5356 170 6

Egil Törnqvist
Between Stage and Screen: Ingmar Bergman Directs, 1996
ISBN paperback 978 90 5356 137 9; ISBN hardcover 978 90 5356 171 3

Thomas Elsaesser (ed.)
A Second Life: German Cinema's First Decades, 1996
ISBN paperback 978 90 5356 172 0; ISBN hardcover 978 90 5356 183 6

Thomas Elsaesser
Fassbinder's Germany: History Identity Subject, 1996
ISBN paperback 978 90 5356 059 4; ISBN hardcover 978 90 5356 184 3

Thomas Elsaesser and Kay Hoffmann (eds.)
Cinema Futures: Cain, Abel or Cable? The Screen Arts in the Digital Age, 1998
ISBN paperback 978 90 5356 282 6; ISBN hardcover 978 90 5356 312 0

Siegfried Zielinski
Audiovisions: Cinema and Television as Entr'Actes in History, 1999
ISBN paperback 978 90 5356 313 7; ISBN hardcover 978 90 5356 303 8

Kees Bakker (ed.)
Joris Ivens and the Documentary Context, 1999
ISBN paperback 978 90 5356 389 2; ISBN hardcover 978 90 5356 425 7

Egil Törnqvist
Ibsen, Strindberg and the Intimate Theatre: Studies in TV Presentation, 1999
ISBN paperback 978 90 5356 350 2; ISBN hardcover 978 90 5356 371 7

Michael Temple and James S. Williams (eds.)
The Cinema Alone: Essays on the Work of Jean-Luc Godard 1985-2000, 2000
ISBN paperback 978 90 5356 455 4; ISBN hardcover 978 90 5356 456 1

Patricia Pisters and Catherine M. Lord (eds.)
Micropolitics of Media Culture: Reading the Rhizomes of Deleuze and Guattari, 2001
ISBN paperback 978 90 5356 472 1; ISBN hardcover 978 90 5356 473 8

William van der Heide
Malaysian Cinema, Asian Film: Border Crossings and National Cultures, 2002
ISBN paperback 978 90 5356 519 3; ISBN hardcover 978 90 5356 580 3

Bernadette Kester
Film Front Weimar: Representations of the First World War in German Films of the Weimar Period (1919-1933), 2002
ISBN paperback 978 90 5356 597 1; ISBN hardcover 978 90 5356 598 8

Richard Allen and Malcolm Turvey (eds.)
Camera Obscura, Camera Lucida: Essays in Honor of Annette Michelson, 2003
ISBN paperback 978 90 5356 494 3

Ivo Blom
Jean Desmet and the Early Dutch Film Trade, 2003
ISBN paperback 978 90 5356 463 9; ISBN hardcover 978 90 5356 570 4

Alastair Phillips
City of Darkness, City of Light: Émigré Filmmakers in Paris 1929-1939, 2003
ISBN paperback 978 90 5356 634 3; ISBN hardcover 978 90 5356 633 6

Thomas Elsaesser, Alexander Horwath and Noel King (eds.)
The Last Great American Picture Show: New Hollywood Cinema in the 1970s, 2004
ISBN paperback 978 90 5356 631 2; ISBN hardcover 978 905356 493 6

Thomas Elsaesser (ed.)
Harun Farocki: Working on the Sight-Lines, 2004
ISBN paperback 978 90 5356 635 0; ISBN hardcover 978 90 5356 636 7

Kristin Thompson
Herr Lubitsch Goes to Hollywood: German and American Film after World War I, 2005
ISBN paperback 978 90 5356 708 1; ISBN hardcover 978 90 5356 709 8

Marijke de Valck and Malte Hagener (eds.)
Cinephilia: Movies, Love and Memory, 2005
ISBN paperback 978 90 5356 768 5; ISBN hardcover 978 90 5356 769 2

Thomas Elsaesser
European Cinema: Face to Face with Hollywood, 2005
ISBN paperback 978 90 5356 594 0; ISBN hardcover 978 90 5356 602 2

Michael Walker
Hitchcock's Motifs, 2005
ISBN paperback 978 90 5356 772 2; ISBN hardcover 978 90 5356 773 9

Nanna Verhoeff
The West in Early Cinema: After the Beginning, 2006
ISBN paperback 978 90 5356 831 6; ISBN hardcover 978 90 5356 832 3

Anat Zanger
Film Remakes as Ritual and Disguise: From Carmen to Ripley, 2006
ISBN paperback 978 90 5356 784 5; ISBN hardcover 978 90 5356 785 2